carbon
nd carbon
urther

er part.
urces of
ng from
spins to
xchange
cterized

(7.144)

ur
ical
(R
nt

=
hen
owards
Bloch
$\hat{x} - \hat{y}$
covery
)]. To

ARCHAEOLOGY AND INTERACTIVE DISCIPLINES

INDIAN ARCHAEOLOGY IN RETROSPECT

VOLUME III

ARCHAEOLOGY AND INTERACTIVE DISCIPLINES

Edited by
S. SETTAR
RAVI KORISETTAR

Indian Council of Historical Research

MANOHAR
2002

First published 2002

ISBN 81-7304-318-3 (Set)
ISBN 81-7304-321-3 (Vol. III)

Published by
Ajay Kumar Jain for
Manohar Publishers & Distributors
4753/23 Ansari Road, Daryaganj
New Delhi 110002

Typeset by
A J Software Publishing Co. Pvt. Ltd.
305 Durga Chambers
1333 D.B. Gupta Road
Karol Bagh, New Delhi 110005

Printed at
Lordson Publishers Pvt. Ltd.
C 5/19 Rana Pratap Bagh
Delhi 110007

Contents

Foreword

As one of the editors of this series and also as one associated with the Indian Council of Historical Research, I am delighted to present the *Indian Archaeology in Retrospect* in four volumes. This series has taken the present form, undergoing several transformations during the last four years. When it was originally planned in 1995 at Dharwad, we had only a limited aim of attempting a historiographical account, covering the Pre and Early history of India in two volumes (from Palaeolithic to the Early Historical Period); we had also somewhat vaguely nourished one-volume retrospect on Indian Art History to complement it. During the early years of the preparation, we kept our options open, sought and considered suggestions from others, tried to involve as many established scholars as possible—all these experiments taught us how much easier it is to write for oneself than get others write for one. Of about a hundred odd scholars with whom we corresponded at the early stages, only about eighty could stand by us till the end. Some could not respond to our invitation and they proved to be the most helpful ones, because their silence remained golden; some others reacted enthusiastically in the beginning, pleaded for more time subsequently, but faded away at the concluding stages. No doubt, the latter should have had justifiable reasons for their withdrawal, but this upset our planning badly, and denied us about a dozen important papers. Critics who notice obvious gaps should not overlook the inherent hazards involved in such collective efforts while assessing the academic content of these volumes.

The four volumes of *Indian Archaeology in Retrospect* are shaped by a combination of factors: our original plan apart, the suggestions and modifications made by colleagues and friends, the range of available scholarship, generous offers and voluntary participations, drop outs and withdrawals, and also accidents of various other kinds, are the most obvious ones among them. All these led to alter the original plan on the one hand and to accommodate new ideas on the other. The latter resulted in the expansion of the series from the original two to four volumes; it also made possible one full volume on the Indus Studies and another on the Interactive Sciences. The most useful addition came from scholars who have more or less devoted their entire lifetime to their respective fields of specialization: this explains the most useful, informative and meticulously prepared Appendices and Bibliographies.

While working on this series with Ravi at Dharwad, I had also initiated several bibliographical projects in the Indian Council of Historical Research at New Delhi. Besides liberally funding such projects (both for their preparation and publication), the ICHR had also made efforts to create opportunities to bring out bibliographical accounts in *The Indian Historical Review*, and in publications brought out under the new monograph series as well as several other publications of the Council. When these volumes were finalised, I thought that a comprehensive bibliography of Indian archaeology, covering the entire nineteenth and twentieth centuries, would be an appropriate complement to this series. I hope Professor V.N. Misra of the Deccan College, who is siezed with this task since 1997, would present it one day. The original plan of making this Bibliography an integral part of this series, as Volume V, had to be, abandoned, however to avoid further delay in the publication of these volumes. I am happy that the Indian Council of Historical Research is able to complement the excellent work done by a community of Dutch, South Asian and South-East Asian scholars under the *ABIA South and Southeast Asian Art and Archaeology Index* project, sponsored by the International Institute of Asian Studies at Leiden, Netherlands. The ABIA offers annotated bibliography of the publications of the year; our volume comprises only bibliographical entries of important publications brought out during the past century and half.

Dr. Ravi Korisettar, Professor and Chairman of the Department of History and Archaeology, Karnatak University, Dharwad, had to bear the major brunt of the responsibility, especially after I took over the Chair of the ICHR and became increasingly involved with the responsibilities of the Council. In fact, his share of contribution is far more than mine. My contribution to it is almost nil. I deem it a privilege to associate myself with these works and to present them on behalf of the ICHR. Both these projects were completed within a reasonable period of time, thanks to the initiative and cooperation of scholars and editors: in fact, the ICHR grant given to it is only nominal and symbolic.

Chairman
Indian Council of Historical Research
New Delhi
30 June 1999

S. SETTAR

Acknowledgements

Edited works are always built on the labour and cooperation of contributing scholars and the *Indian Archaeology in Retrospect* series is no exception to this. Ever since 1995, when this idea was first seriously and systematically formulated, nearly every scholar approached by us responded favourably, contributed his paper well in time and cooperated with us whenever we reached him on editorial details. Some of them helped with the names and addresses of scholars who may be interested to contribute to this series. As valuable as this was the share of experts who carefully went through the papers refereed and helped us ensure the standard.

All the contributors whose names are easily accessible in these volumes, the reviewers of papers who remain invisible, and those who gave us advice to extend the field of enquiry and also suggested names of scholars, deserve to be remembered here.

The project sprouted on the campus of Karnatak University, Dharwad, an old town located on the eastern edge of Western Ghats. Sylvan, quiet, cool though it is, in the mid-nineties, it was hardly suitable for establishing a global communication. This initial handicap was overcome by the electronic mailing facility established in the University. Soon this bug caught us both and invaded into our homes too. From this locale at Dharwad, we maintained contact with more than hundred scholars across the world, and more intensely with about eighty who stood by us till the end. We should recall the facilities generously provided by the authorities of Karnatak University, and in particular, the help given by Dr. S.C. Kendadmath, Librarian, and Mr R.M. Vatnal of the Information Centre. To fill the blanks in the Bibliography and to cross-check references, we had to reach centres within and outside India. The help given by Dorian Fuller, Nicky Boivin, Gregory Possehl, Rabi Mohanty and V. Selvakumar is gratefully remembered here. The Geological Society of India (Bangalore), Indian Society for Prehistoric and Quaternary Studies (Pune), and the Ethnographic and Folk Culture Society (Lucknow), permitted us to reproduce the papers of R.S. Pappu, M.D. Petraliglia, M.K. Dhavalikar and K.A.R. Kennedy published in their respective journals. Professor C. Venugopal of Karnatak University spared his valuable time to read the text and made suggestions to improve the diction. We are obliged to all these individuals and institutions.

The series needed a sponsor and a publisher and there was none in sight at the early stages of its implementation. Even when the volumes were nearing completion in 1998, its institutional base remained uncertain. When we approached the Indian Council of Historical Research, the authorities of the Council accepted to publish these volumes and also met the contingent expenses. The Manohar Publishers & Distributors, especially Mr. Ramesh Jain and Ajay Jain, have done nothing less than a miracle by producing these volumes in a record time. The authorities of the ICHR and the proprietors of Manohar deserve our whole-hearted thanks.

S. Settar
Ravi Korisettar

Introduction

S. SETTAR and RAVI KORISETTAR

Archaeology aims at reconstructing the life-ways of extinct societies. Its roots lie in the disciplines of geology and other natural sciences, while its contemporary conceptual framework is anthropological. The methods advocated by the new or processual archaeology facilitate a better understanding of man-environment relationships as well as adaptive mechanisms of prehistoric communities to a variety of environments and ecosystems. Environmental archaeology, geoarchaeology, archaeological geology, ethnoarchaeology, bioarchaeology, ecological archaeology, human ecology, etc., are not exclusive but mutually complementary disciplines. Specialists in these disciplines produce data which help reconstruct culture history, culture change and culture process, bolstered by a series of physical and chemical dating techniques. These disciplines remain valid and desirable today, as they were four decades ago, despite the paradigm shift from the processual to the post-processual.

The *Quaternary Environments and Geoarchaeology of India*, published in 1995 by the Geological Society of India, Bangalore, has drawn attention to the potential of environmental archaeology in India, but, perhaps, due to the limitation of its scope, several aspects of the Quaternary science could not be included in it. In order to fill such vacuum, the present volume, the third in the *Retrospect* series, has been planned. The fifteen papers presented here make an effort to cover a broad spectrum of research done in interdisciplinary archaeology and highlight the relevance of natural, physical, chemical and biological sciences to archaeology.

'Black Soils of India: a Survey of Pedological Research since 1947' offers pedoloigcal knowledge of the widespread black-brown soils and throws light on their agricultural potentiality during prehistoric times. Black soils (*regur*) are commonly known as black cotton soils, because of their widespread utilization for cotton cultivation. These soils, which constitute one of the most important non-alluvial environmental resources, have played a crucial role in the early phase of agriculture, during the third and second millennia BC. The vast spread of these soils, their suitability for agriculture under the prevailing monsoon regimes, their ability to retain moisture and the 'soil-ploughs-itself' character facilitated simple agricultural operations, especially in the semi-arid, low rainfall regions of the Deccan. They are quite extensive in Madhya Pradesh, Gujarat, Maharashtra, north Karnataka and western Andhra Pradesh—the regions where the early farming communities flourished during the second millennium BC. Pedologically, these soils are known as vertisols: they are characterized by gilgai-relief, surface cracking and slicken-sides. A striking morphological characteristic of these soils is its capacity to swell and shrink under dry and wet conditions respectively. These features as well as that of the associated bioturbation are responsible for the vertical mobility of these soils and also for the maintenance of fertility during repeated cultivation. The high clay content of these soils retain moisture so well as to enable crops to sustain on their own during long dry spells.

'The Indian Monsoon: Roots, Relations and Relevance' examines the progress made in understanding the behaviour of monsoon during the Late Quaternary (the last 125,000 years). Its impact on the ecodiversity as well as food production was obviously considerable as it regulated vital sources of fresh water in major parts of southern Asia. The monsoon exercised absolute control over the food-resources of the hunting gathering tribal communities and thus moulded the agricultural economy of the subcontinent. An attempt is made here to synthesize the multidisciplinary data, drawn from a variety of proxy records preserved in the alluvial, lacustral, littoral and offshore deposits, including pollen spectra as well as isotopic ratios. The palaeomonsoon record, covering the last 2.5 million years, shows that the intensity and fluctuations of Indian palaeomonsoon were in conformity with the long and short term global changes. The segmentation of habitats and forests, leading to differentiation of animal and plant species, were linked with this response to global changes. Expansion and contraction of forest and grasslands, affecting the biological species inhabiting these ecosystems, are a result of such response to fluctuations in the palaeomonsoon regimes. Attempts have been made in the last three decades to relate the archaeological evidence pertaining to the rise and fall in the economic prosperity with long and short term changes in monsoon regimes over much of South Asia.

The paper on 'Bioclimatology and Quaternary Palynology in India' deals with the climates of these two areas of investigation and constitute the thrust areas of Indian palaeoclimatology. Information on past climatic changes is of vital importance to understand the past and present plant life, because most animals are migratory and live in specialized niches created by the forest ecosystems in order to escape the impact of climate. The science of palynology provides a handy tool to reconstruct the past climate and environment, to build archaeological scenarios and also to trace climatic changes which occurred during the Quaternary. The terms 'arid' or 'humid', used often without bearing the intricacies of climate, are re-examined here. Sometimes, pollen grains used as markers of dry or wet conditions are themselves not very faithful indicators, and, in some cases, the change recorded through the pollen spectra is attributed to climate change, ignoring the anthropogenic and other factors that influenced changes in climate, for instance, shifts in river courses. In the Indian subcontinent, where spatial and temporal variations of climate are pronounced, some of the well-known palynological studies have revealed evidential gaps for expressing climate in its multifaceted complex and for deriving inferences on the patterns of climate change. With more radiocarbon dates now available under the International Geosphere-Biosphere Program (IGBP), the author of this study feels that it should be interesting to examine the causative factors that brought about climate change at the global, regional and local levels, to search their interconnectedness and to evaluate the role played by planetary causes—localized factors such as deforestation, etc.

'The Search for Fossil Man in South Asia: Retrospect and Prospect' points out the potential of the study of early man in South Asia. With the discovery of a fossil cranium of early man in the Narmada Valley, Central India, in 1980s, the frustration suffered during a decade-long search by the early explorers seemed to have come to an end. The excitement generated by the Anthropological Survey of India's reported discovery of a clavicle at Hathnora, proved to be short-lived, for a close scrutiny of this find led experts to question its authenticity and thus dampen the early enthusiasm. The author of this paper prefers to reserve his comments on the issue till he would have an opportunity to examine the specimen (personal communication). This account highlights the evidence of Late Pleistocene man associated with the microlithic assemblages in Sri Lanka which rank among the oldest in the world.

Though anthropology as a discipline is about five hundred years old, modern anthropology which deals with human activities, cultural behaviour, structure of language and communication, physical attributes, etc., is not older than a century and half. During the latter period, various sub-disciplines have emerged, including the one that deals with the biology of the extinct and living human populations. The two papers: (a) 'Bio-archaeology of Ancient India: an Integrated Perspective on the Past' and; (b) 'Biological Anthropology of Living Populations in Independent India: a Review', included in this volume, give a detailed account of the bio-anthropological research on both the prehistoric and living populations of India. These papers review the progress made in the area of biological anthropology and evaluate our current understanding. Besides illustrating the past and the present interactions between biology and behaviour, they also examine the environment in which humans live(d). This perspective has brought about a radical change in our understanding of human variability, thanks to the advances made in the fields of genetics, etiology and palaeontology/palaeoanthropology. The biological-anthropologists study living populations to reconstruct the evolutionary path taken by them and the directions towards which they are likely to move in future, adapting themselves to an environment in which they live, create and alter. Here again it has been observed that scientific studies of biological attributes of prehistoric populations have been often treated merely as appendages to excavation reports, mostly because of lack of appreciation of the relevance of biological features of prehistoric populations, derived from skeletal and dental remains. A close collaboration between anthropologists and archaeologists is strongly felt, for such an integrated approach would help establish a meaningful relationship between material culture, subsistence, human biology and environment, besides focusing attention on the role of plant domestication in changing the life-ways of prehistoric South Asians.

Recent studies in this field include dermatoglyphics, genetic markers and their association with diseases, dental anthropology, pattern of physical growth, adaptation and anthropological demography. This paper on the bioanthropology of the living populations traces the development of physical anthropology/biological anthropology in India from the Vedic times. In modern India, bioanthropological studies have tended to blend both Indian and British methodologies, and the history of which goes back to about one and a half centuries. During this period, many aspects of the biological anthropology of living

Indian populations have been explored. Though the first phase of these studies was more or less dominated by issues such as racial classifications and identification of the Negrito substratum of Indian populations, investigators during the recent past have come out of such obsession to focus attention on anthropometry, dermatoglyphics, growth rate in children, demography, dental anthropology, genetic markers and their association with diseases, etc. It is made evident that Indian biological anthropology has not only kept pace with the methodological developments in the West, but has made significant strides on its own. The increasing potential of this discipline is emphasized, besides showing how, in the light of the ever-growing new data, it is now maturing into a multifaceted and problem-oriented field of investigation.

The 'Hunter-Gatherer Studies in India: a Review' evaluates the progress made in this field in South Asia vis-à-vis the changing methodology in the West. The author expresses grave concern at the lack of organized research on the surviving hunter-gatherer populations in India, all the more because these tribal communities have been undergoing so much of transformation and in such rapid pace that their original identity would very soon be beyond recognition. The paper points out that there is a compelling need to redefine the terminology and also to change our outlook towards the so called hunter-gatherers. Areas where problems exist are identified and ways of tackling them at a very primary level have been proposed.

The paper on 'Agro-Pastoralism in Contemporary Ethnography: Its Relevance in Explanation of Archaeological Material in India' shows that there are very few pastoral communities in India which retain their original character. The extant pastoral groups have broadly adapted themselves to the following three ecosystems: (1) the high altitude of the Himalayas (Ladakh, Sikkim and Himachal Pradesh); (2) the Thar desert; and (3) to the semi-arid region of northern Deccan. They are represented by communities such as the Changpas, Gaddis, Bhutias, Raikes and Dhangars. A study of their life-ways as well as the involved man-land relationships indicates that pastoral communities inhabit either areas of low agricultural productivity, or vast stretches of forest/fallow land. It is observed that the labour-intensive, large-scale animal husbandry is achievable only through social manipulations and that transition from nomadism to sedentism is a complex process. Against this background of ethnographic understanding of the surviving pastoral communities, the archaeological record of pastoralism, from sites ranging from the Mesolithic to Chalcolithic cultures (of the second millennium BC) in Rajasthan (Bagor and Tilwara), the Ganga Valley (Dam Dama and Mahagara), the Vindhyas (Adamgarh and Kayatha) and northern Deccan (Inamgaon) has been examined to prove that the pastoral life during prehistoric times was governed as much by environmental factors as by the interactive trade between nomadic and sedentary agricultural populations.

'Fifty Years of Ethnoarchaeological Research in India: a Review' emphasizes the importance of ethnography and ethnoarchaeology in archaeological reconstructions of the life-ways of the prehistoric communities. Though ethnography has a long and independent history of its own, it was integrated into archaeology only during the last few decades. To test the validity of behavioural models, based on material culture studies, it is felt necessary to understand the patterns of prehistoric community life as well as the material culture of surviving primitive societies that bear direct historical link with them. Unfortunately, most ethnographic accounts of recent years lay emphasis on the non-material aspects of primitive societies such as marriage system, religion, etc., and as these have little relevance to archaeological studies, the archaeologists are compelled to conduct fresh surveys on their own to explore the ethnographic analogies. The latter include (a) direct historical analogy, and (b) general comparative analogy. In the former, the analogy is 'considered to provide the highest possibility of being correct because of the conditions of time, space and cultural affinity of the groups who produced the two sets of data are most compared', however, in the latter, an attempt is made to appreciate the analogues anywhere in time and space, on the basis of the present-day ethnographic reality.

During the 1930s-40s, the reconstruction of culture history of India was based predominantly on the Puranas and other Sanskrit literature; gaining further momentum during the closing decades of nationalism, it has now taken a queer twist. In the 1950s, location of Indus and Aryan sites preoccupied archaeologists, leading to the discovery and excavation of several 'protohistoric' sites such as Maheshwar and Navdatoli on the Narmada, and Nevasa and Nashik in the Pravara-Godavari Valleys. Similarity in the blade tool technology among these widely spaced sites and such other features led H.D. Sankalia to think that prehistory should be firmly based on anthropology, especially ethnography. This laid the foundation of Indian ethnoarchaeology. The excavation of Ahar in Rajasthan proved to be a turning point in this study, as it was here that Sankalia observed similarity between ancient Aharian houses and those of the Bhil tribe. The fact that India is a store house of the ethnographic present (with its cultural diversity, range of subsistence, settlement strategies and persistence of traditional crafts, etc.,) has led to gather a large body of ethnographic data both by anthropologists and anthropologists turned archaeologists during the last five decades.

The Stone Age ethnoarchaeological studies in India have paid considerable attention to understand the traditional subsistence and settlement patterns, seasonal mobility, technology and economic resources of surviving hunter gatherer communities. Ethnographic research has revealed that the natural world inhabited by the present tribal populations is not the same which was inhabited during prehistoric times and that modern subsistence patterns do not reflect the entire range of ancient parallels even in the same geographical region. With regard to later prehistoric phases, especially those of the Neolithic and Chalcolithic, ethnographic studies are carried out in conjunction with excavation of sites, be it Ahar in Rajasthan, Inamgaon in Maharashtra or Harappan sites in Gujarat. A study of the present village of Inamgaon, on the opposite banks of the excavated site on the Ghod river from an ethnoarchaeological perspective, has made it possible to identify dwellings/houses of various craftsmen (such as of potters, lapidaries, lime-makers and goldsmiths as well as of a 'ruling chief' of the community). Similarly, a number of floor-plans exposed at Walki have been identified as farmsteads on the basis of surviving parallels. Although this approach has been critically viewed by some, its validity has not been altogether questioned. Ethnographic research in the Inamgaon region was further extended to understand the migratory character as well as the over-night transit camps of the Dhangars who have adapted themselves to the semi-arid environment of Maharashtra. The main goal of this study is to understand the prehistoric settlement organizations both at site specific and regional levels.

Animals constituted an important source of food, especially for the hunting and gathering communities. The paper on 'Quaternary Vertebrate Palaeontology in India: Fifty Years of Research' deals with the vertebrate palaeontological studies in South Asia and traces the development of modern or the New Palaeontology. Unlike general palaeontology, which forms a major branch of geology, Quaternary palaeontology is an important branch of Quaternary science. The latter lays a basis for understanding the origins of animal domestication during the Holocene, and examines the relations between extinct and extant forms of animals, taxonomy, etc. Great strides have already been made in the study of Pleistocene palaeoanthropology of South Asia, with one of the landmark discoveries being the fossil of a partial cranium of advanced *Homo erectus*/archaic *Homo sapiens* from the Narmada Valley. Studies in vertebrate palaeontology have resulted in the identification of three distinct phases—lower, middle and upper—of the Pleistocene. Owing to the mix-up of fossil animal bones and Palaeolithic assemblages in riverine deposits, the precise demarcation of these subdivisions has not been made easy. A large variety of faunal remains, comprising mammals, ostrich egg-shells, reptiles, amphibians, fish and microvertebrates, obtained from such deposits, facilitate better understanding of the palaeoenvironmental conditions. As this assemblage comprises species exotic to South Asia, it has been surmised that the majority of the larger mammals may have migrated to this centre from Egypt, Arabia, Central Asia and North America; similarly, it has been assumed that rhinoceros, horse and camel, all originating in North America, may have evolved further in some countries of Central and West Asia before reaching India. The evolutionary processes, the accompanying animal demographic pressures as well as long term cyclic changes in climate that took place during the last 60 million years in particular, are believed to be the major causative factors which led to the migration of animal communities to suitable habitats across the globe. Palaeontological research in South Asia holds promise for the application of multidisciplinary research for a better understanding of prehistoric man-animal relationship.

Archaeobotany and archaeozoology are complementary disciplines of archaeology; they provide aids to understand man-land relationships of prehistoric times. The archaeobotanist identifies wild and domesticated plants, investigates the origins of domestication of plants and traces the progress made in ancient agricultural practices. The 'Fifty Years of Archaeobotanical Studies in India: Laying a Solid Foundation' traces the growth of this study in South Asia, highlights its current trends and of its future prospects. This is based on the ever increasing wealth of archaeobotanical data obtained from excavation. Both quantitative and qualitative results obtained during the post-Independence period in India are presented here. Among the many interesting aspects of this study are: (a) synthesis of current evidence (as it relates to the origin and spread of food crops during the three millennia BC); (b) examination of the theoretical issues connected with the spread of crops and agriculture in South Asia (colonization of farming communities, by diffusion or by some other factors); and (c) factors responsible for intensification of agriculture, including the relationship between agriculture and climate. Attention is focused on these to establish proper understanding of the 'Neolithic Revolution'. This survey also assesses the present state of our understanding of the origins of agricultural economy as well as the widespread distribution of food crops in prehistoric South Asia.

The paper on the 'Researches in Archaeozoology of the Holocene Period (Including the Harappan Tradition in India and Pakistan)' goes into the development of archaeozoological studies in India vis-a-vis the methodological and theoretical developments in the West. Till mid-1960s, these studies were more or less confined to the identification of species and description of osteological parameters. The metrical approach to the study of animal remains made it possible to distinguish the closely related animal taxa and to develop criteria for identifying domesticated animals, distinguishing them from the rest of the faunal assemblage. After 1960s, the palaeopathology of animals (both diseases and human induced deformities) began to assert an important place. Specialists from the Deccan College, Pune, the M.S. University of Baroda, Vadodara and the University of Allahabad, Allahabad, within the country, the Dutch and American scholars from abroad, are responsible for the growth of this science in India. Faunal remains recovered from a large number of excavated sites have been studied in Indian centres, keeping pace with the methodological developments in the West. The identification of diverse species and intra-site faunal variability in relation to ecological opportunities through time are some of the major achievements of the Indian archaeozoological studies. Determination of the antiquity of domesticated horse, cattle and sheep/goat has been a part of this study. Despite these advances, it is regrettable to note that most of the excavators continue to treat the archaeofaunal data merely as an appendage to their reports and rarely attempt to relate their implications for understanding the man-animal relationship.

'Archaeometallurgical Studies in India: a Review' deals with the progress of research made in this field (the techniques and methods of smelting, alloying, casting, craftsmanship of smiths, etc.) during the last five decades in India. It also explores the prehistoric techniques of procurement (by means of trade, exchange, mining/quarrying, etc.) and sourcing of raw material. The chemical analyses of a variety of metal objects from the Neolithic-Chalcolithic, Chalcolithic, Iron Age and Harappan sites have resulted in provenance studies of metals, mineral resources and alloying techniques. It is now evident that Mature Harappan phase witnessed an upsurge of metallurgical activity and that Harappan copper technology was far superior to that of the Ganga Valley copper hoard culture of later period. Though metal alloying continued in the post-Harappan times, as attested by the Chalcolithic sites in the Deccan and Central India, the casting techniques are found to be far inferior to those of the Harappan. The review goes into these issues, noting the progress made during the pre-Independent and post-Independent periods of our history.

The science of archaeological chemistry provides a set of chemical methods specifically to restore and conserve archaeological artefacts, including stone, soil, metal and organic materials. These methods are also applied to determine the composition, structure and properties of materials used in the past. The conservation and preservation techniques are employed to retrieve the physical and chemical properties of artefactual materials which are closed to visual observation. The 'Progress of Archaeological Chemistry in India' probes into the history of this branch and shows how our knowledge of physical and chemical properties of artefactual material helps explain the ancient methods of production, fabrication, choice and provenance of raw material. It also reveals how research in archaeological chemistry has kept pace not only with the spurt of excavation, but also with the changing methodology evolved from time in the West and how these methods have served the cause of the conservation of monuments, the most visible face of our cultural heritage. The nature and extent of human activity at excavated sites are determined by the chemical analysis of phosphate in the anthrosols (soils associated with human activity); chemical analysis of bones, in terms of their elemental composition, helps reconstruct prehistoric dietary practices; and measurement of fluorine/phosphate ratios from bones serves as a handy tool for determining the relative chronology. These methods have been standardized specially to serve the Indian prehistoric sites.

The paper on 'Dating of Indian Stone Age and Quaternary Deposits' is a brief review of the dating techniques employed in South Asia during the last fifty years, especially after the radiocarbon revolution of the 1950s. The basic principles governing the dating methods such as potassium-argon, radiocarbon, uranium-series, palaeomagnetism and thermoluminescence are given as a backdrop to the list of radiometric dates obtained for the South Asian prehistoric and protohistoric cultures.

Black Soils of India: a Survey of Pedological Research since 1947

G.S. DASOG

INTRODUCTION

Black soils of India are popularly known as 'Regurs'. The term originated from the Telugu word 'Nalla Ragada' meaning sticky black earth. Other vernacular names include gilgai soils (Australia), Smonitzas (Yugoslavia, Austria), Tirs (Morocco) and sols de paluds (France). These soils are referred to as vertisols in Soil Taxonomy developed by U.S. Department of Agriculture (Soil Survey Staff 1975) and in FAO/UNESCO Soil Map of the World. The name 'vertisol' has been coined from the Latin root meaning 'to churn or turn over'. In India black soils constitute an important soil group covering an area of 73 million hectares (Murthy et al. 1982), constituting 22 per cent of the total geographical area of the country (Fig. 1). They are quite extensive in Madhya Pradesh, Gujarat, Maharashtra, north Karnataka and western Andhra Pradesh (Table 1). They also occur in other parts of India but to a smaller extent. Due to their singular properties this soil group had attracted considerable attention from among Indian and overseas pedologists. Considerable work on these soils was reported before India's Independence. Some of the early studies include the works of Bal (1935) on black soils of the erstwhile Central Provinces, Ramaiah (1937) on soils of Tungabhadra project, Desai (1942) on soils of the former Hyderabad State, and Basu and Sirur (1938) on black soils of Deccan Canal areas in Maharashtra. Annet (1910) and Harrison and Ramaswamy Sivan (1912) studied the colour of black soils. After 1947 much work has been done on these soils. The research work done on this subject is reviewed by Dudal (1965), Anon.(1982), Ahmad (1983),

TABLE 1. DISTRIBUTION OF BLACK SOILS IN INDIA

State	Area (m ha)	Area expressed as per cent of total geographical area
Maharashtra	29.9	7.9
Madhya Pradesh	16.7	5.1
Gujarat	8.2	2.6
Andhra Pradesh	7.2	2.2
Karnataka	6.9	2.1

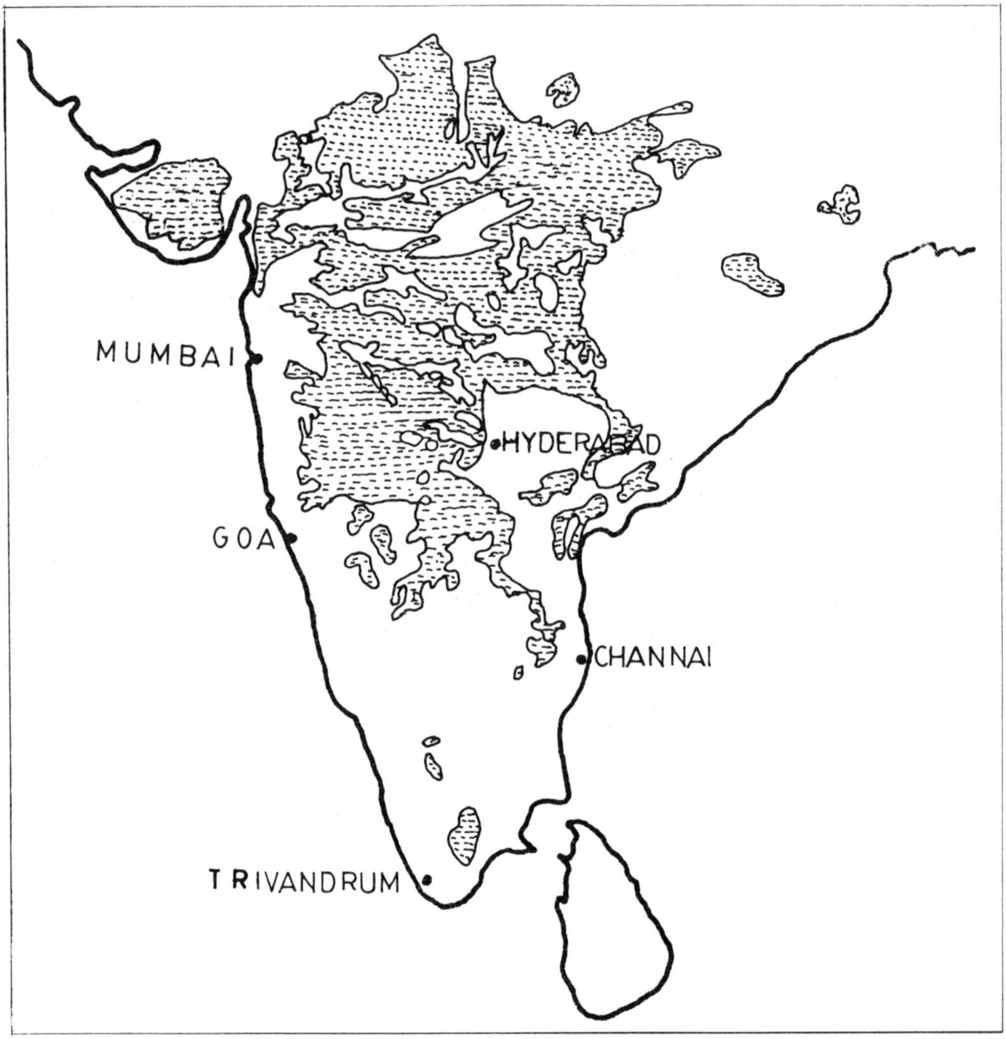

Fig. 1. Distribution of Black soils in India (Redrawn from Dudal and Eswaran 1988).

Murthy (1988), Wilding and Tessier (1988) and by Ahmad and Mermut (1996). The morphology, pedogenesis and classification of these soils with special reference to India is reviewed in the following sections. The word black soils and vertisols are interchangeably used in this review.

MORPHOLOGY

Morphology is the most important feature used to differentiate black soils from others. Indeed, the concept of vertisols is derived from their morphological manifestations (Simonson 1954; Eswaran et al. 1988). The major morphological markers of vertisols are gilgai micro-relief, surface cracking and slickensides (Soil Survey Staff 1992). Other morphological characteristics described in the literature include colour, surface mulching, granular structure and carbonate nodules.

The most striking morphological characteristics are associated with swelling and shrinking on alternate wetting and drying cycles. Vertisols were believed to be remarkably homogeneous. The differences in degree of expression of any morphological characteristics reflect the differences in chemical, physical, mineralogical and environmental conditions.

Gilgai

This is an aboriginal Australian term meaning small water hole for the ground surface characterized by knolls and depressions and is a common feature of many clay soils in subtropical and tropical areas of the world.

The gilgai feature is not found in all black soils. Some do not have them, and with others they have been removed by man due to tillage. Gilgai features are reported in vertisols from U.S.A., the Sudan, India, Australia and several other countries. Spectacular gilgai features are reported in vertisols from Texas. Gilgai formation seems to be dependent, at least in part, on the shrinking, cracking, swelling and heaving characteristics of particular clay types (Probert et al. 1987). However, they are not present in all black soils. For example, gilgai features are not prominent in the semi-arid southern India, compared to central India with a higher rainfall. Sehgal and Bhattacharjee (1988) reported that gilgai features were prominent in the black soils of Maharashtra and Madhya Pradesh which occur in areas receiving rainfall >1000 mm per year. Various types of gilgai features described in detail by Paton (1974).

Cracking

Cracks are another striking morphological feature of vertisols which are used to define this soil order. Partial drying of soil causes the formation of cracks. The open cracks are tortuous and may be 1 cm or more wide at a depth of 50 cm and may extend to a depth of 1 m or more in many vertisols. Due to cultivation and wetting of the surface cracks may not be observed in the plow zone, but those below this zone continue to exist. The depth, frequency, size and shape of the cracks are related to the differential moisture status of the cracking zone (Dudal and Eswaran 1988).

Cracks are formed due to drying of a moist soil when tensile strength exceeds the cohesive strength of the soil (Blokhuis 1982). Studies on evolution of cracks have revealed two stages in the shrinkage process (Hallaire 1984). At first thin cracks (less than 5 mm wide) appear with about 3 cm spacing. Later in the drying process, some of these cracks open wider (more than 1 cm) with about 20 cm spacing while the remaining cracks are partially or even totally closed. On a field scale, it is only the latter types that are measurable.

Data available on cracks in vertisols for different climatic regions of the world are limited. It is obvious that no single parameter can adequately explain cracking intensity. Dasog and Shashidhara (1993) considered crack volume per unit area as the best index of the intensity of cracking as it takes width, depth and spacing of cracks into account. Cracking intensity so measured varied in relation to the moisture depletion by different crops. Cracks are disadvantageous as well as advantageous. Cracks enhance moisture loss from the soil during growing season. On the other hand at the onset of monsoon the open cracks facilitate quick entry of water into the otherwise slowly permeable soil. Soil management practices to prevent cracking during growing season such as mulching will help conserve moisture.

Characterization of cracks is done as part of the profile description and wider and deeper cracks are emphasized. Systematic measurements of crack width, depth and other parameters for an area greater than that of the pedon is very limited and the measurement techniques used are not uniform.

Surface Granular Structure

In several vertisols, the surface 2-10 cm layer is a loose mulch consisting of medium to fine granular aggregates (Blokhuis 1982). As defined by Wenke and Grant (1994) mulching is the ability of a dry remolded soil material to form aggregates (5 mm size) after only a few cycles of drying and gentle wetting. The surface structure of vertisols ranges from the fine granular to the massive (Hubble 1984). The degree of aggregation in the surface layer of a vertisol is a key index of the soils' agricultural potential. For crop production, well aggregated surfaces readily form fine seed beds, and decrease subsoil desiccation by forming a vapour and thermal barrier between the subsoil and air (de Vos and Virgo 1969). The degree of structure development in the whole profile and the profile's suitability for plant growth is said to be reflected in the aggregation of the surface layer as is vertisol's ability to respond to tillage induced structure degradation. There are a few authors who suggest that all vertisols have finely-aggregated surface layers. The surface mulch provides a fine seed bed and partly or fully fills the cracks. It is reported that the thickness of the mulch decreases in passing through semi-arid to humid areas of Sudan (de Vos and Virgo 1969; Blokhuis 1982). In the Sudan, the surface mulch is not well developed where rainfall exceeds 500 mm (Jewitt et al. 1979). Similarly, in India, Sehgal and Bhattacharjee (1988) noted that vertisols of the semi-arid regions had 20-30 mm thick pulverized granular surface mulch. Work on the dynamics of surface structure is not attempted in India unlike in Australia.

Vertisols with finely aggregated surface soil provide a much better medium for plant growth, because the granular topsoil has more porosity, acts as a barrier to vapour transfer from the subsoil and decreases the effect of contraction cracks (Warkentin 1982). On the other hand, those in the sub-humid regions often have a 5-10 mm thick brittle crust which breaks up under the impact of rain. This surface granular mulch may fill cracks during the dry season. Upon wetting, the mulch in the cracks may provide somewhat lower bulk density than the surrounding soil, depending upon the strength of the granules.

Slickensides

The term 'slickenside' refers to a surface that has a polished and shiny appearance and that also may be striated or grooved (Dudal and Eswaran 1988). The term was first used by geologists and is now used to describe the surface of structural aggregates. The term slickenside does not refer to a structural element. Wilding and Tessier (1988) state that slickensides are 'the unifying morphogenetic marker found in all vertisols'. They are actually planes along which failure occurs due to swelling pressure exceeding the shear strength of the soil mass.

The depth at which slickensides start appearing in the profile varies widely. Based on the data for a number of soil profiles from India, Vadivelu and Challa (1985) stated that slickensides occur deeper in regions of high rainfall and at a shallower depth in the drier regions. In semi-arid areas, the slickensides occurred at depths ranging from 22 to 65 cm (average 47 cm) and in the sub-humid to humid regions it varied from 31 to 105 cm (average 60 cm).

In Australian clay soils, slickensides or shear planes are distributed from 0.3 m below the surface to a projected limit of 1.3 to 1.8 m (Knight 1980) although they extend deeper in vertisols of Israel (Yaalon and Kalmar 1978). Knight (1980) states that the ratio of depth of maximum number of slickensides to maximum depth of occurrence is about half in all the cases, an observation that has to be confirmed.

When slickensides intersect, they may form ortho-rhombic structural elements (wedge-shaped natural structural elements or sphenoids) that have their long axis tilted 10-60° from the horizontal. Krishna and Perumal (1948) were among the pioneers who described this unique structure and called it lentil structure.

Colour

Vertisols are generally dark-coloured although they may have a brownish or even brownish-reddish colour depending on their composition, moisture and associated parent material. Despite the fact that the total organic matter content of black soils is not different from other soils occurring under similar environmental conditions, their dark colour is attributed to the complexation or chelation of organic colloids with smectite. Singh (1954) observed that the organic matter was difficult to oxidize in the presence of manganese which contributed to the rapid decomposition of peroxide (H_2O_2). The efficiency of peroxide is related to the exchangeable bases. Only when carbonates were removed was he able to succeed in removing the pigmenting compounds in these soils. Singh (1956) observed that only those clays containing montmorillonite became very dark. The nature of clay mineral is, therefore, a very important factor in the formation of the dark colour.

Worthy of consideration here is that the dark colour associated with many of the vertisols is not due to high organic matter contents but rather due to the intense mixing of organic matter with clay. The organic matter content in these soils is generally less than 1 per cent. Adsorption of organic matter onto the surfaces of clay particles appears to be mediated through anaerobic conditions that are known to exist temporarily during wet seasons. For similar reasons, very dark vertisols generally occur in depressions or experience waterlogged conditions for a part of the wet season. Dudal (1965) suggested that colour of the soil may be controlled by the drainage condition, duration and severity of the dry season, composition and age of the parent material.

Carbonate Nodules

Indurated secondary carbonate nodules are common features of many black soils of India and elsewhere. They may be inherited or pedogenic. The former type is present in several particle sizes. Pedogenic carbonates may form from multiple pathways and require dissolution of primary calcium-bearing minerals or inherited carbonates and subsequent precipitation due to supersaturation of calcium bicarbonate and decrease in partial pressure of carbon dioxide. The depth at which these accumulate is directly related to the amount of rainfall of the area. The black soils in the semi-arid areas of southern India have greater concentration of carbonates than those in central India. For example, in the 20 m ha of deep black cotton soils in Bundelkhand and Malwa plateau and Narmada Valley, 4.8 Pg of $CaCO_3$ stock is estimated as against 24 Pg in about same area in black and associated soils of Maharashtra and northern Karnataka and western Telangana plateau (Pal et al. 1999).

Two morphological types were identified by Mermut and Dasog (1986) and later by Nandi and Dasog (1992) in some vertisols of India. The larger ones were white with irregular surfaces whereas the smaller ones were black with smooth surfaces. The black ones were also more rounded, compact and homogeneous in size. Inorganic radiocarbon dating (Table 2) indicated that both the morphological types were formed as a result of supergene processes. Mean residence time of the nodules was found to increase with depth. Black glaebules from the Bijapur profile yielded radiocarbon ages of 25,000 and 27,050 yr BP which were much older than the white glaebules from the Sultanpur (Kasireddipalli soil) profile. The ages reported in Table 2 indicate the average values of the nodules, not necessarily the real ages of the nodules. However, these suggest that vertisols with only white nodules are considerably younger than those dominated by the black group. The vertisols developed in the sedimentary plains of Sudan are of two types: soft diffuse, and hard discrete carbonate nodules (Blokhuis et al. 1968/69). In the

TABLE 2: INORGANIC RADIOCARBON AGES OF SELECTED CARBONATE GLAEBULES IN THE SULTANPUR AND THE BIJAPUR SOILS, INDIA

Profile	Morphologic group	Horizon	Depth (cm)	Age (MRT)[a] (yr BP)
Sultanpur	White	Ap+A1	0-79	4,085±135
Sultanpur	White	AC	79-130	7,705±210
Bijapur	Black	Ap	0-35	25,000±1150
Bijapur	Black	A1	35-55	27,050±1500
Bijapur	White	Ap	0-35	14,770±790

[a]MRT = Mean residence time.

substratum, segregations consist of both soft with diffuse boundary and hard and discrete. In the solum, however, only the hard ones were found; these increased in size and abundance towards the surface. As in the vertisols of India, mentioned above, part of the carbonate segregations studied in Sudan were also coated with iron manganese. Blokhuis (1982) suggested that non-calcareous Fe-Mn nodules may be formed below the zone of pedoturbation, when hydromorphic conditions prevail in the substratum.

MICROMORPHOLOGY

Micromorphology is a powerful tool to study the microfabrics of soils so as to understand the pedogenic processes operating in these soils. Micromorphological studies were not attempted till recently due to lack of facilities and trained manpower. Kooistra (1982) documented the micromorphological properties of Benchmark soils of India in which were included black soils as well.

Groundmass

Groundmass by definition forms the base material of a thin section excluding the pedofeatures (Bullock et al. 1985). A porphyroskelic related distribution in which the plasma occurs as a dense ground mass and skeleton grains are set after the manner of phynocrysts rock (Brewer 1976) is commonly reported in black soils. The plasma and skeleton grains occur as a dense mass in the soil aggregates resulting in the formation of porphyroskelic fabric. The micromorphological description of black soils include a fine textured ground mass with a porphyric (porphyroskelic) related distribution. The granules are separated by packing and compound packing voids. The subsoil is typically porphyroskelic.

Plasma Separations

The fabric of the fine materials has received considerable attention. This is determined by the interference colour of clay domains under the petrographic microscope. Swelling processes in soils result in micro-shear within the soil fabric. Such stresses reorient the individual clay plates into lineated zones with face to face clay alignment (Wilding and Tessier 1988). Stress-related fabrics such as masepic, skelsepic, vosepic and maybe lattisepic plasmic fabrics are, therefore, commonly observed in black soils. The plasmic fabric of Indian black soils reported by Kooistra (1982) is predominantly vo-masepic (oriented clay around voids and in the matrix) and ma-skelsepic (oriented clay around skeleton grains and matrix). Dasog et al. (1988) reported masepic fabric. Masepic fabrics denote microscale shearing due to unequal stresses acting on peds. Kalbande et al. (1992) observed that black soils from sub-humid regions of India had porostriated (vosepic) plasmic fabric whereas those in semi-arid regions exhibited mosaic-speckled or granostriated (skelsepic) fabric. It is known that drying of unconfined soils do not produce reorganization of clay domains, even under irregular drying of remolded clay (Nettleton et al. 1983). It requires rather a very strong force to produce even a moderately strong preferred orientation; hence distortion (shear), but not compaction, appear to be the significant cause of preferred orientation (Clark 1970). Dalrymple and Jim (1984) also concluded that any well-developed masepic fabric in soils is likely to be formed by processes in addition to wetting and drying.

Voids

The void (pore) type that dominates these soils is planar void with a preferred orientation similar to that of slickensides (Bui and Mermut 1989). Planar voids are interconnected and they play a very important role in water movement in these soils. Methylene blue was added to the percolating water to stain water conducting pores (Bouma and Loveday 1988). Both channels and planar voids are known to conduct water. With the advent of image analysis technique the pore geometry, size distribution, orientation, etc., can be studied using thin sections of these soils (Bui and Mermut 1989).

Pedofeatures

Pedofeatures reported for vertisols include carbonate and Fe-Mn nodules, clay cutans, animal activity, relict features and other neoformations such as gypsum and barite. However, only carbonate nodules are reviewed here as these are the most common features in these soils.

The micromorphology of carbonate nodules, especially in non-calcareous vertisols has been reported by many workers (Blokhuis et al. 1968/69; Govindarajan et al. 1972; Kooistra 1982; Mermut and Dasog 1986; Dasog et al. 1988).

Four Indian vertisols from four different rainfall regions studied by Mermut and Dasog (1986) showed that a considerable proportion of calcitic nodules were impregnated with Fe-Mn oxyhydroxides in the soils from low rainfall regions; however, they were rare or absent in the soil from the high rainfall region. The presence of Fe-Mn oxyhydroxides in calcite nodules was attributed to past hydromorphic conditions. Kooistra (1982) also observed that the nodules exhibited partly or fully accumulations of sesquioxides. Evidence of climatic changes during the soil formation is preserved in the carbonate micromorphological record.

As pointed out by Wilding and Flach (1985), micromorphology is used to determine the direction of pedogenic processes rather than quantify the magnitude of such expressions. They also suggested that micromorphology is most useful when set in context with observations that span the continuum from visible to submicroscopic levels of resolution and when integrated with studies using chemical and physical methods. Such attempts are few in the literature. Thin sections used in fabric analysis of vertisols are made after air drying the soils and it is very difficult to dry the soil without causing any shrinkage (Eswaran et al. 1988). It is stated that there is a need to establish the petrographic changes accompanying changes in moisture status and to establish whether the changes are reversible.

FORMATION OF BLACK SOILS

The genesis of vertisols is strongly influenced by displacement of soil mass due to pedoturbation induced by contraction and expansion of the soil due to drying and wetting. The formation of these specific features are caused by a clayey texture, a dominance of swelling clays in the clay fraction and marked changes in moisture content (Hubble 1984).

Soil-Forming Factors

Soil is formed due to the influence of climate, vegetation, parent rock and topography over a period of time. One or more of these factors may influence the soil formation more than others in any given situation. In respect of black soils the so called passive factors of parent rock and topography are important. The influence of soil forming factors—parent material, topography and climate, are examined below.

PARENT MATERIAL

In India black soils occur extensively on basalt or alluvium derived from it. However, they also occur in other areas covered by granite-gneiss, schist, shale and limestone. Vertisols may develop in situ from the parent materials mentioned earlier, but in general are associated with transported materials (Eswaran et al. 1988). The basic quality of the various parent materials associated with the formation of these soils is that they must have smectites in them (as in the case of marine shales, alluvium) or weathering must produce it as a result of neogenesis or transformation from primary minerals. A situation of high swelling clay content sets the stage for the processes that are discussed later.

The formation and stability of smectites are dependent on the Si activity as well as pH. At high pH, and in the presence of high potentials of Si as well as Mg smectites form, a process which is also favoured by poor drainage conditions. The conditions required for the transformations of other primary or secondary minerals into smectites are also similar. The microenvironmental conditions for this transformation are well established; essentially pH conditions of 7 or higher. Pal and Deshpande (1987a) indicated that smectite is the first weathered product of Deccan basalt. The weathered materials of basalt must have filled the valleys and piedmont areas on which are found black soils. Though basalts are most favourable parent rocks for the formation of black soils, these can undoubtedly form on other rocks as well. As pointed out by Tardy et al. (1973) in the entire climatic range, smectite is the first mineral to form from all rocks that contain weatherable minerals. Smectites do form from the weathering of granite-gneissic rocks as reported by Pal and Deshpande (1987a) and Barabhari (1991). Pal and Deshpande (1987a) reported smectite and kaolinite in red soils and smectite in black soils. They further state that kaolinite is formed at the expense of smectite with progressive weathering.

Many authors have studied the genesis and properties of black soils formed on different parent materials (Tamhane and Namjoshi 1959; Karale et al. 1969; Dasog and Hadimani 1980; Dasog et al. 1990). All these studies have revealed that there are no gross differences in their morphological and clay mineralogical properties. Physical properties are reported to differ among black soils formed from different parent materials (Hirekurubar et al. 1991). Soil chemical properties and fertility status may show subtle differences.

Due to geomorphic instability, there is often no relation between the underlying geology and the black soils formed on them. Often the rocks underlying these soils are considered as the parent rock without close examination. For example, vast stretch of black soils found distributed in the Bhima Basin have an abrupt boundary between the rock and soil. The parent material of these soils may be denuded and transported basalt from the surrounding country (Paddayya and Petraglia 1996). The similarity of texture and other chemical properties among black soils formed on basalts and limestone (unpublished data) attests to the fact that these are formed from transported and redeposited basalt. Similarly, vast stretches of black soils formed in the Malaprabha Basin have no genetic relation with the underlying geology (Barabhari 1991).

Topography and Relief

Black soils are known to occur on nearly level to gently undulating topography. They generally occupy midland and low-lying positions. Simonson (1954) documented that in the Deccan plateau, where black soils commonly occur, the gently undulating land surface consisted of a succession of two ridges with broad crests that are separated by shallow valleys, often fairly wide. Long gentle slopes leading down the ridge crests towards the valleys result in a mildly undulating land form. Large areas in the states of Maharashtra, Madhya Pradesh and Andhra Pradesh are with slopes between 0 to 8 per cent (Simonson 1954). They generally occur in areas with slopes not exceeding 5 per cent.

The effect of relief on the development of black soils assumes importance in a catenary sequence (a chain of soils along a toposequence). The elements of topography have been a decisive factor in the formation of black soils developed on gneiss in Bundelkhand, locally called *mar* and *kabar*. These soils occupied valleys and depressions (Mukherjee and Agarwal 1943). The classic work on catenary soils is that of Biswas and Gawande (1962) who recognized four diverse soils in a catena on sedimentary formations in Chattisgarh Basin in Madhya Pradesh. Drainage conditions and translocation of soluble salts in the lower end of topography favour the formation of smectite and hence favour the formation of black soils. Nagelschmidt et al. (1940) found under the same climate and parent rock soils with kaolinitic mineralogy in soils on slopes and montmorillonitic soils where drainage was poor. The association of red soils on slopes and black soils in valleys is a common phenomenon in many parts of the country more so in peninsular India (Desai 1942; Krishnamoorthy and Govindarajan 1977; Rudramurthy et al. 1997).

Climate

The climate includes two important components, namely, precipitation and temperature which have specific and combined effect on the formation of soil. Precipitation governs the air-moisture regime of the soil and determines the character and extent of leaching to which a soil is subjected. Temperature on the other hand, influences the rate of chemical reaction, organic matter decomposition, microbial activities and finally, the efficiency of rainfall through its control on evapotranspiration. Black soils in India are found extensively in the monsoon semi-arid regions including patches of arid, dry sub-humid and moist sub-humid areas. The rainfall of the black soil regions vary from 300 to 1500 mm (Murthy et al. 1982). The mean annual temperature ranges from 24 to 30 °C. The climate is characterized by hot and dry summers and mild winters. In essence black soils are found in a climate characterized by a period with sufficient moisture deficit to induce cracking followed by a wet period to induce swelling.

Soil Forming Processes

The unique morphological expression of the vertic properties can only occur if there is a moisture deficit of the soil. The genesis of these soils is likely to be more complex than generally recognized (Blokhuis 1982). Of the many processes that operate soil displacement caused by swelling and shrinking is most important.

In black soils there are two main causes of development of slickensides. One is the self-swallowing concept (Buol et al. 1980) referred as pedoturbation model in which surficial soil material is continuously being incorporated into the subsoil through cracks. The varying extents of infilling of the cracks by surficial material during dry seasons prevent these cracks from completely closing up during wet seasons. As a result, the subsoil is pushed upwards and sideways resulting in the formation of slickensides, spenoids and gilgai (Fig. 2). This cycle repeats with time. This homogenization process (pedoturbation) also results in the lack of a distinct horizon development in black soils other than the A and C horizons. However, pedoturbation is a slow process and will not result in a complete mixing of the soil material because they show (i) systematic decrease of organic matter and increase of soluble salts and carbonates with depth as in other soils (Wilding 1985; Dasog et al. 1987) and (ii) systematic increase in the mean residence time of organic matter with depth just as in non-cracking soils (Yaalon and Scharpenseel 1972). El Abedine et al. (1971) reported an annual displacement of 0.33 per cent of the surface material into the subsoil. Such estimates for Indian black soils is not available. The slow rates are considered not to hinder completely the long-term translocation of salts and carbonates and accumulation of organic matter (Wilding 1985).

The other cause is due to generation of swelling pressure upon wetting in the subsoil that exceed the shear strength of the soil resulting in failure planes called slickensides (Fig. 3). This is referred as the soil mechanics model in the literature. The theory underlying the soil mechanics model was presented independently by Yaalon and Kalmar (1978) and Knight (1980). Soil sloughing through cracks is not a pre-requisite to the formation of slickensides as maximum development of slickensides was observed below the depth of maximum seasonal cracking and infilling (Yaalon and Kalmar 1978). The slickensides form at a particular depth range as illustrated in Figures 4 and 5. They are not seen near the surface because the swelling pressures are relieved by the upward movement of the soil. They are not seen deeper in the profile as the swelling pressure is counterd by the overburden weight (pressure) of the soil. They are observed between 50 and 150 cm because of confinement. The relatively small slickensides formed by pedogenesis must not be confused with large slickensides of the substratum associated with alluvial or lacustrine sediments due to large scale land shifting or mass wasting.

It is clear that in many black soils both processes operate. However, their effects on profile development are expected to be somewhat different (Ahmad 1983). The swelling pressures due to 'self-swallowing' are confined to the depth of profile in which the cracking occurs and the vertical component of the swelling pressure could be greater, contributing to heaving and subsidence on wetting and drying. Sufficient shrink-swell activity that would produce sphenoids and slickensides is critical for the formation of vertisols. Most vertisols have a combination of sphenoids and slickensides, but some have only one or the other. Formation of both features require the soil material to be in a plastic state.

Yaalon and Kalmar (1978) postulated that sand grains move upward in the profile in these soils based on their observation in Israel. According to them, during the advancing of the wetting front into a dry soil any moisture reaching a larger sand grain will first wet the clay-rich matrix below the sand grain, causing it to be pushed upwards as the clay swells (Fig. 6). Since drying is a gradual process, this would not return the sand grain to its original position in the solum. The uplift of sand grains by this process is expected to be slow compared to development of slickensides. This and other pedoturbation processes mentioned above are not without implications in archaeological studies as many of the Neolithic objects may have been displaced from their original position in these soils.

CLASSIFICATION

The earlier classification included shallow black soils for those that were less than 30 cm; medium deep black soils that were 30-100 cm deep and deep black soils with a depth of more than 100 cm. Along with depth the presence or absence of gypsum or carbonate layer in the subsoil was also considered by Ramaiah (1937). The discussion in this review is confined to only those soils that are more than 50 cm deep.

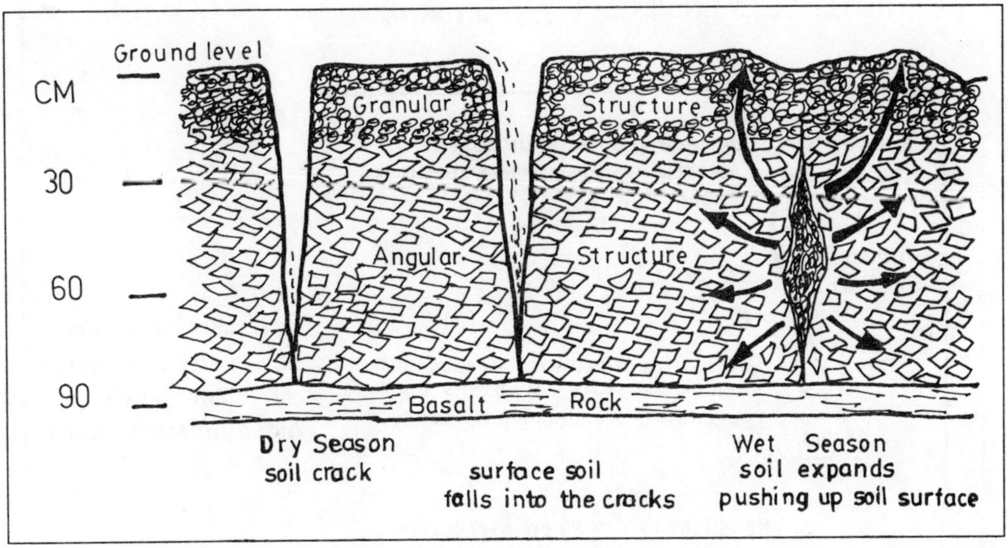

Fig. 2. Pedoturbation or self-swallowing model of formation of spenoids, slickenside and gilgai in black soils (after Buol et al. 1980).

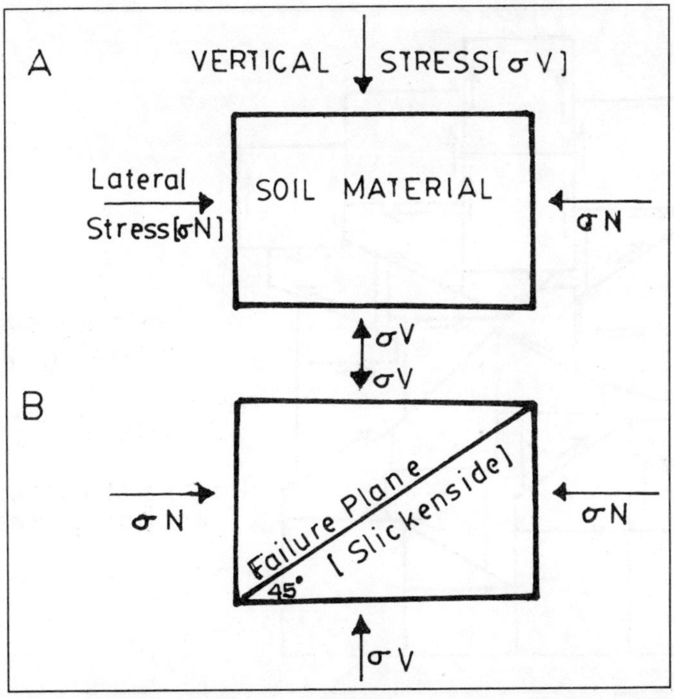

Fig. 3. Soil mechanics model of slickenside formation when confining stresses exceed soil shear strength: (A) Vertical and horizontal stresses acting on a soil ped, and (B) Orientation of shear plane at 45° to the principal stress.

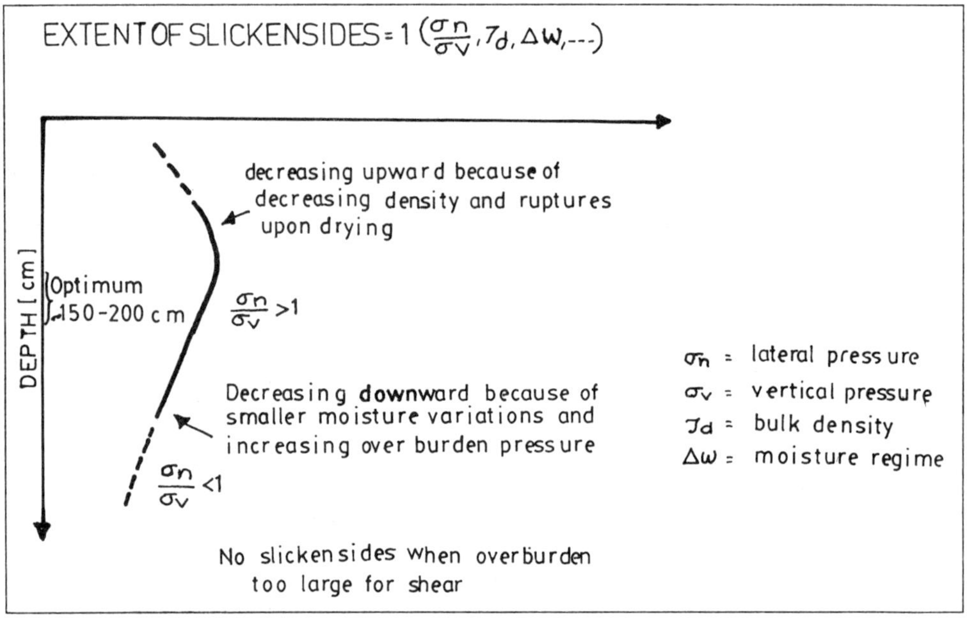

Fig. 4. Effect of stress distribution with depth on extent of slickensides in a vertisol pedon (after Yaalon and Kalmar 1978).

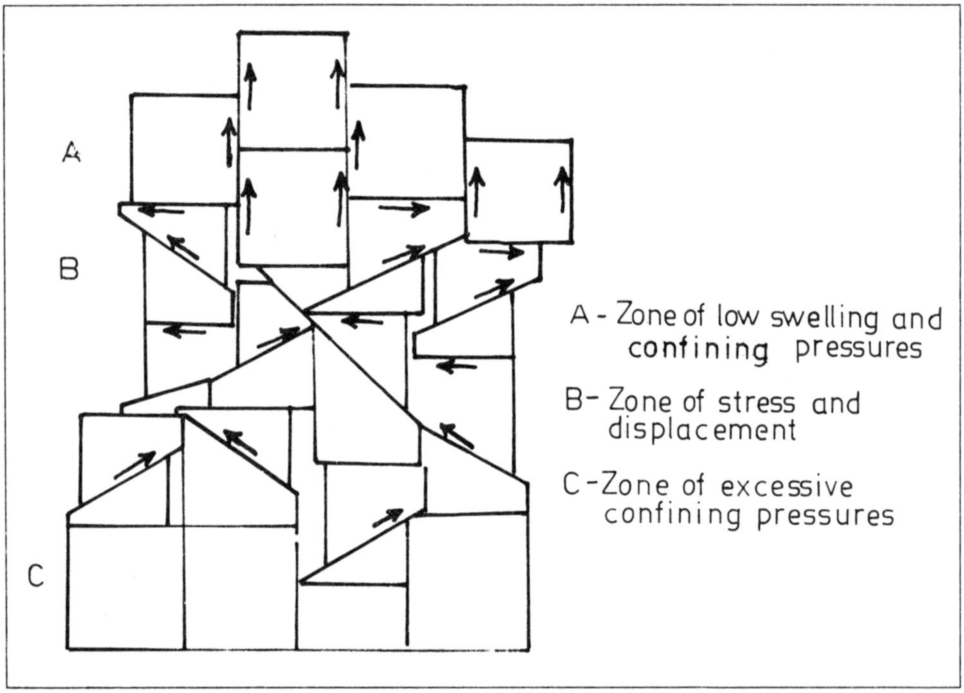

Fig. 5. Simplified shear mechanism in a clay soil containing a number of blocky units. Arrows indicate sense of movement. (A) Zone of low swelling and confining pressures (B) Zone of stress and displacement (C) Zone where no shear or displacement occurs due to excessive confining pressures (after Knight 1980).

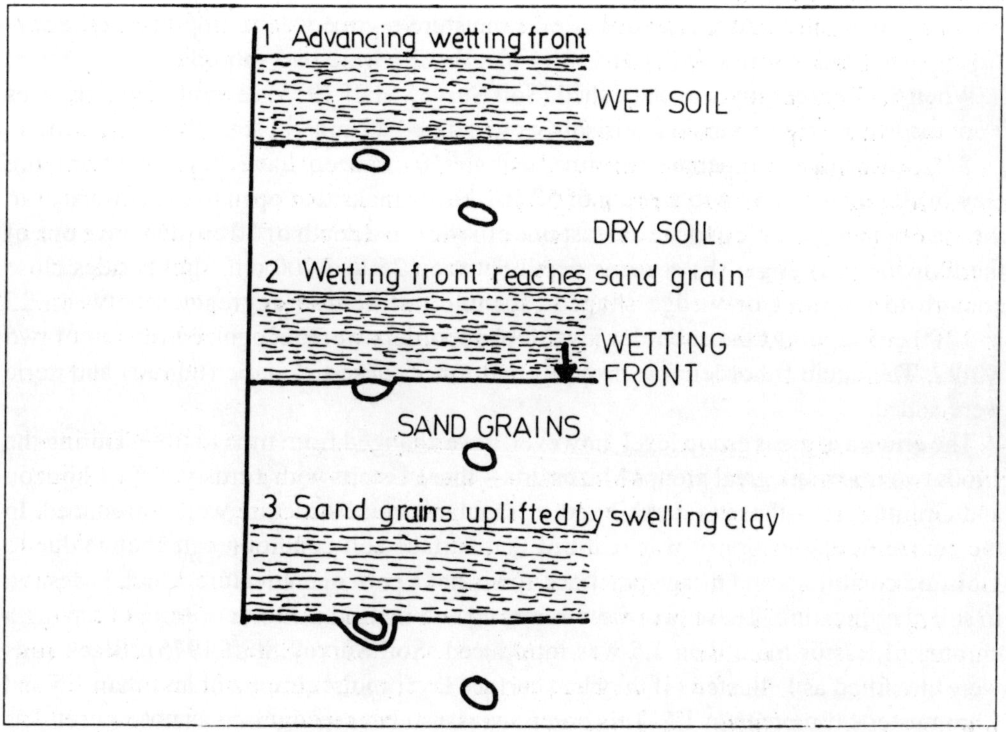

Fig. 6. Uplift of sand grains due to swelling around the grains (after Yaalon and Kalmar 1978).

India does not have its own classification system. As a result the Soil Taxonomy of the U.S. Department of Agriculture is being adopted with some modifications to suit the Indian conditions. During the 6th Congress of the International Society of Soil Science in 1956, the term vertisols was proposed to qualify soils having high shrink-swell characteristics. The term was subsequently adopted in the 7th approximation (Soil Survey Staff 1960) as a soil order. Vertisol was identified to group soils that we know as black cotton soils. The definition of vertisols then included soils with a depth of more than 50 cm, that have 1 cm or more wide cracks for some period during the year and have a clay content of more than 30 per cent and in addition have one of the following: gilgai, or slickensides close enough to intersect between a depth of 25 and 100 cm or wedge shaped structural aggregates. At the suborder level moisture regime was an important criterion. Aquerts (wet black soils) and Usterts (dry black soils) were two suborders.

When Soil Taxonomy was published (Soil Survey Staff 1975) several major changes were made. In the new version vertisols were defined as mineral soils that have a mesic (> 8 °C) or warmer temperature regime; that are 50 cm deep, have 30 per cent or more clay in all horizons down to a depth of 50 cm, have cracks that open to the surface or to the base of plough layer and are at least one cm wide at a depth of 50 cm and have one of the following (a) gilgai (b) at some depth between 25 and 100 cm, slickensides close enough to intersect or wedge shaped (spenoid), structural aggregates between 25 and 100 cm depth. At the suborder level four suborders were recognized instead of two earlier. The aquic suborder was dropped and torric (desertic), udic (humid) and xeric were added.

The criteria at great group level, however, have changed from time to time. During the 1960s two important great groups Mazusterts—those Usterts with a crusty surface horizon and Grumusterts—those that exhibited a granular surface structure were introduced. In the course of application it was realized that surface soil condition can change due to moisture conditions and tillage practices and is not a permanent feature which is desired in soil classification. These taxa were removed and instead a colour criteria of having a chroma of less or more than 1.5 was introduced (Soil Survey Staff 1975). Black soils were classified as Pellusterts if they had surface layer moist chroma of less than 1.5 and Chromusterts if more than 1.5. This criteria was also later recognised as not so useful as it did not separate soils with better drainage from those with poor drainage and many a time soils exhibited chroma of more than 1.5 in one spot and less than 1.5 in another without any apparent reason. Recently, this criteria is removed as well and black soils are classified based on presence of calcic horizon (horizon enriched with calcium carbonate), salinity and other characters. These changes in soil classification reflect the changing concept of soil genesis, and understanding of the use and behaviour of soils with time. The classification is expected to change further as new knowledge accumulates.

Soils that do not exhibit evidences of soil displacement, i.e. slickensides or wedge shaped aggregates but have swell-shrink potential are grouped as vertic intergrades of other orders mainly based on the presence of cracks.

POTENTIALS AND CONSTRAINTS

Though early civilizations believed to have flourished on alluvial soils on river banks, it is argued that grain requirement for the large population in the Deccan may not have been met by cultivation of alluvial soils alone (Dhavalikar 1989). The black soils must have been cultivated since Chalcolithic times. Their self ploughing property is believed to have facilitated their cultivation. It has been stated by Dhavalikar (1989) that black cotton soil seems to have been the most important single factor in the formation of early cultures and that they offered possibilities and limitations also.

These soils have great potential for crop production because of high clay content resulting in a substantial storage of water which supports crops for longer periods. Sinha and Swaminathan (1979) theoretically calculated the maximum production potential in terms of grain equivalents to be of the order of 1,235 million tonnes per year for these soils. The yields obtained in farmers' fields are much lower than those obtained in experimental farms largely on account of the non-adoption of all the recommendations, especially fertilizers.

The yields under dryland conditions present considerable variability due to uncertainties in rainfall. Increased yield levels can be realized under irrigated conditions. Black soils in the semi-arid region invariably have a salt layer in the profile. Experience has shown that due to poor water and crop management good agricultural lands are rendered waterlogged and saline as a result of capillary rise of water containimg dissolved salts. In black soil regions receiving rainfall of >1000 mm, introducing irrigation may not be justified. This encourages farmers to grow heavy water requiring crops like sugarcane and paddy resulting in widespread water-logging in these poorly permeable soils.

Soil erosion is a serious problem in these soils because of high rainfall intensity, lack of vegetative cover at the onset of the monsoon and poor infiltration characteristics (2-6 mm per hour). Kanwar et al. (1982) have estimated a soil loss of around 6 t/ha/yr.

These soils are inherently low in available nitrogen and phosphorus and micronutrients like zinc and iron. The status of available potassium is generally higher.

REFERENCES

Ahmad, N. 1983. Vertisols, in *Pedogenesis and Soil Taxonomy II. The Soil Orders* (L.P. Wilding, N.E. Smeck and G.F. Hall Eds.), pp. 91-123. Amsterdam: Elsevier.

Ahmad, N. and A.R. Mermut 1996. *Vertisols and Technologies for Thier Management*. Amsterdam: Elsevier.

Annet, H.E. 1910. The Nature of the Colour of Black Cotton Soils, *Memoirs Department of Agriculture India, Chemical Series* 1: 185-203.

Anon. 1982. *Vertisols and Rice Soils of the Tropics. Symposium Papers II*. New Delhi: International Society of Soil Science.

Bal, D.V. 1935. Some Aspects of the Black Cotton Soils of the Central Provinces, *Transactions of the 3rd International Congress of Soil Science* 3: 154-8.

Barabhari, M.G. 1991. Soil-Stratigraphic Studies in Dharwad District. M.Sc. Dissertation. Dharwad: University of Agricultural Sciences.

Basu, J.K. and S.S. Sirur 1938. Soils of the Deccan Canals I. Genetic Soil Survey and Soil Classification: Nira Right Bank and Parvara Canals, *Indian Journal of Agricultural Science* 8: 637-97.

Biswas, T.D. and S.P. Gawande 1962. Studies in Genesis of Catenary Soils on Sedimentary Formation in Chattisgarh Basin of Madhya Pradesh I. Morphology and Mechanical Composition, *Journal of the Indian Society of Soil Science* 10: 223-34.

Blokhuis, W.A. 1982. Morphology and Genesis of Vertisols, in *Vertisols and Rice Soils in the Tropics, Symposium Papers II*, pp. 23-47. New Delhi: International Society of Soil Science.

Blokhuis, W.A., Th. Page, and S. Slager 1968/69. Morphology and Distribution of Pedogenic Carbonates in Some Vertisols of the Sudan, *Geoderma* 2: 173-200.

Bouma, J. and J. Loveday 1988. Characterising Soil Water Regimes in Swelling Clay Soils, in *Vertisols: Their Distribution, Properties, Classification and Management* (L.P. Wilding and R. Puentes Eds.), pp. 83-96. College Station: Texas A & M Printing Services.

Brewer, R. 1976. *Fabric and Mineral Analysis of Soils*. New York: Kreiger Publishing Co.

Bui, E.N. and A.R. Mermut 1989. Orientation of Planar Voids in Vertisols and Soils with Vertic Properties, *Soil Science Society of America Journal* 53: 171-8.

Bullock, P., N. Fedoroff, A. Jongerius, G. Stoops and T. Tursina 1985. *Handbook for Soil Thin Section Description*. Wolverhampton: Waine Research Publication.

Buol, S.W., F.D. Hole and R.J. McCracken 1980. *Soil Genesis and Classification*. Ames: Iowa State University Press.

Clark, B.R. 1970. Mechanical Formation of Preferred Orientation in Clays, *American Journal of Science* 269: 250-66.

Dalrymple, J.B. and C.Y. Jim 1984. Experimental Study of Soil Microfabrics Induced by Isotropic Stress of Wetting and Drying, *Geoderma* 34: 43-68.

Dasog, G.S., D.F. Acton and A.R. Mermut 1987. Genesis and Classification of Clay Soils with Vertic Properties in Saskatchewan, *Soil Science Society of America Journal* 51: 1243-50.

Dasog, G.S. and A.S. Hadimani 1980. Genesis and Chemical Properties of Vertisols, *Journal of the Indian Society of Soil Science* 28: 49-56.

Dasog, G.S., A.R. Mermut and D.F. Acton 1988. Micromorphology of Some Vertisols in India, in *Transactions International Workshop on Swell-Shrink Soils* (L.R. Hirekerur, D.K. Pal, J.L. Sehgal and S.B. Deshpande Eds.), pp. 147-9. New Delhi: Oxford-IBH.

Dasog, G.S. and G.B. Shashidhar 1993. Dimension and Volume of Cracks in a Vertisol Under Different Crop Covers, *Soil Science* 156: 424-8.

Dasog, G.S., J. Vishwanath, S.I. Tolanur and T. Satyanarayana 1990. Properties and Genesis of Vertisols Formed on Three Parent Rocks in Northern Karnataka, India, *Transactions of the 14th International Soil Science Congress Commission* V: 391-2.

Desai, A.D. 1942. The Nature and Relationship of Black Cotton Soils and Red Earths of Hyderabad, *Hyderabad Department of Agriculture Bulletin No. 10.*

de Vos, J.H.N.C. and K.J.Virgo 1969. Soil Structure in Vertisols of the Blue Nile Clay Plains, Sudan, *Journal of Soil Science* 20: 189-206.

Dhavalikar, M.K. 1989. Human Ecology in Western India in the Second Millennium BC, *Man and Environment* XIV (1): 83-90.

Dudal, R., 1965. *Dark Clay Soils of Tropical and Subtropical Regions. FAO Agricultural Development Paper, No. 83.* Rome: FAO.

Dudal, R. and H. Eswaran 1988. Distribution, Properties and Classification of Vertisols, in *Vertisols: Their Distribution, Properties, Classification and Management* (L.P. Wilding and R. Puentes Eds.), pp. 1-22. College Station: Texas A & M Printing Services.

El Abedine, Z., G.H. Robinson and A. Commissaris 1971. Approximate Age of the Vertisols of Gezira Central Clay Plain, Sudan, *Soil Science* 111: 200-7.

Eswaran, H., J. Kimble and T. Cook 1988. Properties, Genesis and Classification of Vertisols, in *Transactions International Workshop on Swell-Shrink Soils* (L.R. Hirekerur, D.K. Pal, J.L. Sehgal and S.B. Deshpande Eds.), pp. 1-22. New Delhi: Oxford-IBH.

Govindarajan, S.V.G., R.S. Murthy, A.R. Kalbande and K.R.Venugopal 1972. Micromorphology and Chemistry of Carbonate Concretions in Black Clayey Soils, *Indian Journal of Agricultural Science* 42: 1020-3.

Grant, C.D. and A.V. Blackmore 1991. Self-mulching Behavior in Clay Soils: Its Identification and Measurement, *Australian Journal of Soil Research* 29: 155-73.

Hallaire, V. 1984. Evolution of Crack Networks during Shrinkage of a Clay Soil Under Grass and Winter Wheat Crops, in *Proceedings of International Society of Soil Science Symposium on Water and Solute Movement in Heavy Clay Soils* (J. Bouma and P.A.C. Raats Eds.), pp. 49-54. Wageningen: International Land Reclamation Institute Publication 37.

Harrison, W.H. and M.R. Ramaswamy Sivan 1912. A Contribution to the Knowledge of Cotton Soils of India, *Memoirs Department of Agriculture India Chemical Series* 2: 261-80.

Hirekurubar, B.M., V.S. Doddamani and T. Satyanarayana 1991. Some Physical Properties of Vertisols Derived from Different Parent Materials, *Journal of the Indian Society of Soil Science* 39: 242-5.

Hubble, G.D. 1984. The Cracking Clay Soils: Definition, Distribution, Nature, Genesis and Use, in *The Properties and Utilization of Cracking Clay Soils* (J.W. McGarity, E.H. Hoult and H.B. So Eds.), pp. 3-13. Armidale: University of New England.

Jewitt, T.N., R.D. Law and K.J. Virgo 1979. Vertisol Soils of the Tropics and Subtropics: Their Management and Use, *Outlook on Agriculture* 10: 33-40.

Jim, C.Y. 1986. Experimental Study of Soil Microfabrics Induced by Anisotropic Stresses of Confined Swelling and Shrinking, *Geoderma* 37: 91-112.

Kalbande, A.R., D.K. Pal and S.B. Deshpande 1992. b-fabric of Some Benchmark Vertisols of India in Relation to Their Mineralogy, *Journal of Soil Science* 43: 375-85.

Kanwar, J.S., J. Kampen and S.M. Virmani 1982. Management of Vertisols for Maximising Production. ICRISAT Experience, in *Vertisols and Rice Soils of the Tropics: Symposium Papers* II, pp 94-118. New Delhi: International Society of Soil Science.

Karale, R.L., R.V. Tamhane and S.C. Das 1969. Soil Genesis as Related to Parent Material and Climate I. Morphology, Physical, Chemical and Physico-chemical Properties, *Journal of the Indian Society of Soil Science* 17: 227-39.

Knight, M.J. 1980. Structural Analysis and Mechanical Origins of Gilgai at Boorook, Victoria, Australia, *Geoderma* 23: 245-83.

Kooistra, M.J. 1982. *Micromorphological Analysis and Characterization of 70 Benchmark Soils of India Part III.* Wageningen: The Netherlands Soil Survey Institute.

Krishna, P.G. and S. Perumal 1948. Structure in Black Cotton Soils of the Nizamsagar Project Area, Hyderabad State, *Soil Science* 66: 29-38.

Krishnamoorthy, P. and S.V. Govindarajan 1977. Genesis and Classification of Associated Red and Black Soils under Rajolobhunda Diversion Irrigation Scheme (Andhra Pradesh), *Journal of the Indian Society of Soil Science* 25: 239-46.

Mermut, A.R. and G.S. Dasog 1986. Nature and Micromorphology of Carbonate Glaebules in Some Vertisols of India, *Soil Science Society of America Journal* 50: 382-91.

Mukherjee, B.K. and R.R. Agarwal 1943. Studies on Bundelkhand Soils I. The Genetic Types, *Indian Journal of Agricultural Science* 13: 587-97.

Murthy, A.S.P. 1988. Distribution, Properties and Management of Vertisols of India, *Advances in Soil Science* 8: 152-214.

Murthy, R.S., J.C. Bhattacharjee, R.J. Landey and R.M. Pofali 1982. Distribution, Characteristics and Classification of Vertisols, in *Vertisols and Rice Soils Symposium Papers II*, pp. 1-22. New Delhi: International Society of Soil Science.

Nagelschmidt, G., A.D. Desai and A. Muir 1940. The Minerals in the Clay Fraction of a Black Cotton Soil and a Red Earth from Hyderabad, Deccan State, India, *Agriculture Science* 30: 639-53.

Nandi, S. and G.S. Dasog 1992. Properties, Origin and Distribution of Carbonate Nodules in Some Vertisols, *Journal of the Indian Society of Soil Science* 40: 329-34.

Nettleton, W.D., F.F. Peterson and G. Borst 1983. Micromorphological Evidence of Turbation in Vertisols and Soils with Vertic Subgroups, in *Soil Micromorphology Vol. 2: Soil Genesis* (P. Bullock and C.P. Murphy Eds.), pp. 445-58 Berkamstead: AB Academic Publishers.

Paddayya, K. and M.D. Petraglia 1995. Natural and Cultural Formation Processes of the Acheulian Sites of the Hunsgi and Baichbal Valleys, Karnataka, in *Quaternary Environments and Geoarcheology of India* (S. Wadia, R. Korisettar and V.S. Kale Eds.), pp. 333-51. Bangalore: Geological Society of India.

Pal, D.K. and S.B. Deshpande 1987a. Characteristics and Genesis of Minerals in Some Bench-mark Vertisols of India, *Pedologie* 37: 259-75.

——— 1987b. Genesis of Clay Minerals in Red and Black Soil Complex of Southern India, *Clay Research* 6: 6-13.

Pal, D.K., G.S. Dasog, S. Vadivelu, R.L. Ahuja and T. Bhattacharyya 1999. Secondary Calcium Carbonate in Soils of Arid and Semi-arid Regions of India, in *Global Climate Change and Pedogenic Carbonates* (R. Lal, J.M. Kimble, H. Eswaran and B.A. Stewart Eds.), pp. 145-89. Boca Ratan: Lewis Publishers.

Paton, T.R., 1974. Origin and Terminology for Gilgai in Australia, *Geoderma* 5: 221-42.

Probert, M.E., I.F. Fergus, B.J. Bridge, D. McGary, C.H. Thompson and J.S. Russell 1987. *The Properties and Management of Vertisols*. Oxon: C.A.B. International.

Ramaiah, P.V. 1937. *Report on Soil Survey of Tungabhadra Project*. Madras: Department of Agriculture.

Rudramurthy, H.V. 1994. Studies on Associated Red and Black Soils of North Karnataka. M.Sc. Dissertation. Dharwad: University of Agricultural Sciences.

Sehgal, J.L. and J.C. Bhattacharjee 1988. Typic Vertisols of India and Iraq: Their Characterization and Classification, *Pedologie* 38: 67-95.

Simonson, R.W. 1954. Morphology and Classification of the Regur Soils of India, *Journal of the Soil Science* 5: 275-88.

Singh, S. 1954. A Study of the Black Cotton Soil with Special Reference to Their Coloration, *Journal of Soil Science* 5: 289-93.

Singh, S. 1956. The Formation of Dark Coloured Clay-organic Complexes in Black Soils, *Journal of Soil Science* 7: 45-58.

Sinha, S.K. and M.S. Swaminathan 1979. The Absolute Maximum Food Production Potential in India: an Estimate, *Current Science* 48: 425-9.

Soil Survey Staff 1960. *Soil Classification—a Comprehensive System, 7th Approximation*. Washington, D.C.: Soil Conservation Service. U.S. Department of Agriculture.

——— 1975. *Soil Taxonomy*. Washington, D.C.: Soil Conservation Service. U.S. Department of Agriculture.

——— 1992 (reprinted 1994). *Keys to Soil Taxonomy*. Washington, D.C.: Soil Conservation Service, U.S.Department of Agriculture.

Tamhane, R.V. and N.G. Namjoshi 1959. A Comparative Study of the Black Soils Formed from Different Parent Rocks, *Journal of the Indian Society of Soil Science* 7: 49-63.

Tardy, Y., G. Bocquier, H. Paquet and G. Millot 1973. Formation of Clay from Granite and Its Distribution in Relation to Climate and Topography, *Geoderma* 10: 271-84.

Vadivelu, S. and O. Challa 1985. Depth of Slickenside Occurrence in Vertisols, *Journal of the Indian Society of Soil Science* 33: 452-4.

Warkentin, B.P. 1982. Clay Soil Structure Related to Soil Management, *Tropical Agriculture* (Trinidad) 59: 82-91.

Wenke, J.F. and C.D. Grant 1994. The Index of Self-mulching Behaviour, *Australian Journal of Soil Research* 32: 201-11.

Wilding, L.P. 1985. Genesis of Vertisols, in *Proceedings of 5th International Soil Classification Workshop, Sudan, 1982*, pp. 47-62. Khartoum: Soil Survey Administration.

Wilding, L.P. and K.W. Flach 1985. Micromorphology and Soil Taxonomy, in *Soil Micromorphology and Soil Classification* (L.A. Douglas and M.L. Thompson Eds.), pp. 1-6. Madison: American Society of Soil Science, Special Publication No. 15.

Wilding, L.P. and D. Tessier 1988. Genesis of Vertisols: Shrink-Swell Phenomena, in *Vertisols: Their Distribution, Properties, Classification and Management* (L.P. Wilding and R. Puentes Eds.), pp. 55-82. College Station: Texas A & M University Printing Services.

Yaalon, D.H. and D. Kalmar 1978. Dynamics of Cracking and Swelling Clay Soils: Displacement of Skeletal Grains, Optimum Depth of Slickensides and Rate of Intra-pedonic Turbation, *Earth Surface Processes* 3: 31-42.

Yaalon, D.H. and H.W. Scharpenseel 1972. Radiocarbon Dating of Soil Organic Matter in Israel Soils, *Israel Journal of Agricultural Research* 22: 154-5.

The Indian Monsoon: Roots, Relations and Relevance

RAVI KORISETTAR and R. RAMESH

INTRODUCTION

In recent years the term monsoon has become synonymous with the prevailing patterns of seasonal rainfall over the different continental regions of the world. Among these the Asian monsoon is the largest and most well developed, covering a wide area between East Africa and equatorial South-East Asia and Japan. The larger Asian monsoon system includes the Indian, Malayan, Chinese and Japanese monsoon subsystems. The African, European, Australian and American are the other major monsoon systems. These put together constitute the global monsoon network. Any change in one of these automatically and immediately affects all others proving the fact that all the monsoon systems are interconnected and that climate change is global in magnitude and dimension. 'The world's climate is both unified in itself, and acts as globally integrating drama in which humanity now becomes one of the lead players' (Bolwer et al. 1995: 2). Therefore it is imperative for us to know what were the dynamics that controlled the past changes in the monsoon flow and its intensity and how they influence the monsoon of today and whether prediction of future changes in monsoon conditions be relied upon for a secure future of the humanity and its sustenance. Today the climatologist, in the wake of impending global warming, is deeply concerned with human impact on the initiation of climate change.

The Indian landmass betrays internal variation in accordance with its physiography which governs the prevailing regional variation in the intensity of rainfall. A network of contrasting environmental systems across the landmass has contributed to the regional diversity to the larger cultural unity of India. However, the region as a whole experiences a general weather and climate pattern dictated by the monsoon circulation over South Asia. The Indian monsoons are reversible moisture bound seasonal winds blowing between land and sea in the north Indian Ocean. The reversibility of wind direction has given rise to (a) south-west [SW] monsoon and (b) the north-east [NE] monsoon, during summer and winter respectively.

The Arab traders of the Early Historic period discovered these winds and their facility to voyage between the Arabian Sea and Red Sea. The origin of the name monsoon is credited to the Arabic *mausim* meaning seasons and to the Arab traders who followed the seasonal winds. Their knowledge of maritime tides, currents and winds in the north Indian ocean was a decisive factor in the re-emergence of a flourishing trade and commerce between India and the Arabian Gulf and beyond with the Roman world. The Arab traders used to set out on voyage utilizing the 'Etesian' winds of the Red Sea and the monsoon winds of the Arabian Sea.

Long before Arabs and Romans of the Early Historic period reached the shores of western India traders of the Indus Civilization (2500-2000 BC) went offshore and had established maritime transactions with Egypt and Mesopotamia and the Gulf. Maritime trade between the Harappans and Mesopotamians was necessitated by economic reasons: (a) Mesopotamians possessed surplus food products including oil, and woollen textiles as well as skilled metallurgists and (b) the Harappans possessed huge quantities of metals, semi-precious stones, shells and excellent timber for boat building. With a sizeable population of skilled seafarers in the Indus Valley and that transport of heavy goods in bulk over long distances was easier by waterways, exchange or trade of the surplus and articles of adornment and demand in each of these areas necessitated maritime movements (see Ratnagar 1994; Gupta 1994). Therefore a meticulous knowledge of the wind dynamics and its regularity with the seafarers of the third millennium BC is the positive evidence revealed by archaeological investigations in these regions.

There appears to be a long interlude in the continuity of maritime movement between the end of the Bronze Age Indus Civilization (2000 BC) and the Early Christian era, the so called Dark Age of Indian history. Continuing contact between West Asia and India during this period is reflected in the material culture traits, especially the ceramic types, forms and painted designs, but this archaeological evidence is not clear about the mode of transmission. Continuation of trade is distinctly absent as most of the cultural developments during this interlude were typically agro-pastoral subsistence economy. The Early Vedic literature is silent about the monsoon, whereas in the Later Vedic texts the term *Salilavada* refers to monsoon and the Buddhist texts refer to monsoon winds and monsoon clouds. Much Early Historical literature refers to ports along the Indian seaboard and external and internal trade and trade routes but not on the utility of wind movements for sea trade. Prevalence of trade and trade routes on the hinterland and on the littoral peninsular India is also attested by archaeological evidence and foreign literary and travel accounts throughout Indian history. Classical Indian literature in general is quiet about the movement of winds facilitating maritime movements. On the other hand the Greek literature of the Early Christian era provides us with references to wind movements.

Re-emergence of maritime trade coincides with the rediscovery of the utility and function of monsoon winds by the Arabs, followed by the Romans. It appears that the Arabs had kept their knowledge of the monsoon winds as a trade secret and acted as intermediaries between trading nations. It was the Greek mariner Hippalus who in AD 44 discovered a direct sea route between the two regions for the purpose of procuring Indian spices and facilitate a major exchange of ideas across the seas. This direct and short route was necessary for the Greeks to escape from the sea pirates and the Red Sea shoals. The Egyptians and Greeks at this time were Roman subjects. The *Periplus Maris Erythraei* of an anonymous Greek author and Pliny mention that the month of July was ideal to set sail from Egypt to India and begin the return sail from September onwards.

The early explorers and mariners emphasized on a proper knowledge of the monsoon behaviour to facilitate cultural contact through trade and commerce between the maritime countries. To modern scientific investigators a detailed understanding of monsoon dynamics, its history both in terms of its antiquity and change, the impact of both long and short term global climatic changes on the monsoon intensity, its relationship with the other climate systems of the world are the major areas of concern. Furthermore, India being an essentially agricultural nation stable agriculture is at the pivot of its economy, sustenance and stable demography which in turn are governed by the regular monsoon rainfall and its prognosis. The extent of its impact on the ecodiversity and food production is of fundamental importance. Palaeoclimatic studies have shown that the Indian monsoon responded to the global changes and reveal inverse correlation with glaciations. During the cold glacial the monsoon was weak and strong during the warm interglacial. The monsoon circulation is a major source of fresh water in much of southern Asia. It plays a vital role in shaping the agricultural economy of the people living in the alluvial plains and deserts, and exerts absolute control on the availability of food resources to the hunting-gathering tribal populations living in the hills and forests of the subcontinent. Therefore it is not an exaggeration to say that Indian civilization is largely the gift of the Indian monsoon currents circulating rainfall between the Himalayas in the north and the Indian Ocean in the south during the summer and winter seasons, supporting perennial productivity.

ORIGIN OF INDIAN MONSOON

The SW monsoon sets in around the beginning of June and lasts till mid-September and is followed by the winter north-east monsoon which nearly covers the eastern half of the subcontinent. The SW monsoon rainfall (75-80 per cent of the annual total rainfall) is higher than the winter rainfall. Although the monsoon systems all over the world are interconnected the Indian monsoon betrays individuality in being able to build its circulation between the Himalayas and the Indian Ocean (see for a recent review Webster et al. 1998).

The rise and fall of pressure between the West Pacific and East Pacific oceans in the Southern Hemisphere is called Southern Oscillation which has links with the variations in the tropical east-west circulation. The Southern Oscillation, the Indian monsoon circulation and the elevation of the Tibetan plateau are interactive phenomena. The impact of the tropical easterly jet (TEJ), thermal contrast between land and sea, the existence of monsoon trough over northern India, the winter snow cover on Tibet and obstruction of the advance of polar cold winds by the Himalayas are major parameters causing monsoon over India. During the last 4,500 years the Indian monsoon is periodically experiencing the impact of El Niño, and as such falls in the ambit of El Niño and Southern Oscillation (ENSO) (Deodhar 1988).

After reaching the north Indian Ocean during mid-summer the SW trade winds split into two branches (a) the Bay of Bengal branch arriving earlier and (b) the Arabian Sea branch arriving later. A shift in the heat belt occurs in October (causing moderately hot conditions over the Deccan), this shift takes place from Rajasthan-Punjab to the equator effecting the dominance of NE winds. The NE monsoon is characterized by frequent cyclonic storms arising in the Bay of Bengal. These storms are low pressure systems in which the associated wind rotates in an anti-clockwise direction in the Northern Hemisphere. During the SW monsoon the cyclonic storms forming over the Bay of Bengal (to the north of 18° latitude) move in a north-westerly direction causing heavy rainfall along its transect. Cyclonic depressions in the Bay during active SW monsoon season result in the strengthening of the Arabian Sea monsoon current and cause heavy rainfall over the Western Ghats, largely due to orographic ascent of moisture-laden winds. During intramonsoonal breaks the low pressure monsoon trough shifts towards the Himalayas, causing rainfall over north India (Rakhecha and Pisharoty 1996; also see Naidu 1998).

The total annual rainfall over India at present is ~117 cm. The range of the SW monsoon does not cover Kashmir, the southern tip of the peninsula and the east coast. Within its reach the south-west monsoon progresses with decreasing quantum of rainfall across the mainland. Orographic obstructions on its path render heavy to very heavy rainfall in the Western Ghats, west coast and the Burma mountains; the Deccan plateau is a rain shadow zone; and the air mass inversion between lower shallow moist current and upper drier air mass causes least rainfall in the Thar desert (Deodhar 1988). The varied rainfall and diverse physiographic configurations have created a variety of habitats supporting endemic sets of plants and animal species, and were subject to human colonization from the palaeolithic times onwards. Changes in climate regimes and human interference have caused modification of the ecosystems/habitats.

In this paper an attempt is made to provide an account of our knowledge of the origins of monsoon over the Indian subcontinent, bring out its relations with the other global climate systems and emphasize its relevance in the archaeology of India. Historical records of the monsoon are of the recent past necessitating investigation of proxy records for developing secure predictive capability. Meher-Homji, in this volume, deals with bioclimatology and palynology.

The available rainfall records for India date from 1840. In 1910 Sir Gilbert Walker, Director General of the India Meteorological Department, was the first to utilize these records for analysing the frequency of rainfall variability in India and noted drought years between 1843-60 and 1895-1907 (Walker 1986). For the period beyond 1840 proxy records are the only source involving multidisciplinary investigations for reconstructing the palaeomonsoon over the subcontinent. The proxy records of monsoon rainfall can broadly be grouped into (a) short term records covering a period of less than 2,000 years and (b) long term records covering a period of more than 2 ka. The former can be calibrated with the help of instrumental records going back to ~120 years for major metropolitan cities like Chennai, Mumbai, etc.

Short Term Records

This category includes tree-rings (especially tropical trees such as teak), corals (mainly *Porites*), ice cores from the Himalayas and speleothems from caves (calcitic stalagmites and stalactites).

Teak trees from Thane, near Mumbai analysed by Ramesh et al. (1989) demonstrated that the stable isotopic composition of hydrogen (D/H) in these trees was positively correlated to the monsoon rainfall. G.B. Pant and colleagues at the Indian Institute of Tropical Meteorology, Pune, have collected a large number of teak samples from both the west and east coast of India dating back to a few centuries. Therefore it must be possible to obtain proxy records of the Indian monsoon over this period with a high time resolution of one year or less from these samples, such data being crucial to numerical models aimed at predicting the monsoon.

Corals are marine organisms that live up to a depth of ~50 m, to which depth adequate sun light penetrates. Corals build colonies, made of calcium carbonate (aragonite). Some corals form annual bands, consisting of a dark and a light part, visible in an X-ray photograph. In a live coral, the annual bands can be counted, it is possible to assign dates to each of these bands. The stable isotope ratio of oxygen ($^{18}O/^{16}O$), measured using a mass spectrometer and denoted by $\delta^{18}O$ (per mil units relative to an international standard called the PDB), is a function of both the SST (sea surface temperature) and the $\delta^{18}O$ of sea water. If significant variation in the latter does not occur, one can reconstruct past SSTs using $\delta^{18}O$ of coral bands. The growth rate is typically 1 to 2 cm per year, and the sampling for analysis is done every millimeter, so that a bi-weekly time series of SSTs can be recovered from corals. Corals of the genus *Porites* from the Lakshadweep region are found to be high resolution documents of monsoon.

The South Asian summer monsoon induces mixing of the surface waters of the Arabian Sea leading to a reduction of SST by about 3 to 4 °C. This is recorded in the bands of *Porites* corals growing in the Lakshadweep region (10-13°N; 70-3°E) (Chakraborty and Ramesh 1993). To utilize the coralline $\delta^{18}O$ as a proxy for SST, it is essential to calibrate it with observed SSTs (e.g. COADS: Comprehensive Ocean Atmosphere Data Set). This calibration yielded an equation:

$$SST = 3.0 - 4.68\,(\delta^{18}O_{coral} - \delta^{18}O_{sea\ water})$$

The accuracy of such reconstructions is comparable to that of satellite observations (Chakraborty and Ramesh 1997).

Observation on the rate of exchange of gases between air and sea is another area of monsoon investigation. This exchange of gases is proportional to the wind intensity. For instance, radiocarbon is continuously produced in the earth's atmosphere by interaction of atmospheric nitrogen with cosmic rays. Its natural rate of production was upset by the test explosion of atomic bombs which results in doubling the radiocarbon content in the atmosphere. However, this bomb carbon can be used as a tracer to estimate the air-sea exchange rate of carbon dioxide.

Oceans can store about 60 times as much carbon as the atmosphere. They play a significant role in controlling CO_2 concentration in the atmosphere and thus regulate the greenhouse warming of our planet. The oceans' capacity to take up the excess CO_2 released into the atmosphere by fossil fuel burning, depends on a variety of physical, chemical and biological processes occurring in them. The air-sea exchange can be estimated when we have a time series measurements for the atmospheric and ocean surface radiocarbon. The former can be obtained by analysing the annual growth rings of trees and the latter from the annual bands of corals. These measurements were made for a teak tree (*Tectona grandis*) from the Mumbai region and for a coral (*Favia speciosa*) from Pirotan island (Gulf of Kachchh). Based on these measurements the air-sea exchange rate was calculated to be ~11 millimoles per year. The mean advection velocity from the open Arabian Sea into the Gulf was estimated to be ~28 m/year (Chakraborty et al. 1994).

Calcite deposits found in limestone caves (speleothems) are proxies for the past changes in monsoon precipitation. Two speleothems from tropical India (Madhya Pradesh and Orissa) were analysed for their isotopic composition of oxygen and carbon and were dated by the ^{14}C method (Yadava and Ramesh 1999). Contrary to the high latitude cave deposits, oxygen isotopes from these speleothems in a sub-humid environment show large variations up to 2.5 per cent during the past 3,400 years. These variations are attributed to the regional fluctuation in the monsoon precipitation, which is observed to vary by 33 per cent during the past 3,400 years. Several dry and wet phases were observed, indicating variation in the intensity of the palaeomonsoon. The 3400-3000 BP period witnessed enhanced precipitation. Reduction in rainfall was observed from 3000 to 2900 BP with a sharp dry spell around 2 ka. Low rainfall events documented by meteorological data around AD 1900 were also recorded in the most recent part of the rainfall reconstruction. Similarly isotopic composition of carbon has also responded to varying precipitation regimes as reflected by the changed ratio of the abundance of C3 and C4 type of plants. The sharp dry spell around 2 ka in eastern India compares well with the evidence of abundance of benthic and planktonic foraminiferal morphotypes in a shallow water sediment core from the Arabian Sea shelf off the Karwar coast (Karnataka) (Nigam and Khare 1994). More recent work on the varve thickness of ocean sediments from the northern Arabian Sea, off Karachi has confirmed these observations (von Rad et al. 1999)

The potential of shallow Himalayan ice cores were also studied by Nijampurkar et al. (1986) from this point of view. In the absence of the ice-drilling technology they studied crevasses and found that such samples were not ideally suited for monsoon reconstruction because of thawing and refreezing of ice in the Himalayan glaciers during the summer months.

LONG TERM RECORDS

Role of Tibetan Plateau in the Initiation of Monsoon Circulation

The emergence of orographic landforms across the Asian landmass and the thermal contrast between land and sea have controlled the timing and intensity of the monsoon rainfall. The Western Ghats, Himalayas and the Burma mountains cause the ascent of the monsoon currents and thus help higher precipitation in the orographic belts and low rainfall on the leeward. The Himalayas and the Tibetan plateau on the northern side of the subcontinent anchor the onset of monsoon over South Asia (Figs. 1 and 2).

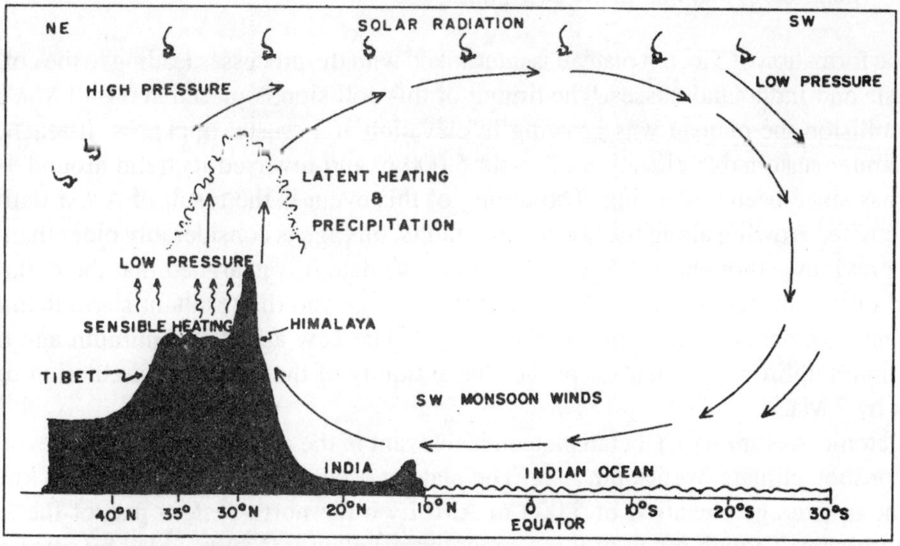

Fig. 1. The Physiography of the South Asian landmass and the monsoon system (after Valdiya 1999).

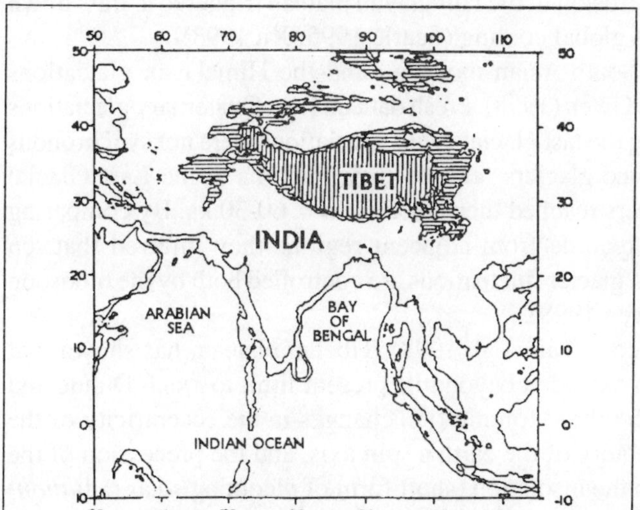

Fig. 2.
The >5000 m high mountain barrier made up of the Himalayas and Tibetan plateau causes not only the change in the wind direction, but also the precipitation of rains and snows (after Valdiya 1999).

The formation of Tibetan plateau is interlinked with the processes leading to the collision of Asia and India landmasses. The timing of this collision is placed at 54-49 Ma. Since the collision the plateau was growing in elevation and crustal thickness. It reached its maximum sustainable elevation of about 5,000 m and reversed its trend around 14 Ma and has since been collapsing. The timing of this event is the result of Ar/Ar dating of muscovites growing along the north-south faults, this age is considerably older than what was previously thought, i.e. 8 Ma. Based on this date it was argued that the collapsing trend of the plateau was coeval with climate change and the resultant strengthening of the Indian monsoon circulation (Searle 1995). The new age (the minimum age of the maximum uplift of the plateau) pushes the antiquity of the monsoon circulation further back by 7 Ma.

Tectonic evolution of Tibetan plateau is relevant in the reconstruction of the evolution of monsoon climate over South Asia. The plateau occupies an area of 2 million km^2 and lies at an average elevation of 5,000 m AMSL on the north-eastern part of the Indian subcontinent. Though much of it is a monotonous plain it is surrounded by some of the world's well known peaks, including the Mount Everest. The monsoon circulation was established following the rise of the plateau to its maximum elevation causing disruption of the west-east air flow across the Northern Hemisphere and initiation of the monsoon driven winds across the continental area with a consequent increase in precipitation along the Himalayas. Higher chemical erosion in the Himalayan plateau triggered a draw down of carbon dioxide and resulted in global cooling (Searle 1995; Xu 1993).

The connection between the South Asian monsoon and the Himalayan glaciations have been addressed by Benn and Owen (1998). Fresh data on Late Quaternary glaciations in the Himalayas show that during the last glacial cycle, glaciations were not synchronous throughout the region: while some glaciers reached their maxima at the Last Glacial Maximum (*c.* 18-20 ka ago), others reached their maxima at *c.* 60-30 ka. By comparing these data with palaeoclimatic records from adjacent regions they inferred that, on millennial time scales, Himalayan glacier fluctuations are controlled both by the monsoon and the westerlies (Benn and Owen 1998).

Palynology of the Dunde ice core (Liu et al. 1998), Tibetan plateau, has shown that during 10 to 4.8 ka the monsoon extended beyond its present limit to reach Dunde and westernmost Tibet in response to orbital forcing [i.e. changes in the eccentricity of the earth's orbit around the sun, obliquity of the earth's spin axis, and the precession of the earth; and consequent changes in the insolation (short form of *in*coming *sol*ar radi*ation*) at the surface of the earth].

The Western Ghats and the Peninsular Monsoon

The uplift of Western Ghats in the Early Neogene effectively changed the peninsular ecosystem from tropical woodland (Early Tertiary) to a network of savanna ecosystems between the west coast and the plateau along with the establishment of allochthonous river systems in peninsular India. The savanna ecosystem became well-defined in the rocky triangle between the Western and Eastern Ghats. This orographic configuration resulted in a progressive decrease in the intensity of rainfall along the path of the SW monsoon, the basic element controlling the habitability of the area. Obviously the structure of food resources between the coastal, upland and plateau ecosystem was very different, the key controlling factor would have been the secular variation in the intensity of SW monsoon across the peninsular region.

Thus the physiographic configuration of India controls the movement of both the SW and NE monsoon during summer and winter respectively. The internal topographic subdivisions do not necessarily coincide with natural ecosystems, the characteristics of which are strongly influenced by the monsoon flow. The orographic barriers in the proximal area of the monsoon flow from the Arabian Sea to the Himalayas and vice versa. Accordingly a network of ecosystems are formed, including deciduous woodlands, tropical evergreen forests, savanna, semi-arid to arid scrub lands and arid sand deserts and periglacial loessic landforms, in response to long term changes in climate.

The Western Ghats and the west coast, being proximal to the Arabian Sea monsoon receive the maximum precipitation in summer and the Western Ghats plateau preserves the climax forest with a distinction of being the one of world's biodiversity hot spots, especially in the region between the mouth of the Tapi in the north and the southern tip of India. Damage to the biodiversity of this region can occur for two reasons (i) secular variation in the monsoon precipitation regimes and (ii) human interference. Impact of the latter is being assessed in order to step up measures to preserve the biodiversity. During the last 4,000 years human interference has steadily increased, more so under the impact of the post-Industrial Revolution developmental programmes and the demographic pressure for increased expansion of agricultural land.

LATERITE AND THE TERTIARY MONSOON

In recent years our understanding of the laterite in southern India has considerably improved in terms of its genesis and climatic significance as well as the associated land form processes coeval with the formation of laterite. Mature well developed laterite situated on the crest of the Western Ghats and on higher denudational surfaces in the peninsular region is dated to the Early Quaternary. This laterite formed under the influence of tropical monsoon and equatorial regime, with longer rainy seasons, was supported by peneplanation processes when the Indian plate was crossing over the equator. During this lateritic phase the existence of tropical woodland ecosystem can be envisaged. The atypical laterite commonly found on the pediments flanking the river valleys in peninsular India is considered to be of Quaternary age. Two broad distinctions are made in the laterite profile. One is a commercial variety and the other is nodular or pisolitic material. Although there are two generations of laterite situated at different altitudes, the highest or plateau laterite dates to the KT boundary and the lower one is dated to Late Tertiary on the basis of palaeolatitude study (Kumar 1986; Sahasrabudhe and Rajaguru 1990; Ollier and Rajaguru 1989; Ollier 1995).

In Konkan and the adjoining high mesa tops of the Western Ghats laterite has developed on Deccan Trap of 60-65 Ma. Southwards in Karnataka it has developed over the pre-

Deccan Trap basement rocks of the Archaean and Proterozoic age, as well as occasional outcrops of Mio-Pliocene age sediments (Widdowson and Gunnel, in press).

Upland and Lowland Laterites as Evidence of Monsoon

Geomorphic analyses of the Konkan (Maharashtra coast) and Kanara (Karnataka coast) laterites have revealed that different generations of laterites are situated between the plateau and the coast. The lowland laterite occurs as clusters of plateaus (Widdowson and Gunnel, in press). The lowland laterite is relevant to our understanding of the geologic, geomorphic processes operating under the seasonal monsoon circulation, which gave rise to this formation in the Late Tertiary period.

The evolution of coastal lowlands along the western seaboard was concomitant with the scarp retreat processes operating along the foot of the Western Ghats during the Neogene, followed by an extensive phase of lateritization of the pediment surface when climatic conditions were conducive for deep weathering. The coastal lowlands are a low relief pediment formed under relative tectonic stability and relative semi-aridity. The present-day monsoonal rainfall is heavy to very heavy with an average of 5,000 mm per annum at the foot of the Ghats. This provides ideal tropical and seasonal hot and humid conditions for the continuation of lateritization, which is observed to have been the case since the Miocene times. Prevalence of tropical climate throughout the Cenozoic is attested by palaeobotanical (Meher-Homji 1989) and palaeoweathering (Bruckner and Bruhn 1992) data. Evidence for hot humid seasonal circulation with greater intensity of rainfall has also been dated to at least 8 Ma (Prell and Niitsuma 1989). Further prevalence of monsoon climate during Miocene and its influence on pedogenesis is attested to by a series of palaeosols in the Siwaliks of Pakistan (Retallack 1995) and the stable isotopic analysis of pedogenic carbonates from the palaeosols of Late Miocene age (Quade and Cerling 1995)

The occurrence of massive lithic calcretes, with relief inversion (rhizoliths and nodules), on laterites and ferricretes of Later Tertiary age in upland western Maharashtra is a good evidence of climatic fluctuation and the onset of semi-arid monsoonal conditions during Late Neogene to Early Pleistocene times. This is consistent with the onset of global cooling around the beginning of the Pleistocene period 2.5 milliom years ago (Vrba 1996; Rajaguru 1997a).

THE PALAEOMONSOON RECORDS IN THE INDIAN OCEAN

While corals provide a high resolution record of one year or less, deep sea sediments provide a coarse resolution of ~1,000 years. Coastal cores may provide a resolution of ~200 years or less. Several species of foraminifera were analysed for their oxygen isotopic ratios, while the layers of the core were assigned ages based on radiocarbon dating. The results (Sarkar et al., 1990) show that the south-west monsoon was weaker during the last ice age (~21ka), whereas the north-east monsoon current enhanced in the Arabian Sea.

In a more recent study of Sarkar et al. (1999) $\delta^{18}O$ and $\delta^{13}C$ of *G. sacculifer* have been measured in five cores from the northern Indian Ocean. In addition, high resolution analysis (1 to 2 cm) was performed on one core (SK 20-185) for both $\delta^{18}O$ and $\delta^{13}C$ in five species of planktonic foraminifera. $CaCO_3$ variation was measured in two cores. The results show that (i) the summer monsoon was weaker during 18 ka and was stronger during 9 ka relative to modern conditions; (ii) $\delta^{13}C$ variations are consistent with independent evidence which shows that during the Last Glacial Maximum (LGM) the upwelling was reduced while during 9 ka it was vigorous; (iii) calculation of $CaCO_3$ flux shows that the LGM was characterized by low biogenic productivity in the Arabian Sea while during the Holocene productivity increased by ~ 65 per cent, as a direct consequence of the changes in upwelling. Similar changes (of lesser magnitude) are also seen in the equatorial Indian Ocean. The amount of terrigenous input into the Arabian Sea doubled during LGM possibly due to the higher erosion rate along the west coast; (iv) $\delta^{18}O$ values indicate that the Arabian Sea was saltier by 1 to 2 per cent during LGM. The northern part was dominated by evaporation while in the equatorial region increased precipitation took place.

In the above studies, radiocarbon dating was done on bulk sediments, which consist of two types of carbonates, hydrogenous (i.e. foraminifera) and terrigenous. The latter is usually a weathered product of continental carbonates belonging to the geological past with imprecise ages. Now in India, thanks to the efforts of B.L.K. Somayajulu and K. Gopalan, the accelerator mass spectrometry (AMS) facility called MUDRA (*MU*lti *D*isciplinary *R*esearch *A*ccelerator) has been set up at the Indian Institute of Physics, Bhubaneswar, Orissa providing facility to date small amounts of foraminifera accurately. For example, several cores collected off the Mangalore coast have been dated (see Somayajulu et al. 1999). These dates indicate high sedimentation rates ranging from 10 to 200 cm/ka. Oxygen isotopic studies from these cores have revealed that during the major part of Holocene, 10 ka to 2 ka, the monsoon steadily increased. This is in direct contrast to observations of aridity in Rajasthan around 4 ka. Such high precision studies underscore the importance of spatial variations of monsoon in the past, as we observe today (e.g. floods in Assam and simultaneously droughts in Gujarat).

Oxygen isotope and carbonate accumulation studies on similar AMS dated cores from the western Arabian Sea spanning the last 24,000 calendar years have shown that the SW monsoon responded to the long term, gradual insolation changes that occurred as several distinct events of less than 300 year duration, at 14,300, 13,500, 13,060, 9,900, 8,800 and 7,300 ^{14}C years BP (Sirocko et al. 1993). It has also been speculated that albedo (percentage of insolation reflected) changes over Asia were mainly the cause of rapid changes in local climate. A good correlation between the high latitude climatic changes (recorded in the Greenland ice cores) and the monsoon (Arabian Sea sediments) has also been found (Schulz et al. 1998).

The marine pollen diagram from the Arabian Sea off the east coast of Africa, shows periodic fluctuation in monsoon conditions that correlated with glacial climatic changes as indicated by Oxygen Isotope Stages. Glacial periods were arid because of decreased monsoon flow and during early interglacial stages the SW monsoon flow was intense resulting in the rise of lake levels in the tropics (Van Campo et al. 1982). An increase in rainfall between 10 and 5 ka was also recorded from lakes in Australia and India. Temperate regions of Australia and China have shown records of major fluctuations in lake levels in response to the onset of glacial aridity during the Last Glacial Maximum, during 25-16 ka. At the end of the Ice Age, 10 ka these lakes were restored to levels a little higher than today (Bowler et al. 1995).

Although a large number of surface and subsurface sediments from the Arabian Sea have been analysed for reconstructing palaeomonsoon fluctuations over the Indian region, this research is generally confined to the period of the Last Glacial Maximum and the latest interglacial. Duplessy (1982) inferred that climate was very arid about 22-18 ka ago and the Asian summer monsoon was weaker during the LGM than it is today, whereas the winter monsoon was stronger. The palynological study of marine cores off the south-west coast of India has revealed two phases of the monsoon. The low mangrove pollen frequency is dated to between 22 and 18 ka, a dry climatic phase, followed by a humid phase at the early post-glacial period (Van Campo 1986). Mineralogical study of the Arabian sea shelf sediments has also shown aridity around 11 ka (Nigam and Hashimi 1995).

Another significant development in the Indian Ocean region is the reconstruction of palaeoclimatic changes for the Middle and Late Pleistocene from the deep sea (DSDP sites) and the continental shelf cores off the eastern coast of India. These cores show marked fluctuation in the population of planktonic foraminifera *Globorotalia menardii* (deep sea species) *Globigerina bulloides*, *Globigerinita glutinata*, *Globigernoides ruber*, *Globogerina falconensis*, etc. (tropical and subtropical shallow marine species) and pteropods (see A.D. Singh 1998, for a recent summary). These species' productivity is sensitive to changes in SST, intensity of upwelling and monsoon strength and therefore the cyclic variation in the abundance of foraminifera and pteropods at these sites is a good record of temperature changes during the Pleistocene. At least three glacial-interglacial cycles from the Upper Pleistocene to Holocene have been identified in these cores (Sarkar and Guha 1993).

The strength of the SW monsoon winds, upwelling in the Arabian Sea and precipitation are strongly interrelated. The upwelled waters are characterized by cooler temperature supporting the productivity of planktonic fauna. The NE monsoon winds in winter suppress upwelling and lower the productivity. Hence upwelling index from the Arabian Sea cores is a good recorder of monsoon conditions. Weak monsoon prevailed during 5,000 and 3,500 years before the present, coinciding with the onset of arid climate of glacial strength over much of the tropics (Naidu 1995, 1997).

Continental shelf cores from the eastern Arabian Sea and the Oman region have been analysed for high resolution reconstruction of oceanographic and climatic changes during the Late Quaternary. Detailed micropalaeontological, and sedimentological study of several gravity cores off Kerala shelf of the Arabian Sea have been carried out by A.D. Singh (1998). While planktonic foraminifera are familiarly used for climatic reconstructions pteropods are found equally suited for this purpose. The pteropods constitute one of the main carbonate components among a variety of micro organisms in the shelf sediments of the eastern Arabian Sea. Like foraminifera pteropod assemblages also respond to upwelling changes which are related to fluctuation in the monsoon intensity. Therefore conjunctive quantitative analyses of foraminifera and pteropod assemblages were examined by A.D. Singh as evidence for the fluctuations in the upwelling intensity and associated changes in the monsoonal strength. Minimum upwelling and weaker monsoon occurred around 23-18 ka. Marked increase in both these took place during 18-15 ka, followed by a weak monsoon and weaker upwelling around 15-12 ka. The monsoon intensified again between 12 and 10 ka. Since 5 ka the monsoon intensity has lowered. This reconstruction is in general agreement with the results of earlier studies of other scholars (mentioned above) in the north Indian Ocean.

LAKE AND OFFSHORE PALYNOLOGY

Palynological studies have been carried out in the lakes of Rajasthan, Uttar Pradesh, Kashmir, Ladakh, Kathmandu and Sikkim. In the Kashmir valley pollen analysis suggests a cooler period around 10,000 years BP followed by a gradual warming between 7,000 and 4,000 years BP. Pollen studies in the Ladakh region indicate that during the last 30,000 years the climate was dry and cold. There were, however, brief periods, when warm climate lasting 200 to 300 years existed. About 1,000 years BP there was a transition from moist to relatively dry conditions in the western Himalayas (see Srinivasan 1998 for an overview).

In Rajasthan a large number of playas and lakes have provided pollen profiles facilitating in the reconstruction of changing vegetation and the corresponding rainfall regimes. The saline lakes of Lunkaransar, Didwana and Sambar were some of the lakes first studied for this purpose. Gurdeep Singh and his colleagues (Singh et al. 1974, 1990; G. Singh 1988) carried out detailed palynological research on these lake sediments and inferred higher rainfall regimes during Early Holocene and attributed the prosperity of the Indus Civilization (2500-1900 BC). Terminal Pleistocene was characterized by hyper arid conditions followed by warm and wet conditions between 10,000 and 6,000 BP. Aridity around 4,000 BP was recorded by the dry phase of the lakes. Similar vegetation change between arboreal and herbaceous ecosystems is observed from the Nal Sarovar pollen spectrum (also see Sharma and Chauhan 1991; Kajale and Deotare 1997).

Bryson and Swain (1981) utilized the pollen spectra from these lakes and estimated a rainfall that was twice the present between 5,000 and 1,500 BP. Later Swain et al. (1983) interpreted the pollen record in terms of 500 mm per annum of rainfall between 10,500 and 3,500 years BP followed by a dry phase leading to increasing salinity of the lakes.

The playas at Bap-Malar (district Jodhpur) and Kanod (Jaisalmer) originated within the structural depressions around 14-15 ka. They carried brackish water between 8 and 6 ka and nearly dried up around 5 ka. These playas in western arid parts of Rajasthan seem to have dried up at least a thousand years earlier than the playas in the eastern parts of the Thar desert. Similar multidisciplinary investigations in the Nal Sarovar in Gujarat (Prasad et al. 1997) show that the lake was almost dry around 6 ka, carried enough water between 4 and 3 ka and again dried up after 3 ka. In general these lake records betray regional variation in hydrological changes during the Early to Mid-Holocene times and that the rainfall was not higher than the present even during relatively wet phase of the Holocene. A possible reason for the discrepancy with other records could be that the core was dominated by sand and radiocarbon and TL dates are of doubtful validity (A.K. Singhvi: personal communication).

A change in the vegetation pattern was documented from the pollen profiles of two cores from the inner shelf of the Arabian Sea off the mouth of the Kalinadi, on the Karnataka coast (Caratini et al. 1994). A decline in the evergreen, deciduous and mangrove forest species in favour of savanna vegetation was observed from 3,200 years ago. This was interpreted as the beginning of a less humid phase under a weaker monsoon.

In a more recent study of Lunkaransar lake sediments, supported by the high precision AMS dates, Enzel et al. (1999) have shown that the lake level abruptly rose around 5 ka and desiccated around 4 ka implying that the early Harappan Civilization began 1000 years after the total dessication of the Lunkaransar lake. As mentioned earlier results from high precision studies seem to contradict earlier coarser dating studies and in a few years time we may have to revise many of the 'well accepted' beliefs entrenched in literature!

Evidence of climatic fluctuations is also reflected in the Nilgiri peat (Sukumar et al. 1993) and the Didwana lake in the Thar desert of India (Singh et al. 1972, 1974; Wasson et al. 1983, 1984). Such changes in lake levels in both the hemispheres can now be shown as uniform and synchronous events (Wasson 1995). Sukumar et al. (1993) analysed the peat bogs of the Nilgiris for variation in the C3 and C4 vegetation. A shift from C3 (forest/grassland) to C4 vegetation took place during 6 and 3.5 ka due to lowering of rainfall and lower carbon dioxide. C4 vegetation is typical of arid climate (the carbon isotopic ratio varying betwen -15 per cent and -11 per cent) and C3 (the carbon isotopic ratio between -26 per cent and -28 per cent) that of humid climate. C4 vegetation explains the expansion of savanna ecosystem on the Nilgiris. This record has since been extended to > 40 ka (Rajagopalan et al. 1997). From prior to 40 to 28 ka, a general decline in the $\delta^{13}C$ values from about -14 per cent to -19 per cent suggests increased dominance of C3 plants concurrent with increasingly moist conditions. During 28 to 18 ka there seems to be relatively little change with $\delta^{13}C$ of about -19 to -18 per cent.

PREHISTORIC RESEARCH AND THE QUATERNARY CLIMATE

Integrated geologic, climatic and prehistoric research in India began with the first discovery of a Palaeolithic tool at Pallavaram near Chennai (Foote 1866). However, until the 1930s not much emphasis was laid on reconstructing palaeoclimate, but it was a productive phase in terms of locating archaeological sites within the British administered domain.

The Yale-Cambridge expedition's primary aim was to document evidence for Pleistocene glaciation in the Himalayan region and bring out its impact on early human cultures (de Terra and Paterson 1939). The expedition covered the Himalayan region, central India and around Madras. Following their fieldwork in the valleys of Kashmir (Jhelum), on the Potwar plateau (Soan Valley), they arrived at a four-fold glacial-interglacial model for north-west India comparable to the European four-fold galcial-interglacial model (Penck and Brückner 1909). De Terra and Paterson's model was based on the sequence of terraces in the Soan Valley (now in Pakistan) and the Jhelum in Kashmir (India).

Around the same time Cammiade and Burkitt (1930) inferred a sequence of alternating succession of wet and dry periods as a climatic background to the sequence of Stone Age cultures in the east coast region (Cammiade and Burkitt 1930). They organized the Stone Age material into Series 1, 2, 3 and 4 cultures with alternating wet and dry climatic cycles, based on the east African model of pluvial-interpluvial cycles implying cyclic variation in the intensity of rainfall. On the west coast K.R.U. Todd (1932) pioneered both prehistoric and Pleistocene research. He extended this east coast model and described the cultural stratigraphy and climate succession on the basis of a depositional sequence on the Kandivli Nala in the Bombay (Mumbai) area (Todd 1932, 1939).

While the laterite (in the coast) and alluvial litho units in the south-east coast were considered as climate sensitive parameters by Cammiade and Burkitt (1930), de Terra and Paterson (1939 and references quoted therein) were the first to highlight the river terraces and related deposits in the Soan Valley as climate indicators. The Siwalik Boulder Conglomerate was assigned to the period of Mindel glaciation and this provided a chronological basis for reconstructing the glacial sequence for the subcontinent. However, Cammiade and Burkitt (1930) and Richards et al. (1932) were clear about the fact that peninsular India did not experience glaciation in the past. The glacial-interglacial and pluvial-interpluvial schemes became standard models for prehistoric and Pleistocene research in India for at least 40 years.

The Boulder Conglomerate zone of the Potwar was considered a marker unit in the Quaternary correlations in India, by Krishnaswami (1947) followed by regional account of Zeuner (1950), Wainwright (1964), Sankalia (1963), Khatri (1961) and Soundara Rajan (1952, 1958). This gradually led to a plethora of climatic interpretations presenting a confused picture of the Pleistocene period. While Sankalia (1964) assigned silt deposition to a dry climate, Soundara Rajan (1958) assigned it to wet conditions and gravels to a dry climate.

Krishnaswami's (1947) synthesis of Stone Age India reveals confusion and uncertainty regarding the age of the laterite and its climatic significance, and was even equated with a glacial stage climate. While emphasizing its importance in climatic and stratigraphic reconstructions and in correlating the Quaternary sequences it was assigned to both Lower Pleistocene (pre-human) and Middle Pleistocene periods. The presence or absence of archaeological evidence on the laterite surface was considered crucial to its dating. This prevailed until Guzder (1980) carried out a detailed study of laterite and Stone Age cultures in the Konkan region of western India. However, Zeuner (1950) and Wainwright (1964) were successful in showing that evidence for more than four cycles of wet and dry phases

TABLE 1. CLIMATIC AND CULTURAL SUCCESSION IN THE SABARMATI VALLEY

Formation	Climate	Culture
Stable dune surface	Relatively wet	Microlithic
Sand dune activity	Dry	—
Erosional phase	Somewhat damper conditions	—
Fine silt and windblown sands	Main dry phase activity	Aeolian activity strong no human
Red soil	Wetter conditions	Alluvial silt, no palaeolithic
Silt	Onset of drier climate	Steeper gradient, palaeolithic man present
Cemented gravel	Rainfall heavier than today	Seasonal flood deposition palaeolithic man present
Mottled clay humid	Relatively less of the Sabarmati	Establishment of the ancient course

existed in the peninsular rivers. This ushered in a new era of geoarchaeology in India that picked up gradual momentum in the late 1970s.

On the basis of a comparative study with the Sabarmati sections Wainwright (1964) suggested that lateritic weathering leading to the formation of lateritic crusts could be of 3rd glacial age and that all the three Pleistocene soils corresponded with the three glacial maxima of the last glaciation (Wainwright 1964; also by Zeuner 1959).

Some examples of regional studies on the Pleistocene climatic and cultural succession in India are: Krishnaswami and Soundara Rajan's (1951) work in the Singrauli Basin (Uttar Pradesh), Subbarao's (1952) work in the Mahi, Orsang and Karjan valleys in central Gujarat, Sankalia's (1956) work in the Godavari and Pravara river Valleys in upland Deccan (Maharashtra), Joshi's (1955) work in the Malaprabha Valley, Karnataka, Bose and Sen's (1948) work in Mayurbhanj (also Bose et al. 1958). Mohapatra's (1962) in the Brahmani Valley (Orissa) and K.V. Soundara Rajan's (1952) in the Gundlakama Valley (Andhra Pradesh).

GEOARCHAEOLOGY AND THE PALAEOMONSOON SINCE 1965

Increased geoarchaeological research during the last three decades has recognized the potential of fluvial deposits for the study of the palaeomonsoon. Although precision is lacking a good dating control essential for the reconstruction of the frequency of monsoon fluctuations, especially from terrestrial environments, where proxy records are seldom continuous and long, has been achieved to some extent. While all the archaeological materials are land-based, its association with datable material is crucial for establishing relationship between culture change and climate change in the past.

Apart from the traditional stratigraphic dating and relative dating based on chemical changes such as fluorine to phosphate ratios in bones from Quaternary sites (Kshirsagar 1993), quite a few radiometric dating techniques with increasing time spans have been successfully employed in the Quaternary studies of India (Korisettar and Rajaguru 1998).

However, owing to natural constraints dating of sites older than the Late Pleistocene (between 40 and 10 ka) is infrequent and as yet not on a secure footing. The Holocene records have an impressive radiocarbon time frame. Since the dating is within the Late Quaternary the land-sea correlation has been possible for a diverse variety of sedimentary environments in western and central India. This has led to a major departure from using archaeological material as an aid to dating Quaternary sequences. Radiometric dating has enabled integration of archaeological and environmental data for delineating man-environment relationships and palaeoecology.

The Thar Desert

In the Thar desert of Rajasthan records of integrated high energy fluvial systems dating back to the Late Teritary and Early Pleistocene have been documented. Other fluvial and aeolian sediments of Late Middle Pleistocene age have provided abundant evidence of Stone Age assemblages and contemporary climate. In the region south of the Aravallis, Mewar, along the tributaries of the Chambal evidence for Acheulian culture has been recorded from the bouldery deposits (Misra 1967). His climatic sequence for the Berach Basin was necessarily based on the standard schemes provided by previous workers.

Semi-arid monsoonal climate continued to prevail over upland Maharashtra and western Rajasthan till the end of the Middle Pleistocene as indicated by calcretes and vertisols preserved in the alluvial, lacustral and aeolian sediments. Ephemeral stream processes, debris flow deposits, colluvial unweathered or weakly weathered deposits intercalating with alluvial and aeolian sediments also suggest relatively dry climate around 300-400 ka. During this time the global climate was glacial arid and Acheulian occupation was adaptation to such an environment (Rajaguru 1997a; Misra and Rajaguru 1987; Misra 1995; Wasson et al. 1984, 1983).

Allchin et al. (1978) covered north Gujarat, Kathiawar and the Pushkar Basin in Rajasthan (Allchin and Goudie 1974). The artefact scatters are associated with hill wash scree, buried under later aeolian sands, generally situated in the vicinity of lakes and streams. Table 2 shows the stratigraphic scheme covering the later Pleistocene and Holocene.

Multidisciplinary studies on the lakes, playas and dune formation around Didwana (Nagaur district, Rajasthan) have helped in establishing the antiquity of dune forming processes and estimating the rate of accumulation as well (Allchin and Goudie 1974; Allchin et al. 1978). The antiquity of dunes goes back to 100 ka and the major dune field of the Thar seems to have formed between 15 and 12 ka (Dhir et al. 1994). Whereas Wasson (1995) on the basis of TL and radiocarbon dates estimated that peak of dune construction was prior to 16 ka and that dune construction was slight by 8 ka, with implications for strengthening of the monsoon by Mid- Holocene times. Geoarchaeological work by Misra and Rajaguru (1987) in the Nagaur district of Rajasthan has shown that during Palaeolithic occupation environmental conditions were congenial and with increasing aridity during Late Pleistocene the expansion of the desert took place.

TABLE 2. CLIMATIC AND CULTURAL SUCCESSION ALONG THE EASTERN MARGIN OF THE THAR DESERT

Lithology	Culture	Climate
Modern land surface (reactivated sand surface)	Microliths	Semi-arid
Calcification and root development	—	Arid
Sand sheet	—	Arid
Buried soil(deep rotlehm type soil)	Middle and Upper Palaeolithic	Moist
Sand sheet	—	Arid
Slope wash scree	Lower Palaeolithic	Semi-arid

The Last Interglacial climate (about 125 ka) was warmer and wetter than the present interglacial (Holocene) in the higher latitude regions of the world. A unique calcic soil horizon has been encountered in the Thar desert at Didwana buried in the classic sand dune at 16R and associated with the Middle Palaeolithic artefacts (Singhvi et al. 1992; Rajaguru et al. 1994). This calcic palaeosol represents a relatively wet phase in the largely semi-arid phase of climate.

The thermoluminescence date (TL) obtained for Rajasthan aeolian sediments and radiocarbon dates for molluscan shells from the alluvial deposits containing archaeological material suggest that wind blown (aeolian) sedimentation was the strongest during the transition from Late Pleistocene to Holocene (Singhvi et al. 1994). Choking of alluvial streams took place in response to arid phase aggradation of the Terminal Pleistocene. Whereas during 40-25 ka channel incision and stabilization of alluvial fill surfaces with vertisol formation upon them took place, when the rainfall was relatively higher than post 25 ka period. Between 22 ka and 16 ka the climate was distinctly dry, in conformity with the Last Glacial Maximum.

The conclusions about the glacial aridity during ~18 ka based on peats from Nilgiris (Sukumar et al. 1993) were recently corroborated by Andrews et al. (1998) by the study of stable isotopes of calcretes in Rajasthan; and by stable isotope ratios of dated ground waters from south India (Sukhija et al. 1998).

Gujarat

In Gujarat Quaternary deposits have been documented from marine, fluvial and aeolian environments (see Chamyal and Merh 1995). The marine sequences are confined to the littoral zones of Kachchh, Saurashtra and mainland Gujarat. The fluvial and aeolian sequences are best exposed in the valleys of Sabarmati, Mahi and Narmada, dating back to the Middle Pleistocene. Miliolites are the conspicuous littoral and aeolian formations and represent transgressive and regressive phases of the sea during the late Middle to Late Pleistocene. Beach rocks, raised mud flats, raised beaches and inland ridges represent a Holocene transgressive sea. The *ranns* of Kachchh also represent a Holocene fluvio-transitional environment.

Lele (1972) and Marathe (1981) have established the relationship of sea level changes with the Stone Age occupation in Saurashtra, determining that the chronology of the Lower Palaeolithic is internlinked with the miliolite formation. During the mid-Quaternary the rivers were flowing 10-15 m below their present bed levels and the Lower Palaeolithic occupation took place at this time—recorded by the evidence of Acheulian artefacts in the gravel conglomerates of buried channels. The fluvial gravel containing Acheulian tools were buried under sediments of a major transgressive phase of the sea, represented by miliolite M-I, occurring at an elevation of 40-60 m AMSL. This phase was followed by a rejuvenation of streams (3-5 m below the present bed of the rivers) at the time of a low sea level. The gravels overlying M-I have yielded Middle Palaeolithic tools. These gravels are in turn overlain by miliolite M-II, representing yet another phase of transgressive sea. Th-U dating of the miliolites suggest that the Lower Palaeolithic occupation took place around 190 ka and the Middle Palaeolithic to around 56 ka (Baskaran et al. 1986). Later Baskaran et al. (1989) dated three episodes of miliolite formations, M-I (56-70 ka), M II (75 to 115 ka) and M-III (140-210 ka). Interruptions in the deposition of miliolite, sedimentary and diagenetic features in it is being interpreted in terms of palaeoclimate changes. Patel and Bhat (1996) while presenting a summary of research on miliolites in Gujarat have identified several palaeoclimatic signatures preserved in them.

Pant and Chamyal (1990) have worked out a detailed composite lithostratigraphy for the Mahi Valley revealing a succession of six units with intervening conglomerate beds. Unit I comprises fine clay (with lateral extent of nearly 30 km) with marly bands and carbonate pipes, overlain by Gravel I containing Lower Palaeolithic artefacts. Unit II is a fractured mud overlain by Gravel II. Unit III is a fine laminated mud. A carbonate crust separates Unit III and IV (fractured mud). Yet another carbonate layer separates Unit IV and V (aeolian silt) which is overlain by Gravel III followed by aeolian silt (Unit VI) and dunal sands (Unit VII) towards the top. Within the section a succession of palaeosols has also been logged. Gravel I yielding Acheulian artefacts has been correlated with the Hiran Valley Acheulian gravel (dated to around 190 ka). The Mahi Valley red palaeosol (Unit V) is equated to Oxygen Isotope Stage 5e and is being considered a marker bed because of its ubiquitous presence in the alluvial sequences of southern Gujarat. Further a detailed pedogenetic analysis of various litho-units in the Mahi Valley by Khadikar et al. (1996) has resulted in identifying a series of palaeosols reflecting cyclic changes in climate between arid and humid phases, but with varying intensity, during the last 300 ka. The lower age limit of the basal clay is extrapolated from the Sabarmati Valley (Sareen et al. 1992).

Acheulian artefacts occur on the surface of a fossil terra rosa (red soil) enclosed between two miliolites (M-I and M-II) at Gopnath in Bhavnagar District of Gujarat. Miliolite II is further overlain unconformably by an aeolianite of the Terminal Pleistocene age. The red soil is ascribed to a humid phase of the Last Interglacial climate when the sea level was higher by 5 m at the time of soil formation (Marathe et al. 1995). The sea level during this phase was 5 m higher than the present (Bruckner et al. 1987).

An erosional buried red soil in the Sabarmati alluvial sequence is TL dated to 50 and 30 ka, the development of gypcrete within the aeolian profile at Kavas (Barmer district, Rajasthan) are a couple of examples of climatic amelioration during the otherwise dry climatic phase of the Late Pleistocene (Sareen et al. 1992; Singhvi et al. 1992).

Central India

In the Son and Belan valleys three widespread alluvial formations have been documented. They range in age from Middle Pleistocene to Holocene, like in the Sabarmati Valley the three oldest formations are capped by aeolian deposits. There is abundant evidence of Stone Age cultures contained in these formations. On the basis of a summary of Quaternary investigation by Williams and Clarke (1995) the following Table 3 presents the Pleistocene sequences in the Son Valley.

In the Belan Valley a similar sequence of sediments has been documented but formal designations have not been designated.

In the central Narmada Basin the stratigraphic construction shows a sequence of four formations arranged in a stratigraphic succession that includes the Palaeolithic succession. They are (a) Shobpur Formation, (b) Narsinghpur Formation (Early Acheulian), (c) Devakachar Formation (Late Acheulian), (d) Jhalon Formation (Middle and Upper Palaeolithic) (Acharyya and Basu 1993). More recently Tiwari and Bhai (1997) have worked out a sequence of seven formations. The basal two, Pilikarar and Dhansi Formations, have been tentatively dated to the Neogene and Early Pleistocene respectively on the basis of degree of oxidation and reversed magnetic polarity stratigraphy. The Pilikarar sediments show a high degree of latosolic weathering under relatively humid conditions. Occurrence of fossil evidence of the hominid and typical Middle Pleistocene

TABLE 3. QUATERNARY ALLUVIAL FORMATION IN THE SON VALLEY, MADHYA PRADESH (after Korisettar and Rajaguru 1998)

Formation	Litho-units	Culture	Age
Khetaunhi	Fine sands silts and clays	Neolithic	—
Baghor	Silts and clays course sands calcreted gravels	Mesolithic Upper Palaeolithic Some Middle Palaeolithic	Holocene Upper Pleistocene
Patpara	Granule sands gravelly clays red-brown clayey gravels	Transitional Lower to Middle Palaeolithic	Upper Pleistocene to Late Mid-Pleistocene
Sihawal Fine	sandy clay Colluvial-alluvial gravels conglomerates	Lower Palaeolithic TL date 103 ka (Clark and Williams 1986)	Middle Pleistocene

fauna such as *Bos namadicus* and *Equus namadicus* typical of the Middle Pleistocene in the highly calcretized members of the Surajkund Formation are suggestive of adaptation to semi arid conditions (Sonakia and Basu 1998).

Late Quaternary fluvial sediments in the central Narmada Valley have also preserved excellent records of prehistoric sites as well as lenses of volcanic ash date to 75 ka (Westgate et al. 1998). By and large the climate was semi-arid almost throughout the Late Quaternary. Geoarchaeological studies of a semi-primary Middle Palaeolithic site preserved in the alluvial sediments of the Narmada at Samnapur in District Narsinghpur have revealed the effect of debris flow/soil creep on the occupation horizon following the ash fall event and the consequent dry phase (Ahsan 1993).

Deccan

Rajaguru and Kale (1985), Kale and Rajaguru (1987) and Mishra et al. (1996) identified aggradational and erosional sequences in the Late Quaternary alluvia of the upland rivers in Maharashtra (Western Ghats), the source region of the Godavari, Pravara, Bhima and Krishna river systems.

On the basis of geomorphological and chronostratigraphic data a detailed lithological, cultural and climatological sequences has been worked out with a possible correlation of deep sea Oxygen Isotope Stages (Rajaguru and Mishra 1997). Two broad groups of sediments are now recognized, (a) colluvial sediments, and (b) alluvial sediments, in order of succession. This sequence has been worked out as a response to changing intensity of monsoon since the Middle Pleistocene (see Table 4).

The prevalence of semi-arid monsoonic conditions prior to the ash fall tephra, dated to 75 ka (Westgate et al. 1998) is attested to by the occurrence of calcretised vertic soils below the ash horizon in the Upland Deccan region (western Maharashtra) (Rajaguru 1997a).

Though the marine cores show a high frequency of warmer and cooler episodes (see below) during the Middle Pleistocene comparable evidence is as yet not revealed either in the alluvial or aeolian stratigraphy in western and peninsular India. In respect of Late Pleistocene-Holocene transitional period much new fluvial data have been collected from the river valleys of western upland alluvial with a new beginning directed towards the palaeomonsoon reconstruction. The northern Deccan and western Indian proxies range in age from 100 to 13-14 ka.

That the Pleistocene-Holocene transition (14-9 ka) witnessed rapid switches in climate pattern is clearly reflected in the alluvial sequences. Episodic and strong gravel aggradation occurred in the Godavari and Bhima valleys in response to intensification of summer monsoon in the Western Ghats. The most distinctive evidence of a dramatic switch to aridity during Late Pleistocene is seen in the form of filled up gorges through which the Pushpawati and Mula rivers flow, at Chilewdi and Bote respectively. The Chilewadi evidence is intriguing as this catchment lies in the high rainfall Western Ghats. This is an instance of aggradation punctuating a long period of quietitude, earlier recorded by Mishra and Rajaguru (1993). Sadakata et al. (1993) have provided a radiocarbon framework

TABLE 4. PROXY RECORDS OF THE MONSOON IN THE UPLAND RIVERS, WESTERN DECCAN

Period	Lithofacies	Geomorphic environment	Radiometric dates	Cultural sequence	Monsoon intensity
Middle Pleistocene	Colluvial gravels	Aggradation active in the piedmont zone	U-series >350 ka	Early Acheulian	Fluctuation between weak and strong discharge
	Alluvial sandy pebbly gravel	same as above		Acheulian	same as above
	Soil Formation or silty alluvium	Erosion	Oxygen Isotope Stage 3, 40-25 ka	monsoon	Relatively strong
LGM	Gravels at Kalas Chandoli and Nevasa	Aggradation and accumulation of colluvium	^{14}C date 18-11 ka	Microliths	Weak monsoon
Terminal Pleistocene	Gravel at Nevasa Inamgaon, Gargaon and Alsa	Aggradation dominant	^{14}C date 13-10 ka Younger Dryas	Microliths	Weak monsoon, episodic floods
Mid-Holocene	Soil Formation on the Pleistocene silts	Erosion	6-4 ka	Microliths	Good monsoon
Late Holocene	Sandy silt deposition	inset fill terrace gully erosion	Minor aggradation within Holocene, 3 ka onwards	Chalcolithic	Weak monsoon

which shows two groups of dates clustering prior to and after the Last Glacial Maximum.

Mishra et al. (1996) have documented evidence for fluvial response to global climatic changes during the Pleistocene-Holocene transition. They have also shown that different sectors of the river respond differently to a particular phase of climatic change, which is again governed by the nature of the catchment. They found that aggradation was dominant during Late Pleistocene in the region west of 75 degrees longitude, whereas in the region towards its east aggradation was dominant during the Early Holocene (prior to 7 ka) (for details see Mishra et al. 1996; Rajaguru 1997a and b).

At Nevasa, Chandoli and Sashtewadi gravels dated to 13-14 ka show an unconformable relationship with the underlying silty alluvium of the Late Pleistocene. The gravels betray maturity as revealed by the degree of roundness and lithology, as compared with the older gravels of 25-14 ka. Mishra et al. (1996) have interpreted these gravels as representing the initiation of a channel incision phase of the Pleistocene-Holocene transition. This according to the authors is comparable to the evidence of deglaciation from the Himalayas (Singh and Agrawal 1976).

Contrasting fluvial responses to climate change are recorded for the period between 12 and 10 ka. While at Inamgaon flood plain aggradation was going on at 12 ka, silty aggradation at Gargaon and erosion to the modern bed level was reached at Asla around 10 ka. Evidence of Early Holocene floods is interpreted by the evidence of burial of microlithic sites at Ranjegaon and Shaksal Pimpri (Mishra et al. 1998).

The majority of radiocarbon dates from this region roughly span the period from 25-14 ka and equated with Oxygen Isotopic Stage 2 and during this period the peninsular rivers were depositing very little sediment on the continental shelf. At Pleistocene-Holocene transition abrupt warming event around 13.5 and 10 ka lead to increasing rainfall and consequently gravel deposition took place as recorded at Nevasa, Chandoli and Sashtewadi (Mishra et al. 1998)

North-Eastern India

Garo Hills and the Manipur Valley provide with a good proxies of the Late Quaternary climatic reocrd. Though the regions are submontane to intermontane valleys they experience much greater humid conditions in comparison with the rest of the subcontinent.

In the Manipur Vaeely Quaternary formations include alluvial fill, colluvio-alluvial cone terraces, rock-cut strath type gravel-terraces and colluvial cones. Supported by archaeological and radiocarbon dates the study lithological and morphological characters of these sediments have recognized five Quaternary formations: Wangu Formation, Imphal Formation, Bishnupur Formation, Supermeina Formation and Loktak Formation. Climatic fluctuations in this region were charaterized by the switch between tropical to subtropical monsoonic and cool and dry-wet phases, good evidence of climate change during the Terminal Pleistocene. In accord with the last glacial maxima cool dry period lasted between 23,000 and 11,000 BP. Lake levels were higher around 25,000-23,000 and 11,000-8,000 years BP.

Although radiocarbon dates are not available for the Garo Hills detailed lithological and sedimentological study of Quaternary formations indicate the prevalence of drier climatic conditions during the Pleistocene (Singh 1987; Medhi 1981).

CONCLUDING REMARKS

In summary one can observe an overall convergence of the palaeomonsoon evidence, from marine, lacustral and terrestrial records, relating to frequency and intensity of monsoonal fluctuations during the Late Quaternary. These while displaying overwhelming synchronity of monsoon conditions in the different regions of India, betray apparent instances of diachronism which has got to be interpreted carefully. The climate of subtropical India during the Last Glacial Maximum of 18 ka reveals a global unity. Though the Kashmir evidence is indicative of an early deglaciation the rest of the subcontinent and the Indian Ocean region were relatively dry. Evidence from sand dunes, desert lakes, alluvial sequences and offshore cores clearly converges to indicate drier conditions between 25 and 18 ka, 16 and 12 ka and again around 9 ka.

The palaeontological assemblages from the riparian environments reveal the symbiosis of herbivorous ungulates with the Lower Palaeolithic inhabitants, and attest to the prevalence of savanna habitats and riverine gallery forests. Fossil fauna, such as *Bos, Sus, Elephas, Equus, Hexaprotodon, Stegodon* and *Cervus* from Middle and Late Pleistocene contexts in India indicate savanna and woodland ecosystems (Badam 1984; Misra 1989: Appendix I).

Palynological and isotopic data, as outlined above, also clearly show that vegetation changes were not primarily controlled by temperature changes, as generally believed, but also by periodic changes in the intensity of precipitation and monsoon upwelling. Such vegetation changes have implications for fragmentation of habitats and forest areas leading to differentiation of animal and plant species. As indicated by palynological studies the montane evergreen forest of the Western Ghats gave way to the expanded grasslands under the arid climate of the Last Glacial Maximum (25-18 ka). The expansion of grasslands as a corollary could have affected biological species endemic to a particular habitat/ecosystem. And the impact of climate on habitat change was determined by the intensity of climate during each of the wet and dry climatic phases.

Increased continentality and low sea levels during glacial epochs as envisaged by Rajaguru and Kale (1985) and Kale and Rajaguru (1987), might have affected the ecosystems across the continental area. During the Last Glacial Maximum the sea level was lower by at least 100 m. In effect the low sea levels must have resulted in the shifting of SW rainfall belts away from the continental region. As evidenced by offshore research, during these periods the NE monsoon was stronger, and perhaps covered a larger area than at present. The present reach of both the monsoons has to be viewed as interglacial high sea level ecoparameter.

Evidence for a prolonged dry period in the subtropical regions of India appears to have had an overriding influence on the ecodiversity and human adaptation to savanna ecosystems. The Last Interglacial wetter conditions supported the Middle Palaeolithic adaptation in the Thar (Rajasthan) and Saurashtra peninsula (Gujarat), while in other areas it was an adaptation to savanna and woodland ecosystems.

The Late Pleistocene aridity is well documented all over India: in Kashmir the loess deposition was dominant (Agrawal et al. 1989; Bronger and Heinkele 1995); dune formation in Rajasthan; aggradation and loess deposition in Gujarat; colluvial cone formation developed over alluvial and lacustral deposits in north-east India (Manipur and Garo Hills) (T.A. Singh 1987; Medhi 1981) and aggradational and colluvial deposition in peninsular India. The formation of calcrete in the present humid tropical region of West Bengal (Basak et al. 1998), in terms of rainfall, is significant, for it indicates decrease in the rainfall during the later Pleistocene. This is further attested by the fossil evidence of a grassland fauna, like *Axis axis, Antelope cervicapra* and *Bos namadicus*. In Tripura extensive development of calcrete in the later Pleistocene alluvial deposits is documented in the Late Pleistocene context (J. Ramesh 1989).

Multidisciplinary palaeoclimate studies carried out on continental and offshore deposits in southern India are suggestive of variation in vegetation cover of the Western Ghats between tropical evergreen and savanna ecosystems. While the evergreen forests were associated with stable humid conditions the spread of savanna vegetation took place during arid to semi-arid transitions. Table 5 gives the summary of Holocene climatic changes.

The Pleistocene stratigraphy reconstructed for the diverse physiographic regions betrays uniformity in the geomorphic processes operating in the past under the prevalent monsoon regimes. The regional environments fluctuated in accordance with these changes between savanna and woodland ecosystem affecting human occupation of the areas. The lithological successions suggest that during Middle Pleistocene bedrock erosion and pedimentation were the dominant processes leading to the formation of debris flow, rubble and colluvial deposits and fan gravels prior to human occupation. Towards the close of the Middle Pleistocene some of these material was incorporated into alluvial systems, leading to the formation of present patterns of drainage in the Late Quaternary.

In the coastal region, particularly along the west coast, the rise in sea level was extremely rapid during the Pleistocene-Holocene transition (Kale and Rajaguru 1985). Oceanographic research off the west coast of India revealed a still stand at 11 ka, with a sea level still 80 m below the present which rapidly rose to a level higher than the present around 6 ka (Hashimi et al. 1995) and gradually reached the present level (Ghate 1988).

Early Holocene was a period of climatic amelioration as well as abrupt changes in the intensity of rainfall. Between 6 and 4 ka the Thar desert received higher rainfall both during summer and winter: playas carried fresh water, the dunes were stabilized and the stream activity was strong in the northern part of the Thar desert. Mesolithic cultures continued to inhabit the region as a whole and the stream banks sheltered the Harappan

TABLE 5. HOLOCENE CLIMATIC CHANGES (after Valdiya 1999)

Area	Warm-Wet (Years BP)	Hot-Dry (Years BP)
Arabian Sea (planktonic forams)	10,500-5,000	3,500
Western coast (terrestrial detritus)	10,500-10,000	
Karwar coast (land-derived pollen)	10,500-5,000	3,500
Nilgiri Hills (δ ^{13}C values of peat)	9,000-8,000	5,000-2,000
Didwana-Lunkaransar lakes in Rajasthan (pollen profiles)	10,800-4,500	4,000-present
Gangotri glacier (pollen in sediments)	6,500-4,000	3,500-3,000
Tsokar Lake, Ladakh (*juniperus* flora)	10,000	
Bangong Co Lake, Aksai Chin (pollen)	6,000 max.	4,000-3,000
Southeastern Tibet (pollen in lakes)	7,500-3,000	3,000-1,500
Bhimtal Basin, south Kumaun (pollen)		3,500±120
Rara Lake, west Nepal (pollen)		4,500
Karewa Lake, Kashmir (pollen)		5,000

settlements. The semi-arid savanna ecosystems across the subcontinent continued to support hunting-gathering and fishing, and agro-pastoral economies and favoured transition to food-producing economy in the Middle Holocene, perhaps human groups were adapting to a decreasing monsoon regime.

The distribution and widespread occurrence of Mesolithic sites in India appear to coincide with the climatic phase characterized by monsoon recovery between 9 and 8 ka after the dry spell. These Mesolithic communities continued to inhabit the region colonized by them and survived the vagaries of monsoonal conditions by developing adaptive capabilities. Delineation of processes responsible for expansion of agricultural economies in the Neolithic and Chalcolithic stages is beyond the scope of the present paper. Beginning of agriculture in the different regions was initially governed by the rainfall regimes and the adoption of suitable introduced and indigenous crops, as well as domestication of cattle, sheep and goat. Sheep and goat possess greater adaptive capability than the cattle. Sheep-goat pastoralism is more viable in low rainfall areas.

In northern Deccan farming was adopted around 3.5 ka. The first farmers settled along the streams exploiting the alluvial strips along the floodplains. However a conspicuous hiatus occurs in the archaeological record of western India (Dhavalikar 1992). This gap is attributed to the onset of severe dry conditions by Dhavalikar (1992) as envisaged by Krishnamurthy et al. (1981). There is supporting evidence for this inference from geological, isotopic, micropalaeontological or palynological analyses, as shown above. The upwelling indices from the Indian Ocean decline further indicating decrease in the monsoon rainfall. Interesting evidence of decreasing lake levels around this period is also reported from Ethiopia and Tibet (Gillesie et al. 1983; Gasse and van Campo 1994). Other meteorological parameteres such as abrupt changes in solar radiation, temperature, and southeasterly winds are cited as good evidence of an abrupt switch in climate causing higher frequency of floods. On the other hand there is evidence of continuation of stabilization of dunes and soil formation on these surfaces. In fact the summer monsoon was weaker between 3.5 and 3 ka the peak of farming activity in the western Deccan. The intensity of monsoon was at its minimum during the period between 4,000 and 1,500 BP (Late Holocene) as compared with the Mid- Holocene (8,000 to 4,000 BP). Great floods occurred between 4,000 and 1,500 BP (Naidu 1995). Kale et al. (1997) have documented a well dated evidence for a 2,000 year old flood on the Narmada in central India. On the other hand the Late Holocene witnessed extreme dynamism of the monsoon and this period also witnessed widespread adoption of agriculture in the Deccan and central India revealing both waxing and waning phases.

Dhavalikar's attempt to relate culture change with climate change in the Late Holocene revealed two phases of cultural efflorescence (i) the Indus Civilization from 3000 to 2000 BC and (ii) Early Historic period from 500 BC to AD 500. He opines that the interval between these two phases of urbanism was marred by erratic and low monsoon regime over South Asia (Contra Enzel et al. 1999) and invokes monsoon as the formidable causative factor in the 'urban decay' of these phases. Steady monsoon was essential for continuing maritime trade with distant Mesopotamia and in the event of erratic wind regimes gradual collapse of trade began and consequently the trade-economy. The second urbanization is attributed to monsoon amelioration during the Early Historic period (Dhavalikar 1992).

At this stage it is not possible to identify a single factor playing a determinant role in the shaping of the cultural complexity of the Holocene Indian subcontinent, but a combination of physiographic, hydrologic, edaphic and seasonal, and cultural factors can safely be envisaged, especially in respect of the introduction of a variety of cereals for agriculture. Wheat, barley, rice, *ragi, jowar*, etc., form the staple foods of the human population living within the different regions of the subcontinent.

Wheat and barley are weedy grasses with lesser adaptive capability. They prosper in areas of disturbed soils such as on hill slopes in the areas of winter rainfall. These plants were domesticated in the region stretching between the eastern Mediterranean and the western borderlands of the Indian subcontinent. This region receives rainfall during the winter that naturally supports their cultivation, and they were adopted by the Harappans in the northern sector of the Harappan domain. Whereas in the southern sector (particularly Gujarat), which is covered by the SW summer monsoon ragi and jowar were introduced for cultivation by the Harappans right in the beginning of the third millennium BC (Possehl 1992).

Ragi and Sorghum are generally summer sown, rainfed crops particularly suited to monsoon seasonality. They are capable of high productivity in areas marginal for wheat and barley. Archaeoethnobotanical research has revealed that none of these cereals are native to the land and were introduced in the cultural landscapes owing to their adaptive capability to the mosaic of climatic regimes across the subcontinent. Cultural processes were primarily responsible for their availability in the Neolithic and Bronze Age contexts. The archaeological evidence shows difference in the timing and spacing of adoption of these cereals in the different Neolithic zones of India.

While evidence of rice cultivation goes back to the middle of second millennium BC at Koldihwa in the Ganga Valley (there is uncertainty regarding its earlier dating), it is also known from Lothal in Gujarat in the Harappan context, but it was introduced in the south beginning in the Megalithic period (Kajale 1991). Since the Early Historic period one observes a continuing expansion of rice cultivation under intensive agriculture in the semi-arid regions. The effective management of rainfed reservoirs across the major river systems has enabled the growth of economic prosperity. Despite this technological control the El Nino years effect drought conditions. However, by virtue of its ability to build itself the monsoon recovers and restores normalcy in about 3-4 years. Regularity of the monsoon is crucial to agro-economic prosperity and stable demography of the Indian civilization. It is interesting to note that during Early Historic period there was growing awareness of territorial integrity and military defense of natural resources by the ruling families leading to the waning and waxing of empires whose agricultural productivity dwindled under falling monsoon intensity and under increased demographic pressure took to looting the booty of the neighbour. Historians have attempted an explanation of urban decay during the post-Gupta period of early Medieval India, but for want of space we would not like to get into the details and would like to refer the readers to Sharma (1987) who alludes to evidence from historical archaeology and literature. Since 2000 BC. The second urbanization and its continuity broadly coincides with the expansion of rice cultivation from the Ganga Valley into much of southern India and a successful exploitation of its mineral and metal resources. With continuing adoption of hardy crops and periodic switch towards an agro-pastoral subsistence economy prehistoric communities could withstand the vagaries of the monsoon.

REFERENCES

Acharyya, S.K. and P.K. Basu 1993. Toba Ash on the Indian Subcontinent and its Implications for Correlation of Late Pleistocene Alluvium, *Quaternary Research* 40: 10-19.

Agrawal, D.P.R. Dodia, B.S. Kotlia, H. Razdan and A. Sahni 1989. The Plio-Pleistocene Geologic and Climatic Record of the Kashmir Valley: a Review and New Data, *Palaeogeography, Palaeoclimatology and Palaeoecology* 73: 267-86.

Ahsan, S.M.K. 1993. A Study of Site Formation Processes in the Sub-Humid Environment of Central India with Special Reference to Samnapur Palaeolithic Site (Madhya Pradesh). Ph.D. Dissertation. Pune: University of Poona.

Allchin, B. and F.R. Allchin 1982. *The Rise of Civilization in India and Pakistan*. Cambridge: Cambridge University Press.

Allchin, B. and A. Goudie 1974. Pushkar: Prehistory and Climatic Change in Western India, *World Archaeology* 5 (3): 359-68.

Allchin, B., A. Goudie and K.T.M. Hegde 1978. *The Prehistory and Palaeogeography of the Great Indian Desert*. London: Academic Press.

Andrews, J.E., A.K. Singhvi, A.J. Kailath, R. Kuhn, P.F. Dennis, S.K. Tandon and R.P. Dhir 1998. Do Stable Isotope Data from Calcrete Record Late Pleistocene Monsoonal Climate Variation in the Thar Desert of India?, *Quaternary Research* 50: 240-51.

Badam, G.L. 1984. The Pleistocene Faunal Succession, in *The Evolution of East Asian Environment* (R.O. White Ed.), pp. 746-75. Hong Kong: University of Hong Kong.

Basak, B., G.L. Badam, A. Kshirsagar and S.N. Rajaguru 1998. Late Quaternary Environment, Palaeontology and Culture of the Tarafeni Valley, Midnapur District, West Bengal: a Preliminary Study, *Journal of the Geological Society of India* 51 (6): 731-40.

Baskaran, M., G. Rajagopalan and B.L.K. Somayajulu 1989. 230Th/234U and 14C Dating of Quaternary Carbonate Deposits of Saurashtra, India, *Chemical Geology* (Isotope Geoscience Section) 13: 505-14.

Benn, D.I. and L.A. Owen 1998. The Role of the Indian Summer Monsoon and the Mid-Latitude Westerlies in Himalayan Glaciation: Review and Speculative Discussion, *Journal of the Geological Society of London* 155: 353-63.

Bose, N.K., D. Sen and G. Ray 1958. Geological and Cultural Evidence of the Stone Age in Mayurbhanj, *Man in India* 38 (1): 49-55.

Bowen, D.Q. 1978. *Quaternary Geology*. Oxford: Pergamon Press.

Bowler, J.M., R. Jones and An Zhisheng 1995. Climate Change in the Western Pacific: Its Implications for Green House Scenarios, in *Quaternary Environments and Geo-archaeology of India* (S. Wadia, R. Korisettar and V.S. Kale Eds.), pp. 1-21. Bangalore: Geological Society of India.

Broecker, W. 1996. Glacial Climate in the Tropics, *Science* 272: 1902-4.

Bronger, A. and T. Heinkele 1995. Loess-Palaeosal Sequences as Witness of Palaeoclimatic

Records?: the Kashmir Valley as an Example, in *Quaternary Environments and Geoarchaeology of India* (S. Wadia, R. Korisettar and V.S. Kale Eds.) pp. 109-23. Bangalore: Geological Society of India.

Bruckner, H. 1987. Milliolite Occurrences off Kathiawar Peninsular (Gujarat) India, *Journal of Archaeological Science* 13: 135-45.

Bruckner, H. and N. Bruhn 1992. Aspects of Weathering and Peneplanation in Southern India, *Zeitschrift für Geomorphology* Supplement Band 91: 43-66.

Bryson, R.A. and A.M. Swain 1981. Holocene Variation of Monsoon in Rajasthan, *Quaternary Research* 16: 35-45.

Caratini, C.B.I., M. Fontugne, M.T. Morzadec-Kerfourn, J.P. Pascal, C. Tissot 1994. A Less Humid Climate Since ca. 3500 yr. B.P. from Marine Cores Off Karwar, Western India, *Palaeogeography, Palaeoclimatology and Palaeoecology* 109: 371-84.

Chakraborty, S. and R. Ramesh 1993. Monsoon Induced Sea Surface Temperature Changes Recorded in Indian Corals, *Terra Nova* 5: 545-51.

——— 1997. Environmental Significance of Carbon and Oxygen Isotope Ratios in Banded Corals from Lakshadweep, India, *Quaternary International* 37: 55-65.

Chakraborty, S., R. Ramesh and S. Krishnaswami 1994. Air-Sea Exchange of CO_2 in the Gulf of Kutch, Northern Arabian Sea Based on Bomb-Carbon in Corals and Tree Rings, *Proceedings of the Indian Academy of Sciences* (Earth and Planetary Science) 103 (2): 329-40.

Chamyal, L.S., and S.S. Merh 1995. The Quaternary Formations of Gujarat, in *Quaternary Environments and Geoarchaeology of India* (S. Wadia, R. Korisettar and V.S. Kale Eds.), pp. 246-57. Bangalore: Geological Society of India.

Corvinus, G. 1981 and 1983. *A Survey of the Pravara River System in Western Maharashtra, India*, 2 Vols. Redaktion, Tubingen: Miller-Bedhek Verlag-Archaeologica Venatoria: Institut fur Ureschte Der Universitat.

Dennell, R.W. and H.M. Rendell 1991. De Terra and Paterson and the Soan Flake Industry: a New Perspective from the Soan Valley, Northern Pakistan, *Man and Environment* XVI (2): 91-9.

Deodhar, H. 1988. *Understanding Monsoons*. Bombay: Nehru Centre.

Deotare, B.C., M.D. Kajale, A.A. Kshirsagar and S.N. Rajaguru 1998. Geoarchaeological and Palaeoenvironmental Studies Around Bap-Malar Playa, District Jodhpur, Rajasthan, *Current Science* 75 (3): 316-20.

Dhavalikar, M. K. 1989. Human Ecology in Western India in the Second Millennium BC, *Man and Environment* XIV (1): 83-90.

——— 1990. *The First Farmers of Deccan*. Pune: Ravish.

——— 1994. Early Farming Communities of Central India, *Man and Environment* XIX (1-2): 159-68.

——— 1992. Culture-Environment Interface: a Historical Perspective. Presidential Address, Historical Archaeology, Epigraphy and Numismatics Section, Indian History Congress, 52nd Session, New Delhi, *Proceedings of the Indian History Congress*: 973-91.

Dhir, R.P., S.N. Rajaguru and A.K. Singhvi 1994. Desert Quaternary Formations and Their Morphostratigraphy: Implications for the Evolutionary History of the Thar, *Journal of the Geological Society of India* 43: 435-47.

Duplessy, J.C. 1982. Glacial and Interglacial Contrasts in the Northern Indian Ocean, *Nature* 295: 494-8.

Enzel, Y., L.L. Ely, S. Mishra, R. Ramesh, R. Amit, S.N. Rajaguru, V.R. Baker, B. Lazar and A.

Sandler 1999. High Resolution Holocene Environmental Change in the Thar Desert, NW India, *Science* (in press).

Gasse, F. and E. van Campo 1994. Abrupt Post Glacial Climate Events in West Asia and North African Monsoon Domains, *Earth and Planetary Science Letters* 126: 435-56.

Ghate, S. 1988. Sea Level Fluctuations in North Konkan with Special Reference to Sopara, *Current Science* 57: 1317-20.

Gillespie, R., F.A. Street-Perrot and R. Switzur 1983. Post-glacial Arid Episodes in Ehiopia: Implications for Climate Prediction, *Nature* 306: 680-3.

Goudeller, L.D. and R. Korisettar 1993. The First Discovery of Acheulian Bifaces in Goa: Implications for the Archaeology of the West Coast of India, *Man and Environment* XVIII, 1: 35-42.

Gupta, S. 1994. Archaeology of Indian Maritime Traditions: the Early Historic Phase, *Man and Environment* XIX (1-2): 217-25.

Guzder, S. 1980. *Quaternary Environments and Stone Age Cultures of the Konkan, Coastal Maharashtra, India*. Pune: Deccan College.

Hashimi, N.H., R. Nigam, R.R. Nair and G. Rajagopalan 1995. Holocene Sea Level Fluctuations Off Western Indian Continental Margin: an Update, *Journal of the Geological Society of India* 46: 157-62

Joshi, R.V. 1970. The Characteristics of Pleistocene Climatic Events in Indian Subcontinent, Land of Monsoon Climate, in *Indian Antiquary 4: Professor H.D. Sankalia Felicitation Volume* (S.B. Deo and M.K. Dhavalikar Eds.), pp. 53-63. Bombay: Popular Prakashan.

——— 1978. *Stone Age Cultures of Central India: Report of the Excavations of Rock-Shelters at Adamgarh, Madhya Pradesh*. Poona: Deccan College.

Joshi, R.V. and B.P. Bopardikar, 1972. Stone Age Cultures of Konkan (Coastal Maharashtra), in *Archaeological Congress and Seminar Papers* (S.B. Deo Ed.), pp. 42-52. Nagpur: Nagpur University.

Joshi, R.V., S.N. Rajaguru, R.S. Pappu and B.P. Bopardikar 1974. Quaternary Glaciation and Palaeolithic Sites in the Liddar Valley (Jammu and Kashmir), *World Archaeology* 5 (3): 369-79.

Kajale, M.D. 1991. Current Status of Indian Palaeoethnobotany: Introduced and Indigenous Food-Plants with a Discussion of the Historical and Evolutionary Developments of Indian Agriculture and Agricultural Systems in General, in *New Light on Early Farming: Recent Developments in Palaeoethnobotany* (Jane M. Renfrew Ed.), pp. 155-89. Edinburgh: Edinburgh University Press.

Kajale, M.D. and B.C. Deotare 1997. Late Quaternary Environmental Studies on Saline Lakes in Western Rajasthan: a Summarised View, *Journal of Quaternary Research* 12 (5): 405-12.

Kale, V.S. and S.N. Rajaguru 1987. Late Quaternary Alluvial History of the North-Western Deccan Upland Region, *Nature* 325: 612-14.

Kale, V.S., Sheila Mishra and V.R. Baker 1997. A 2000-Year Palaeoflood Record from Sakarghat on Narmada, Central India, *Journal of the Geological Society of India* 50 (3): 283-8.

Karve-Corvinus, G. and K.A.R. Kennedy 1964. Preliminary Report on Langhnaj Excavation 1963, *Bulletin of the Deccan College Research Institute* 24: 44-57.

Khadkikar, A.S., L.S. Chamyal, J.N. Malik, D.M. Maurya and S.S. Merh 1996. Arid-Humid Cycles in Mainland Gujarat Over the Past 300 Ka: Evidence from the Mahi River Basin, India, *Journal of Geological Society of India* 47 (3): 383-8.

Kenoyer, J.M. and J.N. Pal 1982. Report on the Excavation and Analysis of an Upper Acheulian Assemblage from Sihawal II, in *Palaeoenvironment and Prehistory in the Middle Son Valley* (G.R. Sharma and J.D. Clark Eds.), pp. 23-38. Allahabad: Abinash Prakashan.

Korisettar, R. and S.N. Rajaguru 1998. Quaternary Stratigraphy, Palaeoclimate and the Lower Palaeolithic Evidence of India, in *Early Human Behaviour in the Global Context: the Rise and Diversity of the Lower Palaeolithic Record* (M.D. Petraglia and Ravi Korisettar Eds.), pp. 304-42. London-New York: Routledge.

Korisettar, R., M.D. Petraglia, J. Schuldenrein and P. LaPorta (in preparation). Geoarchaeology of the Lakhmapur Lower Palaeolithic Site, Karnataka.

Korisettar, R., T.R. Venkatesan, Sheila Mishra, S.N. Rajaguru, B.L.K. Somayajulu, S.K. Tandon, V.D. Gogte, R.K. Ganjoo and V.S. Kale 1989a. Discovery of a Tephra Bed in the Quaternary Alluvial Stratigraphy of Pune District (Maharashtra), Peninsular India, *Current Science* 58 (10): 564-7.

Korisettar, R., S. Mishra, S.N. Rajaguru, V.D. Gogte, R.K. Ganjoo, T.R. Venkatesan, S.K. Tandon, B.L.K. Somayajulu and V.S. Kale 1989b. Age of Bori Volcanic Ash and Acheulian Culture of the Kukdi Valley, *Bulletin of the Deccan College Post-Graduate and Research Institute* 49: 564-7.

Krishnamurthy, R.V., D.P. Agrawal, V.N. Misra and S.N. Rajaguru 1981. Palaeoclimatic Inferences from the Behaviour of Radiocarbon Dates of Carbonates from Sand Dunes of Rajasthan, *Proceedings of the Indian Academy Sciences* (Earth and Planetary Sciences) 90 (2): 155-60.

Krishnaswami, V.D. 1947. Stone Age India, *Ancient India* 3: 11-57.

Kshirsagar, A. 1993. The Role of Fluorine in the Chronometric Dating of Indian Stone Cultures, *Man and Environment* XVIII (2): 23-32.

Kukla, G.J. 1977. Pleistocene Land-Sea Correlations: I Europe, *Earth Science Review* 13: 307-74.

Kumar, A. 1986. Palaeolatitudes and the Age of Indian Laterites, *Palaeogeography, Palaeoclimatology, Palaeoecology* 53: 231-7.

Lele, V.S. 1972. Late Quaternary Studies on the Bahadar Valley Saurashtra. Ph.D. Dissertation. Poona: University of Poona.

Liu, K., Z. Yao and L.G. Thompson 1998. A Pollen Record of Holocene Climatic Changes from the Dunde Ice Cap, Qinghai-Tibetan Plateau, *Geology* 26 (2): 135-8.

Malik, S.C. 1963. Studies in the Prehistory of Western India with Special Reference to Gujarat. Ph.D. Dissertation. Vadodara: the M.S. University of Baroda.

Marathe, A.R. 1981. *Geoarchaeology of the Hiran Valley, Indian*. Pune: Deccan College.

Medhi, D.K. 1981. Quaternary History of the Garo Hills, Meghalaya. Ph.D. Dissertation. Pune: University of Poona.

Meher-Homji, V.M. 1989. History of Vegetation of Peninsular India, *Man and Environment* XIII: 1-10.

Menon, S. and Kamaljit S. Bawa 1997. Application of Geographic Information Systems, Remotesensing, and a Landscape Ecology Approach to Biodiversity Conservation in the Western Ghats, *Current Science* 73 (2): 134-45.

Mishra, S. and S. Ghate 1989. Middle Palaeolithic Site of Ranjani, *Man and Environment* XV: 23-7.

Mishra, S. and S.N. Rajaguru 1993. Quaternary Deposits at Bhedaghat, Near Jabalpur, Madhya Pradesh, *Man and Environment* XVIII (2): 7-12.

Mishra, S., A. Kshirsagar and S.N. Rajaguru 1988. Relative Dating of the Quaternary Record from Upland Western Maharashtra, in *National Seminar on Recent Quaternary Studies in Indian* (M.P. Patel and N. Desai Eds.), pp. 267-78. Vadodara: the M.S. University of Baroda.

Mishra, S., S.N. Rajaguru and S. Ghate 1993. Stone Age Jaisalmer: Implications for Human Adaptation to Deserts, *Bulletin of the Deccan College Post-Graduate and Research Institute* 53: 260-8.

Mishra, S., T.R. Venkatesan, S.N. Rajaguru and B.L.K. Somayajulu 1995. Earliest Acheulian Industry from Peninsular India, *Current Anthropology* 36 (5): 847-51.

Mishra, S., A.A. Kshirsagar, S. Ghate and S. Naik 1998. Fluvial Response to Climatic Change in the Upper Godavari Valley. DST Project Completion Report.

Mishra, S., S.N. Rajaguru, Sonali Naik, Savita Ghate and Anupama Kshirsagar 1996. Climate Change During the Pleistocene/Holocene Transition in Upland Western Maharashtra, Western India, Proceedings of Seminar on Quaternary Environment and Society, Baker Sedget, Israel, 7-12 July 1996.

Misra, V.N. 1971. Two Late Mesolithic Sites in Rajasthan: a Brief Review of Investigations, *Poona University Journal* (Humanities) 35: 59-77.

——— 1973. Bagor: a Mesolithic Settlement in Northwest India, *World Archaeology* 5 (1): 92-110.

——— 1985. The Acheulian Industry of Rock Shelter IIIF-23 at Bhimbetka, Central India, in *Recent Advances in Indo-Pacific Prehistory* (V.N. Misra and Peter Bellwood Eds.), pp. 35-47. Delhi: Oxford-IBH.

——— 1989. Stone Age India, *Man and Environment* XIV (1): 17-64.

——— 1995. Geoarchaeology of the Thar Desert, in *Quaternary Environments and Geoarchaeology of India* (S. Wadia, R. Korisettar and V.S. Kale Eds.), pp. 210-30. Bangalore: Geological Society of India.

Misra, V.N. and Rajaguru, S.N. 1989. Palaeoenvironment and Prehistory of the Thar Desert, Rajasthan, India, in *South Asian Archaeology 1985* (K. Frilfet Ed.), pp. 296-330. Copenhagen: Scandinavian Institute of Asian Studies.

Mohapatra, G.C. 1976. Geotectonic Developments, Sub-Himalayan Lithic Complex and Post-Siwalik Sediments, in *Perspectives in Palaeoanthropology* (A.K. Ghosh Ed.), pp. 31-59. Calcutta: Firma K.L. Mukhopadhyaya.

Murty, M.L.K. 1974. A Late Pleistocene Cave Site in Southern India, *Proceedings of the American Philosophical Society* 118 (2): 196-230.

——— 1979. Recent Research on the Upper Palaeolithic Phase in India, *Journal of Field Archaeology* 6: 301-20.

——— 1981. Hunter-Gatherer Ecosystems and Archaeological Patterns of Subsistence Behaviour in the Southeast Coast of India: an Ethnographic Model, *World Archaeology* 13 (1): 47-58.

Murty, M.L.K. 1989. Pre-Iron Age Settlements in South India: an Ecological Perspective, *Man and Environment* XIV (1): 65-82.

Naidu, P.D. 1995. Onset of an Arid Climate at 3.5 Ka in Tropics: Evidence from Monsoon Upwelling Index, *Current Science* 71: 715-18.

——— 1997. Rapid Climatic Shifts and Its Influence on Ancient Civilizations: Evidence from Marine Records, in *The Indian Heritage* (D. Balasubramanian and N. Appaji Rao Eds.), pp. 69-77. Hyderabad: University Press.

——— 1998. Driving Forces of Indian Summer Monsoon on Milankovitch and Sub-Milankovitch Time Scales: a Reveiw, *Journal of the Geological Society of India* 52: 257-72.

Nijampurkar, V. N., N. Bhandari, S.K. Bhattacharya and R. Ramesh 1986. Climatic Significance of D/H Ratios in a Temperate Glacier in Sikkim, *Current Science* 55 (18): 910-13.

Nigam, R. and N. Khare 1994. Signals of the Change in Monsoonal Precipitation Around 2,000 Years BP in a Sediment Core Off Central West Coast of India, *Current Science* 66 (3): 226-8.

Nigam, R. and N.H. Hashimi 1995. Marine Sediments and Palaeoclimatic Variations Since the Late Pleistocene: an Overview for the Arabian Sea, in *Quaternary Environments and Geoarchaeology of India* (S. Wadia, R. Korisettar and V.S. Kale Eds.), pp. 380-90. Bangalore: Geological Society of India.

Ota, S.B. 1992. Ladakh Evidence of Stone Age Culture, *Himalaya Today* III (3-4): 359-68.

Paddayya, K. 1970. The Blade Tool Industries of Shorapur Doab, in *Indian Antiquary 4: Professor H.D. Sankalia Felicitation Volume* (S.B. Deo and M.K. Dhavalikar Eds.), pp. 165-90. Bombay: Popular Prakashan.

——— 1982. *The Acheulian Culture of the Hunsgi Valley (Peninsular India): a Settlement System Perspective.* Pune: Deccan College.

Pant, P.C. and V. Jayaswal 1991. *Paisra: the Stone Age Settlement of Bihar*. Delhi: Agam Kala.

Pant, R.K. and L.S. Chamyal 1990. Quaternary Sedimentation Pattern and Terrain Evolution in the Mahi River Basin, Gujarat, India, *Proceedings of the Indian National Science Academy* 56A: 501-11.

Pappu, R.S. and S.G. Deo 1994. *Man-Land Relationships During Palaeolithic Times in the Kaladgi Basin, Karnataka*. Pune: Deccan College.

Patel, M.P. and N. Bhat 1996. Evidence of Palaeoclimatic Fluctuations in Miliolite Rocks of Saurashtra, Western India, *Journal of the Geological Society of India* 45: 191-200.

Possehl, G.L. 1992. The Harappan Civilization in Gujarat: the Sorath and the Sindhi Harappans, *The Eastern Anthropologist* 45 (1-2): 117-54.

Prasad, S., S. Kusumgar and S.K. Gupta 1997. A Mid- to Late Holocene Record of Palaeoclimatic Changes from Nal Sarovar: a Palaeodesert Margin Lake in Western India, *Journal of Quaternary Science* 12: 153-9.

Prell, W.L. and E. Vam Campo 1986. Coherent Response of Arabian Sea Upwelling and Pollen Transport to Late Quaternary Monsoonal Winds, *Nature* 322: 526-8.

Prell, W.L. and L. Niitsuma 1989. Introduction, Background and Major Objectives for ODP Leg 117 (Western Arabian Sea) in Search of Ancient Monsoons, in *Proceedings of the Ocean Oil Drilling Program, Initial Reports*, pp. 5-9. Texas: College Station.

Quade J. and T.E. Cerling 1995. Expansion of C4 Grasses in the Late Miocene of Northern Pakistan: Evidence from Stable Isotopes in Palaeosols, *Palaeogeography, Palaeoclimatology, Palaeoecology* 115: 91-116.

Rajagopalan, G., S. Sukumar, R. Ramesh, R.K. Pant, and G. Rajagopalan 1987. Late Quaternary Vegetational and Climatic Changes from Tropical Peats in Southern India—an Extended Record up to 40,000 Years B.P., *Current Science* 73 (1): 60-3.

Rajaguru, S.N. 1970. Studies in the Late Pleistocene Stratigraphy of the Mula-Mutha Valley. Ph.D. Dissertation. Poona: University of Poona.

——— 1997a. Climatic Changes in Western India During the Quaternary: a Palaeopedological Approach. DST- Project Completion Report (unpublished).

——— 1997b. Quaternary Palaeoclimate of Northern Deccan, India. Paper Presented at the

Seminar on Deccan Heritage During the 63rd Meeting of the Indian National Science Academy, National Geophysical Research Institute, Hyderabad, 29-31 September 1997.

Rajaguru, S.N. and V.S. Kale 1985. Changes in Fluvial Regime of Western Maharashtra Upland Rivers During Late Quaternary, *Journal of the Geological Society of India* 26 (1): 16-27.

Rajaguru, S.N. and S. Mishra 1997. Late Quaternary Climatic Changes in India: a Geoarchaeological Approach, *Bulletin of the Indo-Pacific Prehistory Association* 16: 27-32.

Rajendran, P. 1990. The Mesolithic Cultures of Karnataka, Kerala and Tamil Nadu, in *Archaeology in Karnataka* (A. Sundara Ed.), pp. 48-57. Mysore: Directorate of Archaeology and Museums.

Raju, D.R. 1985. The Upper Palaeolithic Industries of the Cuddapah District, Andhra Pradesh, in *Recent Advances in Indo-Pacific Prehistory* (V.N. Misra and P. Bellwood Eds.), pp. 147-56. New Delhi: Oxford-IBH.

Rakhecha, P.R. and P.R. Pisharoty 1996. Heavy Rainfall During Monsoon Season: Point and Spatial Distribution, *Current Science* 71 (3): 179-86.

Ramesh, J. 1989. A Study of Geomorphology, Quaternary Geology and Associated Cultural Remains of West Tripura District, Tripura. Ph.D. Dissertation. Guwahati: Gauhati University.

Ramesh, R., S.K. Bhattacharya and G.B. Pant 1989. Climatic Significance of δD Variations in a Tropical Tree Species from India, *Nature* 337 (6203): 149-50.

Ratnagar, S. 1994. The Harappan Trade in Its 'World Context', *Man and Environment* XIX (1-2): 115-27.

Reddy, K.T. 1977. Billasurgam: an Upper Palaeolithic Cave Site in South India, *Asian Perspectives* 20 (2): 206- 27.

——— 1994. Coastal Ecology and Archaeology: Evidence from the East Coast of India, *Man and Environment* XIX (1-2): 43-55.

Rendell, H.M., R.W. Dennell, and M.A. Halim 1989. Pleistocene and Palaeolithic Investigations in the Soan Valley, Northern Pakistan, in *British Archaeological Mission of Pakistan* (Allchin, F.R., B. Allchin and S.M. Ashfaque Eds.). Oxford: BAR International Series 544.

Retallack, G.J. 1995. Palaeosols of the Siwalik Group as a 15 Myr Record of South Asian Monsoon, in *Quaternary Environments and Geoarchaeology of India* (S. Wadia, R. Korisettar and V.S. Kale Eds.), pp. 36-51. Bangalore: Geological Society of India.

Sadakata, N., H. Maemoko, S.N. Rajaguru, S. Mishra and K. Fujiwara 1995. Late Quaternary Environmental Change in Tropical-Subtropical Northwest Deccan Upland India, in *Proceedings of the International Symposium on Palaeoenvironmental Change in Tropical-Subtropical Monsoon Asia*, pp. 43-56. Hiroshima: Hiroshima University.

Sahasrabudhe, Y. and S.N. Rajaguru 1990. The Laterites of Maharashtra State, *Bulletin of the Deccan College Post-Graduate and Research Institute* 49: 357-70.

Sali, S.A. 1974. The Upper Palaeolithic Since Independence, *Bulletin of the Deccan College Research Institute* 34: 147-60.

——— 1989. *The Upper Palaeolithic and Mesolithic Cultures of Maharashtra*. Pune: Deccan College.

Sankalia, H.D. 1965. *Excavations at Langhnaj: 1944-63, Part I*. Pune: Deccan College.

——— 1974. *Prehistory and Protohistory of India and Pakistan*. Pune: Deccan College.

Sareen, B.K., M. Someshwara Rao, S.K. Tandon and A.K. Singhvi 1992. A Tentative Chronological Framework for the Quaternary Deposits of the Sabarmati Basin of Semi-Arid Western India Using Thermoluminescence: Extended Abstract, in *International Symposium on Evolution of Deserts*, pp. 117-18. Ahmedabad: Physical Research Laboratory.

Sareen, B.K. and S.K. Tandon 1995. Petrology, Micromorphology and Granulometry of Mid-to Late Quaternary Continental Deposits of the Semi-Arid Sabarmati Basin, Western India, in *Quaternary Environments and Geoarchaeology of India* (S. Wadia, R. Korisettar and V.S. Kale Eds.), pp. 258-76. Bangalore: Geological Society of India.

Sarkar, A., R. Ramesh, S.K. Bhattacharya and G. Rajagopalan 1990. Oxygen Isotope Evidence for Enhanced Winter Monsoon Current During the Last Glaciation, *Nature* 343: 549-51.

Sarkar, A., R. Ramesh, S.K. Bhattacharya and N.B. Price 1999. Palaeomonsoon and Palaeoproductivity Records of $\delta^{18}O$, $\delta^{13}C$ and $CaCO_3$ Variations in the Northern Indian Ocean Sediments, in *Professor K. Gopalan Festschrift*. Bangalore: Indian Academy of Sciences (in press).

Sarkar, A. and A.K. Guha 1993. Palaeoceanographic Implications of Planktonic Foraminiferal Abundance at DSDP Sites 219, 220 and 241: an Approach Based on Palaeontologic Time Series, *Journal of the Geological Society of India* 41 (5): 397-416.

Schulz, H., U.V. Rod and H. Erlenkeuser 1998. Correlation Between Arabian Sea and Greenland Climate Oscillations of the Past 110,000 Years, *Nature* 393: 54-7.

Searle, M. 1995. The Rise and Fall of Tibet, *Nature* 374: 17-18.

Shackleton, N.J. 1975. The Stratigraphic Record of Deep-Sea Cores and its Implications for the Assessment of Glacials, Interglacial, Stadials and Interstadials in the Mid-Pleistocene, in *After the Australopithecines* (K.L. Butzer and and G.L. Isaac Eds.), pp. 1-124. The Hague: Mouton Publishers.

Shane, Phil, J. Westgate, M. Williams and R. Korisettar 1995. New Geochemical Evidence for the Youngest Toba Tuff in India, *Quaternary Research* 44: 200-4.

Sharma, G.R. 1973. Mesolithic Lake Cultures in the Ganga Valley, *Proceedings of the Prehistoric Society* 39: 129-46.

Sharma, G.R. and J.D. Clark (Eds.), 1983. *Palaeoenvironment and Prehistory in the Middle Son Valley (Madhya Pradesh, North Central India)*. Allahabad: Abinash Prakashan.

Sharma, G.R., V.D. Misra, D. Mandal, B.B. Misra and J.N. Pal 1980. *Beginnings of Agriculture (Epipalaeolithic to Neolithic): Excavations at Chopani-Mando, Mahadaha and Mahagara*. Allahabad: Abinash Prakashan.

Sharma, J.C. 1977. Palaeolithic Tools from Pleistocene Deposits in Punjab, *Current Anthropology* 18: 94-5.

Sharma, K.K. 1995. Quaternary Stratigraphy and Prehistory of the Upper Indus Valley, Ladakh, in *Quaternary Environments and Geoarchaeology of India* (S. Wadia, R. Korisettar and V.S. Kale Eds.), pp. 98-108. Bangalore: Geological Society of India.

Sharma, C. and M.S. Chauhan 1991. Palaeovegetation and Palaeoenvironmental Inferences from the Quaternary Palynostratigraphy from the Western Indian Plains, *Man and Environment* XVI (1): 65-71.

Sharma, R.S. 1987. *Urban Decay*. Delhi: Munshiram Manoharlal.

Singh, A.D. 1998. Late Quaternary Oceanographic Changes in the Eastern Arabian Sea: Evidence from Planktonic Foraminifera and Pteropods, *Journal of the Geological Society of India* 52 (2): 203-12.

Singh, G. 1988. History of Arid Land Vegetation and Climate: a Global Perspective, *Biological Reviews* 63: 159-95.

Singh, G. and D.P. Agrawal 1976. Radiocarbon Evidence for Climate Change in North-Western Himalaya, India, *Nature* 260: 232.

Singh, G., R.J. Wasson and D.P. Agrawal 1990. Vegetational and Seasonal Climatic Changes since the Last Full Glacial in the Thar Desert, Northwestern India, *Review of Palaeobotany and Palynology* 64: 351-8.

Singh, G., R.D. Joshi and A.B. Singh 1972. Stratigraphic and Radiocarbon Evidence for the Age and Development of Three Salt Lake Deposits in Rajasthan, India, *Quaternary Research* 2: 496.

Singh, G., R.D. Joshi, S.K. Chopra and A.B. Singh 1974. Late Quaternary History and Climate of the Thar Desert, India, *Philosophical Transactions of the Royal Society of London* 276: 467-501.

Singh, Thockchom A. 1987. Quaternary Studies in the Manipur Valley. Ph.D. Dissertation. Pune: Poona University.

Singhvi, A.K., Y.D. Sharma and D.P. Agrawal 1982. Thermoluminescence Dating of Sand Dunes in Rajasthan, *Nature* 295: 313.

Singhvi,, A.K., A. Bronger, R.K. Pant and W. Sauer 1987. Thermoluminescence Dating and Its Implications on the Chronostratigraphy of Loess-Palaeosol-Sequences in the Kashmir Valley (India), *Chemical Geology* (Isotope Geoscience Section) 65: 45-56.

Sirocko, F., M. Sarnthein, H. Erlenkeuser, H. Lange, M. Arnold and J.C. Duplessy 1993. Century-Scale Events in Monsoonal Climate Over the Past 24,000 Years, *Nature* 364: 322-4.

Sirocko, F., D. Garbo-Schoenberg, A. McIntyre and B. Molfino 1996. Teleconnections Between the Subtropical Monsoon and High Latitude Climates During the Last Deglaciation, *Science* 272: 526-9.

Somayajulu, B.L.K., R. Bhushan, A. Sarkar, G.S. Burr and A.J.T. Jull 1999. Sediment Deposition Rates on the Continental Margins of the Eastern Arabian Sea Using Pb-210, Cs-137 and C-14, in *Science of the Total Environment*. Vienna: IAEA (in press).

Sonakia, A. and S. Biswas 1998. Antiquity of the Narmada *Homo erectus*, the Early Man of India, *Current Science* 75 (4): 391-3.

Soundara Rajan, K.V. 1958. Studies in the Stone Age of Nagarjunakonda and Its Neighbourhood, *Ancient India* 14: 49-113.

Srinivasan, J. 1998. The Monsoon Past, Present and Future, *Current Science* 74 (3): 187-9.

Sukhija, B.S., D.V. Reddy and P. Nagabhushanam 1998. Isotopic Fingerprints of Palaeoclimates During the Last 30,000 Years in Deep Confined Ground Waters of Southern India, *Quaternary Research* 50: 252-60.

Sukumar, R., R. Ramesh, R.K. Pant and G. Rajagopalan 1993. A Delta C-13 Record of Late Quaternary Climate Change from Tropical Peats in Southern India, *Nature* 364: 703.

Sundaram, R.M., P. Rakshit and K. Pareek 1996. Regional Stratigraphy of Quaternary Deposits in Parts of Thar Desert, Rajasthan, *Journal of the Geological Society of India* 48: 203-10.

Tiwari, M.P. and H.Y. Bhai 1997. Quaternary Stratigraphy of the Narmada Valley, in *Quaternary Geology in the Narmada Valley: a Multidisciplinary Approach*, pp. 33-63. Calcutta: Geological Survey of India, Special Publication No. 46.

Todd, K.R.U. 1932. Prehistoric Man Around Bombay, *Proceedings of the Prehistoric Society of East Anglia* 7, 9: 35-42.

——— 1939. Palaeolithic Industries of Bombay, *Journal of the Royal Anthropological Institute* LXIX: 257-72.

——— 1950. Microlithic Industries of Bombay, *Ancient India* 6: 4-16.

Valdiya, K.S. 1999. Rising Himalaya: Advent and Intensification of Monsoon, *Current Science* 76 (4): 514-24.

Van Campo. E., 1986. Monsoon Fluctuation in Two 20,000 Yr BP Oxygen Isotope-Pollen Records Off Southwest India, *Quaternary Research* 26 (3): 376-88.

Van Campo, E., J.C. Duplessy and M. Rossignol-Strick, 1982. Climatic Conditions Deduced from a 150 Kyr Oxygen Isotope-Pollen Record from the Arabian Sea, *Nature* 296: 56-9.

Varma, R.K. 1986. *The Mesolithic Age in Mirzapur*. Allahabad: Paramjyoti Prakashan.

Verma, B.C. 1991. Siwalik Stone Age Culture, *Current Science* 61 (8) L: 496.

von Rad U., M. Schaaf, K.H. Michels, H. Schurz, W.H. Berger and F. Sirocko 1999. A 5000-Yr Record of Climate Change in Varved Sediments from the Oxygen Minimum Zone Off Pakistan Northeastern Arabian Sea, *Quaternary Research* 51 (1): 39-63.

Vrba, E.S. 1996. Climate, Heterchrony and Human Evolution, *Journal of Anthropological Archaeology* 52 (1): 1-28.

Walker, Gilbert 1986. On the Meteorological Evidence for the Supposed Changes of Climate in India, in *Long Range Forecasting of Monsoon Rainfall (Collected Papers of Sir Gilbert Walker)*, New Delhi: Indian Meteorological Society.

Wasson, R.J. 1995. The Asian Monsoon During the Late Quaternary, in *Quaternary Environments and Geoarchaeology of India* (S. Wadia, R. Korisettar and V.S. Kale Eds.), pp. 22-35. Bangalore: Geological Society of India.

Wasson, R.J., G.I. Smith and D.P. Agrawal 1984. Late Quaternary Sediments, Minerals and Inferred Geochemical History of Didwana Lake, India, *Palaeogeography, Palaeoclimatology and Palaeoecology* 46: 345-72.

Wasson, R.J., S.N. Rajaguru, V.N. Misra, D.P. Agrawal, R.P. Dhir, A.K. Singhvi and K.K. Rao 1983. Late Quaternary Stratigraphy and Palaeoclimatology of the Thar Dunefield, *Zeitschrift für Geomorphologie* (Supplement) 45: 117-25.

Webster, P. J., V.O. Magana, T.N. Palmer, J. Shukla, R.A. Tomas, M. Yanai and T. Yasunari 1998. Monsoons: Processes, Predictability and the Prospects for Prediction, *Journal of Geophysical Research* 103: 14451-510.

Westgate, J.A., P. Shane, N. J.G. Pearce, W.T. Perkins, R. Korisettar, C.S. Chesner, M.A.J. Williams and S.K. Acharyya 1998. All Toba Tephra Occurrences Across Peninsular India Belong to 75,000 Years Eruption, *Quaternary Research* 50: 107-12.

Williams, M.A.J. and M.F. Clarke 1995. Quaternary Geology and Prehistoric Environments in the Son and Belan Valleys, North Central India, in *Quaternary Environments and Geoarchaeology of India* (S. Wadia, R. Korisettar and V.S. Kale Eds.), pp. 282-308. Bangalore: Geological Society of India.

Widdowson, M. and Y. Gunnel. Tertiary Lateritisation Along the Konkan and Kanara Coastal Lowlands of Western Peninsular India (in press).

Xu, Quiqui 1993. The Appearance of the Himalayas and Its Relation to Global Climatic Events, in *Evolving Landscapes and Evolving Biotas of East Asia Since the Mid-Tertiary* (N.K. Jablonsky Eds.), pp. 115-22. Hong Kong: Centre for East Asian Studies.

Yadava, M.G. and R. Ramesh 1999. Palaeomonsoon Record of the Past 3400 Years from Speleothems of Tropical India, *The Gondwana Society of India* (in press).

Bioclimatology and Quaternary Palynology in India

V.M. MEHER-HOMJI

INTRODUCTION

Bioclimatology is the study of climate in relation to life, especially plant life because most of the animals are migratory and live in specialized niches and thus escape the direct impact of climate. Therefore plants and vegetation remain fidel indicators of climatic conditions.

Flora is the list of plant species encountered in a region, species envisaged in a taxonomic or descriptive manner. Vegetation, on the other hand, is the manner in which the species are grouped to constitute landscapes like forest, grassland, desert. Whereas the flora is the result of phylogenetic evolution, the vegetation reflects the influence of climate.

Palynology is the study of pollen grains and spores of plants. They are like fingerprints as each species or genus or at least family has its own characteristic pollen.

CLIMATES OF THE INDIAN SUBCONTINENT

The climate may be studied at several levels (Soltner 1982) like general climate (tropical climate, mediterranean, montane climate), regional climate (demarcated by relief, altitude, distance from the sea), local climate (determined by the extent of forest-cover, presence of rivers or tanks, topography like hills, valleys, basins and exposure) and micro climate of peculiar sites (shelter provided by a boulder, shade of a slope, interior of a dune) (George 1970).

Climatic Classification of India

A number of classifications are available like those of Köppen (1918, 1936), Lang (1920), de Martonne (1926) and Thornthwaite (1933, 1948), and the latter in particular has been extensively applied by Subrahmanyam (1959, 1972). However, these have not proved successful in explaining the vegetation types.

Bagnouls and Gaussen (1957) suggested a bioclimatic classification in which the climatic regions and sub-regions are formed according to:

- the duration of the dry period (months where precipitation in mm = twice the mean monthly temperature in degree Celsius)
- the duration of frost period (months where the mean temperature is below 0 °C)
- the characteristic values of the temperature
- the regime, i.e. the season of occurrence of precipitation. The main types of regimes

are shown in Figure 1. For details of this classification reference may be made to Bagnouls and Meher-Homji (1959). The climatic types and sub-types prevailing in the subcontinent according to this classification are as follows:

Hot Desertic Climate (12 Months Dry)

The desert occupies an important zone comprising the Thar in India and Pakistan. The valley of Gilgit also experiences desertic climate.

A peculiarity of the desertic climate is that it is of tropical tendency with whatever little rains occurring during long days (i.e. summer) wherever it prevails, except in the north-west corner where it is of irregular tendency (rains without seasonal rhythm). The ombrothermic (rainfall-temperature) diagram of Jacobabad (Fig. 2) illustrates the tropical tendency of desertic climate whereas Panjgur (Fig. 3) presents an irregular tendency.

Hot Sub-Desertic Climate (9-11 Months Dry)

Surrounding the core desertic area is the zone of the sub-desert extending westwards up to the foot of the highlands of Baluchistan and northwards up to the foot of the Himalayas.

This climate offers three tendencies:

(1) Mediterranean, with winter rains, long days (summer) being dry; it is encountered in north-west Pakistan. Figure 4, ombrothermic diagram of Dalbandin, is a graphical representation of this tendency.

(2) Tropical with summer rains and dryness during short days (winter); prevails over the whole of Kachchh, Rajasthan, parts of Sind and Punjab. Figure 6 of Karachi serves as a climate diagram.

(3) The above mentioned two tendencies are separated by a zone having an intermediate transitional character of rainfall exemplified by Figure 5 of Fort Sandeman. This zone receives some rains both during winter and summer.

In southern India, sub-desertic climate is encountered around Bellary (tropical tendency) and around Coimbatore (irregular tendency); the aridity may be explained by the peculiar topographic locations of these stations.

Cold Desertic Climate (the Total of the Dry Months and Frost Months is 11 to 12 Months)

This type is prevalent in the Western Himalayas and the plateau of the Pamir which it borders. The dryness is of two kinds here: one caused by temperatures below 0 °C inhibiting the absorption of water by the roots, and the other caused by the dry months.

Let us examine Figure 7 of Leh, the selected type. Here, we find negative temperature (below 0 °C) for five months (November to March) followed by a dry period of seven months (April to October) with temperatures above 0 °C. In such a case, it is necessary to consider that the precipitation during winter is in the form of snow. If this precipitation is sufficient and if the winds are moderate, the snow would accumulate and melt at the time of the spring thaw. During this melting period there is abundant moisture available to vegetation. This effect of melting of snow, which is capable of reducing the effect of dryness during the early dry period is shown by a dotted line on Figure 7. As a result, the month of April is not considered dry.

Cold Sub-Desertic Climate (the Total of the Dry Months and the Frost Months is 9 to 10 Months)

The Valleys of the Western Himalayas are influenced by this climate. The graph of Kargil (Fig. 8) shows the frost period extending from November to March and the dry period from May to October. By the compensation of melting of snow, we will consider May and June as wet months.

Mediterranean Climate

In the north-west part of the subcontinent, winter rains from the north-west owing their origin to the western disturbances become a decisive factor and this feature along with low temperature creates a climate similar to that of the mediterranean countries. Geographers consider as essential characters of the mediterranean climate a mild winter which does not affect the vegetation, winter-spring-autumn rains, and a dry period in summer which stops the growth of non-woody plants and slows down the growth of woody plants (Gaussen 1955).

The mountainous region of Baluchistan comes under accentuated character with dryness of 8 months (e.g. Quetta in Fig. 9). Drosh (Fig. 10) is an example of moderate character with a dry period of 6 months whereas Srinagar in Kashmir (Fig. 11) is an example of sub-mediterranean climate with a very short dry period.

Cold mediterranean climate with a mean temperature of the coldest month below 0 °C does not exist in India but prevails over the high mountain ranges of Afghanistan. As in is Kabul (Fig. 12).

In order to study the behaviour of the mediterranean climate at its eastern limit in contact with the monsoon climate, the only region suitable is the north-west part of the subcontinent which is remarkable for the vast scale climatic variability it presents both in space and time. This region encompasses climates ranging from desertic and sub-desertic types of the Thar to the less arid and even humid montane type with practically no dry season, or the cold zones with freezing winters in the north. It is also the scene of marked changes in the seasons of occurrence of rains from west to east. In the western part of it, a notable feature of the climate is the winter-spring precipitation originating from the meteorological phenomena called 'western disturbances'; associated with mild winter temperatures, it results in climatic conditions not unlike those prevailing in and around the Mediterranean Basin. This fact was recorded as early as in first century AD by the historian Pliny (André and Filliozat 1980), and the trend of separating the winter precipitation zone from that of the summer rainfall continues in recent publications (Emberger et al. 1963; Labroue et al. 1965; Snead 1968; Meher-Homji 1973a).

Apart from the spatial variations mentioned above, further complications arise because of the temporal fluctuations at one and the same station, so much so that the notion of average climate may be questioned for this region of large scale interannual variability in its climatic parameters. Majority of the individual years may not conform to the average pattern derived from the long-term or even medium-term climatic data especially in what concerns the season(s) of occurrence of rains. It is our aim to precisely determine the degrees and limits of the mediterranean type of climate in the subcontinent both the spatial and temporal variations.

The climate of a place may be characterized by a grade of humidity-aridity into classes ranging from perhumid to hyperarid, by a grade of temperature into frigid to torrid groups and also by its regimes (i.e. season of occurrence of rains) like tropical monsoon (summer rains), mediterranean (winter-spring-autumn rains), bixeric (two dry periods in the year and two rainy seasons) or irregular (rainfall without seasonal rhythm). A rational classification of climate should embrace these three facets of meteorological phenomena.

The limit of the mediterranean climate may be sought where the rains of the cool season(s) are replaced by effective summer rainfall owing its origin to the monsoon phenomenon. For characterizing effective ($P > 2T$) and ineffective monthly rainfall ($P = 2T$), we have retained the definitions of Bagnouls and Gaussen (1957). (P = monthly precipitation in mm; T = mean monthly temperature in degree Celsius.)

Tropical Climate

The situation is diametrically opposite to the mediterranean climate. Short days of the year (winter-spring) are dry and long days (summer months) are rainy. By far this is the most dominant climatic type in the subcontinent.

Subdivisions have been formed on the basis of the number of dry months (1 to 8) and temperature. If the mean of the coldest month (t) is over 15 °C, the climate is referred to as typically tropical, if it is less than 15 °C, the climate is called mesotropical.

The different variations in tropical climate are illustrated in Figures 13 to 18. Mumbai (Bombay, Fig. 13) represents a typical tropical climate with seven months dryness and peak of rains in July. Calcutta (Fig. 14) experiences a dry season of 6 months; Cochin (Fig. 16) of 4 months and Shillong (Fig. 17) of only 2 months. The latter station is also mesotropical as the mean temperature of the coldest month is below 15 °C.

Chennai (Madras, Fig. 15) is an example of dissymmetric tropical regime; the symmetry of the rainfall curve observed in the climate diagram of Mumbai is not noticed in the diagram of Chennai because the peak of rains (due to the depressions formed in the Bay of Bengal during the prevalence of the north-east monsoon) is in November.

Batticaloa (Fig. 18) on the eastern coast of Sri Lanka presents yet another variation of the tropical climate, viz., inverted tropical regime. Long days (May to August) constitute the dry season, reminding us of the mediterranean situation. However, at the latitude of Batticaloa, so close to the equator, there is practically no seasonal difference in the day length and temperature and therefore seasons are not well marked as in northern latitudes.

Bixeric Climate

In the bixeric climates there are two dry seasons in a year. The meso-bixeric variants (t < 15° C) are mostly prevalent along the Sub-himalayan tract and in the Punjab. One of the rainy seasons, that of winter-spring, is due to the western disturbances, the other in summer months is because of the influence of the south-west monsoon. Climatic diagrams of Patiala, Ambala and Rawalpindi (Fig. 20-2) present examples of dryness of 8, 6 and 4 months respectively.

Bixeric climate with mean temperature of the coldest month t > 15 °C is rather rare and is experienced by very few stations of southern India like Madurai and Tiruchirapalli (Fig. 19). One of the two peaks, that of May, due to convectional rains, is not well-marked; the second rainy season is the result of the south-west monsoon followed by rains of depression origin during the prevalence of the north-east winds, as in the case of Chennai explained above.

Axeric Climates Without any Dry Season

Depending on the mean temperature of the coldest month (t), several classes may be distinguished :

Equatorial (t > 20 °C), south-west part of Sri Lanka exemplified by the climate diagram of Colombo (Fig. 23); there are two peaks of rainfall in May and October and two periods of lower rainfall, so very typical of the equatorial climate but no month is dry. The two peaks of May and October correspond to the zenithal position of the sun generating convectional rains which add to the contribution of the monsoon rainfall. Between these two peaks the rainfall of the south-west monsoon (June-September) appears to be depressed and the single peak that should be in July (as for Mumbai) disappears.

Hypothermaxeric (t < 20 °C but > 15 °C); hills of moderate elevation (< 2000 m) near the equator, as those of Sri Lanka are under this climate.

Tropical montane or warm temperate (t < 15 °C but > 10 °C). Hill tops of the Nilgiris and Palnis experience this climate. Graphical example is Kodaikanal (Fig. 24). Meher-Homji (1965b, 1967b) has advanced reasons to refer to the climate of the higher elevation of these south Indian hills as tropical montane type.

It is likely that this type of climate prevails in the eastern Himalayas too but due to paucity of meteorological stations in that area, we could not locate this type.

Temperate type (t < 10 °C but > 0 °C). (Climate of central and northern China. It is likely that this climate prevails in parts of the Himalayas too).

Cold axeric (t < 0 °C) type of climate prevails in the Himalayas between 4,000 and 5,500 m. It is derived from the stations of lower elevation like Darjeeling (2,266 m) at the eastern extremity and Shimla (2,203 m) at the western end by applying thermal gradient of decrease of temperature by 1 °C with every 200 m rise of elevation. The dry period of

1 to 2 months duration of Darjeeling and Shimla would disappear at higher elevation giving rise to cold axeric climate without any dry period and with the mean of the coldest month being below 0 °C.

Glacial (or Cryomeric) Climate

The higher peaks of the Himalayas above 5,500 m with perpetual snow experience glacial climate where the frost period lasts for 12 months (Fig. 1).

CLIMATIC VARIABILITY

So far we have dealt with climatic factors in terms of averages but in quite a few cases, the climatic means conceal facts of practical importance. The inter-yearly fluctuations in rainfall are well-known due to the vagaries of the monsoon. Pondicherry may receive only about 650 mm per annum when the frequency of depressions in the Bay of Bengal is low. In other years with frequent development of depressions, the amount received may be four times higher. The mean rainfall of 1,300 mm has not much bioclimatic significance. In other cases, the length of the dry season may be involved. For example, at Kodaikanal the majority of individual years experience dryness of 1 to 4 months, yet on the basis of averages, the drought period does not come out (Fig. 24) because the dry spells occur in different months in different years. At Murree, the average length of the dry season is 1 month but in actual years it may vary from 0 to 5 months. Rawalpindi with 5 months of dryness on an average basis (Fig. 22) presents the range of 2 to 8 dry months. New Delhi with a range of 5 to 11 months dryness presents an average of 9.

For certain stations of Kashmir and north-west Pakistan, the average rainfall regime turns out to be of mediterranean type but in reality the south-west monsoon is quite important some times, the importance of which is masked by the mean data. In Figure 25 a case is presented of the station of Peshawar where the régime varies from year to year.

The station of Dera Ismail Khan, located in the vicinity of the Harappan Civilization site—Harappa, also presents the full gamut of régime range from tropical to bixeric, irregular and mediterranean types. Such frequent changes in regimes from year to year are to be considered amongst adverse agro-climatological factors. The important question is whether such adverse changes had any role to play in the abandonment of the Indus Valley cultural sites.

PALYNOLOGY

Palynology is the study of pollen grains and spores. Their morphological characteristics lead to the identification of plants at specific, generic or yet family level. Since most of the plant species are indicators of climate or environmental features and since pollen grains remain preserved in certain habitats like peaty soils, fresh water or marine sediments for centuries and even millennia, palynology plays a significant role in deriving the past environmental changes through the dating of the sediments.

Vegetation—the Link Between the Pollen and the Environment

The sequence of succession, i.e. change from forest to grassland to crop land or vice-versa over the past millennia (Holocene period) can be reconstructed by examining the pollen grains in a soil or sediment profile at regular intervals. The timeframe is established through ^{14}C or a more sophisticated method. The Palynologist's role ends with the identification of the taxa. A proper interpretation of the pollenic data in environmental terms requires an ecologist or biogeographer. For example, a species like *Cullenia exarillata* is a sure pointer of evergreen forest and *Careya arborea* of tree savanna. Apart from pointing out vegetation, some species may indicate a definite humid climate, some aridity and yet others may be of intermediate situations and therefore of lesser indicator value. Similarly there are species characteristic of a certain soil type or of human interference. The ecologist has to assess the situation on the merit of the case seeking help from other disciplines like algology, geology, geomorphology, archaeology, etc., as ecology is a multidisciplinary subject.

The lead taken by pioneers like Von Post and Erdtman in Europe in reconstructing vegetational history and consequently also climate changes with study of fossil pollen grains was followed in India by Vishnu-Mittre and his school at the Birbal Sahni Institute of Palaeobotany, Lucknow and by Guinet, Thanikaimoni and Caratini at the French Institute, Pondicherry. Guinet (1966) outlined the value of Palynology to archaeology and ancient history.

Quaternary and the Role of Palynology in Reconstructing the Vegetational History

The fundamental events of the Quaternary were marked fluctuations in temperature in the northern latitudes. These involved three distinct glacial periods followed by warm periods, the interglacials. The altitudinal limit of the eternal snow fluctuated a great deal during the glacials and the interglacials affecting the zonation of the vegetation belts in the Himalayas. The last glaciation terminated about 10,000 years ago.

The temperate species from north, west and east colonized the Himalayas, among these a number of conifers. The glaciation in the Himalayas also helped the migration of a few species from the Himalayas to the higher hill-tops of south India and Sri Lanka. Though no part of peninsular India experienced glaciation, the temperature may have been lowered by about 6 °C. The continuity of the hill ranges from the Himalayas to the Western Ghats through Assam, Bihar, Chhotanagpur, Eastern Ghats, Vindhyas and Satpuras favoured genera like *Rhododendron*, *Gaultheria* and *Mahonia* to reach Ootacamund, Kodaikanal and the mountains of Sri Lanka.

The first glaciation changed the vegetation pattern in the Kashmir Valley according to Vishnu-Mittre (1969). The deodar and the oaks that dominated the hills were replaced by the bluepine, *Pinus wallichiana*. The changing environment due to the glacial and interglacial modification also gave rise to new species and varieties as an example of which Vishnu-Mittre (1969) quotes the case of cedar; and *Cedrus libanica* which spread

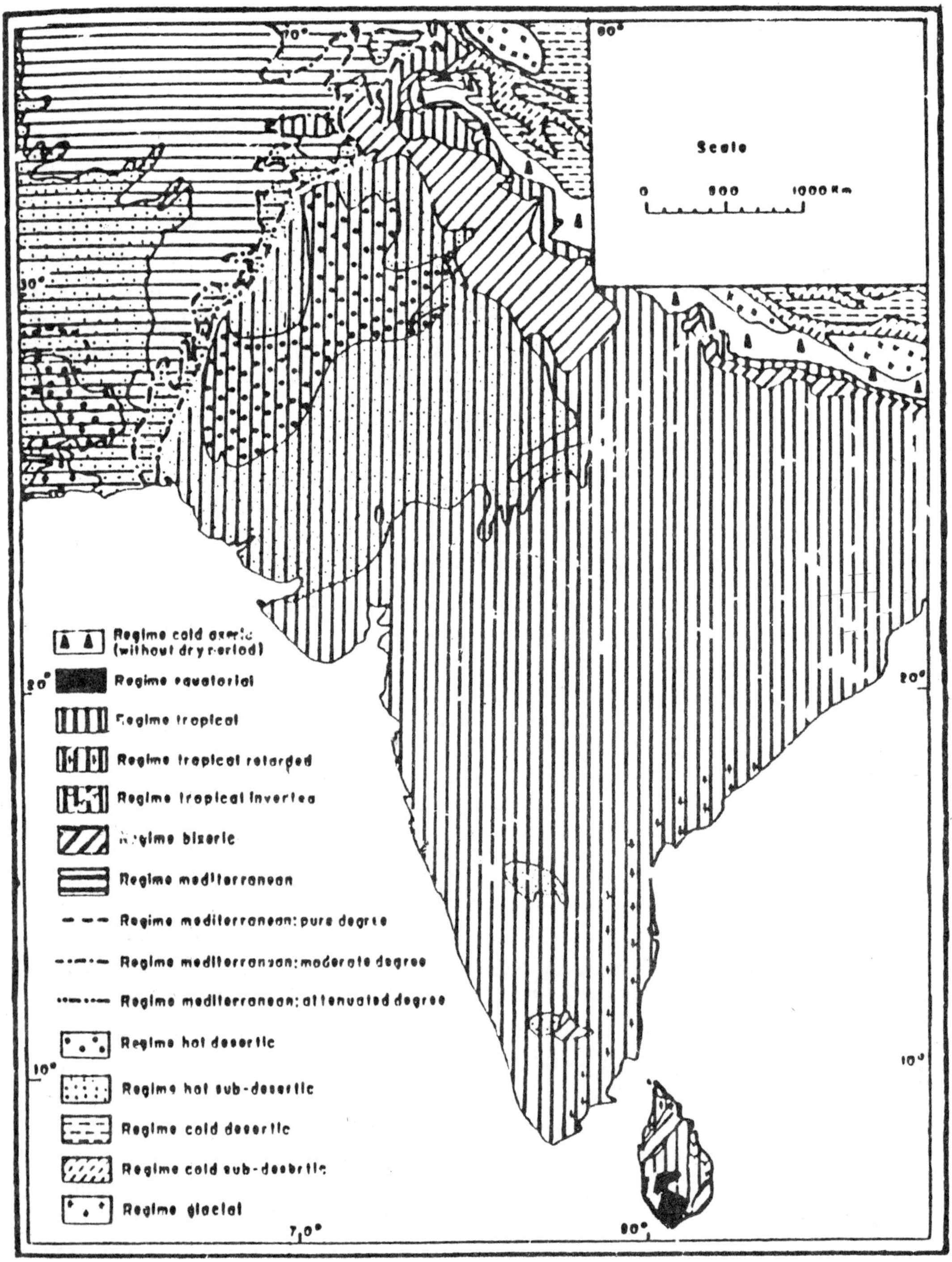

Fig. 1. Indian region: Main types of climatic regimes.

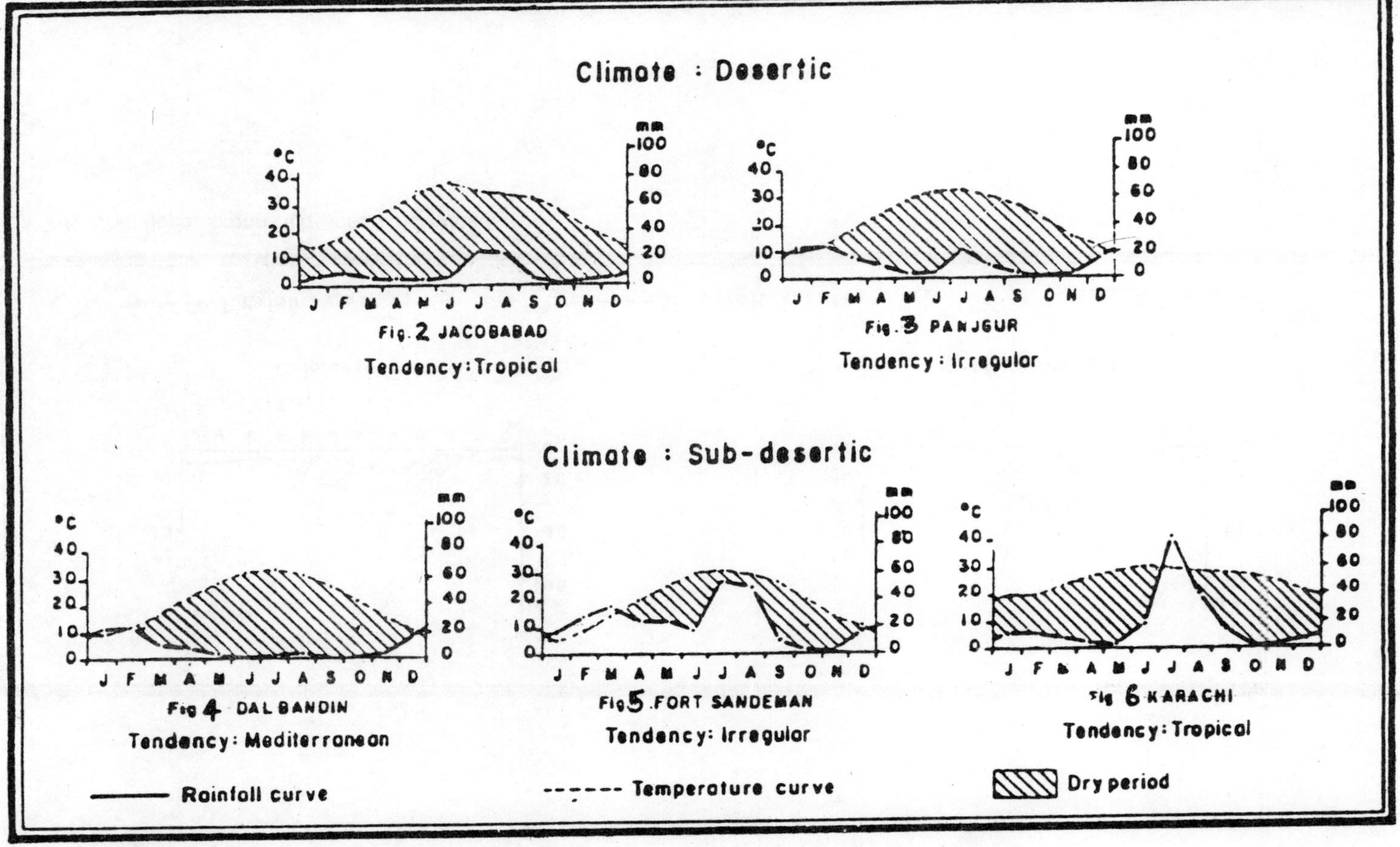

Figs. 2-3. Climate-Desertic.
Figs. 4-6. Climate-Sub-desertic.

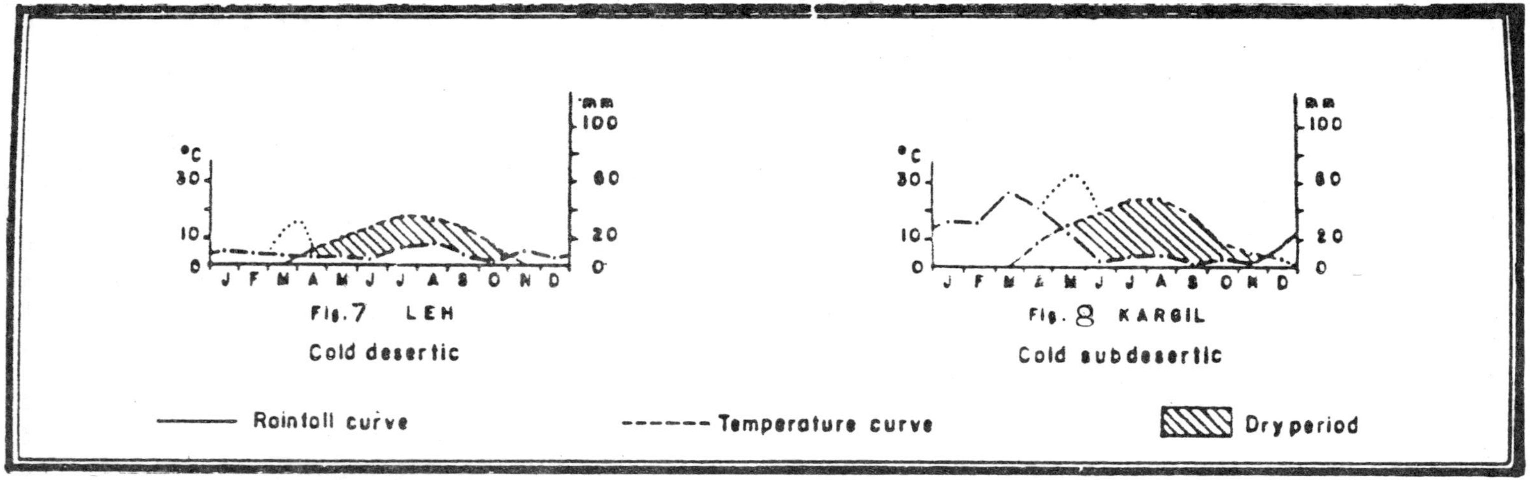

Figs. 7-8. Cold desertic and Sub-desertic climates.

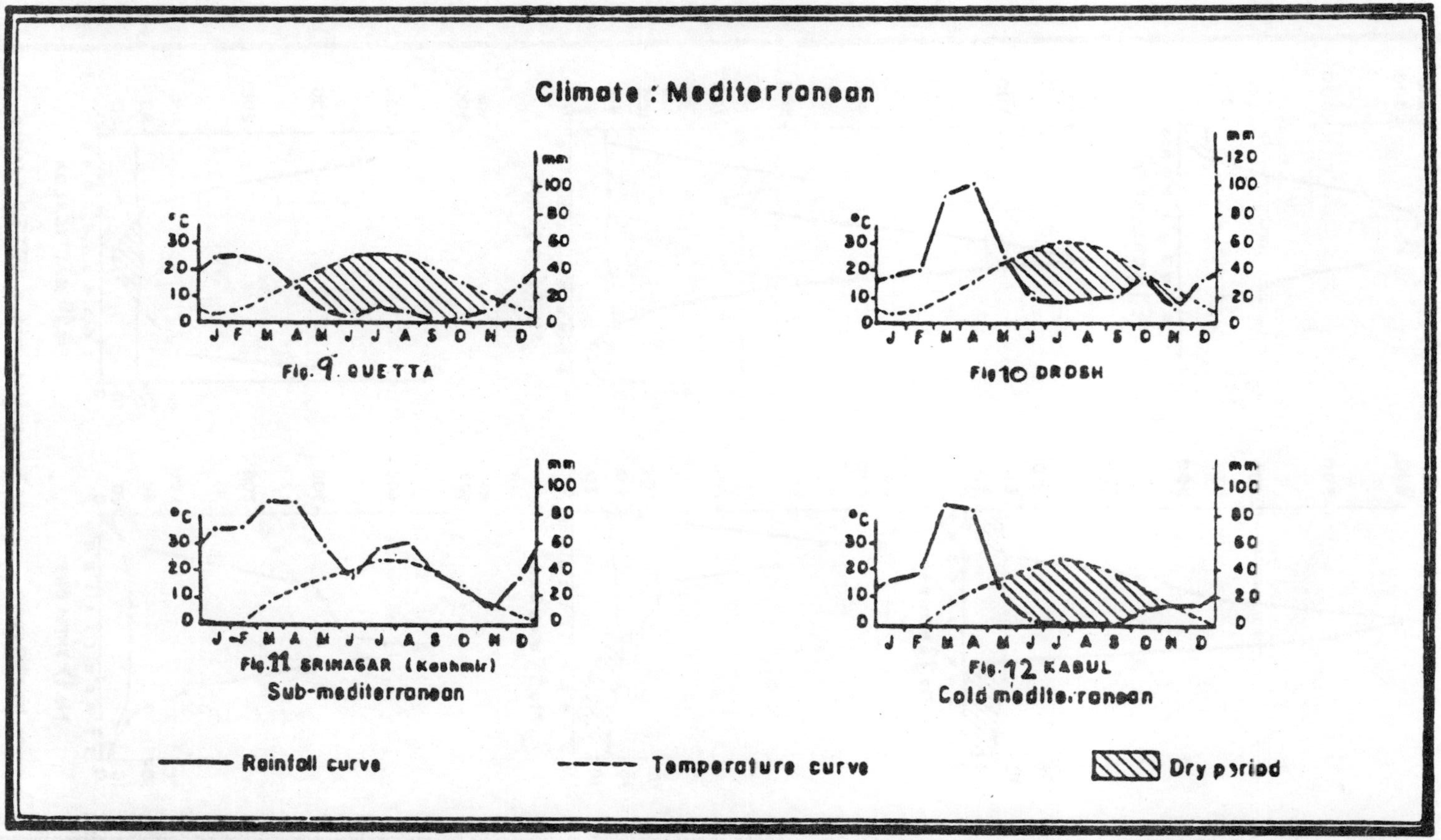

Figs. 9-12. Climate–Mediterranean.

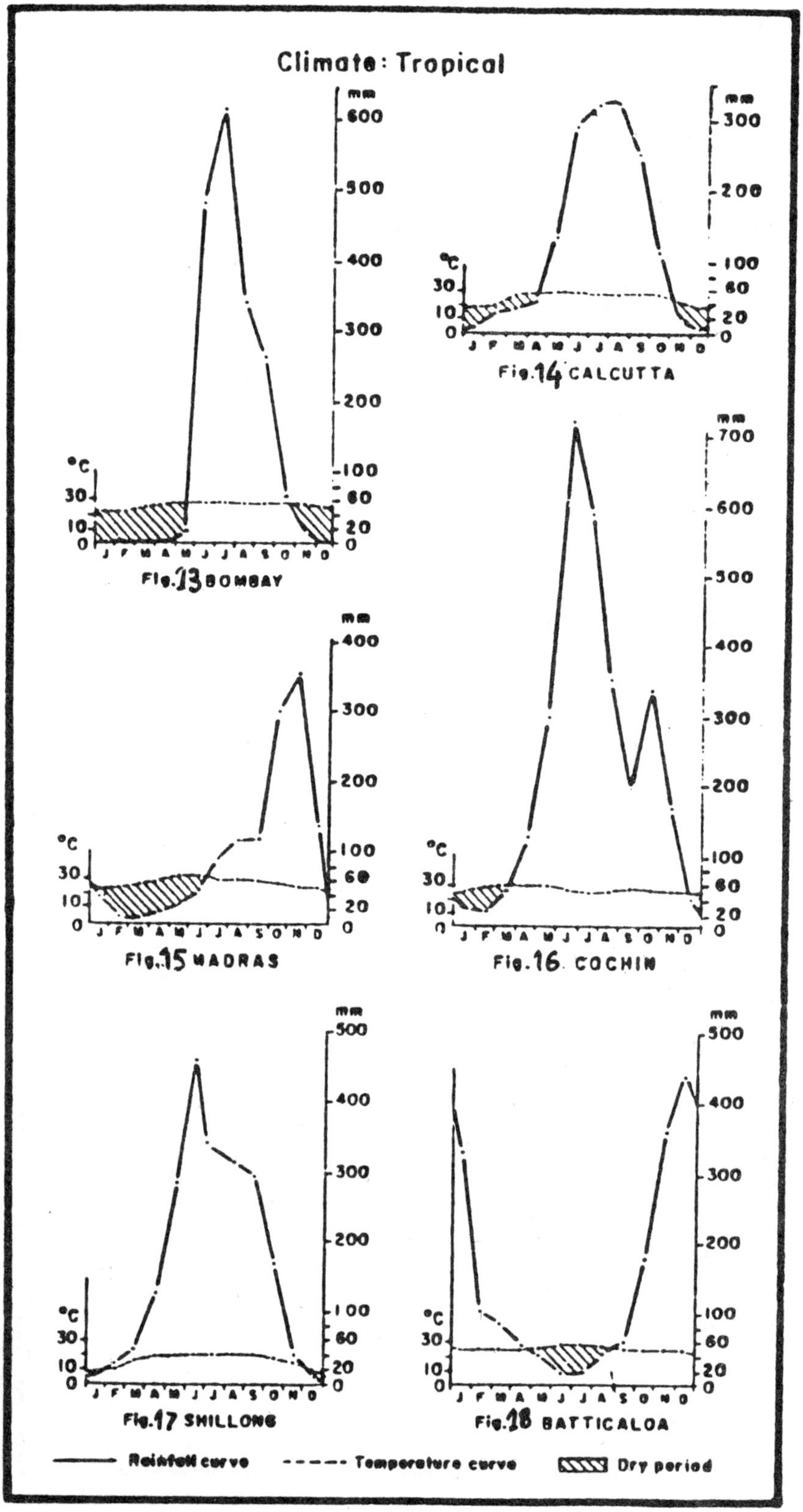

Figs. 13-18. Climate–Tropical.

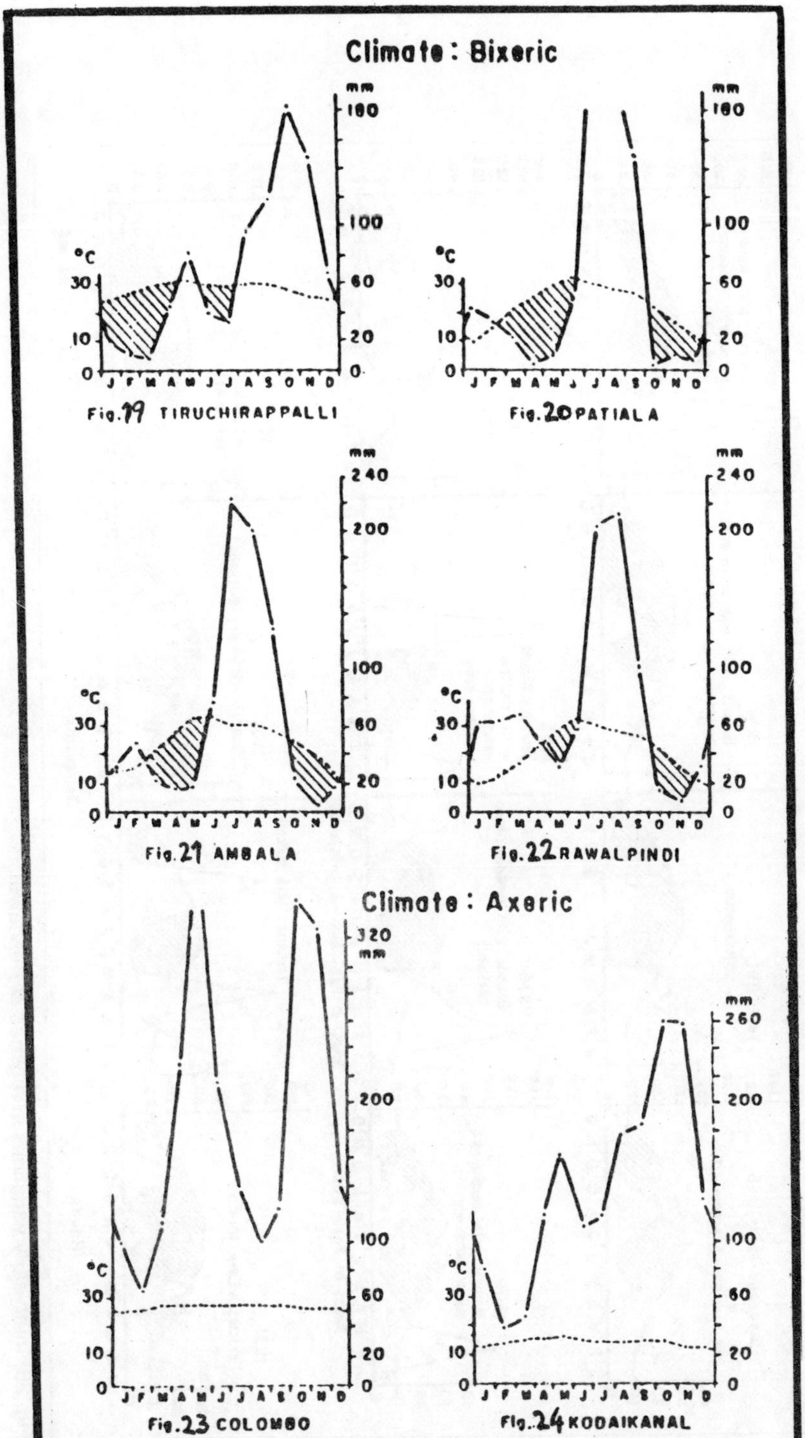

Figs. 19-22. Climate–Bixeric.
Figs. 23-4. Climate–Axeric.

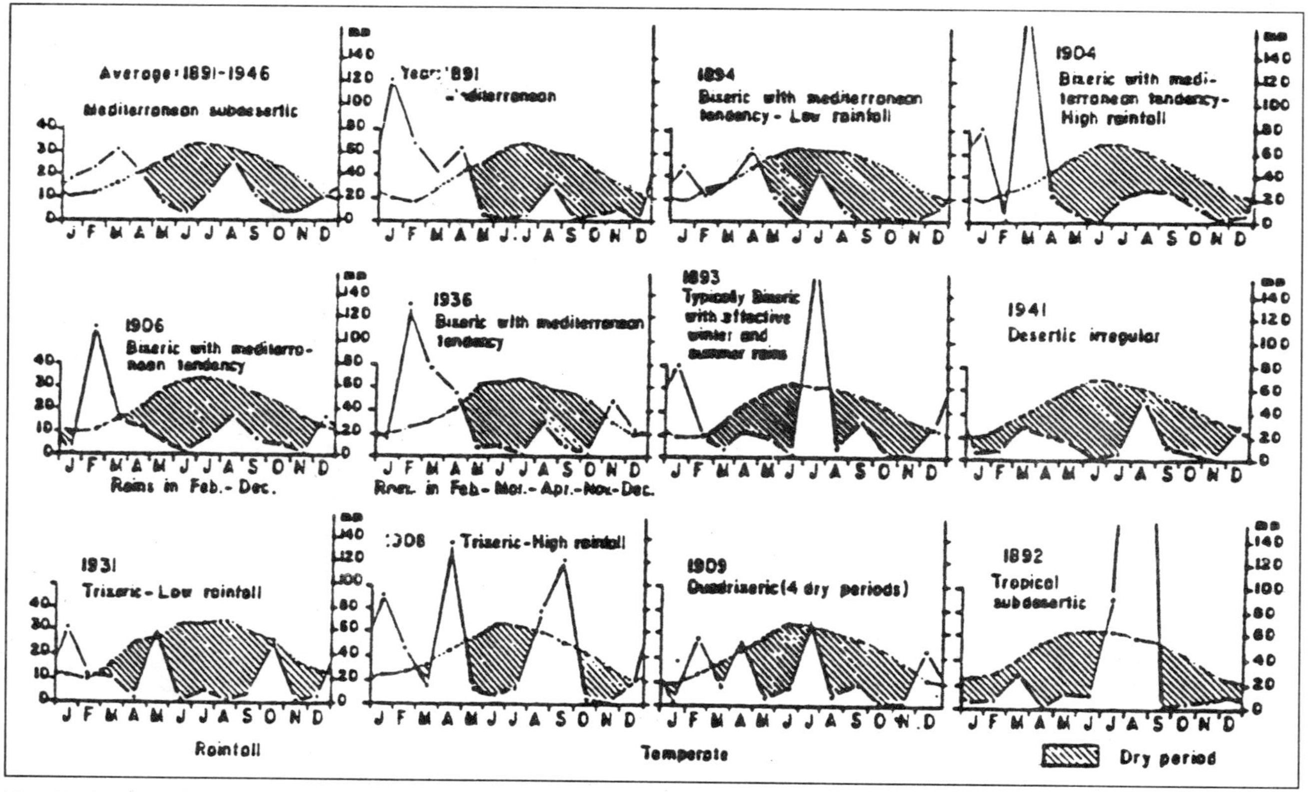

Fig. 25. Interyearly variations in regimes at Peshawar.

from West Asia into India during the Pleistocene and emerged as a distinct species, *Cedrus deodara*.

The glacial history also favours the immigration of the European, Siberian, Chinese and Japanese extra-tropical plants into the Himalayas. Takhtajan (1969) considers the Eastern Himalayas, Assam, Yunnan, Upper Burma, North Vietnam and Eastern Asia as the primary centre of origin of the temperate flora of the Northern Hemisphere, not simply as a refugium of relicts or secondary centre of development. The reason is that in this region are found entire phylogenetic series linking temperate forms with sub-tropical and tropical ones.

Quaternary History of the Flora of the Kashmir Valley, Kumaon

Perhaps in no other part of the country, the Quaternary vegetational history is so well studied as in the Kashmir Valley and Kumaon, thanks to the preservation of mega and micro-fossils in the postglacial deposits of the Lower Karewas and in the peat deposits of the lakes.

The sub-fossil pollen was the object of study by Wodehouse and de Terra as early as 1935. Later Puri (1948a, 1948b, 1957) studied the megafossils. In recent years palynological investigation has gathered momentum and the work of Vishnu-Mittre (1962, 1963a, 1963b, 1964), Singh (1963), Nair (1960) and Vishnu-Mittre et al. (1967) deserve special mention in reconstructing the Quaternary vegetational history of the Kashmir Valley proper, of the Lower Karewas and of the Kumaon Himalayas in the Naini Tal district. According to Puri (1943, 1947) the uplift of the Pir Panjal range which flanks the Kashmir Valley in the south and the south-west, by about 2,000 m has led to the disappearance of plants like oaks, laurels, figs, *Woodfordia*, *Mallotus*, *Pittosporum*, *Myrsine*, *Rhamnus*, *Pinus*, *Cedrus* and *Trapa* which flourished in the valley during the Pleistocene by cutting off the influence of the monsoon.

Vishnu-Mittre (1963a) does not accept this view for three reasons:

(1) Oaks (*Quercus semecarpifolia* and *Q. dilatata*) are recorded for the first time by him in the Kashmir Valley. For *Q. dilatata*, he admits a possible introduced origin as it occurs in a patch around the ruins of a temple near Acchabal but *Q. semecarpifolia* seems a natural escape from the southern slope of Pir Panjal.

(2) There is postglacial evidence of occurrence of oaks (based on pollen grains) on the leeward side of the Pir Panjal. This discredits the hypothesis that oaks disappeared due to climatic change in the wake of the uplift of the Pir Panjal.

(3) The ecological amplitude of the Western Himalayan oaks is sufficiently large; the reduction of monsoon rains would not affect a xerophytic species like *Quercus ilex*. *Q. glauca*, *Q. semecarpifolia* and even *Q. dilatata* have tolerance wide enough to grow in the range of precipitation available in the valley.

Vishnu-Mittre (1966) is of the opinion that the gradual extermination of oaks from the valley is due to the combined action of man and climate. Oaks provide good fuel and so have suffered heavily at the hands of man. He also points out that the successful establishment of some tropical and subtropical species proves that the present climate of the valley is quite suitable to those species.

Whether the Lombardy poplar (*Populus nigra*) is exotic or indigenous in Kashmir is a disputed question. Some botanists (Berry 1923, 1927; Puri 1945) assign to it an oriental origin whereas others consider it as a recent introduction from Europe. Puri (1945) reported the discovery of a few leaf impressions definitely agreeing with the leaves of this poplar. Fotidar (1961) points out the polymorphism of the leaves in this species (FAO 1958) and the absence of female trees, and questions the indigenous nature of the species in Kashmir.

The pollen analytical investigations of the Lower Karewa deposits exposed at Sedau, Laredura, Nichahom, Botapathri and Raithan along the north-eastern slope of the Pir Panjal in the south-west of the Kashmir Valley have been carried out by Vishnu-Mittre and colleagues (1962). The vegetational history begins with the oak woods interrupted by a short phase of the alder woods. The conifers in the forests are *Cedrus deodara*, *Abies*, *Picea* and *Pinus wallichiana*. The herbs and shrubs are poorly represented; this suggests the occurrence of closed woods.

The oak woods are succeeded by the open pine-mixed woods (dominated by *Pinus wallichiana*) which are preceded and followed by phases devoid of vegetation. These phases indicate disastrous changes in the vegetation leading to the destruction of forests. These two phases are referred to as the Lower and the Upper Transition Zones respectively.

The Upper Transition Zone is replaced by a brief phase of oak-mixed woods followed by a phase of Picea-oak woods which are succeeded towards the top of the profile by the Juglanselm phase.

From the lithological studies of the Lower Karewa sediments, de Terra and Paterson (1939) recognized 5 lithozones. The stratigraphy reveals that the climate was temperate wet during the Lithozones 1 and 2, dry in the Lithozone 3 and moist during Lithozone 4. The composite pollen profile also suggests the sequence in the climatic change from wet-dry-moist with progressive cooling while the climate as a whole continued to be temperate.

The age of the Lower Karewa deposits is a controversial question. They are regarded as of Plio-Pleistocene age by some (Wadia 1951) and assigned to the first Interglacial by others (de Terra and Paterson 1939; Pilgrim 1944). The underlying brown to pink gravels and sands are believed by the latter school to be the outwash deposit of the first glaciation.

It is largely held that the Pliocene climate was of subtropical nature and a marked cooling of climate characterized the beginning of the Pleistocene. The pollen analytical sequences shows that the climate during the deposition of Lower Karewas was temperate. The two pines in the Western Himalayas, *P. roxburghii* and *P. wallichiana*, could be taken to be the indicators of subtropical and temperate climates respectively. The pollen of *P. roxburghii* is not recorded in the profiles investigated so far. Vishnu-Mittre et al. (1962) and Vishnu-Mittre (1963b) therefore concluded that the Lower Karewas could neither be referred to the first Interglacial nor to the Pliocene. They may be assigned to the preglacial.

The postglacial vegetational sequence revealed by the pollen diagrams constructed from the Haigam Lake in the Kashmir Valley is divisible into eight vegetational phases (Vishnu-Mittre and Sharma 1966). Here, the vegetational history begins with ash-elm-alder-oak wood phase. With the amelioration of climate, a broad-leaved-conifer mixed forest is established. Probably in response to the deterioration of the climate or under the dual effect of climate and the biotic factor the oak-mixed wood declined and the pine woods are re-established.

This study also brings out with the help of pollen diagrams the evidences of the origin and the progressive development of agriculture during the postglacial period. The earliest forest clearings took place in the conifer mixed woods. The authors also discuss the correspondence between the progressive development of agriculture and the historical and archaeological evidence.

The overall decline of several broad-leaved trees like *Quercus*, *Carpinus*, *Juglans* and the extermination of others (*Alnus*, *Carpinus*, *Betula*) is an important feature in the floristic history of the Kashmir Valley. Their decline is attributed to the onset of the cooler phase but the damage done by the human agency is also assessed from historical and ethnobotanical records.

Another fact of importance is that the postglacial pollen diagrams of Kashmir Valley bring out a more or less similar pattern of vegetation development (conifers-oak woods-conifers) as in the European diagrams (Vishnu-Mittre 1966). However, *Tilia* and *Fagus* so very conspicuous in the European diagrams are not recorded from the pollen spectra of Kashmir. Another remarkable difference is in the low value of *Corylus* which does not rise above 15 per cent in Kashmir whereas in Europe it attains values up to 200 per cent and more.

The Late Quaternary vegetational history of the Kumaon Himalayas is built up through pollen-analytical investigations of two lakes in the subtropical region of outer Himalayas at an elevation of 1,400-1,500 m in the Nainital district (Vishnu-Mittre et al. 1967).

The pollen diagrams seem to slightly predate the Neolithic period and may well extend down to the Mesolithic.

The present-day vegetation consists of oak forests largely comprising *Quercus incana*, *Q. dilatata* and *Q. semecarpifolia* with *Pinus roxburghii* forming mixed or pure associations.

The pollen diagram brings out a succession between *Pinus roxburghii* woods and oak woods. Four distinct vegetational phases from the Early Neolithic to the recent times are recognized and these are designated by the letters a, b, c, d as four stages.

During the stage a, the vegetation largely consisted of *P. roxburghii* with some sprinkling of oak forests. The progressive invasion of the oaks into the pine forests towards the top of stage a ultimately established the mixed oak woods during the stage b. This change seems to correspond to the climate becoming wetter and more humid. Along with the oaks, there was an increase in the broad-leaved elements also.

The oak woods continue to be dominant during the stages c and d although there were some changes in the other broad-leaved species. The appearance of the pollens of temperate trees like *Pinus wallichiana*, *Abies* and *Cedrus* during stage c and their increase in stage d point to the change of climate towards cooler conditions.

The practice of cultivation is not noted in the stage a though a charcoal evidence indicates the destruction of forests by fire in the middle of this stage. Whether the fires were due to the action of man or due to natural causes is not clearly known. Plant economy during the lower half of stage b was moderate but decreased towards the upper half of the stage. During stages c and d there is evidence of considerable increase in plant economy.

Quaternary History of the Nilgiris

Vishnu-Mittre (1962) published a short note on the outline history of the origin and development of the Nilgiri swamps together with past changes in climate comprising three wet and two dry phases. Preliminary pollen analytical investigation revealed the absence of aquatic plants since the origin of the swamps.

The Quaternary microfossil flora of Pykara, Udhagamandalam (Ooty), has been studied by Menon (1966-7). The floral succession at Pykara is shown to be quite unlike postglacial successions elsewhere in that the latter are based on tree elements. This element is shown to be practically absent in Pykara deposits which are composed principally of non-arboreal plants. The only arboreal pollen are shown to belong to Anacardiaceae in low percentage and to Thymeleaceae, Euphorbiaceae, Mimosaceae and Urticaceae in yet lesser percentages. The frequency of the pollen types reveals that Poaceae is the most dominant group followed by *Selaginella* and some other ferns. Cyperaceae, Haemodoraceae, Balsaminaceae, Asteraceae, Scrophulariaceae, Xyridaceae, Chenopodiaceae, Cruciferae and Umbelliferae are the most conspicuous amongst the other families.

A stage with the dominance of Poaceae is succeeded by the abundance of ferns and this stage in turn is again followed by the preponderance of grasses. From these observations, Menon (l.c.) suggests a change from drier climate in the early stage characterized by grasses to a fern dominated moister phase and back to drier climate with continued abundance of Poaceae (grasses).

Vishnu-Mittre and Gupta's (1970) palaeo-palynological work in the Kakathope swamp near Udhagamandalam showed the colonization of the area by *Rhododendron* about 35,000 years ago in the Late Pleistocene, corresponding to the glaciation in the western Himalayas. According to Gupta (1971) grasslands of the Nilgiris were gradually invaded by *Rhododendron* and some other shrubs from this date. Climatic conditions then became wetter and warmer free of frost as indicated by the presence of pollen of *Impatiens* and by preponderance of the pollen of *Gordonia*, *Elaeocarpus*, *Euonymus*. After this phase, pollen record shows decline of forest in favour of grassland. Meher-Homji (1975) pointed out that *Impatiens* spp. do not necessarily indicate frost-free climate. The present-day climate of the south Indian hill-tops is characterized by ground-frost on winter nights (Meher-Homji 1967), yet 36 species of *Impatiens* occur above 1,800 m (Gamble 1915-35). Most of these grow under forest where the canopy does not allow the frost to settle at ground level. At least 3 species (*Impatiens chinensis*, *I. tomentosa* and *I. viscida*) frequent swampy areas or pastures.

For the Konal Ar Basin of the Nilgiri Hills, Vasanthy et al. (1989), found no major change in the vegetation pattern over the last 10,000 years. The present-day grassland-dominated landscape with scattered sholas is in evidence even in the prehistoric time and so man alone cannot be blamed for the creation of the grasslands of the south Indian hills at the expense of forests.

A recent study in progress ăt the French Institute, Pondicherry, points to changes of only minor magnitude in the vegetation and therefore in climate during the Holocene characterized by phases of dominance of *Michaelia*, a forest species at intervals within the general framework of forest grassland mosaic.

Quaternary Climo-Vegetational History of Western Rajasthan

Gurdip Singh and his colleagues (1974) reported large scale vegetation and climatic changes in the now arid Thar desert based on the record of fossil pollen grains from the lakes of western Rajasthan. The palaeo-palynological evidence combined with geomorphological data reveal five arid phases alternating with four moister stages during the Holocene.

The drier phases occurred during (1) Pre-Middle Stone age, (2) Upper Palaeolithic i.e., pre-8000 BC, (3) Pre-Harappan times i.e. 7500 BC to 3000 BC, (4) *c*. 2000 BC to 1400 BC and (5) early centuries AD to the present. In between these phases, there were spells of lesser aridity during (1) the Middle Stone Age, (2) *c*. 8000 BC to 7500 BC, (3) Harappan phase *c*. 3000 BC to 2000 BC, and (4) *c*. 1400 BC to 1000 BC. However, a critical interpretation of the palynological data by Vishnu-Mittre (1974) and Meher-Homji (1973b, 1980) suggests changes in aridity-humidity on a much smaller scale.

Much acclaimed as the study of Gurdip Singh et al. is Bryson and Swain (1981), it does not convince an ecologist of marked changes in the climate because the taxa like *Artemisia, Mimosa rubicaulis, Oldenlandia, Maytenus, Syzygium cumini* and Cyperaceae cited as pointers of humid phases are not very fidel indicators of humidity (Vishnu-Mittre 1974a, 1974b; Meher-Homji 1980). If the climate had changed to humid type in the true sense of the term, pollen of some of the deciduous forest tree species of the Aravallis should have appeared in the profile of the Sambhar Lake.

Syzygium cumini even today grows in the core region of the Indian desert. Others like *Typha* and *Cyperus* can grow in and around the local water bodies in the arid zone.

The study of Deotare et al. (1998) based on palynological, stratigraphical and archaeological evidence around the Bap-Malar playa (Jodhpur district) also suggests marginal changes in climate. The present-day dry core of the Thar experienced semi-arid to arid climate since the early late Pleistocene.

According to Francfort (1987), surface observation of ancient hydrogeographic network and the study of stratigraphy of the unbricked walls of wells clearly show that the dried up rivers were active at the end of the last glaciation, well before the protohistoric settlements in the Indus Valley. Aeolian sands, carbonates, etc., go in favour of arid climate.

The region was populated in a climate not different from today; remnants of canals prove dependence on artificial irrigation for cultivation.

The onset of aridity in the Thar has been a late Tertiary event linked to physiographic causes like the uplift of the Himalayas.

How the glacial and interglacial phases affected the wind directions and the vegetation patterns in the deserts surrounding the Arabian Sea has been brought out by the elegant palynological investigation of Van Campo et al. (1982). Collection of pollen grains with air-filters on ships in the Arabian Sea revealed dominance of Cyperaceae, Euphorbiaceae, *Podocarpus* and *Olea* in summer brought by the south-west winds from East Africa. On the other hand, pollen grains of Chenopodiaceae and *Artemisia* prevailed in winter when the winds blow from the north and north-east over Arabia, Iran and Baluchistan. This pollen pattern linked to seasonal reversal of wind systems has been used by Van Campo et al. (1982) in deciphering the climatic trends and the status of soil salinity in the desert regions through the analysis of the fossil pollen grains obtained from offshore marine cores in the Arabian Sea.

During the period extending from Holocene to 128 ka BP the glacial intervals corresponded to low sea level, increasing the salinity of the littoral zone; this phase is marked by the predominance of halophytic Chenopodiaceae and steppic or arid zone species like *Artemisia*. The glaciation in Central Asia intensified the north-east winds at the expense of the south-west system, depositing large amounts of pollen of Chenopodiaceae and *Artemisia* in the Arabian Sea. The interglacial phases, on the contrary, intensified insolation and low pressures over the tropical continents, strengthening the south-west winds and monsoonal rains; this less dry stage is indicated by an increase in the frequency of the East African pollen taxa in the Arabian Sea core profile.

PALAEO-PALYNOLOGY OF MANGROVE SWAMPS

Based on the pollen representation of the mangrove vegetation in the sediments of two marine cores off the south-west coast of India, Van Campo (1986) recognized two important phases of monsoon climate. The low mangrove pollen frequency in a period dating back to 22,000-18,000 years BP would be indicative of a dry phase when due to a weak monsoon, the run-off of the Western Ghats rivers would be reduced. This dry phase was followed by a humid phase culminating around 11,000 years BP, with very high mangrove pollen representation linked to heavy run-off.

The changes taking place in the mangrove vegetation of the Kaveri delta of southern India over a period of the last 2,000 years due to natural geomorphic processes and anthropogenic interference has been investigated by Tissot (1986).

At Muthupet, four periods have been identified based on the representation of pollen grains of mangrove species and of back-mangroves observed in the sediments; the importance of marine influence has been indicated by a relatively high percentage of foraminifera organic tests and dinoflaggelate cysts.

These periods, from the oldest to the most recent are:

Period A: Mangrove and back-mangrove species are poorly represented, some pollen of Rhizophoraceae and Sonneratiaceae families totally absent from the landscape nowadays, are observed. Marine influence is clear and constant.

Period B: Marine influence increases; gradual expansion of the mangrove is also observed.

Period C: Marine influence decreases substantially, when the mangrove with dominance of *Avicennia* reaches its maximum extension.

Period D: Marine influence is cut off and herbaceous halophytes of the back-mangroves spread over a large area to the detriment of arborescent genera of the mangrove which either decrease (*Avicennia*) or disappear completely (*Rhizophora, Sonneratia*).

The age of the oldest sediment in the Kaveri delta is estimated to be about 2,000 years from various arguments such as ^{14}C dating and the maximum Holocene transgression occurring about 5,000 years BP. The appearance in the cores of pollen of *Casuarina* marks the date of its introduction in India in 1798 (Santapau 1966).

In order to understand the vegetational evolution observed in the cores of Muthupet, Tissot (l.c.) traces the history of the lagoon formation.

According to Ahmed (1972), all along the coast of the Kaveri delta, the dominant action of waves and coastal currents induce the formation of a sand bar, behind which a lagoon is created. Then, this lagoon is filled up more or less quickly by fluvial deposits. Beyond this sand bar fluvial sediments continue to be carried to the sea, and are reworked by the waves leading to the formation of a new sand bar and a new lagoon behind it.

At the bottom of the core (Period A), the site is located near the sea, as indicated by the constant occurrence of marine micro-organisms. In the lagoon, the mangrove which has only limited areas for spreading, expands to a very small extent. As the lagoon fills up with fluvial supplies, the mangrove begins to spread out on the banks of the recently formed channels (Period B); marine influence also increases. Filling up continues, the channels become more and more numerous and the mangroves colonize their banks, reaching its maximum extent, while marine action decreases.

Then, in an area where the sea-water has no influence, arborescent species of mangrove disappear and are replaced by back-mangrove species (Period D). It is possible that, during Period D, human impact has slightly hastened this natural process, but palynological results do not show evidence of it.

At Pichavaram, as at Muthupet, two cores were taken, but in an area closer to the shoreline:

One in the *Avicennia* forest, about 50 m from a channel bank, at a depth of 3.90 m the other, 6.90 m deep, was cored on the opposite bank, very close to the channel, under *Rhizophora*, *Bruguiera* and *Ceriops*.

Tissot (l.c.) observed that the Periods A and B are practically identical to those described for Muthupet. However, from the beginning of Period C, dated from about 200 years BP due to the presence of *Casuarina* pollen, the evolution of palynological assemblages is different. Whereas, in Muthupet, Period C corresponds to the maximum extension of the mangrove, here, pollen percentages of the three main genera, *Sonneratia*, *Rhizophora* and *Avicennia* decrease, while pollen of back-mangrove species show high percentages.

The abundance of marine microfossils in these levels proves that this stage represents the bottom of Period C of Muthupet.

Therefore, Period D, which in Muthupet corresponds to a rapid decrease of arborescent mangrove species and favours large scale extension of back-mangrove species, is not observed in Pichavaram.

The decline of mangrove vegetation at Pichavaram in spite of its being a Reserved Forest since 1880 might be ascribed to heavy anthropic pressure (collection of firewood, grazing, fishing). Besides, the Coleroon river linked to the mangrove lagoon has been dammed for providing irrigation, thus depriving the mangrove of fresh water supply at critical stages and resulting in increase of salinity.

Caratini et al. (1991) analysing a marine core off Karwar, facing the estuary of the Kalinadi river have brought out a convincing palynological evidence of a vegetational change from an evergreen forest type to a savanna (grassland) in the Uttara Kannada district of the Western Ghats around 3,500 years BP. However, the reason assigned for the change, viz., declining humidity, is not entirely convincing. Anthropic interference as a factor for the change also needs consideration.

In the hypothesis of a decrease in rainfall, one would expect a decline in the number of evergreen forest species in favour of those of a moist or dry deciduous forest and even of thorn forest if the decrease in the quantum of rain was drastic. However, the pollen spectrum does not reveal such a change. What it indicates is the establishment of a savanna. It is a known fact that the savannas in the plains and at moderate altitude in the Western Ghats are essentially the result of fire (Pascal 1984). This made us suspect the role of man in bringing about the change from forest to grassland.

The generally accepted date of introduction of cultivation in this region is placed around 1000 BC (3000 BP) after the introduction of iron (Gadgil and Subash Chandran 1988). However, it is likely that clearing the land using fire was an effective method a few centuries earlier. According to Sundara (1990) the Neolithic intruders descended from the upghat region to the downghat region of the Dakshina Kannada district in the last part of the second millennium BC and resorted to cultivation, probably by the slash and burn method.

Reduction in mangrove pollen around 1300 BP is assigned to lessening intensity of humid conditions (Caratini et al. 1991). Gadgil and Subash Chandran (1988) on the other hand point out shrinkage in the mangrove area due to introduction of paddy cultivation in the estuaries. A much lower rate of sedimentation (7cm/100 years) in the recent period compared to the earlier period 3,500-4,500 years ago (18 cm/100 years) has been reported in favour of 'alteration of humid conditions'. However, this is contrary to known facts: one would expect less soil erosion under forested conditions than under grass-savannas occurring 'on slopes' (Caratini et al. 1991). Besides, increase in water yield is linked to the removal of natural forest and burning of grasses (Bruijnzeel 1986), once again an evidence in support of the use of fire. Finally, though the proposed drier phase in Karnataka is shown to be parallel to the one in Rajasthan, actually there is a discrepancy in the dates of onset of the drier phase.

CONCLUDING REMARKS

Though palynology is a useful tool in biogeographic research, there are pitfalls in the interpretation of pollen data.

A point of concern is that the dates proposed for the setting of a drier climate vary not only from continent to continent, from the Himalayas in the north to the Nilgiris in the south, but even from one part of a hill range like the Western Ghats to another part.

Now that more dates would be available under the International Geosphere Biosphere Program, it would be worth investigating whether such changes were global in nature due to planetary causes, regional or merely local, linked to some very localized factor like deforestation which can alter the pattern of rainfall (Meher-Homji 1991).

The merit of the work of Caratini et al. (1991) is that it pinpoints the date of commencement of human activity in the central part of the Western Ghats which changed the forested landscape to savanna type.

Sometimes it happens that the change in vegetation deduced from pollen data is attributed solely to the climate and that too in very broad terms such as humid or arid. There is practically no indication of the quantum of rainfall. Also often ignored is the pattern of rainfall in terms of the length of dry season or season(s) of occurrence of rains (Meher-Homji 1994). The southern part of the Western Ghats in Kerala receives about 3,000 mm per annum, but the dry season is short (of 2 months duration). Agumbe in Karnataka, in the middle part of this hill range, receives rainfall of the order of 7,000 mm but experiences a dry season of 5 months. The tree *Cullenia* is confined to the ghat region where the dry season does not exceed four and a half months.

In certain cases the role of anthropogenic factors, of physiographic changes like shifts in the course of rivers, or yet of a pest in bringing about a change in the density of a species and consequently in vegetation, is ignored, and a climatic interpretation is sought to explain the change in the pattern of plant distribution. The elm (*Ulmus*) in Europe suffered a decline because of a disease, but earlier studies attempted to put the blame on climate change. A marshy area fed by a river would bear a moist forest type but with a shift of the river it would show a change in floristic composition in consonance with the local dry conditions. One may not invoke a climate change in this case.

In some studies (Gurdip Singh et al. 1974) the taxa selected as markers of arid or humid phase are not very faithful indicators of climate and lead to erroneous conclusions.

REFERENCES

Ahmed, E. 1972. *Coastal Geomorphology of India*. New Delhi: Orient Longman.

André, J. and J. Filliozat 1980. *Pline l'Ancien, Histoire Naturelle*, Livre VI, 2e Partie. Société d'Editions Les Belles Lettres.

Bagnouls, F. and H. Gaussen 1957. Les Climats Biologiques et leur Classification, *Annales de Géographie* 3 55: 193-220.

Bagnouls, F. and V.M. Meher-Homji 1959. Bioclimatic Types of South-East Asia, *Institut Français de Pondichér: Travaux de la Section Scientifique et Technique* 1: 207-46.

Berry, E.W. 1923. *Tree Ancestors: a Glimpse into the Past*. Baltimore.

——— 1927. Links with Asia Before the Mountains Brought Aridity to the Western United States, *Scientific Monthly* 25: 324.

Bruijnzeel, P.S. 1986. Environmental Impacts of (De)Forestation in the Humid Tropics—a Watershed Perspective, *Wallaceana* 46: 3-13.

Bryson, R.A. and A.M. Swain 1981. Holocene Variations of Monsoon Rainfall in Rajasthan, *Quaternary Research* 16: 135-45.

Caratini, C., M. Fontugne, J.P. Pascal, C. Tissot and I. Bentaleb 1991. A Major Change at *c*. 3500 Years B.P. in the Vegetation of the Western Ghats in North Kanara, Karnataka, *Current Science* 61: 669-72.

Deotare, B.C., M.D. Kajale, A.A. Kshirsagar and S.N. Rajaguru 1998. Geochronological and Palaeoenvironmental Studies Around Bap-Malar Playa, District Jodhpur, Rajasthan, *Current Science* 75: 316-20.

de Terra, H. and T.T. Paterson 1939. *Studies on the Ice Age in India and Associated Human Cultures*. Washington D.C.: Carnegie Institute.

de Martonne, E. 1926. Areisme et Indice d'Aridité, *Compte Rendu d'Académie des Sciences* 182: 1395-8.

Emberger, L., H. Gaussen, M. Kassas and A. Phillipis 1963. *Carte Bioclimatique de la Zone Méditerranéenne*. Unesco-FAO: Recherche sur la Zone Aride 21.

F.A.O. 1958. *Poplars in Forestry and Land-Use*. FAO Forestry and Forest Products Studies 12.

Fotidar, A.N. 1961. Exotics in Kashmir, *Tenth Silvicultural Conference* 2: 684-90.

Francfort, H.P. 1987. The Indus Civilisation Confronts the Desert, *The World Scientist* 4: 77.

Gadgil, M. and M.D. Subash Chandran 1988. On the History of Uttara Kannada Forests, *in Changing Tropical Forests* (J. Dargavel, K. Dixon and N. Semple Eds.), pp. 47-58. Canberra: Australian National University.

Gamble, J.S. 1915-35. *Flora of the Presidency of Madras*, 3 Vols. London: Adlard and Sons.

Gaussen, H. 1955. Limite et Ecologie des Pays Méditerranées. Extrait du Compte Rendu Géneral de Voyage d'Etudes en France dans la Région Provençale. Document FAO/SCM/55.

George, P. 1970. *Dictionnaire de la Géographie*. Paris: Presses Universitaires de France.

Guinet, P. 1966. What May Afford Palynology to Archaeology and Ancient History in India, *Journal of M.S. University of Baroda* 15: 15-19.

Gupta, H.P. 1971. Quaternary Vegetational History of Ootacamund, Nilgiris, South India. 1. Kakathope and Rees Corner, *The Palaeobotanist* 20: 74-90.

Gurdip Singh, R.D. Joshi, S.K. Chopra and A.B. Singh 1974. Late Quaternary History of Vegetation and Climate of the Rajasthan Desert, *Philosophical Transactions of the Royal Society* 267B: 467-501.

Köppen, W. 1918. Klassification der Klimat nach Temperature, Niederschalag und Jahresverlauf, *Peterm. Mit*. 64: 193-203; 243-8.

——— 1936. *Die Klimat der Erde* in *Handbuch der Klimatologie,* Vol. IC (W. Köppen and Geiger Eds.) Berlin: Verlags-Buchhandlung Gebruder Borntraeger.

Labroue, L., P. Legris and M. Viart 1965. Bioclimats du Sous-Continent Indien, *Institut Français de Pondichéry, Travaux de la Section Scientifique et Technique* 3 (3): 1-32.

Lang, R. 1920. *Ver Witterung und Bodenbuildung als Eifuhrung in die Bodenkunde*. Stuttgart: Schweizerbartsche Verlagsbuchdlg.

Meher-Homji, V.M. 1967. Phytogeography of the South Indian Hill Stations, *Bulletin Torrey Botanical Club* 94: 230-42.

——— 1973a. A Phytoclimatic Approach to the Problem of Mediterraneity in the Indo- Pakistan Subcontinent, *Feddes Repertorium* 83: 757-88.

——— 1973b. Is the Sind-Rajasthan Desert the Result of a Recent Climatic Change?, *Geoforum* 15: 47-57.

——— 1975. On the Montane Species of Kodaikanal, South India, *Phytocoenologia* 2 : 28-39.

——— 1980. The Thar Desert: its Climatic History, *Man and Environment* IV: 1-7.

——— 1991. Probable Impact of Deforestation on Hydrological Processes, *Climatic Change* 19: 163-73.

——— 1994. Climate Changes Over Space and Time: Their Repercussions on the Flora and Vegetation, *Palaeobotanist* 42 (2): 225-40.

Menon, V.K. 1966-7. Pollen Analysis of the Postglacial Deposits from Pykara, Ootacamund, India, *Journal of Palynology* 2 and 3: 1-10.

Nair, P.K.K. 1960. Palynological Investigation of the Quaternary (Karewa) of Kashmir, *Journal of Scientific and Industrial Research* 19: 145-54.

Pascal, J.P. 1984. Les Forêts Denses Humides Semperirentes des Ghâts Occidentaux, *Institut Français de Pondichéry: Travaux de la Section Scientifique et Technique* 20: 1-365.

Pilgrim, G.E. 1944. Lower Limit of the Pleistocene in Europe and India, *Geology Magazine* 81: 28-38.

Puri, G.S. 1943. The Occurrence of *Woodfordia fruticosa* (Linn.) S. Kurz in the Karewa Deposits of Kashmir, with Remarks on Changes of Altitude and Climate During the Pleistocene, *Journal of the Indian Botanical Society* 22: 125-31.

——— 1945. Lombardy Poplar (*Populus nigra* L. *var fastigata* Desf.) in India, *Indian Forester* 71: 423-5.

——— 1947. Fossil Plants and the Himalayan Uplift, *Journal of the Indian Botanical Society* 25: 167-84.

——— 1948a. A preliminary Note on the Pleistocene Flora of the Karewa Formations of Kashmir, *Proceedings of Geological National Society of India* 20: 61-7.

——— 1948b. The Flora of the Karewar Series of Kashmir and Its Phytogeographical Affinities with Chapters on the Methods of Identification, *Indian Forester* 74: 105, 152, 210, 240.

——— 1957. Preliminary Observations on the Phytogeographical Changes in the Kashmir Valley During the Pleistocene, *The Palaeobotanist* 6: 16-18.

Santapau, H. 1966. *Common Trees*. New Delhi: National Book Trust.

Singh, G. 1963. A Preliminary Survey of the Postglacial Vegetational History of Kashmir Valley, *The Palaeobotanist* 12: 73-108.

Snead, R.E. 1968. Weather Patterns in Southern West Pakistan, *Archives für Meteorologie, Geophysique und Bioklimatologie* Serie B-16: 316-46.

Soltner, D. 1982. *Les Bases de la Production Végétale*. Vol. 2—Le Climat. 2e Collection Sciences et Techniques Agricoles.

Subrahmanyam, V.P. 1959. Droughts and Aridity in India: a Climatic Study, in *Proceedings Symposium on Meteorological Aspects of Floods and Droughts in India*. New Delhi.

——— 1972. The Concept of Use of Water Balance in Ecoclimatic Planning, *Publications in Climatology* 35: 46-56.

Sundara, A. 1990. The Neolithic Axe and the Parshurama Legend in the West Coast: Human Response to the Environment. Paper Presented in the Seminar on Rising Trends in Palaeoanthropology, Environmental Change and Human Response (Last Two Million Years).

Tissot, C. 1986. Recent Evolution of Mangrove Vegetation in the Kaveri Delta: a Palynological Study, *Journal of Marine Biological Association of India* 29: 16-22.

Takhtajan, A. 1969. *Flowering Plants: Origin and Dispersal*. Edinburgh: Oliver Boyd.

Thornthwaite, C.W. 1933. The Climates of the Earth, *Geographical Review* 23: 433-40.

——— 1948. An Approach Towards a Rational Classification of Climate, *Geographical Review* 38: 55-94.

Van Campo, E. 1986. Monsoon Fluctuations in Two 20,000 Yr. B.P. Oxygen Isotope Records Off Southwest India, *Quaternary Research* 26: 376-88.

Van Campo, E., J.C. Duplessy and M. Rossignol-Strick 1982. Climatic Conditions Deduced from a 150- Kyr Oxygen Isotope-Pollen Record from the Arabian Sea, *Nature* 296 (5852): 56-9.

Vasanthy, G., C. Caratini and G. Delibrias 1989. Palynological Studies of Clayey Peats of Palni and Nilgiri Hills. Palaeoecological Significance. Fifth International Palynology Conference, Cambridge.

Vishnu-Mittre 1962. Studies of the Vegetational History from the Swamps in the Nilgiris I. The Nilgiri Peat Deposits, *Proceedings Fiftieth Indian Science Congress* 3: 394-5.

——— 1963a. Oaks in the Kashmir Valley with Remarks on their History, *Grana Palynologica* 4: 306-12.

——— 1963b. On the Plio-Pleistocene Boundary in N.W. India, *The Palaeobotanist* 12: 270-6.

——— 1964. Floristic and Ecological Consideration of the Pleistocene Plant Impression from Kashmir, *The Palaeobotanist* 12 (4).

——— 1966. Some Aspects Concerning Pollen-Analytical Investigations in the Kashmir Valley, *The Palaeobotanist* 15: 157-75.

——— 1969. Some Evolutionary Aspects of Indian Flora in *J. Sen Memorial Volume*, pp. 385-94. Calcutta: Sen Memorial Committee and Botanical Society of Bengal.

——— 1974a. Plant Remains and Climate from the Late Harappan and Other Chalcolithic Cultures of India, *Geophytology* 4: 46-53.

——— 1974b. Late Quaternary Palaeobotany and Palynology in India: an Appraisement, in *Symposium Late Quaternary Development in Extra-European Areas*, pp. 16-51. Lucknow: Birbal Sahni Institute of Palaeobotany, Special Publication 5.

Vishnu-Mittre and H.P. Gupta 1968. A Living Fossil Community in South Indian Hills, *Current Science* 37: 671-2.

Vishnu-Mittre, H.P. Gupta and R. Robert 1967. Studies of the Late Quaternary Vegetational History of Kumaon Himalaya, *Current Science* 36: 539-40.

Vishnu-Mittre, Gurdip Singh and K.M.S. Saxena 1962. Pollen Analytical Investigation of the Lower Karewas, *Palaeobotanist* 11: 92-5.

Vishnu-Mittre and B.D. Sharma 1966. Studies of Postglacial Vegetational History from the Kashmir Valley. I. Haigam Lake, *the Palaeobotanist* 15: 185-212.

Wadia, D.N. 1951. The Transitional Passage of Pliocene into the Pleistocene in the North Western India, in *Report of the Eight Session of International Geology Congress* (1948). Pt. II, pp. 43-8. London.

Wodehouse, R.P. and H. de Terra 1935. Pleistocene Pollen of Kashmir, *Memoir Conn. Arts Society* 9.

The Search for Fossil Man in South Asia: Retrospect and Prospect

KENNETH A.R. KENNEDY

Recent discoveries of fossil remains from Pleistocene deposits in Sri Lanka allow for the testing of the hypothesis that there has been a reduction of muscular-skeletal robusticity and tooth size in anatomically modern *Homo sapiens* over the past 125,000 years. Evidence for this trend comes from studies of the skeletal biology of prehistoric human remains from Europe, Africa, western Asia and the Australasian region, but these anatomical changes can now be documented from South Asia as a consequence of recent palaeontological discoveries on the Indian mainland and in island Sri Lanka.

The search for fossil man in South Asia began in the 1830s with discoveries of hominoid and other mammalian palaeontological specimens in the Siwaliks and valleys of the Narmada and Jamuna (Yamuna) rivers, chronologies extending from the Late Micocene to Early Holocene epochs. Since 1863 archaeological finds of Acheulian type handaxes, cleavers and other stone tools in India established that hominids were settled in the Indian subcontinent by Middle Pleistocene times, but the first fossil specimen of this antiquity (*c*. 250,000 years ago) was recovered in 1982 in the middle Narmada Basin (Sonakia 1985; Kennedy et al. 1991)—'Narmada Man'. This calvaria, originally assigned to the taxon *Homo eretus* is now recognized as an anatomically archaic *Homo sapiens*. Early Holocene skeletal and dental hominid remains have been recovered from the Ganga plains and the Vindhyan range in north central India (Kennedy et al. 1992; Lukacs 1992; Lukacs et al. 1996.)

The earliest anatomically modern *H. sapiens* specimens from South Asia were recovered from the cave site of Fa Hien in Sabaragamuva Province, Sri Lanka, by Siran U. Deraniyagala (1992), currently the Director-General of Archaeology of the Government of Sri Lanka. Recently recovered from the site were nongeometric microliths and hearths dating to 34,000 years ago and within this Pleistocene context were found human remains. These skeletal and dental specimens were forwarded to the Human Biology Laboratory at Cornell University where they were examined and a study published (Kennedy and Zahorsky 1996). Other human remains from Fa Hien were found at upper and more recently deposited levels covering a timeframe from 34,000 to 5,400 BP based upon radiocarbon dates calibrated to a half-life of 5,730 BP.

Fa Hien is not the only Sri Lankan site with Late Pleistocene to Early Holocene human remains. Deraniyagala's excavations from the 1970s to the present time have provided a rich osteological and dental record from Batadomba Lena cave, also in Sabargamuva Province. Geometric microliths assigned by the archaeologists to an Early Mesolithic technological tradition occur at levels radiocarbon dated to 28,500 BP within a faunal context that environmental conditions of climate and some narrowly specialized ecological niches have remained relatively stable from the Late Pleistocene to modern times. Glacial activity in the Himalayan range did not have a profound impact upon ecological settings on the island, save for changes of coastline levels during episodes of glacial maxima and recession (Kennedy et al. 1986).

A third Late Pleistocene site in this southernmost portion of the Indian subcontinental landmass is Beli Lena Kitulgala with a Mesolithic tradition of geometric microliths and a human skeletal record extending from 16,000 to 12,000 BP. These specimens were also examined at Cornell University and I have had the privilege of visiting these localities in 1987 (Kennedy et al. 1986). This, too, is a cave site, but the burials at Bellan Bandi Palassa occur in an open-air mortuary deposit with a skeletal record of over 25 individual specimens which I was able to examine some years ago when they were sent to the British Museum of Natural History, London (Kennedy 1965). They have been dated by the thermoluminescence method to 6,500 BP (Wintle and Oakley 1972).

These archaeological localities hold particular interest because they contain one of the earliest examples of a microlithic tool tradition, predating microliths on the Indian mainland from deposits of 10,645 to 9,654 BP and from Africa's Kalemba rock-shelter in Zambia dated to 19,000 to 12,000 BP. Their importance to the study of hominid evolution is that the hominid fossils from Fa Hien are more ancient than those from Dolni and Vestonice in the Czech Republic (29,000 BP), Les Cottes in France (31,000 BP), Mumbwa in Zambia (22,000 BP) and the 25,000 years old fossils from Lake Mungo in Australia (Kennedy and Deraniyagala 1989). In western Europe this was the time when modern-type humans were replacing Neanderthal populations and Cromagnid populations were developing Upper Palaeolithic industries. Archaeological artefacts assigned to a *Ratnapura* cultural tradition of flake and pebble tools may have been manufactured in Sri Lanka as early as 75,000 years ago, and hominid settlement of the Indian subcontinent has been dated on stratigraphic evidence from the Potwar plateau in Pakistan to *c.* 2.2. Ma (Dennell 1991). Thus South Asia can no longer be regarded as a cultural *cul de sac* given its archaeological and palaeontological place in world prehistory.

What do these Late Pleistocene Sri Lankan fossil hominids tell us about changes in muscular-skeletal robusticity and reduced tooth size in the course of evolution of modern-type humans?

Comparisons of cranial and postcranial bones of these ancient Sri Lankan hunter-foragers with Neolithic and later food-producing prehistoric populations in South Asia indicate a retention of pronounced skeletal robusticity and sexual dimorphism in both structural features and reconstructed body size/stature variables, females exhibiting a greater degree of gracility and smaller body size and lower statures than males. When comparisons are made with other prehistoric hunting-foraging populations of Late Pleistocene and Early Holocene epochs, many parallels are found. This has been tested by a principal component analysis (PCA) using 85 cranial measurements for a sample of 160 skulls from South Asian prehistoric sites and an outlier series of 23 European Upper Palaeolithic crania, results showing two clusters: prehistoric hunter-foragers (including

TABLE 1. A CHRONOLOGY OF HUMAN SKELETAL REMAINS FROM SOUTH ASIA

Years BP	Site Location	Dating	Cultural Tradition
Present	Langhnaj	3,875±110	Mesolithic
2,000			
4,000	Mahadaha Fa Hien	4,010±120 4,750±60	Mesolithic
6,000	Bagor Bellanbandi Palassa Fa Hien	6,500±210 6,500±700 7,100±60	Mesolithic Mesolithic Mesolithic
7,000			
8,000	Lekhahia ki Pahari	8,370±75	Mesolithic
9,000			Mesolithic
10,000	Sarai Nahar Rai	10,345± ? (2,860±120)	
11,000			
12,000	Beli Lena Kitulgala	12,260±870	Mesolithic
13,000 14,000 15,000	Batadomba Lena	15,830±1260	Mesolithic
16,000 to 27,000 28,000	Batadomba Lena	28,500±440	Mesolithic
30,000	Darra-l-Kur	30,000±700	Mousterian
34,000	Fa Hein	33,070±410	Pre-Mesolithic
c 2,50,000	Hathnora (Narmada)	Mid-Pleistocene	Acheulian

some Sri Lankan samples) and agricultural-pastoral populations (Kennedy et al. 1984).

There is significant reduction of permanent molar tooth size measured by summed molar tooth crown areas of samples from various Neolithic, Chalcolithic, Bronze Age (Harappan) and Iron Age (Megalithic) sites in South Asia when values from these series are compared with those from Mesolithic Sri Lanka. The dimensions of molar size of the series from Mesolithic Bellanbandi Palassa are nearly twice the dimensions of the Neolithic series from Burzahom in Kashmir (Lukacs 1983; Hemphill et al. 1992).

Tooth sizes of both deciduous and permanent dentitions are a major factor in the complex of adaptive mechanisms whereby hominids encountered their environment (Wolpoff 1971), and measurements of the deciduous teeth from Fa Hien produce bucco-lingual and mesio-distal values which are comparatively large, falling well within the metric values of Neanderthals for the first deciduous molars and within the ranges of Upper Palaeolithic and Mesolithic values for other prehistoric and western Asiatic populations. Lotus ® 1-2-3, release 3, was used to calculate all values and prepare scatter diagrams. The coefficient of variation, expressed in per cent, describes the standard deviation relative to the mean of the sample of deciduous teeth from Fa Hien and comparative series. It was calculated by SD/Mean x 100 (Triola 1989). The formula Ó(x-avg)^2/n-1 was used in this study (Stark 1989; Kennedy and Zahorsky 1996).

The biological affinities of Sri Lanka's Late Pleistocene and Early Holocene hominids with the aboriginal tribal population of the island, the Veddas, and with surviving tribal populations of the Indian mainland have been assessed in earlier studies (Kennedy 1965, 1992, 1993, 1994). Although it would be rash to suggest that the 34,000 years old hominids from Fa Hien or the 16,000 years old hominids from Batadomba Lena are direct ancestors of the Veddas, it may be more than coincidence that many of the morphometric features present in these prehistoric series, as well as those from Bela Lena Kitulgala and Bellanbandi Palassa, are present in cranial and postcranial features of the historic aborigines.

In conclusion, the marked degree of muscular-skeletal robusticity and sexual dimorphism observed in the ancient anatomically modern *Homo sapiens* remains from Sri Lanka may be due to natural selection for the levels of physical strength and stamina demanded in the hunting-foraging life-way of Late Pleistocene and Early Holocene times in Sri Lanka, as in other prehistoric localities outside the island. Reduction of robusticity in later agricultural-pastoral populations may be due to relaxed selection in cultural environments where gracility of skeletal structures and smaller body size no longer placed individuals at disadvantageous levels for survival.

Paralleling the selective advantages for muscular-skeletal robusticity and sexual dimorphism was large (megadont) tooth size. Increase of the size of occlusal surfaces of teeth with consequent greater development of enamel was adaptive under the cultural stresses of food preparation without pottery for cooking. Toughness of certain nutrients and incorporation of gritty substances in the mouth as a result of grinding nuts, seeds and other hard foods in stone querns was a cause of severe dental attrition. Tooth size was reduced after Neolithic technologies were in place as a consequence of improved food preparation techniques and ingestion of domesticated crop and animal resources within farming and pastoral life-ways.

There was no neolithic cultural tradition in Sri Lanka, the Ratnapura and Mesolithic traditions persisting until the middle of the first millennium BC with the introduction of Iron Age farming and pastoral traditions from the Indian mainland and the beginnings of the Historic Period. Nor are there Acheulian traditions nor a Chalcolithic or a Bronze Age tradition on the island. It was a region of relative isolation from cultures and peoples of mainland India and lands bordering the Indian Ocean until well into Holocene times, and even with colonization from India and the diffusion of Buddhism there were areas of the interior that were not penetrated by Sinhala-speaking or Tamil-speaking peoples until the last few centuries. Vedda hunting-foraging populations lived in these relict regions having minimal contact with sedentary village farmers until the middle of the twentieth century. For these reasons, the genetic association of the prehistoric Sri Lankans with the aborigines of the ethnographic present requires further investigation, but affinities are suggested.

Sri Lanka offers the palaeoanthropologist good evidence that as Cromagnid contemporaries they retained many muscular-skeletal and dental features adapative to the hunting-foraging life-way, thus adding support to the hypothesis that it has been relaxed selection that has allowed changes in these variables in later food-producing populations. Significant modifications of body size, form and skeletal structures and tooth size took place in other parts of the world over the past 34,000 years (beginning perhaps as early as 125,000 years ago in Africa and western Asia), but many of the adaptive physical features of Late Pleistocene and Early Holocene human skeletal anatomy continued in that region of relative cultural and demic isolation that is Sri Lanka.

A final word. Sri Lanka and the landmass adjacent to the island stand between the African and Southeast Asian regions and offer the palaeoanthropologist the opportunity to explore this transitional zone of ancient peoples and cultures. South Asia is the new frontier of our discipline and has within the past two decades produced a hominid fossil record of an antiquity of some 250,000 years and an archaeological record of Late Pliocene dates that approximate new dating data of fossil hominid localities in Java (1.8 Ma), the Georgian Caucasus (1.4 Ma), and China (1.6 Ma). Work in South Asia has been conducted by relatively few scientists from the United States, the United Kingdom, France, Italy and Canada. While the numbers of investigators are higher in India than in Pakistan or Sri Lanka, some areas, such as Bangladesh, Nepal and the Himalayan principalities await exploration. Here is a region of high adventure and scientific challenge to which I bid you welcome!

REFERENCES

Dennell, R.W. 1991. A Report of the British Archaeological Missions's Potwar Project for the Year 1989-90, *South Asian Studies* 7: 161-5.

Deraniyagala, S.U. 1992. *The Prehistory of Sri Lanka: an Ecological Perspective*, 2 Vols. Colombo: Memoirs of the Archaeological Survey of Sri Lanka 8.

Hemphill, B.E., J.R. Lukacs and Rami Reddy 1992. Tooth Size Apportionment in Modern India: Factors of Caste, Language and Geography, in *Culture, Ecology and Dental Anthropology* (J.R. Lukacs Ed.), pp. 231-53. Delhi: Kamla-Raj Enterprises.

Kennedy, K.A.R. 1965. Human Skeletal Material from Ceylon, with an Analysis of the Island's Prehistoric and Contemporary Populations, *Bulletin of the British Museum of Natural History* (Geology) 11: 135-213.

——— 1992. Tooth Size Variation of the Veddas and Prehistoric Sri Lankans, in *Culture, Ecology and Dental Anthropology* (J.R. Lukacs Ed.), pp. 171-82. Delhi: Kamal-Raj Enterprises.

——— 1993. Recent Discoveries and Studies of the Human Skeletal Remains of Ancient Sri Lankans: a Palaeoanthropological Update, in *New Perspectives in Anthropology* (P.K. Seth and S. Seth Eds.), pp. 299-342. New Delhi: M.D. Publications.

——— 1994. When the Wild Veddas Came to Edinburgh: a Nineteenth Century Episode in the Development of Sri Lankan Palaeoanthropology, in *From Sumer to Meluhha: Contributions to the Archaeology of West and South Asia in Memory of George F. Dales* (J.M. Kenoyer Ed.), pp. 281-314. Madison: Wisconsin Archaeological Reports 3.

Kennedy, K.A.R. and S.U. Deraniyagala 1989. Fossil Remains of 28,000-Year-Old Hominids from Sri Lanka, *Current Anthropology* 30: 394-9.

Kennedy, K.A.R. and J.L. Zahorsky 1996. Trends in Prehistoric Technology and Biological Adaptations. New Evidence from Pleistocene Deposits at Fa Hien Cave, Sri Lanka, in *South Asian Archaeology 1995* (B. Allchin Ed.), pp. 69-84. New Delhi: Oxford-IBH.

Kennedy, K.A.R., J. Chiment, T. Disotell and D. Meyers 1984. Principal Components Analysis of Prehistoric South Asian Crania, *American Journal of Physical Anthropology* 64 (2): 105-18.

Kennedy, K.A.R., T. Disotell, W.J. Roertgen, J. Chiment and J. Sherry 1986. Biological Anthropology of Upper Pleistocene Hominids from Sri Lanka: Batadomba Lena and Beli Lena Caves, *Ancient Ceylon* 6: 67-168.

Kennedy, K.A.R., A. Sonakia, J. Chiment and K.K. Verma 1991. Is the Narmada Hominid and Indian *Homo etectus*? *American Journal of Physical Anthropology* 86 (4): 475-596.

Kennedy, K.A.R., J.R. Lukacs, R.F. Pastor, T.L. Johnston, N.C. Lovell, J.N. Pal, B.E. Hemphill and C.B. Burrow 1992. *Human Skeletal Remains from Mahadaha: a Gangetic Mesolithic Site.* Ithaca: Occasional Papers and Theses of the South Asia Program, Cornell University 11.

Lukacs, J.R. 1983. Human Dental Remains from Early Neolithic Levels at Mehrgarh, Baluchistan, *Current Anthropology* 24(3): 390-3.

——— 1992. Mesolithic Hunters and Foragers of the Gangetic Plain: a Summary of Current Research in Dental Anthropology, *Dental Anthropology Newsletter* 6 (3): 3-8.

Lukacs, J.R., J.N. Pal, and V.D. Misra 1996. Chronology and Diet in Mesolithic North India: a Preliminary Report of the AMS ^{14}C Dates, ^{13}C Isotope Values and Their Significance. Paper Presented for the International Congress of Pre- and Protohistoric Sciences, September 1996, Forli, Italy.

Sonakia, A. 1985. Early *Homo* from the Narmada Valley, India, in *Ancestors: the Hard Evidence* (E. Delson Ed.), pp. 334-8. New York: Alan R. Liss.

Stark, R. 1989. *Encyclopaedia of Lotus (R) 1-2-3 Realease 3: The Master Reference.* Blue Ridge Summit: Windcrest Books.

Triola, M.F. 1989. *Elementary Statistics*. Redwood City: Bengamin Cummings Publishing Company.

Wintle, A.F. and K.P. Oakley 1972. Thermoluminescence Dating of Fired Rock Crystal from Bellan Bandi Palassa, Ceylon, *Archaeometry* 14: 277-9.

Wolpoff, M.H. 1971. *Metric Trends in Hominid Dental Evolution. Studies in Anthropology, Case Western Reserve University* 2. Cleveland: Case Western Reserve University Press.

Bio-Archaeology of Ancient India: an Integrated Perspective on the Past

JOHN R. LUKACS

INTRODUCTION

Bio-archaeology is a specific research approach to past cultures that requires interdisciplinary cooperation between archaeologists and biological anthropologists. Integration of research designs, concepts, methods, and interpretations from biological anthropology and archaeology is essential to the success of a bio-archaeological research programme. The goal of bio-archaeology is the holistic and unified reconstruction of subsistence economy and behavioural patterns associated with prehistoric cultures, through synthetic integration of biological data from human skeletons with archaeological data from material culture. Also known as the 'bio-cultural' approach, bio-archaeology originated in response to the excavation and analysis of Native American mortuary sites and skeletal remains. This perspective on past cultures has historical depth (Buikstra 1991), a well-established methodology (Huss-Ashmore et al. 1982; Larsen 1987, 1995; Powell et al. 1991), and has dramatically improved our knowledge of the dynamic nature of bio-cultural change in prehistory (Powell 1988; Storey 1992).

While at the cutting edge of anthropological research in North America, the bio-archaeological approach has not been extensively employed in the analysis of Old World cultures, cemeteries and human skeletal samples. In South Asia a few notable exceptions exist, including: (1) the Chalcolithic early farming villages of the Deccan plateau, western Maharashtra, India (Dhavalikar 1988; Lukacs and Walimbe 1986); (2) the cemetery at the Bronze Age urban centre of Harappa, Punjab Province, Pakistan (Dales and Kenoyer 1993; Kenoyer 1998; Lukacs 1992), and (3) the 'mesolithic' hunting and foraging cultures of the Ganga Valley, eastern Uttar Pradesh, India (Lukacs and Pal 1993; Sharma et al. 1980).

The two goals of this contribution are: (1) to introduce the research orientation of bio-archaeology by considering theoretical frameworks and practical methods of study, and (2) to provide two examples of how simultaneous consideration of human biology and culture can yield valuable clues to prehistoric human behaviour.

RESEARCH ORIENTATION: THEORETICAL MODELS METHODS AND TYPES OF DATA

Prehistoric societies are complex dynamic systems composed of three interacting sub-systems: cultural, biological and ecological. These sub-systems are variable and each society relies on a unique integrative 'fit' of the cultural, biological and ecological spheres in response to problems faced in day-to-day living. Subsystem variation and differences in the dynamic interaction of subsystems among societies may be referred to as the 'mode of biocultural integration' (Johnston and Selby 1978). The goal of bio-archaeological research is to move from the independent analysis of individual sub-systems of a prehistoric society, to an integrated and holistic interpretation of the mode of biocultural integration. Parallels exist in other disciplines. The bio-cultural synthesis in medical anthropology advocates melding the ethnomedical approach from cultural anthropology with the epidemiological approach from biological anthropology, all within a modified ecological perspective (Armelagos et al. 1992).

A logical progression from descriptive research to synthetic integration is a fundamental feature of the bio-archaeological approach to prehistoric societies. Initially, research goals strive to document the basic characteristics of each subsystem. This primary phase of research requires basic discipline-specific description and analysis in archaeology, in biological anthropology, and in palaeoecology. When comprehensive documentation of artefacts, human remains, and environments is complete, the ultimate objective of understanding the interactive dynamics of sub-systems is entertained. Realistic re-construction of prehistoric societies requires an holistic analytic perspective in order to understand the dynamic mode of bio-cultural integration.

The array of methods employed in bio-archaeological research include the full compliment of traditional field excavation techniques and standardized laboratory methods of the archaeologist and biological anthropologist. Collaboration of archaeologists and bio-anthropologists in the field is essential if details of context and position of human skeletons are to be well integrated in analytic and interpretive phases of research. Synthetic bio-archaeological research benefits from the archaeologists' contribution of crucial information concerning food preparation technology, plant and animal food refuse, social and economic indication of status, occupational practices, sexual division of labour, and hypotheses on social organization, for example. The biological anthropologist provides complimentary data regarding the demographic structure of the human skeletal series, including age at death, sex, stature, skeletal and dental health, nutritional status, and skeletal indication of habitual activity and occupation pursuits. Careful integration of these two data sets have tremendous potential to improve the clarity of our perception of past patterns of human behaviour in well defined cultural contexts.

CASE 1: THE IMPACT OF AGRICULTURE ON HUMAN HEALTH SHOWS A SEX BIAS[1]

One of the fundamental issues at the forefront of bio-archaeological research concerns changing patterns of health across the subsistence transition from hunting and gathering to agriculture (Cohen 1989; Cohen and Armelagos 1984). Human skeletal samples from diverse cultural contexts and a variety of geographical and temporal settings is essential to answer questions regarding the relationship between health and subsistence in prehistory. Over the past 20 years, the increasingly meticulous recovery of human skeletal remains from prehistoric sites in South Asia provides an abundant source of data for biological

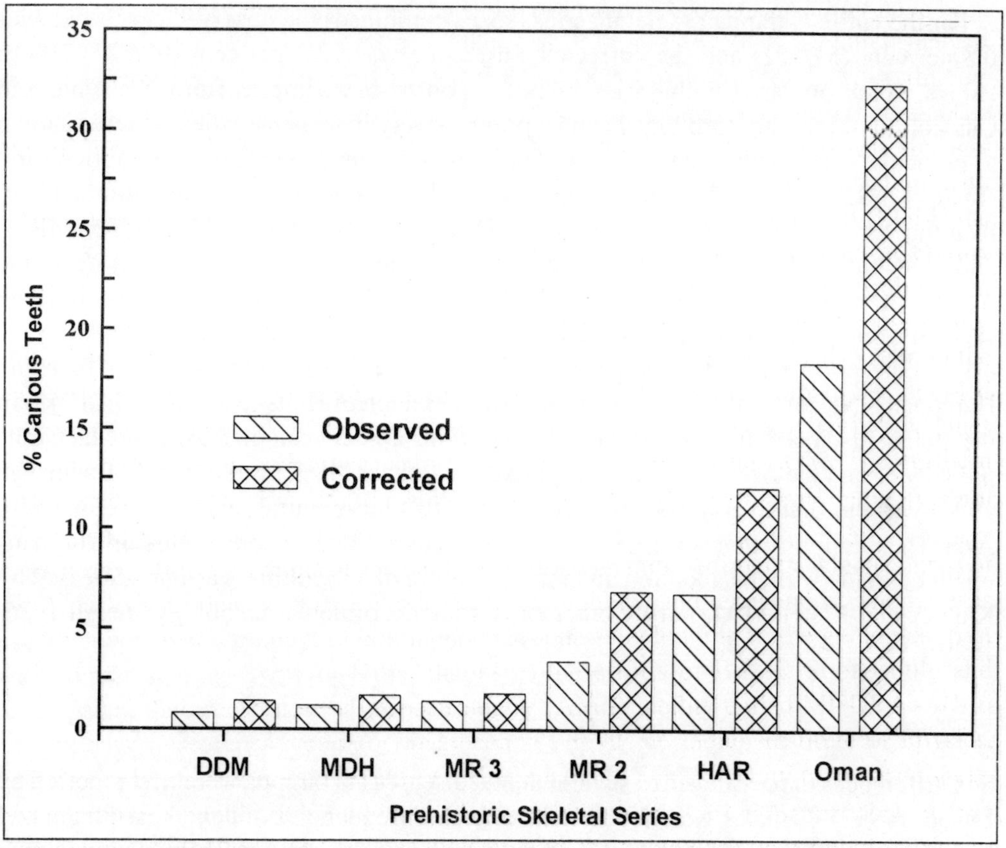

Fig. 1. Caries Prevalence for Sex-Pooled Prehistoric Human Skeletal Samples.

anthropologists. Under careful scrutiny these new data from India and Pakistan have the potential to unravel the complex and dynamic interrelationship of health and culture in earlier human populations. Concerns regarding the impact of agricultural intensification on human health generally, and of sex differences in caries rates at Harappa in particular, represents one small but important component of a broader diachronic evaluation of diet and health in South Asian prehistory.

The physical remains of a complex and well preserved urban society in association with human skeletons at Harappa provide anthropologists with a unique opportunity for investigating the interrelationship between biology and culture in South Asia during the Third Millennium BC. As social organization becomes highly stratified and division of labour and task specialization increases, questions of differential morbidity and mortality between groups arise. For example, can the study of skeletal and dental diseases reveal differences in behaviour between social groups or sexes? The ability to answer such questions will help illuminate bio-behavioural features of socially significant subgroups within Harappan society. This example will address issues concerning sex differences in the prevalence of a dental disease known as caries.

For the entire Harappan skeletal series (sexes combined) the observed caries rate was 6.8 per cent (51/751) and the corrected caries rate was 12.1 per cent (99/821). These values were compared with caries rates for pooled-sex samples from Neolithic and Chalcolithic Mehrgarh (see Fig. 1) and a progressively increasing caries rate was shown to coincide with a subsistence system that was becoming more intensely agricultural (Lukacs 1992: 147, Fig. 7). Note that the observed caries rate increases less dramatically than the corrected rate, from Mesolithic (DDM and MDH), through Neolithic (MR 3) and Chalcolithic (MR 2), to Bronze Age (HAR) and Iron Age (Oman). Please refer to the map for the geographic location of South Asian archaeological sites (Fig. 2). An Iron Age skeletal sample from Oman is included in this graph to show the impact of applying the caries correction factor to groups with higher antemortem tooth loss rates than the Harappans (Nelson et al. 1999). The pioneering research of Klatsky and Klatell (1943) in the 1940s, disclosed the generally parallel relationship between increasing dental caries prevalence and the rise of civilization. However, Lukacs (1992; Lukacs and Minderman 1992) was the first to conclusively demonstrate this bio-cultural relationship for South Asia. The possibility that sex differences in dental caries rates among prehistoric humans might coincide with the adoption and intensification of agriculture was not addressed by Klatsky and Klatell (1943) or by other early students of dental pathology (Leigh 1925, 1929).

Sex Differences in Caries Rates at Harappa

Sex differences in prevalence of several dental diseases at Harappa were first reported by Lukacs (1992). Females were found to have higher frequencies of dental caries, enamel hypoplasia, antemortem tooth loss, and pulp exposure than males. This difference may be attributable to sex-based specialization in economic activities and associated dietary behaviour. These distinctions were based upon the number of individuals afflicted by a dental condition and by the number of teeth that displayed a specific dental lesion. Since dental health tends to increase with age, the *absence* of a significant difference in age at death for males and females at Harappa is an important factor in this analysis. A re-evaluation of the dental caries data for Harappa, using the caries correction factor, yields a more finely tuned assessment of sex differences in caries prevalence. Using the caries correction factor Harappan women have a tooth count caries rate (17.7 per cent) significantly greater than men (10.4 per cent). Figure 3 shows caries rates at Harappa calculated according to the three different methods: (1) Observed Caries Rate, (2) Decayed and Missing Index (over estimates female rate since not all AMTL among females is due to caries), and (3) the corrected caries rate. Reasons for the greater incidence of caries among females than among males may be attributed to a combination of differences in dietary content and distinctive sex-based activity patterns. Faunal analysis suggests that wild animal species may have comprised a portion of the Harappan diet. Cross-culturally hunting is primarily a male activity and one that would allow males a more diverse, eclectic and coarse diet, that overall would be less cariogenic than the female diet.

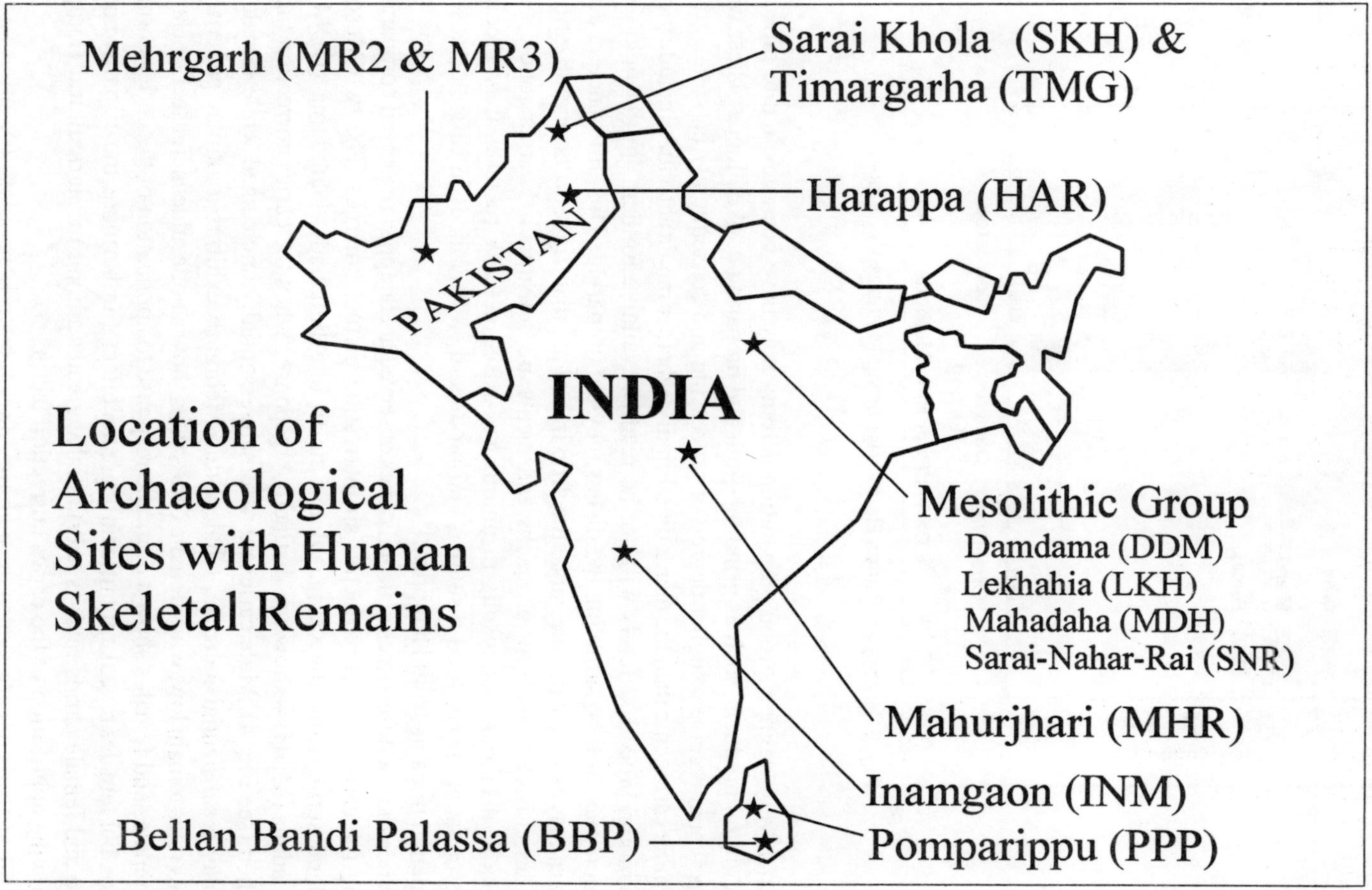

Fig. 2. Location of Archaeological Sites with Human Skeletal Remains.

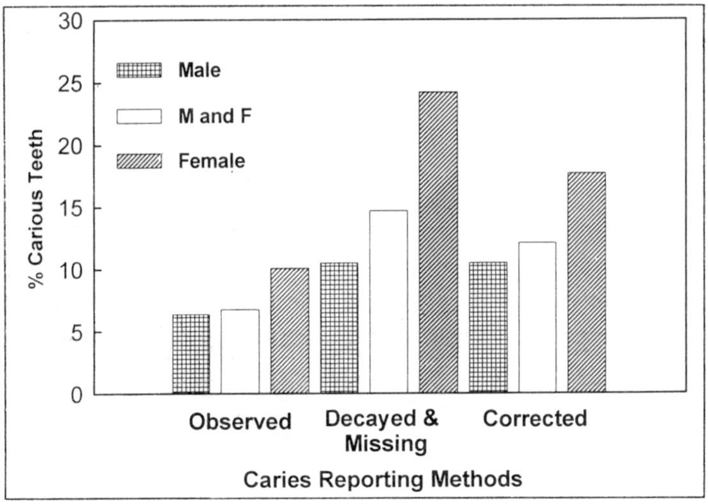

Fig. 3. Harappan Caries Rates: Reporting Methods Compared.

Alternatively, women's food preparation activity may have been devoted to processing agricultural products, such as grinding grain and preparing cooked foods. These dietary items would receive a higher degree of processing and consequently be softer, stickier, and more cariogenic than the men's diet. Finally, whether men's activities include plowing or hunting, processed foods will not be readily available to them 'in the field', while women may well be sampling the dishes they are preparing. This difference in activity pattern may be a crucial one, since the drop in oral pH that triggers demineralization and cavitation occurs every time snacks and meals are consumed (Featherstone 1987). A division of labour that results in unique sex-based activity patterns may precipitate differential access to food resources and produce the differences in caries rates seen in the dental remains from Harappa.

When the sex differences in dental caries observed at Harappa are viewed comparatively using the caries correction factor, an interesting picture emerges. The two Mesolithic skeletal series from the Ganga plains, north of Allahabad—Damdama (DDM) and Mahadaha (MDH)—show sex distinctive responses when the caries correction factor is applied (see Fig. 4). Male caries rates remain essentially unchanged while female rates display a substantial increase. Chalcolithic Mehrgarh exhibits a similar pattern, male caries rates remain low, while female caries rates show a noticeable increase. For Harappa, both males and females show a dramatic response to application of the caries correction factor, but females reveal a significantly greater effect. Furthermore, the disparity between male and female caries rates is substantially greater among the agricultural Harappans following application of the caries correction factor.

This analysis of caries rates through time for prehistoric peoples of South Asia shows that females suffer from carious decay more frequently than males, and that sex

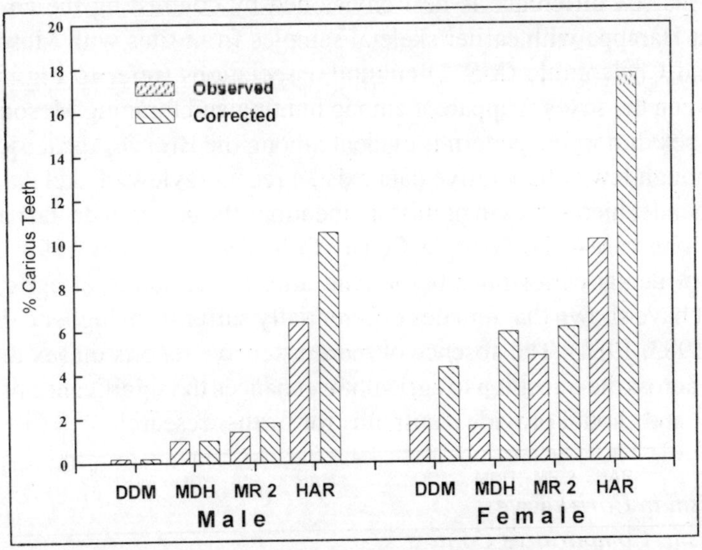

Fig. 4. Observed and Corrected Caries Rates Grouped by Sex.

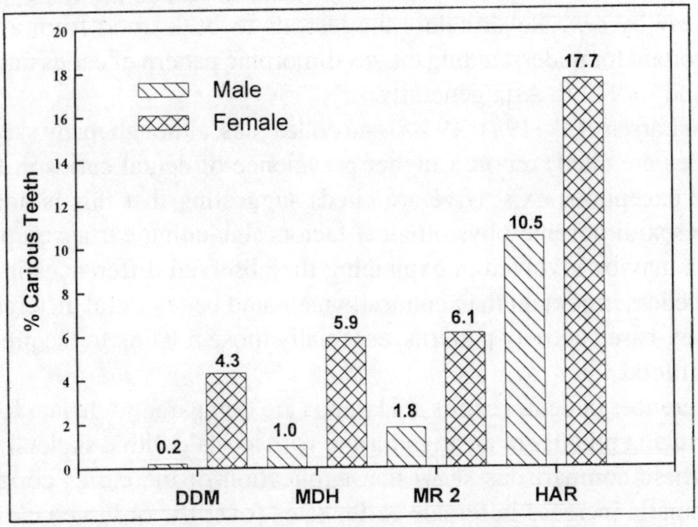

Fig. 5. Corrected Caries Rates by Sex for Selected South Asian Skeletal Series.

dimorphism in caries rates is accentuated with the adoption and intensification of agriculture. This sex difference is best envisioned by contrasting the corrected caries rates by sex at Harappa with earlier skeletal samples from sites with Mesolithic (DDM and MDH) and Chalcolithic (MR 2) cultural associations (refer to Fig. 5). While the disparity between the sexes is apparent among hunting and foraging Mesolithic peoples, an even more sex dimorphic pattern is evident among the Bronze Age agriculturalists of Harappa. Although few collaborative data exist, a recent review of skeletal evidence for sex roles and gender hierarchies in prehistory mentions the utility of dental caries analysis, but cites just one case—the Georgia Coast (Cohen and Bennett 1993: 281). In this investigation of dental caries rates before and after the adoption of agriculture on the Georgia Coast have shown that females differentially suffer from higher caries rates than men (Larsen 1983, 1984). The absence of more extensive reports on sex dimorphism in dental disease across the transition to agriculture enhances the significance of the currently available data, and should provide a stimulus for further research.

Sex Dimorphism in Caries Rates:
the Harappans in Comparative Context

The goal of this brief review of sex differences in dental caries is to provide a comparative picture against which the Harappan pattern can be fruitfully assessed. It is important for the comparison to include investigations of dental caries among living as well as prehistoric skeletal samples, since in many ways they can provide complimentary data. The brevity of the review is partly due to the fact that many studies of dental pathology do not report results separately by sex. Nevertheless the lessons to be learned from a comparative survey are important for understanding the sex dimorphic pattern of caries rates at Harappa in particular, and for South Asia generally.

According to Larsen et al. (1991: 194-5) and colleagues, although many skeletal samples (nineteen studies are cited) report a higher prevalence of dental caries in females than males, notable exceptions exist (five are cited) suggesting that this is not a universal pattern. While sex dimorphic physiological factors, including earlier eruption of teeth and pregnancy, may be involved in explaining the observed differences in caries rates, these seem to be less important than culturally mediated behavioural differences relating to distinctive sex-based activity patterns, especially those relating to the preparation and consumption of food.

The sex differences in dental caries at Harappa are compared with data for Mesolithic hunting and foraging peoples of north India and with a Chalcolithic skeletal sample from Baluchistan. These comparisons show that application of the caries correction factor produces a dramatic increase in female caries rates (over the observed caries rate), but has little affect upon male caries rates. Furthermore, application of the caries correction factor yields a picture of sex dimorphism in dental caries rates from Mesolithic to Bronze Age, and females appear to differentially suffer higher caries rates with the advent and intensification of agriculture.

CASE 2: CLIMATE, SUBSISTENCE, AND CULTURE AT CHALCOLITHIC INAMGAON

The descriptive phase of research on the early farming village of Inamgaon was conducted during the 1970s and 1980s. During this time: (1) archaeological excavations were completed, artefacts analyzed, and a comprehensive picture of Malwa and Jorwe cultures presented, (2) environmental and ecological data were collected, analysed, and interpreted to reveal patterns of climate change, and (3) human skeletal remains were subjected to osteological, dental, palaeodemographic and palaeopathological investigation. As archaeological and environmental perspectives on the village of Inamgaon developed, they were woven into a synthetic interpretation of site history from the perspective of cultural ecology (Dhavalikar 1984, 1988). The geoarchaeological perspective on the florescence and decline of Inamgaon is based on diverse types of data, is well integrated, and reveals a complex interrelationship between environment and culture. Notably absent from this culture ecological interpretative synthesis is the direct evidence of the biological features of the people of Inamgaon. Biological attributes of the inhabitants of Inamgaon have the potential to reveal valuable insights into the nature of diet and nutrition, health and disease, and level of physiological stress. Until recently this potential has been neglected in favour of research questions focusing on: (1) issues of palaeodemography and palaeopathology (Lukacs and Walimbe 1984a; Lukacs et al. 1986), (2) the biological affinities of the people of Inamgaon using data from deciduous (Lukacs and Walimbe 1984b) and permanent teeth (Lukacs 1987), and (3) the relationship between tooth size, subsistence and culture (Lukacs 1981, 1985; Lukacs et al. 1983). The purpose of this example is to illustrate the benefits to be gained from a holistic bio-cultural perspective on climate, culture, and human health status at the early farming village of Inamgaon (see Lukacs and Walimbe 1998a, 1998b for greater details).

Approaches to the origin, character and decline of the Jorwe Culture of prehistoric western India rely heavily on the interpretation of substantial archaeological and palaeoclimatological evidence. A prominent feature of the Jorwe Culture at Inamgaon is the Late Jorwe phase (Period III; 1100-700 BC) which experienced climatic deterioration (aridity), cultural degeneration, and a subsistence shift toward nomadism. The archaeological perspective envisions culture change during the Late Jorwe as an environmentally induced decline in economic status accompanied by a subsistence shift that included greater reliance on hunting and foraging. The language of choice by archaeologists describing the nature of the transition from Early to Late Jorwe has a pejorative tone insinuating that the changes described are largely for the worse.

The objective of this study was to utilize newly gathered data on developmental defects of the primary teeth, a human biological attribute, to evaluate levels of physiological stress in infants and children during the transition from Early to Late Jorwe periods at Inamgaon. Does the degree of documented change in climate, culture and subsistence have a measurable impact on growth and development of primary teeth? How does the prevalence of enamel hypoplastic defects at Inamgaon correlate with other measures of physiological stress and with cultural variations.

To answer these questions a sample of 762 teeth and developing dental germs were observed for evidence of Linear Enamel Hypoplasia (LEH) and Localized Hypoplasia of Primary Canine (LHPC) teeth. Scoring of enamel defects followed standards recommended by the Federation Dentaire Internationale. The primary canine sample comprised a total of 141 teeth, from 66 individuals. All primary teeth were examined with oblique incandescent light and a record was made of all enamel defects, including size and location on affected teeth. This analysis found that primary enamel defects were almost exclusively LHPC, and that very few individuals displayed LEH or other types of enamel defect.

While many aspects of human biology are closely linked to nutritional deprivation and conditions of disease, only a few preserve well in prehistoric human remains. Height for age, lines of arrested growth in long bones (Harris Lines), and developmental defects of teeth are influenced by sickness and malnutrition, and are measurable in prehistoric skeletons.

The trait used in this study is a defect of dental enamel known as hypoplasia. Enamel hypoplasia comes in several different forms—some genetic and some environmental in origin. Two types of environmentally caused enamel defect are considered here (Fig. 4): Linear Enamel Hypoplasia (LEH) and Localized Hypoplasia of Primary Canines (LHPC). In LEH one or more horizontal grooves and/or pits representing deficiencies of enamel formation are present, permanent or primary teeth maybe affected, and each line constitutes a non-specific indicator of growth disruption (Goodman and Rose 1990; Skinner and Goodman 1992). In LHPC an oval 'window' of deficient enamel is visible ONLY on the anterior surface of primary canine teeth (Fig. 4) (Lukacs 1991; Skinner 1986). The clear distinction in the appearance of these defects and their distribution in the dental arcade, symbolizes significant differences in etiology. In a clinical study of LHPC prevalence among Canadian children in the Healthiest Babies Possible Program (consisting of underprivileged, 'at risk' children), Mark Skinner (et al. 1994) found that: (1) it is the most common form of enamel hypoplasia in the primary dentition, (2) it has higher prevalence in nutritionally disadvantaged groups, (3) more severe defects and higher rates of occurrence are evident in people of Asian Indian heritage, and (4) the most significant nutritional factor among affected individuals is lower levels of retinol (Vitamin A).

I first encountered LHPC in 1979 during our analysis of Inamgaon series, subsequently cases were found among children from prehistoric cemeteries at Mehrgarh, Harappa, and Mesolithic Damdama (see Lukacs and Walimbe 1998a for details) (Fig. 5). The defect is pervasive in prehistoric Indian skeletal series that contain infants and children, however, most series have too few young specimens to permit statistical analysis (Fig. 6). Inamgaon, and Deccan Chalcolithic sites generally, are unique in preserving large numbers of sub-adult specimens, facilitating the adoption of a bio-cultural research design. This analysis was conducted in December 1996 at Deccan College, Pune, and involved a re-evaluation of 66 Inamgaon neonates and infants with a total of 141 canine teeth.

Thirty-nine per cent of Inamgaon specimens and 28 per cent of primary canine teeth exhibit evidence of LHPC. Side differences in prevalence do not occur, but mandibular

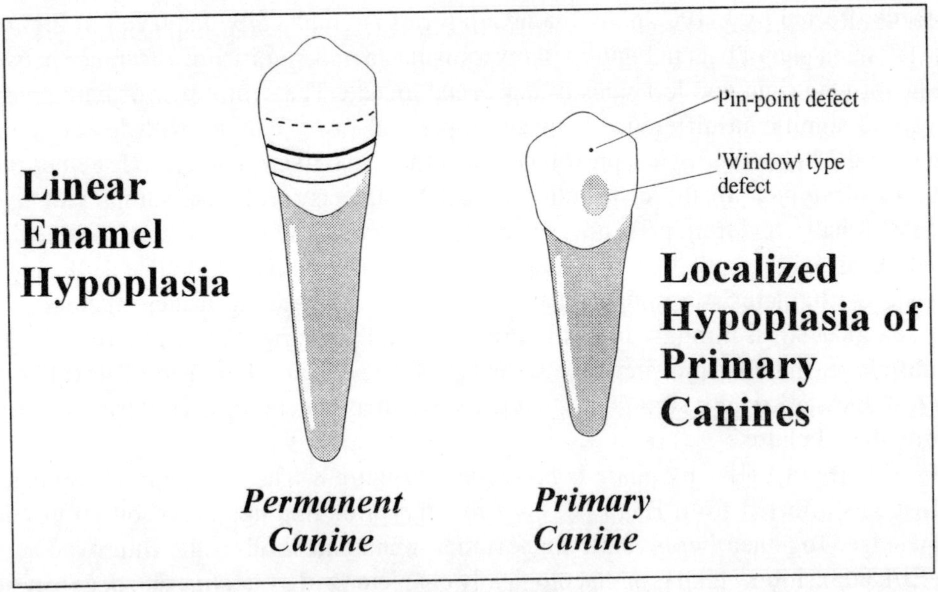

Fig. 6. Two Types of Enamel Defect: LEH and LHPC.

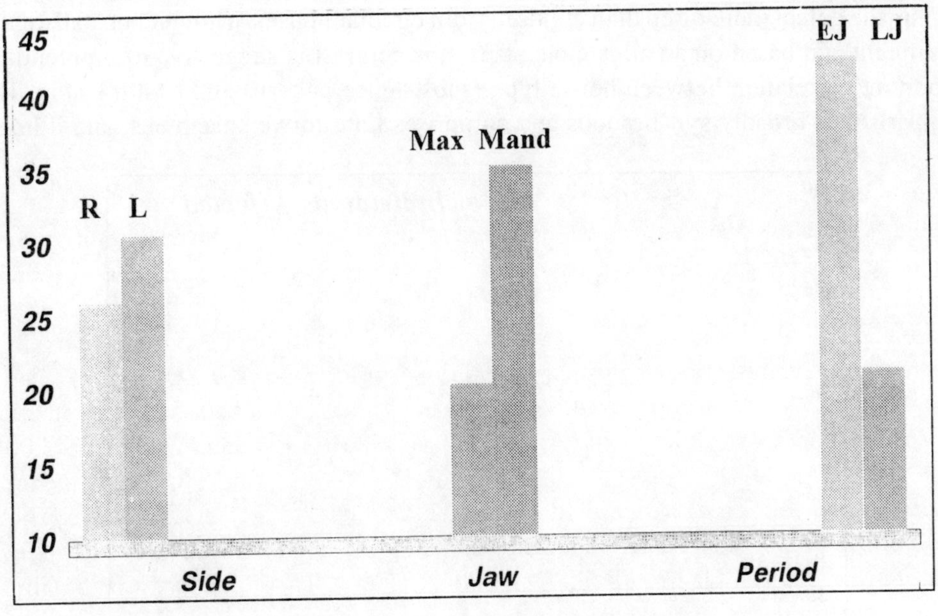

Fig. 7. Prevalence of LHPC at Inamgaon: Tooth Count Percentage.

canines display LHPC significantly more often than maxillary isomeres. The percentage of teeth affected by LHPC in the Inamgaon series is graphically displayed in Figure 7. The left hand pair of bars in Figure 7 show a small and non-significant difference between teeth from the right and left sides of the dental arcade. The centre pair of bars reveal a large and significant difference between upper and lower canine, with lower canines showing a 15 per cent higher prevalence than their maxillary isomeres. Together these patterns are typical of the distribution of LHPC defects in clinical samples of living people globally, and from prehistoric samples from Middle Paleolithic to Neolithic times (see Lukacs and Walimbe 1997 for comparative data). This demonstrates that the Inamgaon sample is characteristic and of adequate size for addressing issues of health and physiological stress through time at Inamgaon. Finally, the right hand pair of bars show the difference in LHPC prevalence between EJ and LJ periods at Inamgaon. The difference is great and statistically significant, with twice as many teeth affected during the EJ as during the LJ phase.

Prevalence of LHPC by phase is presented in Figure 8. The decline in percentage of individuals affected from EJ to LJ, confirms the prior findings based on tooth count percentage. Together these results suggest that infant and child health improved across the EJ/LJ transition which is archaeologically characterized by decline and degeneration. For comparison, the right-hand bar in Figure 8, shows the prevalence of this defect among living school children in the rural town of Harappa, Punjab Province, Pakistan (Lukacs 1991). Data analysis also revealed that burials from different house types show a substantially distinct difference in LHPC prevalence: children from rectangular houses display the defect more often than children from circular houses. Though not statistically significant and based on small sample sizes, this contrast is suggestive of a potentially important correlation between house type (subsistence pattern) and health status. This comparison is broadly synchronous and comprises Late Jorwe specimens, and if house

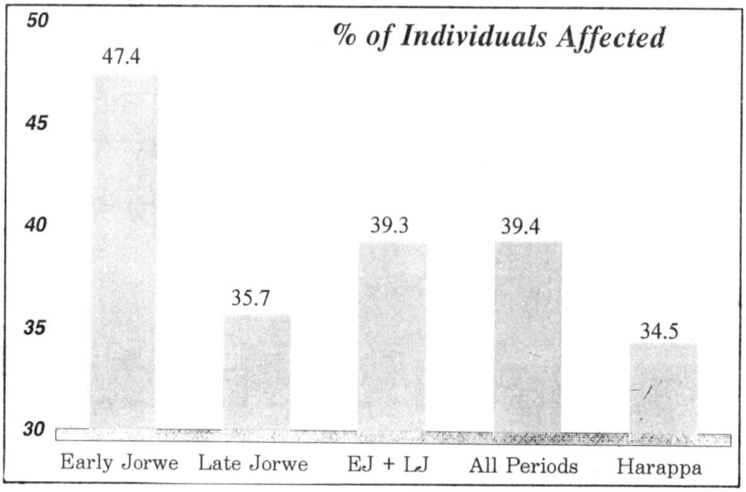

Fig. 8. Prevalence of LHPC at Inamgaon by Phase (per cent of individuals affected).

shape predicts subsistence pattern these data suggest that 'semi-nomadic' 'foragers' were healthier, or at least less commonly affected by physiological stress than their more sedentary, agricultural, neighbours.

Increased dietary diversity during the Late Jorwe is documented by faunal and floral analyses (Kajale 1988; Thomas 1988), greater mobility is implied by house structure and material culture (Dhavalikar 1984, 1988; Shinde 1991, 1994), and climatic change toward aridity has been established. Our results show that these climatic and cultural changes are routinely characterized by archaeologists as 'degenerative' and the LJ people described as 'poorer' than their EJ predecessors. Analysis of developmental enamel defects, however, yields a definite trend toward improved growth of dental tissues, and lower levels of physiological stress. This finding agrees with predictions of the subsistence transition model of Cohen, and conflicts with the archaeological perception of climatic degeneration, cultural decline, and miserable existence during Late Jorwe times.

The archaeological perspective on Inamgaon may constitute a case eco-ethno-centrism, in which climate change and the contingent shift to nomadism, herding, and hunting and foraging subsistence is regarded as less desirable or less successful. Furthermore, by omitting the biological sphere from the bio-cultural integration model the positive benefits of the subsistence change for human health and welfare are not apparent. The picture of health at Inamgaon derived from an analysis of defective enamel in primary teeth is further confirmed by conclusions derived from an analysis of long bone growth among Early and Late Jorwe children (Walimbe and Gambhir 1994). Walimbe and Gambhir have documented long bone growth deficits among Early Jorwe children while the 'impoverished' Late Jorwe children complete a greater percentage of the modern growth standard.

The more numerous Late Jorwe sample shows a significantly lower prevalence of LHPC, an observation that agrees with better bone growth, increased dietary diversity, and higher protein intake. While archaeological reference to climatic, cultural, and subsistence changes at Inamgaon as reflecting degeneration, deterioration, and decadence, may be justified, using these adjectives to describe the health, growth, and nutrition status changes from Early to Late Jorwe is not proper. The Late Jorwe people of Inamgaon may have been 'poorer' in material culture, but display several indicators of improved skeletal and dental development that suggest lower levels of physiological stress.

SUMMARY

These examples of recent research directions in the bio-archaeology of South Asia illustrate the valuable potential to be derived from a synthetic and integrative approach to the past that melds perspectives from both archaeology and bio-anthropology. Continued development of a bio-archaeological research programme in South Asia requires foresight and co-operation of scholars in both disciplines and must include: (1) joint involvement in the planning and conducting field excavation of human skeletal remains, (2) collaboration during laboratory analysis and interpretation of data, and (3) joint participation in presentation of research results at conferences and in the publication process.

ACKNOWLEDGEMENTS

The cooperation and encouragement of present and past directors of the Deccan College Post-Graduate and Research Institute is deeply appreciated (Drs. V.N. Misra, K. Paddayya, S.B. Deo, M.K. Dhavalikar and H.D. Sankalia). The involvement of collaborating Deccan College scholars especially Drs. G.L. Badam and S.R. Walimbe contributed to the success of research in the Inamgaon skeletons.

The late Dr. G.F. Dales conceived the Harappa Excavation Project, now in its 12th season and currently co-directed by Drs. J.M. Kenoyer and R. Meadow. Physical anthropologists Dr. Kenneth Kennedy, Dr. Nancy Lovell and Dr. Brian Hemphill assisted in the excavation and analysis of human skeletons at Harappa during the 1987 and 1988 field seasons.

Financial support for my participation in field and laboratory research on human skeletal and dental remains from South Asia has been provided by the American Institute of Indian Studies, Council for International Exchange of Scholars, National Geographic Society, National Science Foundation (International Programme), Smithsonian Institution (FCP), and the Wenner-Gren Foundation for Anthropological Research.

NOTE

* For further details on methods and interpretation refer to Lukacs (1992) and Lukacs (1996).

REFERENCES

Armelagos, G.J., T. Leatherman, M. Ryan and L. Sibley 1992. Biocultural Synthesis in Medical Anthropology, *Medical Anthropology* 14: 35-52.

Buikstra, J.E. 1991. Out of the Appendix and into the Dirt: Comments on Thirteen Years of Bioarchaeological Research, in *What Mean These Bones?: Studies in Southeastern Bioarchaeology* (M.L. Powell, P.S. Bridges and A.M.W. Mires Eds.), pp. 172-88. Tuscaloosa: University of Alabama Press.

Cohen, M.N. 1989. *Health and the Rise of Civilization.* New Haven: Yale University Press.

Cohen, M.N. and G.J. Armelagos 1984. *Paleopathology at the Origins of Agriculture.* Orlando: Academic Press.

Cohen, M.N. and S. Bennett 1993. Skeletal Evidence for Sex Roles and Gender Hierarchies in Prehistory, in *Sex and Gender Hierarchies* (B.D. Miller Ed.), pp. 273-96. Cambridge: Cambridge University Press.

Dales, G.F., and J.M. Kenoyer 1993. The Harappa Project 1986-89: New Investigation at an Ancient Indus City, in *Harappan Civilization* (G.L. Possehl Ed.), pp. 469-520. Second Edition. New Delhi: Oxford-IBH and the American Institute of Indian Studies.

Dhavalikar, M.K. 1984. Toward an Ecological Model for Chalcolithic Cultures of Central and Western India, *Journal of Anthropological Archaeology* 3: 133-58.

——— 1988. *The First Farmers of the Deccan.* Pune: Ravish.

Featherstone, J.D.B. 1987. The Mechanism of Dental Decay, *Nutrition Today* (May/June): 10-16.

Goodman, A.H. and J.C. Rose 1990. Assessment of Systemic Physiological Perturbations from

Dental Enamel Hypoplasias and Associated Histological Structures, *Yearbook of Physical Anthropology* 33: 59-110.

Huss-Ashmore, R., A.H. Goodman and G.J. Armelagos 1982. Nutritional Inference from Paleopathology, in *Advances in Archaeological Method & Theory* 5 (M.B. Schiffer Ed.), pp. 436-74. New York: Academic Press.

Johnston, F.E. and H. Selby 1978. *Anthropology: the Biocultural View.* Dubuque, Iowa: Wm. C. Brown Publishers.

Kenoyer, J.M. 1998. *Ancient Cities of the Indus Valley Civilization.* Karachi: Oxford University Press and the American Institute of Pakistan Studies.

Klatsky, M. and J.S. Klatell 1943. Anthropological Studies in Dental Caries, *Journal of Dental Research* 22 (4): 267-74.

Larsen, C.S. 1983. Deciduous Tooth Size and Subsistence Change in Prehistoric Georgia Coast Populations, *Current Anthropology* 24 (2): 225-6.

——— 1984. Health and Disease in Prehistoric Georgia: the Transition to Agriculture, in *Paleopathology at the Origins of Agriculture* (M.N. Cohen and G.J. Armelagos Eds.). Orlando: Academic Press, Inc.

——— 1987. Bioarchaeological Interpretations of Subsistence Economy and Behavior from Human Skeletal Remains, *Advances in Archaeological Method & Theory* 10 (M.B. Schiffer Ed.), pp. 339-445. New York: Academic Press.

Larsen, C.S., R. Shavit and M.C. Griffin 1991. Dental Caries Evidence for Dietary Change: an Archaeological Context, in *Advances in Dental Anthropology* (M.A. Kelley and C.S. Larsen Eds.), pp. 179-202. New York: Wiley-Liss.

Leigh, R.W. 1925. Dental Pathology of Indian Tribes of Varied Environmental and Food Conditions, *American Journal of Physical Anthropology* 8 (2): 179-99.

——— 1929. Dental Morphology and Pathology of Prehistoric Guam, *Memoir of the Bernice P. Bishop Museum* XI (3): 3-19.

Lukacs, J.R. 1981. Crown Dimensions of Deciduous Teeth from Prehistoric India, *American Journal of Physical Anthropology* 55: 261-6.

——— 1985. Tooth Size Variation in Prehistoric India, *American Anthropologist* 87: 1-15.

——— 1987. Biological Relationships Derived from Morphology of Permanent Teeth: Recent Evidence from Prehistoric India, *Anthropologischer Anzeiger* 45 (2): 97-116.

——— 1991. Localized Enamel Hypoplasia of Human Deciduous Canine Teeth: Prevalence and Pattern of Expression in Rural Pakistan, *Human Biology* 63 (4): 513-22.

——— 1992. Dental Paleopathology and Agricultural Intensification in South Asia: New Evidence from Bronze Age Harappa, *American Journal of Physical Anthropology* 87 (1): 133-50.

Lukacs, J.R. and L. Minderman 1992. Dental Pathology and Agricultural Intensification from Neolithic to Chalcolithic Periods at Mehrgarh, Baluchistan, in *South Asian Archaeology 1989* (C. Jarrige Ed.), pp. 167-79. Madison: Prehistory Press.

Lukacs, J.R. and J.N. Pal 1993. Mesolithic Subsistence in North India: Inferences from Dental Pathology and Odontometry, *Current Anthropology* 34 (5): 745-65.

Lukacs, J.R. and S.R. Walimbe 1984a. Paleodemography at Inamgaon: an Early Farming Village in Western India, in *The People of South Asia* (J.R. Lukacs Ed.), pp. 105-32. New York: Plenum Press.

——— 1984b. Deciduous Dental Morphology and the Biological Affinities of a Late Chalcolithic Skeletal Series from Western India, *American Journal of Physical Anthropology* 65 (1): 23-30.

——— 1986. *Excavations at Inamgaon Vol. II—The Physical Anthropology of Human Skeletal Remains, Part I—an Osteobiographic Analysis*. Pune: Deccan College.

——— 1998a. Physiological Stress in Prehistoric India: New Data on Localized Hypoplasia of Primary Canines Linked to Climate and Subsistence Change, *Journal Archaeological Science* 25: (in press)

——— 1998b. Health, Climate, and Culture in Prehistoric India: Conflicting Conclusions from Archaeology and Anthropology?, in *South Asian Archaeology 1997* (M. Taddei Ed.). Naples: IsMEO.

Lukacs, J.R., R.K. Bogorad, S.R. Walimbe and D.C. Dunbar 1986. Paleopathology at Inamgaon: a Post-Harappan Agrarian Village in Western India, *Proceedings of the American Philosophical Society* 130 (3): 289-311.

Nelson, G.C., J.R. Lukacs and P. Yule 1999. Dates, Caries and Early Tooth Loss during the Iron Age of Oman, *American Journal of Physical Anthropology* 108 (3): 333-43.

Powell, M.L. 1988. *Status and Health in Prehistory: a Case Study of the Moundville Chiefdom*. Washington, D.C.: Smithsonian Institution Press.

Powell, M.L., P.S. Bridges and A.M.W. Mires 1991. *What Mean These Bones? Studies in Southeastern Bioarchaeology*. Tuscaloosa: University of Alabama Press.

Sharma, G.R., V.D. Mishra, D. Mandel, B.B. Mishra and J.N. Pal 1980. *Beginnings of Agriculture*. Allahabad: Abinash Prakashan.

Skinner, M.F. and A.H. Goodman 1992. Anthropological Uses of Developmental Defects of Enamel, in *Skeletal Biology of Past Peoples: Research Methods* (S.R. Saunders and M.A. Katzenberg Eds.), pp. 153-74. New York: Wiley-Liss.

Skinner, M.F., W. Hadaway and J. Dickie 1994. Effects of Ethnicity and Birth Month on Localized Enamel Hypoplasia of the Primary Canine, *ASCD Journal of Dentistry for Children* 61 (3): 109-13.

Storey, R. 1992. *Life and Death in the Ancient City of Teotihuacan: a Modern Paleodemographic Synthesis*. Tuscaloosa: University of Alabama Press.

Walimbe, S.R. and P.B. Gambhir 1994. *Long Bone Growth in Infants and Children: Assessment of Nutritional Status*. Mangalore: Mujumdar Publications.

Biological Anthropology of Living Populations in Independent India: a Review

RIPUDAMAN SINGH

INTRODUCTION

The paper reviews briefly the direction of bio-anthropological researches on the living populations of India, particularly since 1947, the year of Indian Independence from British rule. Bio-anthropology, in the modern context, with its techniques, methodologies and trends, owes its origins to British scholars in particular, and western thought and approach in general. But some of the areas of study particularly morphometrics, with its applied aspects, was practised in ancient India, during the Vedic period.

Individual perceptions of Independence vary, so do the origins of various fields of study under bio-anthropology. As a sub-field, morphometry was neglected and lost in the interim, but re-emerged incorporating western methodologies, progressed along global trends and later developed its own approaches with a synthesis of native and foreign thoughts to tackle the problems emerging from the population structure in India. New dimensions, like the studies in dermatoglyphics, genetic markers and their associations with diseases, dental anthropology, patterns of physical growth, adaptation and anthropological demography have been added. In this effort, Indian bio-anthropology has kept pace with global trends, as well as developed on its own. It has matured to a stage where many more multifaceted and problem-oriented researches are needed, along with new data being added with every single effort.

Bio-anthropology and bio-anthropologists in India have an enviable field of research in the unique population structure of the region found no where else in the world. Both have done incredibly well and the opportunities for the future are phenomenal so long they maintain the holistic approach.

Anthropology, as it is usually understood in the modern context, is comparatively a new field of study. About five hundred years or so ago, i.e. in the sixteenth century, the word came into existence in reference to understanding and descriptions of various human populations encountered by travellers and explorers. While such accounts were self-serving, modern anthropology moved forward in helping people understand each other and interconnectedness of human activities and functioning (Weiss and Mann 1990). Anthropology, being a comparative science, describes and compares cultural behaviours and creations, language structure and communications, and physical attributes. During the course of a century and a half it has evolved into various subdisciplines and biological anthropology is one of them that deals with the biology of the past and present humans.

Maintaining the scholastic approach, with various sub-branches under study, it is 'the study of the physical aspects of humans: the study of human evolution and biological variation' (Lasker 1976: 4). Since it started with a simple study of physical qualitative aspects of humans, it was named as physical anthropology. With quantitative and biologic aspects, and today, heavily dependent upon the biological aspects of physical attributes, the appellation biological is more preferred. And now biological anthropologists look beyond purely biological phenomena in order to understand how biology and behaviour interact with each other and with the environment in which human populations live, and how these interacting phenomena direct the outcome in terms of variability and adaptability, the limits of human variability as well as the potential for future generations.

In the historical context, descriptive variations of physical attributes received the first attention where a mass of information about non-Europeans gathered in the seventeenth century attracted attention of anatomists like Edward Tyson (1650-1708). Through the dissection of human bodies and apes, he described the similarities between them. But the publication of Darwin's *The Origin of Species* (1959) changed the direction of thinking as well as the approaches to the study of variation in human populations, although not as rapidly as one would like.

The understanding of human variability in the context of the past as well as present has radically changed in the last few decades. This change is partly because of advances in areas like genetics, ethology and palaeontology, and partly because of changes in social values with a better understanding of the demography of human populations, their migrations, isolations and admixtures. We no longer search for the stereotypes for simple classifications and the hierarchies involved, but for interrelatedness and the direction of progression. Intra-group variations are as much evaluated as the intergroup variations in the context of demographic structures, social values, and the working of the social organizations of populations. Biological anthropologists today study real populations to reconstruct the evolutionary path humans have travelled and the direction they are likely to proceed through adaptation to an environment in which we live, create, and alter in order to survive. Human variability is subject to biological as well as cultural adaptations, therefore any study has to account for both the forces operating in their own way under different conditions. The interaction between the two is complicated and the approaches to the study of variation have changed.

However, the concept of the study of human variation is rooted in primeval times, and probably originated from the human quest to know its own kind and identify others. Ancient India gave this quest a scientific garb much earlier than the Westerners could conceive of, 'specially relating to the biological and physical aspects which have been used both for classification and diagnostic purposes' (Singh 1985: 1).

A critical review of this perspective makes it imperative to look for two time sequences. One is the Ancient India from the times of Vedic literature *c.* 3,500 years before the Christian era, where we have references with regard to various physical attributes of certain populations in these times, to the end of the Hindu period in Indian history *c.* 1200 AD. The second time zone is the middle of the twentieth century spanning from 1947 through to the present.

The intervening period is the period of foreign rule and or domination of powers which cannot be called distinctly Indian, though some indigenization did take place in some, particularly during the Muslim period. Here, the variation was seen along religious divide where biological and social boundaries were at times hazy and at times distinct. The concept of a biological population variation was seen only along pedigrees, but there were no studies initiated or attempted.

The western influences leading to modern trends, came largely via the British who ruled India during the nineteenth and twentieth centuries. The British continued to influence and set trends until the late 1930s. However, some of the European continental and American influences got a foothold through Indian scholars trained abroad.

THE ROOTS OF PHYSICAL ANTHROPOLOGY IN ANCIENT INDIA

The earliest references to human diversity in the populations of India can be traced back to Rigvedic literature. *Rigveda* is the earliest of the Vedas dated to *c*. 3,800 BC or even earlier (Rajaram and Frawley 1995; Feuerstein et al. 1995). Controversies with regard to specific antiquity aside, this literature is considered as the earliest in the world, known so far. Between 900 and 500 BC Samhitas, Brahamanas, and Aranyakas came into being. The Upanishads developed from these Rigvedic texts.

These texts cover a vast period, a period in which a profuse development and diffusion of cultures and population movements was occurring, when 'social and cultural norms were being codified' (Kennedy and Singh 1997: 976). The *Dharma*, is continually referred to in relation to stage of life, and class is emphasized, preserved and enforced, implying that it was not the same for all in the society, and there was a hierarchy of social class. In this socio-cultural context, the differences between the 'Aryan' and 'non-Aryan' populations is hardly surprising, and there are references to the *Ayogave*, *Chandala*, *Nishad*, and *Paulakasa* people. Ayogave are considered of mixed ethnic origin, and references to other groups and their specific bodily features are mentioned.

Some aspects of admixture in various population groups referred to, get some support from the human skeletal remains excavated in Harappa, Mohenjo Daro, Lothal (*c*.1500 BC) and Sialk (*c*. 1000 BC).

The *Chandala* is referred in *Yajurveda*, and the *Brhadaranyaka Upanishad* detail *Chandala* and *Paulakasa* as a despised group of people, quite disagreeable to Aryans. They are talked about as people different from the Aryans with respect to facial features and skin colour compared. This indicates that there was some population distinction emphasized on the basis of some physical attributes about these population groups which were possibly one of the earliest (or at least earlier than the so called Aryans) living people of the subcontinent.

Vedic Samhitas and Brahmanas provide evidence to human variations with regard to their physique, body proportions, temperamental dispositions, male-female compatibilities in marriage and sex relations. Some of these were tied down to medicinal approaches as well. The texts, like *Charakasamhita*, *Susrutasamhita* and *Astangasangraka*, provide systematic exposition of variations in humans for diagnostic as well as treatment approaches. Various aspects of humans (e.g. *Prakritti*, *Vikritti*, *Satvasakti*, and *Vayas* among others) were to be considered in a specific background. From a bio-anthropological point of view to understand the *Prakritti*, along with various other factors, was to be considered on the basis of lineage, the caste/group and the region. These factors bring in directly the aspects of heredity and adaptation, and a combination of these is immediately reflected in the consideration of *Varna* (complexion).

Another important aspect of human variation studies is reflected in establishing of *Pramanas* in order to understand and establish *Prakritti* (normal) versus *Vikritti* (abnormal) for various medical and social situations and the responses of an individual. These were seen as basically correct and reasonably accurate.

The study of body build is another aspect where a systematic comparative study appears to have been attempted and the three basic types were established, namely the *Susamhata* (well build), *Madhyama-samhata* (medium build) and *Visamhata* (weakly build). These types approximate to Sheldon's (1940) somatotypes: endomorphs, mesomorphs, and ectomorphs.

Body build and temperament of human male and female have been described in details by Vatsyayana. He classifies them into four basic categories dependent upon their body build, its proportionality and some temperamental attributes. All male categories are named after different animals like *Sasa* (hare), *Mrga* (deer), *Vrsa* (bull) and *Asva* (horse). The female classification gets the nomenclature after animals as well as flowers and specific talents, e.g. *Padmini* (lotus like), *Chitrini* (art-woman), *Shankhini* (conch like) and *Hastini* (elephant like). These four categories of men and women were further reduced to three main types for physical compatibilities in mating, based on the size of the erect penis and the depth of the vagina. Such a study in combination with the practice of medicine, study of behaviour, and considerations in mating capabilities was fairly well known before and after the Christian era. Further extension of this approach is seen in *Ananga Ranga* by Kalyan Malla somewhere between AD 1172-1500. The precise date is not certain as more than one account is available in Sanskrit manuscripts on this piece of literature. Thereafter, no further original work appears on the scene. However, the originals were either translated or paraphrased into many of the modern Indian languages. Some of the translations of these appeared in Persian; in Arabic as *Lizzate-al-Nisa*, or the pleasures of women. It was also translated into Turkish but the Persian and Turkish versions have little changes in them. Within Indian contexts, it was finally reduced to a kind of literature (and attempt) which lost the scientific approach (and flare) and became a populist account of sexual pleasures. Further extension of it can be credited to the European and British scholars through the medium of English in the latter half of the nineteenth century.

FOUNDATIONS OF BIOLOGICAL (PHYSICAL) ANTHROPOLOGY IN MODERN INDIA

The popularity of studies and practice of ancient knowledge in the context of human physical variations having been very much reduced as common knowledge during the entire Muslim period in Indian history, surfaced only after the British firmly established their foothold on the subcontinent. However, their objective was entirely different. On the European continent, after Tyson, there was a spurt in the study of comparative osteology of humans and apes, leading to contrivance of new tools and sets of measurements. The attention was focused, as well, toward the variations in human populations based on the cranial dimensions and later measurements on the cadavour and living individuals through the attempts of Petrus Camper, Blumenbauch, Broca, Virchov and Sergi, among many other leading scholars.

Through the British, came in the European influences in the field of human variation studies exclusively related to population groups, and with emphasis on their similarities and differences in their external physical characteristics. The colonial administrators sowed the seeds of western approaches to the studies in human variations and instituted biological (physical) anthropology as a field of study in Calcutta University as early as in 1921, when the first department of anthropology was established under R.P. Chanda, later joined by L.A.K. Iyer. In 1946 the Anthropological Survey of India came into being. This quarter of the century produced stalwarts like Chanda, Iyer, P. Mitra, Guha, Majumdar, Biswas, Aiyappan, Karve, A. Mitra, B.K. Chatterjee and S.S. Sarkar. They all contributed to the growth of physical anthropology in India. Many of them continued their work in their respective fields in the post-Independence era. In their turn they encouraged and brought forth the younger generation of their students, assistants and as colleagues, a host of people building bio-anthropology on the foundations laid by the pioneers. However, a more eminent role in strengthening the foundations was played by Guha and his associates (A.K. Mitra, P.C. Biswas, B.K. Chatterjee and S.S. Sarker) at Calcutta and D.N. Majumdar at Lucknow. Later, Biswas went over to Delhi University and Sarkar to Calcutta University. From the mid-1950s onward many other University departments with very strong background and serious research programmes in the area came into being and are continuing pioneer work in bio-anthropology. Lucknow could not keep pace with others after about four years of Majumdar's death in 1960, and has lost the place it once held.

Although each one contributed to the growth and establishment of biological anthropology in their own field—from fossil populations to the contemporary living populations—the two stalwarts Guha (in 1931) and Majumdar (in 1941, 1946), did the most important work so far as Indian biological anthropology of living populations is concerned. Under them anthropometry had its hey-day, but after independence and the close of the 1950s almost lost its glamour, because modern physical anthropology shifted its emphasis from typological studies to the population studies involving determinable genetic characteristics, their inheritance patterns and societal as well populational implications including migrations, intermixtures, interrelations and evolutionary trends (Washburn 1951). However, the Anthropological Survey of India did embark on a populational aspect of anthropomometric characters of the Indian populations on an 'all-India' basis, but it basically remained confined to the traditional approaches.

The pre-Independence era also saw the beginnings of the blood-group and dermatoglyphic studies which later formed the basis of the population genetic studies. Thus all work done during these twenty-five years or so is extremely crucial as it forms the solid foundation on which the present day and the future growth of bio-anthropology and the studies of the living populations of India are concerned.

The two major issues of the pre-Independence era were: Racial classification of the

Indian people and Negrito substratum in the population, which, as a matter of fact, was the by-product of the Racial classification.

And both these issues were embedded in the psyche of the academics involved in the studies as a result of western orientation in the first place, and the deep-rooted caste hierarchical concepts further emphasized and formed by the so called Aryan, non-Aryan and the Dravidian divide on the second. Bio-anthropological methods and techniques only provided tools to accumulate empirical physical-trait data for comparisons and sorting out various caste groups from one another. It was not a novel idea to begin with but an extension of the western (European and American) approach. It was but natural for scholars to fall in that trap, so well laid down by Risley (1891) Brockman (1896), Thurston (1909), and some other contemporaries. Though, Guha and Majumdar organized, attempted and interpreted their data, mostly somewhat similarly, but in some respects along different lines. Majumdar (1958), pricked the bubble of the caste myth when he observed that intercaste variations in the same region at times, are less pronounced than the intracaste variations in two different regions. This observation set others thinking differently. Nonetheless, anthropometry occupied a very major portion of the academic activities in bio-anthropology among others, e.g. in population genetics, like blood groups and the related fields, dermatoglyphics, various genetic markers based on certain body fluids, with different trends. These trends are in line with international approaches. To understand these new directions, it is imperative to evaluate the work of the predecessors under the demands of the academic environment, its limitations, as well as the strengths wherein lie the seminal roots for the direction of the progress, its significance, and the status of bio-anthropological studies of the living populations of India.

MORPHOMETRIC VARIATIONS, GROWTH, DENTAL ANTHROPOLOGY AND DERMATOGLYPHICS

Morphometry

It had humble beginnings as a systematic tool for the study of human population variations, irrespective of the objective(s). The approaches followed by ancient Egyptians, Assyrians, Greeks and Romans had quite common features, and mostly concentrated on facial characteristics reflected in their sculpture and other works of art. The pioneers of Ayurveda employed it to study morphological variations in combination with temperamental dispositions based on physique and body build for the practice of medicine. The significant departure was in the critical observations of body proportions (*Pramana*). The tools were not external devices but the fingers. The technique was to measure by the fingers of the body to be measured and to describe the phalangeocorpal indices (Singh 1987). Tied down to Sanskrit texts and the decline of it as a spoken language along with other socio-political factors, this scientific approach, however, went into oblivion.

Modern anthropometry as one of the taxonomic tools employed by the anthropologists for human variation studies has about a one hundred and fifty years old history in India.

It had its debut for the single purpose of understanding the racial composition of Indian populations. Among the earliest efforts in this regard was that of John Shortt (Singh 1986).

In 1864 he measured three Nilgiri tribes—Kotas, Todas and Kurumbas—mostly for their stature, and included only necessary dimensions of head and nose for cephalic and nasal indices. The results were published jointly with Colonel Ouchterlony in 1868 where a phenomenal intra-group variation is noticed (Gupta and Dutta 1966). Risley (1908) followed suit during the census of India in 1891. It was a comprehensive survey for most of British India including Afghanistan, Baluchistan, Burma (now Myanmar) and Sri Lanka (then Ceylon). Drake-Brockman (1896) directed his efforts in Uttar Pradesh (North-Western Provinces) on various castes and tribes, and Thurston (1909) on south Indian populations.

Until this time there were significant deviations in the methods and procedures followed for certain measurements. In other words there was no standardization in techniques, landmarks and methods for taking the measurements, although Paul Topinards procedures were available. The natural outcome was the non-comparability of the metric values of the traits in different populations in the background of unnecessary proliferation of techniques. It was, as a matter of fact, a world-problem, and no exception to India.

After the Monaco Agreement (in 1913) approaches to anthropometric studies and their methodologies became international (at least in spirit) and the data more comparable; some deviations still occurred. Anthropometric data on individual castes and tribes in the Post-Monaco Agreement period was collected by dozens of scholars, e.g. Basu, Biasutti, Chakladar, Chanda, Dixon, Eickstedt, Hutton and Iyer, to name a few, is enormous. In scrutinizing various data for comparative purposes, Mahalanobis (1928) observed several relevant discrepancies and re-emphasized the need for the standardization in measurements on the living. As a result, the significance of the uniformity in techniques and comparability of data was realized by the subsequent census authorities in India. The emphasis was then, on trained personnel, and minimizing the number of individuals responsible for a survey. Thus, during the census operations in 1931, Guha undertook the task for a survey to look into racial affiliations or composition of the Indian population. He selected some groups from a few regions and put forward his classification of the population. He was very much in tune with world trends in biological anthropology. His classification of the population with special observations on the Negrito element as a substratum generated a controversy which finally became an issue between Guha and Majumdar (1946). In 1941, Majumdar was commissioned to undertake an anthropometric survey of Uttar Pradesh, and the results were published in 1949.

During this (almost) first half of the century there was an increasing trend towards the study of individual groups from different regions with an aim to have adequate data for the group under study, whereever feasible. This was imperative because the data was being subjected to standard mathematical formulae for comparative purposes.

A by-product of racial studies during this period had been the hypothesis of a Negrito substratum in the Indian population. Controversy apart, it generated, as well, an enthusiasm among various contemporaries like Sarkar, Aiyappan, Karve, to name a few, to look more intensively into the physical traits, metric as well as non-metric, to understand the nature of populational affiliations in the Indian population. Majumdar, based on his experience with the 1941 survey and in collaboration with Mahalanobis, embarked on another survey of Bengal populations in 1945. A survey of 24 Gujarat groups was undertaken in 1946 by Majumdar for anthropometric as well as serological traits. Comtemporaneous to Majumdar's work in Uttar Pradesh, Karve and Dandekar collected data on 26 groups from Maharashtra; their work spread over five years. Karve also worked in Orissa and Karnataka between the years 1949-50 for 28 and 37 groups respectively. The largest data available and collected by any single researcher is the one by Chatterjee (1948) from Bengal. He measured 9281 individuals from 30 groups for three characters: the stature, the head length and the head breadth. The significance of large scale data was realized in the background of the nature of distribution of populations over large areas and the demands of rigorous mathematical procedures, to which each researcher was made conscious. Nonetheless, most of the data centred around head and face dimensions and the stature was part of the research under all circumstances, but other body dimensions were hardly considered. An opportunity for the study of body proportions was missed. Curiously enough no justification has ever been provided in any of the researches, including the present author, as to why other dimensions were omitted. The underlying thinking was (emphasis mine) that cranio-facial dimensions with stature provide the best results for classificatory studies. Computational costs, however, were also a factor along with the time factor involved in taking the measurements with the cooperation of the subjects and the comparability of the metric dimensions, which had hardly been attended. In hindsight, I now realize that possibly the researchers did not ponder over the significance of body proportions in growth and maturation and as a physical trait subject to adaptive variability under different variables along with genetic heritability. It was a fact of omission or commission? There is no positive answer.

Anthropometry still dominated the scene for another decade after the independence with slightly changing focus. Basically a populational study but with a bias, another large scale data (6,000 individuals) from the convict population in Uttar Pradesh, Lucknow University students (2,000) and Lucknow school children (1,000) was collected under a project jointly sponsored by the Department of Anthropology, Lucknow University and the Indian Statistical Institute, Calcutta. This was conducted by the present author and B.K. Varma, under the supervision of Majumdar. The characters included in the survey were those used by Majumdar in his surveys. The important feature of this study was the standardization of measuring techniques between the two investigators, and the variations worked out before embarking on the fieldwork. The results could not be analyzed and published because of Majumdar's demise in May 1960.

Inter- and intra-observer differences arising from the data for computation purposes were considered serious obstacles for comparative evaluation. A Majumdar, Mahalanobis and Rao collaboration re-emphasized the need for eliminating, if possible, or at least understanding the nature of deviation between the observers under different set of circumstances. This was reflected in the rigorous exercise designed by Rao and his associates at the Statistical Institute in the mid-1950s for a projected all-India anthropometric survey. This rigorous experiment was terminated prematurely because the present author resigned from the Institute (Singh 1987). A reorganized second experiment indicated that the differences did exist between investigators and the time of measurements (Rao 1958). The significance of variations and the reliability of the measurements was tested for sophisticated statistical tools to be applied to anthropometric data.

The Anthropological Survey of India embarked on a very ambitious survey for India as a whole in 1961 starting with the four southern states. One biological anthropologist was assigned to each of the states, thus involving four of us in the Survey. In an initial exercise for the comparability of measurements on the same subjects, we noticed again that at least for one character, significant differences in metric value did exist because of the difference in our methodology. This was ironed out (Rakshit 1965). The data runs into several thousands for hundreds of groups (Rakshit et al. 1988). The reports on some of the individual states were published separately (Ahmad and Sreenath 1992; Sreenath and Ahmad 1989; Sirajuddin, Ahmad and Singh 1992). The underlying theme is the populational study for cephalo-facial characters and the stature with a comparative evaluation of traits and suggested possible distances and nearness among the groups. The emphasis on racial connotations was de-emphasized (although the term race or racial could never be dropped from the texts) in U.P., Bengal, Orissa Maharashtra and Gujarat surveys as well. All these studies may be critically evaluated as regional population studies, and this was a major departure.

All these studies emerged from a background where a few methodological problems in the selection and collection of data, measuring techniques leading to comparability hitches were obvious and serious attempts were made to overcome these drawbacks, yet, not quite successful (Singh 1987). This factor does not reduce the value of these surveys, but certainly it could have been all the more useful for comparative purposes.

Population studies demand rigorous sampling procedures to be followed which yield data truly representative of the group under study, and that the sample size is adequate. Thus, the definition of the group be precise and the methods used in selection of the sample spelled out. Even with honest efforts, at times, the data have remained incomparable, and they do not truly represent the population group(s), or that it has been extended to speak for the population as a whole which it does not represent. Two examples need to be carefully debated in this regard. Chatterjee's (1948) data represents the University students at a time when opportunities to go to such higher levels of learning was limited to a certain class of privileged people (during 1922-8). Guha (1931) extracted the Maratha sample from Ferguson College, Poona (Karve 1948), now Pune. Such a sample is not suitable to stand for the population(s) it belongs, but certainly it does reflect the morphological traits of a section of a particular socio-economic group. At times, over-cautious and most stringent selection of data may prove to be of no extra value as in the case of Karve's data (1951: 44). Random selection of data is adequate (Mahalanobis and Rao 1949: 117). As for the size of the sample, it assumes high importance where groups may have closer resemblance, because 'with increase in sample size, the configuration tends to a stable position' (Rao 1958: 39). Rao demonstrated the validity and importance of it through a comparative study of four Bhil groups. The same point emerges from Shortt's data as referred to earlier.

Certain ambiguities and departures in the techniques of measurements also compounded the problems in the comparative analysis and results of the data from various researchers. Some reluctance on the part of scholars in the description of techniques of measurements exist, is apparent in many cases. The related problems have been adequately commented upon and the significance of clearly spelling out the procedures followed emphasized from time to time (Davenport et al. 1934; Steggerda 1942; Gavan 1950; Hertzberg 1968; Singh 1974, 1987).

The Uttar Pradesh survey followed the basic guidelines. The results indicated that each caste and, or tribe could not be sorted out exclusively on the basis of all the characters observed. Mahalanobis' D^2 statistic analysis sorted out the groups into different clusters with certain combinations of traits (Mahalanobis et al. 1949). Majumdar (1958) observed that intra-group variations in two geographic regions were, sometimes, more magnified than inter-group variations within the same region. Thus, he pointed to the fact that intra-group endogamous units should be treated as Mendelian populations for more meaningful results. Karve and Dandekar (1951) in their study of Maharashtra Brahmins also found intra-group variations, indicating that the Brahmin population was not homogenous (Karve and Malhotra 1968). Rakshit (1966) analysed the available data on Brahmins of India and concluded that the 'variations in the physical features of the Brahmans thus suggest incorporation of more than one physical type . . .' (152). These observations simply re-emphasize that the fundamental unit of the study should be the 'breeding population' within the context of study at hand. These results bring us back to the significance of variables, like the geographic locale of the group, climate and adaptations, migration, inclusion, and or adapting generic names by the people. Social Reform and Social Uplift movements in the twentieth century and breaking down of sub-caste barriers recently in marriage alliances is now changing the earlier caste populational complex of Indian society. The cracks in the inter-caste barriers with regard to marriage practices are likely to introduce further changes in this regard. In other words, the caste/tribe demographic structure is not likely to remain static, but is moving in a direction where the importance of caste and tribe boundaries for such studies may become less important. They may have new dimensions in the realm of intermixtures, and their new import in population studies. It should also be recognized that the size of a population group and its distribution will have their own impact on the nature of the population complex.

In a fairly recent study (Hall and Hall 1995) the effects of geographic factors on the human phenotypic traits have been examined. It confirms the applicability of Bergmann's and Allen's rules, and supports the view that location in geographic variation 'must consider possible confounding effects' (p. 407) of various factors as well. Ecogeographic rules reflect on the relationship between the climate and body proportions as pointed out earlier by Newman (1953, 1960) for body shape, Roberts (1978), Frisancho (1979) and Ruff (1991) on the width of the torso focusing on bi-iliac breadth with various statures. Climatic adaptations of cranial and facial structures seem to follow ecogeographic rules (Weiner 1954; Roberts 1978). With specific reference to early skeletal populations (Carey and Steegman 1981) 'broader noses appear adaptive in moister, warmer climates, whereas projecting and taller, narrower noses appear adaptive in dry and cold climates' (Hall and Hall 1995: 408). Historical background of population migration, settlements in micro-environments and their selective pressures under several other micro-environments are the factors which need to be attended to, as each combination is likely to produce somewhat different results (Little and Baker 1988). By and large major surveys in India have mostly bypassed these considerations in their analysis, though not necessarily in the collection of the data in each case. A few have taken into account the net possible effects of such factors. An analysis of the data along latitude and climatic regions could reflect body size (Hass et al. 1977) in the patterns of adaptation (Frisancho et al. 1997) in body build and proportions (Jantz et al. 1992) as well as health (Lazenby 1997). This dimension has not received full attention in Indian anthropometry. However, some publications do address some of the problems (Basu and Mukhopadhyay 1985; Basu et al. 1985; Bharadwaj 1982; Lahiri 1984; Malik 1979). Individual attempts in the study of the problems of high altitude adaptations, be they physical and/or, physiological are quite few on population groups like the Sherpas (Morpurgo et al. 1976; Weitz 1984), Bhotia (Sidhu et al. 1985), and defense personnel (Salvamurthy et al. 1983). These, and all such researches have kept pace with studies pursued by many (Baker 1969; Baker and Dutt 1972; Baker and Litle 1976; Bhardwaj et al. 1973; Singh et al. 1987).

Human Growth

An offshoot of anthropometric studies in India was the attention towards the growth studies of children after Independence. Although some occasional papers had appeared in journals related with medical sciences, the data was mainly extracted from the routine health examinations of University and college students. The medical health officers, through their routine examinations of eyesight, dental formations and some diseases submitted reports, and these were misappropriately called as growth studies (Majumdar 1951). From bio-anthropological point of view anatomical, physiological and pathological conditions of cultural groups need to be answered in the background of cultural influences which determine the way of life affecting form and function of the body. This was not perceived during the routine medical examinations, or at least not reported. Macfarlane (1937-8) compared the growth rate of children in the background of vegetarian and non-vegetarian diets, in Trivandrum (now Thiruvananthapuram). The results may be considered inconclusive as the sample size of individual groups between the two categories is small; also the characters considered are very few. In a seminal paper Prasad (1949) considered economic and social status as important factors and included somatometric characters like weight, stature, sitting height, chest girth and depth, biacromial diameter, iliac diameter, inter-trochanteric diameter, wrist, arm and calf girths, to assess the nutritional levels of the students in schools of Lucknow. Majumdar was not satisfied with the results, and undertook another inquiry on 1,120 school children. Conscious of the random sampling of data and the nature of distribution of children in various schools from different social groups, he collected data from five educational institutions, which included age-groups from eight to twenty years. Four of them represented only from eight to sixteen years. The minimum sample from one school was 101 and the maximum 547 from another, which adds the age group 16 to 22 years. Ten characters were cranio-facial, and sitting height, stature and weight were the others. Two observations, among many, were of significance and in consonance with later observations on secular trends in growth spurt during the adolescent period (Satyanarayana et al. 1980), and that all parts of the body do not grow at the same rate and at the same time. With reference to hereditary and dietary factors, the Shia students reflected taller stature, longer and thicker bones, a long face and a fine nose (Majumdar and Bahadur 1951). Their argument to Prasada's choice of somatometric criteria leading to no correlation of significance, but selecting a different set of criteria except stature, weight and sitting height, does not help the comparative approach. Possibly, the choice for criteria was to keep in line with Majumdar's earlier surveys. Such a systematic collection of data would have been of immense comparative value if other non-cranio-facial body characters and girths had been included. Indian bio-anthropology missed another opportunity here. A comparative evaluation with Macfarlane's data on the basis of vegetarianism and non-vegetarianism might have provided additional information.

During the middle of the 1950s Majumdar and Biswas collaborated to initiate a study on the growth patterns of north Indian children, under the aegis of the Indian Council of Medical Research. It was to be extended further in the south as well, which, somehow could not be completed. A large set of anthropometric characters were included in the study. This valuable data has only been partially analysed. Since the beginning of the 1960s there has been a phenomenal involvement of scientists, from various fields, in growth studies including nutritional and populational factors, from all over the regions of the country. A few citations in certain specific areas will provide the trends in growth studies. Researches on the birth weight of children in low economic groups (Arora et al. 1963; Banerjee 1969), growth characteristics in upper socio-economic group (Agarwal et al. 1983; Singh and Malhotra 1982), height and weight (Majumdar and Bahadur 1949, 1950; Singh and Bhale 1964; Bhalla et al. 1986), general growth patterns (Murty et al. 1983, Sharma 1970, 1982), have been reported by numerous scholars. General growth patterns have been continuously studied by Sidhu and his collaborators beginning from 1969 onward. Specific height and weight related studies have been addressed by Berry et al. (1968), Bhalla et al. (1987), Bhatnagar et al. 1985. Patterns of growth spurt have been studied by Satyanarayana, et al. (1980). Patterns of heredity of the size of head and other traits (Dash Sharma 1970; Devi and Reddi 1983; Roy 1983; Dasgupta et al. 1997), studies in correlation of some anthropometric characters between mothers and daughters (Bakshi 1975; Kaur and Singh 1981, 1983), genetic components in cephalo-facial dimensions between the newborns and their parents (Annapurna and Murti 1982, 1984; Annapurna et al. 1986) received serious attention. Maternal determinants of birth weight in relation to anthropometric characters attracted the attention of Bhatia and Tyagi (1984), Bhatia et al. (1985). Environment, nutrition, and health are related in a pattern where growth is influenced and this aspect has been attended by many scholars (Aykroyd 1937a, 1937b, 1938; Bhandari et al. 1975; Bhattacharya et al. 1981; Chakravartti 1986; Kaul and Shori 1982; Rao et al. 1978). The significance of body traits in sports and the performance of athletes during adolescent and later is not neglected, and certain correlations in patterns of performance and body build have been reported (Ahluwalia et al. 1987 and many others). Kansal's involvement along with other collaborators in this aspect has been continuous beginning from the nineteen eighties onward.

A majority of the studies referred to here, as well as others (not referred) have been of individual professional or function groups, and those in the area of general growth studies have been cross-sectional where comparisons of morphological traits have been attempted and patterns of growth established (Gupta et al. 1978, 1985; Dasgupta and Das 1997; Dasgupta 1989/90).

Longitudinal studies have been few because of the time factor involved in the collection of the data, loss in samples and various other factors over which a researcher has no control. But these foreseen and unforeseen deterrents did not discourage Das (1985) who considered twenty-two measures in boys and girls of West Bengal—*The Sarsuma Barisha Series*. This is one of the most significant series among the longitudinal studies of the Indian population. Longitudinal studies in physical growth, including birth weight, in relation to sex, period of gestation, maternal age, morbidity and mortality patterns, protein calorie malnutrition, and many of these in relation to socio-economic class have been conducted by Datta Banik and his collaborators, beginning from 1969 to the middle of 1980s. His individual as well as collaborated researches mostly published in *Indian Journal of Paediatrics* provide a wealth of information.

Studies in skeletal growth and maturity did not lag behind, although they are not as many as one would expect. Prakash has been active in this field since 1973 and has carried on his research, some in collaboration, persistently. Singal and Sidhu (1987) studied age changes from twenty to eighty years of age in communities of Punjab, India. Other studies of these two scholars address the problems in growth, maturity and aging. Specifically, Sidhu's involvement in growth studies and body composition has been multi-directional, for over twenty-five years.

DENTAL ANTHROPOLOGY

Fairly recent are the researches in dental anthropology (Lukacs 1984) with regard to their general morphology in different populations, their evolutionary implications (Hassamali 1982; Joshi 1972), sequence of teeth eruption and triat morphology (Banerjee 1967; Bhasin 1974, 1985; Bhatnagar 1986), epidemiological aspects in dental occlusion (Kaul and Corruccini 1984) and decidures and permanent eruptions in different populations.

In this area, researches by J.R. Lukacs, V. Rami Reddi (1986), A. Pal (involved from

1967 onwards) along with their collaborators, deserve special mention for their many faceted extensive work on the past as well as more importantly the living populations. This area of study, as well, has a strong potential to re-establish or reject old and add new concepts in the study of dental morphology, variation and evolution within the context of social and biological environments.

DERMATOGLYPHICS

The study of dermatoglyphic traits can be traced back to several thousand years from ancient China and India in the context of palmistry which dealt with these traits for individual identification, description of their personal attributes, future achievements (familial, social, political, and financial), as well as prediction of future health. Even today, palmistry as an organized branch of study in conjunction with astronomy is fairly well practised and a sizable section of world populations takes it seriously. The basic classifications of pattern types in dermatoglyphic are no different than ancient Sanskrit nomenclature (*Chakra* = whorl; *Shankha* = loop) but their finer sub-classifications and other pattern lines have definitive connection in population studies today. Besides, various dermatoglyphic traits considered currently are the result of elaborate attempts towards the understanding of their biological significance in individuals as well as in populations.

The main objective of bio-anthropologists to study the variations in human population groups based on ethnic and geographic distributions did not remain confined for long to the areas of morphometrics. The development of various sub-branches in the study of population biology, emphasizing more and more the reliable and demonstrable genetic traits came to be duly recognized. The traits of a more stable nature and less subject to environmental influences began to gain priority. From this point of view dermatoglyphic traits received serious attention. These configurations are established around the first quarter of the intra-uterine life and do not alter due to age (except in size) and post-natal environmental influences. The configurations not only vary from individual to individual in their frequencies and details but also from population to population (Rife 1953) in their proportional distributions; within the group, the sexual differences are usually well marked. Their heritability has been demonstrated by the studies of monozygotic twins (MacArthur 1938; Newman 1939).

However, their exact mode of inheritance is not known as in the case of blood-groups. An exact number of genes involved in their inheritance is equally not established, but what is more certain is that multiple genes are responsible for inherited dermatoglyphic variations (Cummins and Midlo 1943). Thus, Rife (1953: 389) considered that 'polygenic variations would seem to offer a distinct advantage over simple variations in the area of population genetics, in that they are less subject to the vagrancies of genetic drift.' Newman (1960) as well emphasized their suitability for their polygenically controlled and putatively non-adaptive nature, and that they do not undergo any post-natal modification on their own, except in cases where skin debilitating diseases cause the epidermic breakdown. Besides, the data collected through any techniques remain analysable as long as it is preserved; and they have a distinct advantage over either anthropometry or serology. Serological or any other genetic marker samples cannot be preserved for long in the first place, and create obstacles in the collection of it during fieldwork in remote areas, in the second, where immediate access to the laboratory or transportation of samples is not always easy to arrange. The analysis demands sophisticated techniques in the lab. A large-scale genetic admixture in the populations can change, or has the potential to change, the genic composition of certain easily detectable traits, even in the second generation. The dermatoglyphic samples and the traits do not seem to present such difficulties, or at least, they are not known so far.

Galton (1982) and Cummins and Midlo (1943) had already emphasized the role of dermatoglyphic traits beyond personal identification and emphasized their use (particularly Cummins and Midlo) and reliability in inheritance of twin diagnosis and racial variations. But, it took some more time to appear on the Indian scene to be used as an additional tool for identifying populations in India. Schlauginhaufen presented the first report in 1906 and Collins in 1913 (Singh and Bhasin 1979). The first major break-through was made by Biswas (1936) and he continued to enrich the dermatoglyphic information on some caste and tribal populations. It must be unequivocally recognized that Biswas was the first Indian physical anthropologist who introduced 'dermatoglyphics to Indian anthropologists. as a field of study, which later attracted the attention of clinicians as well' (Singh and Tyagi 1997: 180). He touched on areas like heredity, criminality, ethno-geographic variations and schizophrenia in relation to dermatoglyphics. Besides his own researches for over three decades (1936-68), he enthused the younger generation of investigators who successfully amassed a wealth of information on dermatoglyphic traits in population groups of India. In this respect the efforts of Buechi (1954), Tewari (1952 to 1983), Sharma (from 1957 to 1977), Mavalwala, Bhasin, Bhanu, Chakravartti, Datta, Kumbnani, Malhotra, Mukherjee, be specifically recognized in enriching this field of study. A host of others not mentioned here have equally contributed in this area and reported data from various regions in India. Most of them are still active in amassing and interpreting the data with current trends in bio-anthropological research.

Since 'racial variations and affiliations' was the theme of the 1930s through 1960s dermatoglyphic traits were visualized as new additional tool for identifying and classifying populations. Therefore, the spurt in growth of dermatoglyphic data took for most of the initial decades was logical. The populational aspect thus enriched by innumerable contributions by a host of researchers provided insight into the frequency distributions of various traits. In the ultimate analysis such frequency distributions failed to clarify the real issues for which they were so much embraced and depended upon. The overall picture of group distinctions and their relatedness remained fuzzy. Various indices, like cephalic and nasal in morphometry, proved to be ineffective. Dankmeijer's index (1938) to obtain dactyloscopical differences in different ethnic groups appeared to be effective (only) in his analysis of some of the data (1947).

In a later analysis, incorporating some available data after 1947, the case for the effectiveness of this arch/whorl index proved to be very weak (Singh 1963). The overall picture of arch/whorl distributions suggested two main constellations comprising populations with diametrically opposed somatic traits. However, they did show differentiation according to geographic location with a suggestion that the trait appeared 'to behave somewhat like blood group gene B' (Singh 1963: 37)—a tangential suggestion for some selective value. The quantitative values of traits in different caste groups did not provide conclusive relatedness or non-relatedness among the groups (Singh 1978, 1982; Sarkar 1976). Despite such inefficacies, data on different population groups is pouring forth from different parts of the country, each time adding an invaluable wealth of information and adding to the population data pool. It is significant in the background of social demography, endogamy, caste hierarchy and subgroups as marriage circles as well as caste concepts with regard to sexual relationships. As for indigenous (so called tribals) populations, along with their own belief systems, their locations in peripheral or remote areas provide them a status of distinct groups in themselves. For population biologists, the data is a gold-mine.

Population surveys, be they morphometric or serologic, indicated that castes differ from one another in some traits and that geographic variations seem to play some role in accentuating the physical variations within the same group. When some geographic trends in the index of pattern intensity were reported (Rife 1953; Newman 1960; Roberts and Coope 1972; Marquer and Jakobi 1976), an attempt was made to collect data from a homogeneous geographic environment to neutralize its effect (if any) but maintaining caste as a reproductively isolated population from other such groups. The emphasis was on the fact that each caste in one region with its subdivisions is a compact social, and biological unit, which regulates, maintains, and perpetuates itself within its framework (Singh 1978). The results did indicate the heterogenous nature of the four castes studied; certain pattern type associations with individual groups were significant, more specifically in their left hands, but the influence of geographic factor could neither find support nor rejection in the variability of the castes. This needed further probing. The question begs to be answered, yet.

The population data from all over the country, whether caste or tribal, does confirm basic findings indicating sexual differences, right and left hand variations in frequencies of pattern configurations, ridge-counts, mainline formulae, terminations of mainlines, positions of tri-radii't' and other general features. But it does not help to sort out clearcut population differences in general, or even in those groups which have diametrically opposite morphometric and serologic traits. Although certain regional or otherwise population groups do suggest some differences in cases like south and central Indian tribes from the Mongoloids for the frequency of their whorls and arches (Singh and Bhasin 1979: 350). These variations, however, are not based on an adequate data, either numerically or representing both the sexes in each case, therefore, inconclusive. So is the case with many other dermatoglyphic traits as well.

Studies on planter dermatoglyphics are very few. As it is, the hindrances in obtaining readable planters prints are more compounded among rural populations due to erosion of configurations and callouses in walking bare-feet. None the less, efforts of P.K. Datta (in the 1960s), R.S. Bali, I. Sachadeva, S.C. Tewari and few others do provide additional data on some caste and tribal groups. It would be rather hasty and inconclusive to plug these results into any definitive biologic measures.

A few studies have also been attempted on the genetic behaviour of the dermatoglyphic traits. These include inheritance of digital patterns, palmer configurations, *a-b* and other interdigital ridge-counts and some calcar configurations. There is no comprehensive study of more than two traits for any single population. More information would only provide some positive direction towards the nature of inheritance patterns in Indian populations. However, efforts of H.K. Kumbnani, H.N. Pateria, P.K. Datta and I.P. Singh, along with others are invaluable. P.C. Biswas (1939) remains the initiator and the source of encouragement for these studies.

With populational variation dermatoglyphics not providing an extremely strong tool for the purpose, and the nature of inheritance mechanism still illusive because of its polygenic nature, the attention has turned towards its clinical applications to understand the patterns of association of traits with diseases. Biswas and Bardhan (1966) reported on the association of palmer configurations and schizophrenia, followed by others (Bhanu et al. 1976; Karmakar and Malhotra 1983), on Down Syndrome (Kolluri et al. 1983, 1984), mental retardation (Bandopadhyay 1969; Roy et al. 1983; Kaur and Singh 1985), diabetes mellitus (Ahuja et al. 1983; Chakravartti 1966; Iqbal et al. 1976; Laha et al. 1975; Sidhu et al. 1985), thalassemia (Mukherjee et al. 1970; Kumar et al. 1971), epilepsi (Sethi 1976), and congenitally deaf and dumb (Mathew et al. 1976; Sharma 1975). In case of Down Syndrome, congenital anomalies are reliably reflected in dermatoglyphic configurations else where as well (Schaumann and Alter 1976). Other positive associations with chromosomal anomalies (Narayanan et al. 1983; Sandhu et al. 1984) have also been reported. Nair and Balkrishnan have investigated the dermatoglyphics in cases of endomyocardial fibrosis (1987).

For some of these cases we certainly need more data, and 'not to accept, in simplistic ways, the definition of a syndrome or other medical condition' (Mavalwala 1983: xxviii). In other words a caution is necessary.

Besides collection of data and analysis of various traits with regard to variations, geographic distributions, association to diseases and inheritance patterns, there have been significant contributions in 'comparative research methodology in palmer dermatoglyphics' (Singh and Bhasin 1979: 372). In this regard A. Sharma should legitimately be regarded as a pioneer to improve and suggest new directions and points of references, finally leading towards more sophisticated approaches in detailing the patterns and their analysis. His contribution to the dermatoglyphic methodologies over a period of about twenty years (beginning in 1959) has elevated the status of dermatoglyphic studies in India. His younger colleagues (J. Mavalwala and K.C. Malhotra) have also pitched in, now that more sophisticated analytical tools are available.

HUMAN BIOLOGY: GENETIC VARIATIONS, ADAPTATION AND DEMOGRAPHY

This subtitle is purposely chosen to bring together various subfields in the study of human population traits by biological anthropologists, as well as others interested researchers with a bio-anthropology orientation in their approach. Bio-anthropology has traditionally borrowed from and been dependent upon the biological sciences. The significant trends, not only in Indian biological anthropology but all over the world, have always influenced its growth and direction. Its synthesizing approach has always kept pace with contemporary researches and methodologies elsewhere, and has added, on its own, new ideas and interpretations through researches on specific human groups and provided new insights into the variations of genetic traits in various populations. Included here are such areas of study as blood groups, vital capacity, basal metabolism, taste sensitivities, deficiencies through genetic inheritance, abnormal haemoglobins, population variation and their susceptibilities to diseases, human chromosomal heteromorphisms and their effects, adaptive and demographic patterns of various genetic traits, etc. Areas of study are many more; similarly, as many categories may be devised for purposes of analyses and critical evaluations.

Genetic Variations and Diseases

Ludwik Hirzsfeld, a Polish serologist, pioneered the studies of ABO blood group distributions in human populations (1919), initiating the beginning of human population biology. The genetic basis of human blood groups provided another strong tool to study population variations. It was anticipated that blood-groups being definitive traits would be more reliable in identifying human populations as races. Thus, the studies were carried forward enthusiastically by a number of researchers in India—most notably like Malone and Lahiri (1929) on blood group distributions in certain castes in India, Pandit (1934) on the Todas of Nilgiris, Aiyappan (1936, 1939) some south Indian tribes, and Basu (1938) reported on the Khasis of Assam. E.W.E. Macfarlane studied a series of groups—castes and tribes—from the Himalayas to south India and Bengal, including even the Tibetans and Bhotia, beginning from 1937 to 1941. Similarly D.N. Majumdar was active for two decades (1932-52) reporting on the blood group distributions of criminal tribes, Bhils, Makranis, Garos and various caste groups in Uttar Pradesh, Bengal and Gujarat. S.S. Sarkar reported on the blood groups of several tribes like the Oraon, Kotas, Andaman Islanders, Kadars and some populations from Bihar and Orissa provinces, including Anglo-Indians from Calcutta for about two decades beginning 1937, Buechi 1942-65, B.M. Das for more than three decades beginning in 1958 on Assam groups. Similarly S.C. Tiwari and S.R. Das worked on various populations and different aspects of blood groups. Significant contributions were made by Narendra Kumar between 1958 and 1985. Most of these studies, as well as by others, focused their attention on blood group distribution patterns for purposes of sorting out population variations along contemporary morphometric studies. The data on population studies continued to be collected until the late 1960s, and occasionally such studies still appear, although they have now lost appeal, but certainly each one enriches the data pool and adds to the information on a new population group among the thousands still unreported.

However, the thrust on population variation studies along traditional lines showed weaknesses because of advanced researches in serological studies and the knowledge of many more other blood groups, e.g. Rh factor, MNSs, Duffy, Kell, Lutheran and others systems, which were, by and large, cross-represented in various frequencies in different populations. Since, most of the later systems involve sophisticated expensive techniques and laboratory settings, all of them have not received equal attention of the scholars. The bulk of the data is on ABO and Rh systems. This data failed to provide the satisfaction of being a wonder-tool to identify and classify populations into neat categories. Nonetheless the gene frequency distributions in populations provided other insights to investigate and analyse the genetics of populations on the basis of their size, matrimonial distances, inbreeding coefficients (Majumdar and Malhotra 1979), gene dispersion (Malhotra 1980) and gene differentiation (Malhotra et al. 1978) in certain caste-clusters. R. Chakraborty, beginning from 1972 onwards, along with some collaborators touched upon population diversity, consanguinous marriage and genetic load (1977), and aspects of gene distributions under various social and geographical conditions. M.K. Bhasin and V. Bhalla have impressive contributions in the area of variations and genetic polymorphisms, Banerjee et al. (1985) and Bangham (1980) on serum protein polymorphisms. Reports on haptoglobins, seretor factors, blood group incompatibilities and neonatal mortality and the like also exist, but not too many. On general aspects of serological studies, the contributions of A.K. Roy Chaudhury, N. Saha, L.D. Sanghvi's, among others, have enriched the field. Sanghvis major contribution lies in the field of blood groups and diseases, with the main thrust on genetic variations and genetic distances between populations. Contributions of S.R. Das are somewhat different than many others. His studies in various aspects of human genetics have been of an intensive kind rather than an extensive one. His in-depth studies of a few selected traits, e.g. P.T.C., blood groups, haemoglobinopathies, erythrocytic enzymes and other blood group proteins, despite their mathematical orientation, have not lost their anthropological perspective and have provided a deeper understanding of genetic traits and their frequency distributions.

Besides the genetic markers referred to above, bio-anthropologists studied glucose-6-phosphate dehydrogenese activity in different groups since the beginning of the nineteen sixties (Ahmad et al. 1972; Baxi et al. 1961, 1969; Bansal et al. 1976; Bhatia and Gupte 1986, among many others). Studies of this trait, with sickle-cell anaemia, have been attempted by Deshmukh and Sharma (1968) and Dey and Seth (1986) in Maharashtra and Himachal Pradesh respectively. Deshmukh and Sharma (1968) also found the deficiency of erythrocyte glucose-6-phosphate dehydrogenese as a cause for neonatal jaundice. Such studies on this marker of clinical significance are not many in bio-anthropological field.

An interaction of B-thalassemia and hereditary persistence of foetal haemoglobins was reported by Bird et al. in 1964. Reports on its occurrence have been made by Ajmani et al. (1976, 1977), Chatterjee (1965, 1968); Chaubisa et al. (1987), and many others. The association of this marker with traits like sickle-cell and glucose-6-phosphate dehydrogenese has also been studied by Jain et al. (1981). But such studies are not many and there appears to be a lack of continuity and extension to many more population groups under different social and physical environmental conditions, which may reflect on the patterns of trait distributions and their associational effects.

The phenomenon of sicklemia, as it was popularly referred to in earlier stages of serological studies, attracted the attention of numerous researchers. Lehmann and Cutbush, during 1952, reported on its presence in some south Indian communities and 'Pre-Dravidians' of southern India, and tried to subdivide the populations on the presence and absence of the trait, an attempt towards the prevailing classificatory approach. Lehmann went a step ahead to suggest that it was not essentially a Negroid feature (1953). From that point onwards, its association with malaria, including malarial climatic conditions, pernicious anaemia along with ABO blood-group system, its heritability, adaptive patterns and population distributions began to be investigated (Agrawal 1964 to 1968; Ahmad 1975, 1980; Babu et al. 1980; Batabyal and Wilson 1958; Bhatia 1986; Brittenham et al. 1977, 1979; Chaubisa et al. 1986; Jain and Goswami 1985 and many others). Negi (1962 onward) focused his sole attention on the distribution of sickle-cell trait in Indian populations. This trait, he observes, appears to be fairly well distributed among many population groups and in certain specific areas. No other anthropologist in India has been so consistent in the study of this trait. His research areas include central India, southern India, western India and the Himalayan foothills. His extensive researches support the view that the trait originated in India as a result of independent mutation in some populations and was gradually introduced into other populations. In favourable environmental conditions, selection in favour of heterozygote sickler resulted in high frequency of the trait (almost 40 per cent) in a few Bastar populations. He, thus, suspects that the distribution of this trait over a wide area in India and in many population groups 'most probably originated in the aboriginal component' (1964: 214) which may have served as a dispersal agent in many of the populations of the Indian region. In the Indian context then, 'malaria-sickle-cell hypothesis has limited validity' (Negi 1975) in the background of its geographical and populational distribution; it appears to have an ethnic basis, and that the adaptation aspect in this context is not as much assertive here as elsewhere. However, the genetic import of the trait for malarial conditions is not minimized.

Studies on haemoglobin variants have focused on medical aspects, but haemoglobin S, E and D have been reported a lot better than others from some regions in India. Anthropological significance of these variants, as well as others is yet to be assessed, except that attempts have been made to analyse the data along regional population basis, or their affiliations; they appear to have some regional distribution (Roy Chaudhury 1975). Das et al. (1983) attempted to look into the fitness of haemoglobin genetypes in Bengali-speaking population.

Researches on many other genetic markers are quite a few, but a closer scrutiny indicates that topics on medical anthropology have not received as much attention as the potential among the bio-anthropologists exists. Although, beginning from the nineteen sixties onward, sporadic researches on various diseases and their associations with some genetic markers have been filling this lacuna. Kaur et al. (1986) studied association aspects of serum immunoglobin and carcinoma, Ramchandraiah et al. (1978) ABO blood groups with Jaundice, filariasis and diabetes mellitus, Reddy and Mukkerjee on glucose-6-phosphate dehydrogenese and colour vision. In this connection reference must be made of Sirajuddin's study (1977) where he combines four genetic markers and the colour blindness among the Chenchus. A comprehensive account of ABO blood groups and diseases has been presented by Chakravartti (1983). Elsewhere he also tackles aspects of selection and fertility.

ANTHROPOLOGICAL DEMOGRAPHY

One area of research, comparatively new in Indian bio-anthropology, and which has remained very much untouched is that of genetic demography. Since 1949 there has been a significant shift away from traditional ethnic variation studies to the demographic patterns of genetic traits. A first serious attempt, apart from census reports, was made by K. Davis (1951) on populations in India and Pakistan; later demographics of pregnancies and childbirth were reported by others. Dandekar (1953) combined fertility and mortality while Majumdar (1952, 1955) investigated demography in a polyandrous society. From wide-scale inbreeding practices in India to localized rural Andhra Pradesh, L.D. Sanghvi (from 1966 to 1978) examined the genetic consequences of inbreeding, outbreeding, and interbreeding. Studies on individual populations on various issues in demography are many. S. Talukder focused on selection intensity and genetic demography between 1971 and 1983. During the past thirty years or so, a great deal of interest developed in this area. Since human societies are the product of both biological and cultural phenomena and they occur together, the social and biological cannot always be neatly sorted out from the tangled web of both. It has come full circle now, and is being realized with the development of population genetics that social networks, segments, and strata in a society influence the inflow and outflow of genes. Hence, consanguinity and marriage define, produce and somewhat limit the genetic boundaries of a population, though not always necessarily as closed breeding units. The Indian population has a caste system, irrespective of the major religious faiths where groupings exist as well; indigenous or so called tribal populations have their own rules of acquiring mates. The result is the numerous population units with varying degrees of inflow and outflow of genetic components. As a population, then, castes have porous boundaries. In order to study the genetic nature of a population, its structure, (caste/tribal structure in the Indian context) must be understood for a meaningful interpretation of a genetic trait, its relationship and the impact on society in the context of new groups being formed and some being eliminated for identification. Thus, a need was felt for the study of population demography with bio-anthropological perspective rather than relying on traditional demographic parameters.

Rakshit (1975, 1976) made a specific case for such an understanding and credit must go to him for establishing the case for anthropological demography. He emphasized that the institution of caste, with all its nuances for selecting mates, must be taken 'into account to understand the consequences of marriage rules' (207) in the formation of population units. Biswas' (1975) analysis of the ABO blood groups of Brahmans from nine provinces of India, and Huq and Rakshit's (1975) study on marriage distance and consanguinity in three Muslim villages of Murshidabad in West Bengal brings the point home. This field of study has attracted the attention of some biological anthropologists in either presenting new data or analysing the existing one and proving the point. Here, mention must be made of Malhotra (1980, 1984), Basu et al. (1985), Barua (1982, 1983), Basu (1985), Kalla (1985), Mavalawala (1984), Mukherjee et al. (1977), Murty and Ramesh (1985), Poddar (1975), Rao (1984), Reddy et al. (1987), Sadhu (1987), Sanghvi's work on inbreeding in the nineteen seventies as referred earlier, and many others.

Whether anthropological demography would survive, flourish and contribute on its own, is not so important as is the bio-anthropological approach to demography to be kept alive. Bio-anthropologists once aware of the potential of it, I am positive, its approach would be incorporated in their future studies on human population variations, selection, adaptation and evolution—the central theme of bio-anthropology.

From this brief review of Indian bio-anthropology researches on the living it is apparent that some areas of inquiry are very well represented, while others are less so, still there are some which have been missed, or, are merged with the major ones. Such a pattern of representation is largely a function of financial resources rather than intellectual priorities. By and large Indian bio-anthropological research reflects world-views and trends. The vitality of the discipline continues to be enhanced by individual and institutional affiliation with the international anthropological community. The native and foreign experiences have blended together and developed an approach of the Indian style to analyse and interpret the data in view of the complexity of the population structure, along with the socio-cultural substrate in which it is immersed. However, there is an imperative need for emphasis on problem-oriented and sustained studies, with changing economic, political, and social configuration, Indian biological anthropology has a unique opportunity to make many more important contributions to the understanding of the natural history of our species as we approach the new millennium. This optimism, expressed earlier elsewhere, I do not hesitate to repeat it within the context of the uniquely complex societal structure on the subcontinent, the way it has been for long, developed, changed and ever-changing populational complex. Recently a few doubts have been expressed about the survival of biological anthropology in terms of its popular appeal and as an integral part of anthropology. It is not only in the context of India alone but on the American continent as well, in the background of tendencies toward fragmentation within anthropology as a discipline. This situation appears to emerge from a social-political-economic-cum-academic reasons. These may be examined under two fundamental facets: One, that biological anthropology had a scientific orientation to begin with, and continued to incorporate and synthesize biological information which always demanded special efforts to lay one's hands on, and present trends of extreme specialization have further removed it from the usual interested intelligentsia. The second facet is that biological anthropologists, confining within themselves, hardly proved to be better and more efficient and aggressive sales-persons of their discipline. This has resulted into some kind of an elitism, as compared to other human sciences.

In the future there may be a dwindling population of bio-anthropologists, if fences are not mended, but the discipline will not disappear or lose its potential so long as it maintains its strongest character of a great synthesizer of human activity and achievements and follows 'biology, society and culture' approach. David Suzuki has a lot more message in this regard. Edward O. Wilson's arguments (1998) on the age of narrow specialization are most commendable. As for Indian bio-anthropology and anthropologists, both have done extremely well; there is an enviable potential with a unique population structure.

ACKNOWLEDGEMENTS

I gratefully acknowledge the permission granted by Dr. Frank Spencer, editor of the *History of Physical Anthropology: An Encyclopedia*, New York and Dr. Nadeem Hasnain, General Secretary of Ethnographic and Folk Culture Society, Lucknow, India, to borrow statements and ideas from my own articles published by them. I am deeply indebted to Ms. Andria Turner, our secretary, for her patient, meticulous efforts to put the manuscript together.

NOTE

* The job of a reviewer is a difficult one, particularly where thousands of researches are involved, covering a period of more than half a century. In a review article like the one attempted here, where the growth, progress, direction and the status of a field of study is the central theme, certain choices had to be made. In this effort, I have concentrated upon the main themes of the subject and briefly discussed those researches which initiated, set trends and contributed in the progress of the discipline. Obviously, the references have been selective, but the contribution of every single researcher is gratefully acknowledged, irrespective of direct, indirect or tangential referring. Certain ideas and emphases in the form of comments are based upon my own perceptions.

REFERENCES

Agarwal, D.K., K.N. Agarwal, S. Mehta, P. Perira, B.B. Khare, G.P. Katiyar and A.M. Tripathi 1983. Physical Growth Characteristics in Adolescent Girls of Upper Socio-Economic Group in Varanasi, *Indian Journal of Medical Research* 77: 839-44.

Ahluwalia, P., R.N. Vasishta and B.S. Kabir 1987. Anthropometric Measurements and Physical Performance in Rural School Girls During Adolescent Age, in *Sports Sciences, Health, Fitness and Performance* (L.S. Sidhu, I.J.S. Bansal, Lakhbir Singh, D.P. Bhatnagar, S.K. Verma, D.K. Kanasal, J.L. Bhanot, M.S. Sohal and P. Singhal Eds.), pp. 109-16. Patiala: Indian Association of Sports Scientists and Physical Educationists.

Ahmad, S.H. 1975. ABO Blood Groups and Sickle Cell Trait Among the Kondh and Nukadora of Karaput District, in *Bio-anthropological Research in India* (H.K. Rakshit Ed.), pp. 119-26. Calcutta: Anthropological Survey of India.

Ahmad, S.H. and D. Chaudhury 1980. ABO Blood Groups and Sickle Cell Trait among the Pardhan of Mandla District, *Man in India* 60: 235-44.

Ahmad, S.H. and J. Sreenath 1992. *All India Anthropometric Survey: South Zone, Tamil Nadu*. Nagpur: Anthropological Survey of India.

Ahmad, S., P. Kumar and V.N. Mittal 1972. A Study of Glucose-6-Phosphate Dehydrogenese Activity in Normal Indian Subjects, *Journal of Association of Physicians of India* 20: 659-65.

Aiyappan, A. 1936. Blood Groups of the Pre-Dravidians of Wyanad Plateau, India, *Man* 36: 191-4.

Aiyappan, A. 1939. Blood Groups of the Nayadis of Malabar, South India, *Man* 39: 200.

Ajmani, M., A. Sharma, G. Talukder and D.K. Bhattacharya 1976. Beta-Thalassemia Trait in West Bengal: a Methodological Study, *Current Science* 45: 461.

Ajmani M., A. Sharma and G. Talukder 1978. Hemoglobin Variants in India, *Acta Geneticae Medicae Et Gemellologiae* 27: 11-30.

Annapurna, V. and J.S. Murty 1982. Anthropometric Variation in the Newborn and Their Parents: Correlation Between the Traits, *Journal of Indian Anthropological Society* 17: 47-55.

——— 1984. Effect of Fetal Age in Cephalo-Facial Measurements, Indian Pediatrics 21: 307-12.

Annapurna, V. and J.S. Murty, M.N. Rao and T. Seetha 1986. The Genetic Component in the Cephalic-Facial Anthropometric Measurements in the Newborn and Their Parents, in *Genetic Research in India* (I.C. Verma Ed.), pp. 215-22. New Delhi: Sagar Printers and Publishers.

Arora, S., N.R. Rao and M.V.R. Rao 1963. Birth Weight of Infants in Low Economic Groups in Bombay, *Indian Journal of Child Health* 12: 612.

Aykroyd, W.R. and B.G. Krishnan 1937a. Diet Survey in South Indian Villages, *Indian Journal of Medical Research* 24: 667-87.

——— 1937b. The State of Nutrition of School Children in South India, Part II. Diet and Deficiency Disease in Residential Hostels, *Indian Journal of Medical Research* 24: 707.

Aykroyd, W.R., K.B. Madhawan and K. Rajgopal 1938. The Detection of Malnutrition by Measurement of Arm, Chest and Hip, *Indian Journal of Medical Research* 26: 55-94.

Babu, M.S., P. Veerraju and J.M. Naidu 1980. A Note on the Sickle Cell Trait in a Tribal Population of Coastal Andhra Pradesh, *Indian Anthropologist* 10: 125-9.

Baker, P.T. 1969. Human Adaptation to High Altitude, *Science* 163: 1149-56.

Baker, P.T. and J.S. Dutt. 1972. Demographic Variables as Measures of Biological Adaptation: a Case Study of High-Altitude Human Population, in *The Structure of Human Populations* (G.A. Harrison and A.J. Boyce Eds.), pp. 352-78. Oxford: Clarendon Press.

Baker, P.T. and M.A. Little (Eds.) 1976. *Man in the Andes: a Multidisciplinary Study of High Altitude Quechua*. Strousburg: Dowden, Hutchinson and Ross, Incorporation.

Bakshi, R. 1975. Correlation of Few Anthropometric Parameters Between Mothers and Daughters, *Research Proceedings*, Delhi 3: 48-50.

Banerjee, A., A. Roy, S.K. Roy, G. Talukder and A. Sharma 1985. Serum Protein Polymorphisms in Selected Areas of West Bengal, India, *Acta Anthropologentica* 9: 216-66.

Banerjee, M.K. and D.K. Bannerjee 1967. ABO Blood Groups Among Jaunsaris, *Man in India* 47: 133-8.

Banerjee, P. 1969. Birth Weight of Bengali Newborns: Effect of the Economic Position of the Mother, *Annals of Human Genetics* 33: 99-108.

Bangham, C.R.M. and S.E. Howarth 1980. Genetic Polymorphisms in Isolated Sherpa Populations of Nepal, *American Journal of Physical Anthropology* 53: 369-73.

Bansal, I.J.S., B. Kaur, P. Singhal and A.J.S. Bhanwer 1976. Glucose-6-Phosphate Dehydrogenese (G-6-PD) Deficiency Among Muslims of Punjab, *Anthropologist* 23: 21-5.

Barua, S. 1982. Bio-Demographic Factors Associated with Offspring Mortality Among the Hajongs of Meghalaya, *Journal of Indian Anthropological Society* 17: 143-6.

——— 1983. The Hajongs of Meghalaya: a Bio-Demographic Study, *Human Science* 32: 190-200.

Basu, A. and B. Mukhopadhyay (Eds.) 1985 *Human Adaptation to Environment*. Calcutta: Indian Anthropological Society.

Basu, A., S. Mukhopadhyay, S. Roy, P. Bharati and R. Gupta 1985. Sherpa Body Dimensions: Further Studies on Altitudinal and Socio-Cultural Effects, *Indian Journal of Physical Anthropology and Human Genetics* 11: 25-31.

Basu, A., R. Gupta, P. Bharati, B. Mukhopadhyay and S.K. Roy 1985. Physical Environmental, Socio-cultural and Ethnic Correlates of Human Biology in Some Populations of West Bengal, India, and Neighbouring Regions; Mortality Differentials, in *Diseases of Complex Itiology in Small Populations: Ethnic Differences and Research Approaches* (R. Chakraborty and E.J.E. Szathmary Eds.), pp. 345-65. New York: Alan R. Liss.

Basu, R.N. 1938. Blood Groups Among the Khasis, *Nature* 142: 797.

Basu, S.K. 1985. Inbreeding in India: Its Genetic Consequences and Implications in Health Care, *Technical Report* 8: 1-97. New Delhi: National Institute of Health and Family Welfare.

Batabyal, J.N. and J.M.G. Wilson 1958. Sickle-Cell Anaemia in Assam, *Journal of Indian Medical Association* 30: 8-11.

Baxi, A.J., V. Balkrishnan and L.D. Sanghvi 1961. Deficiency of Glucose-6-Phosphate Dehydrogenese—Observations on a sample from Bombay, *Current Science* 30: 16-17.

Baxi, A.J., M.P. Parikh and H.I. Jhalla 1969. Incidence of Glucose-6-Phosphate Dehydrogenese Deficiency in Three Gujarati Populations, *Humangenetik* 8: 62-3.

Berry, J.N., H.N. Khattri, P.S. Bidwai and H.D. Gupta 1968. Height and Weight of College and Polytechnique Students in Northern India, *Indian Journal of Medical Research* 56: 1783-99.

Bhalla, A.K., S. Kaul and V. Kumar 1986. A Longitudinal Study of Growth in Length and Weight of Punjabi Infants in Chandigarh, India, *Annals of Human Biology* 13: 427-32.

Bhalla, A.K., V. Kumar and S. Kaul 1987. Longitudinal Growth of Body Weight and Crown Heel Length in Punjabi Infants: Population Comparison, *Indian Journal of Pediatrics* 54: 703-10.

Bhandari, B., A.M. Jain, P. Kerna, A. Mathur and V.K. Sharma 1975. Nutrition and Health Status of Rural School Boys of Udaipur District, *Indian Journal of Pediatrics* 42: 186-93.

Bharadwaj, H. 1972. Effect of Prolonged Stay at High Altitude on Body Fat Content—an Anthropometric Evaluation, *Human Biology* 44: 303-16.

Bharadwaj, H., A.P. Singh and M.S. Malhotra 1973. Body Composition of the High Altitude Natives of Ladakh: a Comparison with Sea-level Residents, *Human Biology* 43: 423-34.

Bharadwaj, H., S.C. Jain, K.P. Chakraborty and Satwanti 1982. Body Composition in Relation to High Altitude Acclimatisation, in *Human Genetics and Adaptation*, Vol. 2 (A. Basu and K.C. Malhotra Eds.), pp. 70-80. Calcutta: Indian Statistical Institute.

Bhasin, M.K., A.K. Sharma and I.P. Singh 1974. Permanent Dental Emergence in the Kuluis of Himachal Pradesh, *Anthropologist* 21: 9-14.

Bhasin, M.K., A. Sharma, I.P. Singh and H. Walter 1985. Morphological and Metric Dental Study on Indians, *Zeitschrift für Morphologie Und Anthropologie* 76: 77-90.

Bhatia, B.D. and N.K. Tyagi 1984. Maternal Determinants of Birth Weight: a Multivariate Analysis, *Indian Pediatrics* 21: 365-71.

Bhatia, B.D., N.K. Tyagi and P. Hemda 1985. Relationship of Low Birth Weight with Anthropometry and Maternal Weight-Height Indices, *Indian Journal of Medical Research* 32: 374.

Bhatia, H.M. and S.C. Gupte 1986. Neonatal Jaundice due to ABO, Rh and G-6-PD Deficiency in Bombay, in *Genetic Research in India* (I.C. Verma Ed.), pp. 106-18. New Delhi: Sagar Printers and Publishers.

Bhatnagar, D.P. and A. Kumar 1986. The Differences in Eruption of Permanent Dentition Among the Individuals of Two Social Groups of Punjabi Origin, *Acta Medica Auxologica* 18: 129.

Bhatnagar, D.P., P. Singal, L.S. Sidhu and J.L. Bhanot 1985. Growth of Weight, Height and Body Surface Area and the Standards in Punjabi Infants and Children, *Journal of Indian Anthropological Society* 20: 169-81.

Bhattacharya, K.K., P. Bharati, R. Gupta and A. Basu 1981. A Study of Diet and Nutritional Anthropometry of the Population of Mirpur, District Midnapur, West Bengal, *Collegium Anthropologicum* 5: 51-8.

Bird, G.W.G., M.I. Hasan, P.O. Malhotra and H. Lehmann 1964. Interaction of B-thalassaemia and Hereditary Persistence of Foetal Haemoglobin, *Journal of Medical Genetics* 1: 24-6.

Biswas, P.C. 1936. Über Hand ünd Finger-leisten von Indern, *Zeitschrift für Morphologie Und Anthropologie* 35: 519-50.

——— 1939-40. Studies on the Heredity of Palmer Pattern, *Journal of Indian Anthropological Institute* 2: 1-10.

Biswas, S. 1975. The Brahmins and Their Blood Groups, in *Bio-Anthropological Research in India* (H.K. Rakshit Ed.), pp. 221-4. Calcutta: Anthropological Survey of India.

Brittenham, G., B. Lozoft, J.W. Harris, V.S. Sharma and S. Narsimhan 1977. Sickle Cell Anemia and Trait in a Population of Southern India, *American Journal of Hematology* 2: 25.

Brittenham, G., B. Lozoft, J.W. Harris, S.M. Mason, A. Miller and T.H.J. Huisman 1979. Sickle Cell Anemia and Trait in Southern India: Further Studies, *American Journal of Hematology* 6: 107-23.

Carey, J.W. and A.T. Steegman Jr. 1981. Human Nasal Protrusion, Latitude and Climate, *American Journal of Physical Anthropology* 56: 313-19.

Chakraborty, R. 1974. Isolate Mixture and Random Mating, *Behaviour Genetics* 4: 91.

Chakraborty, R. and A. Chakravarty 1977. On Consanguineous Marriages and the Genetic Load, *Human Genetics* 36: 47-54.

Chakravartti, M.R. 1983. *Blood Groups and the Diseases in India*. Bombay: Samant & Co.

——— 1986. Health, Nutrition and Environment: Preparing India for the Year 2000 A.D., *Indian Anthropologist* 16: 161-74.

Chatterjee, J.B. 1965. Thalassemia: Clinical and Haematological Aspects, *Triangle the Sandoz Journal of Medical Sciences* 7: 101.

——— 1968. Abnormal Haemoglobins and Thalassemia: Their Geographic Distribution and Genetic Aspects, *Journal of Indian Anthropological Society* 3: 1-15.

Chaubisa, S.L., L. Parmar, M.B. Chauhan and S.L. Sharma 1986. Sickle Cell Trait in the Scheduled

Castes of Rajasthan, *Indian Journal of Pathological Microbiology* 29: 386-90.

Cummins, H. and C. Midlo 1943. *Finger Prints, Palms and Soles: an Introduction to Dermatoglyphics*. Philadelphia: Blakistan Company.

Dandekar, V.M. and K. Dandekar 1953. Survey of Fertility and Mortality in Poona District, *Gokhale Institute Political Economic Publication* 27: 115-87.

Dankmeijer, J. 1938. Some Anthropological Data on Finger Prints, *American Journal of Physical Anthropology* 23 (4): 377-88.

——— 1947. Finger Prints of African Pygmies and Negroes, *American Journal of Physical Anthropology* 5 (4): 458-84.

Das, N.K., J.M. Sarkar, K.K. Bhattacharya and A.K. Ghosh 1983. A Note on Fitness of Haemoglobin Genotypes in Bengali Speaking Population, *Human Heredity* 33: 307-10.

Dasgupta, I., P. Dasgupta and A.B. Dashchaudhury 1997. Familial Resemblance in Height and Weight in an Endogamous Mahisya Caste Population of Rural West Bengal, *American Journal of Human Biology* 9: 7-9.

Dasgupta, J. 1978. Chromosomal and Dermatoglyphic Studies in Schizophrenia, in *Medical Genetics in India*, Vol. 1 (I.C. Verma Ed.), pp. 181-7. Pondicherry: Auroma Enterprises.

Dasgupta, P. and S.R. Das 1997. A Cross-sectional Growth Study of Trunk and Limb Segments of the Bengali Boys of Calcutta, *Annals of Human Biology* 24 (4): 363-9.

Dash Sharma, P. 1970. A Study on the Heredity of the Head Size in Fifty Punjabi Families, *Genetica* 41: 466-70.

Davenport, C.B., M. Steggerda and W. Drager 1936. Critical Examination of Physical Anthropometry on the Living, *Proceedings, American Academy of Arts and Science* 69: 265-84.

Davis, K. 1951. *The Population of India and Pakistan*. Princeton, N.J.: Princeton University Press.

Deshmukh, V.V. and K.D. Sharma 1968. Deficiency of Erythrocyte Glucose-6-Phosphate Dehydrogenase and Sickle Cell Trait: a Survey of Malabar Students at Aurangabad, Maharashtra, *Indian Journal of Medical Research* 56: 821-5.

Deshmukh, V.V. and K.D. Sharma 1968. Deficiency of Erythrocyte G-6-PD as a Cause of Neonatal Jaundice in India, *Indian Pediatrics* 5: 401-5.

Devi, M.R. and G.G. Reddi 1983. Heritability of Body Measurements Among the Jalari Population in Visakhapatnam, *Annals of Human Biology* 10: 483-5.

Dey, S. and S. Seth 1986. Glucose-6-Phosphate Dehydrogenase Deficiency and Sickle Cell Anaemia Among Rajputs of Manali (Himachal Pradesh), *Journal of Indian Anthropological Society* 21: 271-4.

Feuerstein, G., Subhash Kak and David Frawley 1995. *In Search of the Cradle of Civilization*. Wheaton, U.S.A./Madras, India: Quest Books.

Frisancho, A.R. 1979. *Human Adaptation*. St. Louis: Mosby.

Frisancho, A.R., H.G. Frisancho, Rachel Albalak, Mercedes Villain, Enrique Vargas and Rudy Soria 1997. Developmental, Genetic, and Environmental Components of Lung Volumes at High Altitude, *American Journal of Human Biology* 9 (2): 191-203.

Galton, F. 1892. *Finger Prints*. London: Macmillan & Co.

Gavan, J.A. 1950. The Consistency of Anthropometric Measurements, *American Journal of Physical Anthropology* 8: 417-26.

Guha, B.S. 1935. *The Census of India* 1931. Report Vol.1, Part 3 (Ethnographic). Simla: Government of India.

——— 1938. *Racial Elements in Indian Population*. Oxford: Oxford University Press.

Gupta, P. and P.C. Dutta 1966. *Anthropometry in India (1868-1961).* Calcutta: Anthropological Survey of India.

Gupta, P.R., A.K. Dutta and P. Dutta 1978. Growth and Development: a Cross-Sectional Study of Pre-school Children, *Indian Journal of Pediatrics* 45: 189-95.

Gupta, P.P., S.N. Mehrotra, J.N. Bhalla and V.N. Tripathi 1985. Growth and Development in Rural Slums, *Indian Pediatrics* 22: 829.

Hall, R.L. and Don Alan Hall 1995. Geographic Variation of Native People Along the Pacific Coast, *Human Biology* 67: 407-26.

Hass, J.D., P.T. Baker and E. Hunt Jr. 1977. The Affects of High Altitude on Body Size and Composition of the Newborn Infant in Southern Peru, *Human Biology* 49: 611-28.

Hassanali, J. 1982. Incidence of Carabelli's Trait in Kenyan Africans and Asians, *American Journal of Physical Anthropology* 59: 317-19.

Hertzberg, H.T.E. 1968. The Conference on Standardization of Anthropometric Techniques and Terminology, *American Journal of Physical Anthropology* 28: 1-16.

Hirszfeld, L. and H. Hirszfeld 1919. Serological Differences Between the Blood of Different Races, *Lancet*. II: 675-9.

Jain, N. and H.K. Goswami 1985. Genetics of Natural Variants. V. ABO and Sickle Cell Genes in Bharia Tribes of Madhya Pradesh, *Bionature* 5: 23-7.

Jain, R.C., A.M.R. Andrew, S.L. Chaubisa, A. Acharya and K.C. Joshi 1981. Sickle Cell Trait, Thalassemia and G-6-PD Deficiency in Bhil Tribes of South Rajasthan, *Indian Journal of Medical Research* 73: 548-53.

Jantz, R.L., D.R. Hunt, A.B. Falsetti and P.J. Key 1992. Variation Among North Amerindians: Analysis of Boas' Anthropometric Data, *Human Biology* 64: 435-61.

Joshi, M.R., R.N. Godiawala and A. Butia 1972. Carabellis Trait in Hindu Children from Gujarat, *Journal of Dental Research* 51: 706-11.

Kalla, A.K. 1985. *Kashmiri Pandits and Their Diversity*. Delhi: B.R. Publishing Corporation.

Karve, I. 1948. *Anthropometric Measurement of Marathas*. Poona: Deccan College.

Karve, I. and V.M. Dandekar 1951. *Anthropometric Measurements of Maharashtra*. Poona: Deccan College.

Karve, I. and K.C. Malhotra. 1968. A Biological Comparison of Eight Endogamous Groups of the Same Rank, *Current Anthropology* 9: 109-24.

Kaul, S. and R. Shori 1982. Nutritional Status and Growth of Children from Rural Settlement in the Union Territory of Chandigarh, in *Human Biology—Recent Advances*, Vol. 1 (L.S. Sidhu, I.J.S. Bansal, Lakhbir Singh, D.P. Bhatnagar, S.K. Verma, D.K. Kanasal, J.L. Bhanot, M.S. Sohal and P. Singhal Eds.), pp. 191-201. New Delhi: Today and Tomorrow's Printers and Publishers.

Kaul, S.S. and S. Corruccini 1984. The Epidemiological Transition in Dental Occlusion in a North India Population, in *The People of South Asia* (J.R. Lukacs Ed.), pp. 201-16. New York: Plenum Press.

Kaur, D.P. and R. Singh 1981. Parent-Adult Offspring Correlations and Heritability of Body Measurements in a Rural Indian Population, *Annals of Human Biology* 8: 333-9.

——— 1983. Intra-familial Correlations, Heritability Coefficients of Body Measurements in a Rural Indian Population, *Indian Journal of Medical Research* 78: 224-32.

Kaur, H., S.N. Arora and D.N. Bhardwaj 1986. Serum Immunoglobulins in Breast Carcinoma Patients, *Indian Journal of Medical Research* 83: 600-3.

Kennedy, K.A.R. and R.D. Singh 1997. South Asia (India, Pakistan and Sri Lanka), in *History of Physical Anthropology: an Encyclopedia* (Frank Spencer Ed.), pp. 976-87. New York and London: Garland Publishing Inc.

Khanolkar, V.R. and L.D. Sanghvi 1945. Distribution of Rh Factor in Indians, *Acta Anthropogenetica* 2: 57-9.

Kurian, J.C., B.V. Bhanu and P.M. Fulmali 1978. Palmer C-Line Terminations in Schizophrenia, in *Medical Genetics in India*, Vol. 1 (I.C. Verma Ed.), pp. 189-95. Pondicherry: Auroma Enterprises.

Lahiri, S. 1984. Human Adaptation to High Altitude: Lessons from Sherpa Physiology, in *Human Genetics and Adaptation*, Vol. 2 (A. Basu and K.C. Malhotra Eds.), pp. 50. Calcutta: Indian Statistical Institute.

Lasker, G.W. 1976. *Physical Anthropology*. New York: Holt, Rinehart and Winston.

Lazenby, R.A. 1997. Bone Loss, Traditional Diet, and Cold Adaptation in Arctic Populations, *American Journal of Human Biology* 9 (3): 329-42.

Lehmann, H. 1953. Distribution of Sickle-Cell Trait, *Journal of Clinical Pathology* 6: 329.

Lehmann, H. and M. Cutbush 1952. The Findings of the Sickle-Cell Trait in Pre-Dravidians of Southern India, *Man* 53: 10.

Little, M. and P. Baker 1988. Migration and Adaptation, in *Biological Aspects of Human Migration* (C.G.N. Mascie-Taylor and G.W. Lasker Eds.), pp. 167-215. Cambridge: Cambridge University Press.

Lukacs, J.R. 1984. Dental Anthropology of South Asian Populations: a Review, in *The People of South Asia* (J.R. Lukacs Ed.), pp. 133-58. New York: Plenum Press.

Macfarlane, E.W.E. 1937-8. Rate of Growth of Non-vegetarian and Vegetarian Children of Trivandrum, Travancore, *Current Science* 6 (4): 148-51.

Mahalanobis, P.C. 1928. On the Need for Standardization in Measurements on the Living, *Biometrika* 20A: 1-31.

Mahalanobis, P.C., D.N. Majumdar and C.R. Rao 1949. Anthropometric Survey of the United Provinces, 1941: a Statistical Study, *Sankhya* 9: 93-324.

Mahalanobis, P.C. and C.R. Rao 1949. Anthropometric Survey of the United Provinces, 1941: a Statistical Study, *Sankhya* 9.

Majumdar, D.N. 1946: *Races and Cultures of India*. Lucknow: Universal Publishers.

——— 1952. Children in a Polyandrous Society, *The Eastern Anthropologist* 6: 177-89.

——— 1954-5. Demographic Structure in a Polyandrous Village, *The Eeastern Anthropologist* 8: 161-72.

Majumdar, D.N. and S. Bahadur 1949. Correlation of Height and Weight in the Racial Elements of Gujarat, *Journal of Gujarat Research Society* 11: 161.

——— 1950. A Comparative Study of Height and Weight of Castes and Tribes of Gujarat, in *Race Realities in Cultural Gujarat* (D.N. Majumdar Ed.), pp. 65-75. Bombay: Gujarat Research Society.

——— 1951. Anthropological Study of Growth Among School Children in Lucknow, *The Eastern Anthropologist* 5 (1): 1-26.

Majumdar, D.N. and C.R. Rao 1958. *Race Elements in Bengal*. Calcutta: Indian Statistical Institute.

Majumdar, P.P. and K.C. Malhotra 1979. Matrimonial Distance, Inbreeding Coefficient and Population Size: Dhangar Data, *Annals of Human Biology* 6: 17-27.

Malhotra, K.C. 1980. Matrimonial Distances Among the Four Dhangar (Shepherd) Castes of Maharashtra, India: Differences Among Districts, *South Asian Anthropologist* 1: 25-34.

Malhotra, K.C. 1980. Gene Dispersion in Man: the Indian Case, *Current Anthropology* 21: 135-6.

Malhotra, K.C. 1984. Population Structure Among the Dhangar Caste-Cluster of Maharashtra, India, in *The People of South Asia* (J.R. Lukacs Ed.), pp. 295-334. New York: Plenum Press.

Malhotra, K.C., R. Chakraborti and A. Chakravarti 1978. Gene Differentiation Among the Dhangar Caste-Cluster of Maharashtra, India, *Human Heredity* 28: 26-36.

Malik, S.L. 1979. Effect of Altitude on Physical Development: Comparison of Highland and Lowland Bods, *Spectra of Anthropological Progress* 2: 45-50.

Malone R.H. and M.N. Lahiri 1929. The Distribution of Blood Groups in Certain Races and Castes in India, *Indian Journal of Medical Research* 16: 963-72.

Marquer, P. and L. Jakobi 1976. Dermatoglyphics and Endogamy in Bearn, France, *Man* 11: 367-83.

Mavalwala, J. 1984. Culturally Delineating Human Breeding Groups, Their Genesis and Their Complexity, in *Human Genetics and Adaptation*, Vol. 2 (A. Basu and K.C. Malhotra Eds.), pp. 270-82. Calcutta: Indian Statistical Institute.

Morpurgo, G., P. Arese, A. Bosia, G.P. Pescarmona, M. Luzzana, G. Modiano and S.K. Ranjit 1976. Sherpas Living Permanently at High Altitude: a New Pattern of Adaptation, *Proceedings of National Academy of Sciences* (U.S.A.), 73: 747-51.

Mukherjee, D.P., S. Bhaskar and M. Lakshmanudu 1977. Studies on Inbreeding and its Effects in Some Endogamous Populations of Chittoor District, Andhra Pradesh, *Bulletin of the Anthropological Survey of India* 26: 10-22.

Murty, J.S. and A. Ramesh 1985. The Kolam of Andhra Pradesh: a Tribe in the Process of Fission, in *Genetic Micro Differentiation in Human and Other Animal Populations* (Y.R. Ahuja and J.V. Neel Eds.), pp. 118-27. Delhi: Indian Anthropological Association.

Murty, K.J.R., J.S. Rao, M.A. Kabeer, P.S. Raju, S.S. Papiha and D.F. Roberts 1983. Growth in Hyderabad Boys of Various Language Groups, *Anthropologischer Anzeiger* 41: 169-78.

Negi, R.S. 1964. Incidence of Sickle-Cell Trait in Bastar III, *Man* 64: 171-4.

——— 1975. Ethnic Component in the Distribution of Sickle-Cell Trait in India, in *Bio-Anthropological Research in India* (H.K. Rakshit Ed.), pp. 79-89. Calcutta: Anthropological Survey of India.

Newman, M.T. 1953. The Application of Ecological Rules to the Racial Anthropology of the Aboriginal New World, *American Anthropologist* 55: 311-27.

——— 1960. Adaptations in the Physique of American Aborigines to Nutritional Factors, *Human Biology* 32: 288-313.

Pandit, S.R. 1934. Blood Group Distribution in the Todas, *Indian Journal of Medical Research* 21: 613-15.

Poddar, S. 1975. Effect of Birth Order and Mothers Age on Reproductive Wastage, in *Bio-Anthropological Research in India* (H.K. Rakshit Ed.), pp. 208-15. Calcutta: Anthropological Survey of India.

Prasad, B.G. 1949. Assessment of Nutritional Status of School Children of Lucknow, *Indian Journal of Pediatrics* 16: 63.

Rajaram, N.S. and David Frawley 1995. *Vedic 'Aryans' and the Origins of Civilization*. Canada: W.H. Press, Inc.

Rakshit, H.K. 1965. Anthropometry and Personal Error, *Journal of Social Research* 7: 54-60.

Rakshit, H.K. 1966. The Brahmans of India: an Anthropometric Study, *Man in India* 46 (1) 33-58.

——— 1975. Understanding Caste for Demographic Studies, in *Bio-Anthropological Research in India* (H.K. Rakshit Ed.), pp. 195-207. Calcutta: Anthropological Survey of India.

——— 1976. Need for Research in Anthropological Demography in India, in *Physical Anthropology*, Vol. 2 (H.K. Rakshit Ed.), pp. 45-60. Calcutta: Anthropological Survey of India.

Rakshit, H.K., R.D. Singh, D.B. Sastri and S.H. Ahmad 1988. *All India Anthropometric Survey: South Zone, Basic Data.* Calcutta: Anthropological Survey of India.

Ramchandraiah, T., K. Subramaniyam, K.V. Ramalakshmi and B. Shaikshavali 1978. ABO Blood Groups in Relation to Jaundice, Filariasis and Diabetes Mellitus, in *Medical Genetics in India* 2 (I.C. Verma Ed.), pp. 241-57. Pondicherry: Auroma Enterprises.

Rami Reddy, V. 1986. *Dimensions of Anthropology (Dentition, Pathology and Crown Morphology)*, 2 Vols. Delhi: B.R. Publishing Corporation.

Rao, C.R. 1958. Differences Between the Morning and Evening Measurements of Stature, in *Race Elements in Bengal* (D.N. Majumdar and C.R. Rao), pp. 88-92. Calcutta: Indian Statistical Institute.

Rao, K.V., V. Subhadra, P.J. Reddy and T.P. Narayanan 1978. Relative Importance of Factors Affecting Body Weight in Pre-School Children as a Result of Nutritional Status, *Indian Journal of Medical Research* 68: 756-68.

Rao, P.S.S. 1984. Inbreeding in Various Religious and Social Groups in South India, in *Human Genetics and Adaptation* (K.C. Malhotra and A. Basu Eds.), pp. 15-31. Calcutta: Indian Statistical Institute.

Reddy, B.M., V.P. Chopra and K.C. Malhotra 1987. Opportunity for Natural Selection with Special Reference to Population Structural Measures Among the Vedda, *Annals of Human Biology* 14: 249-61.

Rife, D.C., 1953. Finger Prints as Criteria of Ethnic Relationship, *American Journal of Human Genetic* 5: 389-99.

Risley, H.H. 1908. *The People of India.* Calcutta: Thacker-Spink.

Roberts, D.F. 1978. *Climate and Human Variability* (Second Edition). Menlo Park: Cummings.

Roberts, D.F. and E. Coope 1972. Dermatoglyphic Variation in South Midlands, *Heredity* 29: 293-305.

Roy, K. 1983. Inheritance of Some Cephalo-Facial Anthropometric Characters, *Man in India* 63: 399-408.

Roy Chaudhury, S.K. 1975. Haemoglobin Variants and the Thalassemia in India, in *Bio-Anthropological Research in India* (H.K. Rakshit Ed.), pp. 108-14. Calcutta: Anthropological Survey of India.

Ruff, C.B. 1991. Climate, Body Size, and Body Shape in Hominid Evolution, *Journal of Human Evolution* 21: 81-105.

Sadhu, Kanan, K. 1987. *Bio-demographic Study of Kashmiris*. Delhi: Gian Publishing House.

Sarkar, D. 1976. A Dermatoglyphic Study of Four Hindu Castes of Midnapur, *Man in India* 56: 158-64.

Satyanarayana, K., N.A. Naidu, and B.S.N. Rao 1980. Adolescent Growth Spurt Among Rural Indian Boys in Relation to Their Nutritional Status in Early Childhood, *Annals of Human Biology* 7: 359-65.

Schaumann, B. and M. Alter 1976. *Dermatoglyphics in Medical Disorder*. New York-Heidelberg-Berlin: Springer Verlag.

Selvamurthy, W., S.S. Srivastava, R.K., Saxena, N. Krishnamurthy, S.C. Lakhera, C. Venkataraman, H.S. Nayar 1983. To Study the Changes in Lung Functions and Metabolic Parameters with Age and Under Different Environmental Stress, in *DGAFMS Project No. AFMRC 821/76*. New Delhi: Ministry of Defence.

Sharma, J.C. 1970. *Physical Growth and Development of Maharashtrians*. Lucknow: The Ethnographic and Folk Culture Society.

——— 1982. Individual Variations in Physical Growth and Sexual Maturity Among Punjabi Girls: a Study Based on Longitudinal Data, in *Human Biology—Recent Advances*, Vol. 1 (L.S. Sidhu, I.J.S. Bansal, Lakhbir Singh, D.P. Bhatnagar, S.K. Verma, D.K. Kanasal, J.L. Bhanot, M.S. Sohal and P. Singhal Eds.), pp. 47-54. New Delhi: Today and Tomorrow's Printers and Publishers.

Sheldon, W.H., S.S. Stevens and W.D. Tucker 1940. *Varieties of Human Physique: an Introduction to Constitutional Psychology*. New York: Harper.

Shortt, J. and Col. Ouchterlony 1868. *An Account of the Tribes of Neilgherries*. Madras: Government Press.

Sidhu, L.S., P. Singal, D.P. Bhatnagar and S. Jain 1985. Sexual Dimorphism, Physique and Body Composition of Adult Bhotia—a High Altitude Population, *Indian Anthropologist* 15: 115-26.

Singal, P. and L.S. Sidhu 1987. Age Changes in Skeletal Diameters of Two Communities of Punjab (India) from 20 to 80 Years, *Anthropologischer Anzeiger* 45: 71-8.

Singh, I.P. and M.K. Bhasin 1979. Ethnic and Geographic Frequency Distribution of Dermatoglyphic Traits in India—a Review, *Birth Defects: Original Article Series* 15 (6): 347-87.

Singh, I.P., A.K. Kapoor, and S. Kapoor 1987. Morphophysiological and Demographic Status of Western Himalayan Population, *Journal of Indian Anthropological Society* 22: 205-25.

Singh, L., and P. Malhotra 1982. Effect of Socio-Economic Factors on the Patterns of Physical Development in Girls Belonging to Different Socio-Economic Strata, in *Human Biology—Recent Advances*, Vol. 1 (L.S. Sidhu, I.J.S. Bansal, Lakhbir Singh, D.P. Bhatnagar, S.K. Verma, D.K. Kanasal, J.L. Bhanot, M.S. Sohal and P. Singhal. Eds.), pp. 221-35. New Delhi: Today and Tomorrow's Printers and Publishers.

Singh, R.D. 1963. A Note on Arch/Whorl Index as a Tool for Classifying Human Populations, *The Eastern Anthropologist* 16 (1): 28-46.

——— 1974. Problems of Techniques in Anthropometric Studies in India, *American Journal of Physical Anthropology* 40: 221-6.

——— 1978. Dermatoglyphic Variations in Four Castes of Uttar Pradesh, India, *Human Biology* 50 (3): 251-60.

——— 1982. Digital Ridge-count Variations in some Castes of India, *Progress in Clinical and Biological Research* (Bartsokas Ed.) 84: 303-15.

——— 1985. Physical Anthropology in India, *Physical Anthropology News* 4 (2): 1-4. New York.

——— 1986. Physical Anthropology in India, *Physical Anthropology News* 5 (1): 16-19. New York.

——— 1987. Anthropometry in India: Some Aspects, in *Anthropological Perspectives* (K.S. Mathur, U.S. Misra, V.N. Misra, B.R.K. Shukla, R.D. Singh, P.K. Tewari and D. Tyagi Eds.), pp. 1-19. Lucknow: The Ethnographic and Folk Culture Society.

Singh, R.D. and R.B. Bhale 1964. A Study of Stature and Weight—I (The Dubla, the Gamit and the Naika of Gujarat), *The Eastern Anthropologist* 17: 10-18.

Singh, R.D. and D. Tyagi 1997. Biswas, Profulla Chandra (1903-1984), in *History of Physical Anthropology: an Encyclopedia*, Vol.1 (Frank Spencer Ed.), pp. 179-80. New York.

Sirajuddin, S.M. 1977. Blood Groups A_1A_2BO, MN, Rh(D), PTC and Colour Blindness Studies Among Chenchus of Andhra Pradesh, *Anthropologist* 24: 1-20.

Sirajuddin, S.M., S.H. Ahmad and R.D. Singh 1992. *All India Anthropometric Survey: South Zone, Karnataka State*. Nagpur: Anthropological Survey of India.

Sreenath, J. and S.H. Ahmad 1989. *All India Anthropometric Survey: South Zone, Andhra Pradesh*. Nagpur: Anthropological Survey of India.

Steggerda, M. 1942. Anthropometry of the Living: a Study on Checking of Techniques, *Anthropological Briefs* 2: 7-15.

Thurston, E. 1909. *Castes and Tribes of Southern India*, Vol. 1. Madras: Government Press.

Tilak, Bal Gangadhar 1955 (1893). *The Orion, or Researches into the Antiquities of the Vedas*. Poona: Tilak Brothers.

Washburn, S.L. 1951. The New Physical Anthropology, *Transactions of New York Academy of Science* 13: 298-304.

Weiner, J.S. 1954. Nose Shape and Climate, *American Journal of Physical Anthropology* 12: 615-18.

Weiss, M.L. and A.E. Mann 1990. *Human Biology and Behavior: an Anthropological Perspective*. Glenview, Illinois and London, England: Scott, Foresman/Little-Brown.

Weitz, C.A. 1984. Biocultural Adaptations of the High Altitude Sherpas of Nepal, in *The People of South Asia* (J.R. Lukacs Ed.), pp. 387-420. New York: Plenum Press.

Wilson, E.O. 1998. Back From Chaos, *The Atlantic Monthly* (March): 41-62.

Hunter-Gatherer Studies in India: a Review

ALETHA TAVARES

INTRODUCTION

The impetus to tribal research was first felt in Bengal in the latter part of the eigteenth century. Over a period spanning nearly three centuries, much information has been generated, a close scrutiny of which reveals gradual changes in research focus and methodology. There has always been a thin ambiguous dividing line of research on tribes between the disciplines of sociology and social and cultural anthropology. It has thus been a rather difficult task on the part of this author to do full justice to bring to the reader the trends that have occurred and affected research on hunter-gatherers during the past 50 years of India's Independence.

The number of academic journals that deal with tribal studies especially among anthropologists is large. Moreover, these journals, for instance, *Man in India, Indian Anthropologist, The Eastern Anthropologist, Journal of the Indian Anthropological Society, The Journal of Anthropological Survey of India, Man and Environment*, etc., cover a wide range of topics from cultural, social, and physical aspects of all sections of societies and communities and not just the tribals. Compiling information on all tribals in general and hunting-gatherer tribes in particular is a for midable task (not all libraries are known to stock books or journals that could provide regional information). One of the main problems faced by this author is in distinguishing the hunting-gatherer tribes from other tribes that have been well documented and well known. Further, many tribal communities known in the past as hunter-gatherers are today transformed or are in the process of transition to a different occupation, economic subsistence or lifestyle. Moreover, the census figures of tribal communities practising a hunting-gathering lifestyle have never been shown to depict a coherent picture.

One main problem is the ambiguous tribe-caste continuum that makes research focus on tribal communities through time difficult to adhere to. Secondly, very few researches based on a perusal of literature on hunter-gatherer studies present a historical introduction to the tribal community undertaken for research. The hunting-gathering tribe of yesteryear may not necessarily be the same today. With this and several other constraints, in trying to gather and view research trends on hunter-gatherers, the author has tried at a very primary level to highlight the general trends affecting studies on hunter-gatherers, without necessarily specifying any case study on a hunter-gather group. However, it is of vital importance that data on hunter-gatherer tribes should be noted and compiled every few years, so that any student wishing to understand the nature of humans and desirous of knowing which tribe practices hunting-gathering (or any other subsistence method) as a lifestyle, will have a ready reckoner and also information that will at a glance focus on tribes that have transformed or in the process of transformation to a different lifestyle.

Studies on hunter-gatherers have offered researchers a glimpse of past human life in its most primitive state. Most studies of the past have emphasized the cultural and social aspects and these have served as 'yardsticks against which the developments of other more culturally evolved and highly accomplished peoples can be compared' (Bettinger 1991: 2).

WORLDVIEW: STUDIES ON HUNTER-GATHERERS

Early studies on hunter-gatherers were done explicitly to establish a unilinear evolutionary stage of development of human society. Hunter-gatherers have been described and spoken of as 'primitive', 'savage', 'uncivilized', 'undeveloped', 'backward', etc. It was Lubbock in 1872 who had advocated that contemporary hunter-gatherers be used as models of early human society, and Darwin employed his methodology and forwarded a view that the 'primitive people' in certain respects bridged the gap between modern peoples and their closest animal relatives (Bettinger 1991). The archaeological finds in the early eighteenth century were a further impetus for studying 'primitive cultures', who employ a very simple tool technology, live in a forest and utilize the products of the forest for their daily subsistence. The theory that humans progressed from barbarism to savagery to civilisation, advocated by Morgan in 1877 (and later in 1962 by Service), states that 'individual cultures advanced through a well-defined series of stages from band to tribe to chiefdom to state' and justifies the unilinear development of society and the 'primitiveness' of the hunting-gathering way of life (Bettinger 1991: 4).

During the later nineteenth century studies were 'mainly concerned with prehistoric peoples and their cultures, contemporary nonliterates, and the many varieties of non-European cultural traditions. Their objectives . . . were to discover from such studies the psychological laws that underlay and determined human history' (Beals and Hoijer 1970: 16).

During the 1960s and 1970s the concepts of adaptation and homeostasis weaved themselves into the studies on hunter-gatherers and thus was introduced the culture-ecology model. The very concepts of culture underwent a change from the mere listing of static traits to the understanding of the dynamic processes that produced these traits that were tangible to the naked eye. This was also the result of certain methodological changes that affected the discipline of archaeology which is closely allied to anthropology especially in the Western countries. The discipline of archaeology had moved away from the culture-history phase, where identification of cultures and its history was the necessary prerequisite to further excavations, to the questions of 'why' and 'what' prompted changes in culture. Thus 'cultural particularism' gave way to 'ecological functionalism'. Although the evolutionary scheme was still adhered to understand the transition from hunting-gathering to agriculture, the emphasis was not just an observational reference but on the need to know 'why', 'when' and 'how'. Change was sought not as an external factor but within the system itself in accordance with its ecological balance. This led to the entry of archaeologists making forays into the anthropological studies on hunter-gatherers.

Ethnoarchaeology, was on off shout that emerged from this interaction. It was different from ethnography, which studied, observed and recorded, all aspects of a hunter-gatherer community. The basis of ethnoarchaeology arose from problems encountered in the archaeological record, the need to understand the presence of certain artefactual remains, and the processes that influence them, culturally or environmentally. Ethnoarchaeology was the tool to transform the 'static' archaeological record into a 'dynamic' picture. Thus, since the late 1970s archaeologists have taken to studying hunter-gatherers in a more holistic way with a broader perspective to understanding the change that is observed in their lives. Hunter-gatherer studies today lay stress on the economy and diet, their demography and relating their cultural practices to more meaningful aspects of their environmental surroundings. They are no longer viewed as representing 'an antique stage of human culture'. The studies on their subsistence itself has led to further classifying them based on their economic activities. They are either nomadic or settled hunter-gatherers, they practice big game or small game hunting or are either foragers or collectors, and this is dependent on the variability in the quality and seasonal distribution of resources at their disposal (Binford 1980).

Hunter-gatherer studies in archaeology today are influenced by the model developed by Binford where the availability of natural resources is seen to lead to innumerable combinations of social, economic and settlement organization. However, behind these studies is the essential need in archaeology to understand the processes that produce the archaeological record. In the West, especially in America, 'archaeology has been brought into the broader fold of anthropology' (Bettinger 1991: 215). However, this is not the case in India, where not only anthropology and archaeology are observed as distinct disciplines but, within the field of anthropology itself there is segregation, which in itself is seen to inhibit a cohesive and interactive field of study.

TRIBAL STUDIES IN INDIA

The tribal communities found in most of the states of India cover nearly 8 per cent of India's total population. Nearly 80 per cent of the tribals live in the central zone, 12 per cent in the north-eastern zone and the rest in the southern zone (Rao 1996). However, the number of tribes pursuing the hunting-gathering economic subsistence is minimal and confined to southern India, especially to the states of Tamil Nadu and Kerala. Broadly speaking the tribes of north-eastern India follow shifting hill cultivation, those of central and western zones are engaged in cultivation and the economy of a number of tribes of southern regions is based on food gathering. However, categorizing tribal populations on the basis of their economic strategies is a little risky. The most important aspect of tribal economy is that, they rarely depend exclusively on one occupation and usually follow subsidiary occupations, like handicrafts, gathering and labour work (Chaudhuri 1997).

The Early Phase of Hunter-Gatherer Studies

Before the onset of the British administration, there was plenty of literature describing the various customs and beliefs and lifestyles of the so called 'primitive' people of India (see Crooke 1921; Roy 1921; Iyer and Bala Ratnam 1961; Kochar 1970). The term 'primitive' has a long history, and according to Bettinger in its traditional sense denotes

> . . . an evolutionary stage of development and identify peoples whose technologies, organisations and cultures are relatively speaking, 'undeveloped', peoples whose support is dependent on relatively simple tools and strategies—most often lacking benefit of either metal tools or domesticated plants or animals—and whose activities are organized around small local groups that are more or less economically, socially, and politically autonomous. (Bettinger 1991: 2)

Till then not much had been known about the tribal people who lived in the forests or fringes of settled villages.

From the early 1930s to the 1950s research on the tribal communities constituted a descriptive and informative data on the various tribes that many anthropologists or ethnographers worked on. Several physical anthropological studies were carried out in these three decades on bio-genetic features of various tribes in order to determine their racial composition and history which led to identifying various 'racial' groups (see Iyer and Bala Ratnam 1961 for a listing of literature on such studies in the early phase). Besides racial categorization, tribal communities were also divided and studied based on their language affiliations to each other (see Fuchs 1973, for more details).

Most of these studies were descriptive and isolated in nature and carried out without any specific research goal in mind. However, there were a few comparative studies where attempts were made to determine impacts of biological or cultural relations with neighbouring tribal/caste groups (see Jha 1995). Differences or similarities between two tribes of similar regions were used to put forward propositions on 'fusion' or 'fission'. Tribal geographical zones were also introduced into anthropological studies during the 1950s, wherein a listing of the tribes according to their area of occupation was mentioned (see Jha 1995: 34-7). Another noteworthy area of research that was explored during this period was the demographic profile of the various tribal communities spread over the different geographical zones in India (Mamoria 1957), which was only later taken up in the late 1980s (for instance, see Francis 1988). Elwin, a noted anthropologist, took deep interest in the plight of the 'primitive' tribes of India and espoused their cause later in life. His early works are a general documentation of the various tribal communities. But it should be borne in mind that these works are not to be discarded as mere descriptive documentary information. Instead they provide us with insights into tribal lifestyles that are eroding at a very rapid speed.

Majumdar (Jha 1995: 72) identified three phases that led to the development of anthropology, the Formulatory Phase (1774-1911), Constructive (1912-37) and the Critical Phase from 1936 onwards. But L.R. Vidyarthi (Jha 1995: 101) differed in his assessment of the phases of anthropology and suggested that the Third Phase be known as the Analytical Phase beginning when India got her Independence. This phase was seen as analytical based on the exchange of ideas with the West that influenced Indian methodological framework in the field of anthropology. Bera (1995) while reviewing the status of anthropology today, has proposed four phases through which the development of Anthropology can be viewed. The first two phases hold good with the others, while the third phase he refers to as the Empirical phase (1946-78) which is followed by the fourth phase, the Developmental phase (1978-onwards). It was during the time which Vidyarthi formulated his phases, that the concepts of culture ecology, adaptation and homeostasis slowly began to influence anthropological studies on hunter-gatherers in the West. However, in India, the impact had not yet begun to be felt in anthropological studies of hunter-gatherers. The hunting-gathering community were not studied with the prime interest to understand them as an economic unit influenced by its ecological niche. There does not appear to be much work done on whether the ecological niche occupied by them influenced their movements to different areas within a specific territory or not, whether their foraging or gathering techniques, or their nomadic or settled existence, was environmentally induced. No studies explicitly portrayed the different aspects or units of culture of this community being a factor that influenced change or adaptation. The analysis was more of a culture-history documentation, providing information to substantiate the social and physiological development of the more village and urban population, pointing to an 'ethnic continuum' that existed.

Two models appear to have shaped the studies on hunter-gatherers, the Developmental model and the Ecological model. The Developmental model views the hunter-gatherers as primitives. It is derived from the proposition that culture develops from less to more advanced forms and that technology and subsistence are basic to this development. At the centre of this model is the concept of progressive social evolution. This was the more European view that was catered to. The Ecological model viewed the hunter-gatherers in harmony with the environment. This model borrowed heavily from biological and ecological theories. Fundamental to this theory were the concepts of adaptation and homeostasis. Here culture was viewed as being initiated in response to change and evolved as adaptive systems in equilibrium. The concept of primitiveness in this framework was no longer applied (Bettinger 1991).

With respect to Indian anthropological studies on hunter-gatherers, the Developmental model according to this author is seen to apply to the studies during the 1950s on Indian hunter-gatherers, while the ecological model was operative since 1960-70.

Hunter-Gatherer Studies During 1960-80

Adoption of the Ecological Model in hunter-gatherer studies during the 1960s changed the research orientations drastically. Tribes (and more specifically, hunter-gatherers) were no longer seen to be a past extension of contemporary society. They were studied with a keen understanding to know how they operate within the given landscape and that change need not be an external factor but a factor from within the restraints imposed by the community itself.

One of the major works that marked new developments in the anthropological research methodology was Vidyarthi's novel methodological approach to the study of the Maler tribe based on the 'Nature-Man-Spirit-Complex' (Vidyarthi 1963). This approach was in tune with the ecological model developed in the West, but with a difference, the factor of religion and its relationship with nature and man also being accounted for. Tribal classification based on racial elements or linguistic affiliations were no longer the prime focus of anthropologists. With the ecological methodological approach to the study of 'primitive' people, tribals were now classified based on their economic life. The geographical areas into which tribes had been assigned and compared had already been studied (Jha 1995: 34). Again it was Vidyarthi who proposed the eight-fold classification of the tribes in India based on their economic lifestyles. There were other anthropologists before him who had attempted such classifications but Vidyarthi's classification not only amalgamated their work but also introduced certain other classifications, for instance the folk artists who sang and performed their dances, based on the changes that had led to the creation of new classes among the tribal population (Jha 1995: 36). This was based on the changes that affected certain tribal communities due to interaction with the urban communities and the pressure that inevitably forced them to change their lifestyle or occupation as the demands in the socio-economic urban sector seemed to create an imbalance in the relationships they had earlier enjoyed.

Stephen Fuchs who authored *The Aboriginal Tribes of India* in 1973, states in his preface that, 'It is strange that up to the present time no anthropologist has attempted a complete survey and description of the aboriginal population of India'. He attempted to group them according to their 'standard of culture, or occupation, or racial origin' which he found an impossible venture to undertake. He even tried to group them geographically and found that it could not be followed up 'too rigidly'. Unfortunately, till today no anthropologist has ever attempted to update this information. Many of the food-gathering and hunting tribes have undergone much change and have been pulled into the mainstream of India or retreated farther into the interiors (see Upali 1994; Singh 1996). Very few have still been able to preserve their identities, and have maintained a stoic isolation, like the Jarawas and Sentinelese of Andaman Islands. A classic example of how change is being wrought and the hunting-gathering community is being weaned away from the life they have always known is a perusal of literature written on the Onges of the Andamans (see Kulkarni 1987).

Kochar (1970: 228) in an article examining the status of ethnographic research in India referred to the 1950s as an era in which no attempt was made in the books, articles or monographs written, to analyse 'the customs in terms of inter-relationship or function of components. The only theoretical frame which was implicit in these studies was the evolutionary search for survival of archaic customs . . . the other was of cultural or racial origins and affiliations of the tribes'. But, he described the period after the 1950s as a phase where '. . . a new kind of data was collected such as quantitative data by census and genealogical method and data on cultural contact and change . . . and a sporadic evidence of structural-functional analysis'. The aim of this article was to help those interested in the research of social anthropology, especially tribal studies, to focus their research and make such studies more cognisant as compared to studies carried out in isolation with no perspective or goal in mind. His aim was 'to develop a set of priorities so that even a limited number of studies may fruitfully contribute towards cumulative understanding of Indian society' (Kochar 1970: 224). He further states that, '. . . the aim of modern ethnography is not mere description but analytical description for specific understanding' (Kochar 1970: 229). He has not only critically evaluated the past work done, but based on the problems and the Indian scenario with which anthropology is affected, he introduced the 'situational model' upon the lines which ethnographers working with the different tribes across the geographical landscape and the diversity that met the eye could employ in their research methodology.

Post 1980 Hunter-Gatherer Studies

With the introduction of the study of 'primitive' cultures in the discipline of archaeology as a basis to the understanding of cultural processes affecting past societies, a whole new dimension of looking at the tribal population emerged. This sort of work by archaeologists, which goes by the name of 'ethnoarchaeology', should have brought forward an interdisciplinary approach to the study of hunting-gathering populations. Instead, in India, there is a major hiatus between the anthropologists and the archaeologists who study hunting-gathering communities.

In 1981, less than a decade later after the attemptive encyclopaedic work by Fuchs, the Department of Anthropology in Ranchi published a series of books, to provide a 'short but scholarly treatment of key problem areas in anthropology' (see Mann 1981). One of the series introduced the 'Nature-Man-Spirit-Complex in Tribal India' concept that had been developed by Vidyarthi in his study of the Maler tribe (Vidyarthi 1963). This last of the series, attempts to provide the reader a deep insight into tribal life and culture by highlighting how nature is the provider to man's needs and which governs social and religious beliefs that arise out of human interaction with the environment.

Another interesting book that depicts a slight moving away from the traditional explanations and understanding of tribal cultural units is Pandya's study on the Onges of the Andamans (Pandya 1993). He presents here a holistic view of the cultural content and concepts of the cosmological structures and hierarchical systems of the Onges and attempts to understand the movement and the traditional painting of the bodies of the Onges not merely in terms of environment but as their beliefs.

Slowly but steadily a change in the methodology and study of the tribes is undergoing a metamorphosis. New ways of looking at the different tribal aspects that are interdependent on each other is slowly being introduced in anthropological research despite the plea which had been made by W.V. Grigson in 1938 that, 'a culture should be understood as a cohering entity' (Iyer and Bala Ratnam 1961: 63) and is seeing the light today, albeit in a new perspective within the changing methodologies that have been affecting anthropology since its inception.

A review of journals which span the research studies carried out in the various fields of anthropology, produced only a handful of articles on hunting-gathering tribes. Most of the information on tribes centres around their process of assimilation into the Indian mainstream of urban life and the various benefits or disadvantages that they face under the Government Acts. Tribal welfare in the Indian administration was (see Crooke 1921; Roy 1941) and today (see Bera 1995) is the top agenda by most anthropologists studying the tribes and the discussions on the best way for their assimilation. A few that still try to study them without the political emphasis, are summary notes noting the changes in their material culture. Very rarely does one find research articles, books or monographs by anthropologists who study the few hunting-gathering tribes within a historical perspective. Analytical descriptions are few and observations highlighting those changes affecting the community, either as an external factor or an internal factor that wrought such changes, are negligible. Nutritional and health studies are carried out not to determine their status but to 'upgrade' their lifestyles. Observations on diet that is not natural to their lifestyle but introduced to them and its effect on their social customs, their physiology, and even cultural taboos and religion are never clearly analysed. All these have necessarily influenced several aspects of their daily life but anthropological documentation of this is totally negligible. Instead, a series of articles and books by ethnoarchaeologists trying to understand the dynamics of past communities that practises the hunting-gathering lifestyles is more prominent.

Problems to be Tackled

Studies on tribals today have undergone a change. A great deal of information on them is being generated with a view to understanding them and highlight their political rights. We seem to have come a full circle regarding the studies done on the tribals, especially those who have retreated even farther into the interiors and who shy away from being assimilated into the mainstream of the country. Their role in the Indian administration is still a vital topic today, as it was when the British administration decided to administer the Indian territory in the early part of their rule, but the aims and goals were very different. The studies carried out in the early days are, however, not to be relegated to dusty shelves. Instead, they offer valuable documentation, especially when documenting tribes undergoing transformation or under the process of transition to a life different from that lived by their ancestors. But, with changed perspectives, methodologies and attitudes towards the most 'basic' and 'ancient' of subsistence patterns, a need to document them and a solid framework within which studies on them can be carried out is a necessary prerequisite. Below is listed certain points that need to be taken into consideration particularly when hunter-gatherers are studied.

A review of all tribes needs to be undertaken and classified depending on their economic sustenance. This exercise is specially important in understanding the hunting-gathering groups as many of them no longer practise their traditional occupation(s), yet they are still referred to as hunter-gatherers. Because of the increasing contacts with the urbanized world and/or because of the depletion of forest resources and wildlife in recent times all food-gatherers are on the decline and dwindling in numbers. According to Singh,

> (only) about 1/10th of the communities have pursued hunting and gathering as their traditional occupation. About $^1/_2$ of such groups have ceased to be hunters and gatherers because of the depletion of forest resources and wild life. (Singh 1996: 83)

Terminology used while classifying a population is often loosely employed. Therefore, usage of many of the terms like, hunters, gatherers, foragers, collectors, etc., needs to be reviewed and standardized. Moreover, when it comes to classifying human society as hunting, gathering, and pastoral nomads, Burman cites Pathy, who is of the opinion that,

> although the underlying assumption is that the predominant occupation generates specific forms of social relations and its ideological underpinnings and world view . . . this line of thinking does not take care of the relationship with nature and of the total socio-political milieu in which a particular occupation exists. (Burman 1997: 18)

Articles, books or monographs or any fieldwork undertaken should at the onset of their work define explicitly, and lucidly outline widely the concepts, framework, methodology, and approach employed for carrying out research.

Fresh assessment of the tribal populations would assist in economic and other administrative benefits to these segments. The urge to wander and retain the traditional hunting-gathering way of life as seen in some populations was often misunderstood by the then British Government and more surprisingly, the misconception continues even today, at least partially. The British Administration branded such groups as 'Criminal Tribes and Castes'. However, some exceptions were made for certain food-gatherers. The reason as cited by Fuchs (1979: 46) was '. . . because they lived predominantly in 'tribal areas', where their food-gathering activity created less disturbance in the life of the settled population (!)'.

Journals incorporating anthropological research articles should be more streamlined and should insist on review articles every 5 years. A compilation of articles listing topics of research along with an exhaustive bibliography should be introduced. Looking for information on hunting-gathering tribes for instance was (according to this author) like searching a needle in a haystack. Books containing a comprehensive listing of tribes and particularly those practising the hunting-gathering subsistence belong to the 70s. A compilation of such information that provides a database, updated every 5 years, is therefore a pre-requisite for a meaningful research, for it would help avoid duplication or repetition of information.

Research studies by anthropologists on hunter-gatherers are still carried out in isolation and are mere reports on the changes that have occurred to them in terms of dress or other material artefacts and highlighting their political rights. What needs to be really documented with in-depth analysis is how their interaction with neighbouring groups or the changes in the ecosystem have affected their lifestyle, especially their customs and taboos, their kinship ties, their inter- and intra-group social interactions, their technology and skills, their trade, and their knowledge of the environment. This sort of academic exercise would help formulate administrative policies. For example, tribal socio-cultural life is intimately connected with forest ecology and is reflected in the rituals performed. Different plants are often used for specific rituals. Many species in nature are protected from random exploitation as tribals traditionally protect them. In the Report of the Roy Burman Committee on Forest and Tribals, it has been noted that,

> It has been possible for the tribal community to subsist for generations with a reasonable standard of health as the forest provided their food such as fruits, tubers, leafy vegetables, shoots, honey, flowers, juices, grass, game, fish, etc. (Chaudhari 1997)

Medicinal herbs and plants which they have used for treatment of diseases and maintaining health are today the sources of modern medicine. The different Forest Acts restricting the use and exploitation of forest resources are adversely affecting the health and treatment in tribal societies.

No literature cites the declining per cent of these communities. Nowhere is found any comparative literature of such communities occupying different ecological niches yet practising a 'self- efficient' economy. A work that can form a sort of guidelines is the one written by Carleton Coon (1972), who takes up each facet of such communities and introduces the reader to a variety of hunting-gathering communities across the globe, thus highlighting their similarities and yet their differences, and still gathered together under the one umbrella term 'hunter-gatherers'.

Most studies of contemporary hunter-gatherers depict them as the product of a long and timeless past. While no one holds that they are living fossils, their present existence is often explained in terms of extreme isolation. They are assumed to have existed far beyond the reach of farmers, traders and so are thought to retain in their present existence aspects of a distant past that illuminates the evolutionary history of all people (Bettinger 1991: 2). This attitude is slowly undergoing a change and the hunting-gathering lifestyle is now being viewed not as a 'primitive' way of living but viewed as 'a balanced way of living in harmony with nature'. Anthropologists conducting research on hunting-gathering communities need to interact more with archaeologists and thus contribute more fruitfully to the understanding of complexity of the Indian society.

Haimendorf had stated in 1950 that,

> there is a wide field for the Indian anthropologist and if by objective and scientific study of social processes he can help in bridging the gap between the various communities and races he will have done work of national importance. (Danda 1996: 208)

Bettinger in his book states that:

> . . . in response to direct encounters with primitive peoples, many of them hunter-gatherers, that anthropology itself arose. It was hunter-gatherers that prompted the philosophical inquiries and provided the subject matter out of which were built some of the more influential theories of adaptation and evolution in other disciplines. (Bettinger 1991: 2)

Instead of valuing the benefits that studies on hunter-gatherers have provided to disciplines like anthropology and archaeology and even to the discipline of medicine, we tend to treat these fast disappearing ways of life very lightly. A blend rather than trying to force them or draw the hunter-gatherers into today's life would be our way of respecting them and their way of choosing to live with the bare minimum. Singh is of the opinion that,

> There has been a demystification of a kind, a discarding of the traditional way of looking at tribal situation and of existing stereotypes and paradigms; there is a great deal of freshness in analysis and understanding which gives hope.

He further adds, 'In fact every crisis situation tends to accentuate tribal identity instead of destroying it' (Singh 1989: 96-8).

ACKNOWLEDGEMENTS

I would like to thank the Deccan College Library staff for making available to me the vast amount of information that has aided in the preparation of this article. I am also grateful to Dr. S.R. Walimbe for patiently reading this work, and providing me insights and clues to dig up and scan through the pages of journals and books on information pertaining to hunter-gatherers, especially worked upon by anthropologists.

REFERENCES

Beals, R.L. and H. Hoijer 1970. *An Introduction to Anthropology*. London: Collier-Macmillan Ltd.

Bera, G.K. 1995. Development of Indian Anthropology: a Reappraisal, *Journal of Indian Anthropological Society* 30: 229-36.

Bettinger, R.L. 1991. *Hunter-Gatherers: Archaeological and Evolutionary Theory*. New York: Plenum Press.

Binford, L.R. 1980. Willow Smoke and Dogs' Tails: Hunter-Gatherer Settlement Systems and Archaeological Site Formation, *American Antiquity* 45 (1): 4-20.

Burman, B.K.R. 1997. Tribal and Indigenous People: a Global Overview, *The Eastern Anthropologist* 50 (1): 17-25.

Chaudhuri, B. 1997. Forest and Tribals, in *Contemporary Society: Tribal Studies*, Vol. 1: *Structure and Process* (Georg Pfeffer and D.K. Behera Eds.), pp. 231-47. New Delhi: Concept Publishing Company.

Coon, C. 1972. *The Hunting Peoples*. London: Jonathan Cape Thirty.

Crooke, W 1921. A Suggested Programme for Anthropological Investigations in India, *Man in India* 1 (1): 1-5.

Danda, A. 1996. Anthropology in India: in Retrospect and Prospect, *Journal of Anthropological Society* 31: 205-15.

Francis, R. 1988. Tribal Demography of Kerala, *Human Science* 37: 34-42.

Fuchs, S. 1973. *The Aboriginal Tribes of India*. New Delhi: Macmillan.

Haimendorf-F., C.V. 1982. *Tribes of India: the Struggle for Survival*. New Delhi: Oxford University Press.

Jha, M. 1995. *An Introduction to Indian Anthropology*. New Delhi: Vikas Publishing House.

Kochar, V.K. 1970. Strategy and Framework for Ethnographic Research in India, in *Research Programmes on Cultural Anthropology and Allied Disciplines* (S.C. Sinha Ed.), pp. 223-71. Calcutta: Anthropological Survey of India.

Kulkarni, S.M. 1987. Andaman and Nicobar Islands—Bibliography of Recent Literature (Period Covered 1975-86), *Human Science* 36: 300-9.

Mamoria, C.B. 1957. *Tribal Demography in India*. Allahabad: Kitab Mahal.

Mann, R.S. (Ed.) 1981. *Nature-Man-Spirit Complex in Tribal India*. Ranchi Anthropological Series 3. New Delhi: Concept Publishing Company.

Morris, B. 1982. *Forest Traders: a Socio-Economic Study of the Hill Pandaram* (London School of Economics). Monographs on Social Anthropology 55. New Jersey: Athelone Press.

Pandya, V. 1993. *Above the Forest: a Study of Andamanese Ethnoanemology, Cosmology and the Power of Ritual*. New Delhi: Oxford University Press.

Rao, M.K 1996. Perspectives of Tribal Culture with Special Reference to Tribal Community of Andhra, *The Eastern Anthropologist* 49 (2): 101-201.

Roy, S.C. 1921. Anthropological Research in India, *Man in India* 1 (1): 11-55.

——— 1941. Editorial Note, *Man in India*: 247.

Singh, K.S. 1989. Tribal Realm: a Geographical Perspective, *Human Science* 38 (2): 95-101.

Singh, K.S. (Ed.) 1996. *Identity, Ecology, Social Organization, Economics, Linkages and Development Process: a Quantitative Profile. People of India—National Series*, Vol. VII. New Delhi: Oxford University Press.

Upali, A. 1994. Multi-level Analysis for Integrated Resource Planning: a Case Study of the Juangs (Keonjhar District of Orissa), *The Journal of Anthropological Survey of India* 43: 87-100.

Vidyarthi, L.P. 1963. *The Maler*. Calcutta: Bookland (P) Ltd.

Agro-Pastoralism in Contemporary Ethnography: Its Relevance in Explanation of Archaeological Material in India

D.K. BHATTACHARYA and DEEPRA BHATTACHARYA

Man has probably had close enough relationship with animals from as early as 20,000 BP. The numerous archaeological evidences from northern flat land of Europe yielding Hamburgian, Ahrensburgian and Feddermesser culture demonstrates the close man-reindeer relationship (Swabidissen 1954). Whether such relationship can be qualified as domestication is difficult to prove. However, the narrowing down of man's association with a single animal species is significant enough to hypothesize a possible stage which might in course of time develop into animal husbandry. Nearer home, at Catal Huyuk in Turkey (Mellaart 1961) a seventh millennium BC evidence of shrines with animal skulls and horns also shows the persistence of this close relationship. Although at this site, instead of reindeers ibex and other Capra species were chosen. Argissa-Meghula in Greek Thessaly (7000 BC), Starcevo near Belgrade (5800 BC) and finally the important discoveries from Zagros region in Iraq shows a progressively increasing emphasis being given to such domesticates as sheep, goat, pig and cattle.

It is possible that between the third and fourth millennium BC a segment of population in various parts of the world started shifting a major component of their subsistence emphasis on livestock production and thus laid down the foundation of what can be designated as pastoral economy. It is reasonably certain that chronologically such a development could not have emerged before agriculture although culturally there may be some evidence of a hunter-gatherer having slowly evolved into pastoral culture (Crank 1989). Since there is hardly any pure pastoral group known today who does not consume cereals for themselves, one can assume the possibility of a regular symbiotic relation of these communities with neighbouring agricultural groups. Consequently it may not be entirely incorrect to assume that agriculture preceded pastoral economy. However, what is important here is to work out the possible reasons of such a choice made by one segment of a population when the other segment goes for settled village life. For understanding this one needs to study the contemporary pastoral societies and thereby develop a differential pattern of cultural imperatives operative in these two kinds of communities.

Natural curiosity led many early travellers to note these communities and some of their salient cultural features. One of the earliest such works was published from Paris in 1787 by C.F.C. Valoney. The next century saw several such isolated societies of pastorals from Arabia and Africa being reported (Bruckhardt 1831; Duveyrier 1864; Palgrave 1867; Crozals 1883; Rebertson-Smith 1885; Doughty 1888; Hatt 1919 and Jacob 1975). A proper anthropological study on pastoral societies was first attempted by Evans-Pritchard (1940), and this led the way to a thorough investigation of man-animal-society-ecology relationship.

Once most of the travel accounts and some ethnographies from these communities were available, anthropologists tried to develop a suitable definition of pastoral economy which can satisfy the chief socio-economic characters of all societies practicing pastoralism. Unfortunately no such definition was found satisfactory. Consequently it was felt that the term pastoralism probably involves clubbing together of essentially diverse patterns under a single economic category. The UNESCO undertook (1959) the task of listing the nomadic communities and their individual socio-economic features. Federick Barth (1961, 1963) launched an intensive study of a selected group of nomads in south Persia and Afghanistan. Subsequently William Irons and Neville Dyson-Hudson (1972) edited a volume of empirical studies on individual nomadic communities.

These studies of the sixties and seventies are more intensive and address very specific areas of interaction. Yet we seem to be still unable to develop a uniform model of relationship of subsistence to society in these societies. It is not surprising, therefore, that some authors started working on typologies of pastoralism while others concentrated on the taxonomy of the working of the economy. As a result of this the opinions about the pastoral societies also show a great deal of diversity. While one group of scholars thought of them as feudal and the other group took them to be entirely individual family based in production strategy. Khazanov (1984) published a huge compendium of the pastorals from the regions of Eurasia, the Middle East and Africa and tried to develop a comparative evaluation of the various pastoral societies.

Notwithstanding the various criticisms raised against attempts at typological classifications (Sahlins 1961; Meillassoux 1978; Ingold 1985) we might look into the alternatives operative in a pastoral society. Both agriculturists as also pastoralists depend on production from land and water as resource base. The agriculturists manipulate the land and take its products directly and hence is the primary consumer, while pastoralists graze animals on the land produce and take the animals so sustained as his resource base. Hence he is a secondary consumer. The land manipulation requires sedentism as also social and ideological regulatory mechanism. This social input is of cardinal importance because besides regulation regarding storing and redistribution of the produce one has to create laws of inheritance of the source of produce, i.e. the land. Unlike land, which is non-elastic, as resource base number of animals possessed is elastic and can take the risk of fission every generation because soon they can multiply themselves and become equal to the parental stock before fission. Naturally rigorous mechanisms of inheritance of the resource base necessary for a settled agricultural community would seem to be much more relaxed in the pastorals. The total number of animals possessed may be like a capital for a family but it cannot go on increasing the number of animals beyond a limit. Because this will require mounting labour investment as also requirement of good pasturage. An implicit manner of a 'primitive banking' mechanism works in this system and it is also of tremendous benefit for animal breeder. Because any family can dispose of excessive animals at a premium during crisis but the stock has the ability to regenerate itself within a year. These advantages of pastoral economy tends to make them much more individualistic than what an agriculturist can really afford. One of the biggest problems the pastorals face within this relaxed kinship structure, therefore, is mounting need of labour which can no longer be harnessed with kinship obligations. Further, constant requirement of additional pasture land makes it imperative for them to be always moving from one area to another. Consequently, such groups has to come across other settled communities and it becomes important that reasonably good relations with them is maintained. Further, the ever increasing lineages can create a competition for limited availability of pastures in course of time. As such, management of pastures takes up a very important role in their social structure. In most of the pastorals this has given rise to communal pasture land and a strictly maintained regulation about who uses it and how the seasonal rights are rotated. Family ownership of animals is a centripetal force of interest while bending down to communal regulation is a centrefugal force of interest. Evans-Pritchard (1940) argued a specific social system evolved to handle this situation. He called this the segmentary lineage system, and demonstrated how it functions among the Nuer pastorals in Sudan (Fig.1). Subsequently this form of organization was taken as providing a general model of functioning in many 'stateless societies' (Bonte 1978, 1979). Stated in simple manner this form of society pays heavy emphasis on agnatic descent. That is, two brothers can form their individual and separate groups which in course of time can form two territorial groups. Although these lineage segments and territorial groups are genealogically defined, such segmentation may not occur in every generation. The economic group is allowed to maintain all the brothers within one segment to seek their labour in maintaining the animals until an economic stress arises. Segmentation can occur at this phase but a series of obligatory rights control the relations between the junior and the senior lineages. Thus, this built-in tendency of internal disequilibrium is continuously manipulated by creating fission and fusion of the segments at convenience. Since senior members in any lineage are closer to the ancestors they are given a higher ritualistic status and this brings in a political power for this person and his lineage at a subsequent stage of fission. This political power can be harnessed to set out rules for communal pastures and their manner of use. There is always a greater degree of mobility from the junior members to the senior members within a lineage and between two lineages at the level of the seniors there is a obligatory traffic of goods as well as power to negotiate for mates for their respective lineage members (Fig. 2).

Apparently this pattern of social organization may not always be operative unless the territorial groups maintain a manageable space between them. An unmanageable distance can destroy the sense of unity among kinsmen. This is primarily because reciprocal social service is a stronger factor than mere genealogical relationship in maintaining kinship bonds. Consequently pastoral communities normally try to follow a routine in their pattern of transhumance. Ecological and seasonal factors along with such other factors as relations with neigbourhood groups, as such, help to maintain this balance between territorial groups and the relations of production of the genealogical groups.

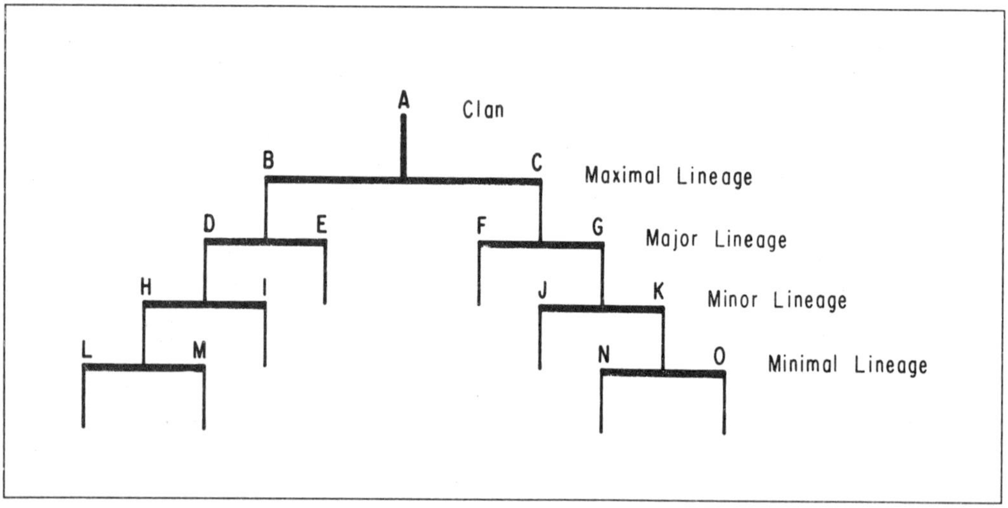

SOURCE: Evan Pritchard, 1940.

Fig. 1. Segmentary Lineage Society Structure.

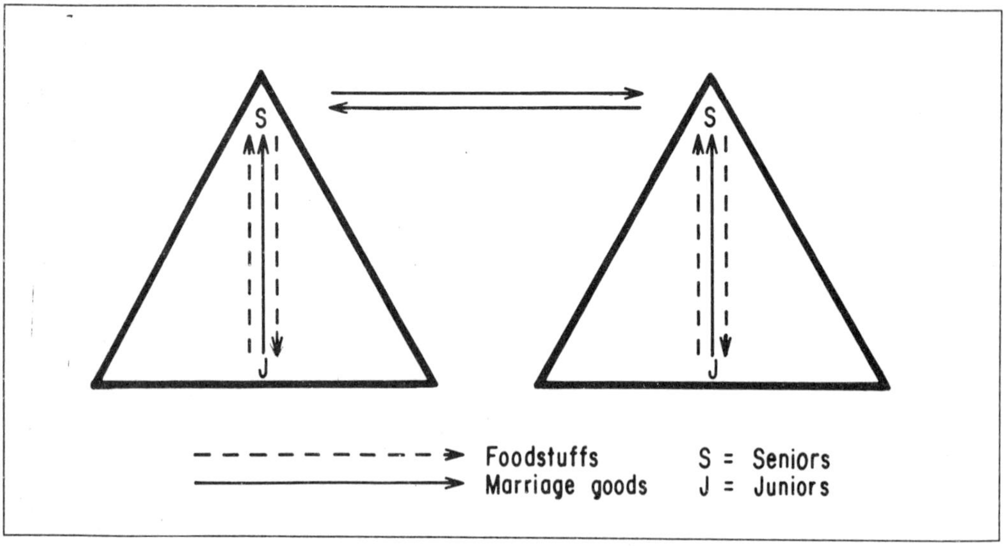

SOURCE: Meillassoux, 1978.

Fig. 2. Mode of Production in Segmentary Lineage Society.

STUDIES ON PASTORAL COMMUNITIES IN INDIA

Studies of pastoral communities in India are not many. In fact there are hardly any purely pastoral groups in existence. However, we might briefly look into the facets of some of those societies who are predominantly pastoral.

Changpas are one such pastoral community adapted to the high altitude pastures of eastern Ladakh across the border of Tibet. Normally this community always maintains a group of animals of more than one species. An average Changpa owns about 5 yaks, 4 demos, 10 sheep and 15 goats. They use fixed and traditionally allotted pastures at the height of 400 to 650 m (Bhasin 1996). Although not very high in altitude the region is extremely frigid in vegetation cover for most part of the year except during the spring. Yet such massive and sturdy mammals as yaks and demos seem to be well adapted to this rarified, cold and dry environment, although mortality rate of the animals—specially sub-adult ones is quite high. The whole household of the Changpas moves with their animals. They live in tents made out of yak-hair blankets. For about 4 months during winter they come down to the lower altitude regions. The animal products like milk (which is usually converted into butter or cheese), animal meat, hide and wool is traded during this season. Some of the special variety of sheep wool produced here fetch very high price in the market because of their very fine texture and light weight. The Changpas buy barley, kerosene and jewellery of coloured stones and other trinkets of silver with this money. It is believed that earlier they could barter these with Tibetans across the border. With the close of this border after India-China war in 1962 the Changpas are getting exposed to the market economy. Their utter inexperience in understanding money economy makes them extremely vulnerable in the hand of the middlemen. So the wool which will cost Rs.10,000 in the capital city in the valley is sold by the Changpas at Rs. 300 to 900 only to the middlemen. One of the most interesting adoption of segmentary lineage system is seen among these people. Probably this indicates a specific type of adaptation which emerged as a subsistence strategy to suit the harsh climate of eastern Ladakh. The Changpas practise polyandry along with polygamy. That is, the bride married to the oldest brother automatically becomes wife for all the other brothers. Families which are rich enough to support larger number of wives may procure one or more sisters of the bride to come and join the household as co-wives. This is an arrangement which allows the brothers to go out all the day with their animals without any mutual conflict of interest. Some times they have to go as far as 10-20 km. in search of suitable pastures. The second important feature of the Changpa social structure is that, the moment the sons are married, the parents pass over the ownership of their flock to the elder son and retire from nomadic life. They would then settle down in the lower valley with minimum number of livestock to maintain themselves. Thus, just in their middle age the Changpas get out of the rigours of transhumance. Consequently if one has to look at the subsistence strategy one can see that the possibility of each brother forming his own line of descent group is skilfully avoided by the system of polyandry and primogeniture. That is, no matter how many sons a couple has the possibility of the subsistence being progressively divided is reduced. The rule of primogeniture further makes the senior brother tied down with the responsibility for his other sibs. Another interesting feature which again shows a specific pattern of adaptation to the region is that unlike most pastoral communities Changpas scarcely follow a common pasture land for many territorial groups. Thus, each household has their own allotted areas for a whole season which their leader can change from time to time. The fierce individuality of pastoral community recorded in Maghreb and Arabia by UNESCO studies would seem to be applicable to some extent in this community as well.

Gaddis in Himachal Pradesh is another pastoral group in western Himalayas. Seen in areal perspective the Changpas are situated in adjoining regions. Yet these two regions differ totally in the height of the ranges, general ambient temperature, rainfall and consequently the vegetation cover. Although identified as a single ethnic group for all practical purposes (Bhasin 1996) the Gaddis are divided into such Hindu caste groups as Brahmins, Rajputs and Sudras. This lends credibility to the fact that probably the term is not referring to an ethnic group but is merely a generic ascription for people who keep a large number of livestock. The Gaddis normally maintain as many as 200-400 sheep and goat in a family and practise both agriculture and pastoralism. Usually the males go out with their animals in the winter months when the females, children and aged males stay back in their houses. These are permanent structures prepared with wood, stones and slates. Usually these are two storied structures and are closely built with similar structures of other families. In winter months the women treat the wool, spin them and weave them besides processing the agricultural products like maize, chilly and pulses, which are harvested just before proper winter sets in. Males are also constantly kept busy minding their huge flocks. This includes milking them, taking them to their grazing pastures, bringing them back to their temporary shelters and caring for the young ones born during this period. Thus, a distinct form of agro-pastoralism develops with visual sexual division of labour. At the end of the winter season (usually around the month of March) the men return with their animals. These are stationed in the field outside their houses in specially fenced enclosures. Around this time the agricultural activities start. Repairing terraces, preparing soil, manuring them, etc., are heavy works and taken up by the males. The livestock is fed on fodder from the earlier harvest for the entire period of March to October. More often than not the stocked fodder is not enough and the animals are let out in the nearby mountain slopes. Shepherds may be hired to take care of them. Gaddis have a real labour intensive economy keeping them busy round the year. The Gaddis show a peculiar custom of elevating the status of a sister's first son to almost the level of a symbolic head. Even if the child is a minor his feet are touched by the elderly brothers of his mother. This appears to be a form of adaptation to keep the web of kinship ties along the daughter's line as well even though she cannot inherit any of her father's movable or immovable properties. The Gaddis are essentially labour hungry because of the two parallel patterns of economy followed. Consequently extending kinship obligation acts as a security of sorts to draw upon at the time of stress. Sister's son also has the privilege of receiving gifts from the second grand parents' source. The inheritance does not show the classic segmentary descent expected in a pastoral society. Neither do they maintain the strong individualistic strand characteristics of such economies. On the contrary there is a constant reciprocation of labour and gifts visible between unrelated families.

Bhutias of north Sikkim are another agro-pastoral group which shows a different form of adaptation. Bhasin (1996) describes at length the two distinct Bhutia groups settled along the rivers at Lachen and Lachung. These two communities follow different migratory habits, speak different languages and are endogamous. They are separated by a range of high mountains. Yet the economy, religion and social structure of the two groups hardly show any difference. Generally they keep yaks, sheep and goats with some horses and ponies to carry them or their belongings. During their migration to the higher altitudes in summer they raise some root crops like turnip, radish and potatoes. When they come back to the lower altitude during winter they combine animal keeping with agriculture. Maize and buckwheat are the usual crops sown during this season. These activities are combined with collection of minor forest produce, firewood or even acting as labour for others at times. Strict rules are followed in allotting land for grazing as also for cultivation. In addition communal grazing fields are also allotted by the Phipun or the village head. Traditionally Bhutias have been trading their produce with Tibet and other settled communities in Sikkim. As such a monetary economy of sorts have emerged in them in the course of the last one hundred years. Earlier they have been known to have barter system to exchange skin, ropes, meat, butter, and cheese for salt, maize, rice and tea. The Bhutia social system organizes itself on equal distribution of wealth to sons and at times a kind of compensatory share even for the daughters. Lineage and kinship are limited to at best two or three generations. Bhasin (1996: 231) summarizes their organization in the following words:

> The indigenous systems of prestige and power in these two societies are based on relative egalitarianism, as these societies are largely unstratified. These systems differ from kinship societies as well as there is no divisive characteristics of kinship system overpowering the socio-political system. . . . Bhutias socio-political system still conforms to the age-old system of community organization.

Polyandry was practised in the past and in many socio-economic features there is a strong comparability of the Bhutias of Sikkim with the Changpas of Ladakh. Here again the view of Bonte (1979) would seem to be substantiated. That is, peripheral and harsher ecology does have the influence on pastoral societies to create shades of different types of organizations.

The Raikas of western Rajasthan provides yet another variety of pastoral adaptation. Srivastava (1997) has recently published a detailed account of Raikas and their simple religion. The high position ascribed to religious renunciation by this community would seem (according to Srivastava) to be linked with the demands of a specific range of adaptations that the community requires for husbanding of camels and sheep which is their primary occupation. Here again we see a segment of retired pastorals preferring to stay back in permanent hamlets with women, sick and children and engage in agriculture. Although the semi-desert conditions of the regions of their settlement afford at best one crop of millet and/or spices a year—their accepting to undertake this alternative economy is significant. The social structure and ideology of a proper peasant society need not evolve within this form of settled life where a major fragment of the community continues with pastoralism with strong ideological back-up of dictates for camel rearing. Raikas are strictly vegetarian and there is strict rule which prevents them from selling milk of the animals. All they can do is to sell camel, its hides and hair. This sets them apart from all pastoral groups discussed above. Yet one can identify segmentary lineage system even though a part of the community is agricultural. Pastoral land available to them today are communal in the sense that only government land is being used. Most of the settled communities do not allow Raikas to bring their animals into the agricultural fields. Wool and skin are directly sold to the agents of city traders who visit their settlements. In a way this has resulted into a complete isolation of the community from the mainstream. Yet their money power puts them in a considerably better position than most of settled villagers. This is because an average peasant in this region can hardly produce enough to sell his agricultural produce after meeting his own needs. Raikas do not mind servicing the draught animals of the farmers for a charge per animal per day.

The Dhangars are another agro-pastoral community spread in the rain shadow rocky regions of Karnataka and Maharashtra (Sontheimer 1976). Again we see a pattern similar to the Raikas. In fact one of the strongest kingdoms in central India-the Holkars during the Maratha period (AD 1600-1700) were Dhangars.

Considering the features available for the Indian situation we might try to seek out certain generalizations for pastoral communities as follows:

1. Pastoralism plays a dominant role in a community which has huge forest or fallow land available around their habitat. Conversely speaking man to land ratio is tilted heavily towards land.
2. In conjunction with this the ecology is so extreme that such land is not suitable for agriculture. Rainfall in such areas is very insignificant. In addition to this the demographic status of community being low attempts of agriculture in such land is not possible.
3. Taking to large scale animal husbandry is also labour intensive but such labour can be harnessed through social manipulation mainly because here the basic resource is elastic in nature and can multiply in number. Thus, gift and repayment with animal heads becomes easy. Often rituals or myths are heavily ingrained in order to give a smooth functioning to the system.
4. Finally it must be stated that the process of sedentism finally culminating into peasantry is a much more complex one (Fig. 3). Here the emphasis is shifted to land as 'seed money' and its inheritance has to be maintained by the evolution of a more complex kinship network and marriage regulation.

CONCLUDING REMARKS

When considering social change in archaeology scholars all through the entire three quarter of this century have got trapped inevitably within evolutionism. Here we wish to argue that such an approach may be convenient for understanding human history within a macro-perspective but certainly the deification of such generalizations to form a rule and then

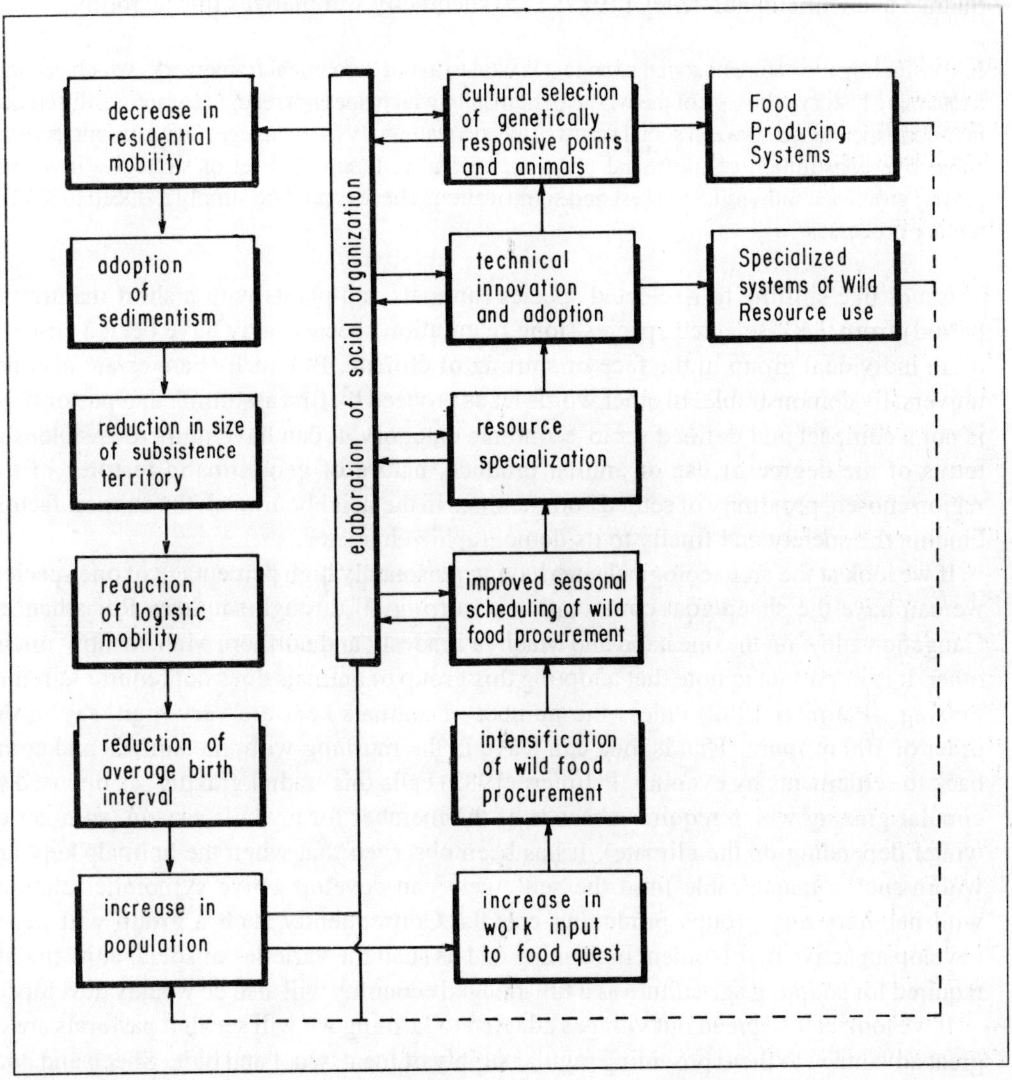

SOURCE: D.H. Harris.

Fig. 3. Transition from Foraging to Dedentary Society.

re-use them to explain micro-level findings is grossly incorrect. Further no social change can be viewed only through the change of technology in isolation. Demography, social complexity, ideology and polity act in combination to result such a change. Michael Shanks and Christopher Tilley (1987: 185) succinctly summarizes this as follows:

> In considering the nature of social change it is vital to avoid theoretical frameworks which produce a totalizing history, a history of the whole of humanity which does not recognize rapture, difference, non-correspondence between social forms. Any adequate analysis of change must take into account subjective constitution of the social as an active and differentiated set of strategies involving power, group and individual interest and signification. These cannot be simply reduced to a set of unitary processes.

Issues like shifting to r-selected species (animals and plants with a short maturation period) from the k-selected species (long maturation species) may have been a strategy of an individual group in the face of shifting of climate. But such changes are also not universally demonstrable. In other words let us proceed by first assuming that pastoralism is not a compact and defined socio-economic category. It can have numerous shades in terms of the degree of use of animal produce, nature of geo-climatic features of the region chosen, proximity of settled communities in the neighbourhood, the cultural factors binding the society and finally to its demographic character.

If we look at the archaeological sites having reasonably high percentage of one species, we can have the sheep/goat combination occurring all through southern Rajasthan[1] to Gangetic valley[2] on the one hand and Madhya Pradesh[3] and northern Maharashtra[4] on the other. It is important to note that adopting this group of animals does not require 'circular grazing' (Palmieri 1982) unless the number of animals kept are very high, say in the order of 100 or more. That is, one can leave in the morning with the animals and come back to settlements by evening. Palmieri (1982) calls this 'radial grazing' as opposed to circular grazing which requires absence of the member for a whole season (summer or winter depending on the climate). It has been observed that when the animals kept are within such a manageable limit the settlement can develop active symbiotic relations with neighbouring groups producing cereals. Consequently such a group will never develop an active involvement in farming and as such the varieties of social adjustments required for adopting agriculture as a full-fledged economy will also be weakly developed.

If we look at the spread out villages adapted to farming we will see that pastorals are of great advantage to them providing regular supply of meat, wool and hide. Sheep and goat not only provide these produces but they soon develop an important status for gifts, exchange for marriage or in various rituals of sacrifices. The pastoral hamlets are likely to show no or very little internal change although products of other economies (cereals, metals and beads) seep in regularly from the neighbourhood. Most pastoral communities prefer round huts to lodge kitchen and other essential belongings, but otherwise stay outside under temporary shelters. This is mainly because they need to keep a vigil on the livestock and protect them from wild animals. For an archaeologist, therefore, analysis of such habitation sites can be frustrating. The lack of change in their tool-kit and clustering of series of similar sites caused by way of fission in the lineage are two possible indicators for an archaeologist to interpret the tilting of emphasis on livestock rearing from farming. Further, such sites are likely to have almost negligible occupational debris. The Ganga Valley evidence from Dam Dama to Sarai Nahar Rai compares very well with these possible indicators. Further, the evidence of cattle from these sites shows that the range of species chosen was broadened as one progressed in time. (That is, early third millennium to late third millennium BC. This date range is surmised by the senior author elsewhere as a more correct possibility.) It is important to mention here that cattle has the lowest water retention capacity out of all the animals chosen for domestication (with the exception of camels). Further, cattle require shade and rest for almost 8 hours in a day to ruminate its food from one stomach to another. Consequently pure cattle breeders have to be fairly restricted in their movement and cannot operate in arid regions.

Tilwara and Bagor are from a much earlier date and could not have been pastoralists. May be during the younger phases they took to animal keeping but the proposed ingradients of their being pastoral even during the younger phases is not present. The Mehsana cluster, on the other hand, does show a wide dispersal and are also about 3,000 years younger than Bagor in date. Yet these sites do not show the bones of the usually adopted domesticated species. It is in Madhya Pradesh and northern Maharashtra that we see evidence of a striking increase of multiple domesticates. Adamgarh lies in the northern extreme of this zone and it is contemporaneous with settled sites in the south and east. Obviously one can see the features of some symbiotic interactions operative in this region. Thus, if a pastoral is encouraged to increase his flock it is not simply decided by the availability of labour in the community or pasture land in the area but also by the degree of demand on it from its settled partners in symbiosis. Possibly the late third millennium BC. Neolithic or Neo-Chalcolithic sites in western India were small peasant settlements, while the pastorals like Dhangars with long range grazing practices made periodic visits to these villages. Such visitations might have resulted into the pastorals taking up grazing services for the livestocks of the peasant group. This kind of system is still practised by many villagers who would pay charges in cash or kind and give their individual holdings to the pastorals for grazing during the entire stretch of summer. If we can consider such a possibility for the past it can create an active force of dispersal of traits. Shaffer and Liechtenstein (1995) in a different context have called this 'palaeo-ethnic' movement.

Shereen Ratnagar (1989) has discussed at length the changes in adaptational strategies at Inamgaon (Dhavalikar et al. 1988), during the phases marking the transition from Early Jorwe (1400-1000 BC) to Late Jorwe (1000-700 BC). Of the many changes which occurred due to increasing aridity in the region the most distinctive one is the shift of emphasis to goat/sheep herding. That such a change in economy could not have been sudden is also indicated by the fact that goat/sheep and cattle are present in the earlier levels of the site as well. In all likelihood such a level of livestock could be maintained with agricultural fodder during these phases (1600-1000 BC). May be during the dry seasons they had to take the animals out for grazing but the shift had not really occurred and one cannot expect the pastoral features to develop at this stage. The tilt of emphasis shifts to animal keeping only after the crop fails to meet the requirement. And with this shift the entire emphasis on dwelling structure, crop storage and other connected activities show a decline. Ratnagar successfully demonstrates these changes in the archaeological material from Inamgaon.

For the Southern Neolithic sites such a shift is hardly demonstrable. This is primarily because these settlements (mid-third millennium BC) from their inception started with a high imperative of large number of livestock maintaining. A Malwa kind of village structure could hardly develop in this zone. The whole area is generally rugged and falls within a rain shadow strip yet the west to east drainage pattern of all the rivers maintain excellent pasture land in patches all over. Livestock maintaining, consequently is not as much of a problem as depending entirely on farming. As a result of this tilt in the resource base one can see that settlement activities always remained in low priority among these people. Even the ceramics found in association lack the kind of refinement in technique or variety when compared with Malwa or Early Jorwe sites. Yet as witnessed earlier one can find beads, metal objects or even semi-precious stones in isolation in many of these sites. Cattle pen and ashmounds found in some of these sites can indicate that animals kept were large enough in number to require circular grazing. Such periodic migrations brings the pastorals in contact with settlements of higher culture through which products of craftsmen find their way in them.

The Todas in the Nilgiris are possibly a completely readapted example of this kind of relationship sought by the pastorals still living in this region. While Todas are cattle breeders they have a sattelite farming community called Kotas with whom they maintain a traditional symbiotic relationship. That such relations must have been operative in the third and second millennium BC in Deccan India is difficult to demonstrate except through the archaeological logic discussed above. The adaptational strategy of these Neolithic settlers must not have been very different from the Lachen and Lachung Bhotias of Sikkim discussed in the earlier section.

That is, migrating groups follow fixed routes for fixed destination and have dual camps. During summer they raise one crop in the higher valleys and this is done parallely with animal grazing. In the winter they come down to lower valleys and again raise another group of produce along with grazing their animals. Such an adaptation can easily undertake the preparation of cow-pens for a season and have one set of activities during one season and another set of activities in the second season. Territorial groups can easily proliferate if the segmentary lineage is adopted. Paddayya (1973) has successfully demonstrated the possibility of such clusters of homogeneity existing in Deccan Neolithic indicating such territorial groups. Possibly the socio-economic reconstruction of the entire cultural scenario in south India during 2,500 to 800 BC will be better understood if we had more information on settlements and habitational remains like we have at Inamgaon.

NOTE

The sites considered for this summary are:

1. Bagor and Tilwara (Misra 1971),
2. Dam Dama yo Mahagara (Sharma et al. 1980a, 1980b),
3. Adamgarh (Joshi 1964),
4. Jorwe to Kayatha (Sankalia et al. 1960; U.V. Singh 1962).

REFERENCES

Barth, F. 1961. *Nomads of South Persia: the Basseri Tribe of the Khamesh Confederacy*. London: Allen and Unwin.

——— 1963. Capital, Investment and Social Structure of a Pastoral Nomad Group in South Persia, in *Capital, Saving and Credit in Peasant Societies* (R. Firth and B.S. Yamey Eds.), pp. 68-81. London: Allen and Unwin.

Bhasin, Veena 1996. *Transhumants of Himalayas: Changpas of Ladakh, Gaddis of Himachal Pradesh and Bhutias of Sikkim*. Delhi: Kamla-Raj Enterprises.

Bonte, Pierre 1979. Pastoral production, Territorial Organization and Kinship in Segmentary Lineage Societies, in *Social and Ecological Systems* (P.C. Burnham and R.F. Ellen Eds.), pp. 203-34. New York: Academic Press.

Burckhardt, J.L. 1831. *Notes on the Bedouins and Wahabys*. London: Colburn and Bentley.

Cronk, Lee 1989. From Hunters to Herders: Subsistence Change as a Reproductive Strategy Among the Mukogoda, *Current Anthropology* 30 (2): 224-34.

Crozals, J. de. 1883. *Les Peulhs: e'tude d'ethnologie Aafricaine*. Paris: Maisonneuve.

Dhavalikar, M.K., H.D. Sankalia and Z.D. Ansari 1988. *Excavations at Inamgaon*, Vol. 1. Pune: Deccan College.

Doughty, C.M. 1888. *Travels in Arabia Desert*. Cambridge (publisher not mentioned).

Duveyrier, H. 1864. *Les Tourage du Nord*. Paris: Challamel Aine'.

Evans-Pritchard, E.E. 1940. *The Nuer*. Oxford: Oxford University Press.

Harris, D.R. 1982. Settling Down: an Evolutionary Model for the Transformation of Mobile Bands into Sedentary Communities, in *The Evolution of Social System* (J. Friedman and M.J. Rowlands Eds.), pp. 401-47. Gloucester Crescent: Duckworth.

Hatt, G. 1919. *Die Nomaden von Tibet*. Vienna: Herold.

Ingold, Tim 1985. Khazanov on Nomads, *Current Anthropology* 26 (3): 384-7.

Jacobs, A.H. 1975. Masai Pastoralism in Historical Perspective, in *Pastoralism in Tropical Africa* (T. Monod, Ed.). Oxford: Oxford University Press.

Joshi, R.V. and M.D. Khare 1966. Microliths Bearing Deposit of Adamgarh Rock-Shelters, in *Studies in Prehistory* (D. Sen and A. Ghosh Eds.), pp. 90-2. Calcutta: Firma K.L. Mukhopadhyaya.

Khazanov, A.M. 1984. *Nomads and the Outside World* (Translated by J. Crookenden). Cambridge: Cambridge University Press.

Meillassoux, C. 1978. The Economy in Agricultural Self-sustaining Societies: a Preliminary Analysis, in *Relations of Production: Marxist Approaches in Anthropology* (D. Seddon Ed.), pp. 127-57. London: Frank Cass.

Mellaart, J. 1961. *Anatolian Studies* (London). Cited by Muller-Karpe, H. 1968, in *Handbuch der Vorgeschichte Zweiter Band*, p. 438. Munchen: C.H. Beck'sche Verlagsbuckhandlung.

Michael Shanks and Christopher Tilly 1987. *Social Theory and Archaeology.* Cambridge: Polity Press.

Misra, V.N. 1971. Two Microlithic Sites in Rajasthan—a Preliminary Investigation, *The Eastern Anthropologist* 24 (3): 237-88.

Newcomer, P.J. 1972. The Nuer are Dinka, *Man* 8: 109-10.

Paddayya, K. 1973. *Investigations into the Neolithic Culture of the Shorapur Doab, South India.* Leiden: E.J. Brill.

Palgrave, W.G. 1867. *Personal Narrative of a Year's Journey Through Central and Eastern Arabia (1862-63).* London: Macmillan.

Palmieri, R.P. 1982. Patterns of Indian Pastoralism, in *India: Culture Patterns and Processes* (Allen G. Noble and Ashok K. Dutt Eds.), pp. 325-36. Colorado: Westview Press.

Ratnagar, Shereen 1989. A Chalcolithic Village in a Famine Belt, *Studies in History* 5 (2): 287-302.

Robertson-Smith, W. 1885. *Kinship and Marriage in Early Arabia.* London: A and C Black.

Sahlins, M. 1961. The Segmentary Lineage: an Organization of Predatory Expansion, *American Anthropologist* 63: 322-45.

Sankalia, H.D. and S.B. Deo 1960. *Report on the Excavations at Nasik and Jorwe, 1950-51.* Poona: Deccan College.

Shaffer, Jim G. and Diane A. Lichtenstein 1995. The Concept of 'Cultural Tradition' and 'Palaeoethnicity' in South Asian Archaeology, in *The Indo-Aryans of Ancient South Asia* (George Erdosy Ed.), pp. 126-54. Berlin: Walter de Gruyter.

Sharma, G.R., V.D. Misra and J.N. Pal 1980a. *Excavations at Mahagara.* Allahabad: Allahabad University.

Sharma, G.R., V.D. Misra, D. Mandal, B.B. Misra and J.N. Pal 1980b. *Beginnings of Agriculture.* Allahabad: Abinash Prakashan.

Sontheimer, G.D. 1976. Biroba, Mhaskoba and Khandoba, *Schriftenreihe des Sudasien Institutes der Uni Heidelberg.* Band 20. Wiesbaden: Franz Steiner Verlag Gmblt.

Schwabedissen, H. 1954. Die Federmesser-Grupen des nordweste uropaischen Flachbandes, Neumunster.

Spooner, Brian 1972. The Status of Nomadism as a Cultural Phenomenon in the Middle East, in *Perspectives on Nomadism* (William Irons and Neville Dyson-Hudson Eds.), pp. 122-30. Leiden: E.J. Brill.

Srivastava, Vinay Kumar 1997. *Religious Renunciation of a Pastoral People.* Delhi: Oxford University Press.

Uday Vir Singh. 1962. Excavations at Eran, *Journal of the Madhya Pradesh Itihasa Parishad* 4: 41-4.

UNESCO. 1959. Nomads and Nomadism in Arid Zone, *International Social Science Journal* 11: 481-585.

Valoney, C.F.C. 1787. *Voyage en Syrie et an Egypte les anne'es.* Paris (publisher not mentioned).

William, Irons and Neville Dyson - Hudson (Eds.) 1972. *Perspectives on Nomadism.* Leiden: E.J. Brill.

Fifty Years of Ethnoarchaeological Research in India: A Review

PRADEEP MOHANTY and JITU MISHRA

INTRODUCTION

During the last four decades ethnoarchaeology has emerged as a powerful organ of archaeological research, thanks to the efforts of a dedicated group of investigators (Kluckhohn 1950; White 1967; Binford 1968, 1978, 1983; Lee and de Vore 1968; Orme 1973, 1981; Jochim 1976; Stiles 1977; Yellen 1977; Kramer 1979, 1980; Watson 1979, 1980, Steensberg 1980; Gould 1978, 1980; Charlton 1981; Hodder 1982a, 1982b; Gould and Watson 1982; Wylie 1982, 1985; Kent 1984; Schrire 1984; Griffin and Solheim II 1990; Cribb 1991; Longrace 1991; Brochier et al. 1992; David 1993; Cameron and Tomka 1993; B. Allchin 1994; MacEachern 1996 and Tilley 1996). Ethnoarchaeology the study of various aspects of contemporary socio-cultural behaviour and material culture to ascertain how certain features of observable behaviour may be reflected in the archaeological record. Such research is therefore relevant to the collection, analysis and interpretation of archaeological remains. The utility of insights into past behaviour derived from observations of contemporary behaviour is greatest when they can be framed as hypotheses and tested.

The major assumptions underlying ethnoarchaeology are as follows:

(a) the present offers a reliable opportunity to the archaeologists to test ideas about the relationship between human behaviour and thought and their material expression;
(b) ethnographic analogies are particularly helpful where there are strong similarities between past and present material cultural forms and;
(c) this value increases further when historical links could be established between present and past cultures. It is possible that in a number of cases the present cultural forms are the outcome of a long historical process. Systematic studies should then make it possible to trace back hundreds even thousands of years (Clark 1951: 51; Kramer 1979: 1, 1980: 1-2; Yellen 1977: 11).

Ethnoarchaeological research involves investigations of the material culture, behaviour and beliefs of present-day populations, with the object of that research being the generation of propositions about the cultural contexts of the residual recovered from archaeological occurrences.

> The goal of ethnoarchaeological research should continue to be the generation of insights, whatever specific or general, direct or indirect, about the cultural workings of ancient human societies. (MacEachern 1996: 250)

Generally, there are two main approaches in ethnoarchaeology, the direct historical approach or analogy and the general comparative analogy. In the former the analogy is generally considered to provide the highest possibility of being correct because the conditions of time, space and cultural affinity of the groups who produced the two sets of compared data are most analogous (Thompson 1991: 235). In the general comparative approach, one seeks appropriate analogues anywhere in time and space, on the basis of present-day ethnographic reality.

With this general background and definition of ethnoarchaeology, we attempt to provide a review of ethnoarchaeological research carried out in India in the last fifty years, using a broad regional and historical approach involving prehistoric, protohistoric and historical archaeology.

INDIAN CONTEXT

India, with its cultural diversity, range of subsistence and settlement strategies and persistence of traditional crafts and arts is an ideal storehouse for ethnoarchaeological research (Sinopoli 1991; Allchin 1998: 32-3). The seeming timelessness of the Indian village, the existence of several tribal communities (living in north-eastern and north-western India, Chhotanagpur plateau, Eastern and Western Ghats including Nilgiri Hills) in the hilly forested zones of India (Fuchs 1973), having considerable antiquity, the apparent stability of social traditions and technological, and the wide range of human adaptations found throughout the subcontinent provide enormous opportunities for data gathering and for generating predictive models.

PREHISTORIC ARCHAEOLOGY

Furer-Haimendorf as early as 1943 wrote:

> Prehistory, although extremely important in establishing the distribution and sequence of ancient civilizations, can seldom do more than unearth material aspects of a culture, and it is the knowledge accumulated through the detailed study of contemporary primitive cultures, which supplements the dry data and breathes life into the fragments brought to light through the spadework of the archaeologist. (1943a: 1, 1948)

Haimendorf's work among the Gadabas and Bondos of Orissa to understand the Megalithic ritual made a good beginning in this direction (Haimendorf 1943b).

M. Nagar has carried out ethnoarchaeological research on the material culture and economic organization of the tribal communities of peninsular India. In the mid-1970s she studied the material culture, religion and socio-economic organization of the Gonds living in villages around the Stone Age site of Bhimbetka in the rank forest of Vindhyan Hills in the Raisen district of Madhya Pradesh (Nagar 1975b). Her study revealed that Gonds in this area raise small stones in memory of their dead. The stones are installed on a stone and mud platform accompanied by elaborate ceremony. The stones called Gantha represent the spirits of dead ancestors and are worshipped on all auspicious occasions.

These ceremonies provide us an insight into the mental templates behind the raising of memorial stones during the early Iron Age in central and south India. Her study of the chief deity of the Gonds who is known as 'Burha Baba' and who is represented by metal weapons like spearheads and daggers revealed that the weapons are kept hidden in the rocks and are taken out by the chief priest for worship only twice a year. Archaeologists coming across these weapons may interpret them to be utilitarian objects in the absence of an archaeological context. But her study showed that they are actually ritual objects. This area is rich in Mesolithic sites as Nagar suggests that the present pattern of tribal subsistence is in part a continuation of the prehistoric tradition (Nagar 1982: 124). Nagar and Misra's (1989, 1990, 1993) work among several semi-nomadic groups such as Aheriya, Baheliya, Bandi, Bangali, Gandhila, Gidiya in the Ganga Valley and Pardhis and Kuchabandhias in central India shows how the hunter-gatherers of this densely populated areas have adapted by supplementing hunting and gathering with a variety of occupations based on their traditional skills of producing material items useful to both farmers and urban dwellers and thus have established a symbiotic relationship, especially with the latter. Most of these communities may not be tribals in the strictest sense; they are more likely to be offshoots of one or more parental stocks which acquired separate names and identities by fission and geographical and cultural isolation (Nagar and Misra 1994: 172). The detailed studies of their subsistence, settlement pattern and social organization over time may not be ethnoarchaeological in the conventional sense, but the survival of hunting-gathering tradition among these mobile groups in a densely populated area which is rich in Mesolithic sites is quite significant.

At times, there is a great mass of ethnographic and ethno-historical research done with little reference to archaeology, but which is yet of undoubted relevance to archaeological investigations. This material may directly increase our knowledge of variation in material culture as with descriptions of artefact types or technological processes. It may provide data on particular societies assumed to be descended from particular prehistoric communities, or it may enhance our understanding of the functioning of past societies, or of technological specialists. This is not ethnoarchaeology, but at times the links among archaeology, ethno-history and ethnography are so intimate that it is impossible to tease them apart. Ajaya Pratap's example is a case in point (Pratap 1987, 1988).

Ethnoarchaeological research in India has primarily focused on surviving hunter-gatherer populations to study the traditional subsistence and settlement patterns. The main reason of such studies has been to apply the data generated from contemporary societies to the interpretation of prehistoric archaeological remains from the same region.

Murty's work among several tribes such as Chenchus, Yanadis, Yerukulas, Kuruvas, Gollas, etc., in Andhra Pradesh shows the immense inexhaustible knowledge of biological environment among these tribes. The accumulation of such an immense amount of knowledge in the tribal groups must have resulted from ecological adaptation and long and continuous exploitation of the resources in the habitat reflecting upon a traditional pattern of economic behaviour. Murty's research not only shows how these tribal groups traditionally exploited a very wide range of plant and animal resources, but also demonstrates the ongoing symbiotic relationship between tribal populations and sedentary agriculturists in the areas of his study in Andhra Pradesh. These relations appear to have considerable antiquity in the region as attested by inscriptional evidence. In yet another attempt Murty and Sontheimer examined local beliefs about origins of particular subsistence and settlement systems in Andhra Pradesh and Karnataka by documenting the ancient Birappa legend they reconstructed the symbiotic relationship between tribal populations and sedentary agriculturists in Andhra Pradesh. These relations appear to have considerable antiquity in the region as attested by inscriptional evidence. The study of Kuruva pastoralism was found to be of considerable relevance for understanding the origins of pastoralism in the third millennium BC. Further Murty's study of historical inscriptions, Medieval literature and colonial accounts helped throw much new light on the dynamics of the hunter-gatherer cultures of the Eastern Ghats (Murty 1978-9, 1981, 1985a, 1985b, 1989, 1994; Murty and Sontheimer 1980).

Following Murty (1966), Bhaskar (1990) surveyed a small area of about 150 sq km in Yarlapudi Kalva Basin of Kalahasti taluk in Chittoor district of Andhra Pradesh and located 16 Lower Palaeolithic sites. With the help of the area dimension, assemblage types, palaeoenvironmental factors and ethnographic parameters, Bhaskar has reconstructed the economic pursuits of the Palaeolithic people. He has studied two tribal communities, viz., the Yanadis and the Chenchus who live in two different geographical settings separated from each other. His assumptions that hominids from Palaeolithic period onwards must have made considerable biological changes, both in macro and micro forms, and the present-day Yanadis and Chenchus are the derivatives of Palaeolithic people is far from convincing considering the vast time gap. Nandini Rao in the course of her survey confined to a small area of Kuntala in Adilabad District of Andhra Pradesh brought to light several Upper Palaeolithic and Mesolithic clusters. She carried out ethnographic research among the Gonds living in the same area to be able to reconstruct past settlement and subsistence patterns. Her ethnographic work revealed how the availability of water evidently influences the location of various types of settlements and a similar thing might have happened in the past too (N. Rao 1987).

Nandini Rao's recent preliminary work along the Tapi Valley in Akkalkuwa taluka, Dhule district of Maharashtra has brought to light several clusters of artefacts. To understand the prehistoric settlement and subsistence patterns Rao studied a community called Vasavas (a subtribe of the Bhils) who are to be displaced from their homeland due to the construction of the Narmada dam. The Vasavas, traditionally hunter-gatherers have been made to accept a settled life with plough agriculture as their mainstay, but continue to practice their traditional occupations. Rao draws a parallel pertaining to settlement and subsistence of the present-day Vasavas to that of the prehistoric population of the area, although she has not identified to which cultural phase her prehistoric clusters belong (N. Rao 1994).

D.R. Raju in the course of his several seasons of field investigation has brought to light scores of Stone Age sites in the Cuddappah district and the Eastern Ghats region of

Andhra Pradesh (Raju 1981, 1983, 1986-7, 1988). To reconstruct the Upper Palaeolithic subsistence and settlement patterns, Raju studied the Yanadi fisher and hunter-gatherer community who inhabit the Gunjana Valley today, very often living on the same sites as were occupied by the Upper Palaeolithic people. Traditionally, they lived in bands of 3 to 20 families in rather haphazard settlements of circular huts with conical roofs, made entirely of plant materials. His research revealed that Yanadis have an expert knowledge of their environment and their economy is based on fishing, hunting and gathering in a traditional manner. This intimate knowledge suggests a long tradition of extensive exploitation. The physical correspondences between the locations of Upper Palaeolithic and present-day Yanadi settlements raised the question of their ethnic link (Raju 1983: 17).

Paddayya's research in Gulbarga district of Karnataka spanning several decades of fieldwork is a guiding example of the use of ethnographic data in the archaeological interpretation of Stone Age hunter-gatherers. His intensive study of the Acheulian culture of the Hunsgi-Baichbal Valleys has yielded an interesting distributional pattern of sites: clustering of a majority of sites in a small patch in the central portion of the valley and random dispersal of the rest in other parts. His observation of the present-day environment of the area along with the drainage patterns, suggests that the clustering of sites in the central part represents dry season aggregation of the Acheulian groups, whereas the scattering of the sites marks the dispersal of groups during the ensuing wet season. His excavations over several seasons in this area have revealed the presence of several contiguous occupation spots, which suggest a band type of social organization. He observes the exploitation of many plant and animal foods by the present-day communities living in the same area in a degenerated forested environment due to agricultural expansion and introduction of irrigation. The present ecological set-up inhabited by contemporary populations is not all the same as the one that was inhabited by the Stone Age peoples of the same region. The wild plant and animal species exploited today may coincide to some extent with those gathered in the past, but the prehistoric people could have chosen from a much wider array of species than do the present populations (Paddayya 1978-9, 1981, 1982). Paddayya is also of the view that there is no need to look for direct historic continuity always, but one can look for cross-cultural parallels.

Z. Cooper's intensive survey in a small area (100 sq km) at Chitrakot Falls in Bastar district of Madhaya Pradesh has brought to light several microlithic clusters belonging to the Mesolithic culture. She has interpreted her archaeological data with the help of ethnographic and ecological parameters. Her study of Kuruk fishermen, who are a subcaste of Maria Gonds demonstrates the juxtaposition of the Mesolithic sites with the settlements of fishermen. The continuation of traditional fishing and collecting methods of procuring food, in spite of the introduction of agriculture provided an excellent insight into the subsistence strategies which might have been used by the makers of microliths. The most interesting result which emerged from her research was that the Kuruks can trace some of their ancestry to their prehistoric counterparts, though a direct line of descent cannot be established because of the fluid structure of the society that has prevailed in the past and which has allowed continuity of local migrations until fairly recently (Cooper 1983a, 1983b, 1986, 1997b). Cooper's work has a marked emphasis on ethnoarchaeology, but not because of any belief that cultural 'backwardness' has predominated in this area, or that the Kuruks are the direct descendants of their prehistoric counterpart. The Kuruks are fishers, hunters, foragers and marginal farmers, but do not place any significance on the microlithic artefacts found in their habitat. Cooper's study of Kuruk subsistence includes details on tools, traps and other facilities and lists of fish, edible plant and medicinal plant species. None of these items are likely to survive in the archaeological record. There is also a diversion on the parameters and changing pattern of mobility, and the Kuruk reinforce the hypothesis on Late Stone Age settlement systems. One of the drawbacks of Cooper's study in this region is that she has put little emphasis on the ethno-history of the Kuruks (Ratnagar 1998: 84-5).

Ethnographic research of hunter-gatherers carried out by archaeologists in India has mainly focused on the general patterns of subsistence and settlement, patterns of seasonal mobility and technology (Misra 1974). Ethnoarchaeologists have noted the intimate knowledge that members of hunting-gathering groups have of their physical and biological environments, and that most groups traditionally exploited a very wide range of plant and animal resources in the dwindling forests of today. Therefore, the natural world inhabited by the present tribal population is not all the same as the one that was inhabited by the prehistoric peoples of the same region. Modern subsistence and settlement patterns do not reflect the whole range of parallels to ancient ones of the same region (Murty 1981, 1985; Paddayya 1982; Nagar 1985; Raju 1988).

Misra's (1990, 1994) several seasons of fieldwork among numerous tribal communities such as Van Vagris, Bhils, Raikas and lower caste Hindus in the semi-arid and arid zone to the west of Aravali Hills in Rajasthan shows the persistence of the hunting and gathering way of life. His detailed study of the subsistence, settlement patterns, social organization and religious practices of these communities, and especially of nomadic Van Vagris, provide invaluable clues for understanding the past human adaptations in this region.

Roy's ethnoarchaeological work in Assam deals with the technological and social aspects of shifting cultivation in the subtropical zone of the Garo Hills. He seeks to document the impact of environmental constraints on labour investment, coordination and of seasonal variations in agricultural activities. Roy also examined the technology of shifting cultivation, such as, the tools used and patterns of usewear. The axes and hoes used by the present shifting cultivators are of metal, but Roy's work has demonstrated that the wear patterns they develop as a result of use in particular activities are quite similar to those found on Neolithic stone tools in the same region, and may result from similar kinds of use. Roy also studied indigenous folktales on the origin of these modern agriculturists and their beliefs pertaining to how cereal crops were introduced into their traditional system of root crop cultivation (Roy 1981).

S.C. Nanda's intensive survey in the Indravati Valley of Koraput district in Orissa which is geographically a part of the Eastern Ghats region, has brought to light a large number of Upper Palaeolithic and Mesolithic sites. Such an intensive survey of a limited geographical area and analyses and interpretation of data on the basis of ethnographic parameters is the first attempt in the Stone Age archaeology of Orissa. Nanda's ethnographic study of several primitive tribes such as Gadabas, Parajas, Saoras and Bondas in the study area showed the continuation of traditional methods of exploiting food resources, in spite of the introduction of agriculture. Nanda has drawn broad parallels of the subsistence pattern of the tribal groups of this area with that of prehistoric peoples in the same region (Nanda 1983, 1988). Following upon Nanda's work Ota (1986) brought to light several Mesolithic sites in the Phulbani district of central Orissa and studied a primitive tribal community known as Khonds to reconstruct the Mesolithic subsistence practices.

P. Mohanty's findings of a series of Mesolithic sites in dense forested region identified during a regional survey of Keonjhar district (Orissa), and a study of contemporary hunter-gatherer-shifting cultivators in the area as typified by the Juang tribe was the first attempt to arrive at an interpretative study of the Mesolithic cultural phase from the settlement system perspective in Orissa (Mohanty 1988, 1989, 1992, 1998). With a view to obtaining ethnographic analogies and parallels that are likely to shed light on the life-ways of the Mesolithic peoples of the area, especially with respect to ecological adaptations and the reconstruction of settlement and subsistence patterns, ethnographic investigations were undertaken among the Juangs. This tribe was considered for detailed study because the Mesolithic sites occur contiguous to Juang settlements. Since environmental conditions of peninsular India are known to have been fairly stable since the Holocene, it is reasonable to assume that the ecological setting during the Mesolithic was similar to that of the Juangs. This in turn implies broad similarities in terms of adaptation. In particular, it was thought best to spend more time to observe the means of exploiting the natural resources that are still available in the depleted forest environment, and to obtain an idea as to the extent to which gathering, hunting and fishing meets the general requirement of the Juangs' food supply. Despite modern influences and 'acculturation', this research revealed the constraints and possibilities of a forest environment, which still regulates the rhythm of Juang life and subsistence, and the Juang's adaptations to it (from dwellings to gathering, hunting, fishing etc.), and offers valid analogies for the reconstruction of adaptation patterns during the Mesolithic. From a holistic perspective, the contemporary Juangs provide a reference grid encompassing all aspects of culture, material as well as non-material, facilitating the reconstruction of human organization and adaptation in the past.

D.K. Chakrabarti in one of his recent articles makes an overview of the archaeological potential, concerning prehistoric, proto-historic and Early Historic cultures, of the Chhotanagpur plateau and its adjoining areas. He also discusses the tribal groups inhabiting this region who are at different levels of economic development such as hunter-gatherers, shifting cultivators and plough agriculturists. Some of these tribal groups continue to adopt traditional technologies in craft production (Chakrabarti 1994). However, Chakrabarti does not make any attempt to link ethnographic data with the prehistoric past in order to understand the archaeological problem of this vast region.

Experimental study is one of the ways by which alternative explanations can be generated to explain the observed archaeological phenomena. Conducting a test or trial and using its results as an aid for interpreting archaeological data is quite old and goes back to the middle of the nineteenth century (Coles 1973: 14). In the Indian context Paddayya through his preliminary observations and experimental work has been advocating and stressing the need for undertaking ethnographic and experimental work for understanding the cultural and natural processes of site formation (Paddayya 1983, 1987; Paddayya and Petraglia 1993, 1995). The range of other experiments carried out so far in India include flint knapping and usewear (Sankalia 1964, 1967, 1974, 1977; Pant 1979a, 1979b; Goerke 1982; Paddayya 1982, 1983; Sinha 1985; Shinde 1988, 1988-9), house structures and taphonomical study of faunal remains (Vacant Land Project 1988-9) and actualistic study (Panja 1995, 1996; Jhaldiyal 1997).

One of the aspects of the natural processes of site formation which has received much attention lately is that of the impact of surface flow on the open-air Stone Age sites. General observations about the impact of this process on the artefact assemblages and the problems in conducting spatial analysis for arriving at meaningful behavioural interpretations about ancient cultures have been recognized and articulated by several workers (e.g. Jacobson 1985; Paddayya 1977, 1978, 1982: Mohanty 1989; S. Pappu 1996a, 1996b). More detailed observations on the nature of impact of surface flow can be seen in the work of Paddayya (Paddayya 1983, 1987; Wandsnider 1991; Paddayya and Petraglia 1995; Paddayya 1978-9). Paddayya's studies of the stone behaviour on the gently sloping land on the Deccan College Campus in Pune, Maharashtra and the Stone Yard at Hunsgi-V and at the Khembhavi observational plot (both located in the Hunsgi-Baichbal Valleys in Karnataka) showed that in 3-4 years there was very little movement of stones. He observed that grass cover and the shallow nature of the runoff were the main factors which inhibited the movement of stone pieces. Some stone showed a tendency to cluster and in some instances were covered by a layer of silt. Thus once buried the stones were unaffected by the process of erosion. Similar observations were also made in the Vacant Land Project. This behaviour of the stones was therefore interpreted as an explanation for the occurrence of several primary Stone Age sites in the Hunsgi Valley, while at the same time it was recognized that these processes did cause considerable rearrangement within the spot (Paddayya 1983, 1991). Though these studies provided a good deal of insight into the nature of behaviour of lithics under the impact of surface flow they were not quantified observations with control on variables like slope and size which are a major determinant on the nature of lithic behaviour.

More recently Jhaldiyal (1997b, 1998) has conducted experimental studies in order to understand the behaviour of stone tools on low angled slopes under the impact of surface wash processes in the semi-arid region of Hunsgi-Baichbal Basins in north Karnataka. The aim of the experimental study was to understand the nature of past sedimentation processes which caused the burial of lithic concentrations and the consequent alterations they may have caused during the process of burial as well as to understand the contemporary processes of sheet wash to assess their role in re-exposing the assemblages to the surface and subsequently causing the spatial rearrangement of the artefacts. Underlying this was the aim of assessing the usefulness of the sites for making behavioural interpretations. Her study quantified the rate of the downslope movement of the artefacts and made observations on the nature of artefact orientation and site sorting on flat *versus* sloped surfaces as well as planar *versus* rilled surfaces. Her study showed that surface wash caused smaller artefacts to undergo greater displacement, though artefact displacement was also determined by their location on the slope. Artefacts located on the parts of the slope underwent greater displacement as compared to those on the upper part of the slope. The artefacts showed a tendency to be oriented parallel to the slope, but since the ground surface is usually uneven the overall orientation was not always directed towards the main slope. Thus it was recognized that orientation angles were not always a useful indicator for assessing slope-wash processes. A need to document microtopographic variations within the site was considered most essential to understand artefact behaviour on low angled slopes.

The second area where experimental work has been conducted to assess the spatial reorganization of artefact assemblages is that of the role of traditional ploughing techniques. In India a large number of Stone Age sites have been found from cultivated tracts of land. Ploughing brings artefacts to the surface and also promote soil erosion, thereby exposing the artefacts to contemporary processes of surface wash erosion (Paddayya 1987; Jhaldiyal 1997b). Paddayya made some observations on the role of these ploughing practices on the preservation of the sites (Paddayya 1996). Experimental work was conducted by Jhaldiyal (1997a) in order to assess the surface ploughzone ratio of artefacts, to study the extent of lateral displacement of artefacts and the nature of breakage undergone by artefacts as a consequence of tillage. Conducted between March 1993 and November 1994 during which six observations were made, the experiment demonstrated that the traditional tillage practices were not very damaging in nature where the maximum lateral displacement undergone by artefacts was under 2 m.

Research on prehistoric and protohistoric rock-art constitutes one of the important aspects of Indian archaeology. Ethnographic studies can help to a great extent in understanding the problems pertaining to various facets of Indian rock-art studies. Despite the great potential for research on this aspect, relatively few ethnoarchaeological studies have focused on this topic. In India, the concentration of rock-art sites is greater in Madhya Pradesh, especially in the districts of Hoshangabad, Narsinghpur, Mandla and Jabalpur, Hazaribag in Bihar and in western Orissa. Ghosh (1984) for the first time has attempted to understand the nature of prehistoric rock-paintings of the region using ethnographic evidence. According to Ghosh the tribals living in these districts make various types of art which may have continued from prehistoric times. Their traditional art form is connected with their respective ecosystem and in many cases the ecorelationship has been transformed into a form of religion. The nature of art is also related with ancestral worship to promote or preserve the fertility of the crops; rituals, to get relief from the diseases, child birth, marriage and death; religious rites representing the shrines of forests, rivers, animals, hills, etc. Ghosh is of the view that parallels can be drawn from the living tradition to understand the prehistoric rock-art and to trace the route of religious beliefs and the ideological determinants. He further opines that the regions with large concentrations of prehistoric rock-art and modern tribal population should be examined from an ethnoarchaeological perspective to understand prehistoric religious and social patterns (Ghosh 1984).

LATER PREHISTORIC AND HISTORICAL ARCHAEOLOGY

Ashmounds are a distinct class of sites forming part of the archaeological record of south India (Paddayya 1991-2: 573). Several scholars have attempted to understand this problem in the past two hundred years. F.R. Allchin's work on ashmounds is undoubtedly the most elaborate treatment of the problem so far. He carried out research on this problem for several years and undertook an excavation of an ashmound site at Utnur (Allchin 1961). Further he carried out extensive ethnographic work in the same area relating to place names, local traditions and various religious practices and ceremonies concerning cattle (Allchin 1963). According to him the ashmounds constitute the Southern Neolithic culture representing the spots of cattle-pens. Each period consisted of several stages: levelling of the site; construction of stockades; cattle occupation and cow-dung accumulation; cow-dung burning and ash deposition. Allchin viewed that some of these pens were forest pens located away from habitation settlements, which were provided with double stockades, with the human community occupying the space between the two lines of stockades. He concluded that cow-dung bearings were intentional, and an annual bonfire ceremony took place in the cattle-pens at the time of leading cattle to hilly tracts in search of summer pastures. These ceremonies were a part of a fertility cult during which cattle were probably driven through a moderate fire of dung. The present-day festivals of Holi, Diwali and Pongal in which cattle still play a dominant role are, according to Allchin, survivals of these Neolithic practices. A few years latter, the Allchins came up with a slightly modified version, i.e. many of the Neolithic ashmounds were employed in the first instance as a means of capturing wild cattle both for immediate purposes and for domestication (Allchin and Allchin 1974: 77). They thus postulated that their interpretation of ashmounds as cattle domestication centres was 'beyond and perhaps additional to that formerly suggested by us' as cattle-pens and even presumed that these centres met the demand for pack-oxen and drought-oxen from the authors of the Indus Civilization.

Paddayya's research in north Karnataka spanning nearly three decades brought new evidence in understanding the ashmound sites in relation to the natural and cultural features of their respective landscape setting (Paddayya 1991-2, 1993a, 1993b, 1998). Paddayya questions Allchin's well known cattle-pen hypothesis, according to which the ashmound represents seasonally occupational cattle-pens where the in situ cow-dung accumulations were being periodically burnt. Relying upon the extensive evidence of human occupation in his own field area, Paddayya visualized these sites as regular Neolithic pastoral sites where human occupation was necessarily involved. The cow-dung accumulations resulting from the overwhelmingly pastoral character of the economy, for want of use as field measure and such other practical purposes, were being burnt regularly; these burnings probably fulfilled a variety of practical as well as ceremonial processes (Paddayya 1993b: 278).

Besides, we find a plethora of information regarding economic organization, social groupings, technology, kinship and family, various forms of marriage and folklore in the general works dealing with cattle and tribes (Thurston 1909; Baines 1912; Iyer 1909-12; Russel and Hiralal 1996; Radcliff-Brown 1922; Roy 1925; McCrindle 1926; Nanjundayya and Iyer 1928-36; Aiyappan 1937, 1948; Ehrenfels 1952; Majumdar 1961; Majumdar and Madan 1961; Cipriani 1966; Williams 1968a, 1968b; Gardener 1968; Fuchs 1973). Here the emphasis is essentially anthropological, but if these customs are to serve as a guide in the prehistoric studies, it should be investigated from an archaeological point of view (Paddayya 1978-9: 76).

In the early 1970s, Nagar carried out ethnoarchaeological studies of the rural population in several villages of Mewar with a view to obtaining similarities, if any, between the second millennium BC Ahar Chalcolithic and the present-day rural culture of the area (Nagar 1966, 1969, 1970, 1973, 1975a). Her study concentrated mainly in the villages around the site of Ahar near the city of Udaipur in Rajasthan. Some fifty sites of the Ahar Culture are known in the valleys of the Banas river and the tributaries. Ahar was a farming culture with copper metallurgy and very limited use of stone technology, plentiful use of painted and incised pottery, and stone and mud structure. The population of the tribes in the area she studied were Bhils and several farming and trading caste Hindus. The economy of these people is based on a combination of agriculture and pastoralism, especially breeding of sheep and camels. Her study revealed that there had been little change in house types, building materials and the techniques between the prehistoric culture and the present-day society. Some of the pottery forms and techniques of surface treatment like slipping and burnishing are common to prehistoric and present-day pottery. A most striking resemblance is seen in some of the Ahar Culture pottery designs with the present-day Bhil clothing designs. The most distinctive Ahar ceramic design is a Black-and-Red Ware with white dotted and linear designs over a black background. Identical designs in white are found on the 'odhnis' of Bhil women. The *odhnis* are also printed in black-and-red and painted designs in white on black borders.

Following upon Nagar's work Hooja (1988, 1994) attempted to understand the symbiotic interactions between the Ahar communities and the contemporary hunter-gatherers classified as Mesolithic using both the archaeological data and ethnographic evidence. She considered both Ahar and Bagor as type sites which coexisted within a common spatio-temporal span. Her analysis of interrelationship between two economies or 'cultures' or 'lifestyles' of present-day agriculturists and hunting-gathering and incipient farming group of Bhils is an example of modern behavioural pattern as direct historical analogy. Work along this line has already been done by Possehl and Kennedy (1979), Possehl and Rissman (1991) and Guha (1994).

Horizontal excavations over several seasons at the Chalcolithic sites of Inamgaon, Kaothe and Walki all in Maharashtra by the Deccan College, Pune, offer a good example on the material culture parallels between ancient and contemporary villages, for example house forms. As many as 130 houses belonging to different cultural periods were exposed at Inamgaon alone along with a rich yield of artefacts. It was possible to identify dwellings of various craftsmen such as potters, lapidaries, lime-makers, and goldsmiths and that of the ruling chief of the community on the basis of architectural and artefactual evidence. Similarly, a number of floor plans were exposed at Walki, which has been identified as a farmstead, possibly of Inamgaon. All these structures provide a good idea of the Chalcolithic architecture and they could only be properly understood to a considerable extent in the light of present-day ethnographic parallels available in the locality (Dhavalikar 1983, 1988, 1994; Dhavalikar et al. 1990a; Dhavalikar et al. 1990b).

Recent actualistic study of the Deccan Chalcolithic (Panja 1995, 1996) has sought to understand the material consequences of human behaviour in order to provide a heuristic device with which to interpret past behaviour from archaeological remains. The Chalcolithic culture of Inamgaon was taken as a case study to assess how earlier researchers have tried to understand mobility change from past material culture. With this archaeological problem ethnoarchaeological work was carried out to examine critically the categories archaeologists use to describe mobility strategies of the past and its relationship with material culture. This is what is known as 'middle-range research', another aspect of processual archaeology which is aimed at understanding how and why the record is formed before we make any statements about the archaeological records themselves (Binford 1983, 1987). What we see in the archaeological record are the static remains of behaviour, but we have to investigate the dynamic behaviour that generated them. Only an ethnographic situation can enable us to perceive different forms of behaviour and their material consequences. Many archaeologists use commonsense notions to interpret past behaviour from material remains, but what we need is a systematic approach to investigate this linkage which is often called 'middle-range research'.

The aim of Panja's actualistic study was to see how and why groups with different mobility strategies use space across the landscape at a local/regional level. This was used as backdrop with which to compare and recognize diverse mobility strategies in the archaeological record. The agro-pastoral Dhangars living in the same semi-arid zone where the archaeological record is found and comprising both sedentary, semi-sedentary and semi-nomadic groups were taken up for study. Her work was aimed at understanding their material culture and its change through time. The aim was to monitor not only how groups use space within a short term (a few years) so as to be able to understand the long-term material consequences of behaviour. Households and field-camps of the sedentary and semi-sedentary groups and Dhangarvadis of the nomadic group were taken up for mapping by a tape/pacing and compass method. The features were described and photographed. Panja made an attempt to follow a group of Dhangars on their migration and record and map their overnight transit camps. Artefact collection was also made from sampled units across the 'sites' of groups with different mobility strategies in order to understand the nature of artefact patterning on a single site and its change through time.

All these observations across a region and a site along with published literature on similar topics were used as heuristic models with which to understand mobility from the archaeological record at Inamgaon.

J.W. Breeks tried to correlate the Megalithic monuments of the Nilgiris with some of the customs and rites of the Todas (Breeks 1873). Walhouse (1874a, 1874b) documented the funeral rites of the Todas. Kapp (1985) studied the Kuruba relationship with the Megalithic cult of Nilgiri Hills.

Nagaraja Rao (1985) studied the house types of the Boyas to reconstruct the Neolithic dwellings of Tekkalakota in Karnataka. He found many similarities between the two. Other ethnoarchaeological works using the food-producing tribal cultures and peasant societies for studying the Neolithic-Chalcolithic cultures are those of Leshnik (1964, 1966) and Paddayya (1969). Cooper's ethno-historical and ethnoarchaeological work in Andaman islands has produced very interesting results concerning the dynamics of site formation processes of the shell midden sites. In the course of her survey, she discovered several shell midden sites on the coast, in the interior inland and in caves. To understand the formation of these middens, she studied the Onge community of the area and found out that the formation of a midden appears to represent two stages: initially as a secondary deposit, and subsequently, when a camp was established over it, as a repository of discard. Although her study pointed out the limitations pertaining to the reconstruction of the social organization, mythological beliefs and linguistic groupings, it nevertheless yielded valuable information on subsistence pattern and local ecological features (Cooper 1993a, 1993b, 1994 and 1997a).

CERAMIC ARCHAEOLOGY

Among the material components of the past, the study of pottery has received maximum attention by the ethnoarchaeologists. From prehistoric till the present-day pottery is one of the essential commodities of daily use and an item of trade. In almost all proto-historic and historical sites ceramics are found in abundance. Their wide distribution, forms and types have led archaeologists to identify them as the signifiers of the past economy, socio-political complexity and the ritual behaviours within the space, time and contextual systematics. The homogeneous characters of various ceramic types in various parts of the country, throughout human history show the routes of penetration and their significance in trade and commerce; both inland and transoceanic.

Ethnographic studies of the present potter communities occupying various rural and urban areas have not only thrown light on the technology of pot making, but have also revealed their social organizations, craft specialization, role of political and social institution and trade mechanism.

Kramar (1991, 1994) studied ceramic ethnoarchaeology at two important cities of Rajasthan, namely Jodhpur and Udaipur keeping the following points in mind: to establish numbers and types of vessels and spatial distribution of potters and shops within two cities of different sizes; to explore relationship among potters and vendors both within and outside those cities; with a view to identifying the role that sociological relationships play in the spatial distribution of ceramics; and to identify the ceramic differences between settlements of varying size which might ultimately be reflected in the archaeological record. Kramar's ethnographic investigations suggest that both scalar differences among settlements may be reflected in material differences between them and that there are complex interactions between sociological and spatial distances. The heterogeneous assemblages, she noticed in the ethnographic set-up, show that different artisans could have congregated at large urban/commercial avenues of the past. Thus, differences in numbers, association and location of particular wares in the archaeological sites may reflect the movement of ceramics between centres of comparable administrative sizes.

Roux (1985-6, 1989a, 1989b) studied the craft specialization of potters at Uttam Nagar, a suburb of New Delhi and the objectives of her study was two-fold: synchronic and diachronic. At the synchronic level, the construction of an ethnographic frame makes it possible to infer the existence of specialists on the basis of ceramic facts, whereas at the diachronic level the ethnographic model helps to describe the phenomenon of craft specialization at the local level, i.e. according to the individual case that each archaeological site represents.

Roux compared her ethnographic data with the archaeological evidence of Amreli, an excavated Harappan site and formulated the hypothesis that the wheel-thrown pottery was observed during fourth-third millennium BC at Amreli could have been practised only by specialists, thus reflecting craft specialization as an important factor in the development of complex societies.

Many of the Harappan sites in Gujarat have revealed a variety of decorative ceramics in abundance. Interestingly, the decorative trend on ceramics has survived till today in many parts of Gujarat, though the contemporary motifs bear no resemblance to those of Harappan Civilization. Archana Choksi (1997) attempts to locate the organizational principles underlying contemporary pottery decoration in Kachchh, and suggests how this contemporary basis could be used to infer similar principles in the archaeological context.

Choksi's work was concentrated around Kachchh, Gundiyali and Lodai. The potting tradition of the former two are rapidly changing to satisfy the demands of urban markets as far as Mumbai, whereas Lodai produces for the conservative, pastoral local markets. These villages have strong decorative traditions which are a function of kinship ties and are highly distinctive, and carry design elements which are similar to those of the Harappan tradition. In both centres, painting is done by women. Her work integrates the design structure with the design rules in the painting process, painter's apprenticeship, the symbolism and the vessel decoration in times of change. She criticizes the trend in the archaeological context, where decorative elements and motifs have always been the centre of attempts to classify vessel sherds, and have generally been understood in terms of art and aesthetics. Her work shows that art and aesthetics form a very small component of the whole design process and that a particular design combination belongs to a particular location.

Choksi in yet another attempt deals with the socio-economic condition of the society in which a potter works. Her work reflects the determination of form, function and shape of the potter's output against the background of her socio-economic condition. She is critical of the archaeologists working on Harappan Culture of Gujarat who have tended to use ceramics to clarify issues of regionality and chronology. Their exclusive use of typologies in this respect has neglected the use of pottery to illuminate social and economic relationships of the past (Choksi 1995). In many archaeological sites, several ritual pots, terracotta mother goddesses and animal figurines occur in substantial numbers. Hashim in an attempt at several places in Gujarat demonstrates the role of clay pots in different social and religious ceremonies and tries to trace their origin and spread through using the ethnographic parallel. Hashim's work shows that the clay pots are specially produced by the traditional potters of Gujarat for uses on the occasion of marriage and ceremonies and on the occasion of festivals of worship (Hashim 1989). Recently, Kar et al. (1993) carried out ethnographic work to understand the manufacturing process of pottery at the village Talasara in Talaza taluka of Bhavnagar district, Gujarat. Their prime objective was to link the present-day pottery of the excavated Harappan site of Padri, located about 2 km north-east of Talasara. Their work covered the technological, functional, socio-economic, distributional and symbolic aspects of pottery. They could draw parallels with the Harappan pottery in certain aspects like the fine Red Ware of the Harappan tradition which were prepared by the people, who had plenty of time and who led a peaceful life.

Krishnan and Veena Rao's combined effort at the workshop of two traditional potters at Muzpur and Borada in Gujarat demonstrate how the various methods used in the preparation of clay paste are reflected in the micro structure of the product. They began their work with making an attempt to produce ceramics of the same type by processing the raw material using the elutriation technique. They further studied the micro structure of the products and the raw materials using their thin sections. Their study revealed the different processes adopted for refining the raw materials, which they could observe in the micro structure of the products.

The result of their work could show the possibility of identifying technological processes in Harappan ceramics from the excavation at Ratnapura (Krishnan and Rao 1994). Miller (1981; 1985) aimed at understanding the factors underlying variability in ceramic artefacts. In many societies, both in the past and present, artefacts produced by the communities reflect the organizational principles of human categorization processes. His work among the Dhangwara potter communities concentrated in a central Indian village concerns the manner in which these organizational principles generate variability in the material forms. Miller's work is quite significant from an ethnoarchaeological perspective, since the variability of material remains in any archaeological site provides an impetus to understanding the past social action and social relations.

His micro-analysis of the ceramic assemblage found in a single village, including the details of rim forms, body angularity and decorative technique throws sufficient light on the contextual setting, which does not survive for the archaeologists. The area in which the Dhangwara settlement is located is rich in Chalcolithic sites. The ceramics found on these sites are divided into two series, the earlier as Malwa and the later as Jorwe. Previously, it had been suggested that the two series merely represented a spatial division, with Malwa named after the present area in which Dhangwara is situated and Jorwe associated with the sites of Maharashtra (Dhavalikar 1979). However, the excavation at Navdatoli produced a varied set of ceramic forms and decoration where the Jorwe types were seen as the continuation of the same ceramic tradition.

Miller analysed the artefacts as categories in three levels: that of the individual pot as representative of a category, that of the pottery categories as constituent elements of a pottery code, and that of a grid in which pottery as code was related to all other codes. Such structure could generate transformation and information of social complexity.

The implication of these for archaeology is that categorization found in material form may be as fully constitutive of society as normative articulated social categories, equivalent to caste. In India, the period between *c.* 500 BC and AD 350 has been considered as the Early Historic period which was most dynamic in terms of state formation. During this period, cities emerged within the context of Buddhism and the changing socio-political and economic framework at various 'integrated estates'. The shift from the sedentary to the urban society had led to the establishment of a network of internal and overseas trade routes and allowed rapid inter-regional distribution of ideas and artefacts through the growth of communication and the increased mobility of people. The religious faiths and institutions had profound impact on language, art and culture. The extension of trade networks had far-reaching implication and were accompanied by the introduction of currency, a wide range of ceramics and specialized art and craft.

Rouletted Ware is one of the distinctive ceramic types of this period, which occurs in a majority of sites on the east coast, thus implying the coastal trade pattern with Sri Lanka and South-East Asia. The ware was discovered for the first time at Arikamedu, the famous port city of Early Historic period located on the Coromandal coast near Pondicherry. Arikamedu has yielded evidence of overseas trade with the Roman-Hellenistic world. Considering the stylistic attributes with those of the Hellenistic region, Wheeler thought that the fine Roulleted Ware arrived at Arikamedu from the Roman territory through the great Indian ocean trade (Wheeler et al. 1946). Subsequently, the ware was found at a majority of sites on both sides of the Bay of Bengal. V. Begley is of the view that this particular ware developed indigenously which she tried to establish through studying the present day pottery tradition (Begley 1986, 1988).

Begley argues that the major thrust of the Rouletted Ware was coastal and in the south-eastern region of the peninsula. Being the major trade centre and having sustained trade with the west, from where the technique of rouletting-chattering was introduced, Arikamedu was the main production centre of the ware. According to Begley, though in the living tradition the technique of rouletting is extinct, it is prevalent at Bijnour, where a group of Muslim communities still make fine lustrous black pottery with rouletting design on them. She claims that the Rouletted pottery decoration at Bijnour provides insight into the other aspects of technology, which may be relevant to Arikamedu. According to her, the Bijnour potters, whose entire families are involved in the process of pottery-making, follow a series of procedures. The delicate pottery produced by them are not meant for daily use, but are used as containers for special items. They use a special different clay and the decoration is added while the vessel is being shaped. They use a roulette (*manka*) made of brass with a detachable wooden handle for the rouletted decoration. The roulette is held to the wall of the vessel firmly, while it is revolving on the wheel, making a band of regularly spaced small stroke. They use mustard oil before firing for the lustrous effect. Begley points out that the use of mustard oil is important and investigation should be carried out to know whether oiling was also used as a method of increasing lustre on Rouletted Ware and Northern Black Polished Ware. Begley's ethnographic work is interesting since it deals with the technological aspect of one of the most important ceramic types of South and Southeast Asia in the living tradition. It strengthens her hypothesis pertaining to the indigenous origin of Rouletted Ware, but it is difficult to agree with her that Arikamedu was the only production centre. Geographical approach involving soil analysis from various localities around Arikamedu has shown that the soil type of south India was not very suitable for making fine wares. In this regard Gogte's argument (1997) for Chandraketugarh-Tamluk region and Krishnan's opinion on multiple production centres (K. Krishnan: personal communication) seem more plausible for identifying the general pattern in the provenance studies of the Rouletted Ware.

Allchin (1978) studied the archaeological significance of the modern Indian potter's technique at Mudgal in Karnataka and Wadkud in Daman. He observed three major groups of forms in the 'proto-historic' and Early Historic ceramic traditions of India. Of these three, the shallow food bowls in Black-and-Red Ware show clear traces of wheel-throwing on the upper parts of the wall, whilst the rounded bases, often below a clearly defined angle, were formed by hand after cutting from the wheel. Similar technique was also employed for the production of Painted Gray Ware, Northern Black Polished Ware and Rouletted Ware. At Mudgal, the modern potters produce shallow bowls without involving wheel but using a rudimentary form of turntable setting as earthen ware saucer. Allchin describes the bowls as poor man's *thalis* and further notices close similarities between Mudgal bowls and shallow bowls of Painted Gray Ware, Northern Black Polished Ware and Black-and-Red Ware traditions. He assumes that similar technology was also adopted during the Iron Age-Early Historic period, which has been misinterpreted by many archaeologists as the products of slow wheel turn technology. Allchin's work at Wadkud has shown an interesting variant of the Mudgal tradition of pottery that shows parallels with another pottery type from the archaeological context. The careful documentation made by him on the technological aspects of ceramic production at Wadkud by both men and women postulate that two different forms such as shallow bowl and the conical lid with knob have considerable archaeological implications. The shallow bowl which is an extension of the *thali* of Mudgal tradition is marked by comparatively heavy rims and sharper angle and shows remarkable parallel with the carinated bowls of the Deccan Chalcolithic culture. The small convex lid with central knob shows similarity with the groove pots in the south Indian Megalithic sites; thus suggesting how ethnographic analogies help us to understand the technological aspects of ceramics from archaeological contexts.

The forgoing discussion pertaining to the works of ceramic ethnoarchaeologists show that their main emphasis was to reconstruct the 'proto-historic' and Early Historic ceramic typology and the institutional framework under which the specialization worked. Laura's work stands apart, since it deals with the present-day ceramic traditions to reconstruct the Medieval ceramic craft system of the Vijayanagara Empire (Laura 1985). Laura studied the morphology, function and style in traditional ceramic at Kamalapura, located in the heartland of Medieval Vijayanagara Empire. The other anthropologists and ethnoarchaeologists who have worked on ceramics are Ansari (1964), Dument (1952) and Bala (1997). Besides, members of the Anthropological Survey of India and the Census of India have carried out large scale documentation projects (cf. Behura 1965, 1967a, 1967b, 1978; Saraswati 1967, 1978; Saraswati and Behura 1966). Their works have provided useful information on regional tradition of craft specialization and the position of craftsmen in the caste-ridden Indian society. To interpret the terracotta art of Early Historic and Historical periods of the Ganga Valley, an intensive documentation of the surviving tradition pertaining to terracotta craft making on the plains of Bihar and eastern Uttar Pradesh was carried out by Jayaswal (1984, 1989); Jayaswal and Krishna (1986) and Jayaswal et al. (1986). They classified the baked clay figurines produced by the hereditary potter communities under three broad categories such as ritualistic, decorative and toys for the children. Among the animal figurines, elephant, horse, and tiger are prominent and elephant is the most common objective of offering. The horse comes next as an object of offering, while the use of the tiger figurine is limited to a smaller pocket in the Gorakhpur area. Elephant figurines are offered during different ritual ceremonies, viz., worship of the Sun god during the Chhatha festival, worship of Ganesha at the time of marriage and sacred thread ceremonies. The horse terracottas are associated with the popular belief in exorcism. In recent years several decorative animal figurines under 'Nauranga style' have been innovated thanks to support from various Government agencies. The terracotta of the 'Nauranga style' are represented by stylized lustrous ochre-coloured figurines of elephant, horse, tiger, camel and rhinoceros.

The manufacturing techniques as described by them involve a series of processes beginning with the preparation of clay, modelling of figurines, working minor details and decorations, prefiring wash or slip, firing and postfiring colouring and painting. In the archaeological records, several terracotta animal figurines have been reported and provide notable analogies with some of the features exhibited by similar figures of present-day eastern Uttar Pradesh and Bihar (middle Ganga Basin). Jayaswal et al. (1986) claim that the archaic looking stylized animal figurines produced by the early societies of the region fulfilled several cultural needs of the society, as evident in the present-day.

BEAD STUDIES

In the archaeological record, the spatial distribution of production materials reflect the segregated production areas, standardization, craft specialization and evidence of complex society. The records also show centralized control over craft specialization, localized production and distribution and in an urban context. Centralized control of production has been used along with political organization, information processing and social stratification, as distinguishing factors of state level-organization. The activities in an urban context is the result of social stratification and intentional urban organization by a state institution or elite groups and this may explain the need of craft groups to reside in close proximity for optimal use of resources and reciprocal exchange of services. This shows that craft specialization has come to be associated with socio-economic stratification and control of production. However, the segregation or isolation of craft indicators in the archaeological record could be attributed to lack of understanding of site formation processes and without a clear understanding of how craft specialization itself is organized in different contexts. It is difficult to define the relationship between occupational specialization and urban segregation of crafts and social structure. With this theoretical outline, Kenoyer et al. (1991, 1994) conducted an intensive study with living bead-makers of Khambat (Cambay) in western India to correlate the dynamics and complex socio-economic relationships with specific archaeological pattern.

Khambat in Gujarat is one of the largest stone bead centres of the world with over two thousand years of documented history and over 4,000 years of archaeological evidence. Presently, Khambat not only provides the continuity of specialized craft, but also in respect of various aspects of social, economic and political organization relating to bead manufacturing, thus reflecting an unique opportunity to study the organization of the specific craft that we find embedded in the archaeological record. Kenoyer et al. describe the various stages of bead manufacturing, beginning with extracting the resources from the mines, drying, heating, chipping, secondary heating, sawing, grinding, drilling, polishing and then final heating. Polishing is the most lengthy process and it requires specialized skill. A highly stratified society controlled by dominant individuals or merchant families characterize the organization of bead production at Khambat. Kenoyer et al. relate them to the complex social stratification of traditional India which is characterized by endogamous castes, occupational specialization and relative levels of ritual purity. They include Hindu, Jaina and Muslim communities and they have established distinct kin networks or alliances with politically powerful individuals or organizations. Through these connections it is possible to control the flow of raw materials, production and distribution of finished commodities.

In Khambat, the major merchant families carefully monitor and control all stages of bead production and often extend their control to the mining of the raw agate nodules. In the archaeological record of Khambat there is clear reflection of centralized control in each stage of production. All types of semi-finished items from each stage of production are found in the archaeological record in or around the merchant's house/workshop. Another interesting observation they make is the common occurrence of broken and unfinished beads from all stages of manufacture in the centralized workshop. They have noted how the administration controls or rejects broken fragments and unfinished beads by counting the number of bead blanks that may serve an archaeological inference. Drilling is done by part-time agriculturalists and polishing is done depending upon the availability of labour and the demand of the object.

Roux et al. (1995) studied to understand the skills involved in knapping of Harappan long carnelian beads using ethnographic parameters. They examined the present stone knapping at Khambat in Gujarat. Their study revealed the procedures of handling the complexity of the task and achieving it and the duration of apprenticeship. They applied the results of their research to differentiate beads on the basis of skills involved in their making, interpret them in terms of intrinsic symbolic value and knapper's socio-economic status.

Indo-Pacific glass beads, which persisted for some two thousand years often in great quantity throughout much of the Eastern Hemisphere is one of the indicators of Early and Medieval Indian ocean trade. The beads are small, usually under 6 mm diameter, undecorated and confined to limited colours. The first Indo-Pacific glass beads were produced at Arikamedu in the south-eastern coast of India and gradually penetrated to Mantai in Sri Lanka, Klong Thom and Oc-Eo in South-East Asia during the later period through the Chola invansion. Fresh evidence from Arikamedu shows an earlier date, *c.* 250-150 BC which is associated with a piece of bead making waste, thus confirming the early age of industry there. However, after the decline of trade at Arikamedu, the bead industry also perished. Soon after Mantai in Sri Lanka emerged as a major manufacturing centre of Indo-Pacific glass beads which is supplied to various southern Indian sites and even the Persian Gulf. Mantai was destroyed by the Cholas in the tenth century AD. Sooner or later, the bead-makers at Mantai moved back to India and later moved to Papanaidupet. Papanaidupet is a semi-urban settlement of about 15,000 people in the Chittoor district of southern Andhra Pradesh. The major occupation of the people of this town is agriculture and bead making. Until recently, Papanaidupet was a major supplier of beads for the Indian market.

Francis's ethnographic investigations at Papanaidupet reveals the craft mechanism, manufacturing process and the business network. The town obtains glass from the large factories of Firozabad in Uttar Pradesh and other ingredients are purchased from the local markets. About 250 men actually make beads, but 5,000 women and girls string them as their part-time pursuit. The technology involves a series of methods beginning with glass making, then glass working, tube drawing, cutting the tubes, reheating the cut segments and finally stringing the beads.

METAL CRAFT

Iron is a very common and profusely distributed mineral deposit in India. The mineral is also found in several river beds in the form of magnetite sand. The knowledge of extraction of iron in different forms was known to the ancient civilizations. One of the simplest ways of obtaining iron was from river beds although it was qualitatively inferior. However, for technical reasons the low grade irons were preferred by ancient iron smiths. The ethnographic work carried out by Tripathi and Mishra (1997), Tripathi and Tripathi (1994) and A. Misra (1997) provide invaluable insights for understanding the ancient technology of iron production.

Tripathi and Mishra (1997) have carried out intensive field studies among the pre-industrial iron working communities of Agaraias in Chattisgarh and Wadruffnagar districts of Madhaya Pradesh. Their observation show that most of the pre-industrial iron workers reside in close proximity to the mineral deposits. They cover about 15-20 km of distance during one trip and collect approximately 45-60 kg of ores necessary for 3-4 days of smelting. This involves group activity comprising several families. Ores are mainly picked up by hand in the form of nodules from exposed surfaces near Nalas or rain-gullies and sometimes also through shallow digging. These communities are experts in identifying the quality of ores.

After the selection of raw materials, arrangements are made for the smelting for which pestles and four-legged querns are used to crush the ores. It is interesting to note that in the Early Historic context four-legged querns have been widely reported from many archaeological sites. Contextually, the functions of these objects have not been properly understood by archaeologists. Thus taking the ethnographic evidence into account their actual relationship with ancient metal technology can be understood.

Tripathi and Mishra further studied the process of iron smelting, the extraction methods, furnaces and forging on the basis of ethnographic analogies for understanding the ancient iron technology of the Ganga Valley.

A.K. Mishra (1997) has attempted to bring a parallel between the ancient iron technology of India and the iron smelting process in the living tradition in the Bastar region in east-central India. Bastar is a part of the ancient Dandakaranya as mentioned in the *Ramayana* and has a well written history and is presently covered with dense forest and inhabited by a large number of tribal communities. The western desisted edge of Bastar plateau lying to the north of the Indravati river is marked by Abujhamar Hills which provides one of the richest iron ore deposits of India at Bailadilla range and this resembles the iron-ore series of Singhbhum of Bihar and Kalahandi of Orissa. The living tribal population spreading over 50 villages are known as Hill Murias. They have been making iron using the ancient technology to prepare arrow-heads, axes, hoe and needle point for tattooing. The Hill Murias believe that tattooing helps them ward off evil spirits.

Mishra discusses the entire process of iron smelting that starts with bringing the iron ores from the nearby available ore deposits. He further shows that the square closed iron smelting furnace with surrounded charcoal and iron slags practised by present Hill Murias closely resemble the evidence reported from Sunga-Kushana level at Khariadih. According to him the smelted iron produced by the Murias are not meteoric iron, which is evident in the archaeological sites at Inca of Peru, Mayas of Yucatan and Aztec of Mexico. In India, meteoric iron has not been reported in any of the archaeological sites. Mishra also discusses the social and religious activities, which take place during the performance of the furnace.

In the Indian subcontinent high tin bronzes have been reported from the Indus Valley site of Mohenjo Daro, the Iron Age site of Taxila and from the megalithic graves of south India. In the present context, the two south Indian states such as Tamil Nadu and Kerala have preserved a rich repertoire of traditional image casting and utilitarian crafts such as mirrors, lamps, bells, vessels and musical instruments in high tin beta (23 per cent) bronze and high tin delta (33 per cent) bronze.

Srinivasan (1994, 1997a, 1997b) and Srinivasan and Glover (1995) carried out systematic investigations to understand the technology of these crafts. Their work demonstrated that these relatively sophisticated high tin bronze crafts are neither anomalous nor 'exotic' crafts within the local milieu, but reflect the existence of a developed copper bronze alloying tradition in the Indian metallurgical record that has not been previously recognized. Their work further showed the employment of a range of copper-base metals from unalloyed copper to bell metal, and techniques such as lost wax process, sand casting, piece mould, and closed crucible casting, annealing, hot forging, quenching, polishing on indigenous lathes and the use of traditional furnaces.

The lost wax casting of Hindu images by *sthapatis* from Tanjavur region has historical significance, since it is described in ancient *Silpasastra* or artistic treatise such as the Gupta *Manasara* and *Silparatna* and later Chalukyan *Manasollasa*. The temple town of Kumbhakonam is a major centre of metal craft, mainly of icons and temple bells of Hindu tradition. The objects are made at Nacharkoli, 8 km away from the town where the lost wax casting of temple bells and lamps and sand casting of cymbals for the classical dance by the Kammalar are observed.

Trichur in Kerala has been considered as a market of highly prized ritual and utilitarian utensils and metal wares for the elite. Srinivasan's fieldwork at several workshops documented the making of large beaten copper vessels by the Chembotti using the traditional methods. She studied the alloying trends and their functions using the latest scientific devices like electron micro probe analysis with wavelength Dispersive X-ray analysis. The result of her work establishes the functional properties of alloys which resembles those of the bronze images of the Chola and Pandya kingdoms, and the high tin bronze bowls of Nilgiri Megalithic, Sonepur Period-II, and from the Historical Period in eastern India, Taxila and Mohenjo Daro. Taking the ethnographic analogy, classical records and the recovery of slags by her from the ancient mining region in the Hassan district of Karnataka, she argues that the indigenous ore sources of tin could have been exploited for south Indian antiquities to make such artefacts. She argues that Kerala represents one of the oldest known metallurgical tradition in the Indian subcontinent.

In India, archaeometallurgical study on ancient metal technology has generally received an evolutionary perspective. The early presence of pure copper and elementary variant objects have always been regarded as 'discrepant' products of alloy metal and craft deficiencies. Lahiri's attempt has shown the value of folk beliefs and memories of historical events around metal and metal related artefacts including slags. Her approach using ethnographic data and literary evidence shows how such elements can be understood as the past cultural signifiers more meaningfully (Lahiri 1995).

Besides, work on socio-religious aspects of a particular metal craft community has been carried out by Suchira Roychoudhury. Roychoudhury has studied the *cire perdue* casting in the living tradition of Bengal among the ancient Dhokra Kamaras. While comparing the present-day social life of the Dhokras with that of past communities, she observes that the earlier Dhokras possessed higher status and were royally patronized. During the Pala-Sena times they were more organized as corporate guilds. At present, their interaction with the established groups have been minimized. Due to their miserable economic condition and other social pressure they are now treated as the fifth caste of the Varna hierarchy (Roychoudhury 1998).

SHELL STUDIES

Molluscan shells have been one of the earliest raw materials to have been used by human beings. In India, shell objects are commonly encountered at a majority of archaeological sites ranging from prehistoric to the Historical period. Most commonly found objects are shell bangles as evident at Harappan sites like Lothal, Kuntasi, Nageshwar, Surkotada, etc. Today shells are not a popular raw material as compared with plastics and metals. However, the ancient craft of shell working is still visible in parts of north-eastern India and in parts of West Bengal like Bankura, Hoogly, Midnapore districts, etc. But the chief centres are Vishnupur, Bankura, Barrakpur, Calcutta, etc. Out of these Vishnupur has been considered suitable because it has an ancient tradition of shell working dating back to the Historic period and it produces good quality objects.

Studies by Hornell (1942), Kenoyer (1983) and Deshpande (1995) brought to light the existence of this particular craft in modern India. The observations of these crafts have helped the archaeologists to gain suitable insights into the nature of shell technology in the past. Deshpande studied the caste which makes these shell objects. The caste known as Shankaries reside within a special locality called Shankaripara consisting of their settlements and working quarters. There are about 200 Shankaries in Vishnupur. All are engaged in making shell bangles and they do not pursue any other trade.

Deshpande's overall study has helped reconstruct the Harappan shell industry at two sites, Kuntasi and Sikharpur in Gujarat. Comparison of both present and past shell working has revealed similarities in both types of shell working, the type of shell used, technology employed, etc. A likeness is observed in the archaeological shell waste and that of Vishnupur revealing the use of a common shell working tradition. It has also provided an insight into the social, religious and economic status of the shell workers. Besides, it has also revealed the deteriorating condition of this ancient craft tradition which is slowly on the decline. This is due to the high cost of shells, poor availability of good quality shells, and preference for plastics as a better raw material. This work of Deshpande constitutes a good example of the general comparative analogy.

In Bengal, the Shankaries procure shells from distant south India, Sri Lanka and the Gulf of Kachchh. In south India and Sri Lanka shell fishing is done by specialized communities of divers who also engage in pearl fishing. In the Gulf of Kachchh shells are collected by shallow dives in the process of pearl fishing. In Bengal Kachchh shells are a craze for their pure white and heavy shell.

Distribution of raw materials is intricately related to the distribution of finished products. Both are a function of socio-economic status of the individuals especially of married Hindu women. Kenoyer (1983) discusses the social and economic parameters of both the merchant class and the user communities, the social and religious significance of shell, tools and manufacturing techniques employed for the making of bangles, and the use of wasters for the lime industry and other shell products produced by these communities.

Evidence of shell ornaments have been widely reported from many Early Historic sites of eastern India. Chandraketugarh is a good example of it, showing its importance in the vast trade networks that traversed the entire subcontinent and across the Indian Ocean. Kenoyer's work shows several regional variations within Bengal in terms of technique, raw material use and decoration, thus having a significant potential for archaeological interpretation. For example, the peripheral centres actually process and manufacture shell objects, which are brought to the large urban markets for selling. In archaeological sites the patterning of debitage styles and manufacturing technique together with raw material differences may throw light on locations of various production centres.

MARITIME ARCHAEOLOGY

Recent years have witnessed a growing use of ethnographic analogies for the reconstruction of seafaring cultures, which offered a long standing stimulus to the maritime trade during the Harappan and Historical times.

Coastal adaptations and exploitation of marine resources in India can be traced to the Mesolithic period, which was prolific among all prehistoric cultural phases. Archaeological evidence indicates that the Mesolithic hunter-gatherer-fishers had expanded and settled in a variety of ecological niches including the coastal tracts; suggesting the exploitation of oceanic resources. The evidence from certain pockets on the east coast indicates a gradual transformation from the hunting-fishing economy of the Mesolithic to the food producing/gathering culture of the Neolithic. Interestingly, the surviving culture, especially in regions like Andaman and Nicobar islands possess many continuation of several prehistoric traits.

In the earlier trend, the colonial model of the transoceanic trade, was more emphasized where long distance seafaring had often been perceived as a luxury trade with the Indian subcontinent, supplying precious commodities to centres further west. Within the colonial framework, the dynamics of sectoral, subsistence based trade have been almost neglected. Recently, the documentation of survival of the boat tradition has emerged as a separate entity within the perspective of ethnoarchaeological research; which helps in understanding not only the prehistoric water crafts, but also some of the pre-Modern boats which were plying in the deep sea for transoceanic trade. With the growth of modern ports, the cargo carrying Masulas lost their relevance and were replaced by smaller boats used mainly for beach seining as at present.

The meticulous recording of the vessels from sixteenth century onwards with the entry of the Portuguese has left valuable records of technological changes in the form of photographic archives, an important ethnographic source, which the ethnoarchaeologists have largely ignored (Ray 1997).

The well known ethnographers of colonial India are Admira Paris (1806-1903) and

Colin Mackenzie (1754-1821). Admira Paris was a trained French navigator, who in the nineteenth century during the course of his voyages in the region catalogued 'extra European craft'. Colin Mackenzie was not a seaman but came to British India in pursuit of a military career. In addition to his official duty he catalogued and illustrated indigenous boats as a part of his quest for the sources of India's past. James Hornel, a marine biologist by profession, but nautical historian by inclination was the last among the British colonials, who published the distillations of a lifetime work in 'Water Transport', which contains an immense amount of ethnographic data (Hornel 1920).

The present decade has witnessed a shift from pan-Indian to regional and subregional levels in pursuit of documentation of the surviving boat tradition to reveal both direct and cross cultural parallel with the Bronze Age and Medieval Europe. In this regard, the combined efforts of Blue, Kentley, McGrail and Umakanta Mishra on documenting the Patia fishing boat of Orissa focus the reverse clinker technique which is rare worldwide in the surviving tradition, but a relic of a much earlier time. Patia is a kind of coastal fishing boat which is built on reverse-clinker technique that has still survived in the northern Orissa coast. In the present century, the use of such a boat is found only in Sweden and Bangladesh and Orissa in the Indian subcontinent. There is also some representational evidence from eastern India dated between twelfth-eighteenth century AD. The most useful information is found in the Jagannath temple at Puri. There are several Medieval examples in Europe, where the reverse-clinker boat has been depicted on seals, in archaeological remains and drawings. The systematic documentation of Patia boats thus have direct bearing on the problem of not only of Medieval boat building tradition of eastern India, but also of Medieval Europe (Blue et al. 1997).

The second season of the fieldwork carried out by Blue, Kentley and McGrail under the documentation programme of 'Boats of South Asia' focuses the surviving boat types on Tamil Nadu coast. Their systematic study of the 'Vattai' boat type at the ship building site of Tuticorin and the boat yard of Atirampattinam shows the use of 'Frame-First' methods. In eastern coast, most of the boat types are built in the traditional 'Plank-First' method. Thus, Vattai constitutes an important technological variation among the surviving boat types of South Asia. Blue et al. (1998) view Vattai boats of south India from a perspective pertaining to the pattern of technological change in Late Medieval Europe when 'Plank-First' methods were increasingly replaced by 'Frame-First' methods.

Kentley's work on the Masula boat of the eastern coast is another good ethnoarchaeological example. Masula is an European term for the sewn boat of the eastern coast. These boats ply in the three modern states of eastern coast, namely Tamil Nadu, Andhra Pradesh and Orissa, exclusively as fishing boats with a few exception as ferries. Technologically the Andhra Pradesh Masula boats are more advanced than those of the neighbouring Tamil Nadu and Orissa, where the boat buildings are carried out by communities specializing in this craft within villages and are mainly found around Bimilipatanam near Visakhapatanam. From here boats are widely exported. Kentley's account gives detailed technological aspects of Masula boats plying in these three states. In the absence of any definite antiquity regarding these boats on the Indian coasts, Kentley attempts to draw cross-cultural parallels with the sewn boats of Bronze Age Britain (Kentely 1996). Guy (1997) studied two relief decorations of boats in Orissa which are attributed to tenth-eleventh century AD. He classified them as boats meant for royal pleasure. Considering ethnographic evidence Guy argues that the depiction of a boat on the sculptural panel of the *Bhoga mandapa* of Jagannath temple at Puri typically shows a ceremonial vessel, which is observed during the annual water festival (the Chandan Yatra) at Narendra tank. This identification is strengthened by the presence of Devadasis, the temple dancers, who perform on the boat.

In the Indian subcontinent, ports were usually located not only on the coast, but at the mouths or on the estuaries, or at some distance from the mouth of major rivers, which also provided convenient trading points and access to the routes of the interior ghats or landing places close to the mouths of the rivers were required for goods to be offloaded and transported. This was possible as a majority of crafts in use did not draw too much water and could easily enter the estuaries. Another practice adopted by large ships was for these to anchor at some distance from the coast and for the commodities to be transported in smaller vessels. This practice too is referred in the early Buddhist texts.

Himanshu Prabha Ray explains the role of ethnographic studies on boat crafts as a close association with the developments of maritime trade. Her theoretical model shows how changes and adaptations in boat types are linked to the purpose for which the boat is used. Demands of maritime trade and the need to adopt to changing circumstances is crucial if the competitive edge is to be maintained. The study of the living boat tradition provides useful information of shifts and changes in routes and commodities. In an explicit attempt, she divides the surviving boat tradition into two sectors—the mainland and the island tradition. In the Indian subcontinent, the large diversity in coastal zones have shown several regional expressions in terms of trade and urbanization during the last four millennia. The overseas trade had always a close association with the regional and subregional exchange and trade networks. The use of traditional water crafts thus provides useful clues in understanding the complexity of past oceanic trade. Ray's ethnographic model serves as an eye-opener for generating a more complete picture within the time, space and the contextual capsule (Ray 1996).

Lajwanti Shahni (1997) carried out ethnographic study of the dhow trade between India and the Persian Gulf to understand the trade and transport mechanism that would serve as a possible model for studying the Harappan sea trade. Her work shows, seasonal sailing is an adaptation to the monsoon system—a practice still continuing in the traditional shipping of Gujarat. The square sail which has been clearly depicted in Harappan representations on amulets, seals and drawings on potsherds is a mechanical device designed to utilize monsoon wind power. The square sail is also known from the ethnographic sources as barchha. Her ethnographic study shows contemporary adaptations in vessel form and navigational aids, the reasons for these changes, the nature of traditional sea trade and the role played both by the seafaring communities and the countries involved in trade in the Arabian sea region, with a view to an understanding of Harappan sea trade.

In many societies, both in the past and the present seafaring and fishing folks have formed a distinct subculture vis-à-vis the generally recognized urban and rural groups. Therefore, maritime activities and their study must constitute an important element in the search for greater understanding of man's past (Muckelroy 1978: 3).

Kirti Jain's holistic study on the Son Kolis on the west coast deals with their social customs, religion, dresses, ornaments, fishing technique, housing pattern and use of space, etc. The community is slowly but steadily getting influenced by the urban mechanized world around them and therefore the acculturation is bringing many changes in their traditions and conventions. Her work emphasizes that the present behavioural studies of the community cannot be taken as a model for reconstructing the past as they are partly or wholly contaminated by the fast growing modernization. She also accepts that the study of Son Kolis in totality did not project any clear evidence in linking seafaring activity of the region to the past. The reasons she has ascribed are the inhospitable terrain of the Konkan coast which discouraged permanent settlements in the past and the shifting of river beds which might have also caused the poor preservation of the archaeological sites (Jain 1989, 1993).

Arunachalam's novel study of traditional knowledge, skills and techniques of navigation in the monsoon dominated Indian ocean has provided impetus to understanding India's maritime past. The oral communication covering a wide area of practical navigational utility reveals knowledge of topography of the littoral sea and the adjoining coasts, sea-circulation including tides, waves and currents, sea-life, sky and weather conditions in different parts of the year, cloud typology, wind, foul weather systems, navigational guide; star recognition in relation to their movement in the sky, etc. According to Arunachalam the craft wisdom falls into different categories; such as information base for memory storage for future use; codified axiomatic truths and astrological prescriptions to be implicitly followed for safe steering and voyage; empirical thumb rules of measurement, and notional estimates of time, distance, directions and depths; and simply ready reckoners of quick field calculations. He argues that the present patterning is an outcome of generations of association with the sea surroundings, which have led to a methodology of nautical charting, integrating time-distances, stellar azimuths, altitude of select stars including the Pole Star, coastal landmarks and select sea-details (Arunachalam 1996).

Saklani's research in the Yamuna Valley of Garhwal Himalaya in Uttar Pradesh among the ethnic communities living in the area shows the typical architectural feature of the multistoried wooden-cum-super structures locally known as *Summer* which are closely associated with the social, cultural and political life of the people of this region from historical times. This research based on epigraphic, numismatic, oral traditions and cross cultural parallels from the neighbouring regions place these multistoried wooden-cum-superstructures in an ethnoarchaeological perspective of a chiefdom society in ancient Garhwal (Saklani 1994; Saklani et al. 1990).

Kashyap identifies Nirmand, an ancient village, some 150 km upstream from Ropar (Rupnagar) on the right bank of the Sutlez as a surviving entity of Harappan Culture. Kashyap's argument is based on epigraphical and archaeological evidence, written records and oral traditions. The surviving citadel associated with a complex of citadel walls is used for special religious rituals showing a parallel with the Harappan town of Ropar located near here. He also finds similarities with the Harrapan architecture and material culture.

CONCLUDING REMARKS

While reviewing and assessing the progress of the ethnoarchaeological research in India in the last fifty years, we are happy to note that this branch of archaeology has made significant strides encompassing many aspects of archaeology from hunter-gatherer to ceramic, bead, metal craft, maritime, rock art, actualistic and experimental studies. This opening of the discipline to a wide array of subjects is perhaps the most important change in 'Indian Ethnoarchaeology' to have occurred during the last few decades. Considering the fact that archaeology as a separate discipline in India has remained esoteric, the use of ethnographic data in understanding the archaeological problems is quite remarkable. If there is anything that we lack, it is in the adaptation of new approaches including those which may be characterized as methodological innovation and theoretical ideas.

To overcome some of the methodological hurdles, it is essential for archaeologists to bear in mind the possibilities and limitations of ethnoarchaeological approach. One should not take for granted that ethnographic parallels exist for any type of artefact, technology or all forms of cultural behaviour for observation in the present (Freeman 1968; Allchin 1985). It only provides a framework for understanding the material consequences of behaviours and technologies as well as a rich laboratory for documenting the diversity and regularities in human behaviour in well defined cultural contexts (Sinopoli 1991: 178). Extant theories about hunter-gatherer adaptations, whether based on economic behaviour (Sahlins 1972), social relationships (Service 1962) or political integration (Fried 1967), all rely on behaviour known from ethnographies. Yet, as numerous authors have pointed out, the ethnographic record does not reflect the full range of variability in human adaptation that existed in the past. So archaeologists utilizing such data are in danger of producing a distorted reconstruction of archaeological record (e.g. Schiffer 1978; Skibo et al. 1989; David 1992). This tendency has been called 'the tryanny of ethnographic record' (cf. Wobst 1978).

To overcome these problems, one should keep in mind the following general safeguards: (a) at the beginning of any proposed programme it is important to limit the time gap between the present living community to be studied and interpreted. It would be best, of course, to relate the most recent archaeological period to the living sites. A big time gap between the ethnographic present and archaeological past involves too many uncontrolled variables and changes, thus severely reducing the likelihood of various interpretation of the latter, (b) it would be wise to limit one's research to living and past communities characterized by a similar stage of economic development, (c) attempts should be made to neutralize the ecological variables by choosing a living community that shares environmental conditions similar to those of archaeological record.

Work carried out along these lines alone will make the discipline richer, fuller and more sophisticated.

ACKNOWLEDGEMENTS

The authors are indebted to Professor K. Paddayya, Dr. John Yellen, Dr. Ajay Pratap, who commented on earlier drafts of this paper. We would also like to thank Dr. Sheena Panja, Dr. Richa Jhaldiyal, Dr. Arti Despande-Mukharjee and Dr. V. Selvakumar for providing us information of their research. As always, all errors of omission and commission are our own responsibility.

REFERENCES

Aiyappan, A. 1937. *Social and Physical Anthropology of Nayadis of Malbar*. Madras. [As Quoted in Fuchs (1973).]

——— 1948. *Report on the Socio-Economic Conditions of the Aboriginal Tribes of Province of Madras.* Madras: Government Press.

Allchin, B. 1957. Australian Stone Industries: Past and Present, *Journal of Royal Anthropological Institute* 87: 115-36.

——— 1985. Ethnoarchaeology in South Asia, in *South Asian Archaeology 1983* (J. Schotsmans and M. Taddei Eds.), pp. 21-33. Naples: Instituto Universitario Orientale.

Allchin, B. (Ed.) 1994. *Living Traditions*. New Delhi: Oxford-IBH.

Allchin, F.R. 1961. *Utnur Excavations*. Hyderabad: Andhra Pradesh Government Archaeological Series 5.

——— 1963. *Neolithic Cattle Keepers of South India: a Case Study of the Deccan Ashmounds.* Cambridge: Cambridge University Press.

——— 1978. The Archaeological Significance of a Modern Indian Potter's Technique, in *History and Society: Essays in Honour of Professor Nihar Ranjan Ray*, pp. 1-14. Calcutta: K.P. Bagchi.

——— 1998. The Interface of Archaeology and History, *Man and Environment* XXIII (1): 19-36.

Allchin, F.R. and B. Allchin 1974. Some New Thoughts on Indian Cattle, in *South Asian Archaeology 1973* (J.E. Van Lohuizen de Leeuw and J.M. Ubughs Eds.), pp. 71-7. Leiden: E.J. Brill.

Arunachalam, B. 1996. Traditional Sea and Sky Wisdom of Indian Seamen and Their Practical Application, in *Tradition and Archaeology* (H.P. Ray and Jean Francois Salles Eds.), pp. 261-82. New Delhi: Manohar.

Ansari, Z.D. 1964. A Potter at Work, *Bulletin of the Deccan College Research Institute* 24: 1-14.

Asher, R. 1962. Ethnography for Archaeology: a Case from the Siri Indians, *Ethnology* 1: 360-9.

——— 1968. Time's Arrow and the Archaeology of a Contemporary Community, in *Settlement Archaeology* (K.C. Chang Ed.), pp. 43-52. Palo Alto: National Press Books.

Baines, A. 1912. *Ethnography (Castes and Tribes).* Strasburg: Karl J. Trubner.

Bala, R. 1997. Ethnography and Archaeology: a Case Study of Earthen Wares, in *Ancient Ceramics: Historical Enquiries and Scientific Approaches* (P.C. Pant and V. Jayaswal Eds.), pp. 157-76. New Delhi: Agam Kala.

Begley, V. 1986. Rouletting and Chattering: Decoration on Ancient and Present Day Pottery in India, *Expedition* 28 (1): 47-54.

——— 1988. Rouletted Ware at Arikamedu: a New Approach, *American Journal of Archaeology* 92: 427-40.

Behura, N.K. 1967a. Social and Cultural Aspects of Pottery in Southern and Southeast India, *Bulletin of the Anthropological Survey of India* 13: 114-23.

——— 1967b. Sociology of Pottery Among Certain Groups of Potters in South India, *Bulletin of the Anthropological Survey of India* 13: 19-38.

——— 1978. *Peasant Potters of Orissa: a Sociological Study*. New Delhi: Sterling.

Bhaskar, S. 1990. *Prehistoric and Primitive Hunter-Gatherers of South India*. New Delhi: Discovering Publishing House.

Blue, L., E. Kentley and S. McGrail 1998. The Vattai Fishing Boat and Related Frame-First Vessels of Tamil Nadu, *South Asian Studies* 14: 41-74.

Blue, L., E. Kentley, S. McGrail and U.K. Misra 1997. The Patia Fishing Boat of Orissa: a Case Study in Ethnoarchaeology, *South Asian Studies* 13: 189-208.

Binford, L.R. 1968. Post-Pleistocene Adaptations, in *New Perspectives in Archaeology* (L.R. Binford and S.R. Binford Eds.), pp. 313-41. Chicago: Aldine.

——— 1978. *Nunamiut Ethnoarchaeology*. New York: Academic Press.

——— 1983. *In Pursuit of the Past*. London: Thames and Hudson.

——— 1987. Researching Ambiguity: Frames of References and Site Structure, in *Method and Theory for Activity Area Research: an Ethnoarchaeological Approach* (S. Kent Ed.), pp. 449-512. New York: Columbia University Press.

Breeks, J.W. 1873. *An Account of the Primitive Tribes and Monuments of the Nilgiris*. London: W.H. Allen and Co.

Brochier, J.A., P. Villa and M. Giacomarra 1992. Shepherds and Sediments: Geoethnoarchaeology of Pastoral Sites, *Journal of Anthropological Archaeology* 11: 47-102.

Cameron, L.M. and S.A. Tomaka 1993. *Abandonment of Settlements and Regions: Ethnoarchaeological and Archaeological Approaches*. Cambridge: Cambridge University Press.

Chakrabarti, D.K. 1994. Some Ethnographic Dimensions of the Archaeology of the Chhotanagpur Plateau and the Adjoining Areas in West Bengal in Eastern India, in *Living Traditions* (B. Allchin Ed.), pp. 219-33. New Delhi: Oxford-IBH.

Charlton, T.H. 1981. Archaeology, Ethnohistory and Ethnology: Interpretive Interfaces, in *Advances in Archaeological Method and Theory* 4 (M.B. Schiffer Ed.), pp. 129-59. New York: Academic Press.

Choski, Archana. 1995. Ceramic Vessels: Their Role in Illuminating Past and Present, Social and Economic Relationships, *Man and Environment* XX (1): 87-108.

——— 1997. Painted Pots: an Expression of Aesthetics or of Social Identity? *South Asian Studies* 13: 227-40.

Cipriani, L. 1966. *The Andaman Islanders*. London: Wiedenfeld and Nicolson.

Clark, J.G.D. 1951. Folk Culture and the Study of European Prehistory, in Aspects of Archaeology, in *Great Britain and Beyond: Essays Presented to O.G.S. Crawford* (W.S. Gnimas Ed.), pp. 49-65. London: Methuen.

Cooper, Zarine 1986. The Kuruk Fishermen of Bastar District, Central India, *The Eastern Anthropologist* 7: 1-30.

——— 1993a. The Origins of the Andaman Islanders: Local Myth and Archaeological Evidence, *Antiquity* 67: 394-9.

——— 1993b. Perceptions of Time in the Andaman Islands, *World Archaeology* 25 (2): 262-7.

——— 1994. Abandoned Onge Encampments and their Relevance in Understanding the Archaeological Record in the Andaman Islands, in *Living Traditions* (B. Allchin Ed.), pp. 235-64. New Delhi: Oxford-IBH.

——— 1997a. The Salient Features of Site Location in the Andaman Islands, Indian Ocean, *Asian Perspectives* 36 (2): 220-31.

——— 1997b. *Prehistory of the Chitrokot Falls, Central India*. Pune: Ravish.

Coles, J. 1973. *Archaeology by Experiment*. London: Hutchinson.

Crib, R. 1991. *Nomads in Archaeology*. Cambridge: Cambridge University Press.

David, N. 1992. Integrating Ethnoarchaeology, *Journal of Anthropological Archaeology* 11 (4): 330-59.

Deshpande, A. 1995. Application of Molluscan Studies in Archaeology with Reference to Western India. Ph.D. Dissertation. Pune: University of Poona.

Dhavalikar, M.K. 1979. Early Farming Cultures of Deccan, in *Essays in Protohistory* (D.P. Agrawal and D. Chakrabarti Eds.), pp. 247-65. Delhi: B.R. Publishing Corporation.

——— 1983. Ethnoarchaeology in India, *Bulletin of the Deccan College Research Institute* 42: 49-68.

——— 1988. *The First Farmers of the Deccan*. Pune: Ravish.

——— 1994. Chalcolithic Architecture at Inamgaon and Walki: an Ethnoarchaeological Study, in *Living Traditions* (B. Allchin Ed.), pp. 31-52. New Delhi: Oxford-IBH.

Dhavalikar, M.K., V.S. Shinde and Shubhangana Atre 1990a. *Excavation at Kaothe*. Pune: Deccan College.

——— 1990b. Small Scale Archaeology: Excavations at Walki, *Bulletin of the Deccan College Post-Graduate and Research Institute* 50: 197-228.

Dumont, L. 1952. A Remarkable Feature of South Indian Pot-Making, *Man* 52: 81-3.

Ehrenfels, U.R. 1952. *Kadar of Cochin*. Madras: University of Madras.

Faculty and Students 1988-9. Archaeology of Vacant Land in Poona: an Experimental Study, *Bulletin of the Deccan College Post-Graduate and Research Institute* 48-9: 240-9.

Fergusson, W.C. 1980. Edge Angle Classification of the Quininup Brook Implements: Testing the Ethnographic Analogy, *Oceania* 15: 56-72.

Francis, P., Jr. 1990. Glass Beads in Asia, Part Two: Indo-Pacific Beads, *Asian Perspectives* 29 (1): 1-23.

Fried, I.M. 1967. *The Evolution of Political Society*. New York: Random House.

Fuchs, S. 1973. *The Aboriginal Tribes of India*. New Delhi: Macmillan.

Furer-Hammendorf C.Von 1943. *The Chenchus—Jungle Folk of the Deccan*. London: Macmillan.

——— 1943. Megalithic Ritual Among the Gadabas and Bondos of Orissa, *Journal of Royal Asiatic Society of Bengal, Letters* 9: 149-78.

——— 1948. Culture Strata in the Deccan, *Man* 48: 87-90.

Gardner, P.M. 1968. Paliyan Social Structure, in *Contributions to Anthropology: Band Societies* (D. Damas Ed.), pp. 153-71. Ottawa: Queen's Printer.

Ghosh, A. 1984. Significance of Rock-Art in the Light of Ethnographic Parallels, in *Rock Art of India* (K.K. Chakravarty Ed.), pp. 106-11. New Delhi: Arnold-Heinemann.

Griffin, P.B. and W.G. Solheim II 1990. Ethnoarchaeological Research in Asia, *Asian Perspectives* 22 (1): 69-86.

Gould, Richard A. 1971. The Archaeologist as Ethnographer: a Case from the Western Desert of Australia, *World Archaeology* 3: 143-77.

——— 1978. Beyond Analogy in Ethnoarchaeology, Exploration in Ethnological Reasoning, *Journal of Anthropological Archaeology* 1 (4): 355-81.

——— 1980. *Living Archaeology*. Cambridge: Cambridge University Press.

Gould, Richard A. and P.J. Watson 1982. A Dialogue on the Meaning and Use of Analogy in

Ethnoarchaeological Reasoning, *Journal of Anthropological Archaeology* 1 (4): 355-81.
Guha, S. 1994. Recognising 'Harappans': a Critical Review of the Position of Hunter-Gatherers within the Harappan Society, *South Asian Studies* 10: 91-8.
Guy, J. 1997. A Sculptural Boat Model from Eastern India, in *South Asian Archaeology 1995* (R. Allchin and B. Allchin Eds.), pp. 769-78. New Delhi: Oxford-IBH.
Hasim, Syed Anis. 1989. Ethnoarchaeology of the Use of Analogy in Ethnoarchaeological Reasoning, *Journal of Anthropological Archaeology* 1 (4): 355-81.
——— 1989. Ethnoarchaeology of the Traditional Ceremonial Pottery of Gujarat, *Puratattva* 19: 60-3.
Hodder, I. 1982a. *Symbols in Action.* Cambridge: Cambridge University Press.
——— 1982b. *The Present Past.* London: Batsford.
Hornell, J. 1920. The Origin and Ethnological Significance of Indian Boat Designs, *Memoirs of the Asiatic Society of Bengal* VII: 139-251.
——— 1942. The Chank Shell Cult of India, *Antiquity* 16: 113-33.
Hooja, R. 1988. *The Ahar Culture and Beyond: Settlements and Frontiers of Mesolithic and Early Agricultural Sites in Rajasthan*. Oxford: BAR International Series 412.
——— 1994. Contacts, Conflicts and Coexistence: Bhils and Non-Bhils in Southeastern Rajasthan, in *Living Traditions* (B. Allchin Ed.), pp. 125-42. New Delhi: Oxford-IBH.
Iyer, L.K. Anantakrishna 1909-12. *Cochin Tribes and Castes*, 2 Vols. Ernakulam: Cochin Government Press.
Jacobson, J. 1985. Acheulian Surface Sites in Central India, in *Recent Advances in Indo-Pacific Prehistory* (V.N. Misra and P. Bellwood Eds.), pp. 49-57. New Delhi: Oxford-IBH.
Jain, K. 1989. Coastal Adaptation in the Konkan: an Ethnohistorical Study of the Son Kolis of Raigad District of Maharashtra. Ph.D. Dissertation. Pune: University of Poona.
——— 1993. Importance of Ethnography for the Archaeological Record: a Case Study of the Son Kolis of Raigad District, Maharashtra, India, in *Current Advances in Indian Archaeology* (R.K. Ganjoo and S.B. Ota Eds.), pp. 1-36. Nagpur: Datsons.
Jayaswal, Vidula 1984. Interpretation of Terracotta Figurines from Archaeological Sites: an Ethnographic Approach, *Jijnasa* 3: 105-10.
——— 1989. Socio-Ritual Significance of Ancient Terracottas in the Gangetic Plains: the Ethnoarchaeological and Literary Evidence, in *Old Problems and New Perspectives in the Archaeology of South Asia* (J.M. Kenoyer Ed.), pp. 253-62. Madison: Wisconsin Archaeological Reports II.
Jayaswal, V. and K. Krishna 1986. *An Ethnoarchaeological View of Indian Terracottas*. New Delhi: Agam Kala.
Jayaswal, V., K. Krishna and P. C. Pant 1986. Ethno-Archaeological Study of Ritual Terracottas of the Ganga Valley, in *Dimensions of Indian Art* (Lokesh Chandra and Jyotindra Jain Eds.), pp. 189-204. Delhi: Agam Kala.
Jhaldiyal, R. 1997a. Traditional Indian Tillage: Methods and Their Impacts on Acheulian Sites in the Hunsgi-Baichbal Valleys, Karnataka, *Man and Environment* XXII (1): 19-30.
——— 1997b. Formation Processes of the Prehistoric Sites in the Hunsgi and Baichbal Basins, Gulbarga District, Karnataka. Ph.D. Dissertation. Pune: University of Poona.
——— 1998. Surface Wash Process and Their Impact on Stone Age Sites, *Man and Environment* XXIII (1): 81-92.
Jochim, M.A. 1976. *Hunter Gatherer Subsistence and Settlement: a Predictive Model*. New York: Academic Press.

Junker, Laura L. 1985. Morphology, Function and Style in Traditional Ceramics: a Study of Contemporary Pottery from Bellary District, Karnataka, in *Vijayanagara: Progress of Research 1983-84* (M.S. Nagaraja Rao Ed.), pp. 144-51. Mysore: Directorate of Archaeology and Museums.

Kamminga, J. 1978. Journey into the Microcosms: a Functional Analysis of Certain Classes of Prehistoric Australian Stone Tools. Ph.D. Dissertation. Sydney: University of Sydney.

Kapp, D.B. 1985. The Kulumas Relationship to the Megalithic Cult of Nilgiri Hills (South India), *Anthropos* 80: 493-534.

Kar, S.B., M. Koiso and E. Thomas 1993. Pottery Making Traditions at Talasara, District Bhavnagar, Gujarat, *Bulletin of the Deccan College Post-Graduate and Research Institute* 53: 143-65.

Kashyap, P.C. 1984. *Surviving Harappan Civilisation*. Atlantic Highlands, N.J: Humanities Press.

Kenoyer, J.M. 1983. Shell Working Industries of the Indus Civilisation: an Archaeological and Ethnographic Perspective. Ph.D. Dissertation. Berkeley: University of California.

Kenoyer, J.M., M. Vidale and K.K. Bhan 1991. Contemporary Stone Bead-making in Khambat, India: Patterns of Craft Specialisation in the Archaeological Record, *World Archaeology* 23 (1): 44-63.

——— 1994. Carnelian Bead Production in Khambat, India: an Ethnoarchaeological Study, in *Living Traditions* (B. Allchin Ed.), pp. 281-306. New Delhi: Oxford-IBH.

Kent, S. 1984. *Analysing Activity Areas*. Alburquerque: University of New Mexico.

Kentley, E. 1996. The Sewn Boats of India's East Coast, in *Tradition and Archaeology: Early Maritime Contacts in the Indian Ocean* (H.P. Ray and Jean-Francois Salles Eds.), pp. 247-60. New Delhi: Manohar.

Kluckhohn, C. 1950. *Mirror for Man*. London.

Kramer, C. 1979. *Ethnoarchaeology*. New York: Columbia University Press.

——— 1980. *Village Ethnoarchaeology: Rural Iran in Archaeological Perspective*. New York: Academic Press.

——— 1991. Ceramics in two Indian Cities, in *Ceramic Ethnoarchaeology* (W.A. Longacre Ed.), pp. 205-30. Tucson: University of Arizona Press.

——— 1994. A Tale of Two Cities: Ceramic Ethnoarchaeology in Rajasthan, in *Living Traditions* (B. Allchin Ed.), pp. 307-22. New Delhi: Oxford-IBH.

Krishnan, K. and V. Rao 1994. A Study of Clay Paste Preparation by Potters Through Grain Size Analysis, *South Asian Studies* 10: 113-17.

Lahiri, N. 1995. Indian Metal and Metal Related Artefacts as Cultural Signifiers: an Ethnographic Perspective, *World Archaeology* 27 (10): 116-32.

Lee, R.B. and I. de Vore 1968. *Man the Hunter*. Chicago: Aldine.

Leshnik, L.S. 1964. Sociological Interpretation in Archaeology: Some Examples from a Village Study in Central India. Ph.D. Dissertation. Chicago: University of Chicago.

Leshnik, L.S. 1966. The System of Dry Farming in the West Nimar District of Central India, *Year Book of the South Asia Institute of Heidelberg*: 56-74.

Lonrace, W.A. (Ed.) 1991. *Ceramic Ethnoarchaeology*. Tucson: University of Arizona Press.

MacEachern, S. 1996. Foreign Countries: the Development of Ethnoarchaeology in Sub-Saharan Africa, *Journal of World Prehistory* 10: 243-304.

Majumdar, D.N. 1961. *Races and Cultures of India*. Bombay: Asia Publishing House.

Majumdar, D.N. and T.N. Madan 1961. *An Introduction to Social Anthropology*. Bombay: Asia Publishing

McCrindle, J.W. 1926. *Ancient India as Described by Megasthenes and Arrian*. Calcutta: Chatterjee and Co.

Miller, D. 1981. The Relationship Between Ceramic Production and Distribution in a Central Indian Village, in *Ceramic Viewpoint* (H. Howard and E. Morris Eds.), pp. 221-8. Oxford: BAR International Series.

——— 1985. *Artefacts as Category: a Study of Ceramic Variability in Central India*. Cambridge: Cambridge University Press.

Misra, A.K. 1997. The Iron Technology in the Bastar Region: an Ethnoarchaeological Study, *Pragdhara* 7: 187-92.

Misra, V. N. 1974. Archaeological and Ethnographic Evidence for the Hafting and Use of Microliths and Related Tools, *Puratattva* 7: 3-12.

——— 1990. The Van Vagrias—Lost Hunters of the Thar Desert, Rajasthan, *Man and Environment* XV (2): 89-108.

——— 1994. Patterns of Human Adaptation in the Semi-Arid and Arid Zone of Rajasthan, in *Living Traditions* (B. Allchin Ed.), pp. 101-24. New Delhi: Oxford-IBH.

Mohanty, P. 1988. Five Seasons of Exploration in Keonjhar District, Orissa, *Bulletin of Indo-Pacific Prehistory Association* 7: 47-53.

——— 1989. Mesolithic Settlement System of Keonjhar District, Orissa. Ph.D. Dissertation. Pune: University of Poona.

——— 1992. Stone Age Research in Orissa: an Overview, *Man in India* 72: 207-32.

——— 1998. The Mesolithic Culture of Keonjhar District, Orissa: a New Perspective, in *New Perspective in History and Archaeology of Eastern India* (A. Datta Ed.), pp. 59-95. New Delhi: Books & Books.

Muckeloroy, Keith 1978. *Maritime Archaeology*. Cambridge: Cambridge University Press.

Murty, M.L.K. 1966. Stone Age Cultures of Chittoor District. Ph.D. Dissertation. Poona: University of Poona.

——— 1978-9. Symbiosis and Traditional Behaviour in the Economics of the Kanchapuri Yerukalas of South India: a Predictive Model, *Puratattva* 10: 50-61.

——— 1981. Hunter-Gatherer Ecosystems and Archaeological Patterns of Subsistence Behaviour on the Southeast Coast of India: an Ethnographic Model, *World Archaeology* 12: 47-58.

——— 1985a. Ethnoarchaeology of the Kurnool Cave Areas, South India, *World Archaeology* 17: 192-205.

——— 1985b. The Use of Plant Foods by Some Hunter-Gatherer Communities in Andhra Pradesh, in *Recent Advances in Indo-Pacific Prehistory* (V.N. Misra and P. Bellwood Eds.), pp. 329-36, Delhi: Oxford-IBH.

——— 1989. Pre-Iron Age Agricultural Settlements in South India: an Ecological Perspective, *Man and Environment* XIV (1): 65-81.

——— 1994. Forest Peoples and Historical Traditions in the Eastern Ghats, South India, in *Living Traditions* (B. Allchin Ed.), pp. 205-18. New Delhi: Oxford-IBH.

Murty, M.L.K. and G.D. Sontheimer 1980. Prehistoric Background to Pastoralism in the Southern Deccan in the Light of Oral Traditions and Cults of Some Pastoral Communities, *Anthropos* 75: 163-84.

Nagar, M. 1969. Clues to Aharian Prehistory in Contemporary Mewar Village Life, *The Eastern Anthropologist* 22: 55-73.

——— 1970. Modern Pottery of Mewar, Rajasthan, in *Indian Antiquary: Professor H.D. Sankalia Felicitation Volume* 4 (S.B. Deo and M.K. Dhavalikar Eds.), pp. 129-40. Bombay: Popular Prakashan.

——— 1973. Folk Ornaments in Mewar, *Bulletin of the Deccan College Research Institute* 31: 168-73.

——— 1975a Folk Religion of Mewar, *Journal of the University of Poona* (Humanities Section) 41: 75-93.

——— 1975. Role of Ethnographic Evidence in the Reconstruction of Archaeological Data, *The Eastern Anthropologist* 29: 13-22.

——— 1977. Living Prehistory Around Bhimbetka, in *Bhimbetka* (V. N. Misra Ed.), pp. 23-6. Poona: Poona Exhibition Souvenir.

——— 1982. Fishing Among the Tribal Communities of Bastar and Its Implications for Archaeology, *Bulletin of the Deccan College Research Institute* 41: 116-24.

——— 1985. The Use of Wild Plant Foods by Aboriginal Communities in Central India, in *Recent Advances in Indo-Pacific Prehistory* (V.N. Misra and P. Bellwood Eds.), pp. 337-42. New Delhi: Oxford-IBH.

Nagar, M. and V.N. Misra 1989. Hunter-Gatherers in an Agrarian Setting: the Nineteenth Century Situation in the Ganga Plains, *Man and Environment* XIII: 65-78.

——— 1990. The Kanjaras—a Hunting-Gathering Community of the Ganga Valley, Uttar Pradesh, *Man and Environment* XV (2): 77-88.

——— 1993. The Pardhis: a Hunting Gathering community of Central and Western India, *Man and Environment* XVIII (1): 115-44.

——— 1994. Survival of the Hunting Gathering Tradition in the Ganga Plains and Central India, in *Living Traditions* (B. Allchin Ed.), pp. 169-92. New Delhi: Oxford-IBH.

Nagaraja Rao, M.S. 1965. Survival of Certain Neolithic Elements Among the Boyas of Tekkalkota, *Anthropos* 60: 480-6.

Nanda, S.C. 1984. Stone Age Cultures of the Indravati Basin, Koraput District, Orissa. Ph.D. Dissertation. Pune: University of Poona.

——— 1985. The Microlithic Cultures of the Indravati Valley, District Koraput, Orissa, in *Recent Advances in Indo-Pacific Prehistory* (V.N. Misra and P. Bellwood Eds.), pp. 159-65. New Delhi: Oxford-IBH.

Nanjundayya, H.V. and L.K.A. Iyer 1928-36. *Mysore Tribes and Castes*, 4 Vols. Bangalore: Government Press.

Orme, B. 1973. Archaeology and Ethnography, in *The Explanation of Cultural Change* (C. Renfrew Ed.), pp. 481-92. London: Duckworth.

——— 1981. *Anthropology for Archaeologists*. London: Duckworth.

Ota, S.B. 1986. Mesolithic Culture of the Phulbani District Orissa: with Special Reference to Heavy Tool Components, *Bulletin of the Deccan College Post-Graduate and Research Institute* 45: 47-66.

Paddayya, K. 1969. On the Form and Function of the Perforated Pottery of the Deccan Neolithic Culture, *Man* 69: 450-3.

——— 1977. An Acheulian Occupation Site at Hunsgi, Peninsular India: a Summary of the Results of Two Seasons of Excavation (1975-6), *World Archaeology* 8: 344-55.

——— 1978. New Research Designs and Field Techniques in the Palaeolithic Archaeology of India, *World Archaeology* 10: 94-100.

——— 1978-9 Palaeoethnography Vis-a-Vis the Stone Age Cultures of India: Some Methodological Considerations, *Bulletin of the Deccan College Research Institute* 38: 63-90.

——— 1981. Water Supply as a Key Determinant in the Acheulian Occupation of the Hunsgi Valley, Peninsular India, *Bulletin of the Deccan College Research Institute* 40: 39-51.

——— 1982. *The Acheulian Culture of the Hunsgi Valley (Peninsular India): a Settlement System Perspective*. Poona: Deccan College.

——— 1983. Relevance of Experimental Approach in Indian Prehistory, in *Rangavalli* (A.V. Narasimha Murthy and B.K. Gururaja Rao Eds.), pp. 1-10. Delhi: Sandeep Prakasan.

——— 1987. The Place and Study of Site Formation in India, in *Natural Formation Processes and the Archaeological Record* (D.T. Nash and M.D. Petraglia Eds.), pp. 74-85. Oxford: BAR International Series 352.

——— 1991. The Acheulian Culture of the Hunsgi-Baichbal Valleys, Peninsular India: a Processual Study, *Quarter* 41-2: 111-38.

——— 1991-2. The Ashmounds of South India: Fresh Evidence and Possible Implications, *Bulletin of the Deccan College Post-Graduate and Research Institute* 51-2: 573-626.

——— 1993a. Ashmound Excavations at Budhihal, Gulbarga District, Karnataka, *Man and Environment* XVIII: 57-87.

——— 1993b. Further Field Investigations at Budhihal, Gulbarga District, Karnataka, *Bulletin of the Deccan College Post-Graduate and Research Institute* 53: 277-322.

——— 1998. Evidence of Neolithic Cattle Penning at Budhihal, Gulbarga District, Karnataka, *South Asian Studies* 13: 141-54.

——— 1996. Modern Impacts on Archaeological Sites in India: a Case Study of the Shorapur Doab, Karnataka, *Man and Environment* XXI (2): 75-88.

Paddayya, K. and M.D. Petraglia 1993. Formation Processes of Acheulian Localities in the Hunsgi-Baichbal Valleys, Peninsular India, in *Formation Processes in Archaeological Context* (D.T. Nash and M.D. Petraglia Eds.), pp. 61-82. Madison: Prehistory Press Monographs in World Archaeology 17.

——— 1995. Natural and Cultural Formation Processes on the Acheulian Sites of the Hunsgi-Baichbal Valleys, Karnataka, in *Quaternary Environments and Geoarchaeology of India* (S. Wadia, R. Korisettar and V.S. Kale Eds.), pp. 333-51. Bangalore: Geological Society of India.

Panja, S. 1995. Mobility Strategies, Site Structure and Subsistence-Settlement Organisations: a Case Study of the Chalcolithic in the Middle Bhima Valley with Special Reference to Inamgaon. Ph.D. Dissertation. Pune: University of Poona.

——— 1996. Mobility Strategies, Site Structure and Settlement Organisation: an Actualistic Perspective, *Man and Environment* XXI (1): 58-73.

Pant, R.K. 1979a. Microwear Studies on Burzahom Neolithic Tools, *Man and Environment* III: 11-17.

——— 1979b. Functional Studies on Stone Blades: Microwear Pattern, *Man and Environment* III: 83-5.

Pappu, S. 1996a. Reinvestigation of the Prehistoric Archaeological Record in the Kortallayar Basin, Tamil Nadu, *Man and Environment* XX (1): 1-23.

——— 1996b. Pleistocene Environments and Stone Age Adaptations in the Kortallyar Basin, Tamil Nadu. Ph.D. Dissertation. Pune: University of Poona.

Possehl, G.L. and K.A.R. Kennedy 1979. Hunter Gatherer/Agriculturalist Exchange in Prehistory: an Indian Example, *Current Anthropology* 20: 592-3.

Possehl, G.L. and P.C. Rissman. 1991. The Chronology of Prehistoric India: from Earliest Times to Iron Age, in *Chronologies in the Old World Archaeology* (R. Ehrich Ed.), pp. 465-90 and 447-72. Third Edition. Chicago: Chicago University Press.

Pratap, A. 1987. Shifting Cultivation in the Rajmahal Hills of India, in *Archaeology as Long-Term*

History (Ian Hodder Ed.), pp. 68-83. Cambridge: Cambridge University Press.

——— 1988. Savaria Pahariya Ethnohistory and the Archaeology of Rajmahal Hills. Ph.D. Dissertation. Cambridge: Cambridge University.

Raju, D.R. 1988. *Stone Age Hunter-Gatherers: an Ethnoarchaeology of Cuddapah Region, South-east India*. Pune: Ravish.

Rao, N.K. 1987. Aspects of the Ethnoarchaeology of Adilabad (Andhra Pradesh), India. Ph.D. Dissertation. Cambridge: The University of Cambridge.

——— 1994. Subsistence and Associated Settlement Patterns in Central India: an Ethnoarchaeological Analysis, in *Living Traditions* (B. Allchin Eds.), pp. 143-68. New Delhi: Oxford-IBH.

Ratnagar, S. 1998. Review: Prehistory of the Chitrokot Falls, Central India by Zarine Cooper, *Marg* 5 (1): 83-5.

Ray, H.P. 1996. Maritime Archaeology: the Ethnographic Evidence, *Man and Environment* XXI (1): 74-85.

——— 1997. Maritime Archaeology and Early Historic Port Sites: the Evidence from the East Coast, in *South Asian Archaeology 1995* (R. Allchin and B. Allchin Eds.), pp. 393-402. New Delhi: Oxford-IBH.

Radcliff-Brown, A.R. 1922. *The Andaman Islanders*. Cambridge. [As Quoted in S. Fuchs (1973).]

Roux, V. 1985-6. Ethnoarchaeological Survey on Ceramic Production, *Puratattva* 16: 63-4.

——— 1989a. *The Potter's Wheel: Craft Specialisation and Technical Competence*. New Delhi: Oxford University Press.

——— 1989b. Preliminary Study of Specialized Craftsmen and Their Socio-Economic Status, in *South Asian Archaeology 1985* (K. Friefelt and P. Søerensen Eds.). London: Curzon Press.

Roux, V. and A.K. Sinha 1986. Ethnoarchaeological Researches in North West Rajasthan, *Man and Environment* X: 117-22.

Roux, V., G. Dietrich. 1995. Skills and Learning Difficulties Involved in Stone Knapping: the Case of Stone Bead Knapping in Khambat, India, *World Archaeology* 27 (1): 63-87.

Roy, S.C. 1925. *The Birhors: a Little Known Jungle Tribe of the Chotanagpur*. Ranchi: Mission Press.

Roy, S.K. 1981. Aspects of Neolithic Agriculture and Shifting Cultivation, Garo Hills, Meghalaya, *Asian Perspectives* 24: 193-221.

Roychoudhury, S. 1998. Cire Perdue Casting in Bengal: a Living Tradition Among the Dhokra Kamars—a Socio Religious Case Study. M.A. Dissertation. Pune: Deccan College.

Russel, P.V. and Hiralal 1916. *The Tribes and Castes of the Provinces of India*, 4 Vols. London: Macmillan. Reprinted in 1969 by the Anthropological Publications, Osterhout (Holland).

Sahlin, M. 1972. *Stone Age Economics*. Chicago: Aldine.

Saklani, P.M., V. Nautiyal and K.P. Nautiyal. 1990. An Ethnoarchaeological Perspective of Mid-Central (Garhwal) Himalaya, *Journal of Himalayan Studies and Regional Development* 13-14: 30-6.

——— 1994. Cultural Adaptability in Garhwal Himalaya: an Ethnoarchaeological Study in Yamuna Valley. Ph.D. Dissertation. Srinagar: H.N. Bahuguna Garhwal University.

Sankalia, H.D. 1964. *Stone Age Tools: Their Technologies, Names and Probable Functions*. Poona: Deccan College.

——— 1967. The Socio-economic Significance of the Lithic Blade Industry of Navdatoli, Madhya Pradesh, India, *Current Anthropology* 8: 262-7.

——— 1974. *Pre and Proto History of India and Pakistan*. Poona: Deccan College.
——— 1979. *The New Archaeology: Its Scope and Application to India*. Lucknow: The Ethnographic and Folk Culture Society.
Saraswati, B. 1967. Social and Cultural Aspects of Pottery Manufacture in Northern and Western India, *Bulletin of the Anthropological Survey of India* 13: 39-49.
——— 1978. *Pottery Making Cultures and Indian Civilisation*. New Delhi: Abhinav Publications.
Saraswati, B. and N.K. Behura 1966. *Pottery Techniques in Peasant India*. Calcutta: Memoirs of Anthropological Survey of India 13.
Schiffer, M. 1978. Methodological Issues in Ethnoarchaeology, in *Exploration in Ethnoarchaeology* (R. Gould Ed.), 229-47. Albuquerque: University of New Mexico Press.
Schrire, L. 1984. *Past and Present in Hunter-Gatherer Studies*. Orlando: Academic Press.
Service, E.R. 1962. *Primitive Social Organisation*. New York: Random House.
Shahani, L. 1997. Ethnoarchaeology of Harappan Sea Trade: a Preliminary Study, *Man and Environment* XXII (I): 9-18.
Shinde, V. 1988. A Microwear Study of the Blade Tools, in *Excavations at Inamgaon*, Vol. 1, Part-II (M.K. Dhavalikar, H.D. Sankalia and Z.D. Ansari Eds.), pp. 543-51. Pune: Deccan College.
——— 1988-9. An Experimental Study of the Technology of Stone Tool Manufacturing, *Bulletin of Deccan College Post-Graduate and Research Institute*: 48-9: 311-17.
Sinha, P. 1985. Microwear Analysis and Its Scope in Indian Context, *Man and Environment* IX: 21-7.
Sinopoli, C.M. 1991 Seeking the Past Through Present: Recent Ethnoarchaeological Research in South Asia, *Asian Perspectives* 30: 177-92.
Skibbo, J., M.B. Schiffer and N. Kowalski 1989. Ceramic Style Analysis in Archaeology and Ethnoarchaeology: Bridging the Analytical Gap, *Journal of Anthropological Archaeology* 8: 388-409.
Srinivasan, S. 1994. High-Tin Bronze Bowl Making in Kerala, South India and its Archaeological Implications, in *South Asian Archaeology 1993* (A. Parapola and P. Koskikallio Eds.), pp. 695-706. Helsinki: Annales Academiae Scientiarum Fennicae, Series B 271.
——— 1997a. High-Tin Bronze Bowl Making in Kerala, in *Archaeometallurgy in India* (V. Tripathy Ed.), pp. 241-250. New Delhi: Sharada Publishing.
——— 1997b. Present and Past of Southern Indian Crafts for Making Mirrors, Lamps, Bells, Vessels, Cymbals and Gongs: Linking with Prehistoric High Tin Bronzes from Mohenjodaro, Taxila, South Indian Megaliths, and Later Finds, *South Asian Studies* 13: 209-25.
Srinivasan, S. and I. Glover 1995. Wrought and Quenched, and Cast High-Tin Bronzes from Kerala, Southern India, *Journal of Historical Metallurgy* (29) 2. London: Institute of Metals.
Steensberg, A. 1980. *New Guinea Gardens: a Study of Husbandry with Parallels in Prehistoric Groups*. London: Academic Press.
Steward, J. 1967. Comments on K.C. Chang's Paper on 'Major Aspects of the Interrelationship of Archaeology and Ethnology', *Current Anthropology* 8: 229-40.
Stiles, D. 1977. Ethnoarchaeology: a Discussion of Method and Application, *Man* 12: 87-103.
Thurston, E. 1909. *The Castes and Tribes of South India*, 7 Vols. Madras: Government Press.
Thompson, R.H. 1991. The Archaeological Purpose of Ethnoarchaeology, in *Ceramic*

Ethnoarchaeology (W.A. Longrace Ed.), pp. 231-45. Tucson: The University of Arizona Press.

Tilley, C. 1996. *An Ethnography of the Neolithic: Early Prehistoric Societies in Southern Scandinavia*. Cambridge: Cambridge University Press.

Tripathi, V. and Arun K. Mishra 1997. Understanding Iron Technology: an Ethnographic Model, *Man and Environment* XXII (1): 59-68.

Tripathi, V. and A. Tripathi 1994. Iron Working in Ancient India: an Ethnoarchaeological Study, in *From Sumer to Meluhha* (J.M. Kenoyer Ed.), pp. 241-51. Madison: Wisconsin Archaeological Reports.

Walhouse, M.J. 1874a. A Toda 'Dry Funeral', *Indian Antiquary* 3: 93-6.

——— 1874b. A Toda 'Green Funeral', *Indian Antiquary* 3: 274-6.

Wandsnider, L. 1991. The Relationship Between Spatial Structure and Temporal Aspects of Site Occupation: an Ethnoarchaeological Study of Indian Ethnographic Sites. Report Submitted to the Govt. of India, Ministry of Human Resource Development. Manuscript on File, University of Nebraska.

Watson, P.T. 1979. *Archaeology and Ethnography in Western Iran*. Tucson: University of Arizona Press.

——— 1980. The Theory and Practice of Ethnoarchaeology with Special Reference to the Near East, *Paleorint* 6 (1): 55-64.

Wheeler, R.E.M., A. Ghosh and Krishna Deva 1945. Arikamedu: an Indo-Roman Trading Station on the East Coast of India, *Ancient India* 2: 17-124.

White, J.P. 1967. Ethnoarchaeology in New Guinea: Two Examples, *Mankind* 6: 409-14.

Wobst, H.M. 1978. The Archaeo-Ethnology of the Hunter-Gatherers or the Tyranny of Ethnographic Record in Archaeology, *American Antiquity* 43: 303-309.

Wylie, A. 1982. An Analogy by Any Other Name in Just as Analogical: a Commentary on the Gould-Watson Dialogue, *Journal of Anthropological Archaeology* 1: 382-405.

Williams, B.J. 1968a. The Birhor of India and Some Comments on Band Organisation, in *Man the Hunter* (R.B. Lee and I. de Vore Eds.), pp. 126-31. Chicago: Aldine.

——— 1968b. The Birhor of Hazaribagh, in *Contribution to Anthropology: Band Societies* (D. Damas Ed.), 142-52. Ottawa: The Queen's Printer.

Wylie, A. 1985. The Reaction Against Analogy, in *Advances in Archaeological Method and Theory* 7 (M. Schiffer Ed.), pp. 68-111. New York: Academic Press.

Yellen, J. 1977. *Archaeological Approaches to the Present: Models for Reconstructing the Past*. New York: Academic Press.

Quaternary Vertebrate Palaeontology in India: Fifty Years of Research

G.L. BADAM

HISTORICAL BACKGROUND

The nature of fossil bones was a subject of various beliefs to the ancient Indians. The first mention of fossils in India was found in a summary of the history of Mughal and Pathan emperors by Ferishta in 1360. This was quoted by Falconer in 1868. According to him bones of 'elephants and men' were discovered by labourers while working on a waterway somewhere in the Siwaliks. 'Some of the bones were petrified, while others were still in the condition of bone'. This was probably the first authentic record of Quaternary fossils in the whole of India. However, between this and the first scientific documentation more than five hundred years elapsed. Whether these discoveries were put on record earlier than 1868 is not known. This goes to show that there was little knowledge or appreciation of the importance of these findings from areas that later turned out to be amongst the richest fossiliferous horizons in the world. This fact is borne out also by the eminent palaeontologist, the late M.R. Sahni who mentions that:

> References to fossils in early Indian literature are, however, few and far between, for our ancients do not appear to have devoted themselves much to the biologic sciences except in so far as these concerned the practice of indigenous medicine. This naturally hampered the initiation of palaeontologic and palaeobotanic research in India. (Sahni 1954)

Though not directly concerned here, it may be mentioned that incidentally the first discovery of plant fossils was reported by John Warren in 1810 (*Asiatick Researches* 1810) from near the village of 'Treevikera in the Carnatic'. No definite identification of this find is available but Sahni (1954) thinks that the discovery might relate to Tamarind. Similarly, the first discovery of an invertebrate fossil was made in 1823 by H.W. Voysey (*Asiatick Researches* 1823) from the intertrappean beds at Melconda. However, there is also an earlier record of a stray find of a marine mollusc from a well in Madras collected by B. Babington in 1818, and which is not well documented. The present synthesis deals only with vertebrate palaeontology of the Quaternary period and lays emphasis on the new techniques employed in the study of fossils during the last few decades.

VERTEBRATE PALAEONTOLOGY

One of the earliest discoveries of vertebrate fossils in India dates to around 1821 when H.T. Colebrooke reported fossils collected from Caribari in Bengal though without assigning a proper identification to them. In fact there are stray references to vertebrate fossils in the early nineteenth century but none of these are of particular importance. In India vertebrate fossils are reported from Permo-Trias, followed by the Mesozoic but it is the Siwaliks which, in terms of diversity and numbers, tops the list in richness of fossils. Obviously most of the earlier discoveries made in India pertained to the Siwaliks.

Capt. W.S. Webb (basically a geographer) was perhaps the first to record vertebrate fossils in the Siwaliks which 'were used as charms by the Tibetans'. An account of this was published by Buckland (1824). Subsequent discoveries were made by Crawford in 1826, who reported remains of hippopotamus, rhinoceros, crocodiles, etc., from the Irrawaddy Valley in Burma (what is now Myanmar) and these were described by Clift (1828). Pentland (1828) described the first anthracothere from the north-eastern borders of Bengal. G.G. Splisbury found an elephant jaw from near Jabalpur which was incidentally the first vertebrate fossil to be sketched (Splisbury 1833). Two army engineers, W.E. Baker and H.M. Durand also collected a lot of faunal material from the north-west and put them on record (Baker and Durand 1836).

Though the above discoveries created an interest amongst scholars and the common man the real breakthrough came when H. Falconer (a surgeon) and P.T. Cautley (an engineer) discovered numerous fossils in the north-west and, with a right understanding of the significance of their discoveries, proceeded to publish these in a series of articles which became landmark publications in so far as the earlier collections are concerned (Falconer and Cautley 1836, 1836-49). This work actually laid the foundation of vertebrate palaeontology in India and Falconer and Cautley came to be regarded as pioneers in the study of Siwalik vertebrates.

During the century that followed a great deal of palaeontological research was carried out in India which became the subject of several monographs and memoirs. Prominent works are those of Falconer (*Palaeontological Memoirs*, 1868, edited after his death in 1865 by R.I. Murchison), Lydekker (*Palaeontologia Indica*, 1881, 1882 etc.) and Pilgrim (1915, 1926, 1932, 1939). During the later part of the nineteenth century some references to vertebrate fossils also came from other parts of the country, e.g. that of *Rhinoceros deccanensis* from Karnataka (Foote 1876) and numerous and diverse fossil forms collected from the Kurnool caves in Andhra Pradesh (Lydekker 1886). All these works indicated considerable advancement over previous studies, the thrust having shifted from the traditional and classic work to more scientific areas of biostratigraphy, correlation, migration and palaeoenvironment. Other works of importance pertained mostly to the Siwaliks and mention may be made of the researches of Matthew (1929), Mook (1932, 1933), Colbert (1935) and Osborn (1935, 1942) whose contributions enriched our understanding of various fossil groups. In fact most of the above works were based on the collections made by Barnum Brown of the American Museum of Natural History who led an expedition to India in 1921-3. It may be of interest to know that the complete fossil of *Colossochelys atlas*, the giant land tortoise and that of a skull of *Sivatherium giganteum*, a distant relative of giraffe, both from Siwaliks (of Pakistan) and displayed in the visitors gallery of the American Museum of Natural History in New York, are from the expedition collection. Similarly there are several museums in the world which display the Indian fossil materials or have them in repositories like the British Museum of Natural History in London. The subsequent Yale-Cambridge expedition of the 1930s resulted in the publication of useful papers and monographs (e.g. Gregory et al. 1938). Later, Chakravarty (1937, 1957), Hooijer (1949, 1955), Deraniyagala (1956,1957) and others worked on proboscidea, hippopotami, bovids, horses, rhinoceroses and other groups bringing out their significance in evolution and palaeoenvironment and also comparing them with the fauna of Sri Lanka, the Malay Archipelago and other parts in the Punjab. More details about the fossil discoveries in the pre-Independence period may be found in the works of Colbert (1935), Sahni (1954) and Badam (1979).

THE LAST FIFTY YEARS

During the last fifty years considerable advances have been made in palaeontological researches in India, particularly in the field of vertebrate palaeontology. By this time several Indian scholars had come on the scene, noteworthy among them being M.R. Sahni, E. Khan, K.N. Prasad, C. Tripathi, P.P. Satsangi and others who concentrated on the Quaternary fossil findings from various areas and published a lot of material. Mention will be made here of only a few publications as much of the material is readily available in libraries.

Sahni and Tripathi (1957) produced a monograph on Indian deinotheres giving descriptions of some new species apart from proposing a new classification of the group. Sahni and Khan, who dominated the scene for almost a decade by carrying out systematic investigations on Siwalik vertebrates described a number of fossils (Sahni and Khan 1961, 1964) with emphasis on their provenance and affinities. It may be emphasized that the fossil collections made by E. Khan and displayed in the museum of Panjab University Geology Department at Chandigarh rank amongst the best in the country, second only to the one displayed in the Indian Museum, Calcutta. Many students, including the writer, have tremendously benefited from these collections and have used part of this material for further study or for comparative research. Prasad (1962, 1970, 1974) studied a number of fossils with special emphasis on primates and also made a detailed stratigraphic and palaeontologic study of the areas around Haritalyangar (Himachal Pradesh) and Perim Island (Gujarat). Prasad and Satsangi (1966) described some mammals and reptiles in addition to a fossil hoof of a bovid from Haritalyangar. Verma (1969) described a fossil primate, *Procynocephalus pinjorii*, from the Siwaliks near Pinjor which happens to be the first record of the genus from the Siwaliks.

Amongst the active workers on Quaternary palaeontology today mention may be made of Ashok Sahni, G.L. Badam, A.C. Nanda, B.S. Kotlia, Rajiv Patnaik, Rajan Gaur, R.N. Vashist, P.K. Basu, S. Biswas, D.C. Dassarma, Arun Sonakia and a few others. It may be mentioned that several students have secured their Ph.D. degrees on various aspects of Quaternary palaeontology under the guidance of some of the above mentioned scholars and have added new dimension to the study of vertebrate palaeontology. There are about twenty of them and references to their work will come in the pages that follow. Also we now have an efficient group of workers doing excellent work on the pre-Quaternary vertebrate palaeontology.

G.L. Badam and A.C. Nanda were the first two students during the last thirty years who worked in the Geology Department of Panjab University for their Ph.D. degrees, that Department being then the only centre of research in vertebrate palaeontology in India. This centre got international recognition as an Advanced Centre in Himalayan Geology and Palaeontology by dint of the efforts of academicians of the calibre of M.R. Sahni who had a host of good students, E. Khan being one in vertebrate palaeontology. Apart from making an excellent collection as stated above, Khan (1962) studied the palaeontology and stratigraphy of the Upper Siwaliks around Chandigarh. Badam's doctoral thesis (1973) is concerned with the geology and palaeontology of the Upper Siwaliks of a part of Pinjor-Nalagarh area and Nanda (1973b) completed a thesis on the stratigraphy and palaeontology of the Upper Siwaliks of a part of Naraingarh tehsil, Ambala. These were the only Ph.D. theses submitted on Quaternary vertebrate palaeontology for a long time and were later published.

At around the same time Ashok Sahni returned from USA after specializing in palaeohistology and the scanning electron microscopy technique for vertebrate material, which he later pioneered in India at Panjab University, Chandigarh, and in which area several students obtained Ph.D. degrees under his guidance. By this time, Badam shifted to Deccan College, Pune, to build up a palaeontological laboratory which houses fossils from the Late Pliocene to the Early Holocene though the collection also includes some from the Miocene period. However, the thrust here is on Quaternary fossils from all over India, found in association with the cultural material. It may be mentioned that already a few fossils had been collected from various areas in Maharashtra (Nevasa, Inamgaon, Rahuri, etc.) by scholars in Deccan College, some of which were identified by the officers of the Zoological Survey of India. The collection was meagre and in the absence of a specialist no detailed study of the material was possible, till the beginning of 1973. Nanda joined the Wadia Institute of Himalayan Geology at Dehra Dun and concentrated on the Siwaliks and on the Ladakh Molasse Group. Hence by 1973 three centres were actively enganged in researches on vertebrate palaeontology, the one at Chandigarh, which of course had a long tradition, and the two new centres at Pune and Dehra Dun which in the years to come also became internationally recognized centres. All these centres have employed new techniques in the study of palaeontology and trained several students. In addition, the Anthropology Department of Panjab University has also produced a few Ph.D. theses on the Siwalik fossils.

PROGRESS IN RESEARCH AND THE APPLICATION OF NEW TECHNIQUES

Palaeobiological research in India in the past had been mostly of the classical and objective type but in the nineteenth century when fossils were first reported, this was then the only method of study (see Falconer and Cautley 1836, 1836-49). The classical palaeontology primarily included descriptive and stratigraphic studies with emphasis on diagnostic features and morphological descriptions. Subsequently, stratigraphical studies were mostly pioneered by Medlicott (1873), Pilgrim (1925, 1944), Colbert (1935) and others which laid emphasis on the stratigraphical position, geographical range and lithological associations. Research progressed gradually to include the ecological and biogeographical aspects of the fossils (Badam 1984 and references therein) and much emphasis was laid on the evolutionary aspects of various animal groups, ancestor-descendant relationship and relationship of one group of animals with the other. In the past three decades or so a change in vertebrate palaeontological research has become evident with the application of several new techniques. Also for research on the Quaternary period the integration of various data from anthropology, archaeozoology, conchology, palaeobotany, palynology and modern ecology has made this field truly inter-disciplinary, interesting and useful.

New workers joined the fray and concentrated on scientific studies in palaeontology with more emphasis on chronology, biostratigraphy, provenance, migration patterns, evolution, etc. Study of microvertebrates, particularly micromammals, techniques of scanning electron microscopy, taphonomy, stable isotope analysis, biomolecular palaeontology (the last one as yet in an experimental stage) started gaining momentum which gave the subject of vertebrate palaeontology a new thrust and it began to be considered at par with palaeontological researches being carried out in some well-known laboratories of the world. Apart from the traditional dating techniques, some sophisticated techniques came to be used on fossils for absolute and relative chronology. Some of the new techniques as applied to vertebrate palaeontology are outlined below.

DATING METHODS

In India, in recent years, a major advance in Quaternary vertebrate palaeontology is seen in the application of absolute dating techniques such as ^{14}C, TL, ESR, K-Ar, U-series, palaeomagnetism, etc. Though this is not the place to go into these dating techniques it is worthwhile to mention that many of the problems of biochronology have been resolved to a great extent by using these methods. Let us take the example of the Neogene/Quaternary boundary problem in north-west India which is one of the most debatable stratigraphical problems in India. Earlier, scholars used to base the delineation of the boundary on stratigraphic, palaeontologic, palaeoclimatic, sedimentary and tectonic considerations. In recent years the application of palaeomagnetic dating techniques has provided a firm basis for correlation of Siwalik beds with the standard magnetic polarity time scale (MPTS). Magneto-stratigraphic studies in the Indian subcontinent were initiated first in Pakistan on the Upper Siwaliks of the Pabbi Hills (Keller et al. 1977) and other parts of northern Pakistan (Opdyke et al. 1979) according to which the Pleistocene epoch commences at the Olduvai Event, dated to 1.8 Ma. Palaeontologically, the N/Q boundary corresponds with the Gauss/Matuyama boundary which has been dated to 2.48 Ma, coinciding with the first appearance of *Equus*, *Elephas*, *Cervus* to mark the beginning of the Pleistocene. Also according to Azzaroli and Napoleone (1982) and

Tandon et al. (1984), who worked on the sites north-east of Chandigarh, the Tatrot/Pinjor boundary corresponds with the G/M transition at 2.48 Ma. Nanda (1973a, 1973b), Badam (1973, 1979) and Gaur and Chopra (1984) documented the presence of *Equus* in the Pinjor beds at various levels falling in the Matuyama epoch. This is the accepted age for the T/P transition. Though there is still a difference of opinion in the use of palaeontologic data and the MPTS in respect of dating the N/Q boundary in north-west India, the INQUA Commission (1991) now accepts the base of Matuyama as the beginning of the Quaternary. Thus absolute dating adds a new dimension to this vexed problem in which fauna does play an important role and the presence of any one of the fossils (*Equus*, *Elephas* or *Cervus*), if in situ, is sufficient proof for assigning a Pleistocene age to the bed yielding it (Hopwood 1935), a fact which is valid even after sixty-five years of researçh.

Another important contribution of dating techniques with regard to palaeontology, based on magnetic polarity stratigraphy, has been made in the Siwaliks whereby the primate fauna at Haritalyangar in Himachal Pradesh is assigned a last appearance datum (LAD) age. The youngest assigned age for *Sivapithecus indicus*, *S. sivalensis* and *Ramapithecus punjabicus* in Asia is 7-7.5 Ma. The age of Holotype specimen of *Gigantopithecus bilaspurensis* is about 6.3 Ma (Johnson et al. 1983).

ESR dating of bone and dental remains was for the first time attempted in India by Gogte and Murty (1986) on a bone sample from the Upper Palaeolithic site of Kurnool caves in Andhra Pradesh. The samples selected for ESR dating belonged to five layers at MCG II in the cave complex. The ESR dates were obtained from two trenches, Trench F and Trench B. The dates for the two levels at Trench F: (1) 893 BP for F 20 cm-40 cm and (2) 5247 BP for F 40 cm -60 cm can provide a time sequence for the upper levels of cave sediments. The date for Trench B4 (120 cm-135 cm) being 9498 BP supports the association of this level with the Mesolithic. The dates for the preceding levels 16,686 BP for B4 (150 cm-165 cm) and 19.224 BP for B4 (165 cm-180 cm) confirm the Upper Palaeolithic age of these levels. The ESR dating for B4 (165 cm-180 cm) is almost in agreement with TL date of 17,390 BP (Murty and Nambi 1983) from burnt clay within the sediment from the same level.

The above dating methods, which have a direct bearing on the fauna, and those like palaeomagnetism, fission-track and TL which have an indirect bearing, have amply demonstrated their usefulness to palaeontology in one way or the other. It has also been confirmed now that the biostratigraphic chronology of the Indian Pleistocene (which was mainly based on taxonomic and morphological studies of fossils and their cultural associations) is erroneous. However, palaeontologic and stratigraphic dating, index fossil assemblages, the first appearance datum (FAD) of an allochthonous faunal element, and the LAD of an index fossil are crucial to building up a biostratigraphical chronology. It is important that these should be supplemented by a number of other parameters which include physical and chemical dating methods.

Fluorine dating of bones and fossils was attempted for the first time in India by Joshi and Kshirsagar (1986) and subsequently on samples collected from various geographic regions (Kshirsagar and Paddayya 1988-9; Kshirsagar and Badam 1990; Kshirsagar 1993).

These studies have established the positive role that fluorine analysis can play in relative dating of faunal material from different geological and archaeological periods. For example the Acheulian sites of Hunsgi (Karnataka) and Chirki (Maharashtra) have f/p ratios in the range of 6.73–8.39 and 8.11–8.29 respectively. Both these ranges indicate a Middle Pleistocene age for the levels yielding fossils. The fluorine/phosphate ratios in Tertiary fossils fall in the range of 8.15–8.67 which is close to the saturation value of 8.92. Another example can be cited from the site of Hathnora in M.P. where the cranium of *Homo erectus narmadiensis* gives a f/p ratio of 7.53 which places the cranium in late Middle Pleistocene time bracket. The range of most of the fossils dated by this method can be favourably compared on the basis of archaeological, geological and palaeontological data. The usefulness of fluorine analysis for establishing a chronological framework for the Indian Quaternary deposits has been realized for the last one and a half decades and this study will continue to occupy an important place in palaeontological researches in the years to come.

Amongst the other relative dating methods in palaeontology nitrogen analysis was attempted on some of the Narmada Valley fossils. This method has some limitations because nitrogen disappears rapidly from bones in a tropical climate and hence may not give accurate results. The figures of 0.97 per cent nitrogen for a fossil from the surface and of 1.20 per cent for a buried fossil, both from the Devakachar area in the central Narmada Valley, were considered by K.P. Oakley to be similar to those of the Upper Pleistocene in Africa and Europe. However, these may not be considered reliable dating evidence (Badam and Grigson 1990).

Recently, Szabo et al. (1990) obtained half a dozen radiometric dates using the U-series technique on a faunal assemblage of the Acheulian culture of the Hunsgi-Biachbal valleys in north Karnataka. These dates confirm the Middle Pleistocene-early Late Pleistocene time bracket for these cultures. The ratios for f/p obtained on bone samples from these sites (8.39–5.06 for Acheulian and 5.28–0.22 for Middle Palaeolithic and Neolithic) confirm the dating (Kshirsagar and Paddayya 1988-9). Two of these dates were calibrated on travertine samples from the site of Kaldevanahalli in the Hunsgi Valley. The remaining four dates were obtained on enamel samples of teeth from Sadab, Teggihalli and Kudalgi in the Baichbal Valley. A fragment of molar of *Elephas* from Sadab has given a date of 2,90,405 BP. The *Bos* sample from Teggihalli gave a date of 2,87,731 BP whereas the *Elephas* sample from the same area came up with a minimum age of 350 ka.

The above new dating techniques have revolutionized our thinking on the chronology of Stone Age cultures in peninsular India. At Bori in the Kukdi Valley typical Acheulian artefacts and fossils of *Bos*, *Elephas* and *Equus* have been recovered from a well from cemented sandy pebbly gravel which is underlain by a compact brown silt, fissured clay and pebble. A 2 m thick tephra layer, now dated to 6,70,000, is embedded in the clay sediments. Fossil samples from different locations at Bori gave a f/p ratio ranging from 8.05–3.22. At location 4 in Bori the value of f/p is close to the saturation point at 8.92, indicating greater antiquity, possibly Middle Pleistocene, for the fossils. The other ratios are in the range of 4 and 5 and comparable with the ratios obtained for the Late Pleistocene period (Kshirsagar and Badam 1990). The Th/Ur dates at Bori also indicate a higher antiquity (400 ka BP). At Nevasa Th/Ur dates, more than 350 ka on calcrete cement of gravels containing Acheulian artefacts along with fossils of *Bos*, *Elephas* and fossil wood indicate an antiquity (Lower to Middle Pleistocene) much higher than assumed earlier. On the whole the application of these dating methods has significantly increased the antiquity of Acheulian in India and also placed some of the fossils in an accurate chronological framework. Of course there is scope for further data and hence more refinement in biochronological studies.

TAPHONOMY

The term taphonomy was proposed by a Russian palaeontologist, J.A. Efremov in 1940 for the study of the transition of animals from the stage of biosphere to that of lithosphere. The word has a Greek origin, *taphos* means burial and *nomos* means law. Literally therefore, taphonomy means laws of burial. It is a process in which animals pass out of different parts of the biosphere, get fossilized and become part of the lithosphere. In fact during the last few years the application of taphonomy and palaeoecology has so widened that they are now considered sister disciplines of archeology (Gifford 1981).

It may be mentioned that taphonomy established itself in palaeontology primarily as a subdiscipline of palaeoecology but it has evolved into a much broader study of the ways in which preservation affects the fossil record (Behrensmeyer and Kidwell 1985). In the US, where such studies have received tremendous attention, there has been a change in emphasis in recent years from descriptive taphonomic studies of fossil assemblages to more experimental, process-oriented multidisciplinary investigations (Behrensmeyer 1990). This research is largely helping to resolve problems in evolution, biogeography, biostratigraphy and palaeoenvironmental reconstruction, and thus to a better overall understanding of the fossil record. However, continuing research in modern analogues and theoretical modelling is critical to the further growth of taphonomy as is the interaction between biological and geological processes.

Taphonomy can be divided into two fields, biostratinomy and diagenesis. Biostratinomy includes the circumstances occurring between the death of an individual and its subsequent burial whereas diagenesis includes the effects upon the interred remains brought about by burial conditions and subsequent exposure until the time of discovery. Gilbert (1979) correlates these fields with events in fossil history as shown below:

Palaeontological	Subdisciplines	Events in Fossil History
		Discovery
	Diagenetic studies	Final burial
Taphonomy	Biostratimony	
		Death
	Palaeoecology	
		Birth

The various stages in taphonomical processes from the death of an animal to its recovery as a fossil have been diagrammatically shown as below:

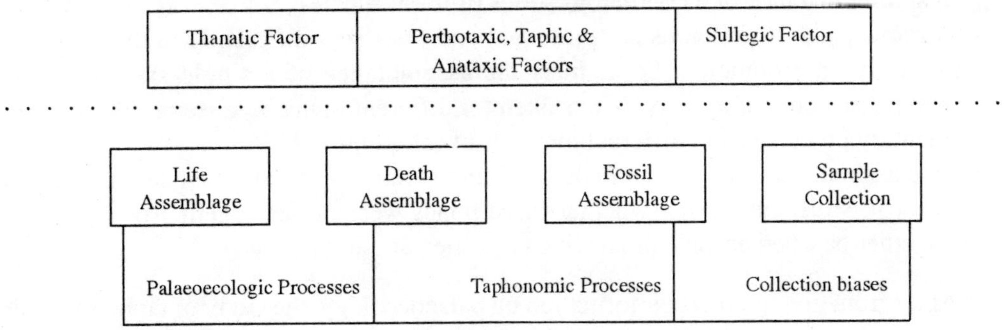

Diagrammatic History of Taphonomy

Explanations for the various terms used in the above figure are given below:

Life Assemblage	Biocoenosis	Population of living animals
Death Assemblage	Thanatocoenosis	Population of dead animals
Fossil Assemblage	Perthotaxic	variables affecting bone preservation subsequent to death but prior to burial
	Taphic	mode of burial of animal remains
	Anataxic	site erosion, nature and rate of sedimentation, depth of burial, sediment chemistry, bioturbation etc.
Collection	Sullegic factor	manner of collecting fossils and the collecting bias

Some of the problems generally connected with fossilization and the role of taphonomy in solving them are given below:

1. Bones from older strata and those from younger strata react differently to the process of fossilization. In the former the state of preservation of fossils is often poor and the number of individuals fewer because chances of destruction increase with time. However, it is the fauna from the younger strata that are more often subject to destruction on account of tectonic events, floods, ploughing, trampling, etc.
2. Faunal assemblages, especially those of vertebrates, may not always be autochthonous. Although a complex of terrestrial mammals found together in one place is usually called a fauna (a term implying that the animals were associated in life), such a complex may have come together accidentally either at or after death.

3. The sudden appearance in the fossil record of a new fauna, without its ancestors in the preceding strata, may or may not reflect a genuinely new group of species. This may be an artefact of preservation. Sometimes strata may be subjected to disturbances resulting in a lack of a continuous series of fossil species.
4. Various parts of skeletons are preserved and fossilized differently in different sedimentary environments. Sometimes the assemblages of a single synchronic and sympatric community may be mistaken for different fauna because of different sedimentary processes and different methods of sampling.
5. In case bones of different animals are found together in a particular sedimentary deposit it is difficult to say whether these bones were buried together or transported together or whether the animals lived and died at the same site.

Apart from giving precise information on palaeoecology, the study of taphonomy also helps to solve the problems of the mode of occurrence, taxonomic diversity and paucity of small mammals (if any) and explains various aspects regarding the concentration of fossils, patterns of disarticulation, varieties of damage, etc.

In recent years taphonomy has been increasingly used in archaeology and geology for a more precise reconstruction of chronology and the palaeoenvironment. Since taphonomy throws light on the autochthonous/allochthonous nature of fossils (primary and secondary context) we can know whether these are related or not to the sediments yielding them. However, in the Indian context discrepancies have crept in while relating fossils to sediments. For example, in the Siwaliks, where earlier collections came from mixed contexts, without a clear-cut stratigraphic control (Badam and Rajaguru 1991), the chronological framework established was somewhat erroneous till the methods of physical and chemical dating became available. In several cases the matrix enclosing the fossils is different from the lithological units from which the fossils are extracted (Saxena 1968). A detailed taphonomy of the Siwalik fossils will help throw new light on the provenance and mode of deposition of these fossils which in turn may have an important bearing on the biochronology of the Siwalik sediments.

A similar difficulty arises in respect of fossils from the central Narmada Valley, where taphonomically, two modes of deposition can be distinguished in the Devakachar area of Narsinghpur district, Madhya Pradesh. The majority of the fossils found in the lag deposit of the bouldery and cobbly horizon are fragmented and seem to have undergone some transportation. Fresh and unabraided fossils are derived from the overlying silty sandy horizon (channel fill and overbank alluvial fill deposits) and probably the animals represented by these fossils were autochthonous.

An interesting case of a redeposited fossil which raises some doubts about its in situ position, is that of the partial cranium of *Homo erectus narmadiensis* found in a channel bar environment at Hathnora in Madhya Pradesh (Sonakia 1984). The cranium is heavily mineralized and has been found associated with Late Acheulian artefacts. Its position in the bar deposits combined with taphonomic features indicates that the cranium was redeposited in this section after having been transported over some distance (Badam 1989). This aspect if overlooked would give erroneous results regarding the dating of the cranium. Thus the sedimentary context and the associated cultural materials warrant a detailed taphonomic study to arrive at a precise chronology and palaeoenvironmental history of the site.

It may be stressed here that research in the new discipline of taphonomy and its related branches on the Quaternary fossils of India, was initiated at Deccan College after a preliminary study of a small collection of fossils from the central Narmada Valley (Badam et al. 1986). Subsequently, additional aspects of this fascinating study were undertaken on collections from Karimnagar, Andhra Pradesh (Badam and Jain 1988), Son Valley in Uttar Pradesh (Badam et al. 1989), and other areas in central and western India (Badam 1990a, 1990b).

Studies on the decomposition and scatter patterns of modern animals have been carried out at various national Parks in Africa. They provide a modern analogue for reconstructing past taphonomic stages leading to their preservation and subsequent fossilization of the skeletal remains. Studies on similar lines have been carried out at the Mudumalai Sanctuary in Tamil Nadu by the author. This preliminary effort is rather broad based but a rigorous follow-up study will help throw more precise light on the chronology and depositional environment of the fossils in relation to archaeological, geological and palaeontological sites in India.

In a more recent work the writer (Badam 1994) presented some of his observations of taphonomic studies from three different situations—modern, archaeological and geological. The integration of the data involving different time periods was thought necessary in order to observe how similar taphonomic processes would operate on assemblages in different ecological settings representing different time periods. It was also demonstrated that individual sites, levels or assemblages have their own taphonomic history. It is necessary, therefore, that as much taphonomic information as possible should be gathered at the site itself for accurate interpretations.

While studying taphonomy as a tool in interpreting fossils and their modes of occurrence Badam (1996) discussed the various processes from biosphere to lithosphere which occur as a result of many interrelated geological, biological and chemical phenomena, viz., causes of death, decomposition and disarticulation, weathering and transport, diagenetic factors, collection and documentation. In addition the writer also gave a brief checklist of vertebrates for taphonomic purposes as below, the careful observation and systematic monitoring of which will ensure a correct picture of the taphonomic losses.

Locality

1. Date of observation
2. Map reference and specific locality with scale
3. General climate (temperature, humidity, etc.) at various times of observation
4. Exposure of specimen to sun (daily, weekly, monthly) depending on the size and weight of the carcass
5. Degree and agent of burial, degree of decay, moisture and organic content, angle of slope, etc.
6. Transport of specimen (water, wind, human, animal, etc.)
7. Proximity of specimen to water source

Biotic Factors

1. Vegetation and its density
2. Predators or scavengers sighted
3. Parts of specimen eaten by scavengers/ predators
4. Tracks, feathers, burrows in proximity of the specimen
5. Evidence of human activity
6. Bioturbation (insect/rodent activity, etc.)
7. Recent fauna and flora in the area

Specimen

1. Specific identification, age and sex
2. Plot of specimen with landmark positions
3. Presence of soft parts including skin and ligaments
4. Distortion due to dehydration
5. Degree of disarticulation and scattering of various parts of the body in relation to rest of the specimen
6. Area of scatter
7. Missing elements
8. Surface features of bones
9. Mechanical breakages, cracking and crushing, fractures
10. Bone flaking and dissolution
11. Abrasion, tooth marks
12. General state of weathering

Finally and importantly, there is a need for more data from recent specimens, as observations of recent skeletons undergoing taphonomic processes show many analogies with fossil occurrences and provide a firm basis for their interpretation. More data will strengthen our understanding and appreciation of taphonomy in vertebrate palaeontology and will also provide a comprehensive data bank for taphonomic research in India.

DENTAL HISTOLOGY AND ENAMEL ULTRASTRUCTURES

As mentioned in the beginning, one of the major advances in palaeontology has been the application of scanning electron microscopic (SEM) studies. These studies were pioneered in India at Panjab University by Ashok Sahni to document the diversity of enamel ultrastructures in various mammalian taxa, to trace the evolution of enamel tissues and to understand the relationship between enamel ultrastructure and functional dental morphology. As mentioned by Badam and Sathe (1995) the results of these studies have given a new dimension to the interpretation of phylogeny, taxonomy, dietary habits, and the diseases from which animals suffered in the past.

SEM studies are of great importance in the field of palaeontology and biomineralization.

The main applications of this instrument are related to micrographic reproduction of the fine morphological features of fossils and living organisms leading to their taxonomic differentiation and the reconstruction of phylogenetic lineages. SEM has also been used to study Precambrian biota, soft-part anatomy of fossil organisms and other microscopic forms of life that cannot ordinarily be studied by light microscopy (Sahni 1989). Furthermore, the biomineralized structure of molluscan shells, vertebrate egg-shells and dental tissue is ideally suited for such studies. However, in India SEM studies have been widely conducted on tooth enamel.

Tomes (1850) was perhaps the first to carry out pioneering work on the dental constituents of the enamel of marsupial and rodent teeth. Poole (1956) suggested that true prismatic enamel originated with the early mammals. On the whole, such studies have brought to light useful information on the evolution and origin of mammalian enamel and its bearing on the problem of phylogeny. It may be mentioned here that the basic prism patterns in mammals have been classified by Boyde (1964) into 3 patterns. Pattern I is found in insectivores, cetacea, sirenia and many extinct mammals whereas Pattern 2 is found generally in ungulates, marsupials and lagomorphs. Pattern 3 is common in carnivores, proboscideans, man, and his anthropoid ancestors. In addition, there are three basic crystallite orientations (structureless, pseudoprismatic, and prismatic) which represent evolutionary trends in the enamel of vertebrates from reptiles to mammals (Sahni 1985). The prismatic arrangement in mammals is controlled by stresses which occur during mastication.

Kozawa (1978) carried out SEM studies on tooth enamel of *Moeritherium*, *Mastodon*, *Stegodon* and *Elephas* and confirmed that *Stegodon* was an evolutionary intermediate stage between *Mastodon* and *Elephas*, something that had been suggested for a long time. Based on changes in the prismatic pattern with respect to tooth morphology, he suggested a gradual transition in the dietary habits of the four elephant species from omnivorous to herbivorous.

Grine et al. (1986) analysed the enamel of *Ovis aries* and *Capra hircus* in order to differentiate these species on a parameter other than dental morphology. Owing to the similarity of the prismatic pattern at the qualitative level, quantitative parameters are shown to be of great value, as they tend to differ in the enamel of intermediate depth. This is an important contribution in the case of such closely related taxa where tooth morphology may not help in a precise identification.

Sahni (1984, 1985, 1989) carried out detailed ultrastructural investigations of cetaceans, rodents, proboscideans, multituberculates and other groups bringing out the evolutionary aspects of enamel development. The dental histology of Subathu vertebrates (Kumar 1983), Siwalik mammals (Tiwari 1983), and rodents from the Karewas of Kashmir (Prakash 1986) are some of the major contributions to our understanding of the dietary habits of ancient vertebrates and their palaeoenvironment. Srivastava (1997) examined, both theoretically and experimentally, chewing stresses in the dentition of a few mammals and reptiles and their relationships with the internal structure of the enamel as observed under the SEM. According to him the internal structure of dental enamel of various mammals has been found to be closely related to chewing stresses produced due to masticatory forces. Also, the biomechanical analyses of various teeth in relation to their shape and enamel microstructure suggest that to dissipate chewing stresses better structural mechanisms have developed in mammalian dental enamel through time.

On the whole it is felt that more research on Pleistocene and contemporary mammals will bring out important aspects like their phylogenetic relationships, dietary habits, palaeopathology and even aspects of domestication. It is of vital importance to document both qualitative and quantitative traits of enamel prismatic patterns for a more precise knowledge of phylogenetic relationships, hitherto based mainly on gross dental morphology and skeletal anatomy (Badam and Sathe 1995).

BIOMOLECULAR STUDIES

During the last decade biomolecular studies have contributed immensely to various aspects of palaeontology and archaeology. In India such studies are still in an experimental stage with regard to earth sciences. This area has great potential and has been briefly discussed by Thomas (1993) while highlighting its inter-disciplinary applications. Molecular biology can contribute to the study of the past in a number of ways, e.g. hominid origins and macro-evolution, the palaeobiology and biogeography of human species, environmental reconstruction, past human diets, etc. Recent successes in recovering DNA from ancient bones have opened up new areas potentially research (Brown and Brown 1992). DNA has been recovered from a fossil leaf of *Magnolia* dating to the Miocene period (Golenberg 1991), from termites fossilized in amber in the Oligocene-Miocene periods (DeSelle et al. 1992), from the skin of Egyptian mummies (Paabo 1985) and from 7,000 year old brain tissue (Paabo et al. 1988). However, at present the results seem to be patchy; even though they are ideal for the study of hominid origins. According to Dover (1991) there is a need for more systematic work on the survival of ancient biomolecules in the whole range of organic materials that can be recovered from archaeological and geological sites and of the effect of age, type of site, context, soil conditions, and macro- and micro-climate. This study promises to make, in the coming years, a significant contribution to the various aspects outlined above.

DNA (deoxyribose nucleic acid) is a macromolecule consisting of two complementary strands of repeating units wrapped around each other in the form of a double helix. The repeating units are of four kinds, each consisting of a base, a sugar and a phosphoric acid. Each one is a nucleotide, and the four bases—thymine, adenine, guanine and cytocine—give infinite variety to the DNA molecule. They also supply genetic information to the cell and the organism and pass it on to offspring. DNA has certain physical and chemical properties. It can be isolated from nearly every organism from viruses to man. Only certain viruses lack DNA and in such viruses DNA is replaced by a comparable molecule, RNA (ribose nucleic acid). No matter where it is found, all DNA has much the same chemical and physical properties.

Collaborative research on the extraction of DNA from ancient bones and fossils with the Centre for Cellular and Molecular Biology, Hyderabad, is gradually bringing out interesting results but not enough for interpretation. It takes a long time to analyse a normal bone; the older the bone, the longer is the time taken. For a better understanding, we may give here examples from the work of Paabo (1993), a pioneer in research on biomolecular palaeontology, according to whom during the past decade scientists have learnt that ancient DNA, sometimes survives the ravages of time. Scholars have used DNA from bone and soft tissues to establish reliable sequences of seven extinct mammals, the oldest being the woolly mammoth found in the permafrost of Siberia. One can learn much more about genetic relations among extinct species by this study. It has also been confirmed that DNA can survive for long periods after the death of an individual. Allan Wilson (University of California, Berkeley) studied the quagga, a member of the horse family, that lived in southern Africa until extinction at the end of the past century. Samples from a 140-year old quagga skin in a German museum yielded bacterial clones containing sequences from the mitochondrial DNA, which exists in many copies outside the cell nucleus. By comparing these clones with sequences of the modern zebra it was shown that the quagga was closely related to the zebra and more distantly related to other equids. These were the first sequences determined from an extinct species.

In 1985 K.B. Mullis introduced a method, the polymerase chain reaction (PCR), that allows the multiplication in the test tube of a particular piece of DNA. This could open up great possibilities for the study of ancient DNA. This technique is extremely sensitive and can generate billions of copies from a single DNA molecule. It was also shown later that PCR can reconstruct intact DNA from several partially degraded ancient molecules. By this method several DNA extractions (leaf of *Magnolia*, termites in amber, etc.) have been successfully carried out. Desalle and his colleagues have shown that their sequences, from termites, are compatible with those from a modern termite.

In future, the study of ancient DNA will 'help us learn more about the dynamics of genetic change in populations over time'. We may be able to understand better the history of ourselves and other species and also 'to frame more rational strategies to limit the ongoing erosion of biodiversity'.

OTHER STUDIES

(a) Isotope studies have recently been initiated in palaeontology to know about the diet of extinct animals. Elsewhere a successful attempt was made at reconstructing cave bear (two species) palaeoecology from skeletons by Stiner et al. (1998) from a cave in Turkey where the nature of wear and breakage to the adult cave bear teeth indicates that extensive mastication was necessary while eating food. The patterns of tooth damage argue for a diet rich in tough, abrasive materials such as nuts, tubers and associated grit. The results also suggest that both species were truly omnivorous and obtained food from terrestrial and fresh water habitats. Also bone pathologies, usually originating from trauma, occur in some of the adult bears, testifying to long lifespans of some individuals in the population.

In India isotopic analysis has been carried out successfully on contemporary elephant populations (Sukumar et al. 1982) and on archaeological bones (Nautiyal et al. 1995).

Similar studies are being experimented in collaboration with scientists of an American university, on extinct and extant animal populations from India ranging from Miocene to Holocene, to work out the dietary habits and other aspects of herbivorous animals.

(b) Population dynamics studies is another area that could be initiated in India but it has its limitations in the context of palaeontological accumulations unless vast in situ thanatocoenoses are available. Kurten (1954) mentioned that this study is a mature branch of ecology with an important bearing on the problem of evolution mechanics. As suggested by him, in order to study the 'survival of the fittest' we need data on actual survival and mortality in natural populations. Badam and Sathe (1995) reaffirm that good results concerning avian populations have been achieved with the 'banding' method by ornithologists. The basic tool of the scientist in this field is the life table which summarizes information on survivorship, rates of mortality and expectation of life within a population. Control on movements, habits and habitats, e.g. that of cave bears, ecological niches and eating habits are areas that could help in a study of population dynamics.

According to Kurten (1954) the sample should be statistically respectable (30–40 individuals can yield good results), relative or absolute age of individuals at death should be known, and some estimate should be made regarding the way in which sample represents the population (biased, comparable to a census record of a living population, or to a mortality record). Kurten (1959) also suggests that taxonomic rates of evolution can be studied on the basis of survival data for taxa on the genus or species level.

(c) Palaeopathological studies have not seriously been undertaken on fossil populations in India (they have been attempted on human and animal skeletal remains) even though some of them do have signatures of diseases as revealed by SEM studies. It is hoped that a beginning would be made soon in this direction.

We expect that more new techniques will be applied to the palaeontological researches in future so as to gather as much precise information as possible on aspects mentioned above. This will give a respectable place to the study of palaeontology in contrast to our knowledge of fossils in the early nineteenth century when they were supposed to be dumb and dead.

NEW DISCOVERIES

Several new fossil complexes, isolated fossil sites, and some new species of animals have come to light during the last few decades. They throw important light on the palaeogeographic distribution of animals in the past, their evolutionary and chronological significance, and migration patterns. We give here examples of three recent discoveries.

(a) The Hominid Fossil

One of the greatest lacunae in Indian palaeontology and prehistoric archaeology has been the absence of the physical remains of pre-*Homo sapiens*. This is rather puzzling considering the fact that cultural material ranging in age from Lower Palaeolithic to

Mesolithic has been found in abundance in various parts of India. In the past there have been reports, though doubtful, about the finding of a human cranium from either the Narmada Valley or from the river Koana in Uttar Pradesh but either the provenance or the identification was not correctly documented. The specimen, first reported by Theobald (1881), was subsequently lost in the collections of the Asiatic Society of Bengal. It may be mentioned here that several primate discoveries have been made in the Siwaliks (Lewis 1934; Gregory et al. 1938; Prasad 1962; Simons and Chopra 1969; Chopra and Kaul 1975) but most of these are from the pre-Quaternary Mio-Pliocene deposits.

It is pertinent to mention here that a project entitled 'Explorations for the Remains of Early Man' was approved by the Council of Scientific and Industrial Research (CSIR) under the direction of the late M.R. Sahni at Panjab University, Chandigarh. This project resulted in the discovery of Lower Palaeolithic tools of the Soanian types from Terrace I of the Middle Pleistocene age and of several Stone Age sites in the valley of the Sirsa. The vertebrate fossils collected under this project are amongst the best found in the country though no fossils of the pre-*Homo sapiens* hominids were discovered.

The CSIR scheme was transferred to the Deccan College Post-Graduate and Research Institute, Pune for further work in the peninsular river valleys under the overall supervision of the late H.D. Sankalia. However, the physical remains of early man continued to elude the scientific community although hundreds of thousands of Stone Age tools and non-primate fossils were collected from various valleys.

It is in the above context that the recent discovery of *Homo erectus narmadiensis* (Sonakia 1984) from Hathnora (22°52' N; 77°53' E), a place 40 km north-east of Hoshangabad in Madhya Pradesh, assumes great significance. Since India holds a critical place between Africa and Java several scholars, e.g. de Chardin (1952), Sahni (1954), Khatri (1961) and Badam (1979) had opined that the physical remains of early man might one day be found in India, particularly in the central Narmada Valley.

At Hathnora in the central Narmada Valley a section of about 15 m is exposed which is distinguishable into five lithological units. The basal unit of 1.5 m thickness comprises greyish, cemented cross bedded sand and matrix supported pebbles at the top. Overlying this unit is cemented bouldery/pebbly gravel, about 0.5 m thick, which has yielded the partial cranium of a fossil hominid. Also fossil bovids, proboscideans and Late Acheulian artefacts have been collected from this horizon. This unit grades into a 5 m thick unconsolidated sandy/pebbly gravel having sub-rounded to rounded and un-imbricated matrix supported pebbles/gravels. This is the most richly fossiliferous unit elsewhere in the central Narmada Valley having also yielded Middle Palaeolithic and Late Acheulian tools. A pebbly/cobbly and silty clay unit of about 2 m thickness overlies the previous unit and this also yielded Middle Palaeolithic artefacts. Capping it is the yellow silty clay of 4 m thickness which is in turn overlain by black cotton soil.

Though there has been controversy with regard to the nomenclature of the Narmada Man, his discovery, which is the first of its kind in India, has provided us with hope of more evidence for an improved hominid record for South Asia. Morphometric and comparative investigations lead to the conclusion that the Narmada man should be designated *Homo sapiens* (Kennedy et al. 1991). While the calvaria shares some anatomical features with Asian *Homo erectus* specimens (about 40 per cent characteristics), it exhibits a broader suite of morphological characteristics (about 60 per cent) suggesting affinity with early *Homo sapiens* fossils from Asia, Europe and Africa.

Even on the basis of archaeological investigations at the hominid site of Hathnora and the close similarity of the associated tools with other Late Acheulian materials in and outside India, a critical investigation into the identification of the specimen was suggested (Badam 1989).

Some scholars have claimed the discovery of pre-*Homo sapiens* hominids from the Pinjor Formation of the Siwaliks (Singh et al. 1988) and from the Narmada Valley (Sankhyan 1997) but the authenticity of these claims is to be confirmed both morphologically and geologically.

(b) Micro-vertebrates in the Narmada Valley

One of the areas in palaeontology that has received tremendous attention in recent years is the study of micro-vertebrates. In the past this area attracted less attention not only because of paucity of such material in geological/ archaeological context but also because of the lack of interest in these vertebrates.

Perhaps the earliest work in this direction was that of Lydekker (1886) who listed a number of rodents (*Tatera, Bandicota, Mus, Millardia, Hystrix, Lepus*) and insectivores (*Sorex*) from Late Pleistocene deposits of the Kurnool caves in Andhra Pradesh. However, no further details about this collection are available. Sahni (1979) and Kumar (1983) studied vast assemblages of micro-vertebrates in Himachal Pradesh, Uttar Pradesh and Jammu and Kashmir, essentially from Lower and Upper Tertiary deposits. This study helped understand better the routes and palaeogeographic distribution of various groups and their chronology.

Quaternary micro-vertebrates have been studied in more detail than the pre-Quaternary vertebrates possibly because of their resemblance to modern microfauna. One of the best works comes from the Siwaliks of north-west India (Sahni and Khare 1976) and Karewas of Kashmir where several insectivore and rodent species, along with fish have been found after intensive bed by bed fossil collection followed by screening (Sahni and Kotlia 1985; Prakash 1986; Kotlia 1991). The microtine rodents have been shown to be of significance both as dating markers as well as indicators of climatic change. The diversity in the enamel pattern of rodents and their significance in the evolutionary framework has also been highlighted in these works.

Recently, micro-vertebrates were, for the first time, recovered from Middle-Late Pleistocene sediments of the central Narmada Valley at Gurariaghat near Devakachar (23°3' N; 79°7' E) in Narsinghpur district of Madhya Pradesh. This assemblage includes micro-mammals, fish, amphibia and reptiles and it is suggested that the small mammals, derived from scats, were deposited by fluvial processes. Rodents like *Millardia* cf. *meltada*, *Bandicota* cf. *bengalensis*, *Tatera* cf. *indica*, and *Gerbillus* sp. indicate an early emergence of these modern rodents in the Indian subcontinent (Patnaik et al. 1995). In addition, the discovery of microfauna assumes importance in the area because so far taphonomical and palaeoecological interpretation of the Narmada Valley was based on large vertebrate assemblages only and now this can provide another and even more precise tool for interpretations. However, because of the meagre record of fossil micromammals no interrelationship between the Narmada and Siwalik rodents can be ascertained. It is hoped that further micro-vertebrate discoveries in the Narmada Valley as well as other river valleys in peninsular India will provide much better evidence for reconstructing a clear picture of biostratigraphy and palaeoenvironmental conditions in peninsular India.

(c) Ostrich in the Indian Pleistocene

An interesting discovery in recent years has been the finding of ostrich egg-shells, plain or engraved, from the Late Pleistocene levels in India, archaeologically equivalent to the Upper Palaeolithic. With several discoveries of such shells various aspects of taxonomy, palaeoecology, distribution of the bird in the past and its importance in archaeological and palaeontological contexts became clearer.

The first discovery of ostrich egg-shells in India was made in 1860s by Archibald Carlyle from the Ken river in Banda district of Uttar Pradesh (Kumar 1988; Neumayer 1990). It was suggested that they resembled those of *Struthio molybdophanes* (the Somali Ostrich). Sali's discovery (1980) of ostrich egg-shells from an Upper Palaeolithic site of Patne in Jalgaon district of Maharashtra evoked a lot of interest followed by the discovery of about sixty sites in Rajasthan, Madhya Pradesh and Maharashtra some of which were dated Patne, Maharashtra: 25,000 BP; Chandresal, Rajasthan: 38,900 BP and 36,500 BP; Ramnagar, M.P.: 31,000 BP. Kumar et al. (1988) and Badam and Sathe (1990) have given a detailed list of egg-shell discoveries in India, the latter authors have also added details about the taxonomy, palaeogeographic distribution and probable ancestry of the ostrich about which there was a difference of opinion amongst some scholars for a long time. Sahni et al. (1990) conducted microstructural studies on an extensive collection of the ostrich egg-shells.

Lydekker (1884) was the first to describe the fossil bones of the ostrich in a geological context (*Struthio asiaticus*) from Dhok Pathan stage of the Middle Siwaliks. This, therefore, is the earliest record (Lower Pliocene) of the fossil ostrich in India. To explain the absence of the ostrich in India during the gap of 6 Ma or more is rather problematic. Whether the evolutionary history of ostrich during this gap is unrecorded, whether the ostrich disappeared from India after the Lower Pliocene and was immigrant to India during the Late Pleistocene and disappeared again during the Holocene are questions that await answers. Overkill hypothesis (Francis 1983), climatic changes at the end of the Pleistocene (Kumar et al. 1988), or spread of an epidemic (Badam and Sathe 1990) are some of the reasons forwarded for the disappearance of the ostrich in the time gap between the Lower Pliocene and Late Pleistocene and during the Holocene. In any case these discoveries have helped us appreciate better the significance of the ostrich in archaeological and geological contexts.

FAUNA AND THE SITES

Since the time when fossils were first discovered in India in the early nineteenth century numerous fossil sites have come to light bearing upon important aspects of chronology, ecology, palaeogeographic distribution, migration patterns, evolution and extinction and other areas which came to light with the application of new techniques as enumerated above. Large collection of fossils have been made in Kashmir; Siwaliks; the alluvial deposits of the Narmada, Godavari and Krishna basins; the Son, Belan, Paimar and Seoti Valleys in the Indo-Ganga region; the Mahanadi Valley (M.P. and Orissa) and Parvati Valley in M.P.; the Susunia and Tarafeni Valleys in West Bengal; and the Kurnool caves in A.P. (see Fig. 1, Table 1). In addition to these faunal complexes a few fossil localities (including solitary occurrences) have been reported from the alluvial deposits in Tamil Nadu and some areas in the north-east (Assam, Manipur, Tripura and Nagaland out of which the Tripura fauna is better known), Tapi Basin, Gujarat, etc. As much of the material is already published, to avoid repetition we will refer only to the latest discoveries and examine their role in the various aspects mentioned above. First, only new sites or those that have not received sufficient attention so far will be discussed. Though references to other river valleys like the Narmada, Godavari and Krishna will be made wherever necessary, they will not be dealt with in great detail. The readers are referred to the work of Badam (1979) for palaeontological and geological information from these and other areas.

(a) The Manjra Valley, Maharashtra

The Manjra, a major southerly tributary of the Godavari, has yielded one of the richest palaeontological treasures of peninsular India. The importance of the fossils with regard to provenance and palaeoecology has been emphasised in earlier publications (e.g. Joshi et al. 1978; Badam 1979, 1984). A reconnaissance survey of the valley carried out as part of a major UGC sponsored project in 1976-7 by a team from Deccan College, Pune, brought to light a host of palaeontological and archaeological sites in the Manjra Valley and also on the main channels of the river Godavari. A large number of fossils of *Elephas hysudricus*, *Stegodon insignis ganesa*, *Sus* sp., *Bos namadicus*, *Bubalus palaeindicus*, *Equus namadicus*, *Axis axis*, *Antilope cervicapra*, *Cervus unicolor*, *Cervus duvauceli*, *Hexaprotodon palaeindicus*, *Crocodylus* sp., and Chelonia were discovered in the low energy overbank flood deposits of the Upper Manjra at Dhanegaon (18°36' N; 76°10' E), Wangdari (18°35' N; 76°25' E), Tadula (18°35' N; 76°25' E) and Ganjur (18°35' N; 76°24' E). The sites are close to each other and it can be presumed that the varied fauna occupied a vast area as an ecological niche. Within this niche there were marked variations, to which the animals adjusted comfortably. It is of interest to note that fossils of Proboscidea

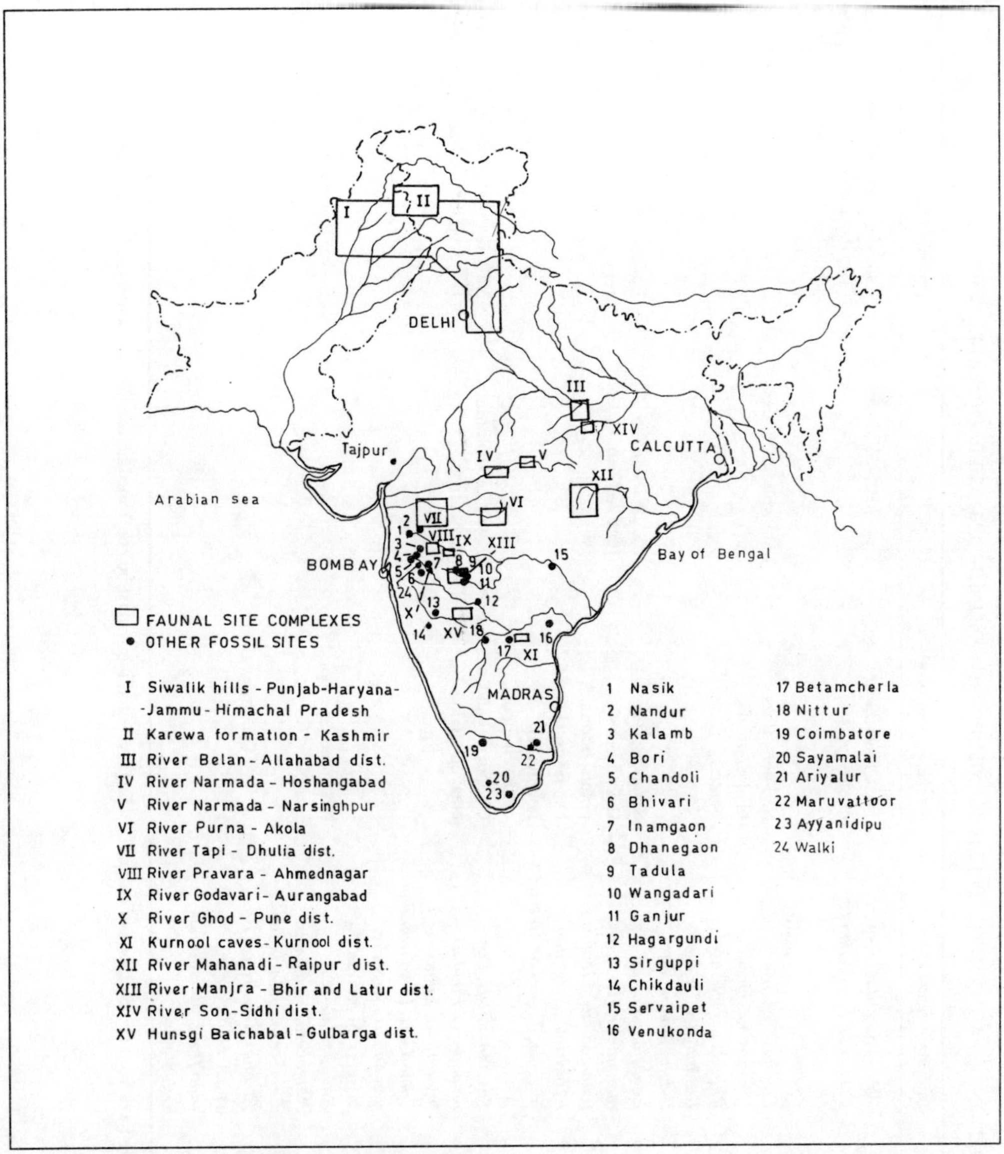

Fig. 1. Important Pleistocene Fossil Bearing Sites.

TABLE 1. DISTRIBUTION OF FAUNA IN THE PLEISTOCENE DEPOSITS OF INDIA AND THEIR PROBABLE AGES

Locality	Important fauna	Associated cultures		Probable age	Environment
Kurnool, Ghod, Manjra, Pravara, Godavari, Krishna	*Canis* sp., *Bubalus* sp., *Cervus* sp., *Bos namadicus*	Bone tools, burins, blades, points.	Upper Palaeolithic	Late Upper Pleistocene (also dated by C-14; 40,000 to 15,000 BP)	Savanna type with pockets of forests and swamps (humid in Kurnool)
	Elephas hysudricus, *Elephas maximus*, *Rhinoceros unicornis*, *Bos indicus*, *Hexaprotodon palaeindicus*.	Scrapers, flakes, blades, points, borers.	Late Middle Palaeolithic		
Central Narmada (Upper group)	*Equus namadicus*, *Bos namadicus*, *Hexaprotodon palaeindicus*, *Elephas hysudricus*, *Stegodon insignis*, *S. ganesa*, *Cervus* sp.	Scrapers, flakes, flake-blades, points, borers, handaxes, cleavers, polyhedrals, discoids, choppers.	Middle Palaeolithic (Late Acheulian)	Early Upper Pleistocene	Savanna grassland interspersed with swamps
Central Narmada (Lower group	*Sus namadicus*, *Bos namadicus*, *Elephas hysudricus*, *Equus namadicus*, *Hexaprotodon namadicus*, *Stegodon insignis*, *S. ganesa*.	Choppers, handaxes, cleavers, flakes.	Lower Palaeolithic (Acheuliean)	Middle Pleistocene (not well established)	Savanna grassland interspersed with swamps
Lower Karewa, Pinjor of Upper Siwaliks	*Equus sivalensis*, *Rhinoceros sivalensis*, *Rhinoceros palaeindicus*, *Elephas hysudricus*, *Bos* sp., *Archidiskodon planifrons*, *Sivatherium giganteum*.	No Stone Age tools*		Lower Pleistocene	Valley and open savanna grassland with lakes swamps.

NOTE: *Although there have been some reports of cultural findings recently, these must be confirmed before their presence can be accepted.

were predominantly found in abandoned ox-bow lake formations near Dhanegaon. The old channel deposits at Wangdari (about 30 km east of Dhanegaon) yielded the maximum number of ungulates out of which fossils of *Bos namadicus* account for nearly 70 per cent of the total collection. The dominance of elephants suggests a heavily vegetated environment, while cattle indicate a savanna landscape. A large number of fresh water molluscan shells, both bivalves and univalves, were also found in the gravel deposits. The total faunal occurrence substantiated by sedimentological studies attests that distribution of these animals was controlled by local ecological factors. Therefore the fauna in the valley has a profound bearing on palaeoecological conditions during the deposition of the sediments. The Manjra Valley enjoyed a good vegetation cover, probably a savanna forest with several deep water pools and generally the climate in the valley was more humid than prevails today in the region. Fossils similar to those found in the Manjra Valley have been found from the yellowish sandy bed of the upper horizon of the central Narmada Valley dated to about 31,750 BP and from parts of the Godavari and Bhima Valleys which date from 40,000 BP onwards. The similarity of faunal material with those of other areas has helped understand better the origin and early history of many vertebrate groups in India. The ^{14}C dates as based on molluscan shells from the Manjra Valley range from 27,000 to 32,000 BP which securely place the findings in late Pleistocene time bracket.

Other sites in the area include Mugaon (18°45' N; 77°27' E) where Middle Palaeolithic tools were found in association with fossils, Deglur (18°34' N; 77°35' E) where a factory site of Middle Palaeolithic tools was located and Salura (18°42' N; 77°47' E), a channel occupation site during Middle Palaeolithic times. Allanadurg, Chitgunda, Metkonda, Latur, Renapur, and Kalamb are some other sites which have yielded Middle Palaeolithic and Mesolithic tools but none in association with fossils which is generally true of many sites in the Manjra valley.

(b) Ghod Valley, Maharashtra

Ghod is a tributary of the Bhima river which is in turn a tributary of the Krishna river. Large scale excavations of a Chalcolithic site on the left bank of the Ghod by Deccan College prompted the discovery of Late Pleistocene faunal material on the opposite bank close to the village of Wangdari. Excavations of the fossil sites for five seasons resulted in the discovery of one of the richest fossil treasures in Maharashtra. Here two litho-units can be identified, about 5 m thick basal sandy pebbly gravel capped by 5-10 m thick unit of fine sands, silts and clays which is in turn overlain by about a metre thick black cotton soil of Early Holocene age.

Fossils identified are those of *Elephas maximus*, *Elephas hysudricus*, *Bos namadicus*, *Bubalus* sp., *Cervus unicolor*, *Canis* sp., *Sus palaeindicus*, *Hexaprotodon palaeindicus*, *Equus namadicus*, *Trionyx* sp., *Unio* sp., *Ceritherium* sp., etc. Some of these fossils were associated with Middle Palaeolithic cultural material and some with Upper Palaeolithic leves while a few were associated with both. It may be mentioned here that Wangdari is perhaps one of the few sites indicating clear-cut separation of Middle and Upper Palaeolithic tools even though the fauna is long ranging.

The discovery of *Hippopotamus palaeindicus* is of special significance as it increases the geographical range of the animal to the south of the Godavari before becoming extinct. This fossil was found in a gravel bed associated with molluscan shells which have been ^{14}C dated to 20,000 BP. This species and *Sus palaeindicus* (dated to 39,000 BP as based on carbonized wood), also reported for the first time in the valley, have an important bearing on the chronology of the sediments and the palaeogeographic distribution of these animals in the past.

The sedimentary formations in the Ghod Valley were deposited by a series of water pools within braid bar or point bar. The periodic flooding of the river is indicated by the occurrence in the pebble gravel of lenticular bands of silt and clay. Such pools, probably with tall grass cover, might have provided suitable habitats for water loving animals like *Hippopotamus palaeindicus*. This animal would have normally inhabited swampy plain areas where sluggish water predominated, although the contemporary presence of fossil elephants, horses, buffaloes, cattle, deer, carnivores, etc., indicates a tropical semi- arid monsoon climate with plateaux and lowlands probably covered by dense grass and stunted trees (Kajale et al. 1976). The presence of Middle and Upper Palaeolithic tools in the same geological layers as the animal bones suggests that biotic factors played an important role in attracting the Palaeolithic settlers to this location. However, the exact role of the prehistoric man in exploiting the contemporary fauna will remain enigmatic until primary/semi primary sites are discovered and excavated in the area.

It may be mentioned in passing here that excavations of the Chalcolithic mound (*c*. 3600-2700 BP) just opposite the fossil site of Wangdari, has yielded important faunal data belonging to both wild and domesticated varieties. Further, a Mesolithic site (*c*. 1200 BP) has also been discovered in the vicinity of the Chalcolithic site (Rajaguru et al. 1980) but a palaeontological record for this period is lacking at present. Otherwise some important light would have been thrown on the process of domestication in this area, if any, as some of the Pleistocene animals discovered here are directly or indirectly related to some of the domesticated animals found at the archaeological site, like cattle, elephant, deer, buffalo, etc.

(c) Tarafeni Valley, West Bengal

The Tarafeni is a west bank tributary of the Kansabati river. It originates in the hills of Bankura which form the north-western border of Midnapur district and flows through a Precambrian terrain. Covering an area of 512 sq km the Tarafeni Valley forms the south-eastern fringe of the Chhotanagpur plateau with Singhbhum district of Bihar as its western boundary.

A systematic study carried out recently in the Tarafeni Valley at Dhuliapur (22°38' N; 86°50'E), brought to light an assemblage of animal fossils dating to Late/Terminal Pleistocene in relation to geology and archaeology. Fossils identified include *Equus* sp., *Bos namadicus*, *Axis axis*, *Antilope cervicapra* and fragments of turtle carapaces, etc.

(Basak et al. 1998). Six other sections were examined and documented in the area but these yielded only microlithic sites and no faunal materials. A detailed palaeoecological study indicates that the region during part of Late Quaternary was sub-humid with savanna habitats, waterpool situations, abundant grass in the foothill region and hard ground towards the watersheet. However, the possibility of the past prevalence of minor environmental fluctuations in the region cannot be ruled out. It is emphasized that even if there were phases of semi-aridity during the Last Glacial Maximum the animals mentioned above would have survived this onslaught reasonably well provided there were sufficient grasslands and water pools present in the area.

It may be mentioned that Das Sarma et al. (1982) had discovered fossil vertebrates from Late Quaternary deposits of several river basins in parts of Bankura, Burdwan and Purulia districts of West Bengal that fall to the north and north-west of the present area. They identified *Bos namadicus*, *Antilope cervicapra*, *Axis axis*, *Sus* sp., *Gavialis* sp., *Batagur* sp., *Hystrix* sp., *Palaeoloxodon* sp., and *Crocuta* sp. (ranging from Late Pleistocene to Holocene). The present fauna of the Dhuliapur region is impoverished due to continuous expansion of cultivation, extermination of the Sal jungle and the anthropogenic factor (O' Malley 1908). However, the collection from Bankura, Burdwan and Purulia districts has also been taken into consideration while suggesting the palaeoecological history of the entire region.

(d) Son Valley, Madhya Pradesh

The Son Valley covers an area of about 14,000 sq km and has a varied Quaternary geology, subdivided into four formations (from top to bottom), the Khetaunhi Formation, Baghor Formation, Patpara Formation and Sihawal Formation. Culturally, Lower Palaeolithic to microlithic tools are found from bottom to top, in a majority of the cases associated with the faunal material (Badam et al. 1989).

A preliminary study of about a thousand fossils (out of a total collection of 6,000 fossils) housed in the Department of Ancient History, Culture and Archaeology of Allahabad University was carried out which brought to light an interesting assemblage of fossils bearing upon biochronology, distribution pattern and palaeoecology during the Quaternary period in the middle Son Valley. However, it is to be admitted that a fuller picture of the faunal wealth of the valley and its various aspects would be known only after the study of the entire collection is complete.

The fauna comprises species referable to *Bos namadicus*, *Bibos gaurus*, *Bubalus* sp., *Antilope cervicapra*, *Boselephas tragocamelus*, *Tetraceros quadricornis*, *Gazella gazella*, *Axis axis*, *Axis porcinus*, *Cervus unicolor*, *Cervus duvauceli*, *Muntiacus muntjak*, *Sus* sp., *Hippopotamus* sp., *Rhinoceros* sp., *Equus namadicus*, *Equus asinus/ hemionus*, *Elephas* sp., *Gavialis* sp., *Trionyx* sp., *Emys* sp., *Panthera* sp., some other carnivores, rodents, etc.

The most fossiliferous horizon is the Baghor Formation (Unit II) and the next in order of abundance is the junction of Patpara and the Baghor Formation (Unit I). The basal and the topmost members in the litholog (Sihawal and Khetaunhi Formations respectively) are almost devoid of fossils.

Taphonomic observations indicate that more than half of the studied fossils are unabraided and less affected by fluvial activity. Most of the fossils (especially from the Baghor Formation) may be treated as autochthonous as there are no appreciable indications of their transport for long distances from their place of death or burial. This formation comprises silts, sands, and clays and represents a channel fill deposit. The junction of the Patpara and Baghor formations may represent a channel lag deposit since it comprises pebbly, gravelly clays and sands with heavier and robust faunal elements. Evidences of bioturbation, gnawing, flaking, splitting, etc., are present in the collection and may be attributed to various taphonomic factors operating on the bones.

It is suggested that some of the fossils ranging from Late Pleistocene to Holocene (e.g. black buck, spotted deer, barking deer, nilgai, four-horned antelope, deer etc.) collected from the Son Valley and also found in the Pleistocene deposits of the Tarafeni Valley (two species), Manjra Valley (three species), and Narmada Valley (four species) are endemic varieties, multiplying in diversity and numbers during the Holocene. A riverine environment, galleria forests along the banks and flood plains of the rivers and tall grasses with sufficient pools along the channels were perhaps some of the factors responsible for the rich faunal survival in the Son Valley. Hill slopes and areas away from the rivers must have been bare or supporting a thin grass, thorn and scrub cover. Flood plain zones, channel pools (water holes) and mixed grassland-woodland environment of the flood plains were the favourable ecological niches. A similar palaeoecological condition emerges from the study of the Narmada Valley fossils many of which, however, were more severely affected by fluvial transport and abrasion than the Son Valley fossils.

(e) Mahanadi Valley, Madhya Pradesh

The Mahanadi is one of the major easterly flowing rivers of peninsular India. The river originates in the hills of Sihawa, about 100 km south of Raipur district in M.P., and traverses through geologically varied landforms before emptying into the Bay of Bengal near Cuttack in Orissa. Palaeolithic sites were discovered in the lower reaches of the river by Mohapatra (1962) and Tripathi (1972). A number of vertebrate fossils (*Bos namadicus*, *Bos* sp., *Cervus* sp., *Equus namadicus* etc.) were for the first time, discovered in the valley at Nandghat (20°01' N; 81°48' E), Sigma (21°37' N; 81°42' E), Somnath (21°34' N; 81°48' E) and Rajnandgaon (21°06' N; 81°02' E) (Pandey 1977; Badam 1979; Joshi et al. 1980). Middle Palaeolithic tools were found associated with the fossils at all the sites except at Rajnandgaon. The presence of the fossils, though scanty in terms of diversity, indicate that the valley supported abundant savannah vegetation and water to support these ungulates. During the Late Pleistocene the nearby forests must have provided a varied assemblage of wild animals. Even today wild animals like jackal, wolf, hare, nilgai, chital, antelope, deer, buffalo, bear, lion, leopard, etc., abound in the hilly and forested areas surrounding the main channel of the Mahanadi and its tributaries.

CONCLUDING REMARKS

One of the landmarks of palaeontological research of the Quaternary period during the last fifty years has been the discovery of a partial cranium of *Homo erectus* in the Narmada Valley. This discovery has filled in, to a great extent, the lacunae in our understanding of hominid evolution in South Asia as a whole. And it is the wish of every anthropologist, archaeologist, geologist, palaeontologist and all those interested in the history of human evolution that more findings of fossil hominids will be discovered in India. The discovery of micro-vertebrates from various sites (Karewas, Siwaliks, Son, Narmada and Kurnool) has its own importance in chronology and palaeoenvironment. It is expected that with concerted efforts and bed to bed dry and wet sieving more micro-vertebrates will be discovered in future and documented.

It is of importance to note that the various subdivisions of the Pleistocene period into Lower, Middle and Upper are essentially based on vertebrate palaeontology and Palaeolithic archaeology. However, there has been a mixing up of various fossils as also the Palaeolithic artefacts through time which has hampered the precise demarcation of subdivisions of geo-time scale as also the archaeo-time scale. With more discoveries of fossils and refinement of techniques, especially the dating techniques, this problem has been resolved to some extent. The Lower Pleistocene deposits in the north-west are generally characterized by the first appearance of *Equus sivalensis*, *Elephas hysudricus*, *Bos acutifrons*, *Cervus punjabiensis* and *Archidiskodon planifrons*. The placement of the Neogene-Quaternary boundary is now accepted to coincide within the time bracket of 1.8 Ma or 2.48 Ma ago—the latter date also accepted by the INQUA Commission of 1991. Lack of appropiate index fossil assemblage, the secondary context of fossils and paucity of radiometric dates (to a large extent this lacuna has also been removed in recent years) has hampered the precise dating of the Middle Pleistocene period which starts with 0.7 Ma at present. On the basis of distribution pattern of some fossils in time and space it has been suggested that *Hexaprotodon namadicus* and *Sus namadicus* be considered as index fossils for the Middle Pleistocene (Badam 1984). Late Pleistocene had a wide range of fossils like several species of deer, blackbuck, nilgai, chital, barking deer, four-horned antelope, etc. (which continue up to Holocene). *Equus namadicus*, *Bos namadicus*, *Bubalus* spp., *Hexaprotodon* spp., *Sus* spp., *Stegodon* spp., etc., range from Middle to Late Pleistocene except the two varieties of *Hexaprotodon* and *Sus* bracketed strictly in Middle Pleistocene. Keeping in view the distribution pattern of animals our concepts of what constitutes an index fossil assemblage for the Late Pleistocene are a matter of further research. However, *Hippopotamus palaeindicus* and *Sus palaeindicus* may be included in Late Pleistocene time bracket in view of the presence of four incisors in the former and the advanced jaw structure in the latter, and their presence in relatively younger sediments.

Discovery of the enormous faunal data comprising mammals, ostrich egg-shells (and also bones in earlier geological periods), reptiles, few amphibians, fish and micro-vertebrates has thrown new light on the depositional environment of the fossil-bearing sediments during the Pleistocene in India which was characterized by one of the most diverse climates—being at times warmer and more humid and at times much drier and cooler than today. In fact during the Plio-Pleistocene there was a transition from tropical humid climate to seasonal monsoonic climate. The climatic changes during the Lower and Middle Pleistocene were reflected by strong to weak fluctuating monsoons. Late Pleistocene was characterized by good monsoons around 1,20,000 BP and moderate to weak monsoons from 75,000 years onwards (see Table 2).

The wide distribution in time and space of some animals in central and southern India may be attributed to a similarity of ecological niches, climatic conditions and geographical history prevailing in these parts. The animals seem to have had a zonal distribution in these areas without any definite ecological barriers between them. Most of these forms are late survivals from the Siwaliks of north-west, having migrated to other suitable areas, e.g. the Narmada-Godavari complex, when the conditions in the north-west became unfavourable on account of Pleistocene glaciation and other factors. As a result of the glaciation the ice-sheet extended repeatedly from the north-west thereby acting as a physical and climatic barrier to the movement of animals northwards and thus forcing them to move southwards. Naturally many of the species became extinct in the course of such migrations because of non-adaptability. Some of them, however, did evolve into advanced forms in the Terminal Pleistocene/Holocene. Interestingly some of the animals like blackbuck, deer, chital, nilgai, etc., range from Late Pleistocene to the present without undergoing appreciable micromorphological changes. Animals like buffalo, cattle, elephant, pig, etc., have direct or indirect bearing on similar genera found during the Pleistocene and reflect minor morphological changes. It is, therefore, suggested that faunal wealth during the later part of Quaternary indicates endemic species having evolved and diversified within the subcontinent.

However, this varied assemblage of animals was not totally indigenous to the subcontinent. Mammals which were shared with the contemporary fauna of Europe were the sabre-toothed cats, the hyaena, wolves, rhinoceros, some horses, some deer, antelope and hippopotamus. The migratory routes lay east and west of the Himalayas (Pilgrim 1925). Most of the larger mammals migrated from Egypt, Arabia, Central Asia and North America through routes across Alaska, Siberia and Mongolia. Hippopotamus and elephants, which had their early origin in Central Africa, migrated outward and entered India during the Tertiary period through Arabia and Iran. Rhinoceros, horse and camel, all originating in North America, evolved in some countries of Central and Western Asia before migrating to India. The elephant and horse populated to almost every country of the world except Australia. The interchange of faunas between India and Africa probably took place more easily. Sufficient evidence indicates the existence of a land bridge at the entrance of the Persian Gulf. Probably a corresponding bridge across the Red Sea provided a ready means of communication between India and Africa through Arabia. Important causes of migration include population pressure, evolutionary pressure and climatic fluctuations throughout the Tertiary (Russell 1962) and of course the glaciation which was a global phenomena. These could also account for the sudden and widespead reduction of vertebrates in India especially in the north-west whereas anthropogenic factors may

TABLE 2. QUATERNARY BIO-CULTURAL AND CHRONO-STRATIGRAPHY IN INDIA

Geo Time Scale	Archeo Time Scale	Approx Age (BP)	Significant Cultural Traits	Fauna	Dominant Climate
Late Holocene	Historical (Iron Age)	3000 BP onwards	Writing, Iron technology, and Advanced agriculture known	Modern animals	Good monsoons prior to AD 1000, Bad monsoons between 14th and 17th *c.* AD
Mid Holocene	Chalcolithic/Neolithic	4500-3000 BP	Use of copper and stone, Beginning of agriculture, Advanced town planning, Knowledge of writing, Polished tool technology	Domesticated and wild animals	Weak Monsoons Around 3000 BP
Early Holocene	Mesolithic	10-12,000 to 4,000 BP	Composite tool technology, Pastoralism and fishing dominant	Beginning of domestication of animals	Very good monsoons (8000-4000 BP), Winter rains strong
Terminal Pleistocene	Upper Palaeolithic	40,000 to 10-12,000 BP	Palaeolithic art and blade tool technology, Hunting and food gathering	Equus Hemionus, Bos Namadicus, Rhinoceros sp., Bubalus sp., Elephas Maximus, Cervus sp., etc.	Poor monsoons
Late Pleistocene	Middle Palaeolithic	130,000 to 40,000 BP	Hunting and food gathering, use of fine grained chalcedony, chert etc. for making scrapers and flake tools, use of quartzite and basalt continues.	Same as Above+Equus Namadicus, Bos Namadicus, Hexaprotodon sp., Elephas Hysudricus, Sus sp., etc.	Good monsoons around 120,000 BP, moderate to weak monsoons from 75,000 yrs onwards
Middle Pleistocene	Lower Palaeolithic (Early to Late Acheulian)	7,00,000-1,30,000 BP	Hunting and food gathering, use of quartzite, basal for making handaxes, Scrapers, cleavers, scrapers, cleavers, flakes, choppers etc	Same as above+Hexaprotodon Namadicus, sus Namadicus, etc.	Fluctuating monsoons, Strong to weak
Lower Pleistocene	Suspected Lower Palaeolithic in Pakistan (Peshawar) and India (Maharashtra)	2.0 My-0.7 My Peshawar: 2 My Bori: 6,70,000 yrs	Hunting and food gathering, use of Basalt for making flakes and choppers	Equus Sivalensis, Bos Acutifrons, Rhinoceros sivalensis, Hexaprotodon Sivalensis, Stegodon Insignis Ganesa, Archidiskodon Planifrons, etc.	Fluctuating monsoons, Strong to weak
Plio-Pleistocene		2.47 My-1.87 My		First Appearance of Equus and Extinction of Hipparion	Transition from tropical humid climate to seasonal monsoonic climate
Pliocene		5 My-2.5 My		Hipparion Predominant	Tropical humid climate
Miocene		20 My-5 My			

NOTES: ^{14}C Dates upto 40,000 BP; UR-th Dates upto 4,00,000 BP; K/AR Dates for period 1 My and Beyond.

REFERENCE: Table Compiled by G.L. Badam and S.N. Rajaguru, Deccan College Postgraduate and Research Institute, Deemed to be University, Pune 411006, India.

A. Classical
1. Systematics: Classification of Fossil organisms (Biological & Genetic)
2. Descriptive (Diagnostic & Morphological) : Reporting of factual data, mostly biological
3. Stratigraphic: Some imagination and interpretation (Biological & Geological)

B. Scientific
4. Evolutionary : Ancestor-descendant relationship
5. Ecological : Relations of fossil organisms to their environment
6. Biogeography : Distribution and contraction of population ranges

C. New
7. Dating Methods
8. Taphonomy
9. Paleohistology
10. Paleopathology
11. Population dynamics
12. Microvertebrates
13. Molecular Studies
14. Isotope Analysis
15. New Discoveries: Sites and Fauna

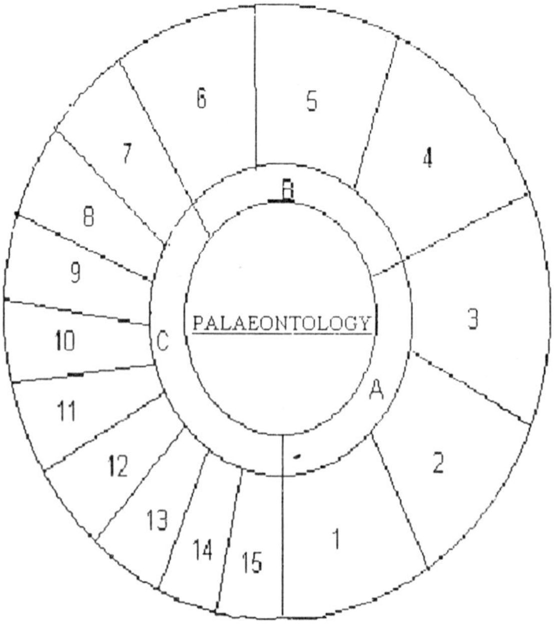

Applications of Palaeontology
a. Geological Sciences : Geology, Geography, Sedimentology, Geomorphology
b. Biological Sciences : Botany, Zoology, Anthropology, Ecology, Limnology, Genetics
c. Historical Sciences : History, Archaeology
d. Physical Sciences : Absolute Dating
e. Chemical Sciences : Relative Dating, Chemical Analysis
f. Quantitative Studies : Computer, Biometry
g. Molecular Studies : Ancient DNA
h. Paleodiet : Isotope Studies
i. Other Areas : Paleohistology, Population Studies, Paleopathology, etc.

Fig. 2. Development of Palaeontology.

have had some role in reduction of animals in the central and peninsular parts of India.

To conclude, Quaternary faunal researches offer a challenging field of investigation to natural and earth scientists. As indicated above several new techniques have been applied to these studies which have become truly multidisciplinary in nature (see Fig. 2). Therefore concerted efforts by archaeologists, anthropologists, geologists, palaeontologists, and other scientists (botanists, biochemists, chemists, etc.) are recommended for applied researches in palaeontology to unravel the mystries of the immediate past with which man is directly concerned.

ACKNOWLEDGEMENTS

I am obliged to Professor S. Settar, Chairman of the Indian Council of Historical Research (New Delhi) for inviting me to write this review article. Thanks are due to Mr. Sandeep Bhonde (Deccan College, Pune) for his help in documentation of the paper and to Mr. Balram Tripathy, and Ms. Arunima Kashyap (Deccan College, Pune) and Ms. Priya Badam for their assistance in compiling the bibliography.

REFERENCES

Azzaroli, A. and G. Napoleone 1982. A Magnetostratigraphic Investigation of the Upper Siwaliks Near Pinjor, India, *Rivista Italiana di Palaeontologia* 87 (4): 739-62.

Badam, G.L. 1973. Geology and Palaeontology of the Upper Siwaliks of a Part of Pinjor-Nalagarh Area. Ph.D. Dissertation. Chandigarh: Panjab University.

——— 1979. *Pleistocene Fauna of India*. Pune: Deccan College.

——— 1984. Pleistocene Faunal Succession of India, in *The Evolution of East Asian Environment* (R.O. Whyte Ed.), pp. 746-75. Hong Kong: University of Hong Kong.

——— 1989. Observations on the Fossil Hominid site at Hathnora, Madhya Pradesh, India. in *Perspectives in Human Evolution* (Ashok Sahni and Rajan Gaur Eds.), pp. 153-71. Delhi: Renaissance Publishing House.

——— 1990a. Taphonomic Implications as Reflected in Large Vertebrates from Quaternary Sites in Western India, Paper Presented at the 6th International Conference of the International Council for Archaeozoology, Smithsonian Institution, Washington D.C. (Abstract).

——— 1990b. Taphonomic Studies of Quaternary Mammalian Fossils in Central and Western India, Paper Presented at the 14th Congress of the Indo-Pacific Prehistory Association, Yogyakarta, Indonesia (Abstract).

——— 1994. Taphonomic Studies of Quaternary Mammalian Fossils and Modern Caracasses from Central, Southern and Western India, *Man and Environment* XIX (1-2): 235-45.

——— 1996. Taphonomy as a Tool in Interpreting Fossils and Their Modes of Occurrence, in *Spectrum of Indian Culture : Professor S.B. Deo Felicitation Volume* (C. Margabandhu and K.S. Ramachandran Eds.), pp. 13-25. Delhi: Agam Kala.

Badam, G.L. and C. Grigson 1990. A Cranium of Gaur, *Bibos gaurus* (Bovidae, Mammalia) from the Pleistocene of India, *Modern Geology* 15: 49-58.

Badam, G.L. and S.L. Jain 1988. First Record of *Bos namadicus* from Middle-Late Pleistocene Deposits of Lower Godavari, Near Servaipet in Karimnagar District, Andhra Pradesh, *Journal of the Palaeontological Society of India* 33: 97-104.

Badam, G.L. and S.N. Rajaguru 1991. Problems of Neogene Litho- and Biostratigraphy of the Siwaliks in Northwest India, *Birbal Sahni Birth Centenary Symposium on Siwalik Basin*, pp. 7-9. Dehra Dun: Wadia Institute of Himalayan Geology.

Badam, G.L. and Vijay Sathe 1990. Geological and Biological Implications of Ostrich in India with Reference to its Importance in Archaeological Context, in *Adaptation and Other Essays* (N.C. Ghosh and S. Chakrabarti Eds.), pp. 75-87. Santiniketan: Visva-Bharati Research Publications.

——— 1995. Palaeontological Research in India: Retrospect and Prospect, in *Quaternary Environments and Geoarchaeology of India* (S. Wadia, R. Korisettar and V.S. Kale Eds.), pp. 473-95. Bangalore: Geological Society of India.

Badam, G.L., R.K. Ganjoo and Salahuddin 1986. Preliminary Taphonomical Studies of Some Pleistocene Fauna from the Central Narmada Valley, Madhya Pradesh, India, *Palaeogeography, Palaeoclimatology and Palaeoecology* 53: 335-48.

Badam, G.L., V.D. Misra, J.N. Pal and J.N. Pande 1989. A Preliminary Study of Pleistocene Fossils from the Middle Son Valley, Madhya Pradesh, *Man and Environment* XIII: 41-7.

Baker, W.E. and H.M. Durand 1836. Fossil Remains of the Smaller Carnivora from the Sub-Himalayas, *Journal of the Asiatic Society of Bengal* 5: 579-84.

Basak, B., G.L. Badam, Anupama Kshirsagar and S.N. Rajaguru 1998. Late Quaternary Environment, Palaeontology and Culture of Tarafeni Valley, Midnapur District, West Bengal—a Preliminary Study, *Journal of the Geological Society of India* 51: 731-40.

Behrensmeyer, A.K. 1990. *Experimental Taphonomy Workshop*. Smithsonian Institution, Washington, D.C.: Internatioanl Council for Archaeozoology.

Behrensmeyer, A.K. and S.M. Kidwell 1985. Taphonomy's Contribution to Palaeobiology, *Palaeobiology* 11: 105-19.

Boyde, A. 1964. The Structure and Development of Mammalian Enamel. Ph.D. Dissertation. London: University of London.

Brown, T.A. and K.A. Brown 1992. Ancient DNA and the Archaeologist, *Antiquity* 66: 10-23.

Buckland, W. 1824. '*Reliquae Diluvianae*': Observations on the Organic Remains Contained in Caves, Fissures and Diluvial Gravel, and on Other Geological Phenomena, Attesting the Action of an Universal Deluge. London.

Chakravarty, D.K. 1937. A New Stage in the Evolution of Stegodons: *Stegodon elephantoides (Clift)*, *Quarterly Journal of the Geological, Mineralogical and Metallurgical Society of India* 9 (2): 33-7.

——— 1957. A Geological, Palaeontological and Phylogenetic Study of the Elephantoidea of India, Pakistan and Burma, Part 1, Gomphotheriidae, *Journal of the Palaeontological Society of India* 2: 83-94.

Chopra, S.R.K. and S. Kaul 1975. New Fossil *Dryopithecus* Material from the Nagri Beds at Haritalyangar (H.P.), India, in *Contemporary Primatology* (S. Kondo et al. Eds.), pp. 2-11: New York: Karger.

Clift, W. 1828. On the Fossil Remains of Two New Species of Mastodon, and of Other Vertebrated Animals Found on the Left Bank of the Irawadi, *Transactions of the Geological Society of London* (Second Series) 2 (3): 369-76.

Colbert, E.H. 1935. Swalik Mammals in the American Museum of Natural History, *Transactions of the American Philosophical Society* (New Series) 26: 1-401.

Das Sarma, D.C., S. Biswas and A. Nandi 1982. Fossil Vertebrates from the Late Quaternary

Deposits of Bankura, Burdwan and Purulia Districts, West Bengal, *Palaeontologia Indica* 44: 1-65.

de Chardin, P.T. 1952. The Idea of Fossil Man, *Anthropology Today* (prepared under the Chairmanship of A.L. Kroeber). Chicago, Illinois.

Deraniyagala, P.E.P. 1956. Some Extinct Hippopotami and Elephants from India and Ceylon, *Journal of the Palaeontological Society of India* 1: 176-8.

——— 1957. Atavistic Characters of Palaeontological Interest in *Elephas maximus* Linn., *Journal of the Palaeontological Society of India.* 2: 190-2.

DeSalle, R.J. Gatesy, W. Wheeler and D. Grimaldi 1992. DNA Sequences from a Fossil Termite in Oligo-Miocene Amber and Their Phylogenetic Implications, *Science* 257: 1933-6.

Dover, G.A. 1991. Contribution to Discussion of Paper by Golenberg (1991), *Philosophical Transactions of the Royal Society of London* (Series B) 333: 427.

Efremov, J.A. 1940. Taphonomy: a New Branch of Palaeontology, *Pan-American Geologist* 74: 81-93.

Falconer, H. 1868. *Palaeontological Memoirs* (Edited by Murchison) 1: 1-556.

Falconer, H. and P.T. Cautley 1836. *Asiatic Researches* 19: 12-200.

——— 1836-49. *Fauna Antiqua Sivalensis*, pp. 1-9. London: Smith Elder & Co.

Foote, R.B. 1876. The Geological Features of the South Mahratta Country and Adjacent Districts, *Memoirs of the Geological Survey of India* 12 (1): 1-265.

Francis, P. 1983. The Ostrich, Ostrich Eggs, and Ostrich Egg-shell Beads, *Man and Environment* VII: 142-6.

Gaur, R. and S.R.K. Chopra 1984. Taphonomy, Fauna, Environment and Ecology of Upper Siwaliks (Plio-Pleistocene) Near Chandigarh, India, *Nature* 308 (5957): 353-5.

Gifford, D.P. 1981. Taphonomy and Palaeoecology: a Critical Review of Archaeology's Sister Disciplines, in *Advances in Archaeological Method and Theory* 4 (M.B. Schiffer Ed.) pp. 365-438. New York: Academic Press.

Gilbert, A.S. 1979. Urban Taphonomy of Mammalian Remains from the Bronze Age of Godin Tepe, Western Iran. Ph.D. Dissertation. Ann Arbor: Columbia University.

Gogte, V.D. and M.L.K. Murty 1986. ESR Dating of Kurnool Caves, South India, *Man and Environment* X: 135-40.

Golenburg, E.M. 1991. Amplification and Analysis of Miocene Plant Fossil DNA, *Philosophical Transactions of the Royal Society of London* (Series B) 333: 419-27.

Gregory, W.K., M. Hellman and G.E. Lewis 1938. *Fossil Anthropoids of the Yale-Cambridge India Expedition of 1935.* Washington: Carnegie Institute.

Grine, F.E., G. Fosse, D.W. Krause and W.L. Jungers 1986. Analysis of Enamel Ultrastructure in Archaeology: the Identification of *Ovis aries* and *Capra hircus* Dental Remains, *Journal of Archaeological Science* 13 (6): 579-95.

Hooijer, D.A. 1949. Observation on a Culvarium of *Equus sivalensis* Falc. et Caut., from the Siwalik of the Punjab, with Craniometrical Notes on Recent Equidae, *Archives Neerlandaises de Zoologie*, 8 (3): 243-67.

——— 1955. *Archidiskodon planifrons* (Falc.et Caut.) from the Tatrot Zone of the Upper Siwaliks, *Leidse Geologische Mededelingen* 20: 110-19.

Hopwood, A.T. 1935. Fossil Elephants and Man, *Proceedings of the Geological Association of London* 46: 46-60.

INQUA Symposium. Proceedings of the International Union for Quaternary Research. 13th Congress, Beijing, 2-9 August 1991.

Johnson, G.D., N.D. Opdyke, S.K. Tandon and A.C. Nanda 1983. The Magnetic Polarity Stratigraphy of the Siwalik Group at Haritalyangar (India) and New Last Appearence Datum for *Ramapithecus* and *Sivapithecus* in India, *Palaeogeography* and *Palaeoclimatology, Palaeoecology* 44: 223-49.

Joshi, R.V. and A.A. Kshirsagar 1986. *Chemical Studies of Archaeological Bones from India: Fluorine and Fossilisation Process*. Pune: Deccan College.

Joshi, R.V., G.L. Badam and R.P. Pandey 1980. Late Pleistocene Animal Fossils and Stone Age Cultures in the Upper Mahanadi Valley, M.P., *The Eastern Anthropologist* 33 (2): 169-75.

Joshi, R.V., G.G. Mujumdar, S.N. Rajaguru, R.S. Pappu and G.L. Badam 1978. Late Pleistocene History of the Upper Godavari Valley, India, *Recent Researches in Geology* 4: 381-7.

Kajale, M.D., G.L. Badam and S.N. Rajaguru 1976. Late Quaternary History of the Ghod Valley, Maharashtra, *Geophytology* 6 (1): 122-32.

Keller, H.M., R.A.K. Tahirkheli, M.A. Mirza, G.D. Johnson, N.M. Johnson and N.D. Opdyke 1977. Magnetic Polarity Stratigraphy of the Upper Siwalik Deposits, Pabbi Hills, Pakistan, *Earth and Planetary Science Letters* 36: 187-201.

Kennedy, K.A.R., J. Chiment, T. Disotell and D. Meyers 1991. Principal-Components Analysis of Prehistoric South Asian Crania, *American Journal of Physical Anthropology* 64: 105-18.

Khan, E. 1962. The Palaeontology and Stratigraphy of the Upper Siwaliks Around Chandigarh. Ph.D. Dissertation. Chandigarh: Panjab University.

Khatri, A.P. 1961. Stone Age and Pleistocene Chronology of the Narmada Valley, *Anthropos* 56: 519-30.

Kotlia, B.S. 1991. Pliocene Soricidae (Insectivora, Mammalia) from Kashmir Intermontane Basin, Northwestern India, *Journal of the Geological Society of India* 38 (3): 253-75.

Kozawa, Y. 1978. Comparative Histology of Proboscidean Molar Enamel, *Journal of the Stomatological Society of Japan* 45: 69-89 (in Japanese).

Kshirsagar, Anupama 1993. The Role of Fluorine in the Chronometric Dating of Indian Stone Age Cultures, *Man and Environment* XVII (2): 23-32.

Kshirsagar, Anupama and G.L. Badam 1990. Biochronology and Fluorine Analysis of Some Pleistocene Fossils from Central and Western India, *Bulletin of the Deccan College Post-Graduate and Research Institute* 49: 199-211.

Kshirsagar, Anupama and K. Paddayya 1988-9. Relative Chronology of Stone Age Cultures of Hunsgi-Baichbal Valley, North Karnataka by Fluorine Analysis, *Bulletin of the Deccan College Post-Graduate and Research Institute* 47-8: 143-6.

Kumar, G. 1988. Ostrich in India and its Relation to Prehistoric Man, in *Culture of the Past* (K.L. Bhowmik Ed.) 101-31. New Delhi: Inter-India Publication.

Kumar, G., Geeta Narware and R. Pancholi 1988. Engraved Ostrich Egg-Shell Object: New Evidences of Upper Palaeolithic Art in India, *Rock Art Research* 5 (1): 43-53.

Kumar, K. 1983. Palaeontological and Palaeohistological Investigation of Subathu Vertebrates of Jammu and Kashmir and Himachal Pradesh. Ph.D. Dissertation. Chandigarh: Panjab University.

Kurten, B. 1954. Population Dynamics—a New Method in Palaeontology, *Journal of Palaeontology* 28 (3): 286-92.

——— 1959. Rates of Evolution in Fossil Mammals, *Cold Spring Harbor Symposia on Quantitative Biology* 24: 205-15.

Lewis, G.E. 1934. Preliminary Notice of New Man-like Apes from India, *American Journal of Science* 27: 161-79.

Lydekker, R. 1881. Siwalik Rhinocerotidae, *Palaeontologia Indica* (Series 10), 2 (1): 1-62.

——— 1882. Siwalik and Narmada Equidae, *Palaeontologia Indica* (Series 10) 2 (3): 67-98.

——— 1884. Siwalik Birds, *Memoirs of the Geological Survey of India* 10 (3): 136-202.

——— 1886. The Fauna of the Kurnool Caves, *Palaeontologia Indica* (Series 10) 4 (2): 23-58.

Matthew, W.D. 1929. Critical Observations upon Siwalik Mammals, *Bulletin of the American Museum of Natural History* 56: 437-560.

Medlicott, H.B. 1873. Sketch of the Geology of the Northwest Provinces, *Records of the Geological Survey of India* 6 (1): 917.

Mohapatra, G.C. 1962. *The Stone Age Cultures of Orissa*. Pune: Deccan College.

Mook, C.C. 1932. A New Species of Fossil Gavial from the Siwalik Beds, *American Museum Novitates* 514: 1-5.

——— 1933. A Skull with Jaws of *Crocodylus Sivalensis* Lydekker, *American Museum Novitates* 670 : 1-10.

Murty M.L.K. and K.S.V. Nambi 1983. An Upper Palaeolithic Fire Place in Kurnool Caves, South India, *Bulletin of the Deccan College Research Institute* 42: 110-16.

Nanda, A.C. 1973a. A Note on the Biostratigraphy of Upper Siwalik of Naraingarh Tehsil, Ambala, *Current Science* 42 (9): 319.

——— 1973b. Contributions to the Stratigraphy and Palaeontology of the Upper Siwaliks of a Part of Naraingarh Tehsil, Ambala (India). Ph.D. Dissertation. Chandigarh: Panjab University.

Nautiyal, V., Y.S. Farswan, A.K. Uniyal 1995. Stable Carbon Isotope Analysis of Archaeological Bones from Garhwal Himalaya, *Science and Culture* 61 (7-9): 139-40.

Neumayer, E. 1990. A Note on Ostriches in India, *Man and Environment* XV (1): 25-8.

O'Malley, L.S.S. 1908. *Bengal District Gazetteers—Bankura*. Calcutta.

Opdyke, N.D., E. Lindsay , G.D. Johnson, N. Johnson, R.A.K. Tahirkheli and M.A. Mirza 1979. Magnetic Polarity Stratigraphy and Vertebrate Palaeontology of the Upper Siwalik Subgroup of Northern Pakistan, *Palaeogeography, Palaeoclimatology and Palaeoecology* 27: 1-34.

Osborn, H.F. 1935 and 1942. Proboscidea, 1 and 2, *American Museum of Natural History*: 1-804 and 805-1676.

Paabo, S. 1985. Preservation of DNA in Ancient Egyptian Mummies, *Journal of Archaeological Science* 12: 411-17.

——— 1993. Ancient DNA, *Scientific American* (November) 86: 92.

Paabo, S., J.A. Gifford and A.C. Wilson 1988. Mitochondrial DNA Sequences from a 7000 Year Old Brain, *Nucleic Acids Research* 16: 9755-87.

Pandey, R.P. 1977. Some New Stone Age Sites in the Upper Mahanadi Valley, Madhya Pradesh, *Current Science* 46 (19): 686.

Patnaik, Rajeev, G.L.Badam and Vijay Sathe 1995. Discovery of Microvertebrates from the Pleistocene Deposits of the Central Narmada Valley, India, *Current Science* 68 (8): 828-30.

Pentland, J.B. 1828. Description of Fossil Remains of Some Animals from the Northeast Border of Bengal, *Transaction of the Geological Society of London* (Second Series) 2: 394-5.

Pilgrim, G. E. 1915. New Siwalik Primates and Their Bearing on the Question of the Evolution of Man and the Anthropoidea, *Records of the Geological Survey of India* 45 (1): 1-74.

——— 1925. The Migration of Indian Mammals. Presidential Address, Section of Geology, 12th Indian Science Congress.

——— 1926. The Fossil Suidae of India, *Palaeontologia Indica* (New Series) 8 (4): 1-65.

——— 1932 .The Fossil Carnivora of India, *Palaeontologia Indica* (New Series) 18: 1-232.

——— 1939. The Fossil Bovidae of India, *Palaeontologia Indica* (New Series), 26 (1): 1-356.

——— 1944. The lower limit of the Pleistocene in Europe and Asia, *Geological Magazine* 81: 28-38.

Poole, D.F. G. 1956. The Structure of the Teeth of Some Mammallike Reptiles, *Quarterly Journal of Microscopic Science* 97: 303-12.

Prakash, B. 1986. Contribution to the Biostratigraphy of Karewa Group (J & K) with Special Reference to Microvertebrates and Associated Microfossils. Ph.D. Dissertation. Chandigarh: Panjab University.

Prasad, K.N. 1962. Fossil Primates from the Siwalik Beds of Haritalyanagar, Himachal Pradesh, India, *Journal of the Geological Society of India* 3: 86-96.

——— 1970. The Vertebrate Fauna from the Siwalik Beds of Haritalyanagar, Himachal Pradesh, India, *Palaeontologia Indica* (New Series) 39: 1-55.

——— 1974. The Vertebrate Fauna from Perim Island, Gujarat, India, *Palaeontologia Indica* (New Series) 41: 9-10.

Prasad, K.N. and P.P. Satsangi 1966. Note on a Fossil Hoof of a Bovid from Haritalyanagar, Himachal Pradesh, *Records of the Geological Survey of India* 94 (2): 317-18.

Rajaguru, S.N., R.S. Pappu, A.R. Marathe and B.C. Deotare 1980. The Terminal Pleistocene Microlithic Industry of Inamgaon, Maharashtra, *Bulletin of the Deccan College Research Institute* 39: 150-9.

Russell, L.S. 1962. Mammalian Migrations in the Pleistocene, *Problems of the Pleistocene Epoch and the Artic Area* 2 (2): 48-55.

Sahni, A. 1979. An Eocene Mammal from the Subathu-Dagshai Transition Zone, Dharampur, Shimla Hills, *Bulletin of the Indian Geologists Association* 12 (2): 259-62.

——— 1984. The Evolution of Mammalian Enamels: Evidence from Multituberculata (Allotheria, Extinct): Primitive Whales (Archaeocete, Cetacea) and Early Rodents in *Tooth Enamel* IV (R.W. Fearnhead and S. Suga Eds.), 457-61. Amesterdam: Elsevier Science Publication.

——— 1985. Enamel Structure of Early Mammals and its Role in Evaluating Relationships Among Rodents, in *Evolutionary Relationships Among Rodents: A Multidisciplinary Analysis* (W.P. Luckett and J.L. Hartenberger Eds.), 133-50. London: Plenum Press.

——— 1989. Application of Electron Microscopy to Problems of Palaeontology and Biomineralisation, in Micropalaeontology of the Shelf Sequences of India, in *Proceedings of 12th Indian Colloquim on Micropalaeontology and Stratigraphy* (P. Kalia Ed.), pp. 1-11, New Delhi : Papyrus Publishing House.

Sahni, A. and B.S. Kotlia 1985. Karewa Microvertebrates: Biostratigraphical annd Palaeoecological Implications, in *Current Trends in Geology Vol. 6 (Climate and Geology of Kashmir)* (D.P. Agarwal, Sheela Kusumgar amd R.V. Krishnamurty Eds.), pp. 29-43. New Delhi: Today & Tomorrow's Printers and Publishers.

Sahni, A. and S.K. Khare 1976. Swalik Insectivora, *Journal of the Geological Society of India* 17: 114-16.

Sahni, A., G. Kumar, Sunil Bajpai and S. Srinivasan 1990. A Review of Late Pleistocene Ostriches (Struthio sp.) in India, *Man and Environment* XV (1): 41-7.

Sahni, M.R. 1954. A Century of Palaeontology, Palaeobotany and Prehistory in India and Adjacent Countries, *Journal of the Palaeontological Society of India* 1: 7-51.

Sahni, M.R. and C. Tripathi 1957. A New Classification of the Indian Deinotheres, *Palaeontologia Indica* (New Series), 33 (4): 133.

Sahni, M.R. and E. Khan 1961. Recent Finds of Siwalik Vertebrates (1-5), *Research Bulletin, Panjab University* (New Series) 12 (3-4): 253-68.

Sahni, M.R. and E. Khan 1964. Stratigraphy, Structure and Correlation of the Upper Siwaliks East of Chandigarh, *Journal of the Palaeontological Society of India* 4: 61-74.

Sali, S.A. 1980. Stone Age Cultures at Patne District Jalgaon, Maharashtra. Ph.D. Dissertation. Pune: University of Poona.

Sankhyan, A.R. 1997. A New Human Fossil Find from the Central Narmada Basin and its Chronology, *Current Science* 73 (12): 25

Saxena, M.N. 1968. A Note on the Validity of the Upper Siwalik Vertebrate Fossils for Stratigraphic Correlation, *The Eastern Anthropologist* 21 (3): 319-21.

Simons, E.L. and S.R.K.Chopra 1969. *Gigantopithecus* (Pongidae, Hominoidea): New species from North India, *Postilla* 138: 1-18.

Singh, M.P., A. Sahni, S. Kaul and S.K. Sharma 1988. Further Evidence of Hominid Remains from the Pinjor Formation, India, *Proceedings Indian National Science Academy* 54 A (4): 564-73.

Sonakia, A. 1984. The Skull Cap of Early Man and Associated Mammalian Fauna from Narmada Valley Alluvium, Hoshangabad Area, M.P. (India), *Records of the Geological Survey of India* 113: 159-72.

Splisbury, G.G. 1833. An Account of the Fossil Bones Discovered in the Bed of the Omar Nadi Near Narsinghpur or Garawarda in the Valley of the Narmada, *Journal of the Asiatic Society of Bengal* 2: 381-95.

Srivastava, R. 1997. Biomechanical Analysis and Load Response in Fossil and Recent Rodent Dentition. Report Submittted to the Department of Science and Technology. New Delhi.

Stiner, M.C., Hema Achyuthan, Guven Arsebuk, F. Clark Howell, Steven C. Josephson, Kenneth, E. Juell, Jeffrey Pigati and Jay Quade 1998. Reconstructing Cave Bear Palaeoecology from Skeletons: a Cross-Disciplinary Study of Middle Pleistocene Bears from Yarimburgar Cave, Turkey, *Palaeobiology* 24 (1): 74-98.

Sukumar, R, S.K. Bhattacharya and R.V. Krishnamurthy 1987. Carbon Isotopic Evidence for Different Feeding Patterns in an Asian Elephant Population *Current Science* 56 (1): 11-14.

Szabo, B.J., Curtis Mckiney, Timothy S. Dalbey and K. Paddayya 1990. On the Age of the Acheulian Culture of the Hunsgi- Baichbal Valleys, Peninusular India, *Bulletin of the Deccan College Post-Graduate and Research Institute* 50: 317-21.

Tandon, S.K., R. Kumar , M. Koyama and N. Nitruma 1984. Magnetic Polarity Stratigraphy of the Upper Siwalik Subgroup, East of Chandigarh, Punjab Sub-Himalaya, India, *Journal of the Geological Society of India* 25 (1): 45-55.

Theobald, W. 1881. The Siwalik Group of the Sub-Himalayan Region, *Records of the Geological Survey of India* 14 (1): 66-125.

Thomas, K.D. 1993. Molecular Biology and Archaeology: A Prospectus for Inter-Disciplinary Research, *World Archaeology* 25 (1): 17.

Tiwari, B.N. 1983. Geology and Vertebrate Palaeontology of the Siwalik Group of Kalagarh-Koti Rao Section, District Pauri, Garhwal, U.P. with Special Reference to Palaeo-histological Studies. Ph.D. Dissertation, Chandigarh: Panjab University.

Tomes, J. 1850. On the Structure of Dental Tissues of the Order Rodentia, Philosophical *Transactions of the Royal Society of London* 140: 529-67.

Tripathy, K.C. 1972. Lithic Industries of Southwestern Orissa. Ph.D. Dissertation Bhubneswar: Utkal University.

Verma, B.C. 1969. *Procynocephalus pinjorii* sp. nov. a New Fossil Primate from Pinjor Beds (Lower Pleistocene), East of Chandigarh, *Journal of the Palaeontological Society of India* 13: 53-7.

Fifty Years of Archaeobotanical Studies in India: Laying a Solid Foundation

DORIAN Q. FULLER

INTRODUCTION

Archaeobotany is a composite discipline, combining botanical knowledge with archaeological materials. The archaeobotanist interprets evidence for human-environment interactions, especially as they pertain to food plants and agricultural activities. Archaeobotany is a young and fast-growing field. As a distinct and systematic enterprise it is younger than Independent India, but its roots penetrate the colonial substrate through its parental disciplines of archaeology and botany. It is my purpose in this chapter, both to trace the growth of this field within India and to highlight current trends and prospects. The archaeobotanical dataset is increasingly rich and recent interpretations of it promise to broaden our understanding of the human past.

After defining archaeobotany in terms of six data types, I briefly sketch the historical development of the discipline. It is possible to trace the growth of archaeobotany through both the quantity and quality of work. Progress through the accumulation of data is clear. This quantitative growth, however, should be understood through a series of qualitative phases (Section 2.1-2.3) in which the methods and interpretative paradigms of archaeobotany were transformed. Archaeobotany began as essentially a descriptive art, performed by a few respected and knowledgeable savants. It has become increasingly quantitative and self-critical, moving it towards a more professionalized and scientific discipline with constructive dialogue and an improved awareness of the limitations and potentials of its unique dataset. Aspects of archaeobotanical analysis which have recently been raised in South Asian publications, namely the application of crop-processing studies, quantification and the reconstruction of agricultural systems, are taken up in Sections 3.1-3.3. One area which still requires more explicit publication, in order to make archaeobotanical analyses replicable, is explicit concern with identification criteria and informative illustration (Section 4). A synthesis of the current evidence as it relates to the origins and spread of crops is provided in Section 5. Approaches to archaeobotany beyond the usual concern with seeds are sketched in Section 6, followed by some comments on theoretical issues (Section 7).

1. A DEFINITION OF ARCHAEOBOTANY AND ITS DATASETS

Archaeobotany is the study of plant remains recovered from or associated with archaeological sites. The study of these botanical remains has often been called palaeobotany (e.g. Sankalia 1975). While this is accurate in a broad sense, archaeobotany is a preferable term, since it distinguishes itself by a focus on plant remains associated with the human past and with archaeological questions, i.e. those of an essentially cultural (including economic) nature. Palaeobotany is more often used to refer to the study of geological fossils for understanding the long term processes of plant evolution (e.g. Stewart and Rothwell 1993). Some workers have come to prefer the term palaeoethnobotany, since it adds the emphasis to the ethnological/human science aspects of the work (e.g. Weber 1991; Lone et al. 1993, in European and American contexts see J. Renfrew 1973; Pearsall 1989). This latter term is sometimes used to refer to the analysis and interpretation, while archaeobotany is used in a restricted sense to refer to the collection of data. Archaeobotany, in addition to being a shorter word, has the advantage of emphasizing the archaeological nature of the data, which should call attention to the exigencies of deposition, preservation and recovery.

Within archaeobotanical research, work can be divided on the basis of the different parts of the plant examined and types of preservation. Although they have not all been studied yet in India, six main lines of evidence can be considered as parts of archaeobotany: seeds, wood, charred parenchyma fragments, plant impressions, pollen and phytoliths. Additional kinds of evidence that are often subsumed within archaeobotany include residue analysis (based on microscopic structure, or identifying distinctive plant chemical products, see Heron and Evershed 1993) and diatom analysis (Battarbee 1988). These different datasets present significant differences and few scholars study all of them. Each derives from different parts of the plant and as a result has different potentials brought about by processes of preservation. Each of these six lines of evidence requires somewhat different techniques of study:

Seeds, which are the most common evidence of archaeobotanists, can be preserved by numerous means, including mineralization, waterlogging, metal oxide preservation (sometimes called pseudomorphs), or as impressions in pottery, although most often seeds are encountered as charred remains. These can generally be identified by examining their external morphology through a low powered binocular microscope (i.e. 6x to 40x). This line of evidence represents the bulk of archaeobotany and will occupy most of this paper. It has now become possible to extract genetic information (DNA) from ancient seeds, and the prospects of this technique are reviewed below (Section 6.5).

Wood charcoal is the most abundant component of archaeobotanical flotation samples. Given the centrality of fire in human cultures, wood charcoal is among the most numerous of cultural by-products. Wood can also be preserved under other circumstances, such as waterlogging (e.g. A. Ghosh 1941; Chowdhury and Ghosh 1946; S. Ghosh 1950). It is identified by looking at anatomical characters in transverse, tangential and radial sections. This kind of study requires higher magnifications, generally 50x to 150x, but sometimes as high as 400x (Section 6.1).

Parenchyma, the starchy storage tissue of plants, which predominates in tubers and other underground storage organs, can also be preserved by charring. Such material has not traditionally been searched for in archaeobotanical samples but studies have found it to be fairly common in a number of regions, including Europe, Southwest Asia, South

America, and the Pacific (Hather 1994a, 1994b; see also Pearsall 1989: 165-73; Hather 1994c). The potential of this line of evidence in India will be discussed below (Section 6.2). Identifications of this material require the high magnifications and depth of field provided by scanning electron microscopy (SEM).

Plant impressions, often preserved in pottery, are one of the traditional sources of archaeobotanical information. However, the study of impressions is often eschewed today when charred remains collected through flotation are available from a site. Impressions can be studied at lower magnifications and often latex casts are prepared from the moulds which can then be submitted to scanning electron microscopy (e.g. Stemler 1990). Most cereal parts such as chaff are preserved in pottery since these readily available by-products of grain production were often used for tempering pottery. Impressions represent the human-caused equivalent to geological plant impression fossils. Natural impression fossils from the Pleistocene are relevant to understanding the environmental context of human culture. Although little such evidence is yet available from South Asia, Korisettar et al. (1977) reported leaf impressions associated with Middle Palaeolithic tools. These specimens were briefly described, and require further examination for identification. Reliable determination of taxonomic affinities from leaf venation has largely developed during the past three decades (Hickey and Wolfe 1975; Hickey 1979).

Pollen is usually collected from geological sediments (palynology) for examining palaeoecology, which is often of relevance for archaeological interpretations. Of particular interest are approaches to identifying the introduction or intensification of agriculture through pollen (Section 5.6). In addition, pollen is sometimes preserved in archaeological sediments (archaeological palynology), and this topic is discussed separately in Section 6.3. The study of pollen requires chemical concentration and slide preparation for examination under magnifications ranging from 400x-1000x.

Phytoliths (sometimes called 'plant opals', silica skeletons, or spodograms) are the silica casts of plant cells formed by the evaporation of silica-laden water through plant transpiration. Being an inorganic glass, these have a high potential for preservation in many sedimentary environments although they are likely to be destroyed by mechanical processes. The study of these remains requires careful collection to avoid contamination by airborne phytoliths, as well as complicated chemical extraction techniques and magnifications from 400x to 1000x or even more (see Section 6.4).

2.1 A FIELD GERMINATES: THE CONSULTANT-PALAEOBOTANICAL PHASE (PRE-1947 TO 1974)

The earliest stage of archaeobotany in India (as elsewhere in the world) consisted of archaeologists sending the few and varied plant remains they had recovered to one botanist or another for identifications. The material recovered was generally small in quantity and collected unsystematically, whenever an excavator noticed a quantity of recognizable plant material, such as a ceramic vessel full of charred grain, or fortuitously preserved pieces of wood (e.g. Ghosh 1950). While this stage began prior to Independence, only five sites had yielded samples, and the total number of plant taxa identified was only nine, three of which were forms of wheat (Table 1). Much of this pre-Independence work revolved around contradictory identifications of the wheat varieties recovered from Mohenjo Daro, Chanu Daro and Harappa (Stapf 1931; Luthra 1941; Burts 1941; also see Section 3.1). Material was often sent to state agricultural officers (e.g. Kumar 1952; Anonymous 1960), who supplied a list of species, often without description or discussion to the archaeologist. In the two subsequent decades much work was carried out by Chowdhury and Ghosh, of the Forest Research Institute, Dehra Dun, who provided a certain emphasis on woods (Chowdhury and Ghosh 1946, 1951, 1952, 1954-5, 1957; Ghosh 1950, 1961; Ghosh and Lal 1958, 1961, 1963). It was these avocational archaeobotanists who began to document the identification process. None of the botanists was primarily concerned with archaeological material or the Quaternary, and such studies formed a minor sideline in careers distinguished for their work elsewhere, in particular for systematizing the anatomy of Indian woods (Chowdhury and Ghosh 1958), as well as contributing to a floristic history of India on a geological timescale, such as Chowdhury's (1965) discussion of Indian palaeobotany in relation to the emergent theory of plate tectonics. They were botanists and palaeobotanists in the strict, traditional sense of such titles.

Coming from a similar background was Vishnu-Mittre (known only by this single name), a pivotal figure in Indian archaeobotany. His earliest work, on which his first Ph.D. focused, was traditionally palaeobotanical. He studied in detail the palaeofloristics of a Jurassic fossil locality at Nipania, district Amrapara, in the Rajamahal Hills, Bihar, and produced systematic descriptions of fossil conifers, ferns (Pteridophytes) and two extinct groups, the Pentoxyleae and Bennetitales, as well as fossil pollen and spores (Vishnu-Mittre 1952, 1954, 1956, 1957a, 1957b). His work on fossil spores and pollen

TABLE 1. PRE-INDEPENDENCE ARCHAEOBOTANY: THE SITES AND SPECIES

Site	Species reported	References
Mohenjo Daro	Free-threshing wheat (*T. aestivum* and *T. compactum*), barley, dates (*Phoenix dactylifera*)	Stapf 1931; Luthra 1936
Chanu Daro	Free-threshing wheat (*T. sphaerococcum* and *T. vulgare [=T. aestivum]*)	Shaw 1943
Harappa	Free-threshing wheat (*T. aestivu*, and *T. sphaerococcum*), barley, *Sesamum indicum*, melon (*Cucumis melo*), dates (*Phoenix dactylifera*)	Burts 1941; Luthra 1941; Vats 1941: 467
Khokhrakot (Early Historic)	Rice (*Oryza sativa*), naked barley (*Hordeum vulgare* var. *nudum*)	Sahni 1936
Arikamedu (Early Historic)	3 wood species; 2 fruit spp.: coconut (*Cocos nucifera*), palmyra palm (*Borassus flabellifer*)	Chowdhury and Ghosh 1946

NOTE: Wheat species level identification are suspect (see Section 3.1)

TABLE 2. Archaeobotanical seed findings: sites sampled without flotation. Based on archaeobotanical reports (some casual reports of plant finds excluded, including numerous reports of rice alone from Chalcolithic, Iron Age and Early Historic sites). Sites from which plant impressions have been studied are also included. Taxa recovered are abbreviated in the fifth column by category, followed by alphabetical abbreviations of genus: C (cereals/possible cereals): Cl (*Coix lachryma-jobi*), Ec (*Echinichloa*), El (*Eleusine*), H (*Hordeum*), O (*Oryza*), Pa (*Panicum*), Pe (*Pennisetum*), Ps (*Paspalum*), Se (*Setaria*), So (*Sorghum*), T (*Triticum*). P (pulses): C (*Cicer*), La (*Lathyrus*), Lb (*Lablab*), Le (*Lens*), M (*Macrotyloma*), Pi (*Pisum*), V (*Vigna radiata/mungo*). Vu (*Vigna unguiculata*) O (others): Ab (*Ablemoschos*), Ar (*Artocarpus*), Br (*Brassica*), Cc (*Curcurbitaceae*), Co (*Coriandrum*), Cr (*Carthamus*), Ct (*Citrus*), G (*Gossypium*), Ln (*Linum*), Mf (*Myristica fragrans*), Ph (*Phoenix*); Pv (*Papaver*), Rc (*Ricinus*), Sm (*Sesamum*), Tf-g (*Trigonella fenugraecum*), Vv (*Vitis vinifera*), Z (*Ziziphus*), ff (other fruits/nuts, with no. of taxa), ww (misc./weeds, with no. of taxa). Taxonomic nomenclature revised as per Tables 5-9 and Section 5. Dates are indicated by the following conditions. bc= dates based on radiocarbon age as reported (often 5570 half-life); BC= dates based calibrated radiocarbon timescale and/or historical chronology; some sites are dated based purely on relative terms by comparison with other dated sites, these probable dates are given in parentheses. *Bracketed taxa represent uncertain/unlikely identifications.* In some cases possible identity of unlikely identifications is indicated by ?=. Some taxa of uncertain crop/weed status are enclosed in parentheses.

Site	Map No.	Period	No. of Samples	No. of Seed Taxa (impressions)	Categories and Taxa	Reference
Ahar, Rajasthan	24	Chalcolithic (to Early Historic)	?	(2)	**C**: O [So]=?Ec	Vishnu-Mittre 1969
Atranjikhera Uttar Pradesh	13	OCP to BRW 2000-1000 BC	?	4	**C**: H O **P**: C La	Chowdhury et al. 1977, 1983
		PGW Phase 1000-500 BC	?	5	**C**: H O T **P**: C La	Chowdhury et al. 1977, 1983
		NBPW Phase 500-250 BC	?	6	**C**: H O T **P**: C La V	Chowdhury et al. 1977, 1983
		Kushan (Early Historic, 250 BC-300 AD)	1	2	**C**: O **O**: ww	Kajale and Deotare 1993
Bhatkuli Maharashtra		Early Historic	2	2	**C**: So **P**: C	Vishnu-Mittre and Gupta 1968b
Bhokardan, Maharashtra	58	Early Historic, (250 BC-300 AD)	20	14 spp.	**C**: [El] So T **P**: C Cj La Lb Le Pi V **O**: Z ff(1) ww(2)	Kajale 1947b
West Bengal sites: Baidipur, Dt. Mayurbhanj; Barudih, Dt. Singhbhum	51, 50	Neolithic (2500-1500 BC?)	?	(1)	**C**: O	after Vishnu-Mittre 1968c
Bir-Kot-Ghwandai, Swat	5	late Chalcolithic, *c.* 1700-1400 BC	?	5spp.	**C**: A H O T **P**: Le	Costantini 1987
Chanu Daro	56	Harappan (2600-2000 BC)	2	3	**C**: H T **P**: Pi	Vishnu-Mittre and Savithri 1982
Chirand, Bihar	45	Neolithic	6(?)	8	**C**: H O T **P**: La Le Pi V **O**: ff(1)	Vishnu-Mittre 1972; Vishnu-Mittre and Savithri 1976
Dangwada, Dt. Ujjain, Madhya Pradesh	59	Chalcolithic (=Malwa/Ahar, 2000-1500 BC)	?	6	**C**: O T **P**: Le V **O**: Z	Vishnu-Mittre et al. 1984
		Early Historic (300 BC-300 AD)	?	5	**C**: O T **P**: La Le **O**: Z	
Daulatpur, Haryana	22	(2200-1700 BC)	1	1 (+1)	**C**: O **P**: V	Vishnu-Mittre and Savithri 1982, 1985

(contd.)

Site	Map No.	Period	No. of Samples	No. of Seed Taxa (impressions)	Categories and Taxa	Reference
Ghaleghay, Swat	6	Chalcolithic I, *c.* 3000-2500 B.C.	6 (?)	1	**O**: ff (1)	Costantini 1987
		Chalcolitic II, *c.* 2500-1900 B.C.	1 (?)	4 + (1)	**C**: (O) T **O**: ff (1) ww (2)	
		Chalcolithic III, *c.* 1900-1700 B.C.	1 (?)	1 + (1)	**C**: H (O)	
Gufkral, Kashmir	2	*c.* 1200 B.C.	?	9	**C**: H O T **P**: Le Pi **O**: Vv ff (2)	(after Kajale 1989c)
Hallur, Karnataka	73	Neolithic-Iron Age	6	4	**C**: [El]=? Se O [Pa] **O** ff (1)	Vishnu-Mittre 1971
		(*c.* 1000 B.C.)	1	6	**C**: O **P**: Lb M V **O**: Z	Kajale 1989a; Kajale and Deotare 1993
Hulas, Dt. Saharanpur, U.P.	12	Late Harappan (1800-1300 B.C.)	?	19	**C**: [El?=Se H O So T **P**: C La Le M Pi V Vu **O**: Cc G Rc ff (2) ww (3)	Saraswat et al. 1992; Saraswat 1993
Hulaskhera, Dt. Lucknow, U.P.	32	(800 B.C.-500 A.D.)	?	27	**C**: (Ec) [El] H O **P**: V **O**: ww (22)	Saraswat and Chanchala 1994; Saraswat 1992
Inamgaon, 1971 season	71	Chalcolithic (Malwa, Late and Early Jorwe)	78	14spp. + 8 indet.	**C**: H O So T **P**: La Lb Le M Pi V **O**: Z ff (2) ww (1)	Vishnu-Mittre and Savithri 1976
Kalibangan	81	Harappan (2600-2000 B.C.	3 (+3)	4 (+1)	**C**: H T **P**: C Pi	Vishnu-Mittre and Savithri 1975; 1982
Kaothe	92	Chalcolithic, *c.* 1900 B.C. (antiquity of seeds uncertain)	45	8 + 2 indet.	**C**: Pe Se So **P**: M V **O**: Sm Z ww (3)	Kajale 1990c
Kaundinyapura, Maharashtra	38	Early Historic	4		**C**: O	Vishnu-Mittre 1968b
		Medieval	1	(Maize)	**P**: La Pi **O**: Z	
Kayatha, Madhya Pradesh	91	Chalcolithic	?	1?	**C**: T	after Vishnu-Mittre 1968*c*, 1977
		(2500-1400 B.C.)	?	2	**C**: T **P**: M	Vishnu Mittre et al. 1985
Khairadih, Dt. Balia, U.P.	33	Iron Age (700-200 B.C.)	?	12	**C**: H O T **P**: C La Pi V **O**: Mf Vv ff (3)	Saraswat et al. 1990
Koldihwa, Dt. Allahabad, U.P.	29	Neolithic (2500-1500 B.C.)	4 (?)	1	**C**: O	Vishnu-Mittre and Savithri 1979c
Lal Qila, U.P.	11	(1800-1200 B.C.)	16	5	**C**: H O T **O**: Cc ww	Kajale and Deotare 1993
Loebanr 3	4	late Chalcolithic, *c.* 1700-1400 B.C.	10	13spp.	**C**: H O T **P**: Le Pi **O**: Cc Ln V ww (6)	Costantini 1987
Lothal Gujarat	10	Chalcolithic, per. II. 2350-2200 B.C.	?	(1)	**C**: O	Ramesh Rao and Lal 1985

(contd.)

Site	Map No.	Period	No. of Samples	No. of Seed Taxa (impressions)	Categories and Taxa	Reference
		Chalcolithic, per. IV 2000-1900 B.C.	1	(2)	C: Se O: Sm	
Magha, Dt. Mirzapur, U.P.	42	Black and Red Ware (1200-600 B.C.)	?	(4)	C: (Ec) O (Ps) O: ww (1)	Vishnu-Mittre et al. 1984
Mahagara, Dt. Allahabad U.P.	30	2000-1300 B.C.	?	2	C: H O O: ww (1)	Vishnu-Mittre et al. 1984; Saraswat 1992
Mahorana, Dt. Sangrur, Punjab	82	Early Bara Culture (2300-2000 B.C.)	1	4	C: H T P: Le O: Vv	Vishnu-Mittre et al. 1986b
			1	1	P: Lb	Saraswat and Chanchala 1994
Manjhi, Dt. Saran Bihar	25	Early Historic (250 BC-250 A.D.)	?	9	C: [El] H O T P: La Le Pi V O: Vv	Saraswat and Chanchala 1997
Mohenjo Daro	55	Harappan (2500-2000 B.C.)	1	4	C: H T P: Pi O: Br	Vishnu-Mittre and Savithri 1982
Nausharo, Baluchistan, Pakistan	54	Harappan (2500-2000 B.C.)	4 (?)	13	C: H T P: Le O: Ln Ph Vv Z ff (1) ww (2)	Costantini 1990a
Navdatoli, Maharashtra	70	Chalcolithic	256	13spp.	C: O T P: La Le V O: Z ff (2) Ln ww	Vishnu-Mittre 1961
Nevasa, Maharashtra (1954-6 season)	62	Early Historic 150 B.C.-200 A.D.)	30	17	C: [El] O Pe Ps So T P: C La Lb Le M Pi V O: Co Cr G Z	Anonymous, in Sankalia et al. 1960: pp. 529-30
(1959-60 season, and 1973 sampling)	Early Historic	150 B.C.-200 A.D.	?	16 + 2 indet	C: El H O [Pe] Ps So T P: C Cj La Lb Pi V O: Cr Z ff (1) ww (3)	Kajale 1977b
		Early Historic?	1	5	C: O P: La Pi V O: Z	Vishnu-Mittre et al. 1985
Noh, Rajasthan	14	Iron Age-Early Historic	4	4	C: H O P: M V	Vishnu-Mittre and Savithri 1974
Pandu Rajar Dhibi, W. Bengal	52	*c.* 1000 B.C.	?	2	C: O T	after Vishnu-Mittre 1968c; 1977
Paunar, Maharashtra	69	Early Historic	?	2	C: O So	Vishnu-Mittre and Gupta 1968a
Peddamudiyam, Andhra Pradesh	96	*c.* 1700-1300 B.C.	3	2spp. (+ unID)	P: Cj O: Ab	Venkatasubbaiah and Kajale 1991
Pirak, Baluchistan	7	Post-Harappan (1950-1550 B.C.)	?	11spp	C: A H O Pa [So] T P: C O: Ln	Costantini 1979
Radhan, U.P.	16	Painted-Grey Ware, Northern Black Polished Ware	1	4 spp.	C: H O P: [Le] Pi	Kajale and Lal 1988, 1989; Kajale and Deotare 1992

(contd.)

Site	Map No.	Period	No. of Samples	No. of Seed Taxa (impressions)	Categories and Taxa	Reference
		Medieval	1	4 spp.	**C**: H O T **P**: [Le]	
Rangpur, Gujarat	9	IIA, 2500-2000 B.C.	Impression	(1)	**C**: o	Ghosh and Lal 1963
Rangpur		III 2000-1700	1	1 (+1)	**C**: O Pe	Ghosh and Lal 1963
Runija, Dt. Ujjain, Madhya Pradesh		Sunga Period	1?	1	**C**: T	Vishnu-Mittre et al. 1984
Rupar, Dt. Ambala Punjab	19	Harappan/Baran (2500-1700 BC)	?	2	**C**: [Ps] T	Vishnu-Mittre and Savithri 1979a
Sanghol, Dt. Ludhiana Punjab	20	Kushana (0-400 AD)	?	9	**C**: H O So T **P**: Le M Pi V **O**: Z	Saraswat et al. 1992
		Late Harappa/Bara (1900-1400 bc)	?	25	**C**: H Se So T **P**: La Lb Le M Pi **O**: Ct Ln Pv Sm ww (10) ff (2)	Saraswat and Chanchala 1997
Senuwar, Dt. Rohtas, Bihar	21	Neolithic (2000 bc-1400 bc)	?	10	**C**: H O Ps T **P**: C La Le Pi V **O**: ww	Saraswat et al. 1992
		IA (2000-1800 bc)	?	20	**C**: Cl [El] H O Se So T **P**: La Le Pi **O**: Z ww (8) ff (1)	Saraswat et al. 1995
		IB (1800-1200 bc)	?	24	**C**: H O Ps Se So T **P**: C La Le Pi V **O**: Z ww (12)	
		II (1200-600 bc)	?	22	**C**: H O Ps Se So T **P**: C La Le Pi V **O**: Cr Ln Sm Z ww (6)	
Shikarpur, Kachchh	84	Harappan (2500-2220 BC)	?	11	**C**: [El] T Se **O**: Z ww (7)	Saraswat et al. 1995
Singh-Bhagwantpur, Dt. Rupnagar, Punjab		(1100-800 AD)	?	2	**C**: T **O**: G	Vishnu-Mittre et al. 1984
Surkotada	90	Harappan/Post-Harappan (2500-1700 BC)	3 from 1 locus (740 seeds)	28	**C**: [El]?=Se Se **P**: ww (25)	Vishnu-Mittre and Savithri 1978, 1979b, 1982; Vishnu-Mittre 1990
Taradih	102	Neolithic (to Late Historical, beginning *c*. 2000-1500 BC?)	?	6	**C**: H T **P**: C Pi V **O**: Z	Kajale 1991
Tekkalakota, Karnataka	93	Neothic (?2000-1500 BC)	?	3	**P**: M [Ph]?=Lb **O**: Z	Vishnu-Mittre and Savithri 1979a
Ter, Maharashtra	64	Early Historic (200 BC-400 AD)	30	12	**C**: H O Ps T **P**: C La Le M Pi V **O**: Z [Rc]?=legum.	Vishnu-Mittre et al. 1971
Watgal, Karnataka	94	IIA (2800-2300 BC)	?	3 reported	**C**: [El] **P**: M **O**: *Areca*	Devaraj et al. 1995 (prelim. site report) -
		2800 BC-1000 BC	?	?	**C**: H Pa Se **P**: M **O**: Z	Kajale 1998 (abstract)

was further stimulated by the pioneering palynologist Gunnar Erdtman, who stayed briefly at the BSIP [Paleobotanical Institute] in Lucknow as a visiting scholar and helped Vishnu-Mittre establish a comparative collection of modern Indian species, and to publish clear terminology for spore and pollen descriptions (Erdtman and Vishnu-Mittre 1956; Vishnu-Mittre 1957c). Having thus distinguished himself, Vishnu-Mittre was awarded a scholarship to pursue a second Ph.D. in Cambridge (Gupta 1994). There he studied Quaternary palynology, completing a Ph.D. on Holocene vegetation change in Cambridgeshire, England (Vishnu-Mittre 1960) under the supervision of Sir Harry Godwin, whose *History of the British Flora* (1956, 1975) laid much of the foundations for British archaeobotany. Vishnu-Mittre's work on the English Quaternary introduced him to the confounding factors of climate change and human intervention in the landscape in the interpretation of Quaternary plant remains, exemplified by the still contentious problem of the catastrophic decline of elms in Britain more or less contemporary with the advent of the Neolithic (Vishnu-Mittre 1965b; for more recent reviews, Scaife 1988; Peglar 1993). Vishnu-Mittre returned to India with interest both in plant evolution (e.g. Vishnu-Mittre 1963) and anthropogenic environmental change. Determined to make positive contributions to the understanding of Quarternary plant evolution and human prehistory, he began a programme in Kashmir of investigating Holocene pollen sequences (Vishnu-Mittre et al. 1962; Vishnu-Mittre and Sharma 1966; Vishnu-Mittre 1966, 1968a), and macrofossils (Vishnu-Mittre 1965a), as well as modern pollen rain (Vishnu-Mittre and Robert 1971). He clearly expressed the potential of pollen for isolating anthropogenic influences on vegetation including the introduction of agriculture in his paper 'Inter-relationship between archaeology and plant sciences' (1968a). Unfortunately the pollen sequences collected in Kashmir during this period were not radiometrically dated, so although they provide a relative sequence of vegetation changes including a likely period for the adoption or intensification of agriculture, they could not be correlated with archaeological phases (Agrawal 1992: 132). Equivalent pollen sequences were subsequently obtained from the Kumaon region which suffered from a similar lack of fixed chronology (Gupta 1975a).

It was during this period (1960s) that Vishnu-Mittre was first called upon to examine archaeobotanical material, consisting of charred lumps of seeds, plant impressions in pottery and mineralized remains preserved in the iron oxide of iron artefacts. His first archaeobotanical publication was a detailed report on material from Chalcolithic Navdatoli (Vishnu-Mittre 1961), in which he identified 13 species from amongst 256 hand-collected charcoal samples. This was the largest number of species identified to that date from an archaeological site, and Vishnu-Mittre used this data to produce the first synthesis of prehistoric Indian agriculture. Although the amount of data available at that time was small, one pattern which was clear was the gradual spread of wheat from the northwest towards the east and south. As more data accumulated, in large part through his own work, Vishnu-Mittre produced additional syntheses of archaeobotany (1968c, 1974, 1977).

Further interpretation of archaeobotany remained quite limited at this stage. The early work had simple taxonomic aims and produced lists of species, which resulted in a vaguely defined study of 'past agriculture' and 'food habits' (Kajale 1974a: 55). As basic components of research, these objectives remain prominent today. Additional interpretation largely focused on plant remains as evidence of past knowledge about plant properties, such as the building properties of various woods (e.g. Chowdhury 1970), or simply the past possession of the knowledge of cultivation: the origins of agriculture was seen simply as a great scientific discovery (e.g. Chowdhury 1969; Vishnu-Mittre 1970b). In some cases archaeobotanical data were combined with geological palaeobotany in discussing the evolution of particular plant groups without giving consideration to the social and cultural associations of the archaeological finds (e.g. Gupta 1975b). In addition, basic ecological assessments were made on the basis of species present, especially trees represented in charcoal, in order to determine whether the environment had varied in the past. The bulk of such assessments concluded that past plant communities around a site were essentially similar to those of today (e.g. Chowdhury and Ghosh 1955; Lal 1963). Little interest was shown in what social patterning might be present in the data nor in the extent to which cultural factors might have encouraged either the adoption of agriculture or other changes in species present in particular regions through time. This narrow approach to plant remains developed in part because specimens were undertaken by botanists lacking expertise in archaeology and anthropology, and in part because of the cultural-historical theories which held sway in archaeological thinking. Archaeological cultures were defined and compared on the basis of checklists of artefact traits, so plant remains too were grouped by site and broad periods. The first assessments of the South Asian archaeobotanical record, which came out close to the end of India's second decade as an independent nation (Chowdhury 1970; Vishnu-Mittre 1968b, 1974), discussed plant domestication in terms of earliest occurrences of crop plants, without systematic consideration of the possible morphological changes involved, or the human activities which would have produced them. Finds from subsequent periods attested to the spread of cultivars, assumed to occur primarily through human migrations. When it was discussed, domestication was described as a typological shift from 'wild' to 'domestic' plants, and their co-occurrence was taken to imply domestication. For example, Vishnu-Mittre (1971) claimed to have identified both domestic finger millet, *Eleusine coracana* (Indian *ragi*) and a wild relative *E. indica* together from Late Neolithic/Iron Age Hallur, Karnataka. However, this claim is dubious on account of both probable mis-identification (see Section 4.2) and strong botanical evidence for an East African origin of finger millet, from a species of *Eleusine* distinct from *E. indica* (see Section 5.2). A similar approach to identify local domestication through co-occurrence was suggested for rice from Belan Valley sites (Sharma et al. 1980; see Vishnu-Mittre 1989).

Over the years the collection of archaeobotanical data became more frequent as archaeologists became increasingly interested in issues relating to plants, especially the origins of agriculture. The consultant-palaeobotanist phase of archaeobotany was greatly encouraged by the burgeoning archaeological research in peninsular India by researchers from Deccan College, Pune, under the guidance of H.D. Sankalia, a guiding light in post-Independence Indian archaeology (e.g. Vishnu-Mittre 1961, 1968a, 1971). As archaeobotanical studies increased, their results had a proportionately increased impact on scholarly views of Indian prehistory. It was this increased demand by archaeologists for botanical consultants that ultimately led to the emergence of the small number of vocational archaeobotanists, specializing only in archaeological plant remains.

2.2 PHASE TWO: FLOTATION AND THE ESTABLISHMENT OF PROFESSIONAL ARCHAEOBOTANISTS (1974-88)

Increasing archaeobotanical evidence from consulting palaeobotanists in the early 1970s corresponded to increased theoretical interest in Indian archaeology, especially within the processual mode of thought, which emphasized cultural ecology and settlement-subsistence systems (e.g. Dhavalikar and Possehl 1974; see Fuller and Boivin, Vol. IV of this series). This led to an increased interest in information on ancient agriculture and environment, and encouraged the growth of archaeobotany. A number of archaeobotanists began their careers during this period. M.D. Kajale at Deccan College produced an important review of the then available evidence (Kajale 1974a) and took up a programme, of sampling at Inamgaon and other excavations. Under the tutelage of Chowdhury, G.M. Buth and K.S. Saraswat entered archaeobotany (e.g. Buth and Chowdhury 1971, 1973; Buth and Saraswat 1972; Chowdhury et al. 1977). During this period, Vishnu-Mittre devoted himself increasingly to the study of archaeological plant remains and took on students of his own, most notably R. Savithri (e.g. Vishnu-Mittre et al. 1971; Vishnu-Mittre and Savithri 1974, 1975, 1976, 1978, 1979, 1982), as well as Chanchala and Saraswat who had come to the Birbal Sahni Institute in Lucknow. This period can be considered the professionalization of archaeobotany. Archaeobotany took on a new status as an integral part of archaeological research in India with the inclusion of a section on 'Palaeobotanical and Pollen Analytical Investigations' in the Archaeological Survey of India's annual *Indian Archaeology—A Review* since 1974-5 (Vishnu-Mittre and Savithri 1979a).

An important new technique, sampling through flotation, was adopted on several sites in South Asia during the later 1970s. Developed in America and Europe in the 1960s initially as a laboratory technique, flotation was transferred to fieldwork situations with the growth of problem-oriented research on the origins of agriculture (Streuver 1968; Helbaek 1969; Jarmon et al. 1972; Stewart and Robertson 1973; for a more detailed review see Pearsall 1989: 19-79). As noted by Kajale (1974a), smaller, less conspicuous seeds could easily be missed in collections made by hand. In 1973, Glover carried out flotation in Island Southeast Asia at Sulawesi (Glover 1979). Flotation was first carried out in India at Daimabad, Naikund and Inamgaon (Kajale 1977a, 197b, 1982, 1988b), and soon came to be applied in a research programme on the Neolithic of Kashmir (Buth et al. 1982, 1986) and later Narhan in the Ganga plains (Saraswat et al. 1994), as well as some Harappan sites (see Table 3, for a comprehensive list of floated sites in South Asia). With flotation, the increase in the amount of botanical data from a single site, even a single trench, increased so dramatically that it requires full-time specialists to work through

TABLE 3. Sites sampled by means of flotation. Taxa recovered are abbreviated in the fifth column by category, followed by alphabetical abbreviations of genus: **C** (cereals/possible cereals): Av (*Avena*), Cl (*Coix lachryma-jobi*), Ec (*Echinochloa*), El (*Eleusine*), H (*Hordeum*), O (*Oryza*), Pa (*Panicum*), Pe (*Pennisetum*), Ps (*Paspalum*), Se (*Setaria*), So (*Sorghum*), T (*Triticum*). **P** (pulses): C (*Cicer*), La (*Lathyrus*), Lb (*Lablab*), Le (*Lens*), **M** (*Macrotyloma*), Pi (*Pisum*), V (*Vigna radiata/mungo*), Vu (*Vigna unguiculata*). **O** (others): Ab (*Ablemoschos*), Ar (*Artocarpus*), Br (*Brassica*), Ca (*Carthamus*), Cc (*Cucurbitaceae*), Ln (*Linum*), Ph (*Pheonix*); Rc (*Ricinus*), Sm (*Sesamum*), Vv (*Vitis*), Z (*Ziziphus*), ff (other fruits/nuts, with quantity), ww (misc./weeds, with quantity); rh (rhizomes). Taxonomic nomenclature revised as per Table 5 and Section 5. Dates are indicated by the following conditions. bc= dates based on radiocarbon age as reported (often 5570 half-line); BC= dates based calibrated radiocarbon timescale and/or historical chronology; some sites are dated based purely on relative terms by comparison with other dated sites, these probable dates are given in parentheses. *Bracketed taxa represent uncertain/unlikely identifications, while parenthetical taxa are of unclear crop/weed status.* In some cases possible identity of unlikely identifications is indicated by ?=. Some taxa of uncertain crop/weed status are enclosed in parentheses.

Site, State	Map No.	Period	No. of Samples	Taxa Reported	Categories and Taxa	Reference
Adam, Maharashtra	65	Microlithic (2000-1500 bc)	2	1	**C**: O	Kajale 1994
		Chalcolithic 1900-900 BC	3	1	**O**: Z	
		Iron Age (100-500 BC	5	2 + 3 indet.	**C**: O **P**: La	
		Pre-Mauryan (*c*. 500-300 BC	2	8 + 9	**C**: [Cl] O Se **P**: Lb Le M V **O**: Z ww (9)	
		Mauryan (300 BC-50 AD)	2	9 + 2	**C**: H O T **P**: La Le Pi V **O**: Ab Z	
		Bhadra (50-150 AD)	2	7	**C**: Cl O **P**: La Lb Le Pi **O**: garlic	
Allhadino, Sindh	88	Harappan, *c*. 2500-2000 BC	?	3	**C**: H T **P**: ?	Fairservis 1982
Apegaon, Maharashtra	103	1600-1000 BC	11	10	**C**: H T **P**: La Lb Le M Pi V **O**: Z	Kajale 1979
Babar Kot, Gujarat	86	2000-1700 BC	200	23	**C**: [El] Pa [Pe] Se **P**: La Le V **O**: Br Ln ww (14)	Reddy 1994
Balakot	89	Harappan, *c*. 2500-2000 BC	? (+ pollen)	1 (+ pollen)	**C**: H pollen: Cc G	cf. Dales 1986; McKean 1983
Balathal, Rajasthan	23	Chalcolithic (2350-1800 bc)	?	22 + 4 indet.	**C**: Cl H Pa Se T **P**: [C] P V **O**: Ab Cc [Ln] Z ww (8)	Kajale 1996a
		Early Historic (500 BC-300 AD)	?	25 + 4 indet.	**C**: Cl H O Pa Ps Se T **P**: C Pi V **O**: Ab [V] Z ww (5)	
Balijapalle, Andhra Pradesh	98	Neolithic (1700-1300 BC)	10	1 + 5 indet.	**O**: Ab ww (5)	Venkatasubbaiah and Kajale 1991
Beli-Lana, Sri Lanka		Mesolithic 10000-8000 B.P.	?	3	**O**: ff (3)=*Ar, Musa, Canarium*	Kajale 1989b
Bhagimohari, Maharashtra	72	First Millennium BC	15	13 + 2 indet.	**C**: (Cl) H O **P**: Cj La Lb Le M Pi V **O**: Z ww (4)	Kajale 1989c; Kajale and Deotare 1992
Burthana Tigrana	18	2500-2000 BC		5	**C**: H T **P**: M V **O**: Z	Willcox 1992

(contd.)

Site, State	Map No.	Period	No. of Samples	Taxa Reported	Categories and Taxa	Reference
Burzahom, Kashmir	3	I 2400-1700 BC	?	12	**C**: H T **P**: Le Pi **O**: ff (3) ww (5)	Lone et al. 1993
		II 1700-1000 BC	?	10	**C**: H T **P**: Le **O**: Vv ff (4) ww (3)	
		III 1000-600 BC	?	14	**C**: H O T **P**: Le Pi **O**: ff (4) ww (5)	
		IV 600 BC-200 AD	?	17	**C**: H O T **P**: Le Pi **O**: ff (5) ww (7)	
Daimabad, Maharashtra	63	Savalda (2000-1700 BC	?	3	**C**: H **P**: Le **O**: Z	Kajale 1977a
		Malwa (1700-1500 BC)	?	7	**C**: H T **P**: La Le M Pi **O**: Z	Kajale 1977a
		Jorwe (1500-1100 BC)	?	14	**C**: [El] H O Ps So T **P**: La Le M Pi V **O**: Cl Ln Z	Kajale 1977a
		Savalda (2000-1800 BC)	14 total, for all periods	2	**C**: H T	Vishnu-Mittre et al. 1986
		Malwa (1700-1500 BC	included above	20	**C**: [El]=? Se H T **P**: La Le M Pi Vu [Ph]=Vu **O**: Z ww (10)	Vishnu-Mittre et al. 1986
		Jorwe 1500-100 BC)	included above	18	**C**: [El]=? Se H Ps Se T **P**: La Le M Pi Vu [Ph]=Vu **O**: Z ww (6)	Vishnu Mittre et al. 1986
Damdama, Pratapgarh, U.P.,	31	Mesolithic (4th M. BC?)	14	8 + 3 indet.	**C**: [O] **O**: ww (10)	Kajale 1990a; Kajale and Deotare 1992
Hallur, Karnaṭaka	73	Neolithic	prelim. 6	10+	**C**: H O T Ec Se Pa **P**: Lb Le M V **O**: ww parenchyma	Fuller et al. forthcoming
Hanumantharao-peta, Andhra Pradesh	99	Neolithic	prelim. 1	4+	**C**: Ec Se **P**: M V **O**: ww parenchyma	Fuller et al. forthcoming
Harappa	7	2400-2350 BC	(100s)	7+	**C**: H T **P**: C La Le Pi **O**: Z ww	Miller and Reddy 1990; Weber 1997
		2200-2000 BC	(100s)	9+	**C**: H O T +'millet' **P**: C La Le Pi **O**: Z ww	
Inamgaon, Maharashtra	71	Malwa 1700-1500 BC	186 total	33	**C**: [El]?=Se H T **P**: Lb Le M Pi **O**: ff (4) ww (9) Cc	Kajale 1988b
		Early Jorwe 1500-1200 BC		30	**C**: [El]?= Se H Se T **P**: La Lb Le M Pi **O**: Ph [Sm] ff (6) ww (13)	
		Late Jorwe 1200-900 BC		31	**C**: (Cl) [El]?=Se H O Pa Se T **P**: C La Lb Le M Pi V **O**: Ph [Sm] ff (5) ww(10)	(also preliminary report, Kajale 1977a)

(contd.)

Site, State	Map No.	Period	No. of Samples	Taxa Reported	Categories and Taxa	Reference
Kuntasi, Gujarat	101	Harappan 2500-2000 BC	?	?	C: [El] H Se T O: ww	Kajale quoted in Dhavalikar 1995
Laduwala, Haryana	near 17, 18	2800-2300 BC	62 (from 5 [?] sites)	2	C: H O: Z	Willcox 1992
Mangali, Luduwala	near 17, 18	(1500-1900 AD)		12	C: H O [Pe] S T P: M V O: Cc G Ss Z Rh	Willcox 1992
Mitathal, Haryana	17	2000-1400 BC		7	C: H O T P: M V O: Z rh	Willcox 1992
Naikund, Maharashtra	75	1st M. BC	7	5	C: T P: Le Pi V O: Z	Kajale 1982
Narhan, Uttar Pradesh	44	Chalcolithic-Iron Age, *c.* 1300 BC-200 BC	54	54	C: (Ec) H O (Pa) Pe Ps T P: C La Lb Le M Pi V O: Ar (Br) Ca (Cc) Ln Ph Ss Vv Z ww (33)	Saraswat et al. 1993; 1994
Oriyo Timbo, Gujarat	85		247	18	C: [El] Pa Se P: V O: Br ww (13)	Reddy 1994
Peddamudiyam, Andhra Pradesh	96	Late Neolithic 1700-1300 BC	prelim. 2	4+	C: Se P: M O: ww Parenchyma	Fuller et al. forthcoming
Ramapuram, Andhra Pradesh	97	Neolitihic (2nd M. BC)	?	3	C: H P:Lb V	Kajale, *IAR* 1980-1
Rohira, Punjab	83	Harappan, (*c.* 2000-1700 BC)	?	5	C: H T P: Le M O: Tf-g	Vishnu-Mittre et al. 1985
Rohira, Punjab		(2300-2000 BC)	Flot. 4	7	C: H So T P: Le M O: Ph Vv	Saraswat 1986
Rojdi, Gujarat	87	A: *c.* 2600-2200 BC	74	22	C: [EI]?=Se H Pa Se P: V O: Z ww (12)	Weber 1991
		B: 2200-2000 BC	59	31	C: [EI]?=Se HPa Se O: Ab (Br) Z ww (20)	
		C: 2000-1700 BC	284	59	C: (Ec) [EI]? Se H Pa (Ps) Se So P: La Le M Pi V O: Ab (Br) Cc Ln ww (38)	
Sanganakallu, Karnataka	95	Neolithic	prelim. 6	9+	C: H T Se Pa P: Cj Lb M V O: Z ww parenchyma	Fuller et al. forthcoming
Semthan, Kashmir	1	I 1500-600 BC	?	8	C: H O T P: Le V O: ff (3)	Lone et al. 1993
		II 600 BC-200 BC	?	12	C: H O T P: Le Pi V O: ff (4) ww (2)	
		III 200-1 BC	?	11	C: Av H O Pa T P: V O: ff (3) ww (2)	
		IV 1-500 AD	?	17	C: Av H O Se T P: Le Pi V	

(contd.)

Site, State	Map No.	Period	No. of Samples	Taxa Reported	Categories and Taxa	Reference
					O: ff (3) ww (6)	
		V 500-1000 AD	?	13	**C**: Av H O T **P**: Le Pi V **O**: ff (3) ww (3)	
Tarakai Qila, NWFP	100	chalcolithic 4th to 3rd M. BC	?	3	**C**: H T **P**: Le	Thomas 1983a, 1983b
Tuljapur Garhi, Maharashtra	68	Chalcolithic	9	15+2 indet.	**C**: H O So T **P**: C Cj La Lb Le M V **O**: ww (5)	Kajale 1988a; Kajale 1996b
Veerapuram, Andhra Pradesh	78	500 BC- 400 AD	44	10	**C**: H O Ps **P**: Lb M Pi V **O**: Cc Z ff (1)	Kajale 1984

all the material. Thus, with flotation, the feasibility of employing botanists only as consultants decreased. It was this rather rapid and revolutionary shift that facilitated future analytical refinements. With fulltime specialists it became possible to consider more carefully the unique nature of archaeobotanical data.

The impact of flotation on the scholarly understanding of ancient Indian agriculture was thus quite dramatic, as a greater number of species came to be identified, and previously attested species became more reliably recorded. A striking example is the case of barley. Barley has long been of interest to Indologists, as the cereal identified with the Sanskrit *Yava*, a cereal widely attested in the Rig Veda (*Rik Samhita*) and it was therefore often connected to the advent of the 'Indo-Aryans.' In relation to this hypothesis Vishnu-Mittre (1970a) reviewed the available evidence for barley, and concluded that it was of minor importance to the Harappans, nor were other archaeological cultures known in which it was a staple, and therefore it was not possible to identify any then sampled sites with the 'Aryans'. Similarly, in a review of the archaeobotanical record, barley was designated 'a distinctly extrapeninsular crop' (Kajale 1974a: 61). Both of the above generalizations, regarding barley as a staple crop and establishing its extra-peninsular distribution, have been clearly disproved by more recent archaeobotany. Indeed, barley is now one of the most widely documented crops on prehistoric sites in India, it is particularly prominent on Chalcolithic sites on the peninsula (see, e.g. Kajale 1988a, 1988b, 1991) and it is known from further south on later Neolithic sites (Fuller et al. n.d.; see Korisettar et al. in Vol. I of this series), Ganga Valley sites and numerous Harappan sites (Vishnu-Mittre and Savithri 1982; Saraswat 1992). This example illustrates the instability of generalizations based on a few haphazard hand-collected samples and the consequent need for flotation.

2.3 PHASE THREE: TOWARDS A SELF CRITICAL ARCHAEOBOTANY THROUGH FORMATION PROCESSES (1988-PRESENT)

For a more judicious use of archaeobotanical data it is necessary to be aware of the processes which brought them to the microscope of the specialists, including recovery, preservation and original depositional processes. The study of depositional and post-depositional factors is called taphonomy, a term borrowed from palaeontology which entered the archaeological literature in the 1970s as increasing attention was paid to the formation of animal bone assemblages. The interest in taphonomic processes developed in archaeology alongside an awareness of pre-depositional factors influencing the formation of assemblages. Archaeobotanical formation processes started to become an issue in the early 1970s in the West after the advent of flotation, although it was some fifteen years before these issues began to be addressed in South Asian contexts.

An important observation was that most archaeobotanical remains represent a particularly limited range of ecological plant communities, most often that of arable fields, and therefore archaeological plant remains were most likely to relate to a limited range of human activities, most notably the harvesting and processing of crops (Knorzer 1971; Hillman 1972). Dennell (1972) took a particular interest in estimating the relative 'value' or importance of the different plant species represented archaeologically. In order to do this he discussed different kinds of archaeological contexts from contemporaneous levels on a site in order to highlight the different depositional and preservational factors involved and their implications for understanding different economic activities. He divided these find-contexts into six main categories: (1) storage jars, storage pits, silos; (2) ovens, hearths; (3) floor deposits; (4) middens or rubbish pits; (5) impressions in pottery (not carbonized remains); and (6) fill deposits. In more recent reviews of archaeobotanical interpretation the importance of the *context* of recovery and the probable *source* (in terms of plant community and human activities) from which the plant came have continued to be emphasized (Pearsall 1988, 1989: 22-225; Kajale 1988b; Weber 1991). Dennell (1972, 1974, 1976) contrasted the assemblages recovered from floor deposits, ovens, and midden deposits from prehistoric Bulgarian sites and found that floor samples had higher proportions of weed seeds and generally smaller cereal grain sizes. He suggested that this came from sieving to remove weeds and accidentally some small grains, which contributed plant remains to floor deposits; oven and midden deposits were interpreted as discard after the grain had been cleaned. Although this study failed to address some problems, such as the question of how the floor deposits were charred, it was important for emphasizing the need to compare similar depositional contexts when making chronological comparisons.

The most common form of archaeological preservation is the carbonization of seeds (and other plant parts such as cereal chaff). Although earlier discussions were not always clear as to how carbonization was assumed to have occurred (including, e.g. Dennell 1972), and there was some belief in natural carbonization in the soil, it is now generally believed that in almost all cases preservation required exposure to fire (Minnis 1981; Hillman 1981, 1984; Pearsall 1989: 202, 224; Zohary and Hopf 1993: 3-4). Thus, as a rule of thumb for sites in most environments, excepting regions of extreme aridity and desiccated preservation, uncharred seeds are generally assumed to represent intrusive, modern contaminants in archaeobotanical assemblages (Pearsall 1989; Weber 1991). As charred grains themselves are not eaten, they must have entered the archaeological record incidentally, and the presence of cereal chaff, which is not eaten, together with seeds of species known to occur as weeds in arable fields, drew attention to the probable roll of crop processing in forming archaeological assemblages (Hillman 1972, 1973; Dennell 1972, 1974, 1976). Hillman (1973, 1981, 1984) pioneered an ethnoarchaeological approach to studying the effects of crop-processing on assemblage formation through his work on traditional cultivation and harvesting of wheat and barley in Turkey. While his work focused on the presence and proportions of different chaff types, in addition to cereals and weeds, Glynis Jones (1983, 1984, 1987) took a different emphasis to her ethnographic study in Greece, in which she focused on the analysis of the weed components of assemblages in order to identify the various processing stages. Such crop-processing studies drew attention to some of the ways in which the remains of crops and their weeds could be routinely exposed to fire, as crop-processing by-products were used as fuel or disposed of in fires. Processing by-products are also frequently used as animal fodder, and therefore seeds can enter fires through the burning of animal dung (Miller 1984, 1991; Miller and Smart 1984; Bottema 1984; Thomas 1989: Fig. 6; Charles 1998). By the mid-1980s discussion of the formation of archaeobotanical assemblages, in particular the effects of crop processing, were a central part of European and Southwest Asian archaeobotany.

The study of formation processes made little impact in South Asian archaeobotany until the late 1980s, and consideration of crop processing was not seriously incorporated until the 1990s, and can be seen as part of a growing awareness of formation processes that developed in South Asian archaeology through the latter half of the 1980s (see Fuller and Boivin in Vol. IV of this series). Kajale (1988b), in his analysis of the evidence from Inamgaon, compared similar contexts from a number of levels, those from the fill and floors of excavated house structures. He found little significant difference, which he interpreted to indicate essentially uniform economic activities between households. However, could not such similarities in assemblages be the result of the same general formation processes of the site deposits and the incorporation of charred plant remains? To argue that the plant remains in a structure are a direct reflection of the activities in that structure one must assume more or less in situ deposition of charred plant remains resulting from human activities rather than the infilling of structures after their abandonment by secondary deposition of rubbish from elsewhere on the site. This example illustrates a problem of equifinality faced by those who interpret plant assemblages in which both human activities and the sedimentary processes on habitation sites affect the composition and location of assemblages. Kajale's report (1988b) also includes the first mention of cereal chaff in a South Asian archaeobotanical report, although it was absent from his samples. He takes its absence to suggest that crop-processing was not carried out in the excavated areas, but perhaps 'off-site' away from the habitation area, although such a claim is also marred by the confounding affects of preservation since chaff is less easily preserved than grains, assuming both regularly come into contact with fire in the first place.

Increasingly, a number of reports have at least discussed briefly the possibility that weed seeds represent the by-products of harvest and processing (e.g. Lone et al. 1993;

Saraswat et al. 1994; see also, Ratanagar 1989). Nevertheless, the insights of archaeobotanical taphonomy have been slow to enter most archaeobotanical discussions in South Asia and a 'utilization falacy' continues. While Weber (1991) took notice of finding comparable contexts, he did not seriously consider the role of crop-processing or the potential contribution of dung-burning. The failure to consider these avenues of seed preservation probably derived from his American archaeobotanical background, as there was generally a lag in American archaeobotany in taking into account crop-processing (Hastorf 1988). Instead, American archaeobotany remained largely under the influence of a utilization fallacy in which most, if not all, recovered species were interpreted in terms of ethnographically documented uses and in terms of the vegetation surrounding a site in the past (e.g. Minnis 1981). Similar assumptions were also already established in Indian archaeobotany (e.g. Vishnu-Mittre and Savithri 1982; Vishnu-Mittre 1985).

In the past decade, the importance of crop-processing has become more widely recognized, and ethnoarchaeological studies of additional crop species have been undertaken. Thompson (1996) has discussed the variations in the processing of rice in Thailand, which includes many general processes relevant to the understanding of rice assemblages in other parts of the world. Within South Asia, the study of the millet processing sequences has been undertaken, by Reddy (1991a, 1994, 1997) in Andhra Pradesh and in Nepal by Lundstrom-Baudais (in press). In addition, Ruth Young (1998) has studied the processing of finger millet in Uganda. Even though it must be accepted that there is a range of potential cultural variations in these operations, many of the basic products and by-products of the processing stages are constrained by the morphology of the crop involved, thus studies in one part of the world can often be transferred to the same or a closely related species in another region (Hillman 1984). Detailed studies of pulse processing are largely lacking, although Butler (1992) supplied a basic framework for considering the cropping, harvesting and processing of traditional pulses in Turkey; in general the processing of pulses can be compared to that of free-threshing wheats.

There remain numerous directions for experimental and ethnoarchaeological research still to pursue to better understand archaeobotanical formation processes. First there are numerous crop types which have not been adequately studied in terms of processing sequences, notably pulses and oil seeds. Another important area for future consideration is the filtering effect of fire and how this may vary in different societies on the basis of customs relating to fire use and hearth-cleaning. The plant remains most often recovered archaeologically are those which have been charred. Thus rather than reflecting ancient plant use on site, the recovered remains represent only a fraction of those 'adventitiously scorched portion' (Saraswat et al. 1994: 256). Thus while the presence of plant remains in a particular soil sample is likely to be more a reflection of charring 'accidents' (Minnis 1981), how particular species repeatedly are subject to such accidents remains poorly understood. At issue is whether we see the archaeobotanical record as the accumulation of a large number of small accidents, which is perhaps more likely in general, or as the dispersal of the products of a few 'accidents' of a larger scale, such as the burning of a large quantity of by-products immediately after large scale threshing and winnowing (this latter case must be assumed in producer/consumer models).

3.1 APPLYING THE INSIGHTS OF CROP-PROCESSING: WEEDS, ARABLE ECOLOGY AND HUMAN ECONOMY

While most archaeobotanical discussion focuses on known food plants, especially crops, there are usually other plant species present in samples, and these are gaining increasing importance as sources of information on the past cultural behaviours. Traditionally, all seeds found on archaeological sites were assumed to represent either human resource use or 'natural' seed rain during occupation (e.g. Minnis 1981; Weber 1991: 16-19). However, considerations of taphonomy (see Section 2.3, above) suggest that most charred plant remains are likely to have originated in arable fields and are likely to have come onto site and into contact with fire through the repetitive activities of crop-processing and food preparation. Indeed, observations that most samples contain crops, often crop chaff, and other herbaceous species that are known to occur as weeds in fields today, led to the reasoning that the weed species could provide insights into the ecology of arable fields (e.g. Knorzer 1971; M. Jones 1988a, 1988b; Hillman 1991; Behre and Jacomet 1991). Thus, in addition to using the weed types present in a sample to understand the stages of crop-processing waste represented by samples (Hillman 1981, 1984; G. Jones 1984, 1987; Reddy 1994, 1997; Thompson 1996), they have come to be considered as data for understanding ecological aspects of agriculture such as soil choice, tillage practices, weeding practices, and irrigation (e.g. Wasylikowa 1981; Hillman 1984, 1991; M. Jones 1988a, 1988b; Behre and Jacomet 1991; G. Jones 1992; G. Jones and Halstead 1995; G. Jones et al. 1995; van der Veen 1992).

Although Weber (1991: 134) recognized that 'weed species are important for our understanding of sowing and harvesting practices and soil fertility patterns', he did not apply this principle in his interpretation of the Rojdi data. Instead he interpreted most of his weedy taxa in terms of 'disturbance in and around a site'. Thus the increase in the number of weed species, and the overall density of weed seeds were taken as indicating increased land disturbance around site due perhaps to deforestation or other human impacts. Unfortunately, such a claim cannot be made from archaeobotanical samples if it is accepted that almost all of the charred seeds represent the incidental inclusions in harvested crops that get separated during crop processing. The changes seem more likely to represent changes either in cultivation practices or else a change in the harvesting/processing regime.

Weed seed assemblages can also provide insight into aspects of social oragnization, as it relates to crop-processing and storage. Several authors have suggested that it may be possible to distinguish sites with local cultivation, 'producer' sites, from sites which received their crops partially processed from elsewhere, 'consumer' sites, although there are serious problems with applying such models. Reddy's ethnoarchaeological models were applied in the analysis of archaeobotanical assemblages from two Late/Post-Harappan sites in Gujarat, Oriyo Timbo and Babor Kot, and she interpreted the lack of most predicted by-products from Oriyo Timbo as evidence that cultivation and preliminary processing were not carried out at this site (Reddy 1994, 1997). Similarly, Thompson (1996) has suggested the rice 'producer' and 'consumer' sites can be distinguished on the basis of archaeobotanical components. Both of these authors base their approach on suggestions by Hillman (1981, 1984), that early processing stage remains should occur on producer sites. Such results are of interest although caution is warranted as there is significant disagreement within European archaeobotany as to whether the composition of by-products in wheat/barley assemblages can be used for distinguishing producer/consumer sites and if so how (M. Jones 1985; van der Veen 1992: 91-9; Stevens 1996). This issue hinges on how one assumes most plant remains came into contact with fire, whether as a result of the burning of processing by-products after the large-scale threshing and winnowing that follows harvest (implicitly assumed in producer consumer models, cf. Hillman 1981, 1984; M. Jones 1985; van der Veen 1992; Reddy 1997), or whether the repeated small-scale processing of crops taken from storage for daily consumption is a more likely route (shown to be the most likely situation for wheat/barley assemblages in prehistoric Britain by Stevens 1996). The difficulty, therefore in interpreting the lack of early processing stages as evidence of consumption without local cultivation, as Reddy (1994, 1997) argues to be the case for Oriyo Timbo, is that it ignores the possibility that cultivating, threshing and winnowing were carried out near but away from the central habitation area and that the products were not burnt. A more general concern with trying to apply a producer/comsumer model to archaeobotanical evidence is whether it is actually realistic to expect village sites where no cultivation and crop-processing was carried out; the ethnographic situation in South Asian villages today suggests that all villages are involved in some amount of food production (Dilip Chakrabarti: personal communication). In the case of Oriyo Timbo, where evidence from cattle teeth suggests repeated, short seasonal occupations (Rissman 1986), it indeed seems likely that cultivation was not practiced locally, but this cannot unambiguously be argued from the archaeobotanical evidence. It is plausible that the population of this site was attached to another more permanent settlement where they were involved in cultivation activities.

Confounding factors that operate against the preservation of all by-products of all stages of the processing sequence. If it is assumed that most seed charring occurs as the result of daily processing of semi-clean stored crops, an attractive assumption since repetitive activities are more likely to produce constant archaeological remains distributed through a site, then the differences in processing stages represented by assemblages may have more to do with decisions about how much processing to do before storage of the crop, which in turn relates to scale of social organization for crop processing (Stevens 1996). If we take this perspective to the material from Rodji (Weber 1991: 135-8), then the change noted to have occurred between Rojdi B and Rojdi C, might be seen as a result of a change in the organization rather than any significant change in the actual cereal cultivated or their relative importance in diet (further discussion in Fuller and Madella in Vol. II of this series). The analysis of non-crop seeds for ecological and social information is a rapidly developing area of archaeobotanical research in many parts of the world, and offers great potential for South Asian archaeology, as the work by Reddy (1994, 1997) demonstrates.

There is no easy formula for interpreting the composition of crop/weed assemblages, but rather a number of consistent factors which need to be thought through for each assemblage. Methods of harvesting, threshing, winnowing and sieving act to separate and group various plant parts, cereal grain, chaff and weed seeds. Only those weeds that are in seed at the time of harvest and are harvested enter the crop-processing filters. At this first filter the harvesting methods (uprooting, sickle reaping at mid-stalk or of individual cereal ears) interact with the growth habit of the weeds (and their seasonality in terms of fruiting) to determine which are harvested (Hillman 1984; Reddy 1994, 1997). Since different crop types are harvested differently, for example *Sorghum*, *Pennisetum* and *ragi* (*Eleusine coracana*) are often harvested by removing individual heads, whereas smaller millets with thinner stalks are gathered in groups and cut near their base (Reddy 1994, 1997), these different crops can be expected to bias weed assemblages in different ways. Another important factor, noted by Reddy (1994, 1997), is whether or not millets are free-threshing, as the case with *Sorghum*, *Pennisetum* and *Eleusine*, or retain an indurate lemma and palea that must be pounded and winnowed off, as in *Panicum*, *Setaria*, *Echinochloa* and *Paspalum*. These latter species therefore will always see more processing and may therefore have a greater likelihood of entering by-product assemblages. In addition, these hulled millets are sometimes parched with fire (or sun-dried) to aid the removal of the lemma/palea (Reddy 1994, 1997; Laundstrom-Baudais et al. in press); this provides another possible route to charring. The range of factors affecting pulse crops, which are also pounded and winnowed and can be harvested either by uprooting or picking individual pods, has yet to be considered seriously.

3.2 ARCHAEOBOTANICAL QUANTIFICATION

Another aspect of archaeobotanical analysis which has been discussed in the past decade is quantification. With the larger assemblages brought about by flotation it becomes necessary to summarize the data numerically in some way. In addition, with an awareness that archaeobotanical remains are not a straightforward reflection of human diet or activities, choosing ways to quantify one's evidence requires making assumptions about the relative significance of different factors in the formation of archaeological assemblages. Issues in quantification revolve around two problems: first, how do we compare the relative importance of different taxa present within a sample; and second, how do we compare the overall contents of different samples. Weber (1991, 1993) addressed the first of these concerns by comparing three common methods for quantifying abundance of archaeobotanical remains: density, percentage, and ubiquity. In general he found that each of the three measures tended to agree in the identification of the few most dominant species at the site of Rojdi, which were *Setaria*, '*Eleusine*' (there is reason for concern over this identification, see Section 4.2), *Panicum sumatrense* (syn. *P. miliare*) and *Chenopdium album*. Density standardizes the number or volume of a taxon in a sample against the total volume of samples (usually of the total sampled sediment, but it could also be against the total charcoal or 'light fraction'), while 'percentage' calculates what percentage of the identified specimens in a sample belong to a given taxon. A potential problem with both of these approaches is that they do not take into account biases related to a particular taxon, such as seed productivity which can vary greatly between species. Those taxa which produce more seeds, or are more likely to produce waste seeds during processing, will be consistently over-represented. Thus it is generally accepted that relative frequencies alone do not lead directly to conclusions about changing plant use in the past (Pearsall 1983; Popper 1988).

A useful alternative to assessing dominance is ubiquity analysis, the third approach employed by Weber (1991, 1993). This approach has been promoted by Hubbard (1975, 1980) as 'presence analysis', in which taxa are scored on the basis of percentage of the total number of samples in which they occur (also Popper 1988; Pearsall 1989: 212-17). There are different scales at which this approach can be applied, such as comparing contexts within a site or sites with a region. This approach may, however, over-emphasize taxa that only occur in samples as rare elements. For particular questions it may then be useful to compare particular taxa through the use of ratios which might highlight trends in the changing relative quantities of particular taxa of interest (Miller 1988; Pearsall 1989: 197-210). Others have utilized various indices, such as species diversity (Pearsall 1983, 1989: 211; Popper 1988; Lone et al. 1993). In general, there is no one correct way to quantify archaeobotanical data. This argues for the full reporting of raw counts so calculations are open to others. Presentation of reasoning for the choice of a particular quantification method should be provided.

Statistical analyses of archaeobotanical data remain contentious amongst archaeobotanists, especially as to whether the data require or preclude complex statistical approaches. Discriminant and multivariate statistical approaches have been increasingly applied to European archaeobotanical assemblages in recent years (e.g. G. Jones 1984, 1987, 1991, 1992; G. Jones et al. 1995; van der Veen 1992, 1995; also Pearsall 1989: 217-21), and this approach appears to be useful for grouping and separating assemblages on the basis of the presence, absence and co-occurrence of taxa. Such groupings have in some cases been interpreted as representing different stages in crop-processing or differences in arable ecology, due to soil types, irrigation or mixed cropping (G. Jones 1987, 1992; G. Jones and Halstead 1992; G. Jones et al. 1995; van der Veen 1992). While these techniques may be useful for highlighting groupings of samples, it remains necessary to understand the basic differences between these groups, such as in the presence or absence of particular taxa, in order to interpret the meaning of statistical groups. However, given the whole range of uncontrollable taphonomic factors that affect assemblage composition, it has been argued that such statistical approaches may be futile and even misleading (Hubbard and Clapham 1992). As Pearsall (1989: 196) recommends: 'do not use approaches that require more rigor than the data are capable of sustaining'.

In general it is accepted that analysis should begin with simple form of quantification such as relative frequencies, ubiquity or ratios. Hubbard and Clapham (1992) advocate the use of simple quantification methods, such as ubiquity, taxa diversity and indices based on ratios, such as their 'rubbish index' that compares the ratio of crop to non-crop species, or ecological indices such as woodland-non-woodland, wetland-non-wetland, etc. The potential of exploring archaeobotanical data through the use of ratios between key taxa or groups of taxa has been discussed by Miller (1988) and Pearsall (1989). In South Asian archaeobotany quantified reports are still few and most that are quantified have relied on basic comparisons of relative proportions (e.g. Kajale 1988b; Weber 1991; Lone et al. 1993, Reddy 1994). These can be problematic to interpret, however. Kajale (1988b: 792) suggested that greater quantities and relative frequencies of most crop types recovered from levels of the Early Jorwe phase indicated a 'richer' plant economy than earlier or later phases. Such an assumption, however, is problemtaic since the difference could be due to changes in taphonomic factors, such as the organization and scheduling of processing (see comments of Ratnagar 1989). Kajale (1988b) is probably right, however, that the marked increase in overall density of plant remains and charred coprolites resulted from some form of intensification.

Lone et al. (1993) attempted to move beyond simple frequency comparisons by also using measures of species diversity and richness in samples. These measures were then tested as to their 'randomness' or 'non-randomness' in order to highlight the taxa which showed chronological patterns. Employing these measures they found relatively little change and it is not clear that such methods were entirely necessary. In addition, they calculated 'standard scores' which downplay absolute counts of taxa but highlight changes, in this case between phases, suggesting a decrease in barley quantities through time with a corresponding increase in rice (Lone et al. 1993: 233). One difficulty with diversity indices, is that there are a range of available methods for calculating 'diversity' not all of which are comparable or necessarily archaeologically meaningful; it is therefore necessary to be clear about the reasoning behind the use of a given index. Unfortunately quantitative approaches in Indian archaeobotany need to be more widely discussed and employed before significant comparisons between sites, regions and periods can be carried out. In the meantime, comparisons will continue to be based on presence/absence and ubiquity assessments.

3.3 RECONSTRUCTING SUBSISTENCE SYSTEMS: SEASONALITY AND RESOURCE CATCHMENT

In the past two decades increasing discussion has been devoted to moving from archaeobotanical evidence to reconstructing systems of agricultural organization, often in conjunction with other sources of evidence. Interest has focused to varying degrees on establishing the seasonality of cultivation activities, the integration of plant-based activities (cultivation and collecting) and animal husbandry, and the extent of the catchment from which sites procured their resources, whether entirely locally (and if so, from how large an area) or whether some form of exchange and movement of resources between sites and regions was in operation. The development of these interests should be seen in the context of a larger shift in archaeological interest towards ecological and economic questions, often associated with the development of processual archaeology, and the increasing interdisciplinary nature of archaeological excavations (see Fuller and Boivin in Vol. IV of this series).

The important contrast between the winter seasonality of crops of Southwest Asian origin and the summer/monsoon seasonality of many other crops of importance in the Indian subcontinent had already been noted by some archaeologists and botanists (e.g. Allchin and Allchin 1968; Fairservis 1971; Hutchinson 1976). More recently, considerations of cropping seasonality in agriculture have been produced by archaeobotanists on the basis of archaeobotanical finds (Costantini and Biasini 1985; Kajale 1988b; Weber 1991, 1997; Saraswat et al. 1994: 321; Reddy 1994; also Thomas 1983b). At Harappa preliminary analysis suggests shift from exclusively winter cultivation to two cropping seasons during the Late Harappan period, *c.* 2200 BC (Weber 1997; see also Meadow 1989, 1996; Franke-Vogt 1995: 32-4; Fuller and Madella in Vol. II of this series).

The importance of *kharif* (summer) cultivation for the establishment of permanent settlements in monsoonal India (i.e. east of the Indus region) has emerged as an issue of particular interest. Possehl attributed the proliferation of sites in Gujarat in the Late Harappan period at the end of the third millennium BC (1980: 8-9, 54) to the availability of summer cultivated (*kharif*) millets, especially those originating in Africa. The importance of *kharif* millet crops in this region has been confirmed by subsequent systematic archaeobotany (Vishnu-Mittre 1990; Weber 1991; Reddy 1994, 1997; Dhavalikar 1995), although most of these are not African in origin (see Section 5.7.2-3). Possehl (1986, 1997: 93) later suggested that African millets paved the way for agricultural development in west-central India in the second millennium BC. However, growing evidence suggests that indigenous summer millets were first (Weber 1998; Fuller et al. n.d.), and also that indigenous summer pulses were important (see Table 8 and Section 5.1). The evidence from Inamgaon (Kajale 1988b) and other Chalcolithic sites from west-central India, points to two cropping seasons, i.e. a synthesis of the monsoonal cropping based on crops of South Asian and African origin and winter crops originating in Southwest Asia. Understanding the relative contribution of these two seasons, the nature of differences between them in terms of irrigation, tillage and crop rotation all remain issues to explore in future research.

One region of India where attempts have been made to model the susbsistence strategy is Maharashtra during the Chalcolithic period. There had already been attempts to estimate populations and the amount of land that would have had to be cultivated to feed them, such as the model of subsistence system of Inamgaon devised by Dhavalikar and Possehl (1974). This model was, however, based on logical deduction from a series of assumptions, rather than trying to develop an understanding of subsistence from an extensive database of bio-archaeological evidence (for an insightful critique of this model and its subsequent incarnations see Ratnagar 1989). Subsequently, once there was a large archaeobotanical data base from Inamgaon and a reconstruction of its subsistence scheduling (Kajale 1988a), Shinde (1987) produced a reconstruction of the Deccan Chalcolithic cultivation system by combing the regional settlement pattern, tillage potential of the soil, based on modern ethnographic analogy, and preserved digging implements, as well as evidence for storage systems and possibly canal irrigation. The latter was perhaps necessary for intensive cultivation of winter crops like wheat, barley, peas and lentils (Kajale 1988a: 308).

Models of the subsistence system of past sites or regions that model the flow of resources between the human community, crops, livestock, and the surrounding environment have been produced for the north-western part of the subcontinent, and as yet few other areas. Working from checklists of find types, including botanical species, Jarrige and Tosi (1981) attempted to reconstruct the spatial areas around the site, whether local or distant, from which plant resources were procured. Thomas (1983a, 1983b) produced a theoretcial model of the subsistence system of the Bannu Basin (Northwest Frontier Province, Pakistan) in the third millennium BC in conjunction with excavations at the sites of Tarakai Qila. Initially, Thomas (1983a) focused on the site of Tarakai Qila and the resources available in its local catchment. He then produced models of different possible ways of obtaining the subsistence base, and its relation to the units of production and consumption, subsequently applied by Weber (1991: 113-16) to the Rojdi data. Thomas (1983b) argued for a 'subsistence economy' in which the village was essentially self-sufficient (i.e. the unit of production was the same as the unit of consumption and the exploited territory was local). This interpretation was based in part on assumptions drawn from producer/consumer interpretations of archaeobotanical assemblages (discussed earlier in Section 2.3), since evidence was found for threshing by-products. Thomas then modelled the flows of energy and products in the entire annual cycle of cultivation and herding. A similar model was produced for Rojdi by Weber (1991). This kind of model was taken a step further by Reddy (1994) who attempted to predict which products and by-products from an agro-pastoral economy might be preserved and recovered archaeologically. Non-equilibrium models, which emphasize historical contingencies and dynamic changes, have become increasingly important in ecology, and challenge us to move beyond the straightforward homeostatic systems that have generally been used to model agricultural systems (Thomas 1989; Blumler 1996; Harris 1996b). In general, more work needs to be put into integrating archaeobotanical evidence with both taphonomic models and models of agricultural systems.

4. PROBLEMS AND DEVELOPMENTS IN IDENTIFICATION

More explicit discussion of identification criteria is immediately needed, especially of seeds. While wood identifications from the earliest reports of Chowdhury and Ghosh were thoroughly documented, with anatomical descriptions, drawings and photographs, seed identifications have not always been as completely reported nor as reliable. Although photographs were often published, they often have failed to convey adequate detail for all seed types, and it has been recommended by some archaeobotanists that drawings provide more reliable reproductions of the criteria relied upon in determinations (Goddard and Nesbitt 1997). Misidentifications have been reported in several instances when specialist examination was not yet complete (see comments of Kajale 1989c: 93), such as the rice reported from Harappan Kalibangan (Sarma 1972; Vishnu-Mittre 1974; unfortunately repeated by Conningham 1995: 67), which further examination revealed to be wheat (Vishnu-Mittre and Savithri 1975). Unlike modern botanical data, where specimens consist of selected pieces of more or less whole plants, selected by the botanist for their information potential, archaeological plant remains are fragments which have survived processes of decay and destruction that have no regard for research questions. Thus systematic characters of plants used by modern taxonomists or agronomic botanists may be of little or no use to the archaeobotanist who is forced to work with whatever plant characteristics are present in the archaeological samples (see Hather 1994d). In order better to recognize certain species, studies of comparative material relevant to what is preserved archaeologically are needed. A few have already appeared in India, such as those by Vishnu-Mittre and Savithri of *Setaria* (1978), *Eleusine indica* and *E. coracana* (Vishnu-Mittre and Savithri 1979b; but see critique of this *Eleusine* study, below), and various forms of wheat (1982; but see reservations below). Subsequently scanning electron microscope (SEM) images were employed to aid identification, especially by revealing epidermal cell patterns when these are preserved (e.g. Korber-Grohne 1981 in Europe; Lone et al. 1993 in India), or wood anatomy (Buth and Bisht 1981). These studies represent the increasing care that was taken with documenting identification procedures from the mid-late 1970s onwards. Nevertheless, there remain some problem areas in archaeobotanical identification which have not received as much attention as they deserve, and will therefore be briefly reviewed here.

Seed measurements often are reported as supporting evidence in identifications (e.g. Vishnu-Mittre 1961; Vishnu-Mittre and Savithri 1982; Kajale 1984, 1988b; Saraswat 1986, 1993). Measurements, and size ratios offer a useful way of comparing both specimens and assemblages. Nevertheless, measurements alone are ambiguous and problematic. As population biology makes clear, contemporary populations include a range of variation in size and form. An individual measured specimen presents an interpretative ambiguity, at best excluding some categories with high probability, as it cannot be determined where the measured individual would fall within the frequency distribution of a past population (Hubbard 1992). Measurements of specimens can only be meaningful when analysed as statistical variation in a population. Fresh seed size and shape may also be affected by various environmental conditions including soil, weather, and disease (Hubbard 1976). More significant still are the effects of charring: seed sizes and shapes change temperatures and durations of heating (Hopf 1955; Hubbard 1976; Boardman and Jones 1990; Lone et al. 1993; Saraswat et al. 1994: 257). Charring ('carbonization') tends to decrease the size of seeds but differentially affects length, width and breadth such that seeds tend towards more spherical forms. This raises particular concerns for the differentiation of some species groups on the basis of length-breadth ratios, such as the Indian *Vigna* pulses (*mung* and *udid*), or kinds of wheat (*Triticum sphaerococcum* as opposed to *T. aestivum* and *T. compactum*). Unfortunately, few experimental carbonization studies have been carried out for most of the crops represented in India, the exception being experiments reported by Lone et al. (1993). However, reported experiments done with other regions in mind can serve as useful guides, since a range of taxa have been charred including, wheat and barley (e.g. Hopf 1955; Jacomet 1987; Boardman and Jones 1990), south-west Asian pulses (Kislev and Rosenzwig 1993), and a selection of Sudanese 'millets' (Magid 1989). Wilson (1984) has explored the effects of charring on the differential representation of taxa in samples due to the tendency of some species to be destroyed more easily by charring. Despite the important implications of these studies for understanding the formation of archaeobotanical assemblages, they have yet to be satisfactorily taken into account when identification is carried out. For example, Lone et al. (1993) describe and illustrate the seeds of weed species in Kashmir including characters such as colour and minute bristles which will not survive charring and are not of use in archaeobotanical identification (except in rare cases of waterlogging or desiccation). In addition they have not taken into account their own charring experiments in the attribution of archaeobotanical rice to varietal level taxa. Problematic for similar reasons are attempts to separate archaeological rice into *indica* or *japonica* varieties such as have been reported from Chinese material (e.g. Oka 1988: Fig. 6.3; Wenming 1991; Chen and Jiang 1997) and from Navdatoli (Vishnu-Mittre 1961) and Swat (Costantini 1987). Such attributions must be considered highly suspect until more reliable charring experiments and morphometric studies are available (Crawford 1992; Glover and Higham 1996). Fruitful discussion regarding how best to approach identification of the rice remains from sites in south/central China is now developing (e.g. Crawford and Shen 1998; Anping 1998), and similar considerations need to be undertaken amongst archaeobotanists working in India.

Beyond the technicalities of identification, there are also theoretical issues about specific identification. There is a danger of imposing the modern situation in terms of species distribution and taxonomy onto the past. As summarized by Hather (1994d: 3):

> The problem for archaeology is that plant remains are often named with reference to, and with influence from, phylogenetic relationships of the *present-day* evolutionary timeplane. The term 'species' should only be used to define a static form of a plant (which itself varies) in a single timeplane (most often the present). If we name an archaeological plant, we are giving a name to a plant of the past, not of the present. If the name is at the species level, and it is the same as the name of an extant plant, we are making a very important statement about the plant's evolution.

While attribution to a modern morphological species is still generally a goal of archaeobotanical research, the presence in the past of extinct varieties or species is likely (Hillman et al. 1996). A few problematic groups of taxa are discussed in the sections that follow.

4.1 WHEAT IDENTIFICATION

One taxon in particular that requires careful archaeobotanical revision is wheat, and a brief review of the difficulties of wheat identification is in order as this has not yet been incorporated into many archaeobotanical studies in South Asia. Table 4 provides a summary of wheat taxonomy, and Figure 1 illustrates general and specific morphological features referred to in this discussion. Systematic considerations of wheat identification in South Asia (e.g. Vishnu-Mittre 1974; Vishnu-Mittre and Savithri 1982; Vishnu-Mittre et al. 1986a; Chowdhury et al. 1977; Lone et al. 1993) must be reconsidered. The re-examination of material from the sites of Harappa, Mohenjo Daro and Chanhu Daro provides a wealth of measurements of modern and archaeological wheat grain dimensions, especially as expressed in length-width ratios (Vishnu-Mittre and Savithri 1982), but raises two important problems. First, the range of wheat types that are considered is limited and therefore assumes which wheat types may or may not have been present in the Indian subcontinent in prehistory. For example, they include only hexaploid forms of free-threshing types (*Tritucm aestivum*, sensu lato). Free-threshing tetraploid wheat, such as the modern *T. durum* Desf. (macoroni wheat or hard wheat) is not even discussed. This is particularly distressing, since *T. durum* constitutes one of most important forms of wheat in parts of India today, notably in Rajasthan, Gujarat, Uttar Pradesh, Madhya Pradesh, Maharashtra and Karnataka (Pal 1966). Furthermore, it is now clear that free-threshing tetraploid wheats played an important role throughout prehistoric Europe and the Near East and probably developed and diffused before hexaploid types (van Zeist 1976; Kislev 1984a, 1984b; Zohary and Hopf 1993: 46; Maier 1996). Second, a comparison of the ratios of different wheat types given by Vishnu-Mittre (1974; Vishnu-Mittre and Savithri 1982; Vishnu-Mittre et al. 1986; Saraswat 1986) with those reported in an extensive compilation of similar measurements from Europe (Jacomet 1987) indicates discrepancies between South Asia and Europe in the metrical characters of the *same* wheat types. Thus the ratios considered adequate to characterize Indian *T. sphaerococcum* are similar to those which were traditionally used for European *T. compactum*. The *T. sphaerococcum* length:breadth ratio advocated by Vishnu-Mittre and Savithri (1982; also Saraswat 1986) would be considered *T. aestivum* or *T. compactum* in traditional European archaeobotany. Standard measurements of archaeological '*T. sphaerococcum*' in the literature easily fall within the range of the free-threshing types documented at extensively sampled sites where there is no suggestion of sphaerococcoid grains, such as Shortugai in Afghanistan (Willcox 1991) and Inamgaon, Maharashtra (Kajale 1988b). However, a more serious problem with this older work is the now established fact that tetraploid and hexaploid free-threshing wheats cannot be distinguished on the basis of grains at all, but rather that distinctions must rely on careful examination of preserved rachis segments (Kislev 1984a; Miller 1992; Zohary and Hopf 1993; Maier 1996; Hillman et al. 1996; Schlumbaum et al. 1998b). As noted by Maier (1996) there is a wide range in the size and shape of a caryopsis of wheat depending on the position of the grain and the number of other grains developing within a spikelet (Fig. 1A). As amply demonstrated by the study of the wheats from Shortugai, Afghanistan (Willcox 1991), free-threshing wheat can take on a wide range of morphological and metrical variation, and the best approach is to try to summarize the variation in the ancient material without trying to impose modern categories, which are themselves often poorly defined in metrical terms. These realizations have profound implications for our understanding of the history of Indian wheats, especially as the tendency with archaeobotanical material from South Asia has been to identify *T. sphaerococcum* more or less everywhere. This attribution seems more likely a product of the fortuitous effects of charring than an actual historical dominance of short wheat.

The best way to approach identifications of wheat is through the examination of 'chaff,'

TABLE 4. TAXONOMY OF *TRITICUM* (WHEAT) (after Zohary and Hopf 1993)

Biological species	Traditional binomial	Ploidy	Common name (glume status)
T. monococcum L.	*T. monococcum* L.	2x (A)	einkorn wheat (glume)
	T. boeticum Boiss. emend. Scheim	2x (A)	wild einkorn (glume)
	T. urartu Tuman.	2x (A)	wild einkorn (glume)
T. turgidum L.	*T. dicoccoides* (Körn.) Aarons.	4x (AB)	wild emmer (glume)
(sensu lato)	**T. dicoccum* Schübl.	4x (AB)	cultivated emmer (glume)
	**T. durum* Desf.	4x (AB)	macaroni wheat (naked)
	T. turgidum L.	4x (AB)	rivet wheat (naked)
	T. polonicum L.	4x (AB)	Polish wheat (naked)
	T. carthlicum Nevski	4x (AB)	persian wheat (naked)
T. araraticum Jakubz.	*T. timopheevi* Zhuk.	4x (AG)	Timopheev's wheat (glume)
T. aestivum L.	*T. spelta* L.	6x (ABD)	spelt (glume)
(sensu lato)	*T. macha* Dekr. and Men.	6x (ABD)	(glume, compact)
	T. vavilovii Tuman.	6x (ABD)	Vavliov's wheat (glume)
	**T. aestivum* (=*T. vulgare* Host.)	6x (ABD)	bread wheat (naked)
	T. compactum Host.	6x (ABD)	club wheat (naked, compact)
	**T. sphaerococcum* Perc.	6x (ABD)	shot wheat (naked, dense)

NOTE: *Wheat types grown in India/Pakistan in recent times (see Pal 1966).

which has almost never been reported nor discussed in South Asian archaeobotany (Fig. 1B-D, with rice and barley shown for comparison). In hulled wheats, the diagnostic element is the spikelet fork in which a rachis segment (or glume forklet) disarticulates cleanly, and it includes a rachis segment with an articulation scar where the next segment would attach), and the basal portions of the glumes on either side of the articulation scar (see Hubbarb 1992; Zohary and Hopf 1993; Nesbitt and Samuel 1996). In free-threshing wheat, rachis segments, sometimes preserved in articulated groups or broken apart (not disarticulating), provide the reliable characters for identification (J. Renfrew 1973; Kislev 1984a; Jacomet 1987; Hubbard 1992; Maier 1996; Hillman et al. 1996). Free-threshing rachis segments will be described as viewed on the abaxial surface. Tetraploid free-threshing wheat (*T. durum*) has swollen glume bases, and the sides of the rachis internode below them are generally more or less straight and converging downwards, the internode often has visible venation, like fine striations (Fig. 1D). Hexaploid free-threshing wheats (*T. aestivum* sensu lato) lack the bulging glume bases and the rachis internode is sometimes (but not always) constricted below the glume bases (Fig. 1B-C). Usually a pronounced vein runs parallel to each side of the internode (Fig. 1B). Free-threshing hexaploids vary widely in terms of how long the internodes are and how much they are constricted. It can be difficult to tell dense-eared *T. aestivum* from *T. compactum* (Willcox 1991; Miller 1992; Hillman et al. 1996). The particular characters that might distinguish *T. sphaerococcum* have yet to be pursued rigorously. Another approach to distinguishing wheat to ploidy level that may be employed in some future studies is through the extraction

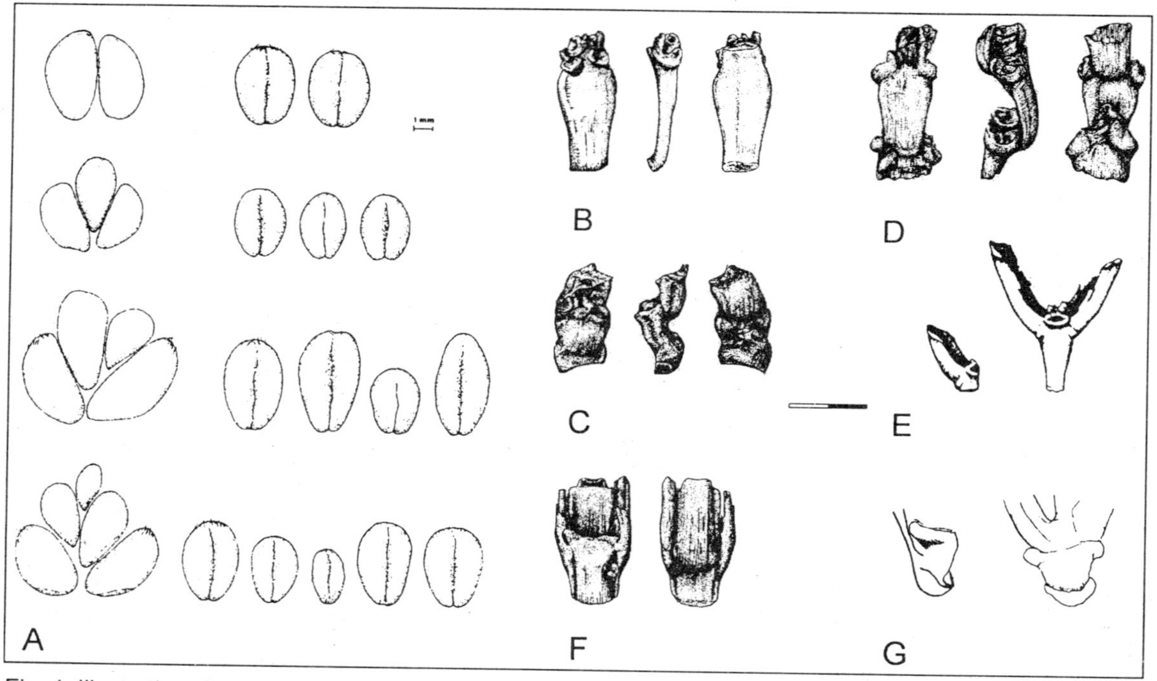

Fig. 1. Illustration showing the problem with attempting to identify wheat species on the basis of grain shape, and useful chaff criteria for identifying the ploidy level of free-threshing wheats, with hulled water, barley and rice chaff for comparison. A. Different grain shapes produced by spikelets with 2, 3, 4, or 5 fertilized florets (after Maier 1996). Note small, roundish grains that could be mistaken *for T. sphaerococcum*. B. Archaeological Free-threshing, loose-eared hexaploid wheat rachis segments (after Goddard and Nesbitt 1997). C. Archaeological, free-threshing, dense-eared hexaploid wheat rachis segment (after Goddard and Nesbitt 1997). D. Free-threshing, tetraploid wheat rachis segment (after Goddard and Nesbitt 1997). E. Typical chaff fragments from hulled wheat, glume base on left, complete spikelet fork on right (after Nesbitt and Samuel 1996). F. Archaeological barley rachis segments (after Goddard and Nesbitt 1997). G. Author's sketch of rice glume base.

of ancient DNA (Sallares et al. 1995; Schlumbaum et al. 1998b), poor DNA preservation in most archaeological samples will probably keep this from becoming a routine technique (see Section 6.5).

Accurately distinguishing these wheat varieties is of interest for both botanical and anthropological reasons. First, it is necessary if the different histories of these wheat species and their evolution is to be understood. Second, species level wheat identification could provide some insights into agricultural ecology, since different species have general ecological tendencies. For example, *T. durum* is generally more drought resistant and has greater disease resistance, which has contributed to its importance in much of central India (Percival 1921; Pal 1966; Zohary and Hopf 1993). However, imposing modern ecological preferences onto ancient remains is problemtic due to the possibility of extinct varieties with different tolerance in the past (T. Miller 1992). In addition, the hulled and the free-threshing varieties would have required different amounts of processing and may have different potential in terms of storage duration or susceptibility to damage during storage. However, within any of the traditional wheat species there is a wide range of variation, with different varieties possessing different characteristics in terms of agricultural and food traits. Unfortunately, most of this variation will remain invisible from traditional archaeobotanical remains.

4.2 MILLETS HULLED AND DE-HULLED: CASES OF MISTAKEN IDENTITY?

Millet identification remains a particular problem. This is due in part to a failure to recognize the differences between charred and fresh material and insufficient comparative collections of millets and related wild species. The purpose of this section is not to provide a comprehensive guide to millet identification but to draw attention to problematic reports. Some identifications require revisions, others may be right, but most lack sufficient documentation in publication for specialists to judge for themselves. There is need for discussion amongst archaeobotanists, and careful documentation, to establish reliable and replicable criteria for distinguishing millets, and not just those species which are most often cultivated today but a whole range of species which could have been utilized in antiquity. (For some preliminary criteria see Fuller et al. n.d.)

'Millets' include a wide range of small-seeded, edible grasses. Most studies take into account the potential presence of perhaps half a dozen millets, including the three African millets (*Eleusine coracana, Pennisetum glaucum, Sorghum bicolor*), foxtail millet (*Setaria italica*), two species of *Panicum*, and *Paspalum scrobiculatum* (e.g. Vishnu-Mittre 1971; 1974, Lone et al. 1993). However, there are a number of additional species of 'millet' both cultivated and gathered wild in parts of India today which have rarely been taken into account when studying ancient material (see Table 5). It is possible therefore that some of these species have not been identified simply because we have not been looking for them. A more fundamental oversight, in many studies, inclduing those of Vishnu-Mittre, was a failure to take into account the effects of charring, which usually destroys the husk that surrounds the grain (i.e. the lemma and palea). While finger millet is free-threshing and easily loses its husk, the other small millets retain theirs and in normal preparation they must be pounded and winnowed to remove these husks. Vishnu-Mittre's (1971: 126) discussion of comparative material of other millets he considered when identifying the Hallur millets, including *Setaria italica*, *Panicum* spp. and *Paspalum scrobiculatum*, indicates that he examined them as hulled seeds. Since he did not take into consideration the form of the dehulled caryopses of these other genera, the attribution to *Eleusine* must have been due to a false process of elimination in which *Eleusine* was the only small, 'free-threshing' millet. Indeed, in cases where its identification criteria are clear, *Setaria* is identified only when it retains its lemma and palea and it raises the possibility that dehusked *Setaria* caryopses have been mis-identified.

Many of the published reports of finger millet need to be reconsidered, as several of them are clearly not *Eleusine.* The published photographs from Hallur (Vishnu-Mittre 1971), although inadequate for identification, are more suggestive of *Setaria* or *Echinochloa*, and a representative of the former genus has been found in quantity in

TABLE 5. 'MILLETS' UTILIZED IN INDIA IN RELATION TO GRASS TAXONOMY

subfamily Chloridoideae: Eragrostideae

[D] *Eleusine coracana* (L.) Gaertn., finger millet, ragi (H.)

subfamily Panicoideae: Paniceae

[W,D] *Brachiaria ramosa* (L.) Stapf. (syn. *Urochloa ramosa* (L.) Nguyen) browntop millet, *pedda-sama*

[W,D] *Digitaria cruiciata* (Ness) A. Camus var. [D] *esculenta* Bor, *raishan* (Khasi)

[W,D] *Echinochloa colona* (L.) Link ssp. [D] *frumentacea*, sawa millet, *sawank*[1]

[W] other *Echinochloa* species (known as 'famine foods'): *E. crusgalli, E. stagnina*

[D] *Panicum mihaceum* L., proso millet

[W,D] *Panicum sumatrense* Roth. (syn. *P. miliare* auct. pl.), little millet, *samai*[2]

[W] other *Panicum* species (known as 'famine foods'):

P. atrosanguineum, P. hippothrix, P. paludosum, P. trypheron, P. trugidum

[W] *Paspalidium flavidum* ('famine food')

[W,D] *Paspalum scrobiculatum* L., kodo millet

[D] *Pennisetum glaucum* (L.) R. Br. (syn. *P. americanum* Leeke; *P. typhoides* Rich.), *bajra*, pearl millet[3]

[W] *Pennisetum alopecurodies* ('famine food')

[D] *Setaria italica* (L.) Beauv., common foxtail millet

[W,D] *Setaria pumila* (Poir.) Roem and Schult. (syn. *S. glauca* auct. pl.), yellow foxtail millet, *korali*[4]

[W] *Setaria verticillata*, bristley foxtail; *Setaria intermedia* Roem and Schult. (syn. Setaria tomentosa (Roxbi) Kunth.)

[W] *Urochloa* spp. ('Famine food')

subfamily Panicoideae: Andropogoneae

[D] *Sorghum bicolor* sorghum, great millet, jowar

NOTE: Species preceded by [D], are those in which a domesticated form has developed, while those preceded by [W] are only known to be gathered from thewild and therefore likely to have undergone little/no genetic change due to human usage.

SOURCES: Rachie 1975; Vishnu-Mittre 1981b; 1985; Rehm and Espig 1991; De Wet 1992; Mehra 1997. Grass taxonomy follows that of Clayton and Renvoize 1982. For additional discussion of taxonomy and current, correct nomenclature see references in the following notes:

[1] Yabuno 1962; De Wet et al. 1983c; Hilu 1994.

[2] De Wet et al. 1983a.

[3] Clayton and Renvoize 1982: 672; De Wet 1995d.

[4] Claytonn 1979; Prasada Rao et al. 1987.

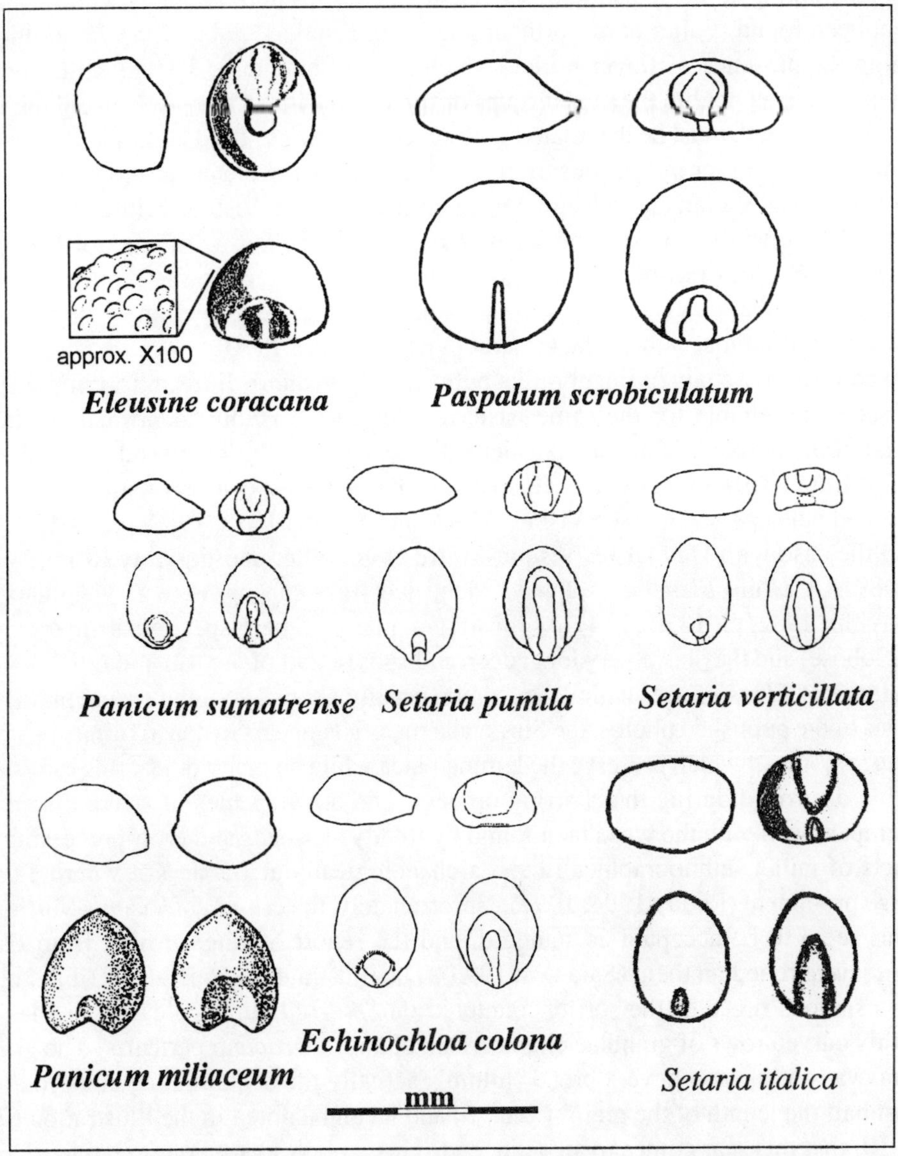

Fig. 2. Schematic drawings of selected small 'millets' showing some of the traits useful for differentiating genera and species. Millets are generally shown in dorsal view (lower right) which shows the size and shape of the embryo/scutellum, ventral view (lower left) which shows the hilum, in longitudinal section (upper left), and 'head on' (apical) looking towards the embryo (upper right). Note that *Eleusine coracana* has a minutely pusticulate surface, shown in schematic form in the inset box. Also in *Eleusine* the hilum is visible in the 'head on' view while the ventral surface is featureless or sometimes transversely furrowed.

recent resampling at the site and other contemporary sites in the regions while *Eleusine* has not been found (Fuller *et al.* forthcoming; also, Kajale 1989b, 1998). In addition to claiming the presence of finger millet (which is so often cited), Vishnu-Mittre argued that it co-occurred, within the same groups of spikelets, with a thinner, more oblong form which, he reasoned, must be the related wild species *E. indica*. The Hallur identifications, as well as the claim for indigenous origins of finger millet, were criticized by Hilu et al. (1979) as well as Harlan (see Vishnu-Mittre 1977: 575, n.1). Vishnu-Mittre and Savithri (1979b) subsequently revoked the identification of *E. indica*, which is not just more oblong than *E. coracana* but has a rugose rather than pusticulate surface (ornamented with small protuberances), although they maintained the identification of *E. coracana* and also identified it at Surkotada, Gujarat (Vishnu-Mittre 1990).

The comparative study of finger millet published by Vishnu-Mittre and Savithri (1979) itself seems unreliable for the same basic reasons as the Hallur identification. In the material from Surkotada, *Setaria* (considered likely to include *S. italica* and *S. verticillata*, Vishnu-Mittre 1990) is identified exclusively on the basis of specimens with intact rugose lemma and palea preserved (see Vishnu-Mittre and Savthri 1978, 1982, pl. 18.4, nos. 1-3; also the case with Daimabad, Vishnu-Mittre et al. 1986; and possibly Rojdi, Weber 1991: 89-90), while *Eleusine* is always identified from caryopses (e.g. Vishnu-Mittre and Savithri 1982, pl. 18.4, no. 4). As illustrated, many of these specimens are too ovate (non-globose) and they have very long, deep embryos (a trait of *Setaria* and *Echinochloa*) while those of *Eleusine* are shallow and short (usually about 1/3 of the grain length). On the basis of the published photos, the Surkotada material appears to consist almost entirely of *Setaria*, some of which preserve the lemma/palea while on many others this is missing, probably destroyed during the charring process. The other species recovered from this site compare well with the weed taxa found by Reddy as weeds and crop-processing by-products of millets ethnographically and archaeologically at Babar Kot where *Setaria* was also prominent (Reddy 1994, 1997). Unfortunately, the criteria of Vishnu-Mittre and Savithri seem to be accepted as standard, and the report of finger millet from Hulas seems to have relied on them (Saraswat 1993). The illustrated rugose 'testa' (ibid., pl. II, 12) has sinuous rugae of the sort encountered on *Setaria* lemma/palea rather than the smoothly curved rows of granulae characeristic of an *E. coracana* pericarp.[1] The grains, as Saraswat notes, each have a broad 'hilum' (actually the scutellum or embryo area), 'almost half the length of the grain' (ibid.: 6) and it can be noted in the illustration (ibid, pl. II, 10) that this scar comes to an acute end. This embryo is too long relative to grain length to be *Eleusine*, and is more probably *Setaria* seen in dorsal view; in addition, if it were *Eleusine*, viewed from the base, one would expect to see the small circular hilum, which occurs immediately below the scutellum in this genus, rather than on the ventral side (as in *Setaria* and other panicoid grasses).

Unfortunately, given the fact that most of the well-illustrated reports of finger millet/ragi in India appear to be mis-identified, one must be circumspect in relying on any of the other reports which are not accompanied by illustrations and may have accepted the approach of earlier workers. Thus compilations for early evidence of millets in South

Asia, as evidence for trade with Yemen/Africa (e.g. Possehl 1998, 1997), must be considered with caution until identification criteria are clarified. For millets photographs are unsatisfactory for illustrating identifications and drawings are probably best. These drawings need to include at least 3, and preferably 4 views of the caryopsis, including dorsal, lateral, apical, and perhaps ventral. Some exemplars, representing a range of small millets are illustrated in Figure 2.

4.2.1 Sorghum Identification: Some Reservations

It is also possible that some of the well-known reports of *Sorghum bicolor*, in South Asia as well as the Arabian peninsula, represent mis-attributions. Several of the prehistoric identifications of *Sorghum* in South Asia have been called into question (Willcox 1992; Rowley-Conwy et al. 1997; Fuller et al. forthcoming). Several of the best known, and most often quoted, examples are based on impressions in pottery, none of which has been convincingly demonstrated to be *Sorghum*. In the case of Ahar in Rajasthan, *Sorghum* was identified on the basis of impressions in pottery which were interspersed with those of rice, rice chaff and straw (Vishnu-Mittre 1969). The attribution to *Sorghum* was largely on the basis of size and the fact that the impressions were round. However, the published photographs (Vishnu-Mittre 1969, pl. XXX) seems to show a long parallel-sided, round-ended embryo on one of the grains, which might suggest *Echinochloa*. Such an attribution may be more logical as *E. colona* and *E. crus-galli* are well known weeds of rice, in particular var. *oryzicola*, a rice mimic which infests paddy cultivation (Hohn et al. 1977; Maun and Barret 1986) and their presence in the pottery along with rice can be understood as the use of rice crop-processing by-products as temper, whereas the inclusion of rice and *Sorghum* in the same ceramics requires assuming two distinct temper sources. The material from Pirak (from the post-Harappan period) was never clearly identified, but reported as simply *Sorghum* sp. with certain reservations expressed (Costantini 1979b).

As noted by Willcox (1992), many archaeologists have overlooked the caution expressed by the original archaeobotanical work and have instead repeatedly cited such reports as well-established scientific fact leading to a general acceptance in the literature. Similar difficulties surround roughly contemporary reports of sorghum from the Arabian peninsula (Rowley-Conwy et al. 1997). The best illustrated example from Yemen is a latex cast made from one of three 'sorghum' seed impressions (Costantini 1990b: pl. 120, c-d). While this is generally large and roundish, and has a small acute projection as sorghum does, there is no evidence of a large embryo/scutellum area, despite this surface being identified as the dorsal surface (ibid.: 193). While this may not have been visible due to the orientation of the impression, without this characteristic feature for the identification of millets and many grasses it is perhaps misleading to attribute this specimen to *Sorghum* as it could come from just about any large, round seeded plant and may not even be a grass. In addition the overall dimensions of these impression are larger than most *Sorghum* grains even of the very large seeded durra varieties (ibid.: 193), which are perhaps unlikely to have been developed at this early date. The best sorghum candidate of any of the published examples is that from Hili IIe in Oman, 2330-2250 BC (Costantini 1979a; Cleuziou and Costantini 1980, 1982; Cleuziou 1989). In addition to the impression, a single charred grain of sorghum is also reported from Hili, phase Ib, although it is not illustrated (see Cleuziou 1989). The impression shows part of a spike (infructescence) in which three rachillae are preserved, each ending in an ovoid structure. As these structures lack evident venation, and arise from triangular-shaped rachillae, they do show similarities with *durra* type *Sorghum*. This specimen is accepted by Doggett and Prasada Rao (1995) as an example of the *durra* race, although there remains room for scepticism until additional material is recovered. To accept any of the reputed *Sorghum* impressions from the Arabian or Indian peninsula requires a leap of faith, a situation which can be contrasted to that of the numerous well-documented impressions of wild-type *Sorghum* from Neolithic sites in the Sudan (e.g. Stemler 1990), or the wheat and barley impressions from Arabia and Baluchistan (Costantini 1979a, 1979b, 1983, 1990a, 1990b). Other archaeobotanical research in the Arabian peninsula has failed to turn up *Sorghum* (e.g. Levkovskaya and Filatenko 1992). Unfortunately *Sorghum* in South Asia has often been discussed in terms of crop diffusion through the far-flung trade contacts of the Harappan period (e.g. Possehl 1986, 1997,1998; Weber 1990, 1991, 1998; Ratnagar 1994; Meadow 1996; Doggett and Prasada Rao 1995), although there is little undisputed evidence to support diffusion either during this period or by this route (see Section 5.7.2, also Fuller and Madella in Vol. IV of this series).

4.3 TROUBLESOME PULSES: THE *VIGNA* SPP.

After cereals, pulses (legumes) are the most common archaeobotanical find in South Asia (Weber 1992), and arguably the next most important category of crop in agricultural terms. When well preserved, identification is quite straightforward, relying on overall shape and placement, size and shape of the hilum. On split legumes, the internal surafce of the cotyledon often preserves a scar where the embryo (plumules) had been. The size, shape and position of the embryo can also be distinctive. Most pulse identification in South Asia is excellent, and what little confusion has surfaced from time to time is largely nomenclatural (for current taxonomy and nomenclature see Section 5.3, footnotes and Tables 6-9; for a review of identification criteria for tropical pulses encountered in Indian archaeobotany, see Fuller et al., n.d.; for pulses of South-West Asian origin see Hopf 1986; Zohary and Hopf 1993).

One genus which has presented some difficulties are pulses in the genus *Vigna* (many formerly considered *Phaseolus*). Green Gram/Mung (*V. radiata*) and Black Gram/Urd (*V. mungo*) share a large number of characters in common and the size and general shape of their seeds overlap. No charring experiments with distinguishing morphometric characters have been presented to validate claims to distinguish them in charred material on the basis of size and shape. Nevertheless, if the hilum is preserved, the distinction between *V. radiata* and *V. mungo* is easily made since Black Gram and its wild progenitor

(*V. mungo*) have a raised hilum with an encirling lip, while in *V. radiata* there is no such lip and the hilum is more or less flush with the seed coat surface (Arora et al. 1973; Lukoki et al.1980). *V. aconitifolia*, the closely related moth bean, can be distinguished by its minute hilum which lies in a slight depression. In addition, these species have distinctive epidermal cell forms on their testas (Chandel et al. 1984). *V. radiata* has rows of very long, thin rectangular cells, whereas those in *V. mungo* are shorter, wider and more ovate. These patterns are readily observable on fresh material at magnifications of 50x or more. *V. aconitifolia* appears to have a much glossier testa and the cells appear to be considerably smaller (author's observation). Other distinctions, on the basis of proportions are probablistic only. On split cotyledons, the embryo in *V. radiata* is generally larger averaging approximately two-thirds the total cotyledon length, whereas in *V. mungo* it tends to be closer to half the cotyledon length; in *V. aconitifolia* it is usually less than half. While most specific level attributions are likely to be correct there is need for more rigour in presenting methods for distinguishing *V. radiata* and *V. Mungo*.

Another species in this genus which has created some confusion is cowpea, *Vigna unguiculata*. This species has so far only been reported from two sites, Hulas (Saraswat 1993) and Daimabad (Vishnu-Mittre et al. 1986)[2]. In the case of Daimabad it is reported as *Vigna sinensis*, a synonym for *V. unguiculata* cv. *biflora* (Westphal 1974; Smartt 1990). Vishnu-Mittre et al. (1986) also tentatively identify a group of other pulses as *Phaseolus* spp., referring to *P. lunatus* and *P. vulgaris*, bean species of New World origin (Debouck and Smartt 1995); these identifications, indicated as uncertain, are undoubtedly mistaken. The photographs show a range of forms which fit well within the variation covered by the several cultivated varieties of *Vigna unguiculata* (see, for example, plates in Westphal 1974).

4.4 A NOTE ON CASTOR

Another mis-identification appears to be the reported *Ricinus communis* from Ter (Vishnu-Mittre et al. 1971: pl. 1.6; Vishnu-Mittre 1977: pl. 5). This identification can be evaluated on the basis of the published photographs which appear to be quite clear. While the seed appears to be elliptic in shape, as is the case in *Ricinus*, the two most distinctive traits of castor seeds appear absent on the illustrated specimen nor are they mentioned in the description (compare, for example, published drawings of castor seeds in general textbooks, e.g. Pandey 1995: 233; Hickey and King 1991: 271) *Ricinus* has a distinctive longitudinal furrow along the length of the seed and a carbuncle at one end (a squarish protuberance). Vishnu-Mittre's illustrated specimen instead shows a trait which suggests a very different identification: the concentric and nearly complete, light-coloured ring. Such rings are characteristic of seeds in some groups of leguminous trees/shrubs (especially of the Mimoseae or Acaciae), such as *Prosopis* or *Acacia*. Even if the archaeological specimens were *Ricinus*, they were so misleadingly represented in the photographs, and incompletely described in the text, as to call their identification into serious doubt.

5. PLANT DOMESTICATION AND ORIGINS: BOTANICAL AND ARCHAEOBOTANICAL CONTRIBUTIONS

Among the questions most often asked of archaeobotanical remains are when and where various crops were domesticated and how they spread. Evidence for the origins of domesticated crops comes largely from the study of modern species, especially through the establishment of genetic relationships between domesticated and wild taxa (Harlan and Zohary 1966; Zohary 1989, 1996; Zohary and Hopf 1993; Harlan 1986, 1992, 1995a; Ladazinsky 1989; Smartt and Simmonds 1995; and see Tables 6-9). The general regions in which these wild progenitors occur today provide a useful guide to regions in which they are likely to have occurred in the past. All regions have not, however, been equally well-documented, with South-West Asia providing the most relaible evidence at present. The first systematic attempts to uncover the geographical origins of crops was the work of Alphonse De Candolle (1886), who drew upon linguistic evidence in addition the botany. While some of his conclusions have stood the test of time, many others have been disproven by work during the past century, especially through plant breeding and genetic studies. During the first half of this century, notably the work by Vavilov (1992 [1950]), studies focused on locating areas of the highest diversity within a crop as regions of origin, although this approach has been superceded by better techniques for assessing the relationships between plants. Ideally, phylogenetic (evolutionary descent) relationships can be established between crops and wild populations; the geographical distribution of these wild populations, in turn, can be used as a base for inferring the *general* ancient distribution of these wild progenitors, and hence crop origin. Vavilov developed the concept of centres of origin , regions in which suites of crop species were domesticated , perhaps at about the same time, and from which they spread to other parts of the world. While Vavilov's studies provided an important baseline from which subsequent research could grow and encouraged the use of modern botanical data for addressing questions of crop histories, his work has been superceded. It is therefore unfortunate that his proclamations about regions of origin are still frequently cited despite more recent research (for example, *Cajanus* and *Lablab* are often mis-attributed in terms of their continent of origin). As additional botanical data has accrued many of Vavilov's centres have been discarded and it has been realized that in some parts of the world, such as sub-Saharan Africa, domestications were more widely dispersed; these latter subcontinental areas have been called 'non-centres' (Harlan 1971, 1986, 1995a). Nevertheless, some groups of crops with a common region of origin can be inferred from the archaeobotanical evidence to have diffused as a suite, such as the cereals and pulses of southwest Asian origin.

5.1 South-West Asian Crops

The crops which have been most extensively studied are cereals of South-West Asian origin, wheat and barley, followed by the pulses from the same region (selected species are given in Table 6). These crops well illustrate the potential of modern botanical evidence as well as debates about its interpretation. Although from the perspective of the Indian subcontinent these species are well established as having originated to the west, the more precise location of their domestications is controversial. Wild stands of einkorn wheat, emmer wheat and barley persist in parts of the 'fertile crescent' although the modern distributions must be considered with reservations because of environmental change, due to both climatic factors and human impact. Through an understanding of environments in which the wild relatives of crops occur today, and by taking into account evidence for vegetational changes in the past, it is possible to model the approximate areas in which crop progenitors may have occurred at the time of domestication (for a reconstruction of pre- and proto-agricultural South-West Asia see Hillman 1996). More detailed genetic screening can help to eliminate some wild populations from progenitor status (Zohary 1989, 1996; Ladazisky 1989). In addition, the genetics of the crops can suggest the minimum number of domestications necessary to account for different genetic groups.

For many of the staple crops, one or very few domestications seem to be indicated, notably for the South-West Asian pulses, emmer wheat, einkorn wheat and barley (Zohary and Hopf 1993; Zohary 1996). Recently, genetic analysis of modern populations of einkorn wheat (*Triticum monococcum*) has suggested a single domestication event from a restricted genetic population, identified with a limited region of south-east Turkey today (Heun et al. 1998; Nesbitt 1998), although controversy continues as to how reliable modern populations are as guides to locating the ancient population from which einkorn was domesticated (Jones et al. 1997; Hole 1998; Nesbitt and Samuel 1998; Nesbitt 1998). On the other hand, recent work on cultivated emmer races suggests the presence of two deep genetic lineages, presumably representing two domestications or domestication from a genetically heterogenous population (Allaby et al. forthcoming); this evidence might challenge the traditional evidence of plant breeding that argued for domestication 'only once, or at most a few times' (Zohary 1996: 155).

Barley also could have been domesticated twice. Evidence for barley indicates two different genes governing the non-shattering rachis (the key domestication trait of cereals) which argues also for at least two domestications of this sepcies (Zohary and Hopf 1993; Zohary 1996; cf. Ladizinsky 1998), although these have yet to be explored through phylogenetic study of genetic data. The restricted genetic diversity of the crop compared to the wider diversity in wild populations of the western fertile crescent (e.g. Israel), coupled with early archaeobotanical finds from the region is usually taken to indicate domestication(s) there in the Early Holocene (Helbaek 1969; Bar-Yosef and Meadow 1995; Harlan 1995; Ladizinsky 1998). Although the distribution of wild barley currently extends in patches eastwards to Afghanistan and Pakistan (Harlan and Zohary 1966), there is no reason at present to believe that barley was domesticated beyond of the 'fertile crescent' given the chronological priority of agricultural sites in the core South-West Asian area (Bar-Yosef and Meadow 1995; Nesbitt and Samuel 1996). Despite the excitement expressed by some with regard to the 'wild' barley impressions identified in early levels at Mehrgarh (Costantini 1983; Costantini and Biasini 1985; Chakrabarti 1988;

TABLE 6. CROPS OF PROBABLE SOUTH-WEST ASIAN ORIGIN, BOTANICAL AND ARCHAEOBOTANICAL SUMMARY

Crop	Vernacular: English, Hindi, others	Frequent synonyms	Region of origin (References)	Early finds, region of origin	Early finds, South Asia
T. diococcum Schubl. (4n)	emmer, durum, gehu	included in *Triticum turgidum* L. sensu lato (hulled)	South-West Asia: Fertile Crescent (*DPOW*)	Asikli Hoyuk, Can Hasan III (Turkey), 7th M. BC; Cafer Hoyuk pre-Pottery Neolithic B (Nesbitt and Samuel 1996)	Mehrgarh (?), 7th M. BC (Costantini 1983); Rohira, 2300-1700 BC (Saraswat 1986); Kalibangan (?), 2600-2000 BC (cf. Vishnu-Mittre and Savithri 1975)
T. durum Desf. (4n)		included in *Triticum turgidum* L. sensu lato (naked)		Can Hasan III (Turkey), 7th M. BC; Tell Aswad (Syria)	not yet reported/presumably represented in many reports of *T. aestivum* (see Sections 4.1. 5.7.1)
Triticum aestivum L. sensu lato (6n)	Bread Wheat, gehu	included *T. compactum* Host.; syn. *T. vulgare* Host.; *T. sativum* Lam.	South-West Asia: West Fertile Crescent	Asikli Hoyuk,Can Hasan III (Turkey), 7th M. BC; Cafer Hoyuk pre-Pottery Neolithic B (Nesbitt and Samuel 1996)	reports probably include *T. durum*: Mehrgarh, Baluchistan, 7th M. BC (Costantini 1983); widespread Harappan era sites, 2500-2000 BC (Vishnu-Mittre and Savithri 1982; Weber 1997); after *c.* 2000 BC in Ganga Basin and Maharashtra
T. aestivum L. subsp. *sphaerococcum* Perc. (6n)	Indian Shot Wheat, gehu	*T. spaerococcum* Perc.	Baluchistan/NW India	?	? identification criteria unclear (see discussion, Section 4.1)
Hordeum vulgare L.	Barley, Yava, Sattu		South-West Asia: West Fertile Crescent and ? second center (*DPOW*)	8th M. BC; Jericho (Palestinian Authority), Tell Aswad, Abu Hureyra (Syria); 7th M. BC; Numerous sites from Iran to Turkey (*DPOW*)	Mehrgarh, Baluchistan, 7th M. BC (Costantini 1983);widespread Harappan era sites, 2500-2000 BC (Vishnu-Mittre and Savithri 1982; Weber 1997); after *c.* 2000 BC in the Ganga Basin and Maharashtra

Lens culinaris L.	Lentil, Masur		South-West Asia (*DPOW*)	8th M. BC; Jericho (Palestinian Authority), Tell Asvad, Abu Hureyra (Syria); 7th M. BC; Numerous sites from Iran to Turkey (*DPOW*)	Harappa, 2500-2000 BC; Kalibangan, 3rd M. BC (Vishnu-Mittre and Savithri 1982; Weber 1997); Rohira, 2300-2000 BC (Saraswat 1986); Burzahom, Kashmir, 2400 BC-1700 BC (Lone et al. 1993); Babar Kot, Gujarat, 2000-1700 BC (Reddy 1994); Maharashtra from *c.* 2000 BC
Pisum sativum L.	Peas, Mattar	include. *P. arvense* L.	South-West Asia (*DPOW*)	8th M. BC; Jericho (Palestinian Authority), Tell Asvad, Abu Hureyra (Syria); 7th M. BC; Numerous sites from Iran to Turkey (*DPOW*)	Harappa 2500-2000 BC (Weber 1997); Burzahom, Kashmir, 2400-1700 BC (Lone et al. 1993); Balathal, Rajastha, 2400-1800 BC (Kajale 1996a)
Cicer arientum L.	Chickpea, Bengal Gram, Chana, kadalai (Tamil)		South-West Asia: North Fertile Crescent (*DPOW*)	8th M. BC: Jericho (Palestinian Authority), Abu Hureyra (Syria); 7th M. BC: Ramad (Syria), Ain Ghazal (Jordan (*DPOW*)	Harappan Civilization: Kalibangan, 3rd M. BC, Harappa, 2500-2000 BC (Vishnu-Mittre, Savithri 1982; Weber 1997); after c. 2000 BC in Ganga Basin and Maharashtra
Lathyrus sativus L.	Grass pea, Khesari		South-West Asia (*DPOW*)	PPNB Gritille (Turkey); 5-6.: sites in Greece and Bulgaria (*DPOW*)	Harappa, 2500-2000 BC; Babar Kot, 2200-2000 BC; Rojdi (Weber 1991), Ganga Valley sites and Maharashtra, 2000-1[illegible]00 BC (Kajale 1991; Saraswat 1992)
Trigonella feonum-graecum L.	Fenugreek, methi		South-West Asia/East Mediterranean (*DPOW*)	Tell Halaf, Iraq, 4000 BC EBA Lachjsh, Israel (DPOW)	Rohira, 2300-1900 BC (Saraswat 1986)
Linum usitatissimum L.	Flax, Alsi		South-West Asia: (*DPOW*)	8th M. BC: Jericho (Israel), Tell Aswad (Syria); 7th M. BC: Ramad (Syria), Ain Ghazal (Jordan) (*DPOW*)	Rojdi C (seeds), 2000-1700 BC (Weber 1991); Pirak (seeds) 1950-1550 BC (Costantini 1979); Navda Toli I-II (seeds), Maharashtra, *c.* 2000-1600 BC (Vishnu-Mittre 1961); Chandoli (thread) 1500-1200 BC (Gulati 1965) (see Janaway and Coningham 1995)

ABBREVIATIONS: *DPOW* = *Domestication of Plants in the Old World*, 2nd edn. (Zohary and Hopf 1993).

Saraswat 1992; R. Singh 1990), caution is warranted, as these may only indicate the spread of wild-type barley as weeds of the crop. In general, crops which originated in South-West Asia, now generally placed more specifically in the western fertile crescent (Israel, Syria, South-East Turkey), spread eastwards as part of an agricultural package which included some livestock, goats and probably sheep, to reach Baluchistan by the end of the eighth millennium BC, although this geographical spread is still relatively poorly documented archaeologically and cannot yet be clearly related to either diffusion or migration, although the latter is currently favoured (Bar-Yosef and Meadow 1995).

By comparison to South-West Asian agriculture, the crops (as well as livestock) with origins in other geographical regions are less well understood both botanically and archaeologically, although there is an increasing body of evidence awaiting synthesis. An attempt to synthesize botanical and archaeological evidence, for major cereals and pulses as well as some oil and fibre crops, is given here. It should be noted that no attempt is made at this time to deal with the plethora of other crop types, including fruits, vegetables and tubers. This is because cereals and pulses are best represented archaeobotanically at present. By incorporating recent, or sometimes obscure data, the claims made here differ from what is current in most of the archaeological literature of South Asia and in some cases from standard reference works of agricultural botany. This summary provides a set of working hypotheses to explore in genetic, biogeographic and archaeobotanical research.

5.2 African Crops in South Asia: Millets and Pulses

A number of crops are established as originating somewhere in Africa (Table 7), but it would be wrong to consider these crops as a package in the way that seems plausible for the South-West Asian crops. Most often discussed have been the three major savanna millets, *Sorghum*, *Pennisetum*, and *Eleusine*. Despite some earlier claims for an Indian origin of *ragi*/finger millet (*Eleusine coracana*, cf. De Candolle 1886; Vavilov 1992 [1950]; Porteres 1976; Vishnu-Mittre 1971; Vishnu-Mittre et al. 1984), the discovery of hybridizing wild tetraploids in the East African highlands provided strong evidence for an African origin, now supported by several genetic studies (Mehra 1962, 1963; Phillips 1972; Hilu and De Wet 1976; Hilu and Johnson 1992; Werth et al. 1994; Hilu 1995; De Wet 1995b). This also indicates that this crop's origins took place in an environment other than the lowland savannas where it is well established today in both India and Africa. Genetic data indicates highly restricted variation in the crop by comparison to its wild progenitor and other wild species; this suggests a single (or very few) domestication (Hilu and Johnson 1992; Werth et al. 1994; Hilu 1995). The racial differentiation of *Eleusine* within India suggests that it was first introduced to the plains of the peninsula and subsequently spread to the northern and north-western part of the subcontinent (Hilu and De Wet 1976; Hilu 1995). Additional suggestive evidence for the region from which finger millet originated comes from linguistics: the root **dègi* in a number of Bantu languages from southern Tanzania and northern Malawi may be the source for *ragi* and

TABLE 7. CROPS OF PROBABLE AFRICAN ORIGIN, BOTANICAL AND ARCHAEOBOTANICAL SUMMARY

Crop	Common names: English, Hindi, others	Frequent synonyms	Region of origin (references)	Early finds, region of Origin	Early finds, South Asia
Sorghum bicolor (L.) Moench.	Sorghum, Great Millet, Jowar	numerous specific epithets in the older literature are all merged as one species (De Wet and Huckabay 1967).	Sudanic Africa (wild), *c.* 6000 BC	Nabta Playa, S. Egypt Hulas (Saraswat 1993), (Wasylikowa and Kubiak-Martens 1995); Khartoum Neolithic (wild) *c.* 3000 BC (Stemler 1990); Qasr Ibrim, Nubia, 100-400 AD (domestic) (Rowley-Conwy 1991; Conwy et al. 1997)	Rojdi C (Weber 1991); Daimabad (Kajale 1977c); 2000-1700 BC (Kajale 1977c); Nevasa 1500-1200 BC, T. Garhi, *c.*1500 BC (Kajale 1988a); ? Inamgaon, c. 1200 BC (Vishnu-Mittre and Savithri 1976)
Eleusine coracana (L.) Gaertn.	Finger Millet, Ragi (Kan. and Hin.), Umi, mandal, mandua		East Africa: Ethiopia-Uganda	Axum, Ethiopia, *c.* 600 AD (S. Boardman: pers. comm.)	all reports need confirmation of identification?: Harappan Rojdi *c.* 2600- (Weber 1991), Kuntasi (Dhavalikar 1995), Shikarpur, Gujarat, 2500-2000 BC; Senuwar, Bihar 2[illegible]0-1800 BC (Saraswat et al. 1995) Babar Kot (Reddy 1994), Harappa (Weber 1998)
Pennisetum glaucum (L.) R. Br.	Pearl Millet, Bajra	*P. americanum* (L.) Leeke, *P. typhoides* Rich	West Africa Mauritania	Mauritania, *c.* 1000 BC (Amblard and Pernes 1989); Khartoum Neolithic, *c.* 3000 BC (wild?) (Stemler 1990)	Daimabad, 2000-1700 BC (Kajale 1977c); Nevasa, *c.* 1500 BC; Rangpur IIC 1800-1700 BC (Ghosh and Lal 1963)
Lablab purpureus (L.) Sweet	Hyacinth Bean, Bonavist, Sem, avarai (Tamil)	*Dolichos lablab* L., *L. niger* Medik.	East Africa (?) (Verdcourt 1970, 71)	Qusr Ibrim, Nubia, 300-500 AD (A. Clapham, unpublished)	Mahorana, Punjab, 2300-2[illegible]00 BC (Saraswat and Chanchala 1994); Chalcolithic Maharashtra, 2nd M. BC (Kajale 1991), Southern Neolithic, Late 3rd/2nd M. BC (Fuller et al. n.d.)

(contd.)

Crop	Common names: English, Hindi, others	Frequent synonyms	Region of origin (references)	Early finds, region of Origin	Early finds, South Asia
Vigna unguiculata (L.) Walp.	Cow Pea, lobia, chowli, karamani (Tamil)	*Dolichos biflorus* L., but *not D. bilforus* in archaeobot. Litt.	West Africa: (Vailencourt and Weeden 1992 Panella et al. 1993)	none; but one report from Old Kingdom Egypt (as wild/weed?)	Hulas, 2000-1700 BC (Saraswat 1993); Daimabad, *c.* 2nd M. BC (Vishnu-Mittre et al. 1986)
Cyamopsis tetragonolobus (L.) Taubert	Cluster Bean, Guar, gaur	*C. psoraloides*	East Africa? (S.C. Hiremath, pers. comm.; also Kajale 1991: 174)	none.	none.
Psophocarpus tetragonolobus (L.) DC.	winged bean, goa bean; chaudhari-phali, charkoni-sem		no conspecific wild. relative identified. Ethiopia? (Smartt 1990)	none.	none.
Ricinus communis L.	Castor, arand		Africa? (De Candolle 1886; Rehm and Espig 1991)	none (?)	uncarbonized fragments, Hulas, 1800-1300 BC (Saraswat 1993)
Gossypium herbaceum L.	Short staple Cotton, 'Asiatic Cotton', Kapas		Africa (?)	Nubia, *c.* 3000 BC (but not cultivated?) (Chowdhury and Buth 1971)	?. See *G. arboreum* in Table 9 for early identifications of this genus

its variants in the Indian subcontinent (Phillippson and Bahuchet 1996). Indeed, the genetic evidence of Hilu (1995), although of limited sampled size, could indicate that some of the most 'primitive' genotypes of the crop come from Tanzania.

The origins of finger millet differ from the sub-Saharan savanna origins suggested by the wild distribution of *Sorghum bicolor* and *Pennisetum glaucum* (Harlan 1971, 1992, 1995a). The origins of *Sorghum* have generally been assigned to the eastern savannas, such as those in Sudan (Harlan 1971, 1992, 1995a), although Ethiopia has also been suggested (Doggett and Prasada Rao 1995). Although the standard interpretation sees the domestication of *Sorghum* between *c.* 5000 BC and 3000 BC (Harlan 1992, 1995a), recent genetic evidence from modern *Sorghum* and archaeological specimens from Qasr Ibrim in Egypt has been used to argue that domestication was quite late, perhaps as late as *c.* AD 0 (Rowley-Conway et al. 1997; Deakin et al. 1998). It can be objected, however, that the genetic locus utilized showed so little variation between modern domesticated and wild varieties (i.e. lacking polymorphism) that they are unlikely to be informative when it comes to assessing phylogenetic divergence between *Sorghum* lineages. In addition, despite a number of questionable reports of Sorghum from prehistoric India and Arabia (Willcox 1992; Rowley-Conway et al. 1997; Section 4.2.1, above), there remain a few finds which appear to have secure archaeological contexts in the second millennium BC and are clearly of domesticated *Sorghum* types. This argues either for an early domestication of sorghum, or else the Haaland (1995) hypthesis whereby wild-type sorghum was transmitted to ancient India and there evolved into the fully domesticated *durra* type.

Recent genetic evidence puts the origins of Pearl Millet/Bajra in the far west of Africa, distantly separated from *Sorghum* (Tostain 1994, 1998); it is argued that Pearl Millet may have been domesticated as early as 6000 BC, although the earliest evidence, in both Africa and India, dates to the mid-second millennium BC (see Table 7).

There are four important pulses in regular cultivation in India today that are of probable African origin, although only two of them have any archaeobotanical record. Guar (*Cyamopsis tetragonoloba*) and winged bean (*Psophocarpus tetragonolobus*) are both of African origin and cultivated in India today, although the former primarily for its seeds' gum. Neither of these two species has yet been recorded archaeobotanically. Cowpea (*Vigna unguiculata*), despite its pan-African wild distribution, appears to have been domesticated from a quite restricted geographical sample of the known genetic populations, approximately restricted to modern Nigeria (Rawal 1975; Vailancourt and Weeden 1992; Panella et al. 1993; Ng 1995). The assemblage of *Vigna unguiculata* illustrated from Daimabad (Vishnu-Mittre et al. 1986, see Section 4.3, above), suggests that a range of varieties of this species were introduced to India quite early. Hyacinth bean (*Lablab purpureus*) is also argued to occur wild in Africa (Verdcourt 1971; Smartt 1990), and as no wild populations have been clearly established in India (cf. Hooker 1872-97; Smartt 1990), it is likely to have originated in eastern Africa. The high diversity of this crop in India (Vavilov 1992 [1950]; Liu 1996), often cited in favour of its origin there, should therefore be seen as the result of an early and extensive radiation in South Asia, and possibly multiple introductions. Nevertheless, *Lablab* appears to have arrived in India relatively early (late third millennium BC) and rapidly became widespread in peninsular India where it has been found on numerous Chalcolithic sites (Kajale 1991) and recently on sites of the Southern Neolithic (Fuller et al.. n.d.; Section 5.3.1).

5.3 South Asian Domesticates

Although not included in the revised centres (or non-centres) of Harlan (1971), there is clear evidence for a number of crop origins in South Asia, most notably amongst tropical pulses as well as several localized millets, tree cotton and possibly sesame (Table 8). Although these crops share origins in the Indian subcontinent, this begs the question as to where more specifically they were domesticated. Unfortunately the modern botanical-geographical evidence is often inadequate to localize these regions with certainty. In addition there are cases in which it seems likely that the wild progenitor has become extinct in its primary habitat due to the extensive spread of agriculture and anthropogenic environmental change on the subcontinent. A possible candidate for such a situation is horsegram (correctly *Macrotyloma uniflorum* (Lam.) Verdcourt, based on *Dolichos uniflorum* Lam., but not *D. biflorus* Linn, nor *Vigna unguiculata*![3]). This pulse is well represented by archaeological finds across India, from the mid-third millennium BC, but is of unclear regional origin since wild populations are not reported in any regional floras. It is also cultivated in Africa, but has not been noted as wild there (Verdcourt 1971; Smartt 1990). Other species of *Macrotyloma* are recognized in Sri Lanka (Maxwell 1991) and Africa (Verdcourt 1971) although it is not clear if they have a close relationship to the domesticated species. Archaeobotanically, *Macrotyloma* is widely reported from Chalcolithic and Neolithic sites, with candidates for the earliest occurrences being Khujhun, in the Vindhyan plateau (Kajale 1991; Saraswat 1992), the Harappan site of Burthana Tigrana in Haryana (Willcox 1992), and Southern Neolithic sites of Andhra and Karnataka (Fuller et al. n.d.; Kajale 1991, 1998), pending more accurate chronology.

An important group of Indian crops is that of three pulses in the genus *Vigna*, a genus which includes two other domesticated species from East Asia.[4] Mungbean, *V. radiata* (L.) R. Wilczek, and Black Gram, *V. mungo* (L.) Hepper,[5] can now be considered to have distinct geographical origins. Formerly they were both considered to derive from the same wild progenitor *Phaseolus sublobatus* Roxb.[6] (syn. *P. trinervius* Heyne, cf. Cooke 1903; Gamble and Fisher 1921-35; Ignacimuthu and Babu 1987), although this has been shown to include two non-hybridizing forms each of which easily crosses with one of the two cultigens and can be linked to the cultigens as wild progenitor on the basis of a wide range of morphological, anatomical, biochemical and genetic data (Arora et al. 1973; Lukoki et al. 1980; Miyazaki 1982; Chandel et al. 1984; Smartt 1985b, 1990; Lawn 1995; Kaga et al. 1996). However, much more work on the ground, collecting these wild taxa, is needed before their primary distribution will be clear. Both occur in the western Himalayan foothills in 'secondary habitats' and the Western Ghats on the Peninsula (Arora et al. 1973). Nevertheless, the primary distribution of wild Green Gram (*V. radiata* var.

TABLE 8. CROPS OF PROBABLE SOUTH ASIAN ORIGIN, ESPECIALLY PENINSULAR, CENTRAL OR NORTHERN INDIA: BOTANICAL AND ARCHAEOBOTANICAL SUMMARY

Crop	Common names: English, Hindi, others indicated	Frequent synonyms	Region of origin (References)	Early finds, region of origin	Other early finds, South Asia
Paspalum scrobiculatum L.	Kodo Millet, kodon, kodu, kodhra, varagu (Tamil), kodo (Munda)		Peninsular India (De Wet et al. 1983; M'Ribu and Hilu 1996)	see next column	Senuwar IB, Bihar, 1800-1200 BC (Saraswat et al. 1995); Rojdi C, Gujarat, 2000-1700 BC (Weber 1991); Daimabad, 1500-1000 BC (Vishnu-Mittre et al. 1986); Narhan, *c.* 1200 BC (Saraswat et al. 1994)
Panicum sumatrense Roth.	Little Millet, shavan, samai (Tamil), gondli (Munda)	*Panicum miliare* nom illeg.	Peninular India:? N. Andhra, (De Wet et al. 1983a; Hiremath et al. 1990; M'Ribu and Hilu 1996)	Southern Neolithic sites, 3rd M. BC (?) (author's data; Fuller et al. n.d.).	Harappan Rojdi from *c.* 2500 BC (Weber 1991), Babar Kot, Oriyo Timbo, Gujarat; 2000-1700 BC (Reddy 1994); Balathal?, by 2000 BC (Kajale 1996a); Inamgaon 1200-900 BC (Kajale 1988b)
Echinochloa colona (L.) Link. ssp. *frumentacea*	Sawa millet, shama, sanwa, sawank	*E. frumentacea* (Roxb.) Link (this species has been used also for the domestic form *of E. crus-galli*)	Peninsular India, multiple domestications (De Wet et al. 1983c; Hilu 1994)	Southern Neolithic sites, 3rd M. BC (?) (author's data; Fuller et al. n.d.).	Narhan (?), *c.* 1200 BC (Saraswat et al. 1994)
Setaria pumila (Poir.) Roem. and Achult.	Yellow Foxtail Millet, bandhra, Korali (Telugu)	*Setaria glauca* nom illeg.	Cult. and Domes., India only (De Wet et al. 1979; De Wet 1995a)	caryopisis not yet clearly distinguished from other *Setaria* species. Study in progress.	*S. pumila*/*S. verticillata* present on Southern Neolithic sites from mid. 3rd M. BC (author's data; Fuller et al. n.d.). Numerous sites with early find of *Setaria* (dating the 2500-1800 BC, could be *S. pumila*, including Balathal, Senuwar IA, Sanghol, Babar Kot, Surkotada
Brachiaria ramosa (L.) Stapf.	Browntop Millet, Pedda Sama (Tel.?)	*Urochloa ramosa* (L.) Nguyen	Cult. and Domes., India only (De Wet 1995a)	none	none

(contd.)

Crop	Common names: English, Hindi, others indicated	Frequent synonyms	Region of origin (References)	Early finds, region of origin	Other early finds, South Asia
Vigna mungo (L.) Hepper	Black Gram, Urid, ulundu (Tamil)	*Phaeseolus mungo* L., *not V. angularis* (Wild.) Ohwi and Ohashi	South Asia: ? Himalayan foothills (Lawn 1995)	see next column	Rodji A (Weber 1991), Balathal (Kajale 1996a), Burthana (?) and Mitathal (?) (Willcox 1992), 2500-2200 BC; Koldihwa; after 2000: Maharashtra sites
Vigna radiata (L.) Wilczek	Green Gram, Mung, hesaru (Kann.)	Phaeseolus radiatus L., P. aureus Roxb.	South Asia: Western Ghats (?) (Lawn 1995)	Southern Neolithic sites, 3rd M. BC (?) (author's data; Fuller et al. n.d.).	Balathal, by 2000 BC (Kajale 1996a); after 2000 BC: Chalcolithic Maharashtra (Kajale 1991); Rojdi C, 2000-1700 BC (Weber 1991)
Vigna aconitifolia (Jacq.) Marechal	Golden Gram, Math, Matki		South Asia: ? (Lawn 1995)	see next column	Narhan, 1000-800 BC (Saraswat et al. 1994); Senuwar, after *c.* 1200 BC (Saraswat et al. 1995)
Cajanus cajan (L.) *Millsp.*	Pigeonpea, Red Gram, Tuvar, Arhar		India: S. Orissa, Bastar, from *C. cajanifolia* (Haines) van der Maeson (1986; 1995)	closest finds in next column	Peddamudiyam, 1300-1700 BC; T. Garhi *c.* 1500 BC; Sanganakallu, Karnataka, mid 2nd M. BC? (author's data, Fuller et al., n.d.)
Macrotyloma uniflorum (Lam.) Verdcourt	Horsegram, Kulthi	*Dolichos biflorus* nom, *Illeg., D. uniflorus* Lam.	South Asia: ? (Verdocurt 1970; Smartt 1985a)	see next column	Harappa Burthana and Mitithal (Willcox 1992); Kunjhun *c.* 2500 BC (Kajale 1991); Rojdi C, 2000-1700 BC (Weber 1991); Chalcolithic Maharashtra sites; Southern Neolithic sites, 3rd M. BC (?) (author's data; Fuller et al. n.d.)
Sesamum indicum L.	Sesame, Til, ellu (Tamil)		South Asia: ? Pakistan (Bedigian and Harlan 1986)	Harappan Makran (Tengberg 1998); Harappa (*c.* 2500-2000 BC)	See previous column. Also, Sanghol, Punjab, 1900-1400 BC (Saraswat and Chanchala 1997); Senuwar ii, 1200-600 BC (Saraswat et al. 1995); Narhan, from *c.* 1200 BC (Saraswat et al. 1994)
Gossypium arboreum L.	Tree Cotton, rapas, rui		South Asia: Gujarat/Sindh? (Santhanam and Hutchinson 1974)	? Mehrgarh Baluchistan? 5000 BC	See prev. (?); Mohenjodaro, Mature Harappan (cloth) 2500-2000 BC (Gulati and Turner 1929; Marshall 1931: 33); Hulas (seed), Late Harappan 1800-1300 BC (Saraswat 1993); Nevasa (thread) 1500-1200 BC (Gulati 1961). (see Janaway and Coningham 1995)

sublobata, formerly *Phaseolus sublobata* Roxb. in part) clearly extends throughout the Western Ghats and into Sri Lanka (Saldhana 1984; Maxwell 1991). Truly wild Black Gram may turn out to be restricted to northern India, although published botanical data is insufficient. Moth Bean (*V. aconitifolia*) also has not been adequately mapped in terms of its wild and weedy distribution, although it is *not* considered native to southern India (Cooke 1903; Gamble 1935; Saldhana 1984), and thus may be northern. Moth may have been a secondary domesticate, evolving from a weed of other crops, as there is no early evidence for it (prior to the later first millennium BC).

Several crops, including two major pulses, have been alternatively attributed to Indian or African origins, although it is now possible to provide more secure origins for some of them. Pigeonpea (*Cajanus cajan*. Hindi: *Tuvar*, *arhar*) has often been referred wrongly to an African origin (e.g. De Candolle 1886; Blench 1991; Langer and Hill 1991; Sundararaj and Thulasidas 1993) on the basis of mistaken botanical evidence and a disputed find of a single archaeological specimen from Egypt. Its wild progenitor, *Cajanus cajanifolia* (formerly *Atylosia cajanifolia*) is now well established through morphological and genetic study and occurs over a very limited area in Bastar and south-eastern coastal Orissa (De 1974; van der Maeson 1980, 1986, 1990, 1995; Smartt 1985a, 1990; Jha and Ohri 1996). Pigeonpea (*Cajanus cajan*) seeds, which appear in a later level at Sanganakallu, show numerous characteristics of putative wild ancestors (Fuller et al. n.d.). This occurrence together with that from Peddamudiyam, Cuddapah district (Venkatasubbaiah and Kajale 1991) and Tuljapur Garhi, Maharashtra (Kajale 1988a, 1996b), suggests that Pigeonpea began to spread out of its region of origin toward the mid-second millennium BC. This could suggest a domestication in the first half of the second millennium. Hyacinth Bean (Hindi *sem*), *Lablab purpureus* (formerly *Dolichos lablab*) has often been suggested to be of Indian origin (e.g. Kajale 1991; Sundararaj and Thulasidas 1993), although current botanical evidence, as inadequate as it is, suggests derivation from East African wild populations (Verdcourt 1970, 1971; Smartt 1985a, 1990).

The geographical origins of cotton and sesame remain disputed. One of the cotton species, *Gossypium arboreum* L. is now considered most likely of South Asian origin. Although disagreement continues to surround the history of the two Old World cotton species, a South Asian origin is supported by a weedy/wild form that is distributed there, although it may no longer be preserved in primary habitat and has perhaps spread together with the early cultivar (Zohary and Hopf 1993; Wendel 1995). This current hypothesis is opposite to the suggestions of De Candolle (1886) who suggested an Indian origin for *G. herbaceum*, now thought to come from Africa, and an African origin for *G. arboreum*. Another crop, now argued by many to have originated in South Asia is sesame, *Sesamum indicum* L. (Bedigian and Harlan 1986; Zohary and Hopf 1993), although doubts persist, with an African origin still preferred by some experts (cf. Nayar 1995). Potentially complicated plant exchanges between India and Africa are highlighted by the example of the vegetable Okra, *Abelmoschos esculentus* (L.) Moench. which appears to be of hybrid origin, with one genome possibly from India (Uttar Pradesh, *A. tuberculatus* Pal and

Singh) and the other from African *A. ficulneus* (cf. Joshi et al. 1974; Hamon and van Sloten 1995). Seeds of an *Abelmoschus* sp. have now been identified from widely separated early third to second millennium BC sites in India (Weber 1991; Venkatasubbaiah and Kajale 1991; Kajale 1996a).

5.3.1 South Indian Neolithic: a Centre of Domestication?

One candidate for domestication in India is the Southern Neolithic, or Ashmound Tradition, which flourished from the beginning of the third millennium BC therefore pre-dating the early Maharashtra villages by at least three to four centuries (Liversage 1991; Possehl and Rissman 1992; Allchin and Allchin 1982, 1997). This chronological priority would make it a candidate area to investigate the initial domestication of several of the indigenous crops. There are still few systematic archaeobotanical collections from this region and period, although the author has recently been involved in a programme to fill this gap (Fuller et al. n.d.; Korisettar et al. in Vol. I of this series). Remains from a number of sites, including Hallur in the west, Sanganakallu and Tekkalakota in the Bellary district, and sites in the Cuddapah district, show the presence of small millets and tropical pulses, with the later addition of *Lablab*, wheat and barley, perhaps in the mid-second millennium BC. The remains appear to be dominated by *Setaria*, perhaps *S. pumila* or *S. verticillata*. *Echinochloa colona* is also tentatively identified from a number of contexts. Small *Panicum* has also been found at a few sites, and is likely to be *P. sumatrense*. The evidence of pulses has implications for the domestication of these crops. *Macrotyloma* and *Vigna* are the most ubiquitous species, and they occur in the early levels at these sites. It is possible that the earliest agriculture in south India relied on grain legumes, like *Macrotyloma* and *Vigna*, and root crops, since parenchyma tissue (as yet unidentified) is also present in Southern Neolithic samples. Most *Dioscorea* spp., of south India are concentrated in the forested hilly tracts along the west and east coasts, the same areas where wild *Cajanus cajan* and *Vigna radiata* were probably located. Thus a tuber and pulse subsistence system is likely to have spread from hilly, forested regions, such as the Western Ghats, onto the drier, savanna grasslands of the Deccan. In these grasslands wild millets would have been readily available and these may then have become the focus of cultivation.

5.4 CHINESE CROPS

In addition there are important crops in India that came from centres of origin in South-East Asia or China (Table 9). Early agriculture in China can be divided into two very different crop complexes. That from south China was based around rice (Wenming 1991; Glover and Higham 1996; Chen and Jiang 1997; Crawford and Shen 1998; Higham and Lu 1998), but this may represent an independent rice culture from that in India (see below). That from north China (the Wei and lower Yellow River Valleys) which included the two best known 'Asian' millets, Proso Millet (*Panicum miliaceum*) and Common

Foxtail Millet (*Setaria italica*) (Bray 1981; Chang 1986: 92; Higham and Lu 1998), but evidence does not suggest that they necessarily diffused together as a package.

Both of the Chinese millet species are widely grown in India today. *S. italica* in South Asia represents one of the three morphological races of the crop (race *indica*) and may derive from mixing between the other two races, *moharia* of South-West Asia and *maxima* of China (Rao et al. 1987; Li et al. 1998). *P. miliaceum* in India falls into the race *patentissimum* which also occurs in Afghanistan, China and the former USSR; it is suggested to have come to India via central Asia or Afghanistan (De Wet 1995a). It is still unclear when, and by what route, these two crops entered the subcontinent. Although both Chinese millets have been identified on Late/Post-Harappan sites in Gujarat, it is unclear how these species were definitively distinguished from indigenous congeneric species, such as the edible *S. verticillata* and *S. pumila* (the latter also domesticated) and the little millet (*Panicum sumatrense*). The work by Weber (1991) and Reddy (1994) appears to have relied on differences of size alone, although no statistical studies of modern samples nor the effects of experimental charring are reported to these support these metrical criteria. *Panicum miliaceum* has positively been identified from Kashmir from the Indo-Greek period, i.e. late first millennium BC (Lone et al. 1993). *Setaria* probably to be indentified with *S. italica* also comes from roughly the same period and region (ibid.). *Panicum miliaceum* is present at Shortugai in Afghanistan but only from the second millennium BC, i.e. after those levels with Harappan affinities, while *S. italica* is absent (Willcox 1991).

The origins of Asian domestic rice, *Oryza sativa*, have been placed by various authorities in India, south China and South-East Asia. The systematics and nomenclature of rice has been subject to a certain amount of confusion, and the taxonomy of Vaughn (1989a) is followed here. In this system two wild species with close affinities to the crop are recognized, *O. rufipogon* Griffith, a perennial, and *O. nivara* Sharma et Shastry, an annual (see also Crawford and Shen 1998). Although Vavilov (1992 [1950]) attributed rice to his Indian centre of origin, wild varieties can also be found across a broad band extending eastwards through South-East Asia and south China (T. Chang 1989, 1995; Oka 1988). Within the crop, three varieties are generally recognized, *japonica* (also called *sinica*), *indica* and *javanica* (sometimes lumped with *japonica* as a tropical offshoot of short-grained rice). The latter is confined largely to South-East Asia while the other two are widespread. The two main divisions can be distinguished on the grounds of morphology and generally ecology (Oka 1988; T. Chang 1989, 1995; Crawford and Shen 1998), with *indica* having long grains and *japonica* possessing short grains. It has long been recognized that crosses between *indica* and *japonica* are usually wholly or partly sterile, although both will readily hybridize with *javanica* (Wan and Ikehashi 1997). While this has long suggested to some authorities two domestications (cf. Chang 1989, 1995), some have also seen these varieties as a rapid divergence after domestication (Oka 1988; White 1989). However, it is now clear that there are a number of substantial genetic distinctions between *indica* and *japonica* (Sano and Morishima 1992; Chen et al. 1993, 1994; Wan and Ikehashi 1997; Crawford and Shen 1998; Sato et al. 1991). Most significant is the

TABLE 9. SELECTRED CROPS OF VARIED ASIAN ORIGIN, INCLUDING EAST AND SOUTH-EAST ASIA, AND NORTH-EASTERN INDIA

Crop	Common names: English, Hindi, others indicated	Frequent synonyms	Region of origin (References)	Early finds, region of origin	Other early finds, South Asia
Oryza sativa L.	Rice, vrihi		cv. *Indica* and *japonica/sinica* separate origins: South China, Yangzi; and ? second centre (could be NE India or Myanmar?)	Peiligang culture, Jiahu, Henan province, China, 7000-6000 BC (Chen and Jiang 1997); Mijiabing culture, Hemudu, SE China, 5000 bc (Glover and Higham 1996)	wild rice at Chopani-Mando, 4th M. BC; domesticated at Mahadaha, 3000-2000 BC? (Sharma et al. 1980). See Sections 5.4, 5.7.4
Coix lacryma-jobi L.	Job's Tears, Gurlu, Giral, Garahedua, Kasi (Munda)		Assam, Auranchal Pradesh (NE India), Myanmar	none	(as weed?): Balathal, 2350-1800 BC (Kajale 1996a); Sunuwar IB, 1800-1200 BC (Saraswat et al. 1995); Inamgaon, 1200-900 BC (Kajale 1988b), Bhagimohari, 1st M. BC (Kajale 1989c)
Digitaria cruciata (Nees) A. Camus	Raishan (Khasi)		Khasi Hills, Assam (NE India)	none	none
Setaria italica (L.) Beauv.	Common Foxtail Millet, Kangni, kangu, kakun, thennai (Tamil)		North China and ? South-East Europe (De Wet et al. 1979) De Wet 1995c)	6th M. BC Peigang and Chishan culture, N. China (Lu 1998); 5th-4th M.: Yangshao culture, N. China (K. Chang 1986)	Harappa (?); Gujarat: Surkotada 2500-2000 BC (Vishnu-Mittre) 1990); Balathal (?), 2000-1700 BC (Reddy 1994); Daimabad (?), *c.* 1500 BC See *S. pumila* (Table 8)
Panicum miliaceum L.	Proso Millet, Chin, Morha, Anu, panivaragu (Tamil)		North China (De Wet 1995a; Zohary and Hopf 1993)	5th-4th M. BC, Georgia sites; 4th M. BC: Yangshao culture, N. China (K. Chang 1986)	?Babar Kot by 2000 BC; ?Pirak after 2000 BC
Echinochloa crusgalli var. *utilis* Ohwi and Yabuno	Barnyard Millet [not cultivated in India; wild form present as weed/wild]	formerly lumped with domesticated *E. colora* as *E. frumentacea* (see Yabuno 1962; Hilu1994)	Japan? and/or North China (Yabuno 1987; Crawford 1992	Middle Jomon culture, Japan, 2000 BC (Crawford 1992, 1997)	none as cultivar (?): Rojdi C, 2000-1700 BC (Weber 1991)
Saccharum officinarum L.	sugarcane, ganna		New Guinea and/or South China (Daniels and Daniels 1993)	none	none, but *Saccharum* sp. fibres from Chirand, 3 M. BC (Vishnu-Mittre 1972); Hastinapur, 1st M. BC (Chowdhury and Ghosh 1955)
Canabis sativa L.	Hemp, ganja, bhang		Central Asia/ Afghanistan?	in N. China by 2500 BC (Li 1974; K. Chang 1986: 143; Crawford 1992)	Senuwar IB (charcoal) 1800-1200 BC;

evidence for a sequence deletion in the chloropast DNA of *indica* cultivars and in wild annual '*O. rufipogon*' (i.e. *O. nivara* in the taxonomy used here), but absent from *japonica* cultivars, perennial *O. rufipogon*, and other wild species (Chen et al. 1993): this evidence indicates clearly that *indica* and *japonica* have distinct phylogenetic origins. It is therefore plausible that they have distinct geographical origins, although it remains to be determined where. Until more detailed genetic markers are recognized and screened for across the range of wild populations, the best evidence comes from archaeobotany. There is strong archaeological evidence for at least one early rice domestication in southern China around the middle Yangzi river area, where on sites of the Hemudu Culture and southern Peiligang Culture of central China, rice is found from seventh and sixth millennia BC (Wenming 1991; Bellwood et al. 1992; Glover and Higham 1996; Chen and Jiang 1997; Anping 1998; Zhao 1998; Crawford and Shen 1998; Higham and Lu 1998). Despite a tradition of distinguishing *japonica* and *indica* within this material on the basis of length:width ratios, these are unlikely to be reliable on charred grains, at least not until we better understand the effects of the charring process (Glover and Higham 1996; Crawford and Shen 1998; see Section 4, above).

5.4.1 Rice Domestication in the Ganga Plains: Evidence and Problems

Plausible botanical arguments for a separate rice domestication in India can be made, although reliable archaeobotanical evidence is still lacking. The wide distribution and diversity of wild rice in India, especially of annual, long-grain *O. nivara* type in northern and north-eastern India, has long suggested that *indica* cultivars may have originated in India and spread from there to South-East Asia and China (Vavilov 1992 [1950]; Shastri and Sharma 1974; Kumar 1988). There is still no convincing archaeobotanical evidence for an in situ domestication, and systematic sampling should be taken up at early sites in regions with large stands of wild rice.

An argument has been put forward for the domestication of rice in the central Ganga Valley, from sites in the Vindhyan palteau (Sharma et al. 1980; Vishnu-Mittre 1989). Unfortunately, the plant remains were not collected systematically by flotation and have been inadequately reported in terms of quantitative and morphometric trends. There is no clear temporal sequence suggesting a move from wild to domestic type rice which would indicate in situ selection for domestic morphology. The Koldihwa material was offered as evidence as both 'wild' and 'domestic' kinds occur together. Initially 'wild' rice was reported (Vishnu-Mittre and Savithri 1979a), but the stratigraphic sequence of rice finds as summarized later (Vishnu-Mitre and Savithri 1979c: 88; Vishnu-Mittre 1989; R. Singh 1990: 30; Kajale 1991: 169-70) has only *O. sativa* in the lower stratum (level 10) while *O. sativa* co-occurs with '*O. rufipogon*' (or a *spontanea* hybrid weed?) and *O. nivara* in levels 8 and 9 above. Thus, in this sequence wild finds actually post-date the earliest reported domesticate (assuming they have been correctly identified). Co-occurrence cannot be used to suggest domestication, since wild species and *spontanea* hybrids often occur as weeds of rice fields (cf. Kumar 1988; Vaughn 1989). This is demonstrated by the co-occurrence of wild and domestic rice in pottery from Late Harappan Hulas, *c.* 1800 BC (Vishnu-Mittre and Sharma 1983; Saraswat et al. 1992) as well as numerous Chalcolithic to Iron Age sites in Uttar Pradesh (Vishnu-Mittre et al. 1984: 106). Indeed at Mahagara, contemporary or later than Koldihwa, domesticated and wild rice continue to co-occur as tempering material, including another rice weed, *Ischaemum rugosum* (Vishnu-Mittre et al. 1984). Thus the evidence from impressions at Koldihwa and Mahagara would appear to indicate only that crop-processing waste from rice cultivation was used as tempering; it says nothing about the evolution of rice cultivation. Burnt clay from Chopani-Mando III (mid-fourth millennium BC) contains charred remains of wild rice (Vishnu-Mittre 1989) which does seem to suggest the utilization of wild grains since querns are also found on the site (Sharma et al. 1980:75). How wild rice use relates to cultivation and later domestication requires research. Recent reviews of the evidence have been skeptical (e.g. Glover and Higham 1996). On the basis of the dearth of finds before the mid-second millennium, Glover and Higham (1996) suggest that cultivation in India did not start prior to this time. However, their compilation of finds by millennium fails to take into account sampling factors. There are very few sites with an archaeobotanical record at all prior to the third millennium in rice-growing areas, while later sites are abundant. This may in itself be significant, indicating that there were few settlements of this period large enough to have been easily detected archaeologically. The occurrence of rice at Harappan sites in Haryana, *c.* 2500-2000 BC (Willcox 1992), at Harappa after *c.* 2200 BC (Fujiwara et al. 1992; Weber 1997; M. Madella: personal communication), Lothal and Rangpur (back to *c.* 2500 cal. BC), suggests that rice must have been cultivated for some time prior to its adoption in Harappan areas which are largely outside its natural range.

Sites in the Vidhyan plateau area have also yielded additional crop species, although these have not drawn much interest. If rice is to be hypothesized as having been domesticated in this area then these other species should be studied as possible companion crops. A *Vigna* pulse, identified as Black Gram *Vigna* cf. *mungo*, and Horsegram (*Macrotyloma uniflorum*) have been reported from Kunjhun and Koldihwa, respectively (see Kajale 1991; Saraswat 1992). More archaeobotanical work in this region is clearly called for. It will also be necessary to systematically reinvestigate the absolute chronology of this region which has been surrounded by controversy and contradiction (cf. Sharma et al. 1980; Sharma and Sharma 1987; Chakrabarti 1988; Possehl and Rissman 1992; Allchin and Allchin 1982, 1997).

5.5 THE PROBLEM OF MAIZE IN INDIA

A controversial issue which emerged during the first era of archaeobotany and has to some extent continued to the present, is that of the antiquity of maize in South Asia (Achaya 1994: 231). Vishnu-Mittre (1968b; 1974) believed that the evidence indicated a pre-colonial adoption of maize (*Zea mays* L.) in India. Earlier suggestions that maize in

South Asia might pre-date Columbus were supported by the fact that some forms of maize, notably popcorn and green vegetable corns, were cultivated by 'primitive peoples' in 'ethnological back corners', such as Assam (Stonor and Anderson 1949: 355). Aside from a flawed view of changeless peoples cut off from modern contact, these arguments hinged on the apparent divergence between maize in Nepal and Assam and elsewhere, especially in the New World (Stonor and Anderson 1949; Nickerson 1953; Jeffreys 1955, 1971). This deep genetic divergence was suggested on the basis of morphological measurements in a period before the availability of direct genetic evidence. In fact, at that time the origins of maize were obscure and Stonor and Anderson (1949) even speculated that maize could have originated in Asia and might be related to *Sorghum*. Today the origins of maize are far better understood and its New World origins are not in doubt (see Goodman 1995; Piperno and Pearsall 1998). Its wild ancestor is almost certainly the grass Teosinte which is indigenous to central America and genetic evidence, breeding experiments and archaeobotanical evidence all indicate its domestication and evolution in central America from *c.* 5000 BC.

Nevertheless, the high diversity in Himalayan maize varieties is remarkable:

> Some primitive Himalayan strains appear to have been isolated from the main stream of maize evolution for a very long time, and the possibility of introduction before the discovery of America by Columbus can not be ruled out. (Hutchinson 1976: 133)

However, population bottlenecks in novel environmental settings could explain this diversity. In addition, it is likely that numerous genetic strains from the New World were transported to Asia during the early centuries of European transoceanic voyaging. And for at least one of these 'primitive' maize types, from Sikkim, a precursor population has been found in South America (Sachan and Sarkar 1986). On the other hand, the genetic diversity in maize from the plains of India (including the peninsular region) is so low as to be certainly of post-Columbian introduction (Sarkar et al. 1974; Hutchinson 1976). Nonetheless, Vishnu-Mittre, citing the diversity noted by Nickerson for *Himalayan* maize, argued for pre-Columbian maize *from the plains* on the basis of maize cob impressions decorating pottery from the late Medieval site of Kaundinyapura, Maharashtra. While his replication experiments strongly support the identification of maize, his argumentation for dating relied on an unsubstantiated assertion of a *terminus ante quem* of AD 1435 on the basis of a coin of this date reported from another contemporary site; in fact this coin can only be considered a *terminus post quem*, since it is unclear how long the coin would have circulated before burial. The inaccuracies of dating these archaeological deposits, however, suggest that a date in the sixteenth century is plausible. In addition, large grass pollen from late in the sequences in Kashmir was attributed to maize on morphometric grounds and suggested to date to the thirteenth or fourteenth centuries (Vishnu-Mittre and Sharma 1966). However, given that there were no absolute dates for this pollen sequence, no reliability can be granted such chronological guesswork. Moreover, some Indian *Coix* spp. were later shown to overlap in size with maize, suggesting that these pollen grains could be native (Vishnu-Mittre and Sharma 1983). Maize pollen from sequences elsewhere in Asia, such as Sulawesi (Indonesia) are also undated (Gremmen 1990).

Other arguments for pre-Columbian maize in peninsular India have been put forward more recently on the basis of supposed artistic depictions of maize in Hoysala temple scenes in Karnataka (Johannessen 1988; Johannessen and Parker 1989; Achaya 1994: 233). These depictions are far from convincing, especially as they lack the distinctive tassels of maize, amongst other incongruencies, such as linguistic evidence in which terms for maize refer to its similarity to the more ancient *Sorghum* (Payak and Sachan 1988; 1993; cf. Veena and Siagamani 1991). Textual evidence from the temples in question and other contemporary written sources do not include the plant name for maize (Payak and Sachan 1993). The Hoysala temple depictions could just as easily be stylized representation of *Sorghum* or may nor even be cereals. Payak and Sachan (1993) suggest that the depictions represent a mythical flower made of pearls, known in Sanskrit as *muktaphala*. The introduction of maize to South and South-East Asia remains a fascinating process to explore, but has so far been subject to more speculation than collection of botanical and archaeobotanical evidence. The hard evidence needed will be lacking until systematic archaeobotany is taken up on later historic sites, and well-dated pollen sequences are available.

5.6 PALYNOLOGICAL INDICATORS FOR THE BEGINNINGS OF AGRICULTURE

Before turning to the evidence of archaeological seeds, for tracing the history of agriculture in South Asia (Section 5.7), some comments on the use of pollen proxy indicators of agriculture is in order. Although the study of pollen from natural deposits, such as lake beds or bogs, are generally analysed in order to reconstruct palaeoecological sequences they can also provide insights into human modification of the landscape (for general reviews, see Faegri and Iversen 1975; Godwin 1975; Behre 1986; Moore et al. 1991; for a discussion of pollen from archaeological sites, see Section 6.3). Perhaps the most significant human landscape modifications came about with agriculture, which cleared and replaced plant communities with arable fields. The first pollen studies that attempted to document the advent of agriculture were conducted in Europe (e.g. Iverson 1949; also Godwin 1956, 1975). Guinet (1963, 1966) and Vishnu-Mittre were the first workers in South Asia to draw attention to palynological indicators for the advent of agriculture (Vishnu-Mittre 1966, 1968a, 1974; Vishnu-Mittre and Sharma 1966; Vishnu-Mittre et al. 1962). As is now becoming apparent from the confrontation of the archaeological and palynological data bases in Europe, the signature of agriculture in pollen record may consistently post-date the actually beginnings of cultivation but reflect instead a subsequent period of agricultural intensification or the crossing of an environmental impact threshold (Willis and Bennett 1994; M. Jones et al. 1996: 93-6).

The biggest difficulty with studying early agriculture through palynological evidence is the recognition of reliable indicators. The most obvious indicator of cultivation would be the presence of pollen that could be identified to domesticated plants, although identification to this level is generally highly problematic. One traditional indicator in Europe is 'cerealia' pollen (taken to include cultivated *Horduem*, *Triticum*, *Avena* and *Secale* as well as some large-grained wild grasses). In general, however, few grass genera let alone species can be separated with certainty on the basis of pollen: grass pollen is all relatively large, single-pored, thin-walled and with relatively-smooth surfaces (Faegri and Iversen 1975; Godwin 1975: 405; Behre 1981; Edwards 1989; Moore et al. 1991). Standard criteria rely on size distinctions in terms of overall pollen grain diameter and pore size (Leroi-Gourhan 1969; Vuorela 1973; Godwin 1975: 405; Andersen 1979; Dickson 1981; Edwards 1989). However, for any given species there is always a range of pollen sizes and the differences that are generally relied are modal tendencies and rarely absolute distinctions. The attribution of pollen to cereals on the basis of size is problematic because of the large pollen of species of wild polyploid grasses in India such as *Coix* spp. (Vishnu-Mittre 1976a, 1976b, 1981a, 1985; Vishnu-Mittre and Guzder 1975; Vishnu-Mittre and Sharma 1983; see also Maloney 1990). Such large grains are known from pollen diagrams in Kashmir and Nepal from the Terminal Pleistocene (Vishnu-Mittre and Sharma 1966; Vishnu-Mittre 1978), which certainly do not indicate domesticates since according to other sources of evidence agriculture does not enter this region until the third millennium BC (cf. Burzahom archaeobotany, Lone et al. 1993). A recent review of the literature on grass pollen studies shows that a large number of genera and species that are common in India have not been taken into account for developing the standard criteria used in European and Near Eastern studies (Bower 1997). Some of these other large-pollen-producing species, however, may be recognized by surface patterning of the pollen and therefore ruled out, such as *Coix* which has distinctive exine (Maloney 1994). In general, further examination of exine sculpturing with a scanning electron microscope may allow specific (or generic) identifications for a number of cultivars, but this technique would seldom be practical for application to pollen cores samples as part of a routine analysis. A further serious problem with identification of cereal pollen in India is that several of the important cereal crops, notably all the small-seeded millets, *Sorghum* and rice, have pollen that falls below the western Eurasian 'cereal' size range and overlaps with a wide range of wild grasses (Vishnu-Mittre 1974, 1975; Vishnu-Mittre and Guzder 1975; Maloney 1990). There are, however, a few other cultivars, e.g. amongst fruit trees, that may be identified in the pollen records (for a review of species utilized in South-East Asia, see Maloney 1994).

The other approach to recognizing early agriculture is by identification of associated weed taxa and inferred forest clearance (Vishnu-Mittre 1968a, 1974; Vishnu-Mittre and Guzder 1975). This approach relies on assuming ecological preference of particular species and plant associations, specifically with crops, can be extended into prehistory. Inevitably such an approach raises difficulties of uniformitarian assumptions; it must assume that plant associations observed today would have held in the past, which may not be the case (Behre 1981; Huntley 1990). Indeed archaeobotanical macrofossils suggest rather the opposite, that arable weed floras have been evolving in response to changes in irrigation, tillage and weeding technologies (M. Jones 1988a, 1988b; Kuster 1991). Also many of the indicator species often used in Europe were present during Pleistocene interglacial long prior to agriculture (Godwin 1975); similar observations were made in Kashmir and the Nilgiri Hills by Vishnu-Mittre (1976a, 1976b, 1978). As Edwards (1979) and Behre (1981) warn, palynologists have been somewhat overzealous in identifying pastoralism and cultivation on the basis of indicator species which often have a range of possible ecological interpretations. A pollen sequence researched in the 1960s from the Nilgiri Hill-station of Ootacamund (Tamil Nadu) initially suggested a period of clearance, attributed to the impact of pastoralism (see Vishnu-Mittre 1968a), although once it was dated it was found to be Pleistocene and was reinterpreted as natural vegetation change and disturbance (Vishnu-Mittre and Gupta 1971; Vishnu-Mittre 1976b). Nevertheless, if used cautiously, evidence for decreasing forest cover and increases in taxa which flourish under regimes of tillage or fallowing can be suggestive of widespread agriculture in a region.

Pollen evidence has been collected from other parts of northern India and the Himalayan region. Vishnu-Mittre discussed the pollen sequence from Kashmir in relation to the origins of agriculture. The decline of forest tree species and the increase in non-tree pollen types together with species associated with disturbed agricultural habitats is often taken as a proxy indicator for agriculture. Vishnu-Mittre attributed the presence of weeds like *Plantago lanceolata*, Chenopodiaceae, as weeds of wheat/barley cultivation. Work in the Kumaon region of the Himalayas (Vishnu-Mittre et al. 1967; Gupta 1975a) correlates well with the Kashmir sequence and indicates a similar phase of agricultural impact on the landscape. In the middle of Zone A of this sequence there is some evidence for burning, but without evidence for 'cerealia' type pollen, so Gupta (1975a) attributes this evidence to natural fires. More certain evidence for agriculture comes from Zone C with greater occurrences of 'cerealia' sized pollen, herbs of disturbed ground, decreasing tree pollen and charcoal. However, these earlier studies remain difficult to utilize for understanding human prehistory as they lack a fixed absolute chronology. More recent work from Sharma and Chauhan (1988) on two lakes in Himachal Pradesh which spans from *c.* 4000 BP to the present has been interpreted to indicate agriculture througout this period. A Holocene pollen sequence is now available from the Garhwal region, between Kumaon and Himachal Pradesh (Sharma and Gupta 1997). This sequence is poorly dated, however, because there is only one radiocarbon date and dates for rest of the sequence must be extrapolated. In Zone II defined by this study there is an apparent increase in non-arboreal pollen as well as several anthropogenic herb groups, some of which were absent from the previous pollen zone. The decline in oak and associated forest elements during the period extrapolated as 4000-3500 BP is interpreted in terms of the local climate cooling, although intensive agriculture is also suggested for this region on the basis of anthropogenic indicators, charcoal and 'Cerealia'-size pollen (ibid.).

Another pollen sequence which has been interpreted in terms of agriculture comes from the salt lakes of Rajasthan (Singh 1971; Singh et al. 1974). The climatic implications of Rajasthan pollen profiles and their implications for understanding the rise and fall of

Harappan Civilization, continue to be debated but will not be dealt with here (Singh 1971; Vishnu-Mittre 1976; Vishnu-Mittre and Savithri 1979c: 109; Meher-Homji 1980; Bryson and Swain 1981; Meadow 1989; Shaffer and Lichtenstein 1989; Agrawal 1992; Kajale and Deotare 1997; also see Fuller and Madella in Vol. IV of this series). On the basis of the occurrence of a few large grass pollen grains (40-50 microns) and an increase in microcharcoal in 'climatic phase' III (8000-4000 cal. BC) Singh (1971) suggested that scrub burning was carried out for 'primitive cereal agriculture'. If accepted, this might be contemporary with or later than the Mehrgarh. Although it is difficult to accept uncritically the attribution of this pollen to domesticated cereals. Given that large quantities of cereal pollen are probably only released through crop processing (Vuorela 1973; Robinson and Hubbard 1977; Behre 1981; Bower 1992), an agricultural hypothesis would suggest human agriculture or settlement very close to the lakes. In the absence of such evidence, as appears to be the case for Rajasthan, a wild source for the pollen seems likely. The *single* occurrence of a supposed anthropogenic weed can not be considered indicative of agriculture (Vishnu-Mittre 1976). The evidence for burning, from microcharcoal in the sediment core, is also ambiguous and could indicate hunter-gatherer management of vegetation to encourage game (Vishnu-Mittre 1985) or an increase in natural burning. The latter position may be supported by the fact that the charcoal level remains consistently high throughout the remaining sequence. This is not accompanied by significant pollen indicators of deforestation (Vishnu-Mittre and Guzder 1975). There is an increase in cereal-sized pollen in latter levels contemporary to Pre-Harappan/ Harappan period. The evidence from this phase is more generally accepted as indicating cultivation because of several clearance herbs (anthropogenic indicators) and larger amounts of cereal-size pollen (Vishnu-Mittre and Guzder 1975).

Additional pollen sequences in South Asia that may have a bearing on agriculture, come from peninsular India. An offshore sequence from the west coast of India is reported by Caratini et al. (1991, 1994). These pollen sequences are assumed to reflect vegetation in the Western Ghats and the adjacent plains carried by rivers to be deposited on the continental shelf. This sequence indicates a dramatic decrease in tree species and an increase in grassland and herbaceous types. While Caratini et al. (1994) prefer to attribute these changes to a climatic change, a weakening of the monsoon and aridification, *c.* 3500 BP (1900-1700 cal. BC), some, if not all, of these changes could be due to forest clearance, for grazing and agriculture, the explanation advocated by Meher-Homji (1996) and Subash Chandran (1997). Certainly, from the emerging archaeobotanical evidence from the Southern Neolithic and the published record for the Maharashtra Chalcolithic (see Sections 5.3.1 and 5.7.5), the early second millennium BC witnessed the proliferation of agricultural villages, and in the case of the Southern Neolithic the adoption of winter crops from external sources, implying agricultural intensification (chronology is still to be resolved). This evidence tends to support an anthropogenic factor. If, however, the change found by Caratini et al. could be shown to have a tight chronological correlation with vegetational changes in other regions (e.g. Rajasthan), then a climatic explanation would gain support. In general, most of available palynological data for the Holocene suffer from the ambiguity of equi-finality with marked changes that could be due to climatic variables or human impact. More discussion of strategies for disentangling these confounding factors should be incorporated in future work. The total quantity of pollen evidence for the Holocene of South Asia is still extremely small and warrants further research, however, there is a need for placing pollen evidence into its broader landscape context by trying to consider archaeological evidence for the scale of settlement and archaeobotanical evidence for agriculture.

5.7 CROP DIFFUSION IN SOUTH ASIA: A CURRENT SYNTHESIS

Starting from the geographical sources of crops outlined earlier (Section 5.5), it is possible to trace in general terms their directions and period of spread in the subcontinent. Liversage (1989) proposed a simple classification of four Neolithic regions in South Asia which can be hypothesized to have had distinct prehistoric agricultural traditions that were based around different but overlapping suites of crops. These regions include Baluchistan, the Indus Valley, the Ganga Valley and a large west-central Indian region that extends from the Aravalli Hills in the north-west down through the peninsula (Deccan). Liversage sees these Neolithic 'complexes' as unified by similar ecological conditions and presumed cultural interaction; a broadly similar division was already discussed by Allchin and Allchin (1968) and Hutchinson (1976). The two river valleys differ from their adjacent regions by the presence of regular alluvial flooding. Liversage suggested that the Indus region formed something of a large, ecological frontier zone where the spread of South-West Asian crops was delayed before spreading into tropical India. As more evidence becomes available these regions are likely to require revision and perhaps a certain amount of subdivision, in particular of the rather large and heterogenous Southern Neolithic. An alternative framework for discussing the Neolithic geography of India is based on the definition of Neolithic cultures as defined by distinctive artefact styles, through which seven Neolithic zones are recognized (Thapar 1974, 1978; Saraswat 1992). There remains a need to evaluate these regional classifications on the basis of archaeobotanical evidence for similarities and differences in ancient agriculture. Some preliminary observations of the geographical distribution of crops in the past on the basis of archaeology are offered below.

The extent to which any or all of these Neolithic zones represent either the independent development of cultivation or the spread of agriculture from elsewhere by migration or diffusion, remains to be determined. A major problem facing Indian archaeologists interested in agricultural origins is an Early Holocene gap in the archaeological record. For the subcontinent as a whole there are very few well-dated sites between the end of the Pleistocene (*c.* 10,000 BC) and the regional Neolithic cultures, which largely appear to date after 3000 BC. While microlithic, 'mesolithic' cultures are assumed to fill this gap, there are still few well-excavated sites that have been sampled archaeobotanically and accurately dated. The filling of this gap is essential, if the roots of Indian agriculture are to be truly understood. Some very promising data that contributes towards filling this gap are the Mesolithic charred assemblage studied by Kajale from Damdama, a Vindhyan plateau site (Kajale 1990a, 1991), in addition to some Mesolithic plant remains from Sri Lanka (Kajale 1989b). More early and pre-neolithic plant assemblages are badly needed.

5.7.1 Spread of South-West Asian Crops

It is conceivable that wheat, barley and four South-West Asian pulses spread together into the subcontinent, although the evidence from the Greater Indus Valley region is too highly fragmentary at present to be sure (Fig. 3). Although the South-West Asian pulse species have not been reported from the early periods at Mehrgarh (Costantini 1984), this cannot be taken to indicate their actual absence as the evidence for wheat and barley comes from pottery and mud-brick impressions, a category of remains which one would not expect to include leguminous crops, since straw, cereal chaff, or dung are the ceramic tempering agents usually documented ethnographically. It is clear however that in regions east and south of the Indus Valley all or most of these crops co-occur in their earliest occurrences which suggests that they spread as a winter crop package. The spread of these crops, usually found together as a package, shows a clear trajectory from the north-west to the east and south, with a discernible delay around the eastern fringes of the Harappan province. Wheat (*Triticum* spp.), barley (*Hordeum vulgare* L.), peas (*Pisum sativum* L.), lentils (*Lens culinaris* Med.), grass pea (*Lathyrus sativus* L.) and chick pea/bengal gram (*Cicer arientinum* L.) are present in the upper Ganga Basin during the Ochre Coloured Pottery phase in the early to mid-second millennium BC (for the dating see Possehl and Rissman 1992; Allchin and Allchin 1997: 214-18, 225-6), e.g. at the sites of Hulas (Saraswat et al. 1992; Saraswat 1993); Atranjikhera (Chowdhury et al. 1977) as well as Lal Qila (excluding *Lathyrus* and *Lens*, Kajale and Deotare 1993; Kajale 1995) and Sringaverapura (excluding *Lathyrus*, *Lens* and *Pisum*, Kajale 1991). In the Ganga Valley these crops were probably adopted into a cultural system in which rice had already been cultivated since at least 2500 cal. BC (Bellwood et al. 1992), and possibly in earlier millennia (Koldihwa and Chapni-Mando: Sharma et al. 1980; Chang 1989; Vishnu-Mittre 1989; Saraswat 1992; but see critical discussion of dating in Possehl and Rissman 1992). In peninsular India they were merged with an agricultural system that utilized summer pulses and millets of peninsular origin.

An unclear aspect of the history of the South-West Asian crops, is the story of different wheat types. As discussed above (Section 4.1), attribution of archaeobotanical material to *Triticum sphaerococcum* has not been reliable. Thus previous reviews of the history of wheat in India (e.g. Vishnu-Mittre 1968c, 1974; Zeven 1978; Randhawa 1980; Kulshrestha 1985; Buth et al. 1987) which emphasize the former dominance of *T. sphaerococcum* should be disregarded until evidence from chaff remains becomes available. Most of the reported evidence for wheat comes from charred caryopses, which are generally inadequate for specific level identifications and the likely presence of free-threshing tetraploid wheat

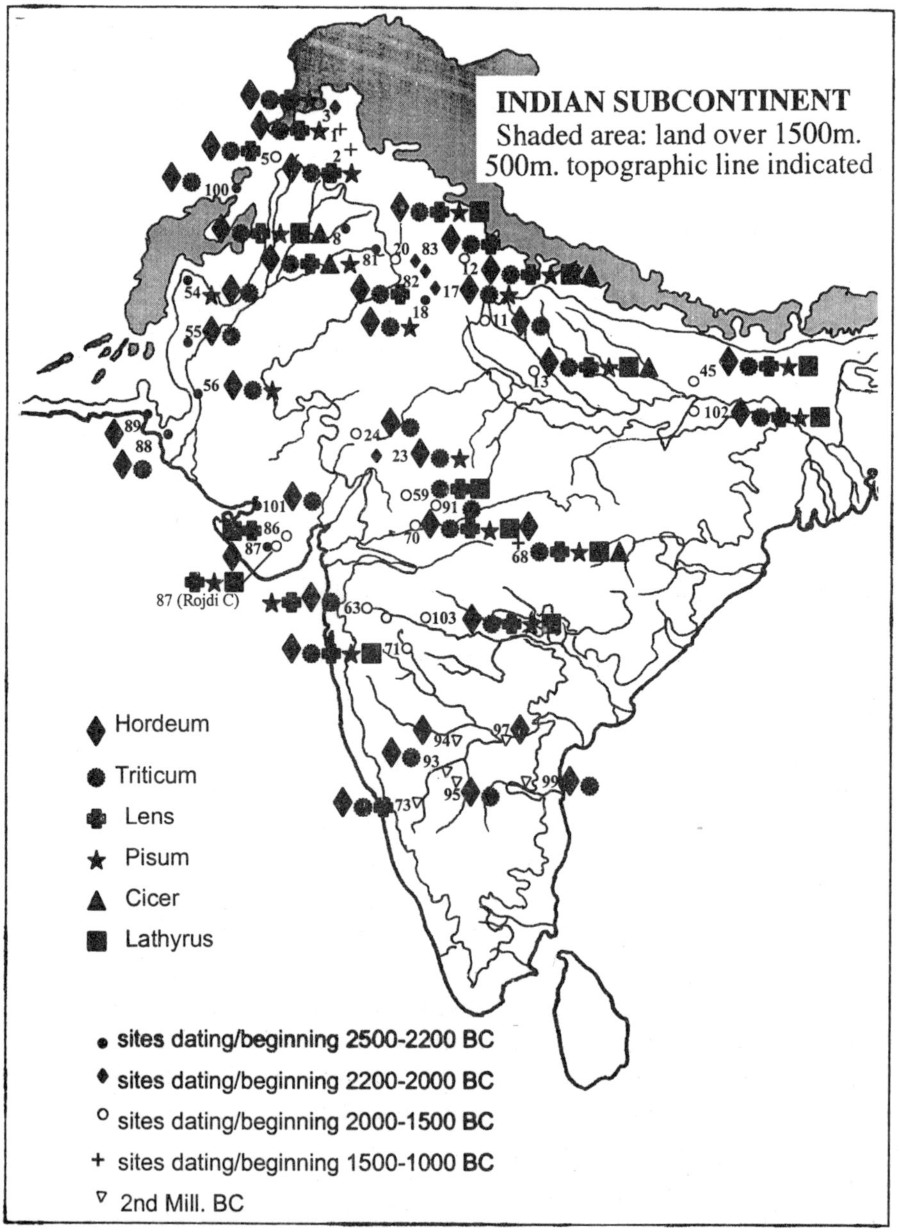

Fig. 3. Map showing the dispersal of the South-West Asian crop suite across South Asia. The representatives of this package (pulses and cereals) are shown next to selected sites plotted according to their approximate archaeological period. Note that only the earliest finds and sites in each region are shown. Site numbers can be found in Tables 2 and 3.

(*T. durum* sensu lato) has been largely ignored (see Section 4.1; Willcox 1992). Thus Vishnu-Mittre's (1986c) suggestion that diploid and tetraploid wheats were introduced to India only in recent times is unfounded. Nevertheless, the bulk of these finds do suggest the widespread presence of free-threshing types (whether hexaploid or tetraploid) in the past, while glume wheats, in particular emmer, would appear to be fairly uncommon. This is perplexing, given the traditional importance of emmer in Karnataka and Tamil Nadu (Pal 1966; Kajale 1974a). Plant impressions in pottery from a few sites have been studied, and as these often include 'chaff' it is possible to suggest plausible specific identifications. For example, glume wheats are present amongst impressions from Pre-Harappan Mehrgarh in Pakistan (Costantini 1983) and from Harappan Kalibangan (cf. Vishnu-Mittre and Savithri 1975). Charred grains of emmer, including in one instance an attached rachis, have come from Rohira, Punjab in the Post-Urban Harappan phase (Saraswat 1986). While in neither case are the illustrated examples adequate for certain identification, there seems a reasonable likelihood for the presence of at least one hulled wheat type, most probably emmer. Other illustrated assemblages, of charred wheat grains, do include specimens that could be emmer (e.g. Early Historic Ter, Vishnu-Mittre et al. 1971: pl. 1.1), although the presentation of the data is usually inadequate to confirm this. It seems plausible that emmer and a free-threshing tetraploid (*T. durum* sensu lato) spread together into peninsular India as part of the 'Harappan package' which included barley and the pulses of South-West Asian origin. The history of *T. sphaerococcum* remains obscure. In the early decades of this century it was cultivated in Punjab, Sindh, parts of Uttar Pradesh and Madhya Pradesh and in pockets of Baluchistan (Ellerton 1939), while today it is more or less extinct (Pal 1966; Kulshrestha 1985). It is not clear whether it represents a relatively recent mutation which has always been of limited local importance, or if indeed it is very ancient and was once more widespread. It showed superior drought resistence in comparison to other wheat types (Percival 1921; Ellerton 1939), which favours the hypothesis of the long history, at least in the north-western part of South Asia. However, this does not provide any reason to expect its more widespread distribution, such as into the Ganga Valley (e.g. Chirand, Bihar; Neolithic Kashmir), as the older archaeobotanical literature suggests. Attempts to estimate the date of its origin, such as a suggestion of 3500 BC (Kulshrestha 1985) seem unwarranted in light of our current knowledge.

Whether flax also spread in South Asia as part of the above-mentioned crop package is unclear, due in part to a sparser archaeological record. The earliest flax evidence came from Late/Post Harappan contexts (i.e. post 2000 BC), at Pirak, Baluchistan (Costantini 1979b) and Rojdi, Gujarat (Weber 1991). Several of these records come from textile fibres, which must be regarded cautiously as evidence for local cultivation as they could be imports. Subsequently, evidence for flax occurs on Chalcolithic sites in Maharashtra from at least the Early Jorwe phase, *c.* 1500 BC (Janaway and Coningham 1995; dating after Possehl and Rissman 1992). Thus, flax appears to lag behind the other South-West Asian crops.

5.7.2 *African Crops and the Hypothesis of a Summer Crop Revolution*

Discussion of African crops in India has focused almost exclusively on millets, to the exclusion of pulses for which there is an equally good archaeobotanical record (Fig. 4). Much interest has been shown in the potential role of African millets in transforming the subsistence systems of ancient India, especially of the Harappan Civilization. Several authors have argued for a 'revolution' in agriculture with the adoption of summer crops, both from East Asia and Africa, around the Harappan sphere in the Late Harappan period, i.e. end of the third/early second millennium BC (Costantini 1981; Costantini and Biasini 1985; Possehl 1980: 33, 1986, 1997,1998; Jarrige 1985, 1997; Meadow 1989, 1996; Franke-Vogt 1995: 32-4; Willcox 1992). This was seen as an agricultural transformation, particularly around the fringes of the Harappan Civilization which corresponds in general to the era of de-urbanization. This *kharif* (monsoon-season) crop revolution opened up new zones to extensive agriculture as opposed to the intensive, presumably irrigated, Harappan system (Possehl 1980: 33, 1997; Meadow 1989, 1996; Franke-Vogt 1995: 32-4). However, this Late Harappan agricultural shift needs to be reconsidered in light of the possibility that earlier dates for the African millets have been overestimated and that *Setaria* and *Panicum* reports relate to indigenous crop species in these genera. The earliest millets cultivated in India are likely to have been entirely indigenous (cf. Weber 1998; Fuller et al. n.d.), and are species that are probably native to the savanna grasslands of the peninsula. This transformation is to be seen, the source of the crops, at least for some regions, such as Gujarat (e.g. Rojdi, Babor Kot, Kuntasi, Surkotada), and at Harappa (Weber 1997, 1998) is likely to have been from the east in inner India, with African crops playing a later and secondary role. The status of east Asian millets, and the possibility of rice coming into northwestern Pakistan from China rather than India in the early second millennium BC (see Jarrige 1997) remain to be critically assessed.

In Gujarat, on the fringes of the Indus Civilization, African millets appeared in India, not as a single package but at different times (Weber 1990, 1991, 1998). Finger millet, *E. coracana*, is the earliest and most widely reported. Although most of these reports are problematic, as discussed earlier in Section 4.2, and some are certainly misidentified. The other African millets are usually thought to arrive by the beginning of the second millennium BC although many early reports are problematic. *Pennisetum* has been reported from a number of Chalcolithic (Malwa Culture) sites in Maharashtra (Kajale 1977c, 1990c, 1991) as well as in Gujarat at Rangpur, Period III, *c.* 1500-1000 cal. BC (Ghosh and Lal 1963; chronology after Possehl and Rissman 1992). A single grain, unidentifiable to species, from Babor Kot in Gujarat (Reddy 1994, 1997) is ambiguous evidence. The timing of the adoption of *Sorghum* is controversial with some doubt being cast as to whether *Sorghum* had even been domesticated before the late first millennium BC (Willcox 1992; Rowley-Conwy et al. 1997). Some tentative reports of *Sorghum* require confirmation, such as those at Pirak and Ahar referred to above (Section 4.2.1). Nevertheless, there are a number of other reports of *Sorghum*, dated on contextual grounds to the first half of the second millennium BC which may constitute support for the earlier origin of

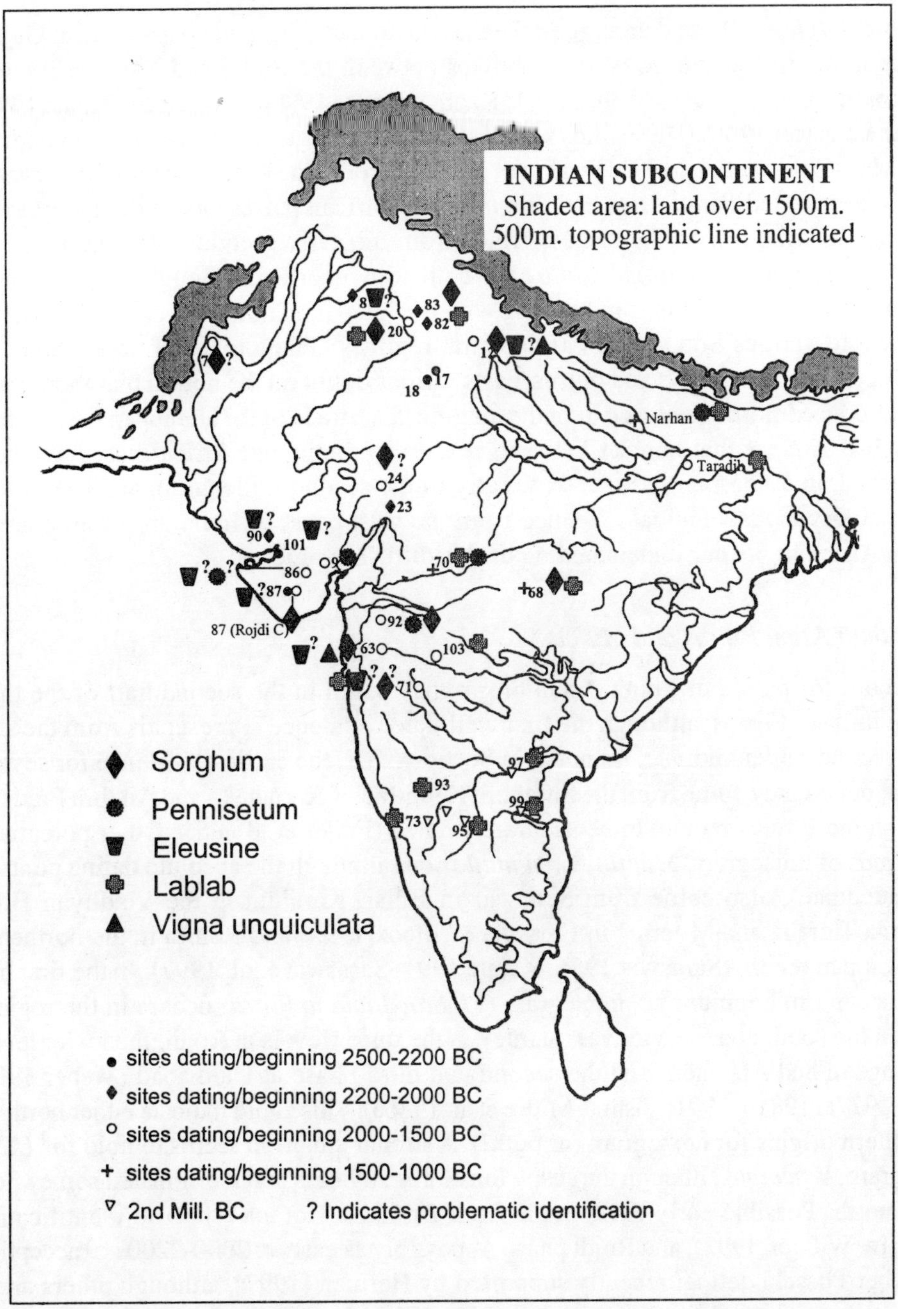

Fig. 4. Map showing the archaeological distribution of African pulses and millets in South Asia. Taxa are shown next to selected sites plotted according to their approximate archaeological period. Questionable identifications are included and indicated by question marks. For discussion of problems with *Eleusine* and *Sorghum* identification, see text, Sections 4.2 and 4.2.1. Site numbers can be found in Tables 2 and 3.

domestic *Sorghum*. These data suggest the introduction of *Sorghum* across parts of Gujarat and the northern Deccan, as well as perhaps between the Sutlej and Yamuna rivers in northern India (e.g. Rojdi C: Weber 1991; Kaothe: Kajale 1990c; Daimabad: Kajale 1977c; Rohira: Saraswat 1986). These finds would seem to argue against accepting the hypothesis of Rowley-Conwy et al. (1997; Deakin et al. 1998) for a late domestication of *Sorghum*.

As with reported *Pennisetum* and *Sorghum*, the African pulses have a distinctly extra-Harappan distribution on the basis of finds from the early second millennium BC (see Fig. 4). *Lablab* and *Vigna unguiculata* have both been recorded, although *Lablab* is much more widely reported. This is in keeping with the idea that *Lablab* diversified relatively quickly into various South Asian agricultural regimes. Taken together as a whole, the evidence of African millets and pulses, casts serious doubt on the notion that these crops were introduced from Africa as part of the long-distance trade of the Harappan Civilization, although it is clear that contact between peninsular India and Africa must have been established, in at least an indirect way, early in the second millennium BC. The lack of contemporary archaeological evidence from the west coast of India and from areas in eastern Africa limits our understanding of this diffusion process.

5.7.3 South Asian Pulses and Millets

The record for pulses of South Asian origin may begin in the second half of the third millennium BC (Fig. 5), although the first well-dated evidence at present is from the start of the second millennium BC. As noted in Section 5.3.1, the earliest evidence for several of these pulses may come from the Southern Neolithic of Karnataka and Andhra Pradesh, although these finds remain to be accurately dated (Fuller et al. n.d.). Other potentially early finds of horsegram, *Macrotyloma uniflorum* (although the absolute dating controls are inadequate), also come from Senuwar in Bihar, Kunjhun in the Vindhyan Hills, Burthana Tigrana and Mitathal in Haryana (Willcox 1992) and Rohira in the northeastern Harappan region (Saraswat 1986; Kajale 1991; Saraswat et al. 1992). In the first half of the second millennium BC, horsegram (*Macrotyloma uniflora*) occurs in the regions between the south and the Vidhyas, namley in the upper levels at Rojdi, the lower levels at Inamgaon and Apegaon, and the second and third phase at Daimabad (Weber 1991; Kajale 1977a, 1988b, 1991; Vishnu-Mittre et al. 1986a). This could indicate either northern or southern origins for horsegram (or both!). A similar situation seems to hold for *Udid/* black gram, *V. mungo*, although the suspicion of this author is that it originated somewhere in the north. Possible early finds come from Birthana Tigrana (specific identification uncertain, Willcox 1992), and Rojdi phase A, possibly as early *c.* 2600-2200 BC (accepting the Weber/Possehl dating; recently supported by Herman [1997], although others argue that this site begins only at the end of the third millennium or the start of the second, i.e. Late Harappan, see Chakrabarti 1995).

The pulses which are more clearly of southern origin are so far only recorded from the second millennium BC. Mung, *Vigna radiata*, however, is widely found on Southern Neolithic sites which await dating but could push its origin back into the early or mid-

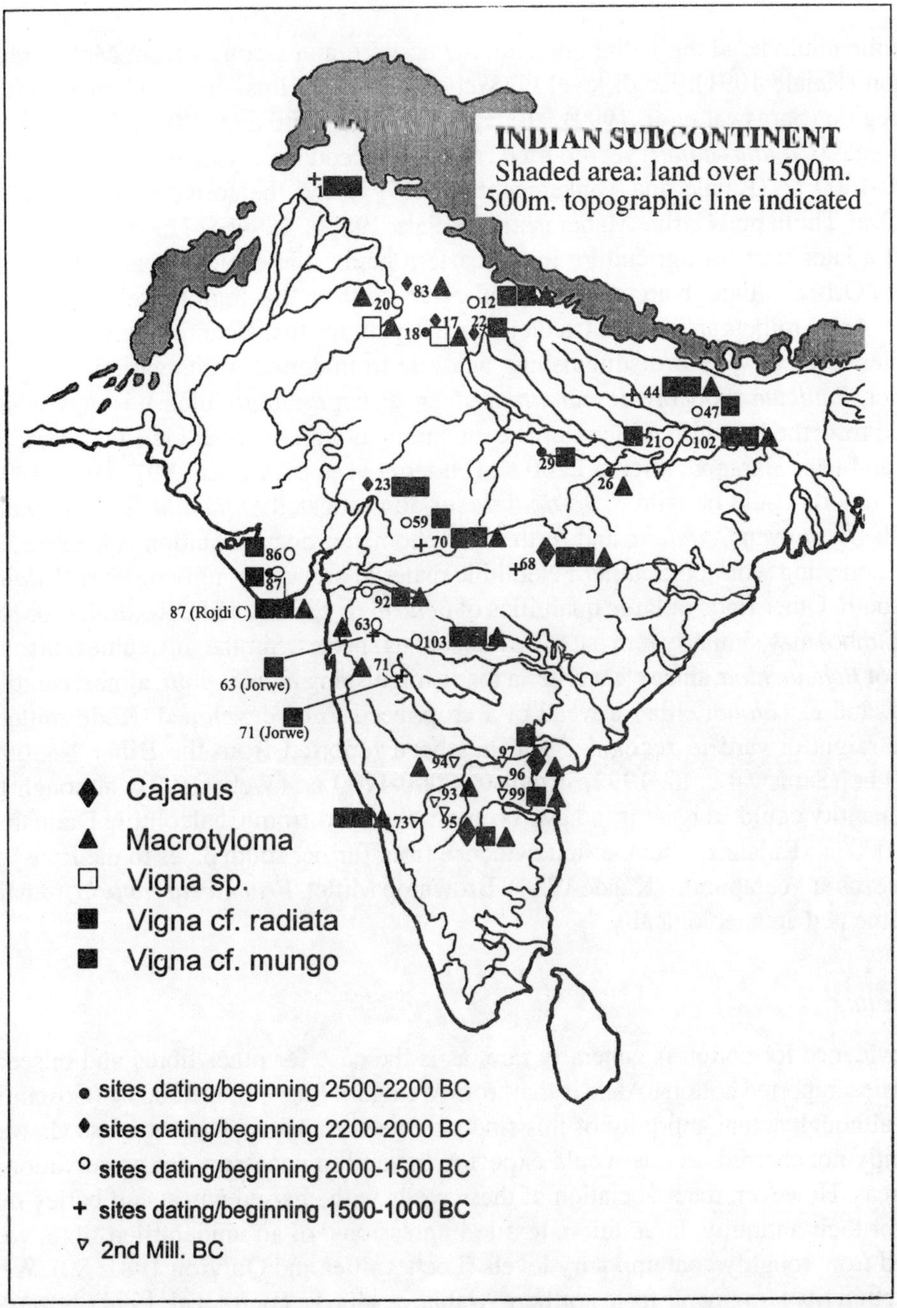

Fig. 5. Map showing the prehistoric distribution of pulses of South Asian origin. Taxa identifications as reported are shown next to selected sites plotted according to their approximate archaeological period. Although *Vigna* finds are reported to species level, it should be recognized that this level of identification is not certain in all cases and requires further confirmation. Site numbers can be found in Tables 2 and 3.

third millennium BC along with horsegram. Otherwise mung comes from Malwa phase Apegaon (Kajale 1991), Rojdi level C (Weber 1991), or Hulas in the Ganga-Yamuna Doab region (Saraswat et al. 1992), all dating between 2000 and 1700 BC. The earliest pigeon-peas (*Cajanus cajan*) yet reported come from Peddamudiyam in Andhra Pradesh, *c.* 1700-1300 BC (Kajale and Venkatasubbaiah 1991) and the Jorwe period (*c.* 1200-900 BC) at Thuljapur Garhi, Maharashtra (Kajale 1988b, 1996b). This would tend to suggest a later start for agriculture in the eastern peninsular region around Bastar and southern Orissa, although archaeobotanical evidence from this region itself is lacking.

South Asian millets are more difficult to trace in part due to difficulties with identifying to species level, as well as distinguishing wild use from domesticated varieties (Fig. 6). However, *Panicum* probably, *P. sumatrense* (syn. *P. miliare* nom. illeg.), is now widely reported from the late third millennium BC, including Southern Neolithic sites, Harappan Rojdi, and later Harappa, after *c.* 2200 BC (Fuller et al. n.d.; Weber 1991, 1997, 1998). *Setaria* reports could be wild *S. verticillata*, or domesticated *S. pumila* (syn. *S. glaüca* nom. illeg.), or even *S. italica*, and further morphometric documentation is needed. The author's ongoing work on Southern Neolithic material argues strongly *against S. italica* in the south. Other finds of large quantities of *Setaria* (e.g. Surkotada, Rojdi, Babor Kot, Oriyo Timbo) may similarly turn out to be indigenous species. Similar difficulties surround reports of *Echinochloa*, since clear criteria for distinguishing *E. crus-galli*, almost ceratinly a weed, and *E. colona*, either a weed or a crop, need to be developed. Kodo millet is fairly straightforward to recognize and has been reported from the Bihar Neolithic *c.* 2000 BC (Saraswat et al. 1992), Rojdi C, 2000-1700 BC (Weber 1991; although the small quantity could suggest it to have been a weed) and from Chalcolithic Daimabad, 1500-1000 BC (Kajale 1977c; the first evidence from further south dates to the Iron Age, *c.* 500 BC, as at Veerapuram (Kajale 1984). Browntop Millet, *Brachiaria ramosa*, remains undocumented archaeologically.

5.7.4 Cotton

Early evidence for cotton is generally rare, as is the case for other fibres and oilseeds. The earliest reported cotton to date is that from Mehrgarh Phase II, *c.* 5000 BC (Costantini 1984), although actual antiquity of this find may need revision. The cotton seeds were apparently not charred, as one would expect to have been necessary for preservation in most areas. However, the association of these seeds with charred wheat and barley may argue for their antiquity. In addition, textile impressions, of an unidentified fibre, were reported from roughly contemporary levels (Lechevallier and Quivron 1981: 80). Well-dated cotton fibre fragments from northern Arabia, *c.* 4400 BC (Betts et al. 1994), however, do suggest that cotton must have been cultivated in the early-mid fifth millennium BC. Cotton seems more likely to have reached Arabia from South Asia then from East Africa, since the limited cotton evidence from Africa (Nubia) does not imply textile production in prehistory (cf. Chowdhury and Buth 1971). Evidence for cotton cloth in South Asia

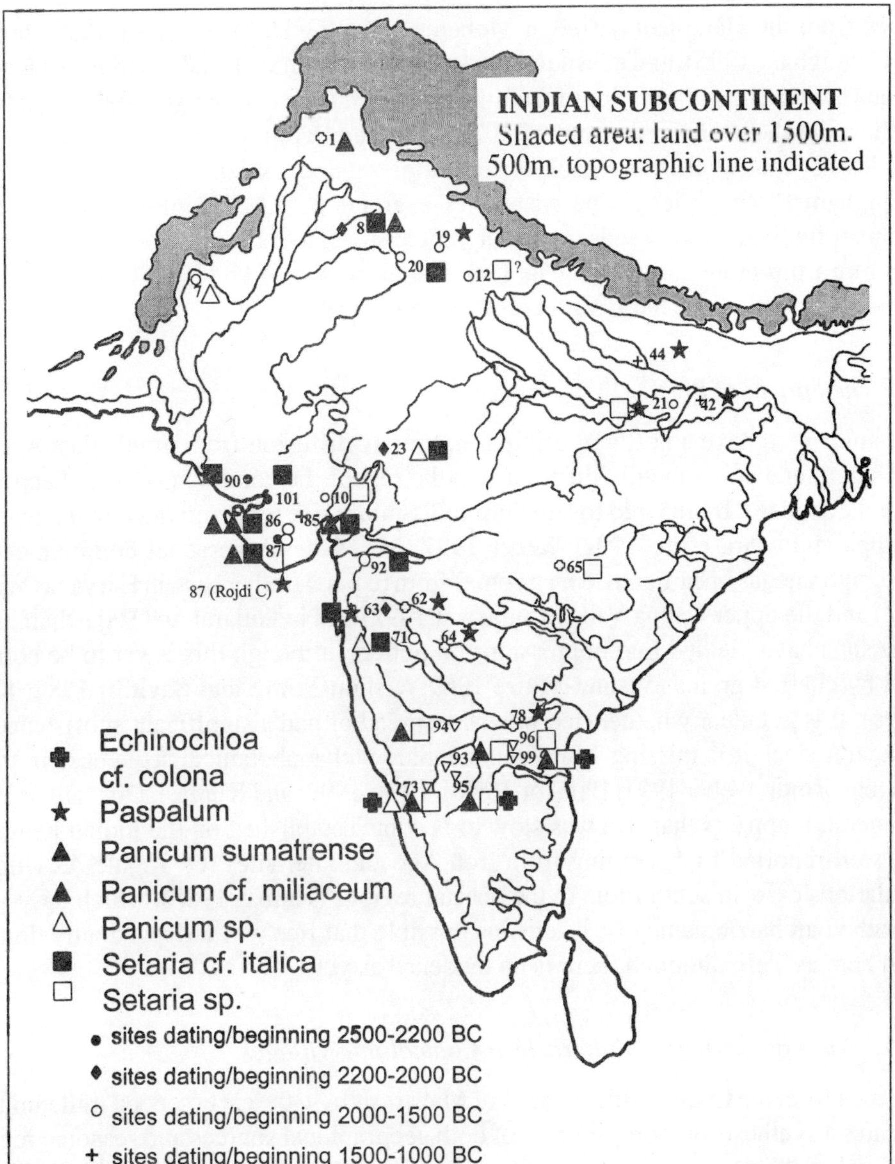

Fig. 6. Map showing the prehistoric distribution of the Asian millets, including those of South Asian and East Asian origins. Reported millet taxa are shown next to selected sites plotted according to their approximate archaeological period. Although reported to species level, it should be recognized that this level of identification is not certain in all cases and requires further confirmation. Site numbers can be found in Tables 2 and 3. ? indicates uncertain identification.

comes from the Harappan period at Mohenjo Daro (Gulati and Turner 1929; Janaway and Coningham 1995), and subsuquently in the Chalcolithic of Maharashtra as Navdatoli (Gulati 1961). Cloth impressions which are presumed to be cotton have been found further south on the Peninsula at the sites of T. Narsipur and Pikhlihal from Late Neolithic/Iron Age levels, that çould date back to the latter second millennium BC (Janaway and Coningham 1995; earlier dating based on Devaraj et al. 1995). Unfortunately archaeobotanical finds of cotton seeds, or better yet capsules, to indicate local cultivation have been rare from prehistoric sites. The Late Harappan site of Hulas (1800-1300 BC?) has produced cotton seeds (Saraswat et al. 1992; Saraswat 1993).

5.7.5 The Spread of Rice

Rice appears to have a northern origin (or an early diffusion from South-East Asia into the Ganga) and subsequently diffused into the rest of the continent (Fig. 7; Section 5.4 and 5.4.1, above). By the mid to late third millennium rice was cultivated in the region of Harappa (Fujiwara et al. 1992; Weber 1997; M. Madella: personal communication). Contemporaneous or earlier evidence comes from regions further east, in Haryana (Willcox 1992) and the upper Ganga Valley (Saraswat 1992) and in Gujarat and Rajasthan, where some sites have yielded rice impressions on pottery, although this is yet to be corroborated by charred grains (Vishnu-Mittre 1969; Vishnu-Mittre and Savithri 1982; Kajale 1989c). It is not clear whether rice was widespread or had a significant subsistence role in Gujarat since it is missing from well sampled archaeobotanical sequences in the region (e.g. Rojdi, Weber 1991; Balakot, Reddy 1994, 1997; and Kuntasi, Dhavalikar 1995). In general, it appears that rice was slow to become established on the Indian Peninsula, with well-reported finds coming from Iron Age and later sites (cf. Kajale As wild rice populations exist in south India in the coastal regions (Kumar 1988), which have yet to be studied archaeobotanically, it remains possible that rice was independently domesticated here as well, although there is no evidence as yet.

5.7.6 A Case of Synthesis: Maharashtra Chalcolithic Villages

Evidence from the Chalcolithic villages of Maharashtra in the early second millennium BC indicates a synthesis of crops in terms of both geographical sources and seasonal regimes (cf Kajale 1989c). Sites like Daimabad (Kajale 1977a; Vishnu-Mittre et al. 1986a), Inamgaon (Kajale 1988b), and Kaothe (Kajale 1990c) indicate that Near Eastern cereals and pulses were grown in the same regions as African millets, indigenous(?) millets and tropical pulses (from both India and Africa). Possehl's (1986) suggestion that African millets were important for opening up peninsular India to agricultural settlement seems controverted on current evidence. Understanding the ways in which different agricultural systems, including diverse crops and cropping systems were integrated in Maharashtra during the late third millennium and early second millennium BC remains a challenge to be addressed in future archaeobotanical work.

6. EMERGING DIRECTIONS AND OTHER DATASETS

Although the focus of most archaeobotanical research are charred seeds from which the spread of crops is reconstructed, there are several other kinds of archaeobotanical evidence. In the sections that follow five other kinds of archaeobotanical evidence are briefly reviewed. First, there is the interpretation of non-crop seeds found in assemblages of agricultural practices. Second, there is the identification of ancient wood remains, including wood charcoal and fragments preserved by other means. Third, there is the study charred parenchyma fragments which have hitherto been overlooked in research on charred plant assemblages. Three other aspects of archaeobotanical work rely on non-charred, microscopic remains. One micro-remain which has been traditionally utilized is the study of pollen from archaeological sediments. Finally I turn to two largely untapped areas of research, phytoliths, and the extraction of ancient DNA preserved in archaeological plant specimens.

6.1 Findings from Wood Identification

The most frequent macrobotanical remains from archaeological sites are fragments of wood charcoal. Wood charcoal is likely to represent primarily the wood which was used to fuel fires, although the burning of other cultural products, such as artefacts or structures, may also contribute. Thus in contrast to seed remains which represent chance/incidental burning, wood is generally considered to be the product of intentional burning (Pearsall 1983, 1989: 203). Since most fuel is likely to come from the vicinity of the site it should provide some reflection of the surrounding vegetation, and numerous studies have utilized changes in the composition of wood taxa to examine changes in the landscape, or to compare the woodland types associated with different archaeological sites (e.g. Minnis 1978; Smart and Hoffman 1988; Pearsall 1983, 1989; Thiebault 1988, 1989,1992; Lone et al. 1988, 1991; Thompson 1994; Saraswat et al. 1994). Admittedly, this reflection will be filtered by cultural processes, such as preferences for certain kinds of wood, and avoidance of others (such as fruit trees, or sacred trees). Indeed, wood choice can relate to political and social concerns as shown by study in Incan Peru (Hastorf and Johannessen 1991: 140-1). Social patterning in the use of fuels, including choices related to the pyrotechnology of different craft activities, can be studied through the analysis of samples from various context on large site excavation, such as that at Harappa (Miller 1991). Despite these biases major changes in woodland composition should be detectable, related in turn to clearance, grazing, or climatic factors. The charcoal record thus combines environmental availability with cultural practices of exploitation. It is difficult to interpret quantification of wood charcoal, even more so than for other charred remains, since large numbers of fragments could originate from the same log or trunk. Nevertheless, relative percentages of different taxa are usually compared (Thiebault 1988, 1989; Lone et al. 1993; Thompson 1994).

In the early decades of Independence, a large number of haphazard, hand-collected

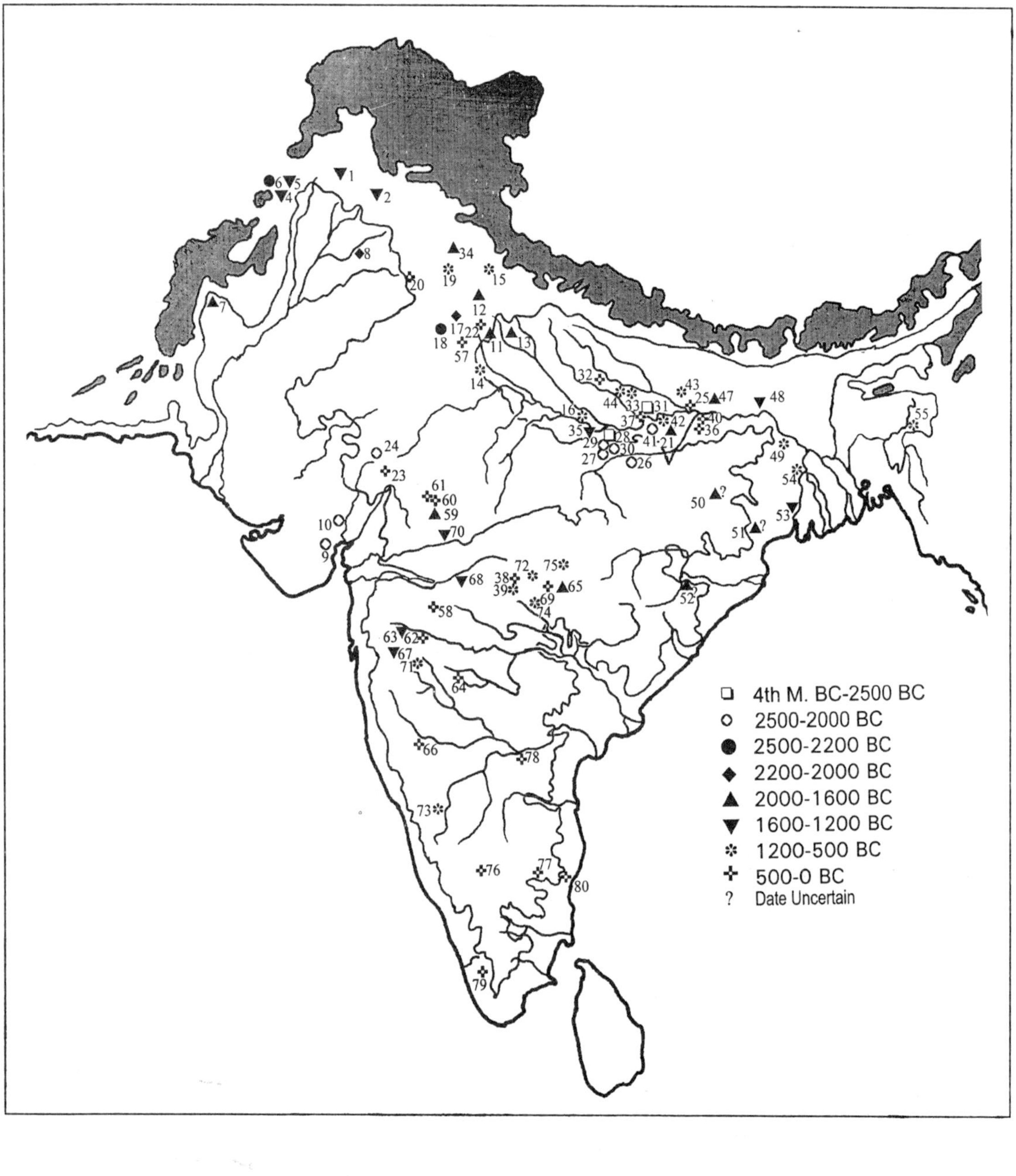

4th M. BC-2500 BC
2500-2000 BC
2500-2200 BC
2200-2000 BC
2000-1600 BC
1600-1200 BC
1200-500 BC
500-0 BC
? Date Uncertain

Fig. 7. Distribution of prehistoric archaeological evidence for rice, including sites of different periods. Sites numbered as per the following list. References for most sites given in Tables 2 and 3. Some additional sites, where rice only has been reported, are plotted on the basis of previous reviews (Vishnu-Mittre 1989, Kajale 1989c; 1991). Only sites not included in the above sources are followed by citations.

1. Semthan
2. Gufkral
3. Burzahom
4. Loebanhr 3
5. Bir-Kot-Ghwandai
6. Ghaleghay
7. Pirak
8. Harappa
9. Rangpur
10. Lothal
11. Lal Quila
12. Hulas
13. Atranjikhera
14. Noh
15. Hastinapura
16. Radhan
17. Mitathal
18. Burthana Trigrana
19. Rupar
20. Sanghol
21. Senuwar
22. Daulatpur (Vishnu-Mittre et al. 1985)
23. Balathal
24. Ahar
25. Manji
26. Kunjhun (Clark & Khanna 1989)
27. Lekhnia
28. Chopani-Mando III
29. Koldihawa
30. Mahagara
31. Damdama
32. Hulashkera
33. Khairadih
34. Un (Vishnu-Mittre et al. 1986)
35. Kausambi
36. Sonepur
37. Patilaputra
38. Kaundinyapur
39. Khairwada
40. Rajgir
41. Baraunha
42. Mahga
43. Sohgaura
44. Narhan
45. Chirand
46. Oriyup
47. Mahisadal
48. Barudih/Singbhum (date uncertain)
49. Baidipur
50. Puri (date uncertain, plotted after Glover and Higham 1996)
51. Baidaypur
52. Pandu Rajar Dhibi
53. Ambri
57. Kokhkrakot
58. Bhokardan
59. Dangwada
60. Ujjain
61. Nagda
62. Nevasa
63. Daimabad
64. Ter
65. Adam
66. Kolhapur
67. Walaki
68. Tuljapur Garhi
69. Paunar
70. Navdatoli
71. Inamgaon
72. Bhagimohari
73. Haliur
74. Kairwada
75. Naikund
76. Koppa
77. Kunnatur
78. Veerapuram
79. Adichanalur
80. Arikamedu

samples of charcoal were examined for taxonomic identification by Chowdhury, Ghosh and colleagues at the Dehra Dun forestry institute (Table 10). Starting from about 1975, Vishnu-Mittre and colleagues began reporting species identified from charcoal samples submitted for radiocarbon dating; this has produced a large number of reports of one or a few species from a site (e.g. Vishnu-Mittre and Savithri 1979c). In most cases only a very few species were identified and rarely were they at all surprising or indicative of significant vegetational differences from the present. A detailed discussion of the vegetational grouping represented in the material from Lothal in Gujarat, concluded that some of the forest communities may have been more widespread in the state in prehistory (Ramesh Rao and Lal 1985). In a few instances, however, charcoal analyses reveal the presence of species which are known to be cultivated or utilized for food; while the use of the wood of these species certainly does not indicate other uses of other plant parts, it at least raises the possibility. For example, sites in Baluchistan, Iran, Kashmir and Punjab have produced *Vitis* (grape) charcoal, which supports the contention that grapes were

TABLE 10. SITES WITH IDENTIFIED WOOD CHARCOAL IN INDIA/PAKISTAN

Site	Period	Sampling notes	Taxa qty.	Reference
Arikamedu	Early Historic	hand	3	Chowdhury and Ghosh 1946
Hastinapura	1000-500 BC	hand	3	Chowdhury and Ghosh 1955
Maski	Neolithic	hand	2	Chowdhury and Ghosh 1957
Kalsi	Early Historic	hand	4	Ghosh and Lal 1961
Rangpur	2500-1000 BC	hand	6	Lal 1962-3
Kandiyapura	Early Historic	hand	1	Vishnu-Mittre 1966
Prakash	1700 BC-600 AD	hand	7	Rao and Sahi 1967
Ter	200 BC-400 AD	hand	6	Vishnu-Mittre et al. 1971
Rojdi	*c*. 2000 BC (?)	hand	1	Vishnu-Mittre and Savithri 1979c
Hallur	1800-1000 BC	hand	5	Vishnu-Mittre and Savithri 1979c
Tekkalakota	2000-1500 BC	hand	1	Vishnu-Mittre and Savithri 1979c
Inamgaon	1800-1000 BC	hand	3	Vishnu-Mittre and Savithri 1979c
Kalibangan	2600-1500 BC	hand	12	Vishnu-Mittre and Savithri 1979c
Ahar	?(2500-1500 BC)	hand	2	Vishnu-Mittre and Savithri 1979c
Rupar	*c*. 500 BC	hand	2	Vishnu-Mittre and Savithri 1979c
Chirand	*c*. 1700 BC	hand	1	Vishnu-Mittre and Savithri 1979c
Lothal	*c*. 1700 BC	hand	4	Chowdhury 1974
		43 samples, by hand	7	Ramesh Rao and Lal 1985
Inamgaon (1971)	1700 BC-*c*. 1000 BC	6 samples, hand collected	8	U. Prakash, in Vishnu-Mittre and Savithri 1975
Atranjikhera	2000-50 BC	hand	10	Chowdhury et al. 1977
Ramapuram	*c*. 1000 BC	hand	1 (+1 later contaminant	Vishnu-Mittre et al. 1985
Veerapuram	*c*. 0 AD	hand	1	Vishnu-Mittre et al. 1985
Kayatha, Madhya Pradesh	(2500-1400 BC)	hand	2	Vishnu-Mittre et al. 1985
Singh-Bhagwantpur, Dt. Kurukshetra, Harayana	?	hand	3	Vishnu-Mittre et al. 1985
Nagara, Dt. Kaira, Gujarat	(*c*. 1500-500 BC)	hand	1	Vishnu-Mittre et al. 1985
Sonegan, Dt. Pune	*c*. 1500-1000 BC	hand	2	Vishnu-Mittre et al. 1985
Besnagar, Dt. Vidisha Madhya Pradesh	Early Historic	hand	2	Vishnu-Mittre et al. 1985
Sringaverapura, Dt. Allahabad, U.P.	*c*. 1000 BC	hand	6	Vishnu-Mittre et al. 1986
Lekhahia, Dt. Mirzapur U.P.	Mesolithis	hand	3	Vishnu-Mittre et al. 1986
Rajgir, Bihar	Iron Age	hand	1	Vishnu-Mittre et al. 1985
Gufkral	2300-1500 BC	hand	2	Vishnu-Mittre et al. 1984
		hand	4	Vishnu-Mittre et al. 1985
		hand	7	Vishnu-Mittre et al. 1986b
Semthan	*c*. 1500 BC	flot	1	Buth and Bisht 1981 (blue pine)
Burzahom	2325-1500 BC	hand?	3	Vishnu-Mittre and Savithri 1979c
	2325-1500 BC	flot	4	Buth and Kaw 1984
	2325-1500 BC	flot		Lone et al. 1993

(contd.)

Site	Period	Sampling notes	Taxa qty.	Reference
Mehrgarh-Nausharo	*c.* 6000-*c.* 2000 BC	sampling hearths, sieving	14	Thiebault 1988, 1989, 1991, 1992
Rohira	2500-1700 BC	?	13	Saraswat et al. 1990; Saraswat and Chanchala 1994
Ahichchhatra, Dist. Bareilly, U.P.	?	hand?	5	Saraswat et al. 1990
Kausambi, Dt. Allahabad, U.P.	Early Historic	hand?	8	Saraswat et al. 1992
Burzhom, Kashmir	2400 BC-200 AD	flot, 4 phases	27	Lone et al. 1993
Semthan, Kashmir	1500 BC-1000 AD	flot, 5 phases	27	Lone et al. 1993
Hulaskhera, Dt. Lucknow U.P.	(800 BC-500 AD)	hand?	6	Saraswat and Chanchala 1994
Narhan	1000-200 BC	flot.	25	Saraswat et al. 1993, 1994
Shikarpur, Kutch	2500-2200 BC	hand(?)	9	Saraswat et al. 1995
Mahorana, Punjab	2300-1900 BC	hand(?)	3	Saraswat and Chanchala 1996
	800-400 BC	hand(?)	1	
	100-200 AD	hand(?)	5	
Senuwar, Bihar	2200-600 BC	hand(?)	20	Saraswat and Chanchala 1996
Sanghol, Punjab	(1900-1400 BC)	?	7	Saraswat and Chanchala 1997
Kot Diji	Harappan	from section scraping		Castelletti et al. 1994

cultivated in these regions in prehistory (Costantini 1979c; Thiebault 1988,1989; Saraswat et al.. 1990; Lone et al. 1993: 180). Similarly, the presence of *Mangifera indica* (mango) wood from Narhan in the early first millennium BC (Period II) raises the possibility that mangoes were cultivated or at least husbanded (Saraswat et al. 1994). Mangoe wood charcoal together with that of the jackfruit tree (*Artocarpus heterophyllus*) were also found from Senuwar, Phase II, *c.* 1200 BC- 600 BC (Saraswat et al. 1996). While charcoal, and in one case fibre impressions, have been identified to the genus *Saccharum*, there remains no evidence for *S. officinarum* L., the cultivated sugarcane (Chowdhury and Ghosh 1955; Vishnu-Mittre 1971, 1974: 26). In addition, wood charcoal can provide evidence for the expansion or contraction of woody species ranges in the past, whether through climatic influence or human action. For example, in Kashmir a number of taxa represented in wood charcoal are not considered native to the Himalaya and must have been adopted through some sort of interaction/contact with cultures to the north in more temperate Asia, including *Platanus orientalis*, *Morus* and *Buxus* (Buth and Bisht 1981; Buth and Kaw 1985; Buth et al. 1987; Lone et al. 1993).

In addition to charcoal, wood is on occasion preserved without charring (see Table 11), often due to waterlogging. The finds in this category are very heterogenous with regard to cultural associations. Nevertheless, these data have provided some important information on long-distance trade either in special woods or wooden products themselves. For example, a wooden coffin excavated from Harappa was found to contain two woods from the Himalayan forests, Elm *(Ulmus* sp.[7]) and cedar (*Cedrus deodara*), the latter known today for its fine scent (Chowdhury and Ghosh 1951). The Indian rosewood (*Dalbergia latifolia*) is restricted today to inner India and may also have been transported some distance to Harappa. However, the reports of *Dalbergia* charcoal from Baluchistan and Iran (Thiebault 1988; Costantini 1979c) in antiquity raises the possibility that this species may have had a broader distribution. This suggests the transport of particular wood types for the production of special objects from regions on periphery of, or indeed beyond, the Harappan Civilization area. In addition, wood represented in preserved furniture fragments, are often from species valued for the hardwoods today and generally rare or absent from studied charcoal assemblages, such as the *Diospyros* from Arikamedu (although there are admittedly few charcoal assemblages published from south India). This does hint at the selection against certain useful species as fuel. More work on reconstructing the distributions of vegetational groups in the past, through systematic charcoal studies and other lines of evidence such as pollen, are needed in South Asia to better understand the distribution and utilization of forest materials. In some coastal areas of the country, notably in the region of Calcutta, waterlogged wood remains (submerged forests) are sometimes preserved which if studied offer detailed information on local natural vegetational communities in the past (e.g. A. Ghosh 1941; for an example of the kinds of analysis that can be made with submerged forests, see Clapham et al. 1997).

6.2 Potential of Parenchyma

Fragments of charred parenchyma, the starchy storage tissue of plants which often comes from tubers (or other storage structures), are a common component of archaeobotanical assemblages. Parenchyma fragments, however, have gone largely unnoticed by archaeobotanists and unstudied until quite recently, especially in the Old World (Pearsall 1989: 165-73; Hather 1992, 1994a, 1996; Hather and Kirch 1991). Two likely sources of these are: firstly, the tubers of weeds used as fuel, which enter the site as crop by-products when harvesting is done by uprooting (as is often the case with south Indian legumes). The second possibility is root foods. Parenchyma can be easily separated during initial sorting of samples, but identification requires high magnification, probably SEM, and may not always provide diagnostic characters. There are no comparative collections, nor to my knowledge literature, on the identification of Indian tubers. Nevertheless, work on European tubers provides useful guides to identification at the family level (Hather 1994b), and some archaeobotanical studies of tubers are available from Island South-East Asia which discuss the major root crop groups of the Old World tropics such as Dioscoreaceae, Araceae and Zingiberaceae (Hather and Kirch 1991; Hather 1994c; cf. Hather 1996). *Dioscorea* spp. have also been identified in samples from West Africa (Paz 1997).

When and where the various root crops or gathered tubers were used remains a large lacuna in our understanding of the past subsistence. In exploring these lines of evidence,

TABLE 11. UNCHARRED WOOD FINDS

Site (Period)	Find type/Context	Taxa	Reference
Arikamedu (Early Historic)	tools, furniture, or timbers	*Heritiera* sp. *Mimusops* sp. *Diospyros* sp.	Chowdhury and Ghosh 1946
Kirari	post	*Casearia* sp.	Ghosh 1950
Harappa (Harappan)	coffin	*Cedrus deodara* *Dalbergia latifolia* *Ulmus* sp.	Chowdhury and Ghosh 1951
	mortar	*Zizyphus* sp.	
Sisulpurgarh (Early Historic)	waterlogged	*Acacia* sp. *Casearia* sp. (?) *Holharrhena* sp. *Boswellia serrata* Bambusaceae	Chowdhury and Ghosh 1952
Pataliputra (Early Historic)	palisade	*Shorea robusta*	Ghosh and Lal 1958
Mula-Dam	fragments from sediments	*Terminalia* sp.	Rajaguru 1970
Chirand	fibre impressions	*Saccharum* cf. *spontaneum*	Vishnu-Mittre 1971
Nirgudsar	from buried channel		Kajale and Rajaguru 1989
Betamcherla (Mesolithic)	fragments from cave sediments	*Cassia* cf. *fistula* L. *Acacia* cf. *chudra* Willd.	Kajale et al. 1991

it will be necessary to consider a large range of indigenous, edible wild tubers, in India. In addition, it has been suggested on modern ethnographic parallels in north-eastern India, that these wild tubers would have served as important food resources of Palaeolithic/Mesolithic hunter-gatherers (Chatterjee and Ghosh 1990; Chatterjee 1991). Many of these species are known as 'famine foods' in floristic or ethnobotanical literature (Gamble and Fischer 1921-35; Vishnu-Mittre 1981,1985; Mehra and Arora 1985; Maheshwari and Singh 1965). There is textual evidence for the use of root foods in the first millennium BC in northern India from the Yajurveda and Brahmanas (Achaya 1994), including *aluka* yams (probably *Dioscorea alata* or *D. esculenta*), originally from northern South-East Asia or Burma(?) (Alexander and Coursey 1969; Hahn 1995); *visa* lotus stem, *shaluka* lotus roots (*Nymphea* sp.?); radishes (*Raphianus sativus* L.) originally from South-West Asia (Crisp 1995); ginger (*Zingiber officinale* Rosc.) which could be native to India, as several wild *Zingiber* species are known and utilized as seasoning (cf. Maheshwari and Singh 1965), although South-East Asia and Pacific Islands are also possibilities from initial domestication and wild *Z. officinale* has not yet been identified (Nayar and Ravindran 1995); garlic/onions (*Allium* spp.) from Iran/Afghanistan? (Zohary and Hopf 1993). Identifying archaeological evidence for these and other species remains a challenge for future archaeobotany.

Archaeobotanical evidence of tubers in South Asia has yet to be fully explored. Small rhizomes have been reported from two sites in Haryana, protohistoric and late historic, although these small tuber types were not necessarily food plants (Willcox 1992). Also, ongoing work on assemblages from Southern Neolithic site by the author (unpublished; see Fuller et al. n.d.) indicates the presence of probable charred parenchyma fragments on most Southern Neolithic sites, especially on the earliest levels. SEM examination of these specimens should allow to assess whether these represent the utilization of edible tuber types such as yams.

6.3 Pollen from Archaeological Sites: Problems of Preservation and Interpretation

The study of pollen from archaeological sediments has received less attention than macro-remains. A few studies have highlighted its potential to fill-out reconstructions of past vegetation and plant use and potential contributions of this dataset have been reviewed by Dimbleby (1985) and Pearsall (1989). But soil pollen and that from archaeological sediments presents serious problems of taphonomy and preservation. Several of difficulties of interpreting archaeological pollen assemblages were outlined by Bottema (1975), including a careful consideration of the representation of insect-pollinated taxa (mostly asteraceaea) which have been reported in large quantities from archaeological sites. Pollen rain, in general, consists of wind-pollinated species, but burrowing bees and other insects can lead to the accumulation of other taxa. In addition, bioturbation of this kind and others will lead to the contamination of ancient layers by more modern pollen. Pollen may even be moved downwards by water percolation. In addition, some soil environments, especially with extremes in pH, pollen is chemically destroyed or damaged, in particular pollen taxa with thinner exines. On the whole these and other factors indicate the need for extreme caution when interpreting archaeological pollen.

The first attempt to extract pollen from archaeological sediments in South Asia was the work on material from Maski (Vishnu-Mittre 1957d). From six soil samples spanning Periods I and II at that site, 10 pollen morphotypes were distinguished, seven of which could be assigned to at least a family level taxon but only a few with certainty to genus. This state of identification resulted both from the early state affairs with regards to the comparative study of the Indian pollen flora as well as the more general difficulties with specific level identification from pollen of several families. Little interpretation is offered for the pollen; while most of the taxa could be readily referred to tree and grassland flora of southern India as it is known today, the presence of pine was noted with interest. Pine pollen, however, is always problematic due to its form which allows dispersal over particularly vast distances. Vishnu-Mittre subsequently became less enthusiastic about pollen analysis from archaeological sediments since many of the sites he sampled over the years yielded very little (Vishnu-Mittre 1989). There has been some renewed interest for testing some archaeological sediments for the presence of pollen apparently preserved due to proximity of copper artefacts (e.g. Kajale and Deotare 1990, 1993, 1996), although the analytical contribution of such pollen is unclear.

Nevertheless, archaeological pollen analysis made some significant contributions to the archaeobotany of the Harappan Civilization through two studies. In conjunction with their study of natural pollen sequences from salt lakes in Rajasthan, Gurdip Singh and his colleagues also examined two sediment samples from the excavations at Kalibangan (Singh 1971; Singh et al. 1974). They compared the pollen constituents with the pollen subzone SM-3a, defined on the basis of the pollen sequence of Sambhar Lake, which corresponded to the Mature Harappan period. Cereal sized grass pollen was recovered from both archaeological samples, with an extremely large presence in one of them (58 per cent of the pollen). This, they suggest must indicate 'very local' occurrence. Indeed, on analogy with a crop processing in which pollen was collected (Vuorela 1973; Richardson and Hubbard 1977; Bower 1992), it can be suggested that the processing of cereal crops is likely to have been carried in the vicinity of the archaeological context sampled. (This assumes that the large grass pollen is correctly identified as that of a cereal; for discussion of some of the difficulties see Section 5.6, above.)

A more extensive study of pollen from the Harappan site of Balakot (in Sindh) was undertaken for a doctoral thesis by McKean (1983; unfortunately unpublished but summarized in Dales 1986). As excavation and flotation had yielded little in the way of macro-remains, although barley was present, pollen provided another means of investigating local environment and agriculture. On the whole, McKean found that the pollen flora represented the local vegetational groups that remain present in the region of the site today, and she concluded that there was therefore no evidence for climatic change in this area since the Harappan period, calling into question the argument by Singh et al. (1974) that Post-Harappan cultural changes were brought about by a rapid climatic change at the end of the Harappan period that was indicated in the Rajasthan lake profiles (for further discussion of this topic see Fuller and Madella in Vol. IV of this series). In addition, she obtained pollen evidence for the presence of crop plants in addition to cereals, including cotton. On the whole, pollen from archaeological sediments has made only minor contributions to the larger archaeobotanical record of South Asia, and, as Vishnu-Mittre (1989) asserted, it seems unlikely to do so in the near future due to the difficulties with predicting which sites will preserve pollen and when they do, interpreting the formation processes of archaeological pollen assemblages.

6.4 Potential of Phytoliths

Phytoliths (called spodograms when cuticle is preserved) are microscopic silica bodies produced by plants. Since opaline silica is a glass it does not usually bio-degrade, although it can be destroyed by physical abrasion and in some soil environments chemical dissolution. The extraction of phytoliths from archaeological sediments is increasingly being used to examine ancient human plant use (Piperno 1988; Pearsall 1989; Kajale et al. 1995). Phytoliths are also deposited in natural environments. After plants decay, phytoliths are deposited in the soil or they can be transported by wind, water, or animals. In principle then they are deposited constantly and should be preserved in palaeosols.

Small samples of soil/sediment can be collected like those for archaeological pollen study (Section 12, above): collection from freshly exposed sediments should be immediately bagged and sealed so as to avoid contamination by modern airborne phytoliths. One important advantage of these over other kinds of samples is that they can be collected from the cleaning of old stratigraphic sections, thus allowing the re-sampling of previously excavated sites, such as a study of Pre-Harappan/Harappan Kot Diji (Madella 1995, 1997). In addition, because samples are very small, they provide the opportunity for comparing discrete archaeological contexts/locales on a single site in order to study spatial variation in past activities which involved plant use (e.g. Madella 1998). The collection and laboratory processing for phytolith extraction must be done to insure against cross-contamination between the sediments of different samples. Numerous extraction techniques have been described, with the important steps being the removal of organics and carbonates in the sediments, usually followed by the separation of the silica fraction from the denser mineral fraction (Powers and Gilbertson 1987; Piperno 1988; Pearsall 1989; Madella et al. 1998; Lentfer and Boyd 1998). Since most processing techniques have the potential to sometimes damage multi-cellular ('articulated') phytoliths, additional slide mountings of sediment without chemical treatment have sometimes been used to scan for multi-cellular preservation (Madella 1995, 1997).

Phytolith studies can trace their roots to the 1830s when 'phytolitharia' were identified amongst other *infusoria*, microscopic organisms or their remains, discovered in wind-carried dust and sediments by the physician/naturalist Christian Ehrenberg (Powers 1992). Nineteenth and early twentieth century German research focused on the morphology of silica bodies produced by different plants while the systematic study of silica from soils was pursued from the late 1930s in Russia and subsequently in the 1950s in Wales, U.K. (Powers 1992). The first palaeobotanical and archaeological applications began in the late 1960s and 1970s, in Japan and America, notable among them are the studies of Watanbe (1968, 1970) to identify prehistoric phytoliths of rice and millets, and the methodological review by Rovner (1971). Archaeological phytolith analysis has yet to be conducted on any appreciable scale in India, although its potential has recently been outlined (Kajale et al. 1995). Phytoliths (although not referred to as such) have already played a part in understanding archaeological site formation. The presence of silicified grass cells was an important factor in arguments in favour of a dung origin for the Neolithic ashmounds of south India made by Zeuner (1959), whose results were repeated at the Kupgal ashmound (Mujumdar and Rajaguru 1966). Both groups of researchers found groups of articulated, silicified long cells, which in light of phytolith studies can be classed as spiny rods, a cell type common in the epidermis of grass, particularly on the glumes, lemma and palea of grass florets. Systematic phytolith studies may have much to contribute to understanding the Neolithic ashmounds or similar dung deposits (as suggested by Kajale et al. 1995), since dung usually incorporates large amounts of well preserved plant silica bodies. Such information may provide evidence relating to layer formation, seasonality and palaeoecology. The phytoliths should reflect the fodder of Neolithic cattle herds, and thus provide insight into the kinds of environments visited by Neolithic herders.

Some phytolith study has been carried on sites in Pakistan of the Harappan period. Fujiwara et al. (1992) reported a preliminary analysis of phytolith samples collected from old exposures at Harappa which included rice forms and possible *Eleusine*. However, the sampling conditions are not clear and the possibility of modern wind-borne contamination must be considered. Nevertheless, additional samples from recently excavated contexts being studied by Marco Madella also contain rive phytoliths (M. Madella: personal communication). It is not as yet clear whether domesticated finger millet, *Eleusine coracana* produces silica bodies which are clearly distinct from wild South Asian relatives, such as *E. indica* or *Dactyloctinum aegyptiacum* (tribe Eragrostideae), both widespread weeds and colonizers of disturbed habitats. Phytolith analysis is now a part of the Italian Archaeological Mission to the Rohri Hills, Pakistan and the Excavations at Harappa (Madella 1995, 1997, 1998: personal communication).

Phytolith identification is complicated by the fact that any given plant produces numerous different forms of phytoliths and similar phytolith forms may be produced by unrelated species. This has led to two different directions of research on phytoliths: one focuses on finding particular phytolith forms specific to a given species or taxonomic group while the alternative approach classifies phytoliths into form categories and uses these morphological types to compare assemblages and therefore highlight changes in the nature of vegetation input to sediments, such as differences in anatomical parts (e.g. leaves, stems, roots, spikelets), or differences in terms of source plant community. There are disagreements amongst specialists about the degree to which the identification of individual plant species is possible. Numerous food plant genera have been sampled for distinctive forms (e.g. Cummings 1992), although there is need for caution until a wider range of non-crop relatives have been sampled. The rice genus (*Oryza*) can be identified by a distinctive bulliform phytolith (Fujiwara 1993; Pearsall et al. 1995), and domesticated rice can be reliably distinguished from wild species through examination of the 'double-peaked glume cell', allowing for a degree of overlap which produces some indeterminate examples in most samples (Pearsall et al. 1995; Zhao et al. 1998). Bananas (*Musa acuminata*) and related plantains produce recognizeble 'volcano' forms (Tomlinson 1969; Wilson 1985). In cases where specific identification is not yet possible, it is often possible to assign phytoliths to larger taxonomic groupings on the basis of certain general forms, such as the wavy rods of grasses or the 'cones' of sedges (Piperno 1988; Pearsall 1989; Ollendorf 1992). It has been suggested that multi-cellular phytoliths from grasses (or cereals) allow specific identification (Rosen 1992), an approach which is akin to more traditional studies of cuticle morphology, such as that used to distinguish wheat chaff temper from that of rice (e.g. Vishnu-Mittre and Savithri 1975). Statistical image-analysis of SEM images of inflorescence phytoliths shows promise for different ploidy levels in wheat (Ball et al. 1996). In general articulated phytoliths (preserved mulitcellular silica skeletons) offer potentially more taxonomic resolution, although individual phtyoliths are far more often preserved. In addition, it is possible to compare ancient phytolith assemblages with those from modern top soils collected in environments or those from modern ungulate faeces (Powers et al. 1989; Powers 1992). Then even if the taxonomic sources of individual phytoliths are unknown they can be compared in terms of ecological suites.

As with other botanical data types phytoliths need to be analysed taphonomically. In addition to potential contamination by extraneous phytoliths analysis may be complicated by problems such as low concentrations of phytoliths or heavily damaged assemblages due to the abrasion or wind transport (for example, in ancient sands from Egypt, Kaplan 1989). Understanding phytolith taphonomy presents important challenges that should direct future research.

Although phytoliths are taphonomically complex, they may also yield insight into numerous categories of sites (Madella 1998). Ultimately suites of phytoliths will represent source plant communities and the particular morphological parts of plants. Thus differences between sites or through time might indicate changes in vegetation or behaviours which bring vegetation onto a site. Madella (1998) has suggested that there will be fundamental differences between the phytolith assemblages on hunter-gatherer sites as opposed to agricultural sites which have much higher frequency of grass lemma, palea, and glume phytoliths (i.e. from chaff). Another important direction for study, being pursued by Madella at Harappa, compares the assemblages of different functional contexts on the site, such as hearths, kilns, pits and domestic floor sediments. The utility of this data set should be assessed in relation to macrobotanical remains from the same contexts.

6.5 The Potential of Molecular Techniques

A new technique which has promise for addressing certain archaeological questions, relating to crop evolution and diversification, is the extraction of ancient genetic material (DNA) from archaeobotanical remains. Over the past decade, since the advent for the laboratory technique of PCR amplification (polymerase chain reaction) it has become possible to work with small quantities of DNA, including that sometimes preserved in carbonized plant remains (Brown and Brown 1992; Brown et al. 1993). The study of ancient DNA poses methodological difficulties, including generally low rates of preservation of DNA in ancient material. A few studies have estimated the rate of recovery of ancient DNA from plant remains at something approaching 5 per cent, i.e. 1 out of every 20 specimens yields positive results (Allaby et al. 1994, 1997; Schulbaum et al. 1998a). While this is likely to preclude DNA analysis from becoming a standard archaeobotanical technique, it remains a powerful tool for large assemblages and can be used to target particular questions, especially of a phylogenetic nature. The first successful extractions of ancient DNA from archaeobotanical materail came from desiccated maize remains from prehistoric America (Rollo et al. 1991). Since then there have been studies on rice from China (Nakamura and Sato 1991); desiccated *Sorghum* from Egypt (Rowley-Conwy et al. 1997; Deakin et al. 1998), a radish seed from the same site (O'Donoghue et al. 1996), as well as wheat from a few prehistoric sites in Europe (Allaby et al. 1994;1997; Blatter et al. 1998; Schlumbaum et al. 1998b). The first studies of ancient wheats were targeted at distinguishing ploidy level, as it is often impossible to do this from charred grains themselves (Brown et al. 1993; Allaby et al. 1994; Sallares et al. 1995; Schlumbaum et al. 1998b). Experimental work is also underway to develop reliable methods for DNA preserved in ancient pollen from sediments in order to trace cereals in the pollen record (Bower 1997).

The most intriguing information to come from ancient DNA relates to phylogenetic questions through the identification of different evolutionary lineages in ancient material. The necessary baseline for such studies comes from gene sequencing of modern plant populations. Studies based on modern plants can be used to produce phylogenetic trees and identify distinct lineages. The historical and geographical spread of different lineages could potentially be traced and correlated with the archaeological sequences and cultural change (M. Jones et al. 1996). In addition, extinct genetic diversity can potentially be identified. This could allow a more detailed understanding of evolution within crops, as pointed out by Allaby et al. (1994: 127-8):

> . . . it could also liberate our thinking from the gross 'genetic events' of 'domestication' to the perspective of a continuous evolutionary dynamic, in which the constant restructuring in human society through space and time is reflected in an equally continuous process of phylogenetic response, sometimes miniscule, sometimes substantial, in the plants and animals with which humans have been most closely associated.

Such detailed information is not yet available, however, for example, two distinct lineages of Asian rice have been identified on the basis of a cpDNA deletion implying separate domestications of *indica* and *japonica* types (Chen et al. 1993). As these are difficult to distinguish on the basis of charred grains alone, screening of ancient DNA may be useful for tracing these lineages in the past. For example, Nakamura and Sato (1991) successfully extracted *japonica* type DNA fragments from rice from China that dates to the first millennium AD. A phylogeny has recently been developed on the basis of modern landraces of emmer (*Triticum diococcum*) which suggests two separate domestications of *Tritcum diococcum* (Allaby et al., forthcoming). These different lineages could now be traced in the archaeobotanical record and they have been identified in archaeological material in Switzerland (Blatter et al. 1998). Similar kinds of study on other crop plants are yet to be carried out in the Old World, but they have much to contribute to our future understanding of the agricultural history of South Asia.

7. DISCUSSION: THEORETICAL ISSUES IN ARCHAEOBOTANY

The history of archaeobotany has been largely the story of improved methods and increasing data, but there is now increasingly an interest in theoretical issues. In general, theoretical questions which can and are grappled with through archaeobotany can be divided into two groups. First, there are those which relate more closely to the kinds of issues explored by botanists, namely questions relating to plant ecology and plant evolution. Second, there are questions which are of archaeological (or anthropological origin), which take an interest in social systems and social change, in this case in terms of plant exploitation and use. Much theoretical consideration has been given to the origins and spread of agriculture, although other issues, such as intensification and hunter-gatherer subsistence modes can also be addressed. While detailed exploration of these issues will not be pursued here, a few general observations may be worthwhile.

Domestication represents an evolutionary process of morphological and genetic change in a plant brought about by a new kind of environment created through human activity. As discussed by Reed (1977) and Rindos (1980, 1984), this can be seen as a form of symbiosis. The nature of this symbiosis depends on the kind of plant involved, which plant part(s) are utilized and ecology. A significant distinction can be made between vegeculture, focused on root crops and seed culture, a distinction that generally correlates with global environmental zones, i.e. biomes (Harris 1972, 1973; Ellen 1994; Hather 1996). Interest has often turned to understanding the interaction of plant reproductive mode (whether self-pollinating, outcrossing, or predominantly vegetative reproduction), plant part utilized by humans, and the ecological setting created by humans (e.g. Harlan et al. 1973; Zohary 1984, 1997; Zohary and Hopf 1993; Rindos 1980,1984; Ladazinsky 1989; Ellen 1994; Blumler and Byrne 1991; Blumler 1996). The symbiotic relationship, changes the plant morphologically, usually leading to the whole or partial dependence on humans for dispersal in seed crops, and loss of toxins or bitterness in root crops, fruits or vegetables. Whether the genetic changes in plants preceded or succeeded cultivation (harvesting, storage and planting) has been one important issue, with the majority of evidence now favouring the former situation in most instances (see Blumer and Byrne 1991, with commentaries). The factors leading to these changes result from the ecological circumstances created through human activity have been much debated, with controlled burning, the creation of refuse heaps and other kinds of disturbance being cited as possible causal settings (Blumler and Byrne 1991; Blumler 1996). There is unlikely to be one universal explanation, but rather a range of human-environment-plant interactions that led to domestication. This needs to be investigated through a combination of modern evidence from ecological and experimental studies (e.g. Hillman and Davies 1990), and available archaeobotanical and palynological evidence.

Taking an anthropological point of view, interest focuses on the nature of the transition in human cultural practices, its relationship to changes in social organization, and the causes of the change to agriculture. Other earlier generations of archaeologists considered the origins of agriculture as the gaining of progressive knowledge, such as Vishnu-Mittre (e.g. 1968c, 1970b, 1975), in his earlier papers, and Chowdhury (1969). However, it is now clear that it was not an obvious or inevitable change, but a contingent one. The change to agriculture can be considered a change from a largely extractive approach to subsistence towards a highly regulative one (Ellen 1994), or a switch from seeking stability in an 'information bank' (knowledge of a range available resources) to a 'labor bank' (the investment in farming for delayed returns) (Binford 1983: 208). However, agriculture was not a sudden revolution but a process that shifted the interaction between societies, plants and animals along a spectrum of possibilities (Rindos 1980, 1984; Harris 1989, 1996a). Early agriculture has often been linked to concepts of ownership and sedentary communities, although it is now clear that in some parts of the world sedentism preceded cultivation and domestication, while in other regions it followed from them (MacNeish

1992; Ellen 1994). It has been suggested that some of the necessary changes in social relationships were dependent on changes in societies already underway in the Upper Palaeolithic (Hodder 1990; cf. Hastorf 1998). Be that as it may there remains a vast literature on not just the pathways to agriculture but the numerous suggested causes, with the most common being some combination of climatic change and population pressure (Blumler and Byrne 1991; MacNeish 1992; Ellen 1994; Bar-Yosef and Meadow 1995; Harris 1996b) but with growing interest in possible social factors such as competition for prestige (Hayden 1990, 1995), social gift exchange between women (Hastorf 1998), or the emergence of a gendered division of labour with the development of pottery and grain-based cooking (Haaland 1995).

Beyond domestication there are additional theoretical problems of an ecological nature. For example there is no clear agreement about the process by which crops and agriculture spread, whether by colonization of agriculturalists or diffusion, and the motivating factors behind this (Rindos 1980, 1984; MacNeish 1992; Hayden 1995; M. Jones et al. 1996; Harris 1996b; Thomas 1996). Another set of theoretical issues revolves around agricultural intensification, how it is defined, detected and caused (Morrison 1994, 1996). Intensification in turn relates to the problem of the relationship between early agriculture and environmental change, e.g. of the sort registered in pollen diagrams, which at least in Europe appears to have occurred two to four millennia after the first agricultural communities occurred on the continent (Willis and Bennett 1994; M. Jones et al. 1996). The relationship between early Neolithic agriculture, later intensification and the formation of the Indian landscape, especially the vast peninsular grasslands, remains an important issue to explore which will require both more empirical data from archaeology and palaeoecology, as well as theoretical bridging arguments to relate this datasets and the processes they represent.

In part due to the development of post-processual and cognitive approaches to archaeology (Hodder 1992; Whitley 1998), there has been an increasing interest in the role of past human perception on behaviour. These theoretical perspectives highlight the need to take into account culturally specific values and frameworks of thought when interpreting past actions, for example the role of culinary preferences, status foods, or taboos on the social processes of the adoption and diffusion of certain crops (see Farb and Armelagos 1980; Weissner and Sciefenhovel 1996; Hosoya and Fuller, forthcoming; Hastorf 1998). This work exemplifies a point emphasized by the archaeologist Gordon Childe that human societies adapt the environment as they perceive it, not necessarily as it truly is (e.g. Childe 1951: 176-7; Trigger 1991). However, studies highlighting the historical constraints on 'adaptation' have yet to arise from South Asian archaeobotany. In addition, the spread of crops and agricultural practices by diffusion (as opposed to actual colonization) was more than just a matter of availability. As with other kinds of diffusion, crop diffusion requires compatibility with the existent cultural and economic system, i.e. social approval (Childe 1951: 172). It is as likely to have been cultural factors, rather than purely ecological factors, which delayed the spread of millets in the central Indus Valley during the Harappan period and perhaps also the lack of wheat/barley cultivation in Gujarat. On the other hand, the rapid and wide distribution of some crops in prehistory, such as wheat and barley in the second millennium BC or *Lablab*, could have had to do with cultural or prestige associations. The difficulty lies in trying to establish such social factors, although they can be inferred in general by contrasts with other crops and ecological predictions.

8. THE FUTURE OF ARCHAEOBOTANY

The history of any discipline, particularly in its early years, is the story of a few enthusiastic and often visionary individuals. The foresters and wood anatomists at the Dehra Dun forestry institute, including K.A. Chowdhury and S.S. Ghosh might be singled out as the founders of archaeobotany in India. More than anything else they must be credited with bringing to the attention of practising archaeologists that plant remains from ancient sites could provide an additional line of evidence on the past. However, the mode of analysis during this period was still largely 'antiquarian' (sensu Trigger 1989) in that it consisted of collecting information, identification of species and compilations of lists, which were largely done for the sake of collecting. It was during the career of Vishnu-Mittre that archaeobotany emerged as a discipline in its own right, a specialization on the plant remains from the human past. As with many pioneers, Vishnu-Mittre's greatest contribution was his wide-ranging involvement and enthusiasm that helped to start research paths in numerous directions. He began to consider seriously the origins and spread of agriculture in South Asia and promoted a 'botanical perspective on the quaternary'. It now appears that in some cases he was somewhat overzealous in his identifications, and critical reassessments of some of this claims are in order. His discussions of early evidence for *ragi* (*Eleusine coracana*) in south India and rice in the Vindhyas attracted interest to possible indigenous domestications of plants but in neither case were the data systematically enough collected or reported to substantiate his claims. The time is ripe for the systematic examination of these issues through the collection and careful documentation of new evidence.

In the following decades, from the mid-1970s to more or less the present-day, a larger number of professional archaeobotanists became involved in research. With systematic collection through flotation and routine publication of results as parts of site reports, the amount of data has grown exponentially. This work has brought us to the stage of greater 'maturity' in which, through a greater awareness of the biases inherent in the archaeobotanical data, a more self-critical and theoretical discipline has emerged. Foreign archaeobotanists only entered the Indian scene in the recent past. For the most part their work has been concentrated in the north-western portion of the subcontinent, in particular on Harappan sites. They have brought with them a number of broader theoretical questions relating to cultural ecology and the rise, maintenance and fall of complex, urban societies. These perspectives have contributed a somewhat larger purview to archaeobotany. It is no longer sufficient to merely record species, but it is now necessary for archaeobotanists, alone or in collaboration, to interpret and explain their data in terms of both ecological understanding and past social activities, such as crop processing, storage, exchange and cooking. International cross-fertilization has contributed to the development of a more reflective, taphonomically-orientated archaeobotany. In time, it is likely that Indian archaeobotany will make important contributions to theoretical problems and thinking abroad. Agriculture on the Indian subcontinent may have included the indigenous development of some small scale cultivation systems based around small, indigenous millets, pulses, and possibly wild root crops which were subsequently transformed by introduction of higher yielding crops such as wheat, barley and *Sorghum*. This may provide an important comparative case for understanding the early agriculture of North America where a number of small-yield, local crops, few of which are of any agricultural significance today, provided the foundations of village life which was subsequently transformed by the adoption of maize (Smith 1989; Fritz 1991). Other indigenous crops in India may turn out to be secondary domesticates whose domestication followed from the establishment of introduced cultivars. By understanding the ecological and social context, these secondary domestications can also be compared with cases elsewhere in the world.

Indian archaeobotany has a bright future but is still quantitatively disadvantaged by comparison to the discipline in some other parts of the world. Archaeobotanists are few and far between, and given the shear size of India, its diversity in terms of natural environments and subsistence strategies (past and present), Indian archaeobotanists have their hands very full indeed. By comparison with the trajectory of the discipline in other parts of the world, we are on brink of increase. In Near Eastern archaeology of the sixties there were only a handful of archaeobotanists, but after the development of flotation there (Hole et al. 1969) there was a proliferation of workers, in the seventies and since. A similar increase can be seen to have occurred in eastern North America in the early 1980s (Watson 1997). Now both of these regions have vast datasets, allowing constant reanalysis and encouraging intricate discussion of ecological, political and social aspects of human-plant relationships. This is marked in particular by the involvement of general archaeologists in debates surrounding archaeobotanical evidence: archaeobotany is no longer peripheral but paramount to many questions of the human past. Food and the plant world are inextricably part of human existence, and something about which archaeobotany has much to say. The opening of the next century may, hopefully, see a similar development in India. The metaphorical tree that is archaeobotany may soon set fruit.

ACKNOWLEDGEMENTS

I would like to acknowledge the encouragement of Professor Martin Jones and Dr. Dilip Chakrabarti in the preparation of this paper. My research has been supported by a Benefactors' Scholarship from St John's College, Cambridge, the Marshall Aid Commemoration Commission, and field work grants from the Faculty of Archaeology and Anthropology, and the Smutts Memorial Fund, Cambridge. I am grateful to several colleagues who commented on earlier drafts of this paper, and whose expertise helped me to clarify several issues, including Mim Bower, Alan Clapham, David Edwards, Tinker Green, Marco Madella, Mark Nesbitt, Victor Paz and Chris Stevens.

NOTES

1 In grasses the outer coat of the grain is a pericarp, usually ornamented or haired, while the testa (true seedcoat), is in a second layer of cells fused with this (Hickey and King 1991; Pandey 1995). The lemma and palea enclose the grain (caryopsis).

2 Reports of *Vigna unguiculata* as the scientific name for horsegram, as at Rojdi (Weber 1991), Babar Kot (Reddy 1994), Watgal (Devaraj et al. 1995), are misnomers. The species usually known as *Dolichos biflorus* in archaeological literature is correctly known as *Macrotyloma uniflorum* (see references in Section 5.3).

3 Although often referred to in Indian floristics and agronomic literature as *Dolichos biflorus* Linn., this species of Linnaeus actually refers to a type specimen of catjang type cowpea (Hindi *chowli*, *lobia*), now placed in the polytypic species *Vigna unguiculata* (L.) Walp. Thus *D. biflrous* Linn. is a synonym for *V. unguiculata*. This equation has, however, been wrongly used by Weber (1991), Reddy (1994), Devaraj et al. (1995) and Kroll (1996; 1997; 1998), since the archaeological finds traditionally described as *D. biflrous* are not cowpeas (Hindi *chowli*)! *D. biflorus* is an invalid name for the horsegram (Hindi *kulthi*), which was first properly described by Lamarck as *Dolichos uniflorum*. It has now been transferred to the genus *Macrotyloma* (Verdcourt 1970; 1971; Smartt 1985a; 1990). The recent suggestion that '*Dolichos uniflorus*' is the wild form of '*Dolichos biflorus*' and localized in the southern and eastern peninsula (Mehra 1997), requires botanical clarification and substantiation.

4 *Vigna umbellata* (Thunb.) Ohwi & Ohashi, rice bean, is cultivated in parts of South-East Asia, while *V. angularis* (Willd.) Ohwi & Ohashi, the adzuki bean, orignated in China or Japan where it is cultivated today. This name was mistakenly applied by Weber (1991) to the Black Gram, *V. mungo* (L.) Hepper!

5 It is indeed unfortunate that Linnaeus mixed-up the common names and therefore assigned the scientific *mungo* to black gram rather than to green gram, known colloquially as 'mung'. But the correct botanical nomenclature can not be helped, even if somewhat confusing to the uninitiated.

6 *Phaseolus aureus* and *P. radiatus* are not domesticated and wild forms, respectively, as suggested by Lone et al. (1993: 135), but older synonyms for the domesticated mung/green gram crop, the wild form of which is *Phaseolus sublobatus* Roxb. As they have all been transferred to *Vigna* and the wild progenitor has been demoted to subspecies following the nomenclatural system of Harlan and De Wet (1971), the wild progenitor is now known as *Vigna radiata* subsp. *sublobata* (Smartt 1985b, 1990). As black gram has a distinct progenitor, it has been removed from *sublobata* to become known as *V. mungo* subsp. *silvestris* (Smartt, ibid.).

7 *Ulmus wallichiana* is also known from Baluchistan as well as from the Himalaya, where *U. villosa* is restricted.

REFERENCES

Achaya, K.T. 1994. *Indian Food: a Historical Companion*. Delhi: Oxford University Press.

Agrawal, D.P. 1992. *Man and Environment Through Ages*. New Delhi: Books & Books.

Allaby, R.G., M.K. Jones and T.A. Brown 1994. DNA in Charred Wheat Grains from the Iron Age Hillfort at Danebury, England, *Antiquity* 68: 126-32.

Allaby, R., Hogben, C. Howe and M.K. Jones (Forthcoming). Biogeographical Distributions of Glutenin Allele Lineages in Cultivated Wheats: Evidence for Two Independent Agricultural Expansions, *Proceedings of the National Academy of Sciences USA*.

Allaby, R.G., K. O'Donoghue, R. Sallares, M.K. Jones and T.A. Brown 1997. Evidence for the Survival of Ancient DNA in Charred Wheat Seeds from European Archaeological Sites, *Ancient Biomolecules* 1: 119-29.

Allchin, Bridget and Raymond Allchin 1968. *The Birth of Indian Civilization*. Harmondsworth: Pelican Books.

——— 1982. *The Rise of Civilization in India and Pakistan*. Cambridge: Cambridge University Press.

——— 1997. *Origins of a Civilization: the Prehistory and Early Archaeology of South Asia.* New Delhi: Viking Penguin Books India.

Amblard, S. and J. Pernes 1989. The Identification of Cultivated Pearl Millet (*Pennisetum*) Amongst Plant Impressions on Pottery from Oued Chebbi (Dhar Oualata, Mauritania), *The African Archaeological Review* 7: 117-26.

Andersen, S.T. 1979. Identification of Wild Grasses and Cereal Pollen, *Danmarks Geologiste Undersøgelse, Årbog* 1978: 69-92.

Anonymous 1960. Identification of Seeds Samples, in *From History to Pre-history at Nevasa (1954-56)* (H.D. Sankalia, S.B. Deo, Z.D. Ansari and S. Ehrhardt Eds.), pp. 529-30. Poona: Deccan College.

Anping, Pei 1998. Notes on New Advancements and Revelations in the Agricultural Archaeology of Early Rice Domestication in the Dongting Lake Region, *Antiquity* 72: 878-85.

Arora, R.K., K.P.S. Chandel and B.S. Joshi 1973. Morphological Diversity in *Phaeseolus sublobatus* Roxb., *Current Science* 42 (10): 359-61.

Ball, T., J.S. Gardner and J.D. Brotherson 1996. Identifying Phytoliths by the Inflorescence Bracts of Three Species of Wheat (*Triticum monococcum* L., *T. dioccon* Schrank. and *T. aestivum* L.) Using Computer-Assisted Image and Statistical Analyses, *Journal of Archaeological Science* 23: 619-32.

Bar-Yosef, O. and R. Meadow 1995. The Origins of Agriculture in the Near East, in *Last Hunters-First Farmers: New Perspectives on the Prehistoric Transition to Agriculture* (T.D. Price and A.B. Gebauer Eds.), pp. 39-94. Santa Fe: New Mexico: School of American Research Advanced Seminar Series.

Battarbee, R.W. 1988. The Use of Diatom Analysis in Archaeology: a Review, *Journal of Archaeological Science* 15: 621-44.

Bedigian, D. and J.R. Harlan 1986. Evidence for Cultivation of Sesame in the Ancient World, *Economic Botany* 40: 137-54.

Behre, K.-E. 1981. The Interpretation of Anthropogenic Indicators in Pollen Diagrams, *Pollen et Spores* 23: 225-45.

Behre, K.-E.(Ed.) 1986. *Anthropogenic Indicators in Pollen Diagrams.* Roterdam: A.A. Balkema.

Behre, K.-E. and S. Jacomet 1991. The Ecological Interpretation of Archaeobotanical Data, *Progress in Old World Palaeoethnobotany* (W. Van Zeist, K. Wasylikowa and K.-E. Behre Eds.), pp. 81-108. Rotterdam: Balkema.

Bellwood, P., R. Gillespie, G.B. Thompson, J.S. Vogel, I.W. Ardika and Ipoi Datan 1992. New Dates for Prehistoric Asian Rice, *Asian Perspectives* 31: 161-70.

Betts, A., K. van der Borg, A. de Jong, C. McClintok and M. van Strydonck 1994. Early Cotton in North Arabia, *Journal of Archaeological Science* 21: 489-99.

Binford, Lewis R. 1983. *In Pursuit of the Past:Decoding the Archaeological Record.* New York: Thames and Hudson.

Blatter, R., S. Jacomet and A. Schlumbaum 1998. How to Study Ancient DNA from Archaeological Wheat—b) Results, Paper Presented at 11th Symposium of the International Work Group for Palaeoethnobotany, 18-23 May 1998, Toulouse, France.

Blench, Roger 1991. Connections Between Egypt and Sub-Saharan Africa. The Evidence of Cultivated Plants, in *Egypt and Africa* (W.V. Davies Ed.), pp. 54-6. London: British Museum Press.

Blumler, M. 1996. Ecology, Evolutionary Theory and Agricultural Origins, in *The Origins and Spread of Agriculture and Pastoralism in Eurasia* (D.R. Harris Ed.), pp. 25-50. London: UCL Press.

Blumler, M. and R. Byrne 1991. The Ecological Genetics of Domestication and the Origins of Agriculture, *Current Anthropology* 32 (1): 23-54.

Boardman, S. and G.E.M. Jones 1990. Experiments on the Effects of Charring on Cereal Plant Components, *Journal of Archaeological Science* 17(1): 1-12

Bottema, S. 1984. The Composition of Modern Charred Seed Assemblages, in *Plants and Ancient Man* (W. van Zeist and W.A. Casparie Eds.), pp. 207-212. Rotterdam: Balkema.

Bower, M.A. 1992. Cereal Pollen Dispersal: a Pilot Study, *Cambridge Archaeological Journal* 2: 236-41.

——— 1997. A Critical Path to the Characterisation of Agriculture Through the Pollen of Cereals. Ph.D. Dissertation. Cambridge: Cambridge University.

Bray, F. 1981. Millet Cultivation in China: a Historical Survey, *Journal d'Agriculture Traditionelle et de Botanique Appliquée* 27 (3-4): 291-307.

Brown, T.A., R.G. Allaby, K.A. Brown and M.K. Jones 1993. Biomolecular Archaeology of Wheat: Past, Present and Future, *World Archaeology* 25 (1): 64-73.

Brown, T.A. and K.A. Brown 1992. Ancient DNA and the Archaeologist, *Antiquity* 66: 10-23.

Burts, B. C. 1941. Comments on Cereals and Fruits, in *Excavations at Mohenjo-Daro* (M.S. Vats), p. 466. New Delhi: Archaeological Survey of India.

Buth, G.M. and R.S. Bisht 1981. SEM Study of Ancient Wood Remains from Kashmir, *Current Science* 50 (16): 728.

Buth, G.M. and K.A. Chowdhury 1971. Plant Remains from Atranjikhera Phase III, *Palaeobotanist* 20: 280-7.

——— 1973. 4,500 Years Old Plant Remains from Egyptian Nubia, *Proceedings of the National Science Academy* 38: 55-71.

Buth, G.M. and R.N. Kaw 1985. Plant Husbandry in Neolithic Burzahom, Kashmir, in *Current Trends in Geology VI* (D.P. Agrawal, S. Kusumgar and R.V. Krishnamurthy Eds.), pp. 109-13. Delhi: Today and Tomorrow Publishers.

Buth, G.M. and K.S. Saraswat 1972. Antiquity of Rice Cultivation, *Research Trends in Plant Anatomy—K.A. Chowdhury Commemoration Volume* in (A.K.M. Ghouse and M. Yunus Eds.), pp. 33-9. New Delhi: Tata McGraw-Hill.

Buth, G.M., R.S. Bisht and G.S. Gaur 1982. Investigations of Palaeoethnobotanical Remains from Semthan, Kashmir, *Man and Environment* VI: 41-5.

Buth, G.M., Maqsooda Khan and Farooq A. Lone1988. Retrieval and Interpretation of Plant Remains from Archaeological Sites, *Man and Environment* X: 45-8.

Buth, G.M., A. Navchoo and A. Navayan 1987. Central Asia and Kashmir: an Appraisal of Past Links, *Journal d'Agriculture Traditionelle et de Botanique Appliquée* 34: 57-64.

Butler, A. 1992. Pulse Agronomy: Traditional Systems and Implications for Early Cultivation, in *Préhistroie L'Agriculture: Nouvelle Approches Expérimentales et Ethnographiques* (P.C. Anderson Ed.), pp 67-78. Monographie du CRA 6. Paris: Editions du CNRS.

Caratini, C., M. Fontugne, J.P. Pascal, C. Tissot, I. Bentaleb 1991. A Major Change at ca. 3500 years BP in the Vegetation of the Western Ghats in North Kanara, Karnataka, *Current Science* 61: 669-72.

Caratini, C., I. Bentaleb, M. Fontugne, M.T. Morzadec-Kerfourn, J.P. Pascal and C. Tissot 1994. A Less Humid Climate Since ca. 3500 years B.P. from Marine Cores Off Karwar, Western

India, *Palaeogeography, Palaeoclimatology and Palaeoecology* 109: 371-84.

Castelletti, L., M. Madella, A. Qayom Mahar 1994. Charcoal Analysis at Kot Diji: a Preliminary Report, *Ancient Sindh* 1: 37-41.

Chakrabarti, Dilip K. 1988. *Theoretical Issues in Indian Archaeology*. New Delhi: Munshiram Manoharlal.

——— 1995. *The Archaeology of Ancient Indian Cities*. Delhi: Oxford University Press.

Chandel, K.P.S., R.N. Lester and R.J. Starlin 1984. The Wild Ancestors of Urid and Mung Beans [*Vigna mungo* (L.) Hepper and *V. radiata* (L.) Wilczek], *Botanical Journal of the Linnean Society* 89: 85-96.

Chang, K.-C. 1986. *The Archaeology of Ancient China*. Fourth Edition. New Haven: Yale University Press.

Chang, T.T. 1989. Domestication and Spread of the Cultivated Rices, in *Foraging and Farming* (D. Harris and G. Hillman Eds.), pp. 408-17. London: Routledge.

Chang, T. T. 1995. Rice (Oryza), in *Evolution of Crop Plants* (J. Smartt and N.W. Simmonds Eds.), pp. 147-55. Harlow: Longman.

Charles, Michael 1998. Fodder from Dung: the Recognition and Interpretation of Dung-Derived Plant Material from Archaeological Sites, *Environmental Archaeology* 1: 111-22.

Chatterjee, P.-G. 1991. Changes in Food Values from Hunting and Gathering to Agriculture; a Reconstruction from Ethnographic Records, in *Indo-Pacific Prehistory 1990*, Vol. 1 (P. Bellwood Ed.), pp. 184-6. Canberra: Indo-Pacific-Prehsitory Association.

Chatterjee, P.G. and A.K. Ghosh 1990. Dioscorea as Food Materials of the Hunter-Gatherer: an Assay on Contents, in *Adaptation and Other Eassays* (N.C. Ghosh and S. Chakrabarti Eds.), pp. 155-61. Santiniketan: Visva-Bharati Research Publications.

Chen, Baozhang and Quinhua Jiang 1997. Antiquity of the Earliest Cultivated Rice in Central China and Its Implications, *Economic Botany* 51 (3): 307-10.

Chen, Wen-Bing, Ikuo Nakamura, Yo-Ichiro Sato and Hirokazu Nakai 1993. Dsitribution of Deletion Type in cpDNA of Cultivated and Wild Rice, *Japanese Journal of Genetics* 68: 597-603.

Chen, Wen-Bing, Yo-Ichiro Sato, Ikuo Nakamura and Hirokazu Nakai 1994. *Indica* and *Japonica* Differentiation in Chinese Landraces, *Euphytica* 75: 195.

Childe, V. Gordon 1951. *Social Evolution*. London: Watts and Co.

Chowdhury, K.A. 1965. The Tertiary Flora of India and Probable Disposition of Continents, *The Palaeobotanist* 14: 172-84.

——— 1969. Archaeological Plant Remains from Pre- and Proto-Historic Periods as a Source of History of Science, *Indian Journal of the History of Science* 4: 5-10.

——— 1970. Wood and Its Use During Pre- and Proto-Historic Times, *Indian Journal of the History of Science* 5(1): 141-3.

Chowdhury, K.A. and S.S. Ghosh 1946. Report on Wood and Fruit Shells (from Arikamedu), *Ancient India* 2: 104-8.

——— 1951. Plant Remains from Harappa Excavations in 1946, *Ancient India* 7: 3-19.

——— 1952. Wood Remains from Sisulpalgarh, *Ancient India* 8: 28-32.

——— 1954-5. Plant Remains from Hastinapur, *Ancient India* 10-11: 121-37.

——— 1957. Charcoal Remains, Maski Excavation, *Ancient India* 13: 133-41.

——— 1958. *Indian Woods* I. Dehra Dun. Forest Research Institute.

Chowdhury, K.A., A.K. Ghosh, K.N. Sen 1972. Botany: Prehistoric Period, in *Concise History of Science in India*, pp. 371-402 and 627-60. Indian National Science Academy.

Chowdhury, K.A., K.S. Saraswat and G.M. Buth 1977. *Ancient Agriculture and Forestry in North India.* New Delhi: Asia Publishing House.

——— 1983. The Plant Remains, in *Excavations at Atranjikhera: Early Civilization of the Upper Ganga Basin* (R.C. Gaur Ed.), pp. 457-9. Delhi: Motilal Banarsidass.

Clark, J.D., G.S. Khanna 1989. The Site of Kunjhun II, Middle Son Valley and Its Relevance, in *Old Problems and New Perspectives in the Archaeology of South Asia* (J.M. Kenoyer Ed.), pp. 29-58. Madison: University of Wisconsin. Wisconsin Archaeological Reports 2.

Clapham, A., T. Clave and T. Wilkinson 1997. A Plant Macrofossil Investigation of a Submerged Forest, in *Archaeological Sciences 1995* (A. Sinclair, E. Slater and J. Gowlett Eds.), pp. 265-70. Oxford: Oxbow Books. Oxbow Monograph 64.

Clayton, W.D. 1979. Notes on *Setaria* (Graminae), *Kew Bulletin* 33 (3): 501-9.

Clayton, W.D. and S.A. Renvoize 1982. *Graminae (Pa:t 3)*, Polhill, J.M. (ed.), *Flora of Tropical East Africa.* Rotterdam: Balkema.

Cleuziou, S. 1989. Excavations at Hili 8: a Preliminary Report on the 4th to 7th Campaigns, *Archaeology of the United Arab Emirates* 5: 61-87.

Cleuziou. S. and L. Constantini 1980. Premiers Éléments sur l'agriculture Protohistorique de l'Arabie orientale, *Paléorient* 6: 245-51.

——— 1982. A l'origine des oasis, *La Recherche* 13 (137): 1180-2.

Coningham, R. 1995. Dark Age of Continuum? an Archaeological Analysis of the Second Emergence of Urbanism in South Asia, in *The Archaeology of Early Historic South Asia: the Emergence of Cities and States* (F.R. Allchin Ed.), pp. 54-72. Cambridge: Cambridge University Press.

Costantini, L. 1979a. Palaeoethnobotany: Identification of Two Rows Barley and Early Domesticated Sorghum, *Archaeology of the United Arab Emirates* 2-3: 70-1.

——— 1979b. Plant Remains at Pirak, in *Fouilles de Pirak*, Vol. 1 (J.F. Jarrige and M. Santoni Eds.), pp. 326-33. Paris: Diffusion de Boccard.

——— 1979c. Wood Remains from Shahr-i-Sokhta: a Source of Information for Ancient Environment and Technology, in *Protohistoric Seistan.*

——— 1981. Palaeoethnobotany at Pirak: a Contribution to the 2nd Millennium BC Agriculture of the Sibi-Kacchi Plain, Pakistan, in *South Asian Archaeology 1979* (H. Härtel Ed.), pp. 271-7. Berlin: Dietrich Reimer Verlag

——— 1983. The Beginning of Agriculture in the Kachi Plain: the Evidence of Mehrgarh, in *South Asian Archaeology 1981* (B. Allchin Ed.), pp. 29-33. Cambridge: Cambridge University Press.

——— 1984. Plant Impressions in Bronze Age Pottery from Yemen Arab Republic, *East and West* 34: 107-15.

——— 1987. Appendix B. Vegetal Remains, in *Prehistoric and Protohistoric Swat Pakistan* (G. Stacul [compiler]), pp. 155-65. Rome: Instituto Italiano per il Medio ed Estremo Oreintale (IsMEO).

——— 1990a Harrapan Agriculture in Pakistan: the Evidence of Nausharo, in *South Asian Archaeology 1987* (M. Taddei Ed.), pp. 321-32. Rome: Estremo Oreintale. (IsMEO)

——— 1990b. Ecology and Farming of the Protohistoric Communities in Central Yemeni Highlands, in *The Bronze Age Culture of Halwan at-Tiyal and Al-Hada (Republic of Yemen)* (A. de Maigret Ed.), pp. 187-204. Rome: IsMEO.

Costantini, L. and L. Baisini 1985. Agriculture in Baluchistan Between the 7th and 3rd Millennium BC, *Newsletter of Baluchistan Studies* 2: 16-37.

Cooke, T. 1903. *The Flora of the Presidency of Bombay*, Volume I. London: Taylor and Francis.

Crawford, G.W. 1992. Prehistoric Plant Domestication in East Asia, in *The Origins of Agriculture: an International Perspective* (C.W. Cowan and P.J. Watson Eds.), pp. 7-38. Washington, D.C.: Smithsonian Institution Press.

——— 1997. Anthropogenesis in Prehistoric Northeastern Japan, in *People, Plants and Landscapes. Studies in Paleoethnobotany* (K.J. Gremillion Ed.), pp. 86-103. Tuscaloosa: University of Alabama Press.

Crawford, G.W. and Chen Shen 1998. The Origins of Rice Agriculture: Recent Progress in East Asia, *Antiquity* 72: 858-66.

Cummings, L.S. 1992. Illustrated Phytoliths from Assorted Food Plants, in *Phytolith Systematics—Emerging Issues* (G. Rapp Jr. and S.C. Mulholland Eds.), pp. 175-92. New York: Plenum Press.

Dales, G.F. 1986. Some Fresh Approaches to Old Problems in Harappan Archaeology, in *Studies in Archaeology of India and Pakistan* (J. Jaboson Ed.), pp. 117-36. New Delhi: Oxford-IBH

Daniels, J. and C. Daniels 1993. Sugarcane in Prehistory, *Archaeology in Oceania* 28: 1-7

De, D.N. 1974. Pigeon-pea, in *Evolutionary Studies in World Crops: Diversity and Change in the Indian Subcontinent* (J. Hutchinson Ed.), pp. 79-88. Cambridge: Cambridge University Press.

De Candolle, A. 1886. *Origin of Cultivated Plants*, Second Edition. London: Keegan Paul, Trench and Co.

De Wet, J.M. 1995a. Minor Cereals, in *Evolution of Crop Plants* (J. Smartt and N.W Simmonds Eds.), pp. 202-7. Essex: Longman Scientific and Technical.

——— 1995b. Finger Millet (*Eleusine coracana*), in *Evolution of Crop Plant* (J. Smartt and N.W. Simmonds Eds.), pp. 137-40. Essex: Longman Scientific and Technical.

——— 1995c. Foxtail Millet (*Setaria italica*), in *Evolution of Crop Plants* (J. Smartt and N.W. Simmonds Eds.), pp. 171-2. Essex: Longman Scientific and Technical.

——— 1995d. Pearl Millet (*Pennisetum glaucum*), in *Evolution of Crop Plants* (J. Smartt and N.W. Simmonds Eds.), pp. 156-9. Essex: Longman Scientific and Technical.

De Wet, J.M.J. and J.P. Huckabay 1967. The Origin of *Sorghum bicolor*: II, Distribution and Domestication, *Evolution* 21: 787-802.

De Wet, J.M.J., L.L. Oestry-Stidd and J.I. Cunero 1979. Origins and Evolution of Foxtail Millets, *Journal d'Agriculture Traditionelle et de Botanique Appliquée* 26: 54-64.

De, Wet, J.M.J., Rao, K.E. Prasada and D.E. Brink 1983a. Systematics and Domestication of *Panicum sumatrense* (Graminae), *Journal d'Agriculture Traditionelle et de Botanique Appliquée* 30 (2): 159-68.

——— 1983b. Diversity in Kodo Millet, *Paspalum scrobiculatum*, *Economic Botany* 37 (2): 159-63.

——— 1983c. Domestication of Sawa Millet (*Echinochloa colona*), *Economic Botany* 37 (3): 283-91.

Deakin, W.J., P. Rowley-Conwy and C.H. Shaw 1998. Amplification and Sequencing of DNA from Preserved Sorghum of up to 2800 Years Antiquity Found at Qasr Ibrim, *Ancient Biomolecules* 2 (1): 27-41.

Debouck, D.G. and J. Smartt 1995. Beans *Phaseolus* spp., in *Evolution of Crop Plants* (J. Smartt and N.W. Simmonds Eds.), pp. 287-94. Essex: Longman Scientific and Technical.

Dennell, R.W. 1972. The Interpretation of Plant Remains: Bulgaria, in *Papers in Economic Pre-*

history (E.S. Higgs Ed.), pp. 149-59. Cambridge: Cambridge University Press.

——— 1974. Botanical Evidence for Prehistoric Crop Processing Activities, *Journal of Archaeological Science* 1: 275-84.

——— 1976. The Economic Importance of Plant Resources Represented on Archaeological Sites, *Journal of Archaeological Science* 3: 229-47.

Devaraj, D.V., J.G. Shaffer, C.S. Patil and Balasubramanya 1995. The Watgal Excavations: an Interim Report, *Man and Environment* XX (2): 57-74.

Dhavalikar, M.K. 1995. *Cultural Imperialism: Indus Civilization in Western India.* New Delhi: Books & Books.

Dhavalikar, M.K. and G.L. Possehl 1974. Subsistence Pattern of an Early Farming Community of Western India, *Puratattva* 7: 39-56.

Dickson, C. 1988. Distinguishing Cereal from Wild Grass Pollen: Some Limitations, *Circaea* 5 (2): 67-71.

Dimbleby, G.W. 1985. *The Palynology of Archaeological Sites.* London: Academic Press.

Doggett, H. and K. Prasada Rao 1995. Sorghum, in *Evolution of Crop Plants* (J. Smartt and N.W Simmonds Eds.), pp. 173-80. Second Edition. Essex: Longman Scientific and Technical.

Edwards, K.J. 1979. Palynological and Temporal Inference in the Context of Prehistory, with Special Reference to the Evidence from Lake and Peat Deposits, *Journal of Archaeological Science* 6: 255-70.

——— 1989. The Cereal Pollen Record and Early Agriculture, in *The Beginnings of Agriculture* (A. Milles, D. Williams and N. Gardner Eds.), pp. 113-35. Oxford: BAR International Series 496.

Ellen, Roy. 1994. Modes of Subsistence: Hunting and Gathering to Agriculture and Pastoralism, in *Companion Encyclopedia of Anthropology. Humanity, Culture and Social Life* (T. Ingold Ed.), pp. 197-225. London: Routledge.

Ellerton, Sydney 1939. The Origin and Geographical Distribution of *Triticum sphaerococcum* Perc. and Its Cytogenegical Behaviour in Crosses with *T. vulgare* Vill., *Journal of Genetics* 38: 307-24.

Erdtman, G. and Vishnu-Mittre 1956. On Terminology in Pollen and Spore Morphology, *The Palaeobotanist* 5 (2): 109-11.

Farb, Peter and George Armelagos 1980. *Consuming Passions: the Anthropology of Eating.* Boston: Houghton Miflin Company.

Faegri, K. and J. Iversen 1975. *A Textbook of Pollen Analysis.* Oxford: Blackwell Scientific.

Fairservis, W.A. 1971. *The Roots of Ancient India.* London: George Allen and Unwin, Ltd.

Franke-Vogt, U. 1995. Cultural Ecology of the Greater Indus Valley and Beyond, *The Archaeological Review* (Karachi) 4: 13-64.

Fritz, Gayle 1991. Multiple Pathways to Farming in Precontact Eastern North America, *Journal of World Prehistory* 5: 387-435.

Fujiwara, H., M.R. Mughal, A. Sasaki and T. Matano 1992. Rice and Ragi at Harappa: Preliminary Results by Plant Opal Analysis, *Pakistan Archaeology* 27: 129-42.

Fujiwara, H. 1993. Research into the History of Rice Cultivation Using Plant Opal Analysis, in *Current Research in Phytolith Analysis: Applications in Archaeology and Palaeoecology* (D.M. Pearsal and D.R. Piperno Eds.), pp. 147-58. Philadelphia: MASCA, University of Pennsylvania Museum.

Fuller, D.Q., R. Korisettar, P.C. Venkatasubbaiah and M.K. Jones (forthcoming). Early Plant Domestications in Southern India: Some Preliminary Archaeobotanical Results, *Vegetation History and Archaeobotany* (submitted).

Gamble, J.S. and C.E.C. Fisher. 1921-35. *Flora of the Madras Presidency*, 3 Vols. London: Adlard and Son.

Ghosh, A.K. 1941. Submerged Forest in Calcutta, *Science and Culture* 6 (2): 669-70.

Ghosh, S.S. 1950. Re-examination of a Wooden Post from Kirari, Madhya Pradesh, *Ancient India* 6: 17-20.

——— 1961. Further Records of Rice (*Oryza* sp.) from Ancient India, *Indian Forest Bulletin* 7 (5): 295-301.

Ghosh, S.S. and K. Lal 1958. On Sal Wood Excavated from Mauryan Pillard Hall, Pataliputra, *Current Science* 27: 136-7.

——— 1961. Plant Remains from Asvamedha Sites Near Kalsi of Dehra Dun District, *Science and Culture* 27: 188.

——— 1963. Plant Remains from Rangpur and Other Explorations in Gujarat, *Ancient India* 18-19: 161-75.

Glover, Ian C. 1979. Prehistoric Plant Remains from Southeast Asia, with Special Reference to Rice, in *South Asian Archaeology 1977* (M. Taddei Ed.), pp. 7-37. Naples: Instituto Universitario Orientale.

Glover, Ian C. and Charles F. W. Higham 1996. New Evidence for Early Rice Cultivation in South, Southeast and East Asia, in *The Origins and Spread of Agriculture and Pastoralism in Eurasia* (D. Harris Ed.), pp. 413-41. London: UCL Press.

Goddard, J. and M. Nesbitt 1997. Why Draw Seeds? Illustrating Archaeobotany, *Graphic Archaeology (the Journal of the Association of Archaeological Illustrators and Surveyors* 1997): 13-21.

Godwin, Harry 1956. *History of the Flora of the British Isles.* Cambridge: Cambridge University Press.

——— 1975. *History of the Flora of the British Isles.* Second Edition. Cambridge: Cambridge University Press

Goodman, Major M. 1995. Maize, *Zea Mays* (Graminae-Maydeae), in *Evolution of Crop Plants* (J. Smartt and N.W. Simmonds Eds.), pp. 192-202. Second Edition. London: Longman Technical and Scientific.

Gremmen, W.H.E. 1990. Palynological Investigations at the Danau Tempe Depressions, Southwest Sulawesi (Celebes), Indonesia, *Modern Quaternary Research in Southeast Asia* 11: 123-34.

Guinet, Ph. 1963. Apports Recents de la Palynologie a l'etude du Quaternaire en Inde, *Bulletin de l'ecole Francaise d' Extreme-Orient* 41: 195-201.

——— 1966. What May Afford Palynology to Archaeology and Ancient History of India, *Journal of the Maharaja Sayoji Rao University*, 15 (1): 15-19.

Gulati, A.N. 1961. A Note on the Early History of Silk in India, in *Technical Reports on Archaeological Remains.* Department of Archaeology and Ancient Indian History, Deccan College and University of Poona Publications 2: 53-9.

——— 1965. A Note on the Early History of Flax, in *Chalcolithic Chandoli* (S.B. Deo and Z.D. Ansari Eds.), pp. 195-201. Pune: Deccan College.

Gulati, A.N. and A.J. Turner 1929. A Note on the Early History of Cotton, *Journal of the Textile Institute*, Transactions XX: 1-9.

Gupta, H.P. 1975a. Pollen Analytical Reconnaissance of Post Glacial Deposits from Subtropical Zone in Naini Tal District, Kumaon Himalaya, *The Palaeobotanist* 24: 215-44.

——— 1975b. History of Fossil Leguminosae in India, *Geophytology* 5 (1): 1-9.

——— 1994. A Tribute to Vishnu-Mittre (1924-91), *The Palaeobotanist* 42 (2): 241.

Haaland, Randi 1995. Sedentism, Cultivation, and Plant Domestication in the Holocene Middle Nile Region, *Journal of Field Archaeology* 22: 157-74.

Hahn, S.K. 1995. Yams. *Dioscorea* spp. (Dioscoreaceae), in *Evolution of Crop Plants*, Second Edition (J. Smartt and N.W. Simmonds Eds.), pp. 112-20. Essex: Longman Scientific and Technical.

Hamon, S. and D.H. van Sloten 1995. Okra, *Abelmoschus esculentus, A. cailei, A manihot, A. oschatus* (Malvaceae), in *Evolution of Crop Plants* (J. Smartt and N.W. Simmonds Eds.), pp. 351-7. Second Edition. Essex: Longman Scientific and Technical.

Harlan, J.R. 1971. Agricultural Origins: Centers and Noncenters, *Science* 174: 468-74.

——— 1977. The Origins of Cereal Cultivation in the Old World, in *Origins of Agriculture* (C. Reed Ed.), pp. 357-83. The Hague-Amsterdam: Elsevier-Mouton Publishers.

——— 1986. Plant Domestications: Diffuse Origins and Diffusion, in *The Origin and Domestication of Cultivated Plants* (C. Barigozzi Ed.), pp. 21-34. Amsterdam: Elsevier.

——— 1992 *Crops and Ancient Man*, Second Edition. New York: American Society for Agronomy.

——— 1995a. *The Living Fields*. Cambridge: Cambridge University Press.

——— 1995b. Barley. *Hordeum vulgare* (Gramineae-Triticinae), in *Evolution of Crop Plants* (J. Smartt and N.W. Simmonds Eds.), pp. 141-7. Second Edition. Essex: Longman Scientific and Technical.

Harlan, J.R. and J.M.J. De Wet 1971. Towards a Rational Classification of Cultivated Plants, *Taxon* 20: 509-17.

Harlan, J.R., J.M.J. De Wet and E.G. Price 1973. Comparative Evolution of Cereals, *Evolution* 27: 311-25.

Harlan, J.R. and D. Zohary 1966. Distribution of Wild Wheats and Barley, *Science* 153: 1074-80.

Harris, D.R. 1972. The Origin of Agriculture in the Tropics, *American Scientist* 60(2): 180-93.

——— 1973. The Prehistory of Tropical Agriculture: an Ethnoecological Model, in *The Explanation of Culture Change* (C. Renfrew Ed.). London: Duckworth.

——— 1989. An Evolutionary Continuum of People-Plant Interaction, in *Foraging and Farming: the Evolution of Plant Exploitation* (D.R. Harris and G.C. Hillman Eds.), pp. 11-26. London: Routledge.

——— 1996a. Introduction: Themes and Concepts in the Study of Early Agriculture, in *The Origins and Spread of Agriculture and Pastoralism in Eurasia* (D. Harris Ed.), pp. 1-9. London: UCL Press.

——— 1996b. The Origins and Spread of Agriculture and Pastoralism in Eurasia: an Overview, in *The Origins and Spread of Agriculture and Pastoralism in Eurasia* (D. Harris Ed.), pp. 552-73. London: UCL Press.

Hastorf, C.A. 1998. The Cultural Life of Early Domestic Plant Use, *Antiquity* 72: 773-782.

Hastorf, C.A. and S. Johannessen 1991. Understanding Changing People Plant Relationships in the Prehispanic Andes, in *Processual and Postprocessual Archaeologies: Multiple Ways of Knowing the Past* (R.W. Preucel Ed.), pp. 140-55. Carbondale: Southern Illinois University Press. Centre for Archaeological Investigations Occasional Paper 10.

Hather, Jon 1992. The Archaeobotany of Subsistence in the Pacific, *World Archaeology* 24: 70-81.

——— 1994a. A Morphological Classification of Roots and Tubers and Its Bearing on the Origins of Agriculture in Southwest Asia and Europe, *Journal of Archaeological Science* 21: 719-24.

——— 1994b. *An Archaeobotanical Guide to Root and Tuber Identification, Volume I. Europe and Southwest Asia.* Oxford: Oxbow Books.

——— 1994c. The Identification of Charred Root and Tuber Crops from Archaeological Sites in the Pacific, in *Tropical Archaeobotany: Applications and New Developments* (J. Hather Ed.), pp. 51-65. London: Routledge.

——— 1994d. Introduction, in *Tropcial Archaeobotany: Applications and New Developments* (J. Hather Ed.), pp. 1-8. London: Routledge.

——— 1996. The Origins of Tropical Vegeculture: Zingiberaceae, Araceae and Dioscoreaceae in Southeast Asia, in *The Origins and Spread of Agriculture and Pastoralism in Eurasia* (D. Harris Ed.), pp. 538-50. London: UCL Press.

Hather, J. and P.V. Kirch 1991. Prehistoric Sweet Potato (*Ipomoea batates*) from Mangaia Island, Central Polynesia, *Antiquity* 65: 887-93.

Hayden, B. 1990. Nimrods, Piscators, Pluckers, and Planters: the Emergence of Food Production, *Journal of Anthropological Archaeology* 9: 31-9.

——— 1995. A New Overview of Domestication, in *Last Hunters First Farmers. New Perspectives on the Prehistoric Transition to Agriculture* (T.D. Price and A.B. Gebauer Eds.), pp. 273-99. Sana Fe, New Mexico: School of Advanced Research Press.

Helbaek, H. 1969. Plant-Collecting, Dry-Farming, and Irrigation Agriculture in Prehistoric Deh Luran, in *Prehistory and Human Ecology of the Deh Luran Plain. An Early Village Sequence from Khuzistan, Iran* (F. Hole, K.V. Flanery and J.A. Neely Eds.), pp. 383-426. Ann Arbor: University of Michigan. Memoirs of the Museum of Anthropology 1.

Herman, C.F. 1997. 'Harappan' Gujarat: the Archaeology-Chronology Connetion, *Paleorient* 22 (2): 77-112.

Heron, C. and R.P. Evershed 1993. The Analysis of Pottery Residues and the Study of Pottery Use, in *Archaeological Method and Theory*, Vol. 5 (M.B. Schiffer Ed.), pp. 242-84. Tucson: University of Arizona Press.

Heun, M., R. Schafer-Pregl, D. Klawan, R. Castagna, M. Accerbi, B. Borghi, and F. Salamini 1997. Site of Einkorn Wheat Domestication Identified by DNA Fingerprinting, *Science* 278: 1312-14.

Hickey, L.J. 1979. A Revised Classification of the Architecture of Dicotyledonous Leaves, in *Anatomy of the Dicotyledons*, Vol. I (C.R. Metcalfe and L. Chalk Eds.), pp. 25-39. Oxford: Clarendon Press.

Hickey, L.J. and J.A. Wolfe 1975. The Bases of Angiosperm Phylogeny: Vegetative Morphology, *Annals of the Missouri Botanical Garden* 62: 538-89.

Hickey, M. and C. King 1991. *100 Families of Flowering Plants*, Second Edition. Cambridge: Cambridge University Press.

Higham, C. and T.L.-D. Lu 1998. The Origins and Dispersal of Rice Cultivation, *Antiquity* 72: 867-77.

Hillman, G.C. 1972. Plant Remains (in D.H. French 'Excavations at Can Hasan III 1969-1970'), in *Papers in Economic Prehistory* (E.S. Higgs Ed.), pp. 182-8. Cambridge: Cambridge University Press.

——— 1973. Crop Husbandry and Food Production: Modern Models for the Interpretation of Plant Remains, *Anatolian Studies* 23: 241-4.

——— 1981. Reconstructing Crop Husbandry Practices from Charred Remains of Crops, in *Farming Practice in British Prehistory* (R. Mercer Ed.), pp. 123-61. Edinburgh: University Press.

——— 1984. Interpretation of Archaeological Plant Remains: the Application of Ethnographic Models from Turkey, in *Plants and Ancient Man—Studies in Paleoethnobotany* (W. Van Zist and W.A. Casparie Eds.), pp. 1-41. Rotterdam: A.A. Balkema.

——— 1991. Phytosociology and Ancient Weed Floras: Taking Account of Taphonomy and Chnages in Cultivation Methods, in *Modelling Ecological Change* (D. Harris and K. Thomas Eds.), pp. 27-40. London: UCL Press.

——— 1996. Late Pleistocene Changes in the Wild Plant-Foods Available to Hunter-Gatherers of the Northern Fertile Crescent: Possible Preludes to Cereal Cultivation, in *The Origins and Spread of Agriculture and Pastoralism in Eurasia* (D. Harris Ed.), pp. 159-203. London: UCL Press.

Hillman, Gordon and M.S. Davis 1990. Measured Domestication Rates in Wild Wheats and Barley Under Primitive Cultivation and Their Archaeological Implications, *Journal of World Prehistory* 4: 157-222.

Hillman, G., S. Mason, D. de Moulins and M. Nesbitt 1996. Identification of Archaeological Remains of Wheat: the 1992 London Workshop, *Circaea* 12 (2): 195-209.

Hilu, K.W. 1994. Evidence from RAPD Markers in the Evolution of *Echinochloa* Millets (Poaceae), *Plant Systematics and Evolution* 189: 247-57.

——— 1995. Evolution of Finger Millet: Evidence from Random Amplified Polymorphic DNA, *Genome* 38: 232-8.

Hilu, K.W. and J.M.J. De Wet 1976. Racial Evolution in *Eleusine coracana* ssp. *coracana* (Finger Millet), *American Journal of Botany* 63 (10): 1311-18.

Hilu, K.W., J.M.J. De Wet and J.R. Harlan1979. Archaeobotanical Studies of *Eleusine coracana* ssp. *coracana* (Finger Millet), *American Journal of Botany* 66: 330-3.

Hilu, K.W. and J.L. Johnson 1992. Ribosomal DNA Variation in Finger Millet and Wild Species of *Eleusine* (Poaceae), *Theoretical and Applied Genetics* 83: 895-902.

Hiremath, S.C., G.N.V. Patil and S.S. Salimath 1990. Genome Homology and Origin of *Panicum sumatrense* (Graminae), *Cytologia* 55: 315-19.

Hodder, Ian 1992. *Theory and Practice in Archaeology.* London: Routledge.

Hohn, L.G.D., D.L. Plucknett, J.V. Pancho and J.P. Herberger, 1977. *The World's Worst Weeds. Distribution and Biology.* Honolulu: University Press of Hawaii.

Hole, Frank 1998. Wheat Domestication, *Science* 279 (5349): 303.

Hole, F., K.V. Flannery, and J.A. Neeley 1969. *Prehistory and Human Ecology of the Deh Luran Plain: an Early Village Sequence from Khuzistan, Iran.* Ann Arbor: Museum of Anthropology, University of Michigan Memoir 1.

Hodder, I. 1990. *The Domestication of Europe.* Oxford: Blackwell.

——— 1992. *Theory and Method in Archaeology.* London: Routledge.

Hooker, J.D. 1872-97. *Flora of British India*, 7 Vols. London: Reeve and Co.

Hopf, M. 1955. Form veranderunga van Getreide-Kornern beim Verkohlen, *Berischte der Deutschen Bontanischen Geselleshasaft* 68: 191-3.

——— 1986. Archaeological Evidence of the Spread and Use of Some Members of the Leguminosae Family, in *The Origin and Domestication of Cultivated Plants* (C. Barigozzi Ed.), pp. 35-60. Amsterdam: Elsevier. Developments in Agricultural and Managed-Forest Ecology 16.

Hosoya, Leo-Aoi and Dorian Q. Fuller (Eds.) 1999. *Cuisine, Culture and Culinary Archaeology. Archaeological Review from Cambridge* 17 (1) (in press).

Hubbard, R.N.L.B. 1975. Assessing the Botanical Component of Human Palaeoeconomies, *Bulletin of the Institute of Archaeology* (London) 12: 197-205.

——— 1976. On the Strength of the Evidence for Prehistoric Crop Processing Activities, *Journal of Archaeological Science* 3: 257-65.

——— 1980. Development of Agriculture in Europe and the Near East: Evidence from Quantitative Studies, *Economic Botany* 34 (1): 51-67.

——— 1992. Dichotomous Keys for the Identification of the Major Old World Crops, *Review of Palaeobotany and Palynology* 73: 105-15.

Hubbard, R.N.L.B. and A. Clapham 1992. Quantifying Macroscopic Plant Remains, *Review of Palaeobotany and Palynology* 73: 117-32.

Huntley, B. 1990. Dissimilarity Mapping Between Fossil and Contemporary Pollen Spectra in Europe for the last 13,000 Years, *Quaternary Research* 33: 360-76.

Hutchinson, Joseph B. 1976. India: Local and Introduced Crops, *Philosophical Transactions of the Royal Society, London B* 275: 129-41.

Ignacimuthu, S. and Babu, R. 1987. *Vigna radiata* var. *sublobata* (Fabaceae): Economically Useful Wild Relatives of Urd and Mung Beans, *Economic Botany* 41: 418-22.

Iverson, J. 1949. The Influence of Prehistoric Man on Vegetation, *Danmarks Geologiske Undersoegelse* (series IV), 3 (6): 1-25.

Jacomet, S. 1987. *Prahistorische Geteidefunde. Eine Anleteitung zur Bestimmung prahistorischer Gersten- und Weizen-Funde.* Basel: Botanisches Institut der Universitat, Abeitlung Pflanzensystematik und Geobotanik.

Janaway, R.C. and R.A.E. Coningham 1995. A Review of Archaeological Textile Evidence from South Asia, *South Asian Studies* 11: 157-74.

Jarrige, J.F. 1981. Economy and Society in the Early Chalcolithic/Bronze Age of Baluchistan, in *South Asian Archaeology 1979* (H. Hartel Ed.). Berlin: Deitrich Reimer.

——— 1985. Continuity and Change in the North Kachi Plain (Baluchistan, Pakistan) at the Beginning of the Second Millennium BC, in *South Asian Archaeology 1983* (J. Schotmans and M. Taddei Eds.), pp. 35-68. Naples: Instituto Universitario Orientale. Dipartmento di Studi Asiatici.

——— 1997. From Nausharo to Pirak: Continuity and Change in the Kachi/Bolan Region from the 3rd to the 2nd Millennium BC, in *South Asian Archaeology 1995*, Vol. 1 (R. Allchin and B. Allchin Eds.), pp. 11-32. New Delhi: Oxfrod-IBH.

Jarrige, J.F. and M. Tosi 1981. The Natural Resources of Mundigak, in *South Asian Archaeology 1979* (H. Hartel Ed.), pp. 115-42. Berlin: Dietrich Reimer.

Jha, S.S. and D. Ohri 1996. Phylogenetic Relationships of *Cajanus* and its Wild Relatives Based on Seed Protein Profiles, *Genetic Resources and Crop Evolution* 43: 275-81.

Jeffreys, M.D.W. 1955. Pre-Columbian Maize in Asia, *Eastern Anthropologist* 9 (1): 21-8.

——— 1971. Pre-Columbian Maize in Asia, *Man across the Sea. Problems of Pre-Columbian Contacts* (C.L. Riley, J.C. Kelley, C.W. Pennington, and R.L. Rands Eds.), pp. 376-400. Austin: University of Texas Press.

Johannessen, C.L. 1988. Indian Maize in the Twelfth Century BC [*sic*], *Nature* 332: 587.

Johannessen, C.L. and A.Z. Parker 1989. Maize Ears Sculptured in 12th and 13th Century AD India as Indicators of Pre-Columbian Diffusion, *Economic Botany* 43 (2): 164-80.

Jones, G.E.M. 1983. The Ethnoarchaeology of Crop Processing: Seeds of a Middle Range Methodology, *Archaeological Review from Cambridge* 2 (2): 17-26.

——— 1984. Interpretation of Archaeological Plant Remains: Ethnographic Models from Greece, in *Plants and Ancient Man—Studies in Paleoethnobotany* (W. van Ziest and W. A. Casparie Eds.), pp. 42-61. Rotterdam: Balkema.

——— 1987. A Statistical Approach to the Archaeological Identification of Crop Processing, *Journal of Archaeological Science* 14: 311-23.

——— 1991. Numerical Analysis in Archaeobotany, in *Progress in Old World Palaeoethnobotany* (W. van Zeist, K. Wasylikowsa and K.E. Behre Eds.), pp. 63-80. Rotterdam: Balkema.

——— 1992. Weed Phytosociology and Crop Husbandry: Identifying a Contrast Between Ancient and Modern Practice, *Review of Palaeobotany and Palynology* 73: 133-43.

Jones, G.E.M. and P. Halstead 1995. Maslins, Mixtures and Monocrops: on the Interpretation of Archaeobotanical Crop Samples of Heterogenous Composition, *Journal of Archaeological Science* 22: 103-14.

Jones, G.E.M., M. Charles, Sue Colledge and P. Halstead 1995. Towards the Archaeobotanical Recognition of Winter-Cereal Irrigation: an Investigation of Modern Weed Ecology in Northern Spain, in *Res Archaeobotanicae* (H. Kroll and R. Pasternak Eds.), pp. 49-68. Kiel: Institut fur Ur- und Fruhgeschichte der Christian- Albrecht- Universitat (Kiel).

Jones, Martin K. 1985. Archaeobotany Beyond Subsistence Reconstruction, in *Beyond Domestication in Prehistoric Europe* (G.W. Barker and C. Gamble Eds.), pp. 107-28. New York and London: Academic Press.

——— 1988a. The Arable Field: a Botanical Battleground, in *Archaeology and the Flora of the British Isles—Human Influence on the Evolution of Plant Communities* (M.K. Jones Ed.), pp. 86-92. Oxford: Oxford University Committee for Archaeology Monograph 14.

——— 1988b.The Phytosociology of Early Arable Weed Communities with Special Reference to Southern England, in *Der Prahistorische Mensch und Seine Umwelt, Forschungen und Berichtezur vor-und Fruhgeschichte in Baden-Wurttemberg, Band 31* (H. Kuster Ed.), pp. 43-51. Stuttgart: Theiss.

Jones, M.K., T. Brown and R. Allaby 1996. Tracking Early Crops and Early Farmers: the Potential of Biomolecular Archaeology, in *The Origins and Spread of Agriculture and Pastoralism in Eurasia* (D.R. Harris Ed.), pp. 93-100. London: UCL Press.

Jones, M.K., R.G. Allaby, T.A. Brown 1998. Wheat Domestication, *Science* 279 (5349): 302-3.

Joshi, A.B., V.R. Gadwal and M.W. Hardas 1974. Okra, in *Evolutionary Studies in World Crops. Diversity and Change in the Indian Subcontinent* (J. Hutchinson Ed.), pp. 101-7. Cambridge: Cambridge University Press.

Kaga, A., N. Tomooka, Y. Egawa, K. Hosaka and O. Kamijima 1996. Species Relationships in the Subgenus *Ceratropis* (Genus *Vigna*) as Revealed by RAPD Analysis, *Euphytica* 88: 17-24.

Kajale, Mukund D. 1974a. Ancient Grains from India, , *Bulletin of the Deccan College Research Institute* 34 (1): 55-74.

——— 1974b. Plant Economy at Bhokardan, in *Excavations at Bhokardan (Bhogavardhana)* (S.B. Deo and R.S. Gupte), pp. 217-24. Nagpur–Aurangabad: Nagpur University-Marathwada University.

——— 1975. A Note on Grain Remains from Excavations at Ter (District Osmanbad) in 1975, *Bulletin of the Deccan College Research Institute* 35: 62-5.

——— 1977a. Plant Economy at Inamgaon, *Man and Environment* I: 64-6.

——— 1977b. Ancient Plant Economy at Nevasa during Satavahana and Indo-Roman Period, *Bulletin of the Deccan College Research Institute* 36: 48-61.

——— 1977c. On the Botanical Findings from Excavations at Daimabad, a Chalcholithic Site in Western Maharashtra, India, *Current Science* 46: 818-19.

——— 1977d. Barley Grains from Chalcolithic Songaon, Maharashtra, *Man and Environment* 2: 64-7.

——— 1979. On the Occurrence of Ancient Agricultural Patterns during the Chalcolithic Periods (*c.* 1600-1000 BC) at Apegaon, District Aurangabad in Central Godavari Valley, Maharashtra, in *Apegaon Excavations* (S.B. Deo, M.K. Dhavalikar and Z.D. Ansari Eds.), pp. 50-6. Pune: Deccan College.

——— 1982. First Record of Ancient Grains at Naikund, in *Excavations at Naikund 1978-1980* (S.B. Deo and A.P. Jamkhedkar), pp. 60-3. Bombay: Department of Archaeology and Museums, Government of Maharashtra.

——— 1984. New Light on Agricultural Plant Economy During 1st Millennium BC: Palaeobotanical Study of Plant Remains from Excavations at Veerapuram, District Kurnool, Andhra Pradesh, in *Veerapuram: a Type Site for Cultural Study in the Krishna Valley* (T.V.G. Sastri, M. Kasturibai and J. Vara Prasada Rao (Eds.), Appendix B. Hyderabad: Birla Archaeological and Cultural Research Institute.

——— 1988a. Ancient Plant Economy at Chalcolithic Tuljapur Garhi, District Amraoti, Maharashtra, *Current Science* 57: 377-9.

——— 1988b. Plant Economy, in *Excavations at Inamgaon*, Vol. 1, Part ii (M.K. Dhavalikar, H.D. Sankalia and Z.D. Ansari Eds.) pp. 727-821, Pune: Deccan College.

——— 1989a. Palaeobotanical Findings from Excavations at Hallur (Second Season), District Dharwar, Karnataka, *Bulletin of the Deccan College Post-Graduate and Research Institute* 47-8: 123-8.

——— 1989b. Mesolithic Exploitation of Wild Plants in Sri Lanka: Archaeobotanical Study at the Cave Site of Beli-Lena, in *Foraging and Farming: the Evolution of Plant Exploitation* (D.R. and G.C. Hillman Eds.), pp. 269-81. London: Routledge.

——— 1989c. Archaeobotanical Investigation on Megalithic Bhagimohari and its Significance for Ancient Indian Agricultural System, *Man and Environment* XIII: 87-96.

——— 1990a. Some Initial Observations on Palaeobotanical Evidence for Mesolithic Plant Economy from Excavations at Damdama, Pratapgarh, Uttar Pradesh, in *Adaptation and Other Essays* (N.C. Ghosh and S. Chakrabarti Eds.), pp. 98-102. Santiniketan: Visva-Bharati Research Publications.

——— 1990b. Early Village Farming in Western Maharashtra, India: Palaeobotanical Evidence, *Ancient Ceylon* 7: 249-62.

——— 1990c. Observations on the Plant Remains from Excavation at Chalcolithic Kaothe, District Dhule, Maharashtra with Cautionary Remarks on Their Interpretations, in *Excavations at Kaothe* (M.K. Dhavalikar, V.S. Shinde and S.M. Atre Eds.), pp. 265-280. Pune: Deccan College.

——— 1991. Current Status of Indian Palaeoethnobotany: Introduced and Indigenous Food Plants with a Discussion of the Historical and Evolutionary Development of Indian Agriculture and Agricultural Systems in General, in *New Light on Early Farming—Recent Developments in Palaeoethnobotany* (Jane Renfew Ed.), pp. 155-89. Edinburgh: University Press.

——— 1994. Archaeobotanical Investigations on a Multicultural Site at Adam, Maharashtra, with Special Reference to the Development of Tropical Agriculture in Parts of India, in *Tropical Archaeobotany: Applications and New Developments* (J. Hather Ed.), pp. 34-50. London: Routledge.

——— 1995. Plant Remains from Lal Quila, in *Excavations at Lal Quila* (R.C. Gaur Ed.), pp. 189-93. Jaipur: Publication Scheme.

——— 1996a. Palaeobotanical Investigations at Balathal: Preliminary Results, *Man and Environment* XXI (1): 98-102.

——— 1996b. Palaeobotanical Investigations on Chalcolithic Tuljapur Garhi, in *Excavations at Tuljapur Garhi 1984-1985 (Vidarbha, Mahrashtra)* (B.P. Bopardikar Ed.), pp. 47-61. New Delhi: Memoirs of the Archaeological Survey of India 95.

——— 1998. Initial Palaeoethnobotanical Results from Neolithic Watgal, South India in Relation to Data from Contemporary Sites, Abstract Submitted to the 11th International Workgroup for Palaeoethnobotany, Toulouse, France, 18-23 May

Kajale. M.D. and B.C. Deotare 1990. On the Preservation of Microfossils in Association with Copper Objects from Megalithic Sites, *Bulletin of the Deccan College Post-Graduate and Research Institute* 49: 127-9.

——— 1993. Palaeobotanical and Pollen Analytical Investigations 2-5, 9-10, *Indian Archaeology 1986-1987–A Review*: 129-31.

——— 1993. Palaeobotanical and Pollen Analytical Investigations 1-4, *Indian Archaeology 1987-1988–A Review*: 150-1.

——— 1996. Pollen Analysis of Habitational Deposits Associated with Copper Objects from Excavations at Adam in Vidarbha, Maharashtra, *Bulletin of the Deccan College Post-Graduate and Research Institute* 54-5 (for 1994-5): 391-5.

——— 1997. Late Quaternary Environmental Studies on Salt Lakes in Western Rajasthan, India: a Summarised View, *Journal of Quaternary Science* 12 (5): 405-12.

Kajale, M.D. and M. Lal 1988. On the Botanical Findings from a Multicultural Site at Radhan, District Kanpur, Uttar Pradesh, in *Archaeological Studies* (P. Singh and O.P. Tandon Eds.), pp. 88-91. Varanasi: Banaras Hindu University.

——— 1989. On the Botanical Findings from a Multiciltural Site at Radhan, District Kanpur, Uttar Pradesh, *Bulletin of the Deccan College Research Institute* 47-8: 109-11.

Kajale, K.D., S. Mulhollad and George Rapp, Jr. 1995. Applications of Phytolith Analysis: a Potential Tool for Quaternary Environmental and Archaeological Investigations in the Indian Subcontinent, in *Quaternary Environments and Geoarchaeology of India* (S. Wadia, R. Korisettar and V. S. Kale Eds.), pp. 530-44. Bangalore: Geological Society of India.

Kajale, M.D., M.L.K. Murty, B.L. Sharma, R. Dayal and R. Vijendra Rao 1991. Archaeological Wood Remains from the Prehistoric Cave Site at Betamcherla (Muchchatla Chintamanu Gavi), District Kurnool, Andhra Pradesh, *Man and Environment* XVI (2): 115-19.

Kaplan, Lawrence. 1989. Phytolith Analysis at Wadi Kubbaniya, in *The Prehistory of Wadi Kubbaniya Volume 2. Stratigraphy, Paleoeconomy, and Environment* (F. Wendorf, R. Schild and A.E. Close Eds.), pp. 267-9. Dallas: Southern Methodist University Press.

Kislev, M.E. 1984a. Botanical Evidence for Naked Wheats in the Near East, in *Plants and Ancient Man* (W. van Zeist and W.A. Casparie Eds.), pp. 141-52. Roterdam: A.A. Balkema.

——— 1984b. Emergence of Wheat Agriculture, *Paleoorient* 10 (2): 61-70.

Kislev, M. E. and S. Rosenzweig 1991. Influence of Experimental Charring on Seed Dimensions of Pulses, in *Palaeoethnobotany and Archaeology: International Work-Group for Palaeoethnobotany 8th Symposium* (E. Hajnalova Ed.), pp. 143-57. Archaeological Institute of the Slovak Academy of Sciences (Nitra): Acta Interdisciplinaria Archaeologia 7.

Knorzer, K.-H. 1971. Urgeschichtliche Unkrauter im Rheinland. Ein Beitrag zur Entstehung der Segetalgesellschaften, *Vegetatio* 23: 89-11.

Korber-Grohne, U. 1981. Distinguishing Prehistoric Grains of *Triticum* and *Secale* on the Basis of Their Surface Patterns Using Scanning Electron Microscopy, *Journal of Archaeological Science* 8: 197-204.

Korisettar, R., M.D. Kajale, S.N. Rajaguru and K. Paddayya 1977. On the Occurrence of Plant Fossils Along with Middle Palaeolithic Tools at Wajjal, Dist. Gulbarga, Karnataka, *Bulletin of the Deccan College Research Institute* 36: 62-4.

Kroll, H. 1996. Literature on Archaeological Remains of Cultivated Plants (1994/95), *Vegetation History and Archaeobotany* 5: 169-200.

——— 1997. Literature on Archaeological Remains of Cultivated Plants (1995/96), *Vegetation History and Archaeobotany* 6: 25-67.

——— 1998. Literature on Archaeological Remains of Cultivated Plants (1996/97), *Vegetation History and Archaeobotany* 7: 23-56.

Kulshrestha, V.P. 1985. History and Ethnobotany of Wheat in India, *Journal d'Agriculture Traditionelle et de Botanique Appliquée* 32: 61-71.

Kumar, L.S.S. 1952. Identification of Charred Ragi and Rice Grains from the Excavations at Kolhapur, 1945-6, *Bulletin of the Deccan College Research Institute* 14: 79-80.

Kumar, Tuk-Tuk 1988. *History of Rice in India—Mythology, Culture and Agriculture.* Delhi: Gian Publishing House.

Kuster, H. 1991. Phytosociology and Archaeobotany, in *Modelling Ecological Change* (D.R. Haris and K.D. Thomas Eds.), pp. 17-25. London: UCL Press.

Ladizinsky, G. 1989. Origin and Domestication of Southwest Asian Grain Legumes, in *Foraging and Farming* (D.R. Harris and G. Hillman Eds.), pp. 374-89. London: Routledge.

——— 1998. How Many Tough-Rachis Mutants Gave Rise to Domesticated Barley? *Genetic Resources and Crop Evolution* 45: 411-14.

Langer, R.H.M. and Hill, G.D. 1991. *Agricultural Plants.* Second Edition. Cambridge: Cambridge University Press.

Lawn, R.J. 1995. The Asiatic Vigna Species, in *Evolution of Crop Plants*, Second Edition (J. Smartt and N.W. Simmonds Eds.), pp 321-6. Essex: Longman Scientific and Technical.

Lechevallier, M. and G. Quivron 1981. The Neolithic in Baluchistan: New Evidence from Mehrgarh, in *South Asian Archaeology 1981* (H. Hartel Ed.), pp. 93-114. Berlin: Deitrich Reimer.

Lentfer, C.J. and W.E. Boyd 1998. A Comparison of Three Methods for the Extraction of Phytoliths from Sediments, *Journal of Archaeological Science* 25 (12): 1159-84.

Leroi-Gourhan, A. 1969. Pollen Grains of Graminae and Cerealia from Shanidar and Zaw Chemi, in *Domestication and Exploitation of Plants and Animals* (P.J. Ucko and G.W. Dimbleby Eds.), pp. 143-8. London: Duckworth.

Levkovskaya, G.M. and A.A. Filatenko 1992. Palaeobotanical and Palynological Studies in South Arabia, *Review of Palaeobotany and Palynology* 73: 241-57.

Li, H.-L. 1974. An Archaeological and Historical Account of *Cannabis* in China, *Economic Botany* 28 (4): 437-8.

Li, Yu, Jizeng Jia, Yaru Wang and Shuzhi Wu 1998. Intraspecific and Interspecific Variation in *Setaria* Revealed by RAPD Analysis, *Genetic Resources and Crop Evolution* 45: 279-85.

Liu, C.J. 1996. Genetic Diversity and Relationships among *Lablab purpureus* Genotypes Evaluated Using RAPD as Markers, *Euphytica* 90: 115-19.

Liversage, D. 1989. The Spread of Food Production into India—Some Questions of Interpretation, in *South Asian Archaeology 1985* (K. Frifelt and P. Sorensen Eds.), pp. 292-5. London: Curzon Press.

——— 1991. South Asian Radiocarbon Datings; Calibration and Computer Garphics, *Bulletin of the Indo-Pacific Prehistory Association* 10: 198-205.

Lone, Farooq A., Maqsooda Khan and G. M. Buth 1988. Five Thousand Years of Vegetational Changes in Kashmir: the Impact of the Biotic Factor, *Proceedings of the Indian National Science Academy* 54A: 497-500.

——— 1993. *Palaeoethnobotany—Plants and Ancient Man in Kashmir.* Rotterdam: Balkema.

Lukoki, L., R. Marechal, E. Otoul. 1980. Les Ancestres Sauvages Des Haricots Cultivees: *Vigna radiata* (L.) Wilczek et *V. mungo* (L.) Hepper, *Bulletin du Jardin Botanique de Belgique* 50: 385-91.

Lundsrom-Baudais, K., A.-M. Rachoud-Scheinder, D. Baudais and B. Poissonnier (in press). Le Broyage Dans la Chaine de Transformation du Millet Commun (*Panicum miliaceum*) au Nepal et en Vendee: Outils, Gestes et Ecofacts, in *Actes du collque Moudre et Broyer, Clement-Ferrand 30 nov. – 2 dec. 1995.* Valbonne: Monographies du CRA.

Lu T. L.-D. 1988, Some Botanical Characteristics of Green Foxtail (*Setaria viridis*) and Harvesting Experiments on the Grass, *Antiquity* 72: 902-7.

Luthra, J.C. 1936. Ancient Wheat and Its Variability, *Current Science* 4 (7): 489.

——— 1941. [Letter Quoted], in *Excavations at Mohenjo-Daro* (M.S. Vats), p. 467. Delhi: Manager of Publications.

M'Ribu, H.K. and K.W. Hilu 1996. Application of Random Amplified Polymorphic DNA to Study Genetic Diversity in *Paspalum scrobiculatum* L. (Kodo Millet, Poaceae), *Genetic Resources and Crop Evolution* 43: 203-10.

Mackay, E.J.H. 1943. *Chanhu-daro Excavations 1935-36.* New Haven: Connecticut: American Oritental Society.

MacNeish, R.S. 1992. *The Origins of Agriculture.* Norman: University of Oklahoma Press.

Madella, Marco 1995. A Preliminary Study of Phytolith Analysis, Agriculture and Use of Plants at Kot Diji (Sindh–Pakistan), *Ancient Sindh* 2: 93-108.

——— 1997. Phytolith Analysis from the Indus Valley Site of Kot Diji, Sind, Pakistan, in *Archaeological Sciences 1995* (A. Sinclair, E. Slater and J. Gowlett Eds.), pp. 294-302. Oxford: Oxbow Books, Oxbow Monograph 64.

——— 1998. Morphological Analysis of Phytoliths: a Botanical Tool for the Interpretation of Archaeological and Geological Sediments from Eurasia. Ph.D. Dissertation. Cambridge: Cambridge University.

Madella, M., A.H. Powers-Jones and M.K. Jones 1998. A Simple Method of Extraction of Opal Phytoliths from Sediments Using a Non-Toxic Heavy Liquid, *Journal of Archaeological Science* 25: 801-3.

Maier, Ursula 1996. Morphological Studies of Wheat Free-Threshing Ears from a Neolithic Site in Southwest Germany, and the History of Naked Wheats, *Vegetation History and Archaeobotany* 5: 39-55.

Magid, A.A. 1989. *Plant Domestication in the Middle Nile Basin—an Archaeobotanical Case Study.* Oxford: BAR International Series 523.

Maheshwari, P. and U. Singh 1965. *Dictionary of Economic Plants in India.* New Delhi: Indian Council for Agricultural Research.

Mujumdar and S.N. Rajaguru 1966. *Kupgal Excavations.* Poona: Deccan College.

Maloney, B.K. 1990. Grass Pollen and the Origins of Rice Agriculture in North Sumatra, *Modern Quaternary Research in Southeast Asia* 11: 163-6.

——— 1994. The Prospects and Problems of Using Palynology to Trace Origins of Tropical Agriculture: the Case of Southeast Asia, in *Tropical Archaeobotany:Applications and New Developments* (J.G. Hather Ed.), pp. 139-71. London: Routledge.

Marshall, J. 1931. *Mohenjo-daro and the Indus Civilization.* London: Arthur Probsthain.

Maun, M.A. and S.C.H. Barrett 1986. The Biology of Canadian Weeds 77. *Echinochloa crus-galli* (L.) Beauv., *Canadian Journal of Plant Science* 66: 739-59.

Maxwell, R.H. 1991. Tribe Phaseoleae, in *A Revised Handbook of the Flora of Ceylon*, Vol. VII (M.D. Dassanayake and F.R. Fosberg Eds.), pp. 236-381. Washington, D.C.: Smithsonian Institution.

Meadow, Richard 1989. Continuity and Change in the Agriculture of the Greater Indus Valley: the Palaeoethnobotanical and Zooarchaeological Evidence, in *Old Problems and New Perspectives in the Archaeology of South Asia* (J.M. Kenoyer Ed.), pp. 61-74. Madison: University of Wisconsin. Wisconsin Archaeological Reports 2.

——— 1996. The Origins and Spread of Agriculture and Pastoralism in Northwestern South Asia, in *The Origins and Spread of Agriculture and Pastoralism in Eurasia* (D. Harris Ed.), pp. 390-412. London: UCL Press.

Meher-Homji, V.M. 1980. The Thar Desert: Its Climatic History, *Man and Environment* IV: 1-7.

——— 1996. Monsoon: a Bioclimatologist's Point of View, *Current Science* 71: 352-7.

Mehra, K.L. 1962. Study of 35 Herbarium Specimens of African *Eleusine*, *Journal of Indian Botanical Society* 41: 531.

——— 1963. Considerations on the African Origin of *Eleusine coracana* (L.) Gaertn., *Current Science* 32: 300-1.

——— 1997. Biodiversity and Subsistence Changes in India: the Neolithic and Chalcolithic age, *Asian Agri-history* 1 (2): 105-26.

Mehra, K.L. and R.K. Arora 1985. Some Considerations on the Domestication of Plants in India, in *Recent Advances in Indo-Pacific Prehistory* (V.N. Misra and Peter Bellwood Eds.), pp. 275-9. Leiden: E.J. Brill.

Miller, H. 1991. Urban Palaeoethnobotany at Harappa, in *Harappa Excavations 1986-1990* (R. H. Meadow Ed.), pp. 121-6. Madison: Prehistory Press.

Miller, N.F. 1984. The Use of Dung as Fuel: an Ethnographic Example and an Archaeological Application, *Paleorient* 10 (2): 71-9.

——— 1988. Ratios in Paleoethnobotanical Analysis, in *Current Paleoethnobotany* (C.A. Hastorf and V.S. Popper Eds.), pp. 72-85. Chicago: University of Chicago Press.

——— 1991. The Near East, in *Progress in Old World Palaeoethnobotany* (W. Van Zeist, K. Wasylikowsa and K.-E. Behre Eds.), pp. 133-60. Rotterdam: Balkema.

Miller, N.F. and T.L. Smart. 1984. Intentional Burning of Dung as Fuel: a Mechanism for the Incorporation of Charred Seeds into the Archaeological Record, *Journal of Ethnobiology* 4: 15-28.

Miller, T.E. 1992. A Cautionary Note on the Use of Morphological Characters for Recognising Taxa in Wheat (Genus *Triticum*), in *Prehistoire de l'Agriculture: Nouvelles Appreoaches Experimentales et Ethnographiques* (P.C. Anderson Ed.), pp. 249-53. Paris: Editions CNRS. Monographie du Centre de Recherches Archeologiques 6.

Minnis, Paul 1978. Palaeoethnobotanical Indicators of Prehistoric Environmental Disturbance: a Case Study, in *The Nature and Status of Ethnobotany* (R.I. Fords, M.F. Brown, M. Hodge, W.L. Merrill Eds.), pp. 347-66. Michigan: Museum of Anthropology, University of Michigan. Anthropological Papers 67.

——— 1981. Seeds in Archaeological Sites: Sources and Some Interpretive Problems, *American Antiquity* 46: 143-51.

Miyazaki, S. 1982. Classification and Phylogenetic Relationships of the *Vigna radiata-mungo-sublobata* Complex [in Japanese with English Summary], *Bulletin of the National Institute of Agricultural Science* (Japan) D. 33: 1-61.

Moore, P.D., J.A. Webb, and M.E. Collinson 1991. *Pollen Analysis*, Second Edition. Oxford: Blackwell.

Morrison, K. 1994. Intensification of Production: Archaeological Approaches, *Journal of Archaeological Method and Theory* 1: 111-59.

——— 1996. Typological Scheme and Agricultural Change: Beyond Boserup in Precolonial South India, *Current Anthropology* 37 (4): 583-608.

M' Ribu H.K. and K.W. Hilu 1994. Detection of Interspecific and Polymorphic DNA, *Theoretical and Applied Genetics* 88: 412-16.

Nakamura, Ikuo and Yo-Ichiro Sato 1991. Amplification of DNA Fragments Isolated from a Single Seed of Ancient Rice (AD 800) by Polymerase Chain Reaction, *Chinese Journal of Rice Science* 5(4): 175-9.

Nayar, N.M. 1995. Sesame, *Seasmum indicum* L. (Pedaliaceae), in *Evolution of Crop Plants* (J. Smartt and N.W. Simmonds Eds.), pp. 404-7. Essex: Longman Scientific and Technical.

Nayar, N.M. and P.N. Ravindran 1995. Herb Spices, in *Evolution of Crop Plants*, Second Edition (J. Smartt and N.W. Simmonds Eds.), pp. 491-4. Essex: Longman Scientific and Technical.

Nesbitt, M. 1998. Where was Einkorn Wheat Domesticated? *Trends in Plant Science* 3 (3): 82-3.

Nesbitt, M. and D. Samuel 1996. From Staple Crop to Extinction? The Archaeology and History of the Hulled Wheats, in *Hulled Wheats. Proceedings of the First International Workshop on Hulled Wheats 21-22 July 1995, Castelvecchio Pascoli, Tuscany, Italy* (S. Padulosi, K. Hammer and J. Heller Eds.), pp. 41-100. Rome: International Plant Genetic Resources Institute.

——— 1998. Wheat Domestication: Archaeobotanical Evidence, *Science* 279 (5356): 1433.

Nickerson, N.H. 1953. Variation in Cob Morphology among Certain Archaeological and Ethnological Races of Maize, *Annals of the Missouri Botanical Garden* 40: 79.

Ng, N.Q. 1995. Cowpea. *Vigna unguiculata* (Leguminosae- Papilionideae), in *Evolution of Crop Plants*, Second Edition (J. Smartt and N.W. Simmonds Eds.), pp. 326-32. Essex: Longman Scientific and Technical.

O'Donoghue, K., A. Clapham, R.P. Evershed and T.A. Borwn 1996. Remarkable Preservation of Biomolecules in Ancient Radish Seeds, *Proceedings of the Royal Society* (London) B 263: 541-7.

Oka, H.I. 1988. *Origin of Cultivated Rice*. Amsterdam: Elsevier. Developments in Crop Science 14.

Ollendorf, Amy L. 1992. Toward a Classification Scheme of Sedge (Cyperaceae) Phytoliths, in *Phytolith Systematics—Emerging Issues* (G. Rapp Jr. and S.C. Mulholland Eds.), pp. 91-111. New York: Plenum Press.

Pal, B.P. 1966. *Wheat.* New Delhi: Indian Council for Agricultural Research.

Pandey, B.P. 1995. *Modern Practical Botany*, Vol. II, Fourth Edition. New Delhi: S. Chand and Co. Ltd.

Panella, L., Kami, J. and Gepts P. 1993. Vignin Diversity in Wild and Cultivated Taxa of *Vigna unguiculata* (L.) Walp. (Fabaceae), *Economic Botany* 47: 371-86.

Payak, M.M. and J.K.S. Sachan 1988. Maize in Somnathpur, an Indian Mediaeval Temple, *Nature* 335: 773-4.

——— 1993. Maize Ears not Sculpted in 13th Century Somnathpur Temple in India, *Economic Botany* 47 (2): 202-5.

Paz, Victor 1997. *Tubers in Their Cultural and Taphonomic Context: a Contribution to the Archaeology of Adansemanso.* M.Phil. Dissertation. Cambridge: University of Cambridge.

Pearsall, Deborah 1983. Evaluating the Stability of Subsistence Strategies by Use of Palaeo-ethnobotanical Data, *Journal of Ethnobiology* 3: 121-37.

——— 1988. Interpreting the Meaning of Macroremain Abundance: the Impact of Source and Context, in *Current Palaeoethnobotany: Analytical Methods and Cultural Interpretations of Archaeological Plant Remains* (C.A. Hastorf and V.S. Popper Eds.), pp. 97-118. Chicago: University of Chicago Press.

——— 1989. *Palaeoethnobotany.* New York: Academic Press.

Pearsall, D., D.R. Piperno, E.H. Dinan, M. Umlauf, Z. Zhao and R.A. Benfer Jr. 1998. Distinguishing Rice (*Oryza sativa* Poaceae) from Wild *Oryza* Species Through Phytolith Analysis: Results of Preliminary Research, *Economic Botany* 49 (2): 183-96.

Peglar, S.M. 1993. The Mid-Holocene Ulmus Decline at Diss Mere, Norfolk, UK: a Year-by-Year Pollen Stratigraphy from Annual Laminations, *The Holocene* 3: 1-13.

Percival, John 1921. *The Wheat Plant.* London: Duckworth and Co.

Phillippson, G. and S. Bahuchet 1996. Cultivated Crops and Bantu Migrations in Central and Eastern Africa: a Linguistic Approach, in *The Growth of Farming Communities in Africa from the Equator Southwards. Azania* 29-30 (J.E.G. Sutton Ed.), pp. 103-20. Nairobi: British Institute of East Africa.

Phillips, S.M. 1972. A Survey of the Genus *Eleusine* Gaertn. (Graminae) in Africa, *Kew Bulletin* 27 (2): 251-70.

Piperno, Dolores. 1988. *Phytolith Analysis: an Archaeological and Geological Perspective.* New York: Academic Press.

Piperno, D.R. and D.M. Pearsall 1998. *The Origins of Agriculture in the Lowland Neotropics.* New York: Academic Press.

Popper, V.S. 1988. Selecting Quantitative Measurements in Palaeoethnobotany, in *Current Paleoethnobotany* (C.A. Hastorf and V.S. Popper Eds.), pp. 53-71. Chicago: University of Chicago Press.

Porteres, R. 1976. African Cereals: Eleusine, Fonio, Black Fonio, Teff, Brachiaria, Paspalum, Pennisetum, and African Rice, in *Origins of Africa Plant Domestication* (J.R. Harlan, J.M.J. De Wet and A.B.L. Stemler Eds.), pp. 409-52. The Hague: Mouton Publishers.

Possehl, G.L. 1980. *Indus Civilization in Saurashtra.* Delhi: B.R. Publishing Corporation.

——— 1986. African Millets in South Asian Prehistory, in *Studies in the Archaeology of India and Pakistan* (J. Jacobson Ed.), pp. 237-56. New Delhi: Oxford-IBH.

——— 1997. The Seafaring Merchants of Meluhha, in *South Asian Archaeology 1995* (R. Allchin and B. Allchin Eds.), pp. 87-100. New Delhi: Oxford-IBH and the American Institute of Indian Studies.

——— 1998. The Introduction of African Millets to Indian Subcontinent, in *Plants for Food and Medicine* (H.D.V. Prendergast, N.L. Etkin, D.P. Harris and P.J. Houghton Eds.), pp. 107-121. London: Kew Botanical Gardens.

Possehl, G.L. and P. Rissman 1992. The Chronology of Prehistoric India from Earliest Times to the Iron Age, in *Chronologies in Old World Archaeology*, Vol. 1 (R.W. Ehrich Ed.), pp. 465-90,Vol. 2, pp. 447-74. Chicago-London: University of Chicago Press.

Powers, A.H. and D.D. Gilbertson 1987. A Simple Preparation Technique for the Study of Opal Phytoliths from Archaeological and Quaternary Sediments, *Journal of Archaeological Science* 14: 529-35.

Powers, A.H., J. Padmore, and D.D. Gilbertson 1989. Studies of Late Prehistoric and Modern Opal Phytoliths from Coastal Sand Dunes and Machair in Northwest Britain, *Journal of Archaeological Science* 16: 37-45.

Powers, A.H. 1992. Great Expectations: a Short Historical Review of European Phytolith Systematics, in *Phytolith Systematics—Emerging Issues* (G. Rapp Jr. and S.C. Mulholland Eds.), pp. 15-35. New York: Plenum Press.

Rachie, K.O. 1975. *The Millets. Importance, Utilization and Outlook.* Hyderabad: International Crops Research Institute for the Semi-Arid Tropics.

Ramesh Rao and Lal 1985. Plant Remains, in *Lothal* (S.R. Rao Ed.), pp. 667-84. Delhi: Archaeological Surevy of India.

Randhawa, M.S. 1980. *A History of Agriculture in India: Beginning to 12th Century.* New Delhi: Indian Council for Agricultural Research.

Rao, K.E. Prasada , J.N.J. De Wet, D.E. Brink., and M.H. Mengesha 1987. Infraspecific Variation and Systematics of Cultivated *Setaria italica*, Foxtail Millet (Poaceae), *Economic Botany* 41 (1): 108-16.

Rao, K.R. and R. Sahi 1967. Plant Remains: Prakash, *Ancient India* 20-1: 139-53.

Ratnagar, S. 1989. A Chalcolithic Village in the Famine Belt, *Studies in History* (New Series) 5 (2): 287-302.

Ratnagar, S. 1994. Harappan Trade in Its 'World' Context, *Man and Environment* XIX (1-2): 115-28.

Rawal, K.M. 1975. Natural Hyybridization Among Wild, Weedy and Cultivated *Vigna unguiculata* (L.) Walp., *Euphytica* 24: 699-707.

Reddy, Seetha N. 1991a. Complementary Approaches to Late Harappan Subsistence: an Example from Oriyo Timbo, in *Harappa Excavations 1986-1990—a Multidisciplinary Approach to Third Millennium Urbanism* (R.H. Meadow Ed.), pp. 127-35. Madison: Prehistory Press.

——— 1991b. On the Banks of the River: Opportunistic Cultivation in South India, *Expedition* 33 (3): 18-26.

——— 1991c. Archaeobotany at Oriyo Timbo 1989-1990: a Post Urban Site in Gujarat, *Man and Environment* 16 (1): 73-84.

——— 1994. Plant Usage and Subsistence Modelling: an Ethnoarchaeological Approach to the Late Harappan of Northwest India. Ph.D. Dissertation. Ann Arbor Michagan: University of Wiscosin. University Microfilms.

——— 1997. If the Threshing Floor could Talk: Integration of Agriculture and Pastoralism During the Late Harappan in Gujarat, India, *Journal of Anthropological Archaeology* 16: 162-87.

Reed, C.A. 1977. Introduction: Prologue, in *Origins of Agriculture* (C.A. Reed Ed.), pp. 1-21. The Hague: Mouton.

Rehm, S. and G. Espig 1991. *The Cultivated Plants of the Tropics and Subtropics: Cultivation, Economic Value, Utilization.* Weikersheim: Verlag Josef Margraf.

Renfrew, Jane. 1973. *Palaeoethnobotany.* London: Methuen and Co. Ltd.

Rindos, D. 1980. Symbiosis, Instability, and the Origins and Spread of Agriculture: a New Model, *Current Anthropology* 21: 751-72.

——— 1984. *The Origins of Agriculture: an Evolutionary Perspective.* New York: Academic Press.

Rissman, P. 1986. Seasonal Aspects of Man/Cattle Interaction in Bronze Age Western India, *Journal of Ethnobiology* 6: 257-77.

Robinson, M. and R.N. Hubbard 1977. The Transport of Pollen in the Bracts of Hulled Cereals, *Journal of Archaeological Science* 4: 197-9.

Rollo, F., F.M. Venanzi and A. Amici 1991. Nucleic Acids in Mummified Plant Seeds: Biochemistry and Molecular Genetics of Pre-Columbian Maize, *Genetical Research* 58: 193-201.

Rosen, Arlene Miller 1992. Preliminary Identification of Silica Skeletons from Near Eastern Archaeological Sites: an Anatomical Approach, in *Phytoliths Systematics: Emerging Issues* (G. Rapp Jr. and S. Mulholland Eds.), pp. 129-47. New York: Plenum Press. Advances in Archaeological and Museum Science 1.

Rovner, I. 1971. Potential of Opal Phytoliths for Use in Paleoecological Reconstruction, *Quaternary Research* 1: 343-59.

Rowley-Conwy, P. 1991. The Sorghum from Qasr Ibrim, Egyptian Nubia, *c.* 800 BC–AD 1811: a Preliminary View, in *New Light on Early Farming* (Jane Refrew Ed.), pp. 191-212. Edinburgh: Edinburgh University Press.

Rowley-Conwy, P., W. Deakin and C.H. Shaw. 1997. Ancient DNA from Archaeological Sorghum (*Sorghum bicolor)* from Qasr Ibrim, Nubia: Implications for Domestication and Evolution and a Review of the Archaeological Evidence, *Sahara* 9: 23-34.

Sachan, J.K.S. and K.R. Sarkar 1986. Discovery of Sikkim Primitive Precursor in the Americas, *Maize Genetics Cooperative Newsletter* 60: 104-6.

Sahni, B. 1936. Antiquities from Khokhrakot mount at Rohtak in the Jumna Valley, *Current Science* 4 (11): 796-801.

Saldanha, C.J. 1984. *Flora of Karnataka*, Vol. I. New Delhi: Oxford-IBH.

Sallares, R, R.G. Allaby and T.A. Brown 1995. PCR-Based Identification of Wheat Genomes, *Molecular Ecology* 4: 509-14.

Sankalia, H.D. 1975. *Prehistory of India.* New Delhi: Munshiram Manoharlal.

Sankalia, H.D., S.B. Deo, Z.D. Ansari and S. Ehrhardt 1960. *Form History to Prehistory at Nevasa (1954-56)*, Poona: Deccan College.

Sano, R. and H. Morishima 1992. Indica-Japonica Differentiation of Rice Cultivars Viewed from Variations in Key Characters of Isozyme, with Species Reference to Himalayan Hilly Areas, *Theoretical and Applied Genetics* 84: 266-74.

Santhanam, V and J.B. Hutchinson 1974. Cotton, in *Evolutionary Studies in World Crops. Diversity and Change in the Indian Subcontinent* (J. Hutchinson Ed.), pp. 89-100. Cambridge: Cambridge University Press.

Saraswat, K.S. 1986. Ancient Crop-economy of Harappans from Rohira, Punjab (c. 2000-1700 B.C.), *The Palaeobotanist* 35: 32-8.

——— 1992. Archaeobotanical Remains in Ancient Cultural and Socio-Economical Dynamics of the Indian Subcontinent, *The Palaeobotanist* 40: 514-45.

——— 1993. Plant Economy of Late Harappan at Hulas, *Puratattva* 23: 1-12.

——— 1994. Palaeobotanical and Pollen Analytical Investigations, *Indian Archaeology 1989-1990—A Review*: 132-3.

Saraswat, K.S. and Chanchala Srivastava 1994. Palaeobotanical and Pollen Analytical Investigations, *Indian Archaeology 1989-90—A Review*: 132-3.

——— 1995. Palaeobotanical and Pollen Analytical Investigations, *Indian Archaeology 1990-91—A Review*: 103-4.

——— 1996. Palaeobotanical and Pollen Analytical Investigations, *Indian Archaeology 1991-92—A Review*: 139-40.

——— 1997. Palaeobotanical and Pollen Analytical Investigations, *Indian Archaeology 1992-93—A Review*: 123-4.

Saraswat, K.S., N.K. Sharma and D.C. Saini 1994. Plant Economy ay Ancient Narhan (c. 1300 B.C.-300/400 A.D.), in *Excavations at Narhan (1984-1989)* (Purushottam Singh Ed.), pp. 255-346. Varanasi: Banaras Hindu University.

Saraswat, K.S., D.C. Saini, M.K. Sharma and Chanchala Srivastava 1990. Palaeobotanical and Pollen Analytical Investigation, *Indian Archaeology 1985-86—A Review*: 122-5.

——— 1992. Palaeobotanical and Pollen Analytical Investigations 1, 6-8, 11, *Indian Archaeology 1986-87—A Review*: 129-32.

——— 1993. Palaeobotanical and Pollen Analytical Investigations, 5-7, *Indian Archaeology 1987-88—A Review*: 151-3.

Sarkar, K.R., B.K. Mukherjee, D. Gupta and H.K. Jain 1974. Maize, in *Evolutionary Studies in World Crops. Diversity and Change in the Indian Subcontinent* (J. Hutchinson Ed.), pp. 121-8. Cambridge: Cambridge University Press.

Sarma, I.K. 1972. South-east Asia, India and West Asia (a Study on the Beginnings of the Food Producing Stage), in *Archaeological Congress and Seminar Papers. Papers Presented at the 4th Annual Congress of the Indian Archaeological Society and the Seminars Held at Nagpur, 1970* (S.B. Deo Ed.), pp. 95-112. Nagpur: Nagpur University.

Sato, Yo-Ichiro, Ryuuji Ishikawa and Hiroko Morishima 1990. Nonrandom Association of Genes and Characters Found in *indica* x *japonica* Hybrids of Rice, *Heredity* 65: 75-9.

Scaife, Robert G. 1988. The Elm Decline in the Pollen Record of South East England and Its Relationship to Early Agriculture, in *Archaeology and the Flora of the British Isles. Human Influence on the Evolution of Plant Communitites* (M.K. Jones Ed.), pp. 21-33. Oxford: Oxford University Committee for Archaeology Monograph 14.

Schlumbaum, A., R. Blatter and S. Jacomet 1998a. How to Study Ancient DNA from Archaeological Wheat—a) Methods, Paper Presented at 11th Symposium of the International Work Group for Palaeoethnobotany, 18-23 May 1998, Toulouse, France.

Schlumbaum, A., S. Jacomet and J.-M. Neuhaus 1998b. Coexistence of Tetraploid and Hexaploid Naked Wheat in a Neolithic Lake Dwelling of Central Europe: Evidence from Morphology and Ancient DNA, *Journal of Archaeological Science* 25: 1111-18.

Shaffer, J.G. and D.A. Lichtenstein 1989. Ethnicity and Change in the Indus Valley Cultural Tradition, in *Old Problems and New Perspectives in the Archaeology of South Asia* (J.M. Kenoyer Ed.), pp. 117-26. Madison: Department of Archaeology, University of Wisconsin. Wiscosin Archaeological Reports 2.

Sharma, C. and M.S. Chauhan 1988. Palaeoenvironmental Inferences from the Quarternary Palynostratigraphy of Himachal Pradesh and Kumaon, India, *Proceedgins of the Indian National Science Academy* 54 A (3): 510-23.

Sharma, C. and A. Gupta 1997. Vegetation and Climate in Garhwal Himalaya during Early Holocene: Deoria Tal, *The Palaeobotanist* 46 (3): 111-16.

Sharma, D.P. and Madhuri Sharma 1987. A Reappraisal of the Chronology of Mesolithic and Neolithic Cultures of the Vindhyas and Middle Ganga Valley, in *Archaeology and History—Essays in Memory of Shri A. Ghosh* (B.M. Pande and B.D. Chattopadhyaya Eds.), pp. 57-66. Delhi: Agam Kala.

Sharma, G.R., V.D. Misra, D. Mandal, B.B. Misra and J.N. Pal 1980. *Beginnings of Agriculture (Epi-Palaeolithic to Neolithic: Excavations at Chopani-Mando, Mahadaha, and Mahagara)*. Allahabad: Abinash Prakashan.

Shastri, S.V.S. and S.D. Sharma 1974. Rice, in *Evolutionary Studies in World Crops. Diversity and Change in the Indian Subcontinent* (J. Hutchinson Ed.), pp. 55-61. Cambridge: Cambridge University Press.

Shaw, F.J.F. 1943. Vegetable Remains, in *Chanhudaro Excavations* (E.J.H. Mackay), pp. 250-251. New Haven, Connecticut: Yale University Press.

Shinde, V. 1987. Farming in the Chalcolithic Deccan, India, *Tools and Tillage* 5 (4): 214-27.

Singh, Gurdip 1971. The Indus Valley Culture Seen in the Context of Postglacial Climatic and Ecological Studies in North-West India, *Archaeology and Physical Anthropology of Oceania* 6: 177-89.

Singh, Gurdip, R. Joshi, S. Chopra and A.B. Singh 1974. Late Qauternary History of Vegetation and Climate in the Rajasthan Desert, India, *Philosophical Transactions of the Royal Society London* 267: 467-501.

Singh, Ranjit Pratap 1990. *Agriculture in Protohistoric India*. Delhi: Pratibha Prakashan.

Smart, T.L. and E.S. Hoffman 1988. Environmental Interpretation of Archaeological Charcoal, in *Current Palaeoethnobotany: Analytical Methods and Cultural Interpretations of Archaeological Plant Remains* (C.A. Hastorf and V.S. Popper Eds.), pp. 167-205. Chicago: University of Chicago Press.

Smartt, J. 1985a. Evolution of Grain Legumes. II. Old and New World Pulses of Lesser Economic Importance, *Experimental Agriculture* 21: 1-18.

——— 1985b. Evolution of Grain Legumes. III. Pulses in the Genus *Vigna*, *Experimental Agriculture* 21: 87-100.

——— 1990. *Grain Legumes: Evolution and Genetic Resources*. Cambridge: Cambridge University Press.

Smartt, J. and N.W. Simmonds (Eds.) 1995. *Evolution of Crop Plants*, Second Edition. London: Longman Scientific and Technical.

Smith, Bruce D. 1989. The Origins of Agriculture in Eastern North America, *Science* 246: 1566-71.

Stemler, Ann B. 1990. A Scanning Electron Microscopic Analysis of Plant Impressions in Pottery from Sites of Kadero, El Zakiab, Um Direiwa and El Kadada, *Archeologie du Nil Moyen* 4: 87-106.

Stapf, O. 1931. [Comments Quoted], in *Mohenjo-daro and the Indus Civilization* (J. Marshall Ed.), p. 586. London: Arthur Probsthain.

Stevens, C.J. 1996. Iron Age and Roman Agriculture in the Upper Thames Valley: Archaeobotanical and Social Perspectives. Ph.D. Dissertation. Cambridge: University of Cambridge.

Stewart, R.B. and William Robertson IV 1973. Application of Flotation Technique in Arid Areas, *Economic Botany* 27 (1): 114-16.

Stewart, Wilson N. and Gar W. Rothwell 1993. *Palaeobotany and the Evolution of Plants*, Second Edition. Cambridge: Cambridge University Press.

Stonor, C.R. and Edgar Anderson 1949. Maize Among the Hill Peoples of Assam, *Annals of the Missouri Botanical Garden* 36: 355-404.

Struever, Stuart 1968. Flotation Techniques for the Recovery of Small-Scale Archaeological Remains, *American Antiquity* 33: 353-62.

Subash Chandran, M.D. 1997. On the Ecological History of the Western Ghats, *Current Science* 73 (2): 146-55.

Sundararaj, D.D. and G. Thulasidas 1993. *Botany of Field Crops*. Second Edition. Delhi: Macmillan.

Tengberg, M. 1998. Plant Husbandry in the Makran (Pakistan, 4000 BC—2000 BC), Paper Presented at the 11th Symposium of the International Work Group for Palaeoethnobotany, 18-23 May 1998, Toulouse, France.

Thapar, B.K. 1974. Problems of the Neolithic Cultures in India: a Retrospect, *Puratattva* 7: 61-5.

——— 1978. Early Agricultural Communities in India, *Journal of Human Evolution*. 7: 11-22.

Thiebault, S. 1988. Palaeoenvironment and Ancient Vegetation of Baluchistan Based on Charcoal Analysis of Archaeological Sites, *Proceedings of the Indian National Science Aacademy* 54A: 501-9.

——— 1989. A Note on the Ancient Vegetation of Baluchistan Based on Charcoal Analysis of the Latest Periods from Mehrgarh, Pakistan, in *South Asian Archaeology 1985* (K. Frifelt and P. Sorensen Eds.), pp. 186-8. London: Curzon Press.

——— 1992. Complementary Results in Anthracological Analysis from Sites in Baluchistan, in *South Asian Archaeology 1989* (C. Jarrige Ed.), pp. 271-6. Madison: Prehistory Press. Monographs in World Archaeology 14.

Thomas, Julian 1996. The Cultural Context of the First Use of Domesticates in Continental Central and Northwest Europe, in *The Origins and Spread of Agriculture and Pastoralism in Eurasia* (D.R. Harris Ed.), pp. 310-22. London: UCL Press.

Thomas, K.D. 1983a. Tarakai Qila: Site, Economy and Environment, in *Site, Environment and Economy* (B. Proudfoot Ed.), pp. 127-44. Oxford: BAR International Series 173.

——— 1983b. Agricultural and Subsistence Systems of the Third Millennium B.C. in North-West Pakistan: a Speculative Outline, in *Integrating the Subsistence Economy* (M.K. Jones Ed.), pp. 279-314. Oxford: BAR International Series 181.

——— 1989. Hierarchical Approaches to the Evolution of Complex Agricultural Systems, in *The Beginnings of Agriculture* (A. Milles, D. Williams and N. Gardner Eds.), pp. 55-73. Oxford: BAR International Series 496.

Tomlinson, P.B. 1969. *Anatomy of the Monocotyledons: III. Commelinales-Zingiberales.* Oxford: Oxford University Press.

Thompson, G.B. 1994. Wood Charcoals from Tropical Sites: a Contribution to Methodology and Interpretation, in *Tropical Archaeobotany: Applications and New Developments* (J.G. Hather Ed.), pp. 9-33. London: Routledge.

——— 1996. Ethnographic Models for Interpreting Rice Remains, in *The Excavation of Khok Phanom Di a Prehistoric Site in Central Thailand. Volume IV: Subsistence and Environment: the Botanical Evidence (the Biological Remains Part II)* (C. Higham and R. Thosarat Eds.), pp. 119-50. London: The Society of Antiquaries of London.

Tostain, S. 1994. Isozymic Classification of Pearl Millet (*Pennisetum glaucum, Poaceae*) Landraces from Niger (West Africa), *Plant Systematics and Evolution* 193: 81-93.

——— 1998. Le mil, une Longue Histoire: Hypotheses sur sa Domestication et ses Migrations, in *Plantes et Paysages d'Afrique. Une Histoire a Explorer* (M. Chastanet Ed.), pp. 461-90. Paris: Editions Karthala and Centre de Recherches Africaines.

Trigger, B.G. 1989. *A History of Archaeological Thought.* Cambridge: Cambridge University Press.

——— 1991. Distinguished Lecture in Archaeology: Constraint and Freedom: a New Synthesis for Archaeological Explanation, *American Anthropologist* 93: 551-69.

Vaillancourt, R.E. and N.F. Weeden 1992. Chloroplast DNA Polymorphism Suggests Nigerian Center of Domestication for the Cowpea, *Vigna unguiculata*, Leguminosae, *American Journal of Botany* 79: 1194-9.

Van der Maeson, L.J.G. 1980. India is the Native Home of the Pigeonpea, in *Libergratulatorius in Honorem H.C.D. de wit* (J.C. Arends, G. Boelema, C.T. de Groot and A.J.M. Leeuwenberg Eds.), pp. 257-62. Wageningen: Netherlands: H. Veenman and B.V. Zonen. Landbouwhoge school Miscellaneous Paper 19.

——— 1986. *Cajanus DC. and Atylosia W & A.(Leguminosae)*, Agricultural University Wageningen Papers 84-5. Wageningen, Netherlands: Agricultural University, 255pp.

——— 1990. Pigeonpea: Origin, History, Evolution, and Taxonomy, in *The Pigeonpea* (Nene, Y.L., S.D. Hall and V.K. Sheila Eds.), pp. 15-46. Wallingford: CAB International.

——— 1995. Pigeonpea *Cajanus cajan*, in *Evolution of Crop Plants*, Second Edition (J.S. Smartt and N. Simmonds Eds.), pp. 251-5. London: Longman Scientific and Technical.

Van der Veen, M. 1992. *Crop Husbandry Regimes. An Archaeobotanical Study of Farming in Northern England 1000 BC-AD 500*. Sheffield: University of Sheffield. Sheffield Archaeological Monographs 3. J.R. Collis Publications.

——— 1995. The Identification of Maslin Crops, in *Res Archaeobotanica. International Workgroup for Palaeoethnobotany, Proceedings of the Ninth Symposium, Kiel 1992* (H. Kroll and R. Pasternak Eds.), pp. 335-44. Kiel: Oetker-Voges-Verlag.

Van Zeist, W. 1976. On Macroscopic Traces of Food Plants in Southwestern Asia (with Some Reference to Pollen Data), *Philosophical Transactions of the Royal Society London* (Biological Sciences) 273: 27-41.

Vats, M.S. 1940. *Excavations at Harappa* I. Calcutta: Archaeological Survey of India.

Vaughan, D.A. The Genus *Oryza* L. Current Status of Taxonomy, *The International Rice Research Institute Research Paper Series* 138: 21pp.

Vavilov, N.I. 1992 [originally 1950]. *The Origin, Variation, Immunity, and Breeding of Cultivated Plants*. Cambridge: Cambridge University Press.

Veena, T. and N. Sigamani 1991. Do Objects in Friezes of Somnathpur Temple (1268 AD) in South India Represent Maize Ears?, *Current Science* 61 (6): 395-7.

Venkatasubbaiah, P.C and M.D. Kajale 1991. Biological remains from Neolithic and Early Historic Sites in Cuddapah District, Andhra Pradesh, *Man and Environment* 16: 85-97.

Verdcourt, B. 1970. Studies in the *Leguminosae-Papilionidae* for the 'Flora of Tropical East Africa': III, *Kew Bulletin* 24 (3): 379-443.

——— 1971. Phaeseoleae, in *Flora of Tropical East Africa, Leguminosae (Part 4), Papilionidae (2)* (E. Milne-Redhead and R.M. Polhill Eds.). London: Crown Agents for Overseas Governments and Administrations.

Vishnu-Mittre 1952. Charophyte Remains from the Jurassic of Rajmahal Hills, Bihar, *Current Science* 21: 41-2.

——— 1954. Petrified Spores and Pollen Grains from the Jurassic Rocks of Rajmahal Hills, Bihar, *The Palaeobotanist* 3: 117-27.

——— 1956. Studies on the Fossil Flora of Nipania (Rajmahal Series), India– Bennettitales, *The Palaeobotanist* 5 (2): 95-9.

——— 1957a. Studies on the Fossil Flora of Nipania (Rajmahal Series), India– Pentoxyleae, *The Palaeobotanist* 6: 31-46.

——— 1957b. Studies on the Fossil Flora of Nipania (Rajmahal Series), Bihar– Coniferales, *The Palaeobotanist* 6: 82-112.

——— 1957c. Abnormal Pollen Grains in Some Indian Gymnosperms with Remarks on the Significance of the Abnormalities, *Journal of the Indian Botanical Society* 36 (4): 548-63.

——— 1957d. Pollen Analysis (Maski), *Ancient India* 13: 129-33.

——— 1960. Post-Glacial History of the Whittlesey Mere Region of East Anglian Fenland, 2 Vols. Ph.D. Dissertation. Cambridge: University of Cambridge.

——— 1961. Plant Economy in Ancient Navdatoli-Maheshwar. *Technical Report on Archaeological Remains.* Poona: Department of Archaeology and Ancient Indian History, Deccan College and University of Poona Publications 2: 13-52.

——— 1963. The Ice Ages and the Evolutionary History of the Indian Gymnosperms, *Journal of the Indian Botanical Society* 42 (2): 301-8.

——— 1965a. Floristic and Ecological Reconsiderations of the Pleistocene Plant Impressions from Kashmir, *The Palaeobotanist* 13: 308-27.

——— 1965b. Comments and Suggestions Towards Various Interpretations of the Postglacial Elm Decline, *Meddelelser fra Dansk Geologisk Forening* 15 (4): 32-45.

——— 1966. Some Aspects Concerning Pollen-Analytical Investigations in the Kashmir Valley, *The Palaeobotanist* 15: 157-75.

——— 1968a. Inter-Relationship Between Archaeology and Plant Sciences, *Puratattva* 1: 4-15.

——— 1968b. Kaundinyapura Plant Economy in Pre-historic and Historic Times, in *Excavations at Kaundinyapura* (M.G. Dikshit), pp. 140-7. Bombay: Government Central Press.

——— 1968c. Protohistoric Records of Agriculture in India, *Transactions of the Bose Research Institute* 31 (3): 87-106.

——— 1969. Remains of Rice and Millet, in *Excavations at Ahar (Tambavati)* (H.D. Sankalia, S.B. Deo and Z.D. Ansari), pp. 229-35. Poona: Deccan College.

——— 1970a. Status of Barley in Indian Archaeology with Remarks on the Aryan Hypothesis, *Puratattva* 3: 1-2.

——— 1970b. Agriculture. Biological Concepts and Agriculture in Ancient India, *Indian Journal of the History of Science* 5: 144-61.

——— 1971. Ancient Plant Economy at Hallur, in *Protohistoric Cultures of the Tungabhadra Valley (Hallur Excavations)* (M.S. Nagaraja Rao), pp. 1-9. Dharwar: Published by Author.

——— 1972. The Neolithic Plant Economy of Chirand, Bihar, *The Palaeobotanist* 21: 18-22.

——— 1974. Palaeobotanical Evidence in India, in *Evolutionary Studies in World Crops. Diversity and Change in the Indian Subcontinent* (J. Hutchinson Ed.), pp. 3-30. Cambridge: Cambridge University Press.

——— 1976a. Palaeoecology of the Rajasthan Desert During the Last 10,000 Years, *The Palaeobotanist* 25: 549-58.

——— 1976b. The Archaeobotanical and Palynological Evidence for the Early Origin of Agriculture in South and Southeast Asia, in *Gastronomy* (M.I. Arnott Ed.), pp. 13-21. The Hague: Mouton and Co.

——— 1977. Changing Economy in Ancient India, in *Origins of Agriculture* (C. Reed Ed.), pp. 569-88. Paris: Mouton.

——— 1978. Origins and History of Agriculture in the Indian Sub-continent, *Journal of Human Evolution* 7: 31-6.

——— 1979. Palaeobotanical Evidences of the Environment of Early Man in Northwestern and Western India, *Grana* 18: 167-81.

——— 1981a. Botanical Perspective on the Quaternary, *The Palaeobotanist* 28-9: 402-12.

——— 1981b. Wild Plants in Indian Folk Life: a Historical Perspective, in *Glimpses of Indian Ethnobotany* (S.K. Jain Ed.), pp. 37-58. New Delhi: Oxford-IBH.

——— 1982. The Harappan Civilization and the Need for a New Approach, in *Harrapan Civilization* (G.L. Possehl Ed.), pp. 31-9. New Delhi: Oxford-IBH.

——— 1985. The Uses of Wild Plants and the Processes of Domestication in the Indian Subcontinent, in *Recent Advances in Indo-Pacific Prehistory* (V.N. Misra and P. Bellwood Eds.), pp. 281-91. New Delhi: Oxford-IBH.

——— 1989. Forty Years of Archaeobotanical Research in South Asia, *Man and Environment* 14: 1-16.

——— 1990. Plant Remains, in *Excavations at Surkotada* (J.P. Joshi Ed.), pp. 388-92. New Delhi: Memoirs of the Archaeological Survey of India 87.

Vishnu-Mittre and H.P. Gupta 1968a. Ancient Plant Economy at Paunar, Maharashtra, in *Paunar Excavations 1967* (S.B. Deo and M.K. Dhavalikar Eds.), pp. 128-34. Nagpur: University Press.

——— 1968b. Plant Remains from Ancient Bhatkuli, District Amraoti, Maharashtra, *Puratattva* 2: 21-2.

——— 1971. The Origin of Shola Forest in the Nilgiris, South India, *The Palaeobotanist* 19: 110-14.

Vishnu-Mittre and Statira Guzder 1975. The Early Domestication of Plants in South and Southeast Asia—a Critical Review, *The Palaeobotanist* 22: 83-8.

Vishnu-Mittre and R.D. Robert 1971. Studies of Pollen Content of Moss Cushions in Relation to Forest Composition in the Kashmir Valley, *Geophytology* 1 (1): 84-96.

Vishnu-Mittre and R. Savithri. 1974. Ancient Plant Economy at Noh, Rajasthan, *Puratattva* 7: 77-80.

——— 1975. Supposed Remains of Rice (*Oryza* sp.) in the Terracotta Cakes and Pai at Kalibangan, Rajasthan, *The Palaeobotanist* 22: 124-6.

——— 1976. Ancient Plant Economy at Inamgaon, *Puratattva* 8: 55-63.

——— 1978. Setaria in Ancient Plant Economy of India, *The Palaeobotanist* 25: 559-64.

——— 1979a. Palaeobotanical and Pollen Analytical Investigations, *Indian Archaeology 1974-75—A Review:* 78-81.

——— 1979b. Further Contribution on Protohistoric Ragi—*Eleusine coracana* Gaertn., *The Palaeobotanist* 26: 10-15.

——— 1979c. Palaeobotanical and Pollen Analytical Investigations, *Indian Archaeology 1975-76—A Review:* 86-8.

——— 1981. Palaeobotanical and Pollen Analytical Investigations, *Indian Archaeology 1978-79—A Review:* 108-10.

——— 1982. Food Economy of the Harappans, in *Harappan Civilization* (G.L. Possehl Ed.), pp. 205-21. New Delhi: Oxford-IBH.

——— 1990. The Environment and Economy of the Neolithic Cultures of South India: Palaeobotanical Evidence, in *Archaeology in Karnataka* (A. Sundara Ed.), pp. 100-12. Mysore: Directorate of Archaeology and Museums.

Vishnu-Mittre and B.D. Sharma 1966. Studies of Postglacial Vegetational History from the Kashmir Valley-1. Haigam Lake, *The Palaeobotanist* 15: 185-212.

Vishnu-Mittre and K.A. Sharma 1983. Palaeobotanical and Pollen Analytical Investigations, *Indian Archaeology 1979-80—A Review*: 113-14.

Vishnu-Mittre, Statira Guzder and R.D. Robert 1967. Studies of the Late Quaternary Vegetational History of Kumaon Himalaya, *Current Science* 36 (2): 539-40.

Vishnu-Mittre, U. Prakash and N. Awasthi. 1971. Ancient Plant Economy at Ter, Maharashtra, *Geophytology* 1 (2): 170-7.

Vishnu-Mittre, A. Sharma and Chanchala Srivastava 1984. Palaeobotanical and Pollen Analytical Investigations, *Indian Archaeology 1981-82—A Review:* 105-6.

——— 1986a. Ancient Plant Economy at Daimabad, in *Daimabad 1976-1979* (S.A. Sali), pp. 588-626. New Delhi: Archaeological Survey of India.

Vishnu-Mittre, G. Singh, K.M.S. Saxena 1962. Pollen Analytical Investigations of the Lower Karewas, *The Palaeobotanist* 11: 92-5.

Vishnu-Mittre, K.S. Saraswat, A. Sharma and Chanchala Srivastava 1985. Palaeobotanical and Pollen Analytical Investigations, *Indian Archaeology 1982-83—A Review*: 146-50.

——— 1986b. Palaeobotanical and Pollen Analytical Investigations, *Indian Archaeology 1983-84—A Review*: 174-8.

Vuorela, I. 1973. Relative Pollen Rain Around Cultivated Fields, *Acta Botanica Fennica* 102: 1-27.

Wan, J. and H. Ikehashi 1997. Identification of Two Types of Differentiation in Cultivated Rice (*Oryza sativa* L.) Detected by Polymorphism of Isozymes and Hybrid Sterility, *Euphytica* 94: 151-61.

Wasylikowa, K. 1981. The Role of Fossil Weeds for the Study of Former Agriculture, *Zeitschrift fur Archaologie* 15: 11-23.

Wasylikowa, K. and L. Kubiak-Martens 1995. Wild Sorghum from Early Neolithic Site at Nabta Playa, South Egypt, in *Res archaeobotaicae* (H. Kroll and R. Pasternak Eds.), pp. 345-58. Oetker-Voges-Verlag, Kiel.

Watabe, T. 1984. Origin and Dispersal of Rice in Asia, *East Asian Cultural Studies* 24: 33-9.

Watanabe, N. 1968. Spodographic Evidence of Rice in Prehistoric Japan, *Journal of the Faculty of Sciences* (Tokyo) 3: 217-35.

——— 1970. A Spodographic Analysis of Millet from Prehistoric Japan, *Journal of the Faculty of Sciences* (Tokyo) 5: 357-84.

Watson, Patty Jo. 1997. The Shaping of Modern Palaeoethnobotany, in *People, Plants and Landscapes—Studies in Paleoethnobotany* (K. Gremillon Ed.), pp. 13-22. Tuscaloosa: The University of Alabama Press.

Weber, Steven A. 1990. Millets in South Asia: Rojdi as a Case Study, in *South Asian Archaeology 1987* (M. Taddei Ed.), pp. 333-48. Rome: IsMEO

——— 1991. *Plants and Harappan Subsistence—an Example of Stability and Change from Rojdi.* New Delhi: Oxford-IBH.

——— 1992. South Asian Archaeobotanical Variability, in *South Asian Archaeology 1989* (C. Jarrige Ed.), pp. 283-90. Madison, Wisconsin: Prehistory Press

——— 1993. Changes in Plant Use at Rojdi: Implications for Early South Asian Subsistence Systems, in *Harappan Civilization: a Recent Perspective* (G.L. Possehl Ed.), pp. 287-94. New Delhi: Oxford-IBH and the American Institute of Indian Studies.

——— 1996. Distinguishing Change in the Subsistence and the Material Records: the Interplay of Environment and Culture, *Asian Perspectives* 35 (2): 155-63.

——— 1997. Harappa Archaeobotany: a Model for Subsistence, in *South Asian Archaeology 1995* (R. Allchin and B. Allchin Eds.), pp. 115-17. New Delhi: Oxford-IBH.

——— 1998. Out of Africa: the Initial Impact of Millets in South Asia, *Current Anthropology* 39 (2): 267-74.

Weissner, Polly and Wulf Schiefenhovel (Eds.) 1996. *Food and the Status Quest: an Interdisciplinary Perspective.* Oxford: Berghahn Books.

Wendel, J.F. 1995. Cottòn, *Gossypium* (Malvaceae), in *The Evolution of Crop Plants*, Second Edition (J. Smartt and N.W. Simmonds Eds.), pp. 358-66. Essex: Longman Scientific and Technical.

Wenming, Yan 1991. China's Earliest Rice Agriculture Remains, *Indo-Pacific Prehistory 1990, 1*, Papers from the 14th IPPA Congress, Yokyakarta: 118-26

Werth, C.R., K.W. Hilu and C.L. Langner 1994. Isozymes of *Eleusine* (Gramineae) and the Origin of Finger Millet, *American Journal of Botany* 81 (8): 1186-97.

Westphal, E. 1974. *Pulses in Ethiopia, Their Taxonomy and Agricultural Significance*. Wageningen: Centre for Agricultural Publishing and Documentation. Agricultural Research Reports 815.

Whitley, David S. 1998. (Ed.) *Reader in Archaeological Theory: Post-Processual and Cognitive Approaches*. London: Routledge.

Willcox, G. 1991. Carbonised Plant Remains from Shortugai, Afghanistan, in *New Light on Early Farming. Recent Developments in Palaeoethnobotany* (J.M. Renfrew Ed.), pp. 139-53. Edinburgh: Edinburgh University Press.

——— 1992. Some Differences Between Crops of Near Eastern Origin and Those from the Tropics, in *South Asian Archaeology 1989* (C. Jarrige Ed.), pp. 291-9. Madison: Prehistory Press. Monographs in World Archaeology 14.

Willis, K.J. and K.D. Bennett 1994. The Neolithic Transition—Fact or Fiction? Palaeoecological Evidence from the Balkans, *The Holocene* 4: 326-30.

Wilson, S.M. 1985. Phytolith Analysis at Kuk, an Early Agricultural Site in Papua, New Guinea, *Archaeology in Oceania* 20 (3): 90-7.

Yabuno, T. 1962. Cytotaxonomic Studies on the Two Cultivated Species and the Wild Relatives in the Genus *Echinochloa*, *Cytologia* 27: 296-305.

——— 1987. Japanese Barnyard Millet (*Echinochloa utilis*, Poaceae) in Japan, *Economic Botany* 41 (4): 484-93.

Young, Ruth 1998. Ethnobotanical Observations: Finger Millet Processing in East Africa, Paper Presented at the 11th Symposium of the International Work Group for Palaeoethnobotany, 18-23 May 1998, Toulouse, France.

Zeuner, F.E. 1959. On the Origin of the Cinder Mounds of the Bellary District, India, *Bulletin of the Institute of Archaeology* (London) 2: 37-44.

Zeven, A.C. 1978. The Prehistoric Spread of Bread Wheat into Asia, in *Proceedings of the Fifth International Wheat Genetics Symposium*, Vol. 1 (S. Ramanujam Ed.), pp. 103-7. New Delhi: Indian Society of Genetics and Plant Breeding.

Zhao, Zhijun 1998. The Middle Yangtze Region in China is One Place Where Rice was Domesticated: Phytolith Evidence from the Diaotonghuan Cave, Northern Jaingxi, *Antiquity* 72: 885-97.

Zhao, Z.D., M. Pearsall, R.A. Benfer Jr. and D.R. Piperno 1998. Distinguishing Rice (*Oryze sativa* Poaceae) from wild *Oryza* Species Through Phytolith Analysis, II: Finilized Method, *Economic Botany* 52 (2): 134-45.

Zohary, Daniel 1969. The Progenitors of Wheat and Barley in Relation to Domestication and Agricultural Dispersal in the Old World, in *The Domestication and Exploitation of Plants and Animals* (P.J. Ucko and G.W. Dimbleby Eds.), pp. 47-66. London: Duckworth.

——— 1984. Modes of Evolution in Plants under Domestication, in *Plant Biosystematics* (W.F. Grant Ed.), pp. 579-86. New York: Academic Press.

——— 1989. Domestication of the Southwest Asian Neolithic Crop Assemblage of Cereals, Pulses, and Flax: the Evidence from the Living Plants, in *Foraging and Farming* (D. Harris and G. Hillman Eds.), pp. 358-73. London: Unwin Hyman.

——— 1996. The Mode of Domestication of the Founder Crops of Southwest Asian Agriculture, in *The Origins and Spread of Agriculture and Pastoralism in Eurasia* (D. Harris Ed.), pp. 142-58. London: UCL Press.

——— 1997. Genetic Systems: an Overview, in *Proceedings of the Workshop on Conservation of the Wild Relatives of European Cultivated Plants* [*Bocconea* 7] (B. Valdes, V.H. Heywood, F.M. Raimondo and D. Zohary Eds.), pp. 127-31. Palermo: Herbarium Mediterraneum Panormitamanum.

Zohary, Daniel and Maria Hopf 1993. *Domestication of Plants in the Old World*, Cambridge: Cambridge University Press.

Researches in Archaeozoology of the Holocene Period (Including the Harappan Tradition in India and Pakistan)

U.C. CHATTOPADHYAYA

1. INTRODUCTION

The study of animal remains constitutes, by common consent, a theme essential to an integrated ecological approach to the past. Archaeozoology is the term most popularly used to deal with such studies, although Zooarchaeology and, to a lesser extent, Palaeozoology are also often used. However, the appropriateness of treating this pursuit under a separate technical category or sub-discipline has rightly been questioned (Legge 1978). It is beyond the scope of the present discussion to engage in this debate, so I shall retain these terms. Archaeo-faunal study, another term, though not without problem, will however be used more frequently. Suffice it to say that there lies much substance in the arguments of veteran archaeologists like Lewis Binford, Eric Higgs, Tony Legge, Clive Gamble, Geoff Bailey, and Peter Rowley-Conwy in favour of incorporating such studies within mainstream archaeology.

Before attempting to present the main results of Holocene archaeo-faunal studies in the Indian subcontinent, it is important to outline the evolution of such studies outside India. It is by situating archaeo-faunal studies in India within the global trend of research that we will be able to better appreciate our achievements and limitations, and chalk out future lines of research. This will be followed by a brief review of archaeo-faunal studies in India along with an introduction to the specialists and their approaches.

2. ARCHAEOZOOLOGICAL RESEARCH IN THE WEST

The study of archaeological faunal remains began in north-western Europe in the second half of the nineteenth century, mostly with mere taxonomical lists (Chattopadhyaya 1985a). The last four decades witnessed a phenomenal progress in such studies. Objectives now became borader in range, and analyses more detailed and focused (Ucko and Dimbleby 1969; Olsen 1971; Clason 1975; Meadow and Zeder 1978; Davis 1987; Rackham 1994; Hesse and Wapnish 1985). The latter meant in-depth study of specific problems such as the origins of animal husbandry/domestication with particular reference to West Asia and Middle East (Braidwood and Howe 1960; Reed 1959, 1969, 1983; Perkins 1964,1969; Perkins and Daly 1968; Meadow and Zeder 1978; Hecker 1982; Braidwood et al. 1983; Davis 1987). Different analytical techniques emerged in view of changing needs of the research (Uerpmann 1973; Wilson et al. 1982; Klein and Cruz-Uribe 1984). The criteria for recognizing animal domestication in archaeological assemblages were defined and methods were worked out and debated from time to time (Bökönyi 1969, 1973; Chaplin

1971; Meadow and Zeder 1978; Olsen 1979; Ucko and Dimbleby 1969). Initially, osteomorphological change and size variation in the skeletons of the potential domesticates were the main criteria for ascertaining domestication, and the method soon included age and sex identification of the animal bones with a view to reconstructing their mortality profiles. Such profiles, supposed to be different for different economies, were treated as reflections of the state of human-animal relatioships (cf. Higgs and Jarman 1972; Chattopadhyaya 1985a, for a critique). Thus the central problem of inquiry, particularly for West Asia and Middle East, did not greatly deviate from identifying animal domestication, retaining the age-old culture-historical methodology. Gordon Childe's influence was paramount as archaeozoologists began to talk of the 'Hearth Area' of domestication and dispersal of domestication to adjacent regions and beyond. We also know that one of the main lines of departure of the New Archaeology from the culture-historical approach rested on the debate whether innovation is region-specific and reaches out to non-centres through dispersal, or involves independent centres (Clarke 1968; Binford 1972; Renfrew 1978). With the success of the New Archaeology, the trend in faunal studies took a distinctive turn, away from the Childean approach that highlighted diffusion/migration as the sole explanation for culture change.

It was in the early seventies that archaeologists at Cambridge, led by Eric Higgs, formally established an independent school of archaeo-faunal studies under the banner of 'Palaeoeconomy' (Higgs 1972, 1975; Jarman et al. 1982; Bailey 1983). Critical as they were to the zoologists' understanding of archaeological problems, including animal husbandry and methods of its recognition, their purpose was to situate such studies within mainstream archaeology. The late 1970s also witnessed the rise of yet another novel line of research, with C.K. Brain's taphonomic study (1976, 1981) in southern Africa that has indeed revolutionized faunal studies in recent years. It is now becoming clear that without incorporating taphonomy, faunal studies have only a limited scope. In other words, the future of archaeo-faunal studies lies in taphonomy. I shall come back to this point later in the article.

The need for a standardization of methodology was realized as early as 1970 (Chattopadhyaya 1985a) and a blueprint of the sort of data that should be collected and the sort of interpretation that might be presented was subsequently prepared by Caroline Grigson (1978). According to her the ideal kind of faunal report should consist of three sections: (a) introduction, (b) presentation of the data, and (c) interpretation. She gave special emphasis to the second section, constituting the most vital part of the faunal report this should be open to objective evaluation by future workers. Data presentation also includes metrical data on standard lines suggested by Driesch (1976), and quantification (Chaplin 1971; Grayson 1984).

3. DEVELOPMENT OF ARCHAEO-FAUNAL STUDIES IN THE INDIAN SUBCONTINENT

In India the faunal studies as a meaningful approach in archaeology took off with the famous sites of Mohenjo Daro (Sewell and Guha 1931) and Harappa (Prashad 1936). The principal objective in these studies was to know about the representation of animal taxa at sites and to present a systematic description of the identified species. The momentum geared up only after Independence and faunal assemblages from more and more sites were studied by zoologists. Bhola Nath of the Zoological Survey of India took the initial lead and was, in a sense, the torchbearer of post-Independence archaeo-faunal studies in the country. George (1955, 1958) and Eapen (1960) were other early post-Independence workers in the field. The reports of Sewell and Guha (1931) and Prashad (1936) became models for most early studies. However, these technical reports were tagged by directors of excavations as appendices to the main reports, a practice that by and large continues till today.

While the objectives in early archaeo-faunal studies were the identification of elements and species and systematic zoological description of the identified taxa, the post-Independence scenario witnessed gradual changes in objectives and methods, the acceleration, however, attaining new heights only recently. While Bhola Nath and D.R. Shah followed more or less the line of Sewell and Guha (1931), Juliet Clutton-Brock (1965) was the first to show the importance of bone measurements in faunal studies as an aid to distinguish closely related species or wild from domesticated ones. R. Conrad (1966) and Anneka Clason (1974, 1979, 1984) were other archaeozoologists to have made substantial contributions to archaeo-faunal studies. Clason exclusively used metrical data on standard lines, prescribed by Driesch (1976), for distinguishing closely related animal taxa (1979). K.R. Alur introduced new objectives and techniques in faunal studies during the 1960s and 1970s (Alur 1990). Specializing in veterinary science, palaeo-pathology became one of his most favourite concerns and he exclusively dealt with pathological disorders (disease and human-induced deformities) discernible on bones. Herein lies the potential of such studies in understanding the secondary utilization of animals for traction or as beasts of burden (see Section 4.2). Alur also visualized the importance of understanding animal for the economy of the past people, but could not apply this technique, except in a most general sense. A.K. Sharma, K.K. Bhan, S. Banerjee, M.K. Biswas, V.V. Rao, and G.V. Sreenivasa Rao have also made useful contributions.

Archaeozoological studies have flourished at Deccan College over the last three decades or more. Among its archaeozoologists, a special mention may be made of P.K. Thomas, who has taken the lead in such studies in the country and has examined, independently as well as jointly with P.P. Joglekar, faunal assemblages from a large number of archaeological sites, with fruitful results. Some of his important contributions to Indian archaeozoology include the study of species diversity and intra-site faunal variability over time in relation to ecological opportunities. Other experts of this institution are G.L. Badam, essentially a palaeontologist, V.G. Sathe, and S.J. Pawankar.

It may be pointed out that over the last decade or so, archaeo-faunal studies in India have made some progress in the sense that (a) archaeologists are taking an active interest in this branch and (b) new methods and techniques in faunal studies are being used to address archaeological problems, in sharp contrast to the traditional approaches involving mainly taxonomical resolutions. These include, amongst others, seasonality of site occupation, hunter-gatherer subsistence and settlement patterns, site functions, industrial activities, and pastoralism (Kane 1989; Rissman and Chitalwala 1990; I. Chattopadhyaya 1990, 1999; Chattopadhyaya and Chattopadhyaya 1990; Chattopadhyaya 1991, 1996;

Thomas 1989; Patel 1997). Besides, for some archaeologists the faunal evidence constitutes an important aspect, which is most encouraging (Sahu 1988;Varma 1991). BP Singh of Banaras Hindu University is another leading archaeologist with a good understanding of archaeozoological techniques.

In Pakistan, Richard Meadow of Peabody Museum, Harvard, has been the main expert engaged in the study of faunal remains from prehistoric and protohistoric sites of the greater Indus Valley. His work on the fauna of Mehrgarh with long cultural sequence, has been outstanding. He is one of the most competent zoo-archaeologists of the world and has introduced several innovative techniques in tackling problems relating to subsistence practices including the domestication of cattle,[1] goats and sheep (Meadow 1981, 1984a, 1984b, 1986, 1987, 1989a, 1989b, 1991). With him the future of archaeo-zoological studies in Pakistan is bright. Other faunal specialists working in Pakistan include Bruno Compagnoni (Rome) and Priscilla Turnbull (Chicago) and Laura Miller (New York).

It may be mentioned here that, bearing a few exceptions, the faunal specialists in India did not pay much attention to the the suggestions of Grigson about the standardization of methodology. The conventional practice in Indian faunal studies has been to present lists of animal taxa or comparative charts, i.e. cross-tabulations of archaeological sites and different animal taxa identified therefrom, with marginal comments about terminological confusion on zoological names, or distinctions between a domesticated species and its wild progenitor. Such tables, though devoid of quantified data, make some very broad suggestions about the animals present at sites, the overall status of the economy, and the palaeoenvironmental conditions prevalent in the region. However, it should be noted that without taphonomical studies, such lists, even with quantified data, are generally unreliable guides to past subsistence practices. Papers reviewing archaeozoological studies in India with such cross-tabular charts have been published from time to time and the latest one on Holocene faunal studies appeared a few years ago (Thomas and Joglekar 1994). So it is desirable to present here these earlier results with minor modifications, along with certain fresh entries, though this constitutes neither the main concern nor the thrust of the present contribution. The emphasis, rather, will be on new faunal methods and techniques that are being worked out over the last couple of decades in view of alternative research objectives, and some theoretical issues. For general taxonomical and other details from individual sites some reviews may be useful (Thomas and Joglekar 1994; Badam 1984; Badam and Sathe 1991; Meadow 1989a,1993; Thomas (n.d.) and Thomas, in Vol. 2 of this series).

4. THE HOLOCENE FAUNA

The advent of the Holocene marked the beginning of cultural adaptations in response to environmental changes in most parts of South Asia leading to the emergence of what archaeologists define as the Mesolithic phase. The 'transition' however was neither concurrent nor uniform. It is unlikely that the Upper Palaeolithic tradition came to an abrupt end after the Pleistocene. In fact, late Upper Palaeolithic traditions continued in all probability into the Holocene. Were this to be confirmed by future radiocarbon evidence, we still lack the relevant faunal evidence. The study of palaeontological assemblages from the Terminal Pleistocene alluvial deposits of the river Son, for example, shows the predominance of the populations of large bovids, including the now extinct wild cattle, *Bos namadicus*, over other ungulates (Blumenschine and Chattopadhyaya 1983; Chattopadhyaya 1991). It may, however, be inferred from the available palaeo-environmental and palaeontological evidence, particularly from the northern half of India, that the faunal composition during the Early Holocene would have been different from the preceding Pleistocene because of the expansion of the forest cover as a result of higher levels of precipitation (Williams and Royce 1982, 1983; Clark and Sharma 1983). In other words, the populations of different species of deer in nature might have increased from the Terminal Pleistocene to Early Holocene. Mahagara II, an Epipalaeolithic site in the Belan Valley, flourished during the transition between the Terminal Pleistocene and Holocene (Sharma et al. 1980). Animal taxa identified in this assemblage by the present author include both large bovids (continuing from the preceding period) and medium—as well as small-sized deer in almost equal proportions (Chattopadhyaya 1991). However, we shall see in the sections that follow that, although deer remains are the most numerous in some of the Early Holocene faunal assemblages, cattle soon started playing an important role. All this all happened between the Mesolithic and the Early Neolithic.

In certain ways, *the history of Indian archaeo-fauna is the evolution of the zebu* from its wild progenitor *Bos namadicus*. An important problem of investigation therefore is to trace the changing pattern of human–cattle relationships during different cultural phases of the Holocene and concentrate on those archaeological strata where this animal began to substitute deer/antelopes in the overall economy of the relevant groups. According to Richard Meadow (1989a), in certain respects, what sheep and goats meant to the civilizations of West Asia and the Near East, cattle meant to South Asia. The singular character of South Asian culture was shaped, to a large extent, by man's unique relationship with cattle that developed over the millennia. As man's dependence on cattle became total by the time of the Bronze Age Harappan Civilization, and as the faunal assemblages of later cultural traditions exhibit, by and large, a repetition of the late Harappan faunal composition, the following discussion is confined to the Mesolithic, Neolithic, and Harappan periods. Later periods, like the Chalcolithic and Early Historic, will be discussed only briefly, touching upon certain important points.

In the absence of proper sieving techniques coupled with a bias among collectors towards larger/identifiable bones, a greater emphasis will be given here to mammalian fauna in comparison with others. I shall also discuss in passing the non-mammalian fauna wherever the available information would permit so doing.

4.1 The Mesolithic

The Mesolithic, a broad archaeological tradition, is defined on chronological, economic, and technological criteria. It is also described as a transitional phase between the 'hunting-gathering' and 'food production' patterns of subsistence (Thomas and Joglekar 1994;

Thomas et al. 1996), a generalized statement stemming from the 'linear' evolutionary model. 'Transition' is a vaguely-defined term, often used in archaeology to simplify a rather complex process. Yet, as we shall see below, the available archaeo-faunal evidence at Mesolithic sites has little osteomorphological change or other evidence to suggest local genetic domestication of cattle, sheep, goat or pig. In fact, biological concepts alone are inadequate to explain the origins of animal husbandry and a broader theoretical framework, incorporating ideas from social sciences, is needed for the purpose (Chattopadhyaya 1999b, 1999c).

Mesolithic sites in India have a wide spatial range and fairly long temporal span. These have been discovered in most parts of the Indian subcontinent[2] and the tradition flourished from the Early to the Late Holocene, cross-cutting in certain cases Bronze Age or Chalcolithic traditions. However, faunal remains were recovered only from certain sites of Gujarat, Rajasthan, Madhya Pradesh and the central Ganga plains and Vindhya regions of southern Uttar Pradesh.

A. *Western and West-Central India*

The relevant Mesolithic sites are Langhnaj, Kanewal (Gujarat), Bagor, Tilwara (Rajasthan), and Adamgarh and Bhimbetka (western M.P.). Recently two more such sites, Ratanpura and Loteshwar, have been reported in north Gujarat (Bhan 1994). It may be noted that these sites lie in different ecological niches and temporal contexts. The faunal assemblages from the first six sites were studied by zoologists during the 1960s and 1970s. The aims and methods were limited largely to taxonomical identification. The present author's observations here will necessarily be brief, reflecting on the taxonomical composition and the possible roles played by the identified animals in the economy, on the one hand, and broad palaeoenvironmental conditions, on the other. In the following discussions the common names of animals will be used which will be supplemented by the zoological names only when necessary. Table 1 provides the common names and zoological nomenclature of mammals under consideration.

The animal species identified at these six sites are generally of wild category, though domestic cattle, sheep, goats and pigs are also reported except at Langhnaj (see Table 2).

GUJARAT

The animal taxa identified at Langhnaj by Clutton-Brock (1965) include a canid (most probably wolf: (*Canis* cf. *lupus* Sykes 1831), mongoose (*Herpestes edwardsi* cf. *ferrugineus* Blanford, 1874), rhinoceros, wild boar (*Sus scrofa cristatus*), chital, hog deer, swamp deer, nilgai, blackbuck, and an undetermined bovine species. Misra (1973) suggests the presence of Indian wild buffalo on the testimony of Zeuner without, however, mentioning the elements in this identification. Therefore, it is not clear whether this identification is based on the same element(s) as that of the undetermined *bovini* of the assemblage studied by Clutton-Brock or others. Thomas and Joglekar prefer to identify

TABLE 1. LIST OF SOME ANIMAL TAXA DISCUSSED IN THE TEXT

Genus	Species/Race(s)	Common Name(s)
Bos	*namadicus* Falconer	Wild cattle (extinct since Midddle Holocene)
	indicus Linnaeus	Indian humped cattle or Zebu
Bos (bibos)	*gaurus* Smith	Indian bison or Gaur
Bubalus	*arnee*	Wild water buffalo
	bubalus Linnaeus	Domestic water buffalo
Ovis	*Orientalis* Gmelin	Wild sheep: The Shapu or Urial
	aries Linnaeus	Domestic sheep
Capra	*ibex* Linnaeus	Ibex
	falconeri Wagner	Markhor
	aegagrus Gmelin	Wild goat
	hircus Linnaeus	Domestic goat
Hemitragus	*jemlahicus* Smith	Himalayn Tahr
Capricornis	*sumatraensis* Bechstein	Serow
Nemorhaedus	*goral* Hardwicke	Goral
Gazella	*gazella* Pallas	Indian gazelle or Chinkara
	bennetti Sykes	-do- (another race)
Antilope	*Cervicapra* Linnaeus	Blackbuck
Boselaphus	*tragocamelus* Pallas	Blue bull or Nilgai
Tetracerus	*quadricornis* Blainville	Fourhorned deer or Chowsingha
Axis	*axis* Erxleben	Spotted deer or Chital
	porcinus Zimmermann	Hog deer or Para
Cervus	*elephus hanglu* Wagner	Kashmir stag or Hangul
	duvauceli duvauceli Cuvier	Swamp deer or Barasingha
	duvauceli branderi Pocock	-do- (the central Indian race)
	unicolor Kerr	Sambar
Muntiacus	*muntjak* Zimmermann	The barking deer or Muntjac
Moschus	*moschiferus* Linnaeus	Musk deer
Tragulus	*meminna Erxleben*	Indian chevrotain or Mouse-deer
Camelus	*dromedarius* Linnaeus	One-humped camel
Sus	*scrofa* Linnaeus	Indian wild boar
	domesticus	Pig
	silvanius Hodgson	Pygmy hog
Equus	*hemious Pallas*	The Asiatic wild ass
	asinus Linnaeus	Donkey
	caballus Linnaeus	Horse
Elephas	maximus Linnaeus	Indian elephant
Hystrix	*indica* Kerr	Indian porcupine
Lepus	*nigricollis* Cuvier	Indian hare
Rattus	*rattus* Linnaeus	Common house rat
Bandicota	*indica* Bechstein	Bandicoot rat
	bengalensis Grey & Hardwicke	Mole rat
Suncus	*stoliczkanuus*	Yellow-throated shrew
Presbytis	*entellus* Dufresne	Common langur or Hanuman monkey
Panthera	*tigris* Linnaeus	Tiger
Felis	chaus Güldenstaedt	Jungle cat
	libyca Forster	Desert cat
	catus	Domestic cat
Hyaena	*hyaena* Linnaeus	Striped hyaena
Canis	*lupus* Linnaeus	Wolf
	aureus Linnaeus	Jackal
	familiaris Linnaeus	Domestic dog

(contd.)

Genus	Species/Race(s)	Common Name(s)
Cuon	*alpinus* Pallas	Indian wild dog or Dhol
Vulpes	*bengalensis* Shaw	Indian fox
Melursus	ursinus Shaw	Sloth bear
Herpestes	edwardsi Geoffroy	Common mongoose
	auropunctatus Hodgson	Small Indian mongoose

TABLE 2. MAMMALIAN TAXA IDENTIFIED FROM MESOLITHIC SITES

TAXON	BGR			TLW		LNG		KNW	ADG	BMB	CPM		SNR		DDM		MHD	
	1	2	3	4	5	6	7	8	9	10	11	12	13	14	15	16	17	18
Bos indicus	-	+	+	+	+	-	-	+	+	+	-	-	?+	-	-	-	-	-
Bubakus sp.	-	-	+	-	-	-	+	+	+	-	-	-	-	+	-	+	-	+
Capra hircus	-	+	+	+	-	-	-	+	+	-	-	-	?+	-	-	$	-	-
Ovis aries/vignei	-	+	+	-	-	-	-	+	+	-	-	-	+	?-	-	-	-	-
Sus domesticus	-	-	+	-	-	-	-	-	+	-	-	-	-	-	-	-	-	-
Canis familiaris	-	-	-	-	-	-	-	-	+	-	-	-	-	-	-	-	-	-
Canis fam./aureus	-	-	-	+	-	-	-	-	-	-	-	-	-	-	-	-	-	-
Camelus sp.	-	-	-	-	-	-	-	+	-	-	-	-	-	-	-	-	-	-
Bos sp.	-	+	-	-	-	-	-	-	-	-	+	+	+	+	+	+	+	+
Bovini	+	-	-	-	-	+	-	-	-	-	-	-	-	-	-	-	-	-
Bos (bibos)gaurus	-	-	-	-	-	-	-	-	-	-	-	-	+	+	+	+	+	+
Capra sp.	-	-	-	-	-	-	-	-	-	-	-	-	-	-	-	+	-	-
Capra/Ovis	-	-	-	-	+	-	-	-	-	-	+	-	?+	-	-	-	+	-
Boselaphus tragocamelus	-	-	-	-	-	+	-	+	-	-	-	-	-	-	-	+	-	-
Tetracerus quadricornis	-	-	-	-	-	-	-	-	-	-	-	-	-	-	-	+	-	-
Antilope cervicapra	-	-	+	-	-	+	-	-	-	-	-	-	-	-	+	+	+	+
Gazella gazella/bennetti	-	-	+	-	-	-	-	-	-	-	-	-	-	-	-	+	-	-
Axis axis	-	-	+	+	-	+	-	+	+	-	-	-	?+	-	+	+	-	+
Axis porcinus	+	-	-	+	-	+	+	-	-	+	-	-	-	+	+	+	-	+
Axis/Cervus	-	-	-	-	-	-	-	-	-	-	-	+	-	-	-	-	+	-
Cercus duvauceli	+	-	-	-	-	+	-	+	+	-	-	-	+	+	+	+#	-	+
Cervus unicolor	-	-	+	-	-	-	-	-	+	+	-	-	-	-	-	+	-	+
Muntiacus muntjak	-	-	-	-	-	-	-	-	-	-	-	-	-	-	+	+	-	+
Moschus moschiferus	-	-	-	-	-	-	-	-	-	-	-	-	-	-	-	+	-	-
Tragulus meminna	-	-	-	-	-	-	-	-	-	-	-	-	-	-	-	+	-	-
Equus sp.	-	-	-	-	-	-	-	-	+	-	-	-	-	-	+	-	+	+
Rhinoceros sp.	-	-	-	-	-	+	-	+	-	+	-	-	-	+	+	+	-	+
Sus scrofa	+	-	+	+	-	+	-	+	-	-	-	-	-	-	+	+	+	+
Sus salvanius	-	-	-	-	-	-	-	-	-	-	-	-	-	-	-	+	-	-
Hippopotamus sp.	-	-	-	-	-	-	-	-	-	-	-	-	-	-	-	+	-	-
Elephas maximus	-	-	-	-	-	-	-	-	-	-	-	-	+	-	-	+	-	-
Canis lupuss	-	-	-	-	-	?+	-	-	-	-	-	-	-	-	?+	+	-	?+
Canis aureus	+	-	-	-	-	-	-	-	-	-	-	-	-	-	-	+	-	-
Vulpes bengalensis	-	-	+	-	-	-	-	-	-	-	-	-	-	-	+#	+#	-	+#
Melursus ursinus	-	-	-	-	-	-	-	-	-	-	-	-	-	-	-	+	-	-

(contd.)

TAXON	BGR			TLW		LNG		KNW	ADG	BMB	CPM		SNR		DDM		MHD	
	1	2	3	4	5	6	7	8	9	10	11	12	13	14	15	16	17	18
Felis sp	-	-	-	-	-	-	-	-	-	-	-	-	-	-	-	-	-	+
Hystrix indica/cristata	-	-	+	-	-	-	-	-	+	-	-	-	-	-	-	+	-	-
Rattus rattus	+	-	+	-	-	-	-	-	-	-	-	-	-	-	-	+	-	-
Bandicota sp.	-	-	-	-	-	-	-	-	-	-	-	-	-	-	+	+	-	+
Lepus nigricollis	-	-	+	-	-	-	-	-	+	-	-	-	-	-	+	-	-	-
Herpestes sp.	-	-	+	+	-	+	-	-	-	-	-	-	-	-	-	-	-	-

NOTES: + Present- Absent ? Doubtful $ Stratigraphy uncertain/Later intrusion # Species uncertain

BGR=Bagor (1. Shah 1971, 2. Alur in Misra 1973, 3.Thomas 1975); TLW=Tilwara (4. Shah in Misra 1971, 5.Thomas 1975); LNG=Langhnaj (6. Clutton-Brock 1965; 7. Zeuner in Misra 1973); KNW=Kanewal (8. Shah 1980); BMB=Bhimbetka; 9. ADG=Adamgadh Nath 1967 (10. Misra 1989); CPM=Chopani-Mando (11. Alur 1980, 12. Chattopadhyaya 1991); SNR=Sarai-Nahar Rai (13. Alur 1980, 14. Chattopadhyaya 1991); DDM=Damdama (15. Chattopadhyaya 1991, 16.Thomas et al. 1995, 1996); MHD=Mahadaha (17. Alur 1980, 18. Chattopadhyaya 1991).

Clutton-Brock's bovini as wild cattle (Thomas and Joglekar 1994). Misra (1973) suggests arid climatic conditions for Langhnaj during the Mesolithic habitation, i.e. around 3875±105 BP.[3] (calibrated to 2550-2185 BC). If the climate was indeed arid, the narrow stretch of the Luni River Valley would have been like a linear oasis and, therefore, unlikely to have supported the population of rhinoceros, as Misra would argue, again on the testimony of Zeuner. The rhinoceros prefers wide stretches of marshland and grassland (Prater 1971). The fact that the occurrence of rhinoceros at Langhnaj is not an isolated or regionally restricted phenomenon, is supported by the identification of its remains from a number of contemporaneous Harappan sites like Lothal, Surkotada, Kuntasi, Khanpur, Shikarpur, and also possibly Oriyo Timbo, covering the whole of Gujarat and Saurashtra (see Section 4.3 and Table 4B). But if one accepts Zeuner's identification, then the presence of the Indian wild buffalo, along with the rhinoceros, at Langhnaj would certainly imply wetter conditions and hence greater carrying capacity during the period under consideration than suggested (see Nath 1968a: 6, for a similar view). The available faunal evidence would indicate a mosaic topography of savanna and forest cover with interspersed wetlands in northern Gujarat during the Mesolithic occupation of Langhnaj.

The non-reporting of smaller fauna, such as fish and turtle, at Langhnaj is disturbing and shows bias in either the method of, or attitude towards, recovery. It is unthinkable that the aquatic resources of the nearby Luni River were not utilized by the Mesolithic occupants of the site.

The excavations at the Mesolithic site of Kanewal, situated north-east of Langhnaj, too have produced faunal materials in appreciable numbers (Shah 1980). As at Langhnaj, the presence of rhinoceros and buffalo has been reported. Other wild species include spotted deer, swamp deer, nilgai and wild boar. The assemblage also includes domestic animals like cattle, sheep and goats. The occurrence of camel bones is interesting and is indicative of cultural contacts with camel using peoples.

RAJASTHAN

The site of Bagor lies on a prominent dune on the left bank of the river Kothari, 25 km west of Bhilwara in eastern Rajasthan. The faunal remains from the Mesolithic phase at the site (Period I), datable between the fifth and fourth millennium BC, have been studied by Shah (1971), Alur (quoted in Misra 1973) and Thomas (1975). Thomas presented quantified data showing the relative proportions of twelve species using the NISP[4] quantification method (*N*=1774), that however excludes carpals, vertebrae and ribs (Thomas 1975). The presence of domestic animals like cattle (15.7 per cent) and sheep/goats (64.4 per cent) has been claimed by Thomas (1975), Shah is silent on the presence of such animals. Again, in the latter group, the identification of sheep alone has been confirmed by Thomas (1975). Stock-rearing is said to be the main basis of the economy at Bagor. The swine bones (3.7 per cent) belong to both wild boar as well as pigs, and the probability of small-scale pig herding has been suggested by Thomas. The buffalo is represented by 14 cranial (including a horn core fragment) and post-cranial bones (together 0.8 per cent) and is said to have been hunted for food. Other wild animals include the blackbuck and gazelle (together constituting 4.4 per cent), spotted deer (4.8 per cent), sambar (4.3 per cent), hare (0.6 per cent), Indian grey mongoose (0.8 per cent) and Indian fox (0.5 per cent). The unquantified species include porcupine, rat, tortoise, fish and frog (Thomas 1975). The bones of rats are completely intact and said to have been intrusive into the mound at a post-occupational date. About 70 per cent of the faunal elements are charred. Bagor is the only Mesolithic site of this region where bone quantification has been carried out, but to make this effort more meaningful, detailed taphonomic analysis was necessary

In addition to the above taxa, the river turtle (*Lissemys punctata* Bonnaterre) and the monitor lizard (*Varanus flavescence* Gray) were identified (Shah 1971).

At Tilwara (Barmer district), a small bone assemblage of the Mesolithic phase has been recovered. The chronology of the site is insecure in the absence of radiocarbon dates; but the excavator has described Phase I as Late Mesolithic (Misra 1971). On the basis of an unpublished report of Shah, Misra (1971: 73) lists the presence of humped cattle (domesticated), goat (*Capra hircus aegagrus* Erxl.), a canid (jackal or dog), pig (*Sus scrofa cristatus* Wagner), spotted deer, hog deer and mongoose (*Herpestes auropunctatus* Hodgson). The assemblage is dominated by cattle bones and 'the economy appears to have been a combination of hunting and stock-raising' (Misra 1971: 73). Thomas too is understood to have studied the Tilwara faunal assemblage but reports the presence of only cattle and *Ovis/Capra* (1975).

MADHYA PRADESH

The Adamgarh rock-shelter, in Hoshangabad district, is another important site at which domestic animals such as cattle, sheep, goats, pigs and dogs have been reported along with wild mammals like spotted deer, barasingha, sambar, porcupine, hare and an unknown species of the genus *Equus* (Nath 1967). Besides, the lizard (*Varanus grisius* Daud) has been identified on the basis of an incomplete lumbar vertebra. There are two conflicting radiocarbon dates. One, in the sixth millennium BC (7,240±125 BP), was dated on a shell sample collected at a depth only of 0.15 - 0.20 m, whereas the much younger date in the first millennium BC (2,765±105 BP) came from an uncharred bone recovered from a much lower level, 1.90 m below the surface. Therefore, the dates are inconsistent with stratigraphy. The authenticity of the sixth millennium BC date is doubtful because it is possible that the sample involved in this dating might have entered the site not as a living organism, but in its long dead form. Finally, such as faunal composition is uncharacteristic of the early Mesolithic tradition. Therefore, the alleged Adamgarh evidence for the origins of animal husbandry during the 'early' Mesolithic phase does not stand on sound footing.

In the limited faunal assemblage recovered from the Mesolithic level at Bhimbetka, Raisen district, the following animal species have been identified: domestic cattle, barasingha, hog deer, and rhinoceros (Misra 1989). The Mesolithic at this site has been radiometrically dated to the fifth millennium BC. The importance of Bhimbetka lies in the fact that a large number prehistoric paintings have been discovered in numerous rock shelters of this region (Neumayer 1983). Some of the early paintings have been placed in the Mesolithic period. Here one finds the depiction of humped Indian cattle (zebu) along with its humpless, wild progenitor, *Bos namadicus*. Local domestication of cattle in western M.P. may perhaps be inferred (Chattopadhyaya 1991). This finds some support from the claim regarding the presence of domestic cattle in the Mesolithic faunal assemblage (Misra 1989). However, this suggestion needs more convincing archaeological support. First, the anatomical elements need fresh examination and second, one has to study intra-site assemblage variability to confirm the possibility of evolution of this species from its wild progenitor (see Section 5B).

B. The Ganga Valley and the Eastern Vindhyas

The faunal assemblages recovered from excavations at the Mesolithic sites in this region, with radiocarbon dates touching the Early Holocene, were studied in three stages. The first of this series of studies was carried out by K.R. Alur (1980), who covered, besides others, the sites of the Ganga Valley: Sarai-Nahar Rai and Mahadaha (first of the two seasons' excavated materials) and the adjacent Vindhyan plateau: Chopani-Mando. This was followed by the present author's work on the same materials as well as on the second season's (1978-9) excavated faunal assemblage from Mahadaha and first two seasons' (1983-5) materials from Damdama, as part of his doctoral study at Cambridge (Chattopadhyaya 1991, 1996). In the final phase, Thomas and Joglekar completed the study of the entire assemblage (Thomas et al. 1995, 1996) from Damdama. The taxonomical identifications carried out in these studies are compared in Table 2.

In their review of the Holocene fauna, Thomas and Joglekar (1994: 182) discredited and dismissed Alur's work on Sarai-Nahar Rai and Mahadaha assemblages on the alleged ground that he 'had identified bones of domestic animals', a fact not well supported by their own findings at Damdama. It is strange to note that whenever one reports the presence of sheep or goats at archaeological sites, people infer they are the domesticated species. An instance of this tendency can be seen in Agrawal's misinterpretation of Alur's identification of sheep-goat at Sarai-Nahar Rai to prove a lower antiquity for the site (Agrawal 1982). Alur did identify both cattle and sheep/goat at these sites, but was totally unambiguous about their wild affinity in the discussions on individual taxa. It may, however, be mentioned that Thomas and Joglekar (1994) have confirmed the presence of an unknown species of goat—*Capra* sp. from Damdama. If this is a wild goat one has to explain its arrival at Damdama, radiometrically dated to the early seventh millennium BC from its natural habitat in western Himalayan ranges without the human protection.

The study of the assemblages from the above sites by this author, however, presents a picture of faunal composition somewhat different from that reported by Alur and later workers. Some general observations of the present author can be briefly summarized as follows:

(i) The presence of sheep/goats, wild or domesticated, could not be confirmed in the three assemblages studied by this author. Again, an earlier identification of a sheep/goat 'horn core' from the Vindhyan site of Chopani-Mando has been revised to be that of an antler of *Axis* sp. Large bovids identified from the three Ganga Valley sites are: *Bos* cf. *namadicus*, wild buffalo (*Bubalus* cf. *arnee*) and gaur (*Bos bibos gaurus*) (Chattopadhyaya 1991, 1999b). Perhaps, 'horse' (*Equidae*) identified by Alur on the basis of a lone incisor from Mahadaha was meant to be a general term to indicate a species of the genus *Equus* and not any specific one. This along with a few other elements of this genus belonged to either *Equus namadicus/hemionus* or *Equus asinus*, but certainly not *Equus caballus*. But this raises a serious problem: the former three species prefer arid climatic conditions and the remains of *Equus namadicus* and *Equus hemionus* have been recovered from the Terminal Pleistocene deposits of the rivers Belan and Son, witnessing dry conditions (Chattopadhyaya 1991; Blumenschine and Chattopadhyaya 1983). So in all probability this non-caballine species of *Equus* was not a local inhabitant of the wet, low plains of the Ganga Valley (Gupta 1976). If it was of Vindhyan origin, how its skeletal elements were recovered from the Ganga Valley is a problem that requires investigation. It may be noted, however, that all the animal species identified by the present author at these sites are wild, as was the original view of Alur. The purpose behind making some of the above observations is to eradicate certain unnecessary confusions in the minds of archaeologists and *not* to discredit Alur's contribution; in fact, he worked under severe constraints which not many of his critics understand.

(ii) To assess the overall economy or relative dependence on various resources, niche-width analysis is often quite useful. Niche-width (W) is essentially an index of 'evenness' of resource use and is mathematically expressed as:

$$W = (\Sigma p_i^{2})^{-1}$$

where p_i is the proportion of resource i in the diet. The lower the value of W, the more likely it is that people practised a specialized economy, depending on fewer resources even when a large number of species were used at the site. The variation of resource diversity with niche-width at all the three Mesolithic sites suggests a broad-spectrum, rather than specialized economy, characteristic of a hunting, or rather non-agricultural, way of life (Chattopadhyaya 1991, 1996). However, a greater dependence on a few species of deer like swamp deer and hog deer, on the one hand, and aquatic resources like tortoise and fish, on the other, has been suggested for Mahadaha as well as Damdama (Chattopadhyaya and Chattopadhyaya 1990). This was inferred from (a) the combination of three methods of quantification: NISP (Number of Identified Specimens), MNI (Minimum Number of Individuals) and Caloric Contributions by MNI of individual taxa, as no single method is in itself reliable, and (b) taphonomic considerations. It is pertinent to mention here that two races of swamp deer are found in India: (a) *Cervus duvauceli duvauceli* (Cuvier) distributed in the terai of U.P., Assam and the Sunderbans and (b) *Cervus duvauceli branderi* (Pocock) inhabiting the 'hard' open grounds of Madhya Pradesh and peninsular India (Prater 1971). The former is distinguished by its splayed hooves and larger skull and body. The Mesolithic Ganga Valley taxon has been identified by this author as belonging to the 'swamp-dwelling' race of *Cervus duvauceli duvauceli* Cuvier, which is consistent with the environment of the Mesolithic sites with its large number of lakes, as well as palaeoenvironmental conditions of Pratapgarh district during Early-/Mid-Holocene times, as inferred from the combined palynological and satellite remote sensing evidence (Chattopadhyaya 1995). It has also been suggested by me that the ecological features of the present-day *terai* region, which includes tall grasses of the genus *Saccharum*, was more extensive and covered parts of central plains of the Ganga Valley during Early-/Mid-Holocene times (Chattopadhyaya 1988; cf. Mishra 1982; Wemmer 1987). Therefore, hog deer populations, preferring such ecological surroundings (Prater 1971; Roberts 1977) were not distant from the archaeological sites under consideration. The presence of these two species in greater proportions at these archaeological sites is, therefore, not surprising. In fact, the reason behind the exploitation of hog deer was its special type of antlers (see below). Finally, this animal was more hefty and larger during earlier times in this region than its present-day populations and, therefore, its archaeological remains from the Ganga Valley Mesolithic sites are likely to be confused with spotted deer, a species of the same genus (Chattopadhyaya 1999b).

(iii) The Mesolithic settlement pattern in the Ganga Valley involved 'logistic mobility' as opposed to residential mobility and the excavated Mesolithic sites were special purpose sites.

Rather than carrying out mere taxonomical identifications, the main objective in my study, with the valuable assistance of Indrani Chattopadhyaya, was to understand and situate in global context the subsistence-settlement patterns of the Mesolithic peoples of the Ganga Valley using faunal data (Chattopadhyaya 1988, 1991; I. Chattopadhyaya 1990; Chattopadhyaya and Chattopadhyaya 1990). However, the taphonomic analyses raised some new problems for investigation, and, as a result, presented a fresh set of evidence on hunter-gatherer patterns of behaviour (Chattopadhyaya 1991, 1996). A brief account of this study is summarized below.

The initial purpose was to evaluate a global predictive model of hunter-gatherer subsistence-settlement pattern, in relation to environmental parameters, as put forward by Lewis Binford (1980, 1983b) on the basis of cross-cultural generalization. According to the predictions of the model, hunter-gatherer mobility strategy and associated subsistence would vary directly with the effective temperature and hence the latitude. This meant that hunter-gatherers in warm tropical/sub-tropical regions, including north-central India, would tend to be nomadic rather than sedentary. G.R. Sharma's view that the Mesolithic sites of the Ganga Valley were temporary camp sites seasonally occupied by peoples of Vindhyan origin during the summer months (Sharma 1975), was in conformity with Binford's model. It was thought necessary to probe the matter with the help of faunal analysis, the potential of which had not yet been tapped in India.

The faunal assemblages from Mahadaha contained a sufficiently large number of ageable cheek teeth of both hog deer and swamp deer. The cheek tooth wear-sequence pattern was computed following the study by Koike and Ohtaishi (1985). Again, crown height measurements were taken on slightly worn lower molars of these two species to age specimens (Chattopadhyaya 1985a) and compute the mortality profiles, and also determine the seasons in which these animals were killed. This was possible because (1) the seasons of birth in these two species are fairly fixed and known (Mishra 1982; Schaller 1967; Wemmer 1987) and (2) the ages when unworn molars erupt to their full height are known (Chattopadhyaya 1991). The periods of hog deer and swamp deer killing at Mahadaha, derived from this absolute age calculations, are distributed in all the principal seasons: spring, summer, autumn and winter. If the results have interpretative significance and if the ages, and hence the seasons represented by individual teeth and mandibles, are a reflection of the actual seasons when these animals were killed, then it is interesting to note that killing of hog deer in summer months was slightly more frequent in comparison with other seasons. This is also the time when hog deer prefer riverine grassplains (Mishra 1982), and might have been close to the sites. Likewise, the exploitation of swamp deer has been a year-round pattern, but the proportion killed was highest between July and September.

An alternative simpler method of determining the seasonality problem consists of identifying fully erupted but unworn molars of certain animals, for which the ages at which wear commences are known. The Mahadaha assemblage contains several unworn, fully erupted lower molars of these species and the mere presence of such molars of hog deer indicates August (M1), April (M2) and December (M3) as the periods of occupation at Mahadaha (see Chattopadhyaya 1991, 1996 for details). Likewise, July and January as the months of occupation are indicated by the presence of such molars of swamp deer. This faunal evidence, in conjunction with astro-archaeological evidence derived from human grave orientations in relation to annual solar paths across horizons, are sufficient to disprove Sharma's hypothesis of the temporary nature of Mesolithic settlements in the Ganga Valley (Chattopadhyaya and Chattopadhyaya 1990). However, it was suggested on the basis of combined archaeological (including faunal) and ethnographic evidence that rather than being a sedentary settlement of the type one normally associates with agricultural societies, settlement in the Ganga Valley showed 'logistic mobility', on residential stability at home-based camps with fluctuating annual populations; task specific groups making periodic journeys out in connection with the food quest or for other reasons.

This evidence from the Mesolithic Ganga Valley of residential stability under warm tropical conditions certainly shows deviation from the predictions of the global model, based on the controversial principle of 'techno-environmental determinism', and allows a reconsideration of the complex nature of human adaptations in post-Pleistocene times. Some explanation is necessary for this unusual pattern within the overall hunting-gathering mode of subsistence. One factor favouring residential stability in the Ganga Valley may relate to the aquatic resource potential of the region. But such explanations, often called the 'pull argument' or 'Garden of Eden' proposition, are not beyond controversy (Binford 1983a). It has been argued, instead, that the Ganga Valley presented a very special case where the cultural continuity of societies depended upon the influx of stone raw materials (a limiting resource) from the Vindhyas, and that residential stability among the Mesolithic Ganga Valley populations was part of an adaptive process (under threatened conditions of reproduction), directed towards securing control over economic/industrial productivity that would, in turn, either facilitate large-scale acquisition of exotic stones or minimize such a dependence. The second possibility is indicated by the taphonomic evidence, a discussion of which is now in order.

Taphonomy relates to 'the study of the transition (in all its details) of animal remains from the biosphere into the lithospheres' (Efremov 1940: 85) and thus explores post-mortem relations between organic remains and their external environment (Noe-Nygaard 1977). Initially a sub-discipline of palaeontology, it has been found to be a useful tool for the archaeological interpretation of the differential preservation of organic remains. The first step in taphonomical study consists of observations on the physical condition of bones, such as relative hardness, colour and the fragmentation patterns. The next step is to identify traces of carnivore activities on bone—gnawing marks in particular (Binford 1981). This is followed by the application of analytical techniques to evaluate the recovery quality, i.e. sample bias due to the techniques of recovery (Payne 1972; Maltby 1985) and the differential survival of bones—Brain's method (1976, 1981), for example. Without going into details of analyses carried out on the above lines (see Chattopadhyaya 1991), the main results are:

(a) Most of the bones from Sarai-Nahar Rai, Mahadaha and Damdama are hard and heavily charred. The overall preservation conditions at the sites appear to be fairly good. Despite the presence of carnivore remains at these sites, traces of gnawing and pitting on the bones are rare. The high degree of long bone fragmentation may not be entirely due to natural forces such as exposure to unfavourable climatic conditions, or carnivore activities, or eating habits. The differential representation of the anatomical elements resulted, rather, to a large extent from bone modification by human agency: some 'special activities'.

(b) Despite conventional methods of recovery (dry sieving), the level of sample bias during bone retrieval was minimum for the Mahadaha and Damdama assemblages. Even small spikes and rodent bones were carefully collected. But the same is not true of the Sarai-Nahar Rai assemblage in which a clear bias is evident towards the collection of larger bones. The application of Maltby's method (1985) of comparing closely occurring elements of dissimilar size, such as first and second phalanges, of hog deer and swamp deer from Mahadaha and Damdama implies that (a) the faunal assemblages from these sites are generally speaking representative and fairly reliable indications of the relative abundance of animal taxa, particularly ungulates, at these sites, and (b) carcasses of deer were subject to regular skinning for extracting hides (see also Binford 1981).

(c) Brain's method of taphonomical analysis consists of plotting the percentage survival of different skeletal elements from the expected values, calculated on the basis of the Minimum Number of Individuals for a species (Brain 1976, 1981). The assemblage having undergone the natural process of decay and loss (including carnivore activities) has a distinctive pattern of variation in ascendance from caudal vertebrae (minimum representation) to mandibles (maximum representation). Any deviation from this ascendancy curve of differential survivorship in an archaeological pattern needs to be interpreted by incorporating factors other than natural agencies. This method was used for large bovids, swamp deer and hog deer from Mahadaha and Damdama. The conclusion was that the role of human activities in creating the archaeological assemblage was far greater than that of natural factors. The overall pattern at Mahadaha also suggests that most of the butchery of swamp deer and hog deer carcasses was done at or close to the site. Again the underrepresentation of mandibles in these species of deer has been explained in terms of the possible practice of trampling or skull fragmentation for the purpose of dismantling antlers. A separate faunal technique of calculating Tooth-Bone Index (TBi) (for details see Levine 1986) was also used on the Mahadaha assemblage, which led to a similar conclusion. It may be mentioned that the short and compact brow tines of hog deer antlers were particularly favoured as a material for tools at all the three excavated sites.

(d) The study of animal skeletal element frequencies using the Percentage Minimum Anatomical Units (per cent MAU) method (Binford 1978, 1984) has been used by this author on swamp deer and hog deer assemblages from Mahadaha and Damdama to see if any light could be shed on site function and the logistical use of the landscape (Chattopadhyaya 1991, 1996: 471-3). Detailed analysis of the data shows a remarkable similarity of the per centMAU variations between Mahadaha and Damdama, and that the patterns from these sites do not match those noted for the three ideal site categories, hunting camps, kill-butchery sites and base camps, associated with logistically mobile hunter-gatherers. Ideally one would expect a similarity in the patterns between these archaeological sites and the ethnographic base camps. This negative finding, nonetheless, gives an important clue to what might have happened at these archaeological sites. Mahadaha and Damdama, where numerous activities were carried out, including human burial and what has been described as 'ritual' hearths containing charred animal bones (Sharma et al. 1980), might have been more complex in nature than the ethnographical examples described by Binford. It is just possible that the taphonomic model used hitherto is oversimplified. To explain the above disparity we have to reconsider the taphonomic factors other than the natural ones, i.e. large-scale bone modification by 'human' agencies. Perhaps the so called ritual hearths were not associated with 'rituals' in the usual sense of the word. They could have constituted centres of large-scale bone modification for an industrial purpose (see below).

(e) The large-scale burning of animal bones at Damdama has been interpreted as something to do with periodic site clearance process (Thomas et al. 1996). But the taphonomic studies by the present author provide a different explanation. It has been argued elsewhere, following Cornwall's description of archaeological bone chemistry (1956), that controlled firing of these bones contributed to their excellent preservation at these sites. A comparison of the colours of archaeological bones from these Mesolithic sites (matched with the Munsell Colour Chart) with the experimental burning of fresh bones at different temperatures (Gilchrist and Mytum 1986) shows that a large majority of the archaeological bones were fired between 300 and 400 ^{0}C (I. Chattopadhyaya 1999). The heating of bones to such a high temperature range would have been counterproductive if the sole purpose behind this practice was cooking. The large-scale firing of bones seems to have been a regular feature at these sites and involved a special purpose. A number of medium- to large-sized pit hearths containing burnt and longitudinally split long bones of large ungulates, as well as bone and antler tools have been recovered from these three excavated sites. At Mahadaha a bone/antler 'dump' (earlier described as the 'butchery area') has been located. Both tools (scrapers, points, awls and daggers, sledge-hammer) and objects (drinking vessel, ornaments) fashioned on long bones and antlers in various stages of manufacture have been recovered (see Sharma et al. 1980: Pls. MDH.XXIV, XXVa-b; Alur 1980). It may be mentioned here that controlled heating of these organic raw materials not only facilitates smooth flaking in comparison with raw bones, but also provides hardness and durability to such artefacts (Cornwall 1956; cf. Narain 1972). The most plausible explanation for this combined taphonomic and archaeological evidence is that the Mesolithic populations of the Ganga Valley engaged in the regular manufacture of bone and antler artefacts and that Sarai-Nahar Rai, Mahadaha and Damdama were essentially the bone-antler 'factory sites'. This was perhaps necessitated by the local absence of stones, this alternative technology certainly supplemented the conventional stone tools. This argument in favour of an alternative industrial activity provides an additional explanation for residential stability at some sites.

The study of the entire faunal assemblage from Damdama by Thomas and Joglekar is a commendable effort and, despite certain divergence in taxonomical identification, supports some of the above conclusions (Thomas et al. 1995, 1996). They have succeeded in identifying more than thirty species of animals, comprising mammals (NISP-77.4 per cent), reptiles, birds, fish and molluscs. Among the mammal remains, deer bones, belonging to six different species, predominate (71 per cent). Initially, swamp deer was not identified, though subsequently the possibility of its presence was suggested on metrical evidence. In course of the long existence of Damdama, the '. . . faunal exploitation pattern indicated a cyclical trend in resource management where changes in mammalian resources were mainly compensated by parallel changes in avian and, to some extent, aquatic fauna' (Thomas et al. 1996: 255). This brilliant conclusion came after a detailed analysis of the proportional distribution patterns of faunal remains at different strata of the site. However, the usefulness of this theory could be enhanced, provided a stratum-wise taphonomic analysis, on standard lines was carried out.

As far as the Mesolithic sites of the eastern Vindhyas are concerned, the faunal evidence is meagre. The identification of only two taxa from the advanced Mesolithic phase at Chopani-Mando in the Belan Valley has been mentioned earlier. Again, *cervidae* has been identified from Lekhahia rock-shelter in the Kaimur Range (Mirzapur District of U.P.) and cattle, on the basis of a lone lower third molar, from Baghor II in the middle Son Valley, dated to the seventh millennium BC. The only other species that was associated with Baghor II was sambar, though the evidence is non-osteological: the hoof marks that were identified in the context of a short stratigraphic break when the site was temporarily abandoned.

4.2 The Neolithic

The Neolithic of India has been divided into six regional traditions: (i) Northern, covering the Kashmir Valley, (ii) Belan Valley, (iii) Northern Bihar or Mid-eastern, (iv) North-eastern, covering Assam and the Subhimalayan regions, (v) Central-eastern, covering Chhotanagpur plateau with its peneplains extending to Orissa and West Bengal, and (vi) Southern (Thapar 1987). From the point of view of faunal remains, only the first three and the last groups are discussed below, along with another significant area outside the present-day boundary of India: Mehrgarh in the tip of the Kachi plain in Baluchistan. Of these, the Mehrgarh tradition is the earliest and most important from the point of view of the origins of animal domestication. The cultural deposit at this site shows continuity from the seventh through to the third millennium BC, and presents the best evidence on the intra-site changing pattern of human-cattle relationships (Jarrige and Meadow 1980; Meadow 1981, 1984a, 1984b, 1986, 1989a). Though a separate and original account of the archaeo-zoological researches in the greater Indus Valley by Richard Meadow and Ajita Patel is available in Vol. 2 of this series, it was thought appropriate to incorporate his contributions, even at the risk of repetition, towards presenting a connected account of the development of this branch of study in South Asia.

The Mehrgarh tradition

Mehrgarh is the only site in the whole of South Asia where the beginnings of animal husbandry and its subsequent development can be identified with confidence. The site is situated at the foot of the Bolan pass, and thus lies on major communications route between the Baluchistan-Afghanistan highlands and the lower Indus Valley. Being useful towards shedding light on the development of agriculture in the Greater Indus Valley, the site is also crucial to our understanding of the rise of the Harappan Civilization (Allchin and Allchin 1982).

Of a total of seven cultural periods identified at Mehrgarh, Periods I and II are Neolithic. The faunal assemblage from the earliest (aceramic) Neolithic levels (Sub-period IA: seventh millennium BC) shows the overwhelming majority of wild ungulates, some of which are extinct today (Table 3). Such animals include gazelle (*Gazella dorcas/bennetti*), wild sheep (*Ovis ?orientalis*), wild goat (*Capra ?aegagrus*), swamp deer, nilgai and wild cattle (most probably, *Bos namadicus*). Gazelle remains occur most frequently and alone constitute about 42 per cent (Standardized Counts) of the assemblage from this period. Other wild animals identified are water buffalo (*Bubalus bubalis*), spotted deer, wild Asiatic ass (*Equus hemionus*), wild boar (*Sus scrofa*) and most probably the elephant. Also infrequently occur the remains of two domesticates (*Capra hircus*) and (*Bos ?indicus*), which have been distinguished from their wild relatives on the basis of their much smaller size. The presence of a few such smaller bones of *Capra hircus* along with the remains of five very young goats in each of two human burials is taken to indicate that 'some of these animals were being kept and herded by the inhabitants of the site early in the Neolithic period' (Meadow 1989a: 67). A few remains of carnivores, as also birds, fish and turtle complete the assemblage, but 'little use was apparently made of what must have been abundantly available avian and fresh water resources' (ibid.). This is somewhat strange and has to be understood perhaps in the light of taphonomic factors affecting the survival of smaller bones. The result of a thorough taphonomical analysis on differential survival of faunal remains needs to be discussed, as that alone will tell us about the representativeness of the material.

In the subsequent Period IB, there is a substantial decrease in the frequency of gazelle remains, a minor decrease in that of *Capra*, and a corresponding increase in those of *Bos* and *Ovis*. This decline in gazelle bones is significant as people concentrated more and more on potential domesticates. By the end of the Aceramic Neolithic (*c*. 5500 BC), there is a majority of domestic animals. Gazelle disappears in Period II (Ceramic Neolithic), only to reappear in all subsequent periods though in very small proportions. The decrease in the representation of wild mammals at the later aceramic level of Mehrgarh compares well with the situation at aceramic Kili Gul Mohammad I (Fairservis 1956: Appendix 4, quoted in Meadow 1986). The significance of Period II lies in the fact that most of the faunal remains now belong to domestic animals like sheep, goats and cattle (most probably zebu: Meadow 1984b). In fact, the cattle remains outnumber those of all other animals and constitute about 65 per cent of the assemblage by the middle of the Ceramic Neolithic (Period II: *c*. 5000 BC), though it never touched this record percentage in subsequent periods. The cattle remains increase four-fold in Period IB and eight-fold in Period II from their initial occurrence in Period IA. It should be noted that while discerning intra-site variability one has to consider two factors. First, the preservation conditions in different strata might not have been the same. Second, the faunal remains that archaeologists dig up are the residues that escape the regular clearing practices by ancient dwellers and their carnivorous pets, and this cleaning process might not have been uniform in all the periods. However, in the absence of any evidence to the contrary one has to discount that any possibility of disproportionate preservation conditions in these periods, or a sample bias. The above trend in cattle remains may, therefore, be taken as significant. The overall increasing representation of these potential domesticates—sheep, goats, and particularly cattle—through the course of the aceramic Neolithic has been interpreted as indicating the development of animal keeping and herding around the beginning of the Chalcolithic (Period III: *c.* 4500 BC). The relative proportions between (i) domesticated and wild ungulates and (ii) those within the domesticated category formed a pattern that by and large stabilized not only throughout the occupation of the site till around the third millennium BC (Period VII), but also in several Chalcolithic settlements of the Indus Valley. Marginal variations, if any, have been explained in terms of local ecological factors.

This is not the whole argument about the recognition of animal domestication at Mehrgarh. As will be seen from the following discussion, the increase in the representation of these potential domesticates is in conformity with another criterion—the progressive body size decrease, particularly among cattle and sheep over time. To establish intra-site body size reductions in cattle, sheep and goats, Meadow devised a method using the standard metrical data approved by Angela von den Driesch (1976). Due to the limited nature of the sample size of measurable bones at a site, it is difficult to show size reduction element by element. So 'whereby points representing the dimensions of different elements can be plotted on the same axis' (Meadow 1981: 160). For this he used a standard skeleton each of a cow, a sheep and a goat, from the collections of the Museum of Comparative Zoology, Harvard, as the points of reference. The metrical dimensions of the standard skeletons and the archaeological specimens were converted into logarithms and then the differences between the two categories were plotted for different archaeological periods. His method is essentially an adaptation of the 'ratio diagram' developed by G.G. Simpson to graphically display similarities or differences of body proportion. The method was used for cattle, sheep and goat remains from Mehrgarh (Meadow 1981). The graphical presentation for cattle indicates an overall size decrease in its body size from the Aceramic Neolithic to the Late Neolithic. This evidence along with that of the progressive increase in the representation of cattle, as discussed above, is 'consistent with an interpretation of local domestication of this animal' (Meadow 1989a: 67). The same conclusion has been drawn for sheep. By the beginning of the Chalcolithic, i.e. Period III: *c.* 4500 BC, 'size decrease in all three animals had largely come to an end with bones from later pre- and proto-historic levels of sites throughout the Greater Indus Valley indicating the keeping of animals little different from those of Period III Mehrgarh' (ibid.).

The Northern Tradition

This is represented by a large number of sites in the Kashmir Valley. The Kashmir Neolithic has been dated to the second half of the third millennium BC to the mid-second millennium BC. Faunal remains have been studied from two sites, Burzahom (Nath 1969) and

Gufkral (A.K. Sharma 1979-80, 1980-1). Both domestic and wild animals have been identified from these sites (Table 3). Domestic animals like cattle, sheep, goats and dogs are common to both assemblages, but the pig (domestic) has been identified at Burzahom alone. The complete or partial skeleton of a dog is buried with human skeletons at Burzahom, showing man's close relationship with this animal. In addition the presence of the buffalo, wild boar, red deer (hangul), swamp deer and sambar has been reported at Burzahom. At Gufkral, wild sheep, wild goats and wild cattle too have been identified, as also ibex, Himalayan tahr, serow, wild boar, and wolf. At Burzahom bone tools, such as harpoons, eyed needles, arrow heads and points have been recovered.

The Swat Valley too has yielded evidence of a comparatively Late Neolithic tradition as represented by sites like Loebanr and Aligrama, dated to the first half of second millennium BC. The faunal assemblages from these sites are dominated by cattle remains

TABLE 3. MAMMALIAN TAXA IDENTIFIED FROM SOME MAJOR NEOLITHIC SITES

TAXON	MHR	BZM	GFK	LBR	ALG	BLN	KDW	MGR	CRD	PHL	UTN	TLK	KDK	HLR	TNP	VPR	PYP
Bos indicus	+	+	+	+	+	+	+	+	+	+	+	+	+	+	+	+	?+
Bubalus bubalis	-	+	-	+	-	-	-	-	+	-	-	-	+	?+	-	-	?+
Capra hircus	+	+	+	+	+	-	-	-	+	+	+	+	?+	?+	+	-	
Ovis aries	+	+	+	+	+	-	-	-	+	+	?+	+	-	-	?+	+	+
Sus domesticus	-	+	-	+	+	-	-	-	+	-	-	-	+	+	-	+	+
Canis familiaris	?+	+	+	-	-	-	-	+	+	-	-	-	+	-	?+	+	-
Camelus sp.	-	-	-	-	+	-	-	-	-	-	-	-	-	-	-	-	-
Equus caballus	-	-	-	+	+	?+	-	-	-	-	-	-	-	+	-	-	-
Equus asinus	-	-	-	+	+	-	-	-	-	-	-	-	+	-	-	-	-
Bos sp.	-	-	+	-	-	+	-	-	-	-	-	-	-	-	-	-	-
Bos cf. *namadicus*	+	-	-	-	-	-	-	-	-	-	-	-	-	-	-	-	-
Bos (bibos) gaurus	-	-	-	-	-	-	-	-	-	-	-	-	-	-	+	+	-
Bubalus arnee	+	-	-	-	-	-	-	-	-	-	-	-	-	-	-	-	-
Capra sp.	-	-	+	-	-	-	-	-	-	-	-	-	-	-	-	-	-
Capra aegagrus	+	-	-	-	-	-	-	-	-	-	-	-	-	-	-	-	-
Capra falconeri	-	-	-	+	-	-	-	-	-	-	-	-	-	-	-	-	-
Capra ibex	-	-	+	-	-	-	-	-	-	-	-	-	-	-	-	-	-
Ovis sp.	-	-	+	-	-	-	-	-	-	-	-	-	-	-	-	-	-
Ovis orientalis	+	-	-	-	-	-	-	-	-	-	-	-	-	-	-	-	-
Capra/Ovis	-	-	-	-	-	+	-	+	-	-	-	-	-	-	-	-	-
Nemorhaedus goral	-	-	-	+	-	-	-	-	-	-	-	-	-	-	-	-	-
Capricornis sumatraensis	-	-	+	-	-	-	-	-	-	-	-	-	-	-	-	-	-
Hemitragus jemlahicus	-	-	+	-	-	-	-	-	-	-	-	-	-	-	-	-	-
Boselaphus tragocamelus	+	-	-	-	-	-	-	-	-	-	-	-	-	-	-	-	-
Antilope cervicapra	+	-	-	-	-	-	-	+	-	-	-	-	-	+	-	+	-
Gazella dorcas/bennetti	+	-	-	-	-	-	-	-	-	-	-	-	-	-	-	-	-
Axis axis	+	-	-	-	-	-	+	+	+	-	-	-	+	-	-	+	+
Cervus elephas hanglu	-	+	-	-	-	-	-	-	-	-	-	-	-	-	-	-	-
Cervus duvauceli	+	+	-	-	-	+	+	+	+	-	-	-	+	-	-	-	-
Cervus unicolor	-	+	-	-	-	-	-	-	-	-	-	-	-	-	+	+	-

(contd.)

TAXON	MHR	BZM	GFK	LBR	ALG	BLN	KDW	MGR	CRD	PHL	UTN	TLK	KDK	HLR	TNP	VPR	PYP
Muntiacus muntjak	-	-	-	-	-	-	-	-	-	-	-	-	-	-	-	-	-
Cervidae	-	-	-	+	+	-	-	-	-	-	+	+	-	-	-	-	-
Sus scrofa	+	+	+	+	+	+	-	+	+	-	-	+	-	+	-	+	-
Equus sp.	-	-	-	+	+	-	-	-	-	-	-	-	-	-	-	-	-
Equus hemionus	+	-	-	-	-	-	-	-	-	-	-	-	-	-	-	-	-
Rhinoceros unicornis	-	-	-	-	-	-	-	-	+	-	-	-	-	-	-	-	-
Elephas maximus	+	-	-	-	-	-	-	-	+	+	-	-	-	-	-	-	-
Canis lupus	-	-	+	-	-	-	-	+	-	-	-	-	-	-	-	-	-
Canis aureus	+	-	-	-	-	-	-	-	-	-	-	-	-	-	-	-	-
Felis silvestris ornata	-	-	-	+	-	-	-	-	-	-	-	-	-	-	-	-	-
Felis chaus	+	-	-	-	-	-	-	-	-	-	-	-	-	-	-	-	+
Felis caracal	?+	-	-	-	-	-	-	-	-	-	-	-	-	-	-	-	-
Panthera tigris	-	-	-	+	+	-	-	-	-	-	-	-	-	-	-	-	-
Hystrix indica	-	-	-	+	-	-	-	+	-	-	-	-	-	-	-	+	-
Lepus nigricollis	-	-	-	+	-	-	-	-	-	-	-	-	-	-	-	-	-
Rattus sp.	-	-	-	-	-	-	+	+	-	-	-	+	+	-	-	-	-
Squirrel	-	-	-	-	-	-	-	-	-	-	-	+	-	-	-	-	-

+ Present - Absent ? Doubtful

MHR=Mehrgarh: aceramic and ceramic (Meadow 1981, 1989a); BZM=Burzahom (Nath 1969); GFK=Gufkral (Sharma 1979-80,1980-81); LBR=Loebnar (Campagnoni 1979); ALG=Aligrama (Campagnoni 1979); BLN=Belan valley: Koldihwa and Mahagara combined (Alur 1980); KDW=Koldihwa (Chattopadhyaya 1991); MGR=Mahagara (Chattopadhyaya 1991); CRD=Chirand (Nath and Biswas 1980); PHL=Piklihal (Allchin 1960); UTN=Utnur (Allchin 1961; Alur 1990); TLK=Tekkalakota (Nagaraja Rao and Malhotra 1965); KDK=Kodekal (Shah 1973; Paddayya 1975; Clason 1979); HLR=Hallur (Alur 1971a); TNP=T. Narsipur (Alur 1971c); VPR=Veerapuram (Thomas 1984b); PYP=Paiyampalli (*IAR* 1967-8).

(Campagnoni 1979) and the taxonomical list shows broad similarity, particularly in view of a mixture of domestic and wild animals, with that of the Kashmir Valley. Domestic animals include—apart from cattle (zebu)—sheep, goats and pigs from both the Swat Valley sites, with buffalo confined to Loebanr. Additionally domestic animals include the camel, donkey and horse at Aligrama. These animals, except the camel, are also reported at Loebanr. This is suggestive of long distance movement of people or goods between the Swat Valley and other regions during the first half of the second millennium BC. Some of the wild animals from the Swat Valley sites, not reported for the Kashmir Valley, include markhor, goral, tiger, porcupine and hare (Table 3).

The Eastern Vindhyas

The archaeological investigations carried out by the University of Allahabad in the eastern Vindhyas, drained by the river Belan, have been of tremendous importance (G.R. Sharma et al. 1980). Koldihwa and Mahagara, situated on either bank of the river, furnished the evidence of a distinctive Neolithic tradition, which probably had its origin in the earlier Mesolithic tradition (Chopani Mando) of the region (ibid.). Two conflicting sets of dates from these Neolithic sites are puzzling. The first is a series of three ^{14}C dates from Koldihwa, viz., 6570±210 BC, 5440±240 BC and 4530±85 BC. The other is a series of six dates, four ^{14}C and two TL, from Mahagara, none of which predate the late third millennium BC. The excavators have dismissed the younger dates on the ground that they are inconsistent with the corresponding stratigraphic sequence and that the dating samples are contaminated (see ibid: 194-200, for a fuller discussion).

While Mahagara and Koldihwa (Phase I) witnessed the existence of a pure food-producing Neolithic economy, an earlier phase, termed Proto-Neolithic or Advanced Mesolithic, has been documented at the neighbouring site of Chopani Mando. Due to poor preservation conditions at these sites the recovery of faunal remains has not been satisfactory. Out of a total of 4,455 brittle bone fragments from the Advanced Mesolithic phase at Chopani Mando, only two were identifiable (see Section 4.1). The situation at Koldihwa and Mahagara was not that bad. These assemblages were studied in two phases: first by K.R. Alur between 1978 and 1980 and subsequently by the author. The taphonomic studies carried out by this author suggest that the differential survival of animal remains from these sites was the result of unfavourable natural conditions between the long process of bone discard and archaeological recovery, and that the samples thus retrieved may not be taken as representative (Chattopadhyaya 1991). Therefore any theorization on relative taxonomical abundance will be misleading. Cattle remains being large and comparatively less susceptible to environmental hazards, expectedly survived best.

The major objective in the early study of faunal remains from the Vindhyas (and the Ganga Valley) by Alur (1980) was to trace the 'evolution' of human-animal relationships in a long time perspective from the terminal Pleistocene to the Neolithic period, and to investigate the origins of the domestication of cattle. While presenting the faunal report for the Neolithic Vindhyas, Alur did not present separate accounts from Koldihwa and Mahagara. This has resulted in misrepresentation of his identification in certain other sources (Thomas and Joglekar 1994: Table 5, p. 191), and some clarification is necessary. The animals identified by Alur in the combined report are: cattle (*Bos indicus*), sheep/goats, horse, deer, wild boar, tortoise and fish. Of these, the horse and wild boar are exclusive to Mahagara. A detailed study of these two assemblages by the present author confirms some of the above identifications, such as cattle, sheep/goats, fish and tortoise (Chattopadhyaya 1991). As far as deer are concerned, two species, viz., barasingha and spotted deer, have been identified in both assemblages. Additional species identified at both sites are chicken and rat. Blackbuck, porcupine, wolf, possibly dog and molluscs are some of the other taxa identified by this author at Mahagara. The horse, caballine or otherwise, identified by Alur at Mahagara, could not be confirmed. The caballine horse first appears in this region during the Chalcolithic phase at Koldihwa (see Section 4.4).

On the basis of osteomorphological characters, Alur argued for the emergence of cattle husbandry at these Neolithic sites. He distinguished cattle of two different sizes, but the argument that the larger belongs to the wild variety is not convincing. A detailed metrical analysis by this author on the lines of Meadow (see above), shows that none of the cattle remains are comparable in size to wild cattle either of Mehrgarh Period IA or the remains of *Bos namadicus* (the progenitor of zebu) in terminal Pleistocene deposits of the river Son (Chattopadhyaya 1991). The size variability noticed by Alur may at best be explained in terms of sexual dimorphism within the same species, which is on the whole comparable in size with modern cattle of the region.

The possibility that the cattle at these sites were domesticated may not be questioned because of (i) the similarity of its bone morphology and size with present-day cattle and (ii) the archaeological evidence of a cattle pen at Mahagara with hoof marks. The hoof prints indicate a population comprising individuals of different age groups (G.R. Sharma et al. 1980). If domestication had been a local development in this region during Neolithic times, Alur's method based on osteomorphological criteria and size variation (without recourse to metrical analysis) could not convincingly establish any 'gradual' change in cattle osteomorphology from the Upper Palaeolithic through to the Neolithic in this region. No evidence on intra-site change, either in body size or morphological characters, is established either. However, the variation of the faunal resource diversity with niche-width does suggests a specialized economy or overall dependence on a single species, characteristic of an agricultural way of life (Chattopadhyaya 1991).

Another feature of these sites is the occurrence of bone/antler tools, though in a limited number.

The Eastern Tradition

Given the vast area of distribution of the eastern Neolithic sites from Bihar, Orissa and West Bengal to Assam, this Neolithic tradition, despite certain common features, including rectangular variety of celts and adzes, should ideally be divided into a few regional sub-groups. Thapar does talk of three distinctive groups, as noted above. His comments about the distinctive status to be given to the north-eastern group certainly holds good, but the separation of the mid-eastern (north Bihar, represented in the main by Chirand) and central-eastern (Chhotanagpur plateau) is debatable. It now appears on the basis of archaeological (including faunal) evidence that Chirand represented a special type of adaptation of people not different from those of the Neolithic tradition of the plateau regions (Chattopadhyaya 1999d). Chirand, situated on the left bank of the river Ghaghra (close to its confluence with the Ganga) in Saran district of north Bihar, is the only Neolithic site in the whole of the eastern region that has produced any appreciable quantity of faunal evidence (Narain 1970). Again, in the light of recent discoveries of sites like Chechar, Sonpur, Taradih and Senuwar in western Bihar and Kunjhun II in the middle Son Valley (Sidhi district of M.P.), it now seems probable that the Neolithic of Bihar (including Chirand) was not unconnected with that of the Vindhyas, and that this linkage was along Son and not the Ganga (Chattopadhyaya 1999d). The beginning of the Neolithic phase at Chirand can be placed around the late third millennium BC on the basis of calibrated radiocarbon dates.

The faunal evidence presented by Nath and Biswas (1980) is interesting and represents, in a sense, a combination of the faunal economies of Neolithic Vindhyas, on the one hand, and Mesolithic central Ganga Valley, on the other. Though the remains of domestic animals like cattle, buffalo, sheep and goats, pig and dogs were found (Table 3), as also carbonised grains, including rice, lentils and legumes, a major occupation of the people appears to have been hunting-fishing (Prasad 1997; cf. Narayan 1996). This does not portray a picture of the 'classic' Neolithic as one understands the term. Chirand was inhabited on a regular basis by small-scale agricultural communities associated with animal husbandry, hunting-fishing, as well as some industrial activities (bone tool/object industries). The last feature has also been noted for the Mesolithic sites of the central Ganga Valley. This was necessary for microlith using communities in a region where stone is not available. The occurrence of a large number and variety of tools and objects fashioned on limb bones of large bovids as well as antlers and turtle plastrons, and also with taphonomic consideration, suggest that bone tools were not meant for local use alone. There is a great degree of probability that these items had a wider range of distribution in order to negotiate the exchange of other items of use from surrounding areas. For obtaining the raw materials, therefore, there was an additional pressure on stock-raising of large bovids like cattle and buffalo, on the one hand, and hunting of deer like barasingha, on the other. Narain (1972) has outlined the methods of bone tool making at the site, which also include beforehand boiling of bones to provide durability and hardness, which is comparable to the controlled firing of bones in the Mesolithic Ganga Valley, as discussed above. The reason behind the difference in the new bone heating technique at Neolithic Chirand was the availability of earthen vessels. The excavation has also produced the remains of multiple ovens which might have been used not only for cooking purpose, but also for large-scale manufacture of bone artefacts. Apart from mammalian fauna, aquatic resources like fish and turtles were also consumed by the Neolithic communities of Chirand (Nath and Biswas 1980).

Animal remains have also been recovered from sites like Bharatpur and Mahisadal in West Bengal, which may be placed, as per Thapar's scheme of classification, in the wide central-eastern Neolithic zone. Yet most archaeologists tend to classify these sites as Neolithic-Chalcolithic or Chalcolithic, rather than as pure Neolithic (Ghosh 1986). The identification of animal taxa carried out by Banerjee (1979-80) shows the presence of both domestic and wild animals at both these sites. Domestic animals like cattle, sheep, goats and pig are common to both the sites and buffalo has been reported from Bharatpur alone. The wild species include nilgai, barasingha, red deer and barking deer from Bharatpur and spotted deer, barasingha, sambar, wild boar, wolf and jungle cat from Mahisadal.

The Southern Tradition

A substantial number of Neolithic sites have been reported from peninsular India, covering parts of Karnataka, Andhra Pradesh and Tamil Nadu, dated on radiometric evidence between *c.* 2500 and 1000 BC (Paddayya 1975). The identification of faunal remains in eight representative sites of southern India has been listed in Table 3. These sites are Piklihal, Tekkalakota, Kodekal, Hallur, T. Narsipur, Veerapuram, Utnur and Paiyampalli. Other sites are Brahmagiri (Nath 1968a, b), Maski (Nath 1957), Nagarjunakonda (Nath 1968a), Sanganakallu (Alur 1969), Terdal (Alur 1971), and Palavoy (Reddy 1978), where the faunal picture is similar to that of the eight sites listed in Table 3. Budihal in Gulbarga district of Karnataka is another promising site in respect of faunal remains being studied by Thomas (Paddayya 1993). Rather than describe the results from individual sites, the salient features of the faunal evidence will be outlined below.

Throughout its existence for about 1,500 years, this Neolithic tradition, usually associated with 'ashmounds', shows a picture of continuity not only in the overall material culture patterns but also in the faunal economy, which is essentially dominated by cattle. On the basis of osteomorphological characters, this animal has been identified as of a domesticated type. This is further supported by its hoof-impressions from the floor of a cattle pen exposed at Utnur (Allchin 1961). On the basis of horn cores, two breeds have been distinguished: one is the long-horned, slender-built, with a developed humps and the other is a massively built type (Shah 1973; Paddayya 1975). The faunal assemblages contain about 80-5 per cent remains of cattle (Paddayya 1975). Cattle would have been a source, not only of food, but also fuel, fertiliser, power, and bone artefacts. The ashmounds which are generally associated with these Neolithic sites, are essentially deposits of ash/ decomposed cow-dung. Cattle also formed the main theme for rock paintings as at Piklihal (Allchin 1963). The possibility that cattle were used for heavy draught work or weight-bearing purposes, is indicated by such pathological features as anchylosis and exostosis, that Alur recognized on certain limb bones of cattle from Utnur, Sanganakallu, Palavoy, and Hallur (Alur 1969, 1971a, 1990; Allchin 1969). According to Paddayya cattle-breeding constituted the main occupation of the people.

Other domestic animals include buffalo, sheep, goats, pig, horse, donkey, dog and domestic fowl or chicken; horse remains come from the upper levels of the Neolithic site of Hallur (Alur 1971a). It is highly probable that the donkey was used as a beast of burden. The elephant is represented by a solitary bone fragment, from the Upper Neolithic phase at Piklihal; whether domestic or wild, it is not known (Allchin 1960). (From its representation of the elephant being driven by a man on the famous cylinder-seal from Maski, one might infer that elephant was tamed during Neolithic times.) The wild taxa include sambar, spotted deer, barasingha, nilgai, blackbuck, gazelle (*Gazella gazella* Pallas), hare, common house rat, monitor lizard, tortoise, fish and invertebrates like freshwater mussel and banded pond-snail. It may be mentioned that barasingha, described in reports as *Cervus duvauceli* Cuvier, should be more appropriately identified as *Cervus duvauceli branderi* Pocock, a race of central India and peninsular India (Prater 1971: 289). The pictorial evidence suggests that snakes and peacocks were known to these Neolithic communities, but their bones have not been reported from any of these sites. Another important feature of the south Indian Neolithic tradition is the occurrence of artefacts fashioned on the bones of cattle, antlers, and shell. While cattle bones provided raw materials for points, chisel-ended pieces, and axe-shaped scrapers, beads and pendants were made of shell. On faunal evidence, Paddayya suggests that the climatic conditions during Neolithic times was more humid than that in the present (also see Korisettar et al. in Vol. I of this series).

It has also been observed in the context of southern Neolithic that the pattern of faunal representation shows a continuity at succeeding levels, associated with metals.

Discussion

The Neolithic faunal evidence from different regional traditions of the subcontinent is useful towards an understanding of human-cattle relationships and latter's domestication. Though the problem of the origins of cattle domestication in South Asia will be elaborated in Section 5A, it is suggested on the basis of available evidence that zebu or humped cattle (*Bos indicus*) evolved out of its, now extinct, South Asian progenitor—*Bos namadicus*, and not from prehistoric *Bos primigenius*, which is regarded as the ancestor of the humpless *Bos taurus* of Europe. The archaeological evidence from Mehrgarh suggests that *Bos indicus* was independently domesticated around the first half of the sixth millennium, not much later than the earliest domestication of *Bos taurus* in Thessaly and Anatolia (Meadow 1981,1989a; Chattopadhyaya 1991). A comparative study of blood group factors and the haemoglobin variants between several Indian breeds of zebu and some humpless cattle breeds of western origin supports a separate ancestry (Naik 1978; Naik et al. 1969; Braend 1971). The following remarks of Naik are relevant: 'the northern and southern zebu . . . , because of their contemporary existence and distinctly different morphology depicted from ancient times, suggest different centres of domestication in India' (Naik 1978: 25). His genetic findings also support this hypothesis. In this light, it now seems that Mehrgarh, despite being the earliest centre of cattle domestication, was not the only such centre in South Asia. The presence of two breeds of cattle at Southern Neolithic sites, as noted above, points to the possibility that cattle domestication in southern India was a local development. Another possible centre seems to be the vast stretch of uplands from the eastern Vindhyas to western Madhya Pradesh. This is indicated to some extent by the prehistoric rock art evidence of this macro-region (see Section 5B, below). However, we need more concrete archaeological evidence to support this possibility than is presently available (see Korisettar et al. in Vol. I of this series).

4.3 The Pre-/Early Harappan and Harappan Traditions

The Harappan Civilization flourishing between *c.* 2500 BC and 1750 BC primarily in the Indus Valley, but also extending to adjoining regions, has been the most intriguing and most intensely researched subject in the archaeology of the subcontinent. A large number of sites excavated in Pakistan and India (Punjab, Haryana, Rajasthan, Gujarat), have furnished faunal material which 'is probably one of the best sources of information in archaeozoological context' (Badam and Sathe 1991). However, the results of the early studies on these materials have not been as enlightening as those from other areas of Harappan researches. Again, barring a few recent exceptions (see Meadow and Patel, and Thomas, Vol. II of this series), the conventional archaeozoological research on the Harappan period have not been as interesting as those on earlier periods. The conventional approach in Harappan archaeozoology has been to determine the range of animal species known to the Harappans, which is in a sense corroboration of prior knowledge gathered from representations on seals, sealings, or pottery. However, archaeozoology did assume importance in identifying the camel and various equid species.

The importance of the available Harappan faunal evidence can, however, be better appreciated and explained in the light of two major economic changes, or what Meadow calls 'distinct agricultural revolutions', that occurred in the north-western regions of South Asia between sixth and second millennia BC (Meadow 1989a). The first involved the emergence in the sixth millennium BC of a farming complex based principally on the *rabi* crops (barley and wheat), on the one hand, and domestic bovids like zebu, sheep and goats, on the other. The second involved the addition by the early second millennium BC of *kharif* cereals, such as sorghum, various millets, and rice (*Oryza sativa*) (cf. Possehl 1992). This second development also coincided with the use of certain new domestic animals like camels, horses and donkeys. In this connection, Meadow makes an important point:

> new agricultural opportunities resulting from the introduction of the summer-sown cereal crops, when combined with the new means of animal-based traction, transport, and communication, facilitated widespread settlement in areas previously marginal to food production as well as realignment of settlement in already occupied areas. (1989a: 61)

These points have an important bearing on the origins of the Harappan Civilization, as also on the transformation of its Mature form in the early second millennium BC.

The Harappan faunal economy, characterized by a fairly large-scale use of cattle, with a possible exception at Mohenjo Daro, was the culmination of a trend set in motion at Mehrgarh II and continuing in the intervening period, not only at Mehrgarh itself, but also at certain Pre-Harappan and Early Harappan sites in Pakistan (Meadow 1986). At Mehrgarh (Periods III-VII) the decrease in the proportional representation of wild mammals by the later Aceramic Neolithic (Period II), and corresponding increase in that of domesticates like cattle, sheep and goats, reflects a distinctive cultural pattern that also finds corroboration from a similar evidence described for the Aceramic Kili Gul Mohammad I (Fairservis 1956, quoted in Meadow 1986). The Chalcolithic periods (III-VII) at the former site shows continuation of this pattern to the end of the occupation of the site around the mid-second millennium BC.

Balakot, a site located about 16 km inland from the Arabian Sea off the south-eastern corner of the Las Bela Plain, with an altogether different ecological zone, has produced interesting faunal evidence in two of its distinctive phases: I, a Pre-Harappan tradition, termed as the 'Balakotian' (late fourth millennium BC) and II, the Harappan tradition, though with a stratigraphic break (Meadow 1979). The Balakotian faunal evidence reflects a cultural adaptation based mainly on a well developed cattle economy, rather than on aquatic or marine resources as would be expected from its location. The faunal assemblage is dominated by cattle remains, which constitute as high as 75 per cent of bones of all mammalian fauna. The remaining one quarter of the assemblage includes the remains of sheep, goats, gazelle, wild boar and wild asiatic ass; the representation of the last two taxa is only marginal (Table 4A). Fish bones are almost conspicuous by their absence and the shells of molluscs are rare. The situation in the Harappan phase, though different on certain key points, is similar in the broad sense that the same domestic cattle is represented in appreciable proportion and almost the same combination of ungulates reappear, along with water buffalo and nilgai. The contrast, however, lies in the facts that (i) despite the appreciable representation of cattle (little less than 40 per cent) in phase II, small ruminants like sheep and goats become more abundant, together making up about 60 per cent of the collection, and (ii) during the Harappan phase fish (particularly the species, *Pomadasys hasta*) became a very important resource, so much so that its

TABLE 4A. MAMMALIAN TAXA IDENTIFIED FROM SOME MAJOR PRE-/EARLY HARAPPAN AND HARAPPAN SITES (OUTSIDE GUJARAT)

Taxon	MG*	BK-1	BK-2	JLP	NSR	HRP	MJD	KLB	RPR	BAR	AGP
Bos indicus	+	+	+	+	+	+	+	+	+	+	+
Bos taurus	-	?	-	-	?	+	?	-	-	-	-
Bubalus bubalis	?	?	+	-	?	+	+	+	+	+	+
Capra hircus	+	+	+	+	+	+	-	+	+	+	+
Ovis aries	+	+	+	+	+	+	+	+	+	+	+
Sus domesticus	?+	?+	?+	-	-	+	+	+	+	+	+
Camelus dromedarius	-	-	-	-	-	?+	?+	?+	-	-	-
Equus caballus	-	-	-	-	-	+	+	?+	-	-	-
Equus asinus	-	-	-	-	-	+	-	+	-	-	-
Canis familiaris	-	-	-	-	-	+	+	+	+	-	+
Felis catus	-	-	-	-	-	+	-	-	-	-	-
Bos sp.	-	-	-	-	-	-	-	-	-	-	-
Bubalus arnee	?	?	?	?	-	?	?	-	-	-	-
Capra/Ovis	-	-	-	-	-	-	-	-	-	-	-
Capra aegagrus	-	?	-	-	?	-	-	-	-	-	-
Ovis orientalis	?	?	-	-	+	-	-	-	-	-	-
Boselaphus tragocamelus	-	-	+	-	-	+	-	-	-	-	-
Gazella bennetti/gazella	+	+	+	+	+	+	+	-	-	-	-
Tetraceros quadricornis	-	-	-	-	-	-	-	-	-	-	-
Antilope cervicapra	+	+	-	-	-	-	-				
Axis axis	-	-	-	-	-	+	+	+	-	-	+
Axis porcinus	-	-	-	-	-	+	+	-	-	-	-
Cervus elephas hanglu	-	-	-	-	-	-	+	-	-	-	-
Cervus duvauceli	+	-	-	-	-	+	-	+	-	-	+
Cervus unicolor	-	-	-	-	-	-	+	-	-	-	-
Muntiacus muntjak	-	-	-	-	-	-	-	-	-	-	-
Sus scrofa	+	+	+	+	+	+	+	-	-	-	-
Equus hemionus	+	+	+	-	+	?	?	-	-	-	-
Rhinoceros unicornis	-	-	-	-	+	+	-	+	-	-	-
Elephas maximus	-	-	-	-	-	+	+	+	+	+	-
Presbytis entellus	-	-	-	-	-	-	-	-	-	-	-
Hyaena hyaena	-	-	-	-	-	-	-	-	-	-	-
Canis lupus	-	-	-	-	-	+	-	-	-	-	-
Canis aureus	-	-	-	-	-	+	-	-	-	-	-
Cuon alpinus	-	-	-	-	-	-	-	-	-	-	-
Felis libyca	-	-	-	-	-	-	-	-	-	-	-
Felis chaus	-	-	-	-	-	-	-	-	-	-	-
Herpestes edwardsi	-	-	-	-	-	+	+	-	-	-	-
Hystrix indica	-	-	-	-	-	-	-	-	-	-	-
Bandicota bengalensis	-	-	-	-	-	-	-	-	?+	-	-
Rattus rattus	-	-	-	-	-	+	+	-	+	-	-
Suncus stoliczkanuus	-	-	-	-	-	+	-	-	-	-	-

+ Present - Absent/Not Reported ? Doubtful

MG*=Mehrgarh III-VII (Meadow 1981, 1986, 1989a); BK-1=Balakot I: Balakotian (Meadow 1979, 1986, 1989a); BK-2=Balakot II-III: Harappan (Meadow 1979, 1986); JLP=Jalilpur (Meadow 1986, 1989a); NSR-Nausharo (Meadow 1989a); HRP=Harappa (Prashad 1936; Meadow 1991); MJD= Mohenjo Daro (Sewell and Guha 1931); KLB=Kalibangan (Nath 1969); RPR=Rupar (Nath 1968a, c); BAR=Bara (Nath 1968c); AGP=Alamgirpur (Nath and Biswas 1969).

proportion by weight in the total assemblage surpassed in some sieved lots. Molluscs too now became an important aquatic resource. The most frequently occurring species are *Terebralia palustris* (a gastropod) and *Callista* (*Meretrix*) *casta* (a bivalve), in that order. It may be mentioned that the shells of the latter species were used as a raw material for a unique and well developed shell bangle industry (Meadow 1979; Dales and Kenoyer 1977; Bhan et al., in Vol. II of this series). The population of the Harappan period at this site: 'used a much wider range of resources than did their predecessors at the same site, exploiting not only the alluvial area immediately around the settlement but also mangrove swamps, lagoons, estuaries, and the open sea coast' (Meadow 1989a: 68).

Jalilpur, a site in southern Pakistani Punjab, provides the faunal evidence for an Early Harappan tradition. The 1971 excavation by M.R. Mughal yielded a small bone assemblage that included only so-called 'identifiable' remains. However, a greater recovery control maintained in the 1974 excavation of the site resulted in the recovery of a much larger assemblage. The mammalian assemblage of the 1971 excavation was dominated by cattle remains (90 per cent); other mammals identified are sheep, goats and gazelle (together constituting the remaining 10 per cent). However, the preliminary analysis of the 1974 materials by Meadow indicates that the representation of sheep, goats and gazelle is more than 10 per cent but probably less than 25 per cent, the latter being the proportion noted for the Balakotian level.

By Harappan times, though cattle still constituted an important source of diet, one can find a perceptible decrease in the proportional representation of its remains at a number of sites, or at clusters of area at a particular sites. Again, in contrast to earlier periods, the remains of fish, land tortoise, river turtle, and birds are abundant at most sites, be it Harappa itself, Mohenjo Daro, Nausharo (near Mehrgarh) or others. Molluscs too were increasingly used as items of food. During Harappan times the representation of wild animals like deer, gazelle, blackbuck and nilgai were on the increase (25 per cent of a faunal assemblage from Mound AB, Harappa, for example). At sites in northern India, such as Rupar (Rupnagar), Bara, Alamgirpur and Kalibangan, antelope remains are not found, though they occur regularly at sites of Gujarat and Saurashtra (Tables 4A, 4B). Large mammals like elephant and rhinoceros have been reported at a number of sites in Gujarat as well as northern regions, but their contribution to food is doubtful. Thomas is of the opinion that the remains of these animals were associated with the manufacture of bone/ivory tools or craft items. Another interesting development during the Harappan period is the regular presence of water buffalo in the faunal assemblages of most sites; its presence in earlier periods is doubtful. Its representation in various seals also shows its importance. Prashad (1936) believes that the elephant was domesticated and that the Sindh Valley constituted one of the centres, if not the sole centre of its domestication. Zeuner (1963) too holds a similar view. Given these new economic emphases, it is not surprising then that cattle that had dominated assemblages of earlier periods in a big way, had a comparatively reduced proportional representation, from most Harappan sites. However, some sites in Gujarat and Saurashtra may be taken as exceptions. The representation of other domesticates like sheep and goats marginally increase in this

TABLE 4B. MAMMALIAN TAXA IDENTIFIED FROM SOME MAJOR HARAPPAN SITES OF GUJARAT

Taxon	DV	RG	LT	SK	KS	NG	RJ	KP	MV	BK	PD	SP	OT
Bos indicus	+	+	+	+	+	+	+	+	+	+	+	+	+
Bubalus bubalis	+	+	+	-	+	+	+	+	-	+	+	+	+
Capra hircus	+	+	+	+	+	+	+	+	+	+	+	+	+
Ovis aries	+	+	+	+	+	+	+	+	+	+	+	+	+
Sus domesticus	?+	+	+	+	+	+	+	+	-	+	+	+	+
Camelus dromedarius	-	-	-	+	+$	-	?+	-	-	-	-	-	-
Equus caballus	?+	-	+	+	+	-	-	-	+	-	-	+	-
Equus asinus	?+	+	-	+	+	-	-	-	-	-	-	-	-
Canis familiaris	-	+	+	+	+	+	+	-	+	+	+	+	-
Felis catus	-	-	-	-	-	-	?+	-	-	-	-	-	-
Bos sp.	-	-	-	-	+	-	-	-	-	-	-	+	-
Bubalus arnee	-	-	-	-	+	-	-	-	-	-	-	+	-
Capra/Ovis	-	-	-	-	-	-	-	-	-	-	-	-	-
Boselaphus tragocamelus	-	-	+	-	+	+	+	-	-	+	+	+	+
Gazella bennetti/gazella	+	-	-	-	+	+	?+	+	-	+	-	+	?+
Tetraceros quadricornis	-	-	-	-	+	-	?+	-	-	+	-	+	-
Antilope cervicapra	?+	-	-	-	+	+	?+	-	-	+	+	+	?+
Axis axis	-	-	+	+	+	+	+	-	+	+	+	+	-
Axis porcinus	-	-	-	-	+	-	+	-	-	-	-	+	-
Cervus duvauceli	-	-	-	-	?+	-	?+	-	+	-	-	-	-
Cervus unicolor	-	+	+	-	+	+	?+	-	-	-	-	+	?+
Muntiacus muntjak	-	-	-	-	+	-	-	-	-	-	-	+	-
Cervidae	+	-	-	-	-	-	-	-	-	-	+	+	-
Sus scrofa	?+	-	-	-	+	-	+	+	+	+	+	+	-
Equus hemionus	-	-	-	+	+	-	+	-	-	-	-	+	-
Rhinoceros unicornis	-	-	+	+	+	-	-	+	-	-	-	+	?+
Elephas maximus	-	-	+	+	-	-	?+	-	-	-	-	-	-
Presbytis entellus	-	-	-	-	?+	-	-	-	-	-	-	-	-
Hyaena hyaena	-	-	-	-	+	-	-	-	-	-	-	-	-
Cuon alpinus	-	-	-	-	-	-	+	-	-	-	-	-	-
Canis lupus	-	-	-	+	?+	-	-	-	-	-	+	-	-
Canis aureus	-	-	+	+	-	-	+	-	-	-	+	+	-
Canis aureus/familiaris	+	-	-	-	-	-	-	-	-	-	-	-	-
Felis libyca	-	-	-	-	-	-	?+	-	-	-	-	-	-
Felis chaus	-	-	-	-	?+	-	-	-	-	-	-	-	-
Herpestes edwardsi	-	-	+	+	+	-	-	-	-	+	+	-	-
Hystrix indica	-	-	-	-	+	-	+	-	-	-	-	-	-
Lepus nigricollis	+	-	+	+	+	+	+	-	-	+	+	+	+
Bandicota bengalensis	-	-	-	-	-	+	-	-	-	-	-	-	-
Rattus rattus	-	-	+	+	-	+	+	-	-	+	+	+	-
Suncus stoliczkanuus	-	-	-	+	-	-	-	-	-	-	-	-	-

\+ Present - Absent ? Doubtful $ Stratigraphy uncertain

DV=Dholavira (Roy 1993; Patel 1997); RG=Rangpur (Nath 1962-63); LT=Lothal (Nath and Rao 1985); SK=Surkotada (A.K. Sharma 1974, 1990); KS=Kuntasi (Thomas and Joglekar 1994); NG=Nageshwar (Shah and Bhan 1992); RJ=Rojdi (Possehl et al. 1985; Kane 1989); KP=Khanpur (Chitalwala and Thomas 1977-78); MV=Malvan (Alur 1990); BK=Babarkot (Ryan, quoted in Thomas and Joglekar 1994); PD=Padri (Thomas and Joglekar 1994); SP=Shikarpur (Thomas and Joglekar 1994); OT=Oriyo Timbo (Rissman and Chitalwala 1990).

period. In fact it is the remains of domestic pig that outnumbered those of cattle at Mohenjo Daro (Badam and Sathe 1991: 136).

The taxonomical identifications carried out at various Harappan sites in Gujarat (Table 4B) are not too dissimilar from the one described earlier (Table 4A), and some minor variations can be explained in terms of ecological differences between this and the northern regions. While a separate contribution by Thomas on the archaeozoology of the Harappan period in western India is available in Vol. II of this series, the faunal evidence from the famous urban site of Dholavira alone may be briefly discussed (also see Meadow and Patel in Vol. II of this Series). The faunal assemblage from the 1990-2 excavations were studied by Roy (1993), as part of his dissertation at the Institute of Archaeology, New Delhi. He reported the presence of ungulates like cattle, sheep, and goats, beside horse and donkey. Non-mammalian fauna included fowl, fish, turtle, prawns and lobsters. However, the study by Ajita Patel (1997) of a much larger assemblage belonging to the cultural Stages III and IV (Mature Harappan) and V (subsequent period of decline) from two sectors, the Middle Town and the Bailey (inside the Citadel) of the site shows the presence of wild asiatic ass and not that of the horse or donkey. Other mammalian taxa identified by her include cattle, buffalo, antelopes like blackbuck and gazelle, pig/wild boar, cervids, the genus *Lepus*, rodents and *Canis* (dog or jackal). Beside, bones of birds and fish are also represented. An important observation is the patterned distribution of bovine remains. For example, these remains constitute 74 per cent of the identified assemblage from the Middle Town. This stands in sharp contrast to the situation in the Bailey area with 51 per cent of such remains; here the remains of pig and small bovids are more common (Patel 1997). There exist differences in some other taxonomical combinations. For example, Patel notices a much higher proportion of wild fauna in the Bailey in Stage III, and of some small bovids and pigs in Stage IV, in comparison with the corresponding stages in the Middle Town. This spatial pattern of relative taxonomical abundance within Dholavira is highly significant and has been interpreted in terms of socio-economic differences between the inhabitants of these two sectors (Patel 1997: 108). Another interesting feature of the faunal evidence from Dholavira relates to the temporal variability in relative taxonomical abundance, particularly involving cattle and buffalo. At the Bailey, the ration of cattle to buffalo is almost constant as 3:1, in Stages III and IV, though a complete reversal in this ratio takes place in Stage V. In the Middle Town, buffalo remains are relatively rare in Stage III, but become more common in the subsequent stage. The above analyses of Patel is of great importance and suggest: (i) beef eating was more common in the Middle Town in comparison with that in the Bailey, and (ii) in course of time buffalo was substituting cattle as a source of meat.

A comparatively low representation of cattle is also documented at the three Periods (IA-IC) of Surkotada, dated between 2315 to 1700 BC (A.K. Sharma 1990; cf. Allchin and Allchin 1982: 218). For example, the proportion of cattle in the total identifiable taxa drops from 39.2 per cent in Period IA to 29.8 per cent in Period IB, but finally reaches the height of 45.6 per cent. Again at Nageshwar, the proportionate representation of cattle drops from 49.87 per cent in Phase a to 34.01 per cent in Phase b (Shah and Bhan 1992).

These figures are much lower than those noted for Pre-Early Harappan sites.

Another feature of the Harappan fauna was the identification of camel and certain equid remains. While camel remains have been reported from a number of Harappan sites, they are either from the upper levels or doubtful stratigraphic contexts (Badam and Sathe 1991). Meadow concludes that camels were first used during the early second millennium BC. We have discussed about the camel bones in the Late Neolithic site of Aligrama in the Swat Valley around the same time. It is not yet clearly established whether the camel of the archaeozoological record was one-humped or two-humped.

While the presence of wild asiatic ass and donkey has been confirmed at a number of Harappan sites, that of the horse (*Equus caballus*) has remained a subject of controversy for a long time. This is largely because of the osteomorphological similarities between different species of the genus *Equus* (including donkey, wild Asiatic ass or onager, mule, etc.). The identification of the horse at Rana Ghundai by Ross is not generally taken seriously by scholars (Allchin 1969). Again, a few remains of the true horse, including a skull, from the uppermost level at Mohenjo Daro did not clear the picture as Marshall (1931) thought them to be later intrusives. However, the identification of horse at Surkotada from all the three periods, IA-IC, from such elements as phalanges, distal end of cannon and teeth, has been taken by many archaeologists and historians as conclusive evidence for the presence of this animal during the Harappan period (A.K. Sharma 1990, 1994). Horse remains are also reported from Harappa, Mohenjo Daro, Lothal, Malvan and Kuntasi (Tables 4A and 4B). Though the authenticity of some of the identifications of caballine horse at such Harappan sites is not being contested here, the association of horse remains with the mature Harappan phase, including that at Surkotada, has been questioned by Richard Meadow on the ground that the stratigraphical and contextual positions are far from secure (Meadow and Patel 1997; cf. Anthony 1997). For Meadow the true horse first appeared in South Asia around 1800 BC at Pirak (Meadow 1989a). The absence of horses on Harappan seals points to the possibility that this animal was either unknown to the Harappans during the mature phase, or else was too insignificant to demand attention. South Asia never had wild horses, so the ancestry of the proto-historic domestic horses has to be sought outside. The horse was first domesticated in southern Russian steppes, possibly from its wild ancestor *Equus ferus*, around 4000 BC (Davis 1987). If we leave open the question of the association of horse with the Harappan mature phase, it does not necessarily alter the views of Marshall (1931) and K. Chattopadhyaya (1975, 1976) regarding the difference between the Harappans and the Vedic 'Aryans', respectively with iconic and non-iconic forms of religions. It may not be surprising that the horse was introduced from Central Asia to a region in South Asia with a flourishing civilization and that the animal existed in certain pockets of the vast Harappan territory. But certainly, towards the later phase, this animal not only made its appearance felt, but also became widespread.

Finally, a few words on the exploitation of molluscs for the purpose of shell working and the associated trade during Harappan times may be mentioned (for details see Bhan et al. in Vol. II of this series). This practice has a long history in the region beginning somewhere along the Sindh or Makran coasts in early Neolithic times (Kenoyer 1989). But by Harappan times the centralized regime seems to have had a greater control, direct or indirect, over the marine resources and the necessary raw materials for shell working. The evidence from Balakot (Phase II) has already been mentioned. Some major urban centres like Mohenjo Daro, Chanhu Daro and Harappa were associated with the local production of shell objects for local market and perhaps also for nearby rural communities. Coastal sites like Balakot and Allahdino provided the necessary raw materials as also certain finished products like bangles. Nageshwar is another such coastal site in Gujarat where the shells of marine gastropods like *Turbinella pyrum* and *Chicoreus ramosus* were used for the manufacture of various kinds of ornaments and utensils, and the site was most probably 'geared towards the supply of raw material and production of finished goods like bangles and ladles for trade to regional and inter-regional markets' (Bhan 1992: 133; Bhan and Kenoyer 1984). Lothal, another Harappan urban centre associated with such shell products, seems to have been directly linked with Nageshwar.

Discussion

If the above faunal evidence gets through standard taphonomic test regarding the representativeness of samples, perhaps we can present a new interpretation of the available evidence. The data pointing to a somewhat decreased representation of cattle remains and hence, slightly higher niche-width at some of the Harappan sites in northern regions in comparison with that in certain Pre-/Early Harappan sites should not be interpreted as decrease in the importance of this animal. The fact that a broader spectrum of faunal resources was being utilized by the Harappans 'is consistent with efforts to mitigate risks attendant upon the use of a restricted range of agricultural products by relatively larger or concentrated populations' (Meadow 1989a: 68). What seems to have happened at the Harappan as well as Early Harappan sites was a qualitative change in attitudes toward cattle. Some scholars have emphasized that it was the bull rather than the cow that received greater importance in Harappan society, and that certain special body traits like the hump and dewlap (non-existent in non-zebu cattle), were the result of cultural selection rather than natural selection. In the light of the purposive artistic representation of developed dewlap and hump on a large number of seals, it can be inferred that cattle had special status at the emotional or religious/ideological level, the latter not unconnected with social pride and power. The frequent representation on seals also of the mythical 'unicorn', conceptually not unconnected with cattle, further supports the importance of the latter. The representation of cattle on seals has been in much greater proportion than that of other animals; it is positively disproportionate to the actual representation of this animal in the osteological record. Again, the representation of bulls in the terracotta form and on pottery also has antecedents in several Early Harappan sites which implies that the extra-economic importance of cattle was an ongoing process in certain culture pockets prior to their integration into a unified urban Harappan tradition. Cattle, associated with certain human sentiments, might well have been one of the ideological factors responsible for this integration. The ideas expressed in this paragraph constitute only *an initial hypothesis* requires further examination (Chattopadhyaya 1999c).

In fact during Harappan times the importance of cattle might have risen from the utilitarian to the ideological level associated with what Miller (1985) calls the insurmountable and non-challengeable Harappan 'order' or 'style'—a social construct for the larger socio-political integration and successful reproduction of the unique Harappan tradition. One certainly cannot argue in favour of any 'sacred' status of the Harappan cattle, but it seems highly probable that a special bond developed between humans and this animal. At the same time, cattle remained part and parcel of peoples' diet. But given the other forms of its importance, not only at the mundane plane such as traction, transport and communications over a vast stretch of land, but also in non-material, cultural plane, it is most likely that some of its role as an item of diet (meat), and hence, the pressure on its slaughter, were carefully bypassed to other animals. This practice got a further momentum towards the end of the mature phase or in early second millennium BC, as is shown by the Dholavira evidence. This proposed small-scale calculated move in resource management was perhaps a thoughtful effort or strategy towards a long term goal—the preservation of cattle wealth leading to the continuity of a 'Great' tradition that also survived, though in diffused forms, through to the historical period and beyond (Chattopadhyaya 1999c). Or else, there was a socio-economic factor involved in this process: the central control on the cattle wealth was on the decline by the turn of the millennium and decentralizing social forces were in operation.

In this context Meadow raises a pertinent question regarding the means by which the non-cattle (including wild mammalian and aquatic) resources, were integrated into the Harappan domestic economy. He thus asks:

> did an occupational specialisation of hunter and fisherman come to be established to supply agricultural and urban communities or did previously segregated specialist occupational groups, so far invisible to archaeology, come to be included in Harappan communities or integrated into the Harappan system? (Meadow 1989a: 68)

In the light of Miller's insightful views on the Harappan 'order' playing the ideological role for continuity and group integration, the second point seems to be a fair possibility. This is thought provoking and Meadow has been seriously engaged in addressing this important issue. While the integration into the Harappan mainstream of diverse occupational groups like segregated hunter-gatherers, sheep and goats pastoralists and fishermen seems to have been a great possibility, the present author would like to suggest that one of the factors responsible for the rise of this situation was either inadequate supply of slaughtered cattle for food or the increasing concern among Harappans for the long term survival of the cattle populations.

We have stated above that cattle played a pivotal role in shaping Indian civilization. The conventional practice in history and archaeology has always been to catch the dominant trend and highlight the mainstream or the 'core' tradition. But the task of an investigator should not be limited to this line alone; it should also consider less abundant and 'hidden' data. In other words, human relationships with other animals, domestic or wild, need to be unfolded as far as is possible, despite the limited nature of the data. The roles played by wild animals as well as domesticates like sheep, goats, camels, donkeys and horses, or by the anonymous peoples associated with them, for example, in the development of South Asian civilizations were also important and cannot be overlooked (see Section 5C).

4.4 The Chalcolithic and the Iron Age

While high level human activities took place during much of the early and Mid-Holocene in north-western and western regions, the remaining parts of the subcontinent were no *terra incognita*. We have discussed the Neolithic farming communities of southern and north-central India cereal cultivation and cattle rearing being the common preoccupation. The use of copper was not exclusive to the Harappan tradition. The alternative copper ores of eastern India, the Chhotanagpur plateau, for example, were utilized by the ancient communities of Bihar, Orissa and West Bengal. This is reflected from the material culture uncovered at several eastern Neolithic-Chalcolithic sites, also associated with rice cultivation and domestic cattle. It is possible that by the late third millennium BC the knowledge as well as practice of rice cultivation was widespread in regions beyond the eastern fringes of the Harappan Civilization. In the previous section we had discussed shift in economic practices around the early second millennium BC in which (a) certain *kharif* cereals, including rice, began to be grown and (b) new domesticates like camel, donkey and horse found a prominent place in the society. This economic shift associated with new summer-sown cereals (also reflecting a greater utilization of annual harvesting seasons) on the one hand, and new means of animal-based traction, transport and communications was indicative of either rise in populations towards the beginning of the second millennium BC, or the lowering of the resource base or both, and thus facilitated movements of peoples and rise of new settlements outside the eastern and southern peripheries of the Harappan 'empire'. This second shift is consistent with the recent claims about environmental changes and the drying up of the ancient bed of the river Ghagghar by this time.

We have also discussed the possibility that Rajasthan and the highlands of Madhya Pradesh became the new cradle by the fifth millennium BC of cattle- and sheep/goats-based pastoralism that not only continued in subsequent millennia but also spread across a larger area of the country. So by the end of the mature phase of the Harappan Civilization, say around 2000 BC, a new phase of interaction began between the Harappans (including materially less distinguished non-urban folks) and archaeologically less-stamped communities of different regions: Gujarat, eastern Rajasthan, western Madhya Pradesh and Deccan, on the one hand, and western Uttar Pradesh on the other. In fact the rise of 'distinctive' Chalcolithic traditions in these regions between c. 2000 BC and 1500 BC generally coincided with the gradual phasing out of the homogeneous, mature Harappan tradition.

What were the common traits between the Harappan or its diluted, Late Harappan tradition and these diverse traditions? This has been a matter of inconclusive debates in archaeology. As far as the faunal evidence is concerned, a few animals—cattle in the main, but also others like horse and donkey, might have constituted the link, though in an indirect way.

A large number of Chalcolithic and Iron Age sites in these diverse settings have been excavated with the recovery of faunal remains. Some of the important such sites are Ahar in south-eastern Rajasthan, Kayatha, Navdatoli in western Madhya Pradesh; Nashik, Nevasa, Inamgaon, Daimabad, Walki and Kaothe in the Deccan; and Hastinapura, Lal Qila, Atranjikhera, and Jhusi in the Ganga-Yamuna Doab. While the general pattern of animal exploitation at these sites is characterised by the predominant position of domestic cattle, other domesticates like sheep, goats and pig were also kept and slaughtered for food. Dog remains, though certainly not abundant, are associated with most of these sites, and this animal had a close symbiotic tie with human society. Wild ungulates include a number of species of deer, such as spotted deer, sambar and barasingha, and antelopes like blackbuck. Turtle and fish are the other frequently reported resources.

The faunal compositions somewhat vary at different sites depending upon the (a) taphonomic factors affecting the differential survival of bones, (b) local social and ecological factors, and to a lesser extent, (c) temporal factor. However, the general scenario is essentially a repetition of the pattern we have noted in the Harappan context.

(a) Central and Western India

Ahar in south-eastern Rajasthan and Kayatha in north-western Madhya Pradesh are the early Chalcolithic sites with distinctive material culture traits that developed around the late third millennium BC outside the eastern fringes of the Harappan domain. The 'Ahar Culture' (*c.* 2200-1800 BC) and the 'Kayatha Culture' (*c.* 2000-1800 BC) were followed by another distinctive Chalcolithic tradition (Malwa Culture) discovered at Maheshwar and Navdatoli (*c.*1800-1200 BC). Animal remains recovered from above sites, as well from some Iron age sites like Nagda and Ujjain have been examined by experts and constitute the subject of the present discussion.

The Ahar faunal assemblage, examined by Shah (1969), contained the remains mostly of domestic animals like cattle, buffalo, sheep, goats, pig, dog. The only wild ungulate identified at the site is barasingha. From Kayatha the animals identified are domestic animals like cattle, sheep, goats, pig and horse. In addition, elephant and blackbuck have also been identified (Alur 1975; Clason 1979). The faunal remains from Navdatoli (Malwa tradition) have been studied initially by George (1958) and then by Clason (1974, 1979). The faunal spectrum is broader than that noted for the Ahar and Kayatha traditions. Here the same typical range of domestic animals, viz., cattle, buffalo, sheep, goats and pig has been identified. Also was identified the presence of the horse and donkey. The wild fauna includes antelopes like nilgai, blackbuck, gazelle, and some of the cervids like sambar, barasingha, spotted deer and hog deer. At all these sites, cattle remains dominate.

The recent excavations at Balathal, a site in the Mewar region of Rajasthan, have thrown new light on the early Chalcolithic (Misra 1997). The excavation has revealed two cultural periods: the Chalcolithic, similar to that noted for Ahar, and the Maurya-Kushana. The beginning of the site may be placed on radiocarbon evidence in the late third millennium BC Animal bones from both the periods have been recovered and examined in detail (Thomas and Joglekar 1996). As many as 38 species comprising mammals, reptiles, aves, fish and molluscs have been identified. However, cattle remains alone constitute a large majority (about 65 per cent) in the entire collection. This animal was an important source of meat in both the periods. An important feature of this site is what has been described as the intentional burials of cattle skulls, and the entire body of cats and blackbucks in both the periods.

The faunal remains from Early Iron age traditions of this broad region have been recovered mainly from Ujjain and Nagda and studied by Nath (1968a). The twelve species identified from Ujjain are cattle, buffalo, sheep, goats, pig, horse, donkey, elephant, chital, blackbuck, mongoose and the chank shell *Xancus pyrum* L. According to Nath the elephant and mongoose remains are akin to those from Harappa and Mohenjo Daro. The animals represented at Nagda are cattle, buffalo, sheep, goats, barasingha, sambar, Great Indian crocodile (*Crocodilus palustris*) and three species of river turtle: *Lissemys punctata*, *Chitra indica* and *Trionyx gangeticus*. This is the first report of *Crocodilus palustris* in Indian archaeology.

(b) The Deccan

In the Deccan the major Chalcolithic traditions are the Savalda (*c.* 2200-2000 BC) and the Jorwe (*c.*1400-700 BC), the latter being preceded by the Malwa tradition at several sites in northern Deccan. A sizeable number of Chalcolithic sites (some of which also yielding Iron age materials) in the valleys of the rivers Tapi, Godavari and Bhima have been reported and excavated. Faunal remains were recovered from most of these sites and studied. Such sites include Nashik, Jokha, Kaothe, Dhatva, Walki, Daimabad, Nevasa, Apegaon, Inamgaon and Tuljapur Garhi (Thomas n.d.). Detailed faunal reports are, however, available for three sites: Inamgaon, Walki, and Kaothe. Some observations on these results is being presented below; for the remaining sites, detailed reviews by Thomas (1984a) and Thomas and Joglekar (1994) may be consulted. Inamgaon materials have in fact been most intensively studied by at least four faunal experts over the last couple of decades (Badam 1977; Clason 1979; Thomas 1988; Pawankar and Thomas 1997). The importance, therefore, of the archaeozoological study of Inamgaon cannot be over-emphasized.

The high point of some of these detailed faunal studies lies in the proposed evolution of human-animal relationships in relation to environmental changes. At Inamgaon, for example, the assemblage from the first two periods (Malwa and Early Jorwe, *c.* 1800-1000 BC) contained a large majority of cattle remains (more than 60 per cent), which dropped to as low as 20 per cent in the subsequent Late Jorwe period beginning around 1000 BC. The taxa with increased representation in the Late Jorwe period are antelopes and other small ruminants, including sheep/goats. This drastic change in the relative taxonomical abundance and hence in the nature of economy has been explained in terms of environmental changes by the end of the second millennium BC Naturally cattle-based farming communities at the site paved the way for sheep/goats herders and the material culture associated with the Late Jorwe period shows marked changes from that in the preceding period. This is a classic example of interpretations based on environmental determinism on culture change and a reflection of the growing influence of the New Archaeology in India (Dhavalikar et al. 1988). Also intensive are the faunal studies of Walki and Kaothe where the presence of most of the known domestic animals and a large number of wild ungulates has been documented, as at Inamgaon (Thomas and Joglekar 1994). At Walki, for example, apart from the usual domesticates like cattle, buffalo, sheep, goats, and pig, common pets like dog and cat, as also horse and donkey have been identified. The wild animals here include wild Indian buffalo, gaur, four species each of antelopes and deer, wild boar and carnivores like leopard, tiger, wolf, and jackal, as also hare. At Kaothe, sloth bear, the small Indian civet (*Viverricula indica*), porcupine, and common house rat have been identified (Thomas and Joglekar 1990).

Another early Chalcolithic tradition in south Gujarat is represented by the site Prabhas Patan (*c.*1700-1200 BC), which is not far from the concentration zone of the Deccan Chalcolithic. The animals identified from the site include domestic animals like cattle, buffalo, sheep, goats, pig and wild ungulates like gazelle, barasingha, chital, wild boar and porcupine (Thomas and Joglekar 1994). Cattle again is the most frequently represented animal.

From the Vidarbha and southern India a substantial number of Iron age and Megalithic sites have been located and excavated. However, the faunal assemblages from these sites are limited in number and their examinations have not provided any information that could be of much help for the reconstruction of past economic practices (see Thomas and Joglekar 1994 for details).

(c) The Ganga Plain

The cultural sequence in the Ganga-Yamuna Doab and the middle Ganga Valley came to light from some of the excavations at sites of U.P. like Ahichchhatra (Bareilly district), Hastinapura (Meerut district), Kaushambi near Allahabad (now in Kaushambi district), Atranjikhera (Etah district), Lal Qila (Bulandshahr district) and Sringaverapura (Allahabad district). Ochre Coloured Pottery (OCP) constitutes the earliest Post-Harappan Chalcolithic tradition that flourished between the early and mid-second millennium BC, though some isolated cases tend to indicate its origin in the late third millennium BC It covered an area from the doab (maximum concentration of sites) in the east to Rajasthan and Haryana/ Punjab in the west. There is a strong correlation between the OCP and the enigmatic Copper-Hoard tradition.This is followed in the doab region by the Black-and-Red Ware (BRW) tradition, as at Atranjikhera, and the Painted Grey Ware tradition at other sites like Hastinapura. But at Atranjikhera, the former tradition precedes the PGW one. These two cultural traditions can be dated between mid-second and mid-first millennium BC and both are associated with iron technology. This is followed by the Northern Black Polished Ware (NBPW) tradition (seventh/sixth to first centuries BC). Chalcolithic and Iron age sites also emerged along certain tributaries of the Ganga in its middle reaches, particularly in the Belan Valley (Koldihwa), and in districts Gorakhpur (Imlidih Khurd, Narhan) and Basti (Siswania). The painted Black-and-Red Ware occurring in many such northern sites has been ascribed to the 'Narhan' tradition, dated to *c.* 1300 BC and later (Singh 1994). Chalcolithic traditions with regional variations are also reported from Bihar and West Bengal along the lower Ganga Valley.

The faunal evidence connected with the OCP tradition is available from two sites, Atranjikhera and Lal Qila (Shah 1983, 1997). The faunal sample size from the former was very small and only two taxa could be identified, domestic cattle, represented by thoracic and lumbar vertebrae, thoracic rib and humerus, and tiger (*Panthera tigris*), represented by a lone ulnar fragment. This gives a highly biased picture of the faunal economy. But the recent study of the Lal Qila assemblage led to the identification of nine taxa, eight mammalian and an avian (*Gallus* sp). The mammals include one wild species, nilgai, and seven domestic species: cattle, buffalo, sheep, goats, pig, dog and horse. As per NISP values, the representation of cattle is highest (74.2 per cent), followed by buffalo (14.4 per cent), sheep and goats (together 4.1 per cent), pig (3.4 per cent), nilgai (2.2 per cent), dog (1 per cent), horse (0.5 per cent) and fowl (0.2 per cent). As no taphonomic analyses have been carried out, one is not sure about the representativeness of the faunal data. The sample recovered in fact shows a bias towards large bones and it is not safe to draw any serious conclusion about relative taxonomical abundance. The only conclusion that could be drawn is the fact that the OCP people practised animal husbandry involving a number of domesticates, and that they were familiar with the horse. Another important feature was the use of arrowheads, points and styluses of bones.

The faunal remains from the next cultural tradition in the Ganga-Yamuna Doab, the Black-and-Red Ware, come from Atranjikhera alone. Shah (1983) reports the presence of mammals like cattle, buffalo, sheep, dog and barasingha, and the river turtle *Lissemys punctata granosa* and bonyfish. The sample size being small, the percentage representation of these species does not make much sense. Not unexpectedly, cattle remains dominate the limited faunal assemblage.

Faunal remains from PGW contexts were first recovered at Hastinapura (Period II) and were studied by Nath (1954-5). Bhagawanpura (district Kurukshetra, Haryana) and Atranjikhera are the two other principal sites with faunal evidence. At Hastinapura Nath identified the remains of cattle, buffalo, sheep, pig, and horse. For Nath, the bones of these species resemble those from Harappa and Mohenjo Daro. The same five species are also reported by Shah (1983) from the corresponding period at Atranjikhera, in addition to goats, dog, barasingha, nilgai, leopard, fowl, monitor lizard (*Varanus flavescens*), three species of river turtle, and the bivalve. At Bhagawanpura, five species, viz., cattle, sheep, goats, dog, and horse have been identified (Joshi 1978), whereas at Rupar (Ambala district, Haryana) the horse and donkey have been reported (Nath 1968a). At Atranjikhera the remains of young individuals of most of the domestic animals are also represented in the assemblage and people were essentially cattle-breeders who at times took to hunting (Shah 1983). The significant point is the peoples' association with the horse.

The classic PGW tradition of the Doab is rare at sites around Allahabad or regions further east and northeast. A local variant termed as pre-NBPW tradition is more common as one finds at Jhusi and Siswania on the bank of the Kuwano in Basti district. Further east along the Kuwano is situated the site Imlidih Khurd (Gorakhpur district) where a regional variant of BRW—the painted BRW, associated with the Narhan culture of *c*. 1300-1000 BC has been identified. Painted BRW was first brought to light at the excavation at Narhan, located in the Ghaghra Valley, again in Gorakhpur district. At Imlidih, BRW overlies a different local ceramic of the early/mid-second millennium BC, associated with corded ware and described as the Pre-Narhan tradition. The present author examined the faunal assemblages not only from Siswania, but those also Narhan, Imlidih and Koldihwa (Chalcolithic and Iron Age) (Chattopadhyaya 1985b, 1991, 1994, n.d.a-c). While cattle bones are as usual the most frequent, a common feature of the Koldihwa Chalcolithic phase associated with (unpainted) BRW, the 'Narhan' phases at Narhan and Imlidih, and the pre-NBPW phase at Siswania, is the caballine horse of a uniform build.

Faunal remains of NBPW levels have been examined from a number of sites: Hastinapur, Atranjikhera, Rajghat in Varanasi District (Narain and Agrawala 1978) and Siswania in Basti District (Chattopadhyaya n.d.a). The present author is also studying the faunal assemblages from Jhusi (Allahabad), and Amil Koni (Rewa district). The mammalian fauna identified at these sites are cattle, buffalo, sheep, goats, pig, dog, horse, donkey, elephant, barasingha, blackbuck, and nilgai. Non-mammalian fauna include bivalve and three species of turtle (*Lissemys punctata*, *Trionyx gangeticus*, *Chitra indica*). The NBPW assemblage at Siswania also contains skeletal remains of at least two species of fish, spotted deer, hog deer, pygmy hog (*Sus salvanius* Hodgson), and most probably the wild boar (Chattopadhyaya n.d.c). The only other site which has yielded the remains of the pygmy hog is Damdama (Table 2).

Despite marked changes in pottery types, there is little perceptible change in the faunal composition between the NBPW and the subsequent Sunga-Kushana periods. The same combination of domestic animals—cattle, buffalo, sheep, goats, pig, dog, etc.—along with turtle, fish and a few species of deer/antelope appear during the Sunga-Kushana period. Nath (1954-5, 1968a) has reported the presence of the elephant at Hastinapura and the horse and donkey at Taxila. He writes that 'two distinct forms of humped cattle have been found at Taxila as at Harappa' (1968a: 11). On the basis of study of faunal remains from Siswania, Jhusi and Lal Kot (an early Medieval and Medieval site in Delhi, excavated by B.R. Mani), a few observations may be made. The complete and careful burial of a cow in a circular grave at Siswania suggests an intimate relationship that humans had developed with this animal by the Kushana period. Although cattle remains continue to appear during the Gupta period at Jhusi, the proportional representation of this animal shows a substantial decrease from the preceding NBPW period. The limited faunal assemblage from the medieval levels at Lal Kot is dominated by sheep and goats bones, and curiously no cattle remains occur at the site before the Sultanate period. This last point requires corroboration in the light of fresh evidence from other such sites.

Discussion

The horse, appearing initially appearing in later Harappan phases in Gujarat as well as northern regions and subsequently in the central Indian sites of Kayatha and Navdatoli, on the one hand, and the Ganga-Yamuna Doab, on the other, is then noticed in north-central India towards the late second and early first millennium BC. It may be postulated that it played an important role in the rapid 'transportation' of various peoples and associated material cultures across a wider landscape, which strongly correlates with the later Vedic evidence of the eastern expansion of the Indo-Aryan language speaking peoples.

5. SOME THEORETICAL ISSUES

A. Origins of Cattle Domestication in South Asia

The earliest available evidence of cattle domestication (humpless, *Bos taurus* of Western Asia and Europe) comes from Argissa-Magula in Thessaly in the seventh millennium BC, and Çatal Hüyük (Anatolia), towards the late seventh millennium, but interestingly, not from the 'hearth' of animal domestication in West Asia (Chattopadhyaya 1999c). The geographical separation of the early domestication of two different groups of animals—cattle and sheep/goats—reinforces the claim that there can be more than one centre of domestication, involving different types of specialization. The cattle of Thessaly and Anatolia evolved from *Bos primigenius* of the same region. The Mehrgarh evidence is conclusive the domestication of *Bos indicus*, or zebu around a similar time range, and Meadow is confident that this development in the Kachi Plain was independent of that noted for Europe and Asia Minor. The question is, what is the ancestry of the zebu?

Grigson (1980) has set aside the possibility of zebu deriving from the gaur, banteng or kouprey. Some zoologists believe that, like the *Bos taurus*, *Bos indicus* too evolved from *Bos primigenius*. However, according to Zeuner (1963), the huge *Bos namadicus*, represented in Pleistocene fossil assemblages from various river deposits in India, should be regarded as the direct ancestor of *Bos indicus*. Although Epstein and Mason (1984) question whether *Bos primigenius* and *Bos namadicus* are as separate species, but Grigson has convincingly justified such a distinction on the basis of comparative cranial morphology and morphometric analyses. In *Bos namadicus* the supracristal portion of the occipit overhangs the infracristal, a feature also noticed in *Bos indicus*, but absent in *Bos primigenius*, and its derivative, *Bos taurus* (Grigson 1980). This has been taken as strong evidence of two distinct lines in cattle phylogeny. Two implications of Grigson's study are worth mentioning. First, *Bos namadicus* must have survived throughout India in the Terminal Pleistocene and into the Holocene. Second, *Bos indicus* originated in India: 'either there was autochthonous domestication or *Bos taurus* was imported into India and crossed with the surviving *namadicus* to give rise to *Bos indicus*' (Grigson 1985: 427). The comparative study of blood group factors and haemoglobin variants between several breeds of zebu and some humpless cattle breeds of western origin support this theory of separate ancestry and origins (Naik 1978). It is of some interest to note that 'hill cattle' examined by Naik, still found in the wild in the Kumaon region, show a much greater resemblance to the Indian breeds than to the western ones. Beside, there is a karyotypic difference in their Y chromosomes: the former has an acrocentric Y chromosome, while the latter has a submetacentric Y chromosome (Kiefer and Cartwright 1968; Hsu and Benirschke 1967-77). This observable chromosomal difference provides 'additional support to the theory of their independent origin' (Naik 1978: 27). Thus the combined evidence—morphological and genetic—clearly refutes the hypothesis of Epstein and Mason and lends considerable support to Zeuner's original suggestion that zebu originated from a separate South Asian progenitor, the now extinct *Bos namadicus*.

The Mehrgarh evidence reflects this metamorphosis quite convincingly (Meadow 1981, 1986, 1989a,b). What is not explicit in the archaeological evidence, and may be a fair possibility, is that the inhabitants of Mehrgarh were not necessarily involved directly in the domestication of all the three animal taxa: cattle, sheep and goats. Rather, domestication was the result of an ongoing human-animal symbiotic relationships involving specialized, mobile or semi-sedentary communities (for respective species) operating in wide areas around the site (Chattopadhyaya 1999c). Directly involved or not, Mehrgarh just one, reported, site that developed access to and capitalized on, these new resources and handed down to the posterity that essential component (humped cattle, for example), which helped in building the singular character of the Indian tradition. However, cultural attitudes toward this animal seems to have undergone a qualitative change during the Harappan period.

B. The Mesolithic Origins of Animal Husbandry

The much talked-about question of the Mesolithic origins of animal husbandry requires discussion. We have seen the lack of any such evidence from Langhnaj or the Ganga Valley sites. The presence of domestic animals, like cattle, sheep and goats, has been claimed from the early Mesolithic phases at Bagor and Bhimbetka (both being placed in the fifth millennia). If we accept for a while the high antiquity of Adamgarh rock-shelter site as a supporting argument for the above claims regarding the rise of animal husbandry during the early Mesolithic period, the combined evidence is indeed interesting. Because of the fact that these sites lie outside the range of the natural habitats of wild sheep and goats, the domestic status of sheep and goats from Bagor and Adamgarh may not be doubted. But was domestication invented in this region during the Mesolithic period? The possibility can be ruled out, as there is no evidence for within-site evolution of domestic from wild forms. The natural habitats of the wild progenitors is the distant ranges of the western Himalayas. Why and how these wild animals came to plains as far as Rajasthan and Madhya Pradesh in the absence of human protection, remains the question. But we now know for certain that domestication of sheep/goats (as also cattle) had already taken place in the north-western (Mehrgarh) during the sixth millennium. It is likely that pastoral communities of Baluchistan associated with cattle and/or sheep/goats became more widespread during late sixth and fifth millennia and made their influence felt as far as Rajasthan and the uplands of Madhya Pradesh. So rather than explaining animal herding/domestication at Bagor or Adamgarh as a locally developed phenomenon, the wider archaeological evidence may be interpreted as suggesting the presence of a north-west–south-east *mobility axis* of sheep/goat herders and cattle pastoralists. This mobility of populations and their possible diversification in terms of additional specialization in course of a *cladogenetic* mode of evolution served, in all likelihood, as the initial impetus and necessary basis for the rise and development of various Chalcolithic village settlements (including the Early Harappans), thus cross-cutting this long mobility axis during the intervening period between the Neolithic Mehrgarh and the Bronze Age Harappan Civilization.

This possibility is based on the culture-historical perspective in which an invention, like animal domestication has a single centre of origin and spreads through human migration or diffusion. There can be another possibility. We have discussed Naik's suggestion regarding the presence of more than one centre of cattle domestication in the subcontinent. The early prehistoric paintings at Bhimbetka and other rock-shelter sites of central India and the eastern Vindhyas, dated to a time span of Early- to Mid-Holocene, depict both humpless, large cattle with long horns (identified with the extinct *Bos namadicus*), and smaller humped cattle (zebu), the former predating the latter (Neumayer 1983; Chattopadhyaya 1991). Despite the existence of the said mobility axis, it may be possible that central India was an independent region of close human-cattle symbiotic relationships leading to cattle husbandry. In that case, the domestic cattle of Bagor, Bhimbetka or Adamgarh might have been of central Indian rather than Mehrgarh origin. But the same cannot be suggested for sheep and goats.

C. On the Social Dimension of Animal Husbandry

A few words on certain social dimensions of animal husbandry, including its formative stages (Chattopadhyaya 1999c). History is witness to the fact that there have been innumerable, peripheral or marginal groups in the past with no less contribution towards the growth of civilization, than core groups. The Bronze Age civilization in the Indus Valley was certainly built on a highly evolved agricultural economy based on, amongst others, domestic cattle. But in no point of time was human society monolithic. It has been argued elsewhere that in regions with environmental/topographic heterogeneity, coupled with population pressure, human groups diversify in terms of specialization to form a 'partitioned social network system' and that this kind of system, based on ecological complementarity, developed early in the central Ganga Valley and adjoining plateau (Chattopadhyaya 1991). The north-western region including the Indus Valley was another such region where cladogenesis was in motion at least since the Early Holocene. In fact, Shaffer and Lichtenstein (1989) have argued that throughout the third and second millennia the Indus Valley witnessed the development of a complex cultural mosaic of related but distinct ethnic groups and it is highly probable that this socio-cultural diversity had a longer history. Strait-jacket explanations in archaeology on changes from hunting-gathering to domestication have their limitations. Implicit in such explanations is the idea that one brilliant group gradually succeeded in taming a number of wild animals and inventing the cultivation of plants, thus changing the course of history. But in practical terms it may not be possible for a single group to do everything necessary for its long term survival. A study of animal behaviour reveals that the responses of different animal species toward humans are not alike and that no single mental formula, on the part of humans, works in taming all potential domesticates or capturing and exploiting wild animals. What seems more plausible, is that under differing conditions, human groups diversify in terms of specialization on one or other natural resource or a limited combination of them, be it individual animal groups like cattle, donkey, camel, deer, snake, fish, or various plants, or even inorganic substances like stones, thus forming a systems network in which specialized products move between different groups (Chattopadhyaya 1991; cf. Gadgil and Malhotra 1983). There is a great possibility that the faunal picture at Mehrgarh or for that matter various Mesolithic sites of India reflects the presence of several interesting groups specializing in different resources, some of which may not even have been local residents. It is management which is crucial to this mechanism. The complementarity may not be symmetrical across the social boundary and the process may lead to the emergence of a powerful group, such as sedentary cereal agriculturalists, or a social formation involving different groups (with a common value), which can skilfully manage the socio-economic proceedings and dominate the course of history. The development from the early Neolithic through to the rise of the centralized mature Harappan Civilization may be better understood with the help of this cladogenetic mode of evolution. Cattle were, no doubt, integral to Harappan culture, and it is highly probable that there was considerable amount of control on cattle wealth by skilful managers. But it was individual marginal cattle pastoral groups, despite their peripheral existence and historical anonymity, contributed significantly to the origins and growth of the civilization. It is heartening, indeed, to find the application of faunal data to address the problem of cattle pastoralism in Gujarat in the second millennium BC (Varma 1991; see also Rissman and Chitalwala1990 for cattle pastoralism from Oriyo Timbo). Again given the social compulsion among Harappans to use a broader spectrum animal resource than what was practised in Pre- or Early Harappan times, a number of specialist occupational groups—hunter-gatherers, sheep and goats pastoralists, fishing communities—might have been integrated into the Harappan system, as Meadow has suggested. Identifying such important, but invisible to archaeology, groups constitutes a challenging area of research.

D. The Continuity of Traditions

The evidence from the Mesolithic site of Langhnaj is interesting in the sense that, despite its contemporaneity with the Harappan sites of the region and probable cultural contact with agricultural communities (Possehl and Kennedy 1979), the faunal spectrum here does not include domestic animals. This shows that culture contact does not necessarily mean acculturation or shifts in the lifestyles of hunter-gatherers. It contradicts the commonly held view that hunter-gatherers would necessarily take advantage of the knowledge of more sophisticated economic practices and right away adapt to this 'improved' way of life, should such opportunities come their way. Conservatism associated with such traditional peoples is of the essence that should be taken into consideration while theorizing on hunter-gatherer adaptation.

In the context of the Southern Neolithic it has been observed that the pattern of faunal representation does not change at succeeding levels associated with metals. This faunal evidence goes hand in hand with the overall archaeological evidence, as far as the question of continuity is concerned. Bhattacharya (1989) correctly observes the lack of change in the character of the sites either in habitation or the overall material culture even after the arrival of metals. This observation on conservatism is consistent with present author's views of hunting-gathering society at Langhnaj. For Bhattacharya, however, 'culturally such an unchanged status inspite of the knowledge of a new and better technology is untenable' (ibid.: 138). This is a classic example where one finds a clear glimpse of technological determinism (a modernist bias, associated with the New Archaeology), increasingly advocated by scholars dealing with traditional societies. As a matter of fact, untenability lies not in the preservation of cultural values, but perhaps in the simplistic understanding of culture change, characteristic of 'scientistic' archaeologists. The long argument built up by Bhattacharya to explain this lack of change was uncalled for (ibid: 138-9), as explanation might have been required only in the contrary situation. The simple reasons for the above noted prehistoric behavioural pattern, which some scholars find as 'abnormal', are that not all peoples are unhappy with the present or unnecessarily concerned about their future, and that mental deprivation is largely a modernist virus! Despite the fact that the World Wars have been viewed as symbolizing the end of modernism (Mills 1959; cf. Spengler, quoted in Wood 1997), archaeologists are making untiring efforts towards perpetuating the conventional status of archaeology as a modernist discourse. In fact, we could study prehistoric societies with the understanding that primitive economics is the reverse of modern economic orthodoxy centering on the culture-specific notion of 'progress' (cf. Sahlins 1974).

6. FUTURE PROSPECTS

Archaeo-faunal studies in India have certainly made some headway since Independence, yet a lot remains to be achieved, particularly in the areas of alternative research design, methodology (including taphonomy) and interpretation. A glance at the archaeozoological literature shows that most of the work in India comprises are either faunal reports or short papers discussing technical details on animals, humans being relegated to the background. Very few works are available that centre around faunal data to address archaeological problems. Specialization is certainly important but it has to come forward to join hands with archaeology: a revisionist one, involving fundamental research. The present wave of interdisciplinary studies should not be taken to imply an arithmetic addition of different parts of the whole, as the whole is much more than sum of the constituent parts. The problems being tackled by technical experts should originate from the core, archaeology in the present case, and the results of the analyses should be meaningfully interpreted and situated in a unified research framework. In other words, a core–periphery–core path has to be followed, otherwise the core itself might be lost in the peripheral jungle. For this, continuous feedback is essential, thus breaking the artificially created boundaries between hard core sciences and archaeology.

Archaeologists too need to interact more intensely with experts. They have to discuss the problems that they raise from time to time and to work out jointly as to how this technique could usefully address their problems. It is not enough to say that so many domestic animals were present at a site. If domestication, be it its origin or dispersal, is the focus of research, one should be able to define criteria for identifying the domestic status of certain animals and carrying out analysis on statistically significant sample size. But archaeologists and faunal experts need to realize that this line of inquiry was influenced by the anagenetic mode of evolution and is certainly not the only problem to engage us. There are other important archaeological issues like site formation process (Binford 1978), settlement pattern (Rowley-Conwy 1980; Chattopadhyaya 1991), hunter-gatherer decision making (Mithen 1990), inter- and intra-site assemblage variability and within-site social hierarchy or ranking (Hesse and Wapnish 1985) or even social and symbolic dimensions of human action, as suggested by post-processual archaeologists like Ian Hodder and Chris Tilley, which could be usefully addressed with the help of faunal analysis. It is re-emphasized that, whatever be the objective of an archaeo-faunal study, taphonomy should be the initial as well as central part of faunal analysis for the reasons outlined above. Finally, it is in the self-interest of archaeologists, particularly those of the younger generation, to study the faunal remains directly, with the background technical knowledge that they routinely receive during their formative period of studies.

Unfortunately, however, the future does not appear very bright. While taking stock of archaeological studies over the fifty years of Independence, one finds that the discipline witnessed two generations of dedicated workers. It is an irony of civilization that the 'developmental' work in a newly independent nation, such as ours, has been detrimental to the preservation of archaeological heritage. The first generation archaeologists had more opportunities to select suitable sites for excavation, though, barring a few exceptions, they did not pay adequate attention to the optimum recovery of faunal remains. Even if they did, recovery was partial. But the last quarter of the present century has witnessed all-round 'development' including intensive agricultural practices, population encroachments on vacant lands, and construction of dams. In fact, the map of the country visualized on a satellite imagery is dreadful; the first thing that comes to our attention is the countless dragon-like dark patches, interpreted as water reservoirs, filling up a substantial part of the landscape. All this has caused destruction of archaeological sites, and the present archaeologists have to be satisfied with rescue archaeology of sites already partially destroyed, for example, by canal diggers or construction workers. Archaeological sites that existed in hundreds in certain areas a few years ago are being destroyed in an alarming rate. Under such circumstances, one cannot hope to recover large assemblages of animal remains for systematic study. This is not the concern of faunal experts alone; it is a collective problem. Post-modernism, which is more dangerous modernism, has already set in motion and will rule the next century. Being anti-historical, post-modernism vehemently denies past and tradition (Chattopadhyaya 1999a). Archaeology now stands at the threshold of modernism and post-modernism; waiting to be dislodged by post-modern agencies.

REFERENCES

Agrawal, D.P. 1982. *The Archaeology of India*. London: Curzon Press.

Allchin, B. and R. Allchin 1982. *The Rise of Civilization in India and Pakistan*. Cambridge: Cambridge University Press.

Allchin, F.R. 1960. *Piklihal Excavations*. Hyderabad: Government of Andhra Pradesh.

——— 1961. Utnur Excavations. Hyderabad: Government of Andhra Pradesh.

——— 1963. *Neolithic Cattle Keepers of South India: a Study of the Deccan Ashmounds*. Cambridge: Cambridge University Press.

——— 1969. Early Domestic Animals in India and Pakistan, in *Domestication and Exploitation of Plants and Animals* (P.J. Ucko and G.W. Dimbleby Eds.), pp. 317-22. London: Duckworth.

Alur, K.R. 1969. Animal Remains from Sanganakallu, in *Excavations at Sanganakallu 1964-65* (Z.D. Ansari and M.S. Nagaraja Rao), pp. 29-38. Poona: Deccan College.

——— 1971a. Skeletal Remains, in *Protohistoric Cultures of Tungabhadra Valley* (M.S. Nagaraja Rao), pp. 107-24. Dharwad: M.S. Nagaraja Rao.

——— 1971b. A Note on the Animal Bones from Terdal Excavation 1966, in *Studies in Indian History and Culture* (S. Ritti and B.R. Gopal Eds.), pp. 23-30. Dharwad.

——— 1971c. Report on the Animal Remain, in *Report on the Excavation at T. Narsipur* (M. Seshadri), pp. 19-104. Mysore: Department of Archaeology and Museums.

——— 1975. Animal Remains from Kayatha, in Excavations at Kayatha (Z.D. Ansari and M.K. Dhavalikar Eds.), pp. 157-63. Pune: Deccan College.

——— 1980. Faunal Remains from the Vindhyas and the Ganga Valley, in *Beginnings of Agriculture* (G.R. Sharma, V.D. Misra, D. Mandal, B.B. Misra and J.N. Pal Eds.), pp. 201-30. Allahabad: University of Allahabad.

——— 1990. *Studies in Indian Archaeology and Palaeontology*. Dharwad: Srihari Prakashana.

Anthony, D. 1997. Current Thoughts on the Domestication of the Horse in Asia, *South Asian Studies* 13: 315-16.

Badam, G.L. 1977. Faunal Remains from Chalcolithic Inamgaon, *Man and Environment* I: 58-60.

——— 1984. Holocene Faunal Material from India with Special Reference to Domesticated Animals, in *Animals and Archaeology 3: Early Herders and Their Flocks* (J. Clutton-Brock and C. Grigson Eds.), pp. 339-54. Oxford: BAR International Series 202.

Badam, G.L. and V.G. Sathe 1991. Subsistence Economy of the Indus Civilization, in *Indian Archaeological Heritage: Sh. K.V. Soundara Rajan Felicitation Volume* (C. Margabandhu, K.S. Ramachandran, A.P. Sagar and D.K. Sinha Eds.), pp. 135-43. Delhi: Agam Kala.

Bailey, G. (Ed.) 1983. *Hunter-Gatherer Economy in Prehistory: a European Perspective*. Cambridge: Cambridge University Press.

Banerjee, S. 1979-80. The Archaeological Material from West Bengal in the Zoological Survey of India, *Puratattva* 11: 162-4.
Bhan, Kuldeep K. 1992. Shell Industry, in *Excavation at Nageshwar, Gujarat: a Harappan Shell Working Site on the Gulf of Kutch* (K.T.M. Hegde, K.K. Bhan, V.H. Sonawane, K. Krishnan and D.R. Shah Eds.), pp. 125-36. Vadodara: the M.S. University of Baroda.
——— 1994. Cultural Development of the Prehistoric Period in North Gujarat with Reference to Western India, *South Asian Studies* 10: 71-90.
Bhan, K.K. and J.M. Kenoyer 1984. Nageshwar: a Mature Shell Working Site on the Gulf of Kutch (Gujarat), *Journal of the Oriental Institute of Baroda* 34: 67-75.
Bhattacharya, D.K. 1989. *An Outline of Indian Prehistory*. Delhi: Palaka Prakashan.
Binford, L.R. 1972. *An Archaeological Perspective*. New York: Seminar Press.
——— 1978. *Nunamiut Ethnoarchaeology*, New York: Academic Press.
——— 1980. Willow Smoke and Dogs' Tails: Hunter-gatherer Settlement Systems and Archaeological Site Formation, *American Antiquity* 45: 4-20.
——— 1981. *Bones: Ancient Men and Modern Myths*. New York: Academic Press.
——— 1983a. *In Pursuit of the Past: Decoding the Archaeological Past*. London: Thames and Hudson.
——— 1983b. *Working at Archaeology*. Orlando: Academic Press.
——— 1984. *Faunal Remains from Klasies River Mouth*. Orlando: Academic Press.
Blumenschine, R.J. and U.C. Chattopadhyaya 1983. A Preliminary Report on the Terminal Pleistocene Fauna of the Middle Son Valley, in *Palaeoenvironments and Prehistory in the Middle Son Valley* (G.R. Sharma and J.D. Clark Eds.), pp. 281-4. Allahabad: University of Allahabad.
Bökönyi, S. 1969. Archaeological Problems and Methods of Animal Domestication, in *Domestication and Exploitation of Plants and Animals* (P.J. Ucko and G.W. Dimbleby Eds.), pp. 219-29. London: Duckworth.
——— 1973. Some Problems of Animal Domestication in the Middle East, in *Domestikationsforschung und Geschichte der Haustiere* (J. Matolcsi Ed.), pp. 69-75. Budapest: Kiado.
Braend, M. 1971. Haemoglobin Variants in Cattle, *Animal Blood Groups and Biochemical Genetics* 2: 15-21.
Braidwood, L.S., R.J. Braidwood, B. Howe, C.A. Reed and P.J. Watson (Eds.) 1983. *Prehistoric Archaeology Along the Zagros Flanks*. Chicago: The Oriental Institute.
Braidwood, R.J. and B. Howe 1960. *Prehistoric Investigations in Iraqi Kurdistan*. Chicago: Oriental Institute Studies in Ancient Oriental Civilization 31.
Brain, C.K. 1976. Some Principles in the Interpretation of Bone Accumulations Associated with Man, in *Human Origins: Louis Leakey and the East African Evidence* (G.Ll. Isaac and E.R. McCown Eds.), pp. 97-116. Menlo Park (California): Staples Press.
——— 1981. *Hunters or the Hunted? an Introduction to African Cave Taphonomy*. Chicago: University of Chicago Press.
Campagnoni, B. 1979. Preliminary Reports on the Faunal Remains from Protohistoric Settlements in Swat, in *South Asian Archaeology 1977* (M. Taddei Ed.), pp. 697-700. Naples: Instituto Universitare Orientale.
Chaplin, R.E. 1971. *The Study of Animal Bones from Archaeological Sites*. London: Seminar Press.
Chattopadhyaya, I. 1990. 'Seasonality of Occupation in the Mesolithic Ganges Valley: the Faunal

Evidence', Paper Presented at the 6th Conference of the International Council of Archaeozoology held at the Smithsonian Institution, Washington, D.C., 1990 (Abstract).

——— 1999. 'Writing' in Space: an Interpretation of Prehistoric Mortuary Practices in the Central Ganga Valley (in press).

Chattopadhyaya, I. and U.C. Chattopadhyaya 1990. The Spatial Organization of Mortuary Practices in Mesolithic Ganga Valley: Implications for Territoriality, in *Adaptation and Other Essays* (N.C. Ghosh and S. Chakrabarti Eds.), pp. 103-21. Shantiniketan: Vishva-Bharati.

Chattopadhyaya, K. 1975. *The Vedic Religion*. Varanasi: Centre of Advanced Study in Philosophy. Banaras Hindu University.

——— 1976. *Studies in Vedic and Indo-Iranian Religion and Literature*, Vol. 1. Varanasi: Bharatiya Vidya Prakashan.

Chattopadhyaya, U.C. 1985a. Faunal Studies in Archaeology: Current Trends in Methods and Concepts, *Man and Environment* IX: 3-20.

——— 1985b. A Preliminary Report on Faunal Remains from Narhan, Gorakhpur, *Bharati* (New Series) 3: 177-84.

——— 1988. Subsistence Variability and Complex Social Formations in Prehistoric Ganga Valley: Problems and Prospect, *Man and Environment* XII: 135-152.

——— 1991. A Study of Subsistence and Settlement Patterns during the Late Prehistory of North-central India. Ph.D. Dissertation. Cambridge: University of Cambridge.

——— 1995. Application of Satellite Remote Sensing to the Study of Mid-Ganga Palaeochannels and Its Archaeological Implications. Project Report Submitted to the National Remote Sensing Agency, Department of Space, Hyderabad.

——— 1996. Settlement Pattern and the Spatial Organization of Subsistence and Mortuary Practices in the Mesolithic Ganges Valley, North-central India, *World Archaeology* 27(3): 461-76.

——— 1999a. The Post-Modern Denial of the Past: Challenges Before Archaeology in the Twenty-first Century, in *Sraddhanjali: G.R. Sharma Memorial Volume* (S.C. Bhattacharya Ed.). Allahabad: Department of Ancient History. University of Allahabad.

——— 1999b. The Mesolithic Fauna of India, with Special Reference to Central Ganga Valley, in *Mesolithic Cultures of India* (V.D. Misra Ed.). Allahabad: Department of Ancient History, University of Allahabad (in Press).

——— 1999c. Domestication of Cattle in the Ancient World, in *History of Indian Science, Philosophy and Culture*, Vol. V: *History of Agriculture in India* (L. Gopal Ed.). New Delhi: Indian Council of Philosophical Research (in press).

——— 1999d. The Ganges Neolithic, in *Encyclopedia of Prehistory* (M. Ember and P.N. Peregrine Eds.). New Haven: Human Relations Area Files Inc. (in press).

——— (n.d.a.) Faunal Remains from Lal Kot Excavations (1991-94). Submitted for publication to the Director of Excavation.

——— (n.d.b.) A Preliminary Report on the Faunal Remains from Imlidih Khurd, District Gorakhpur (U.P.) (in preparation).

——— (n.d.c.) Faunal Remains from Siswania, District Basti (U.P.) (in preparation).

Chitalwala, Y. M. and P.K. Thomas 1977-8. Faunal Remains from Khanpur and Their Bearing on the Culture, Economy and Environment, *Bulletin of the Deccan College Research Institute* 37: 11-14.

Clark, J.D. and G.R. Sharma 1983. A Discussion of Preliminary Results and Assessment of Future Research Potential, in *Palaeoenvironments and Prehistory in the Middle Son Valley* (G.R. Sharma and J.D. Clark Eds.), pp. 261-8. Allahabad: University of Allahabad.

Clarke, D.L. 1968. *Analytical Archaeology*. London: Methuen.
Clason, A.T. 1974. Archaeozoological Study in India, in *South Asian Archaeology 1973* (J.E. Lohuizen de Leeuw and J.M.M. Ubaghs Eds.), pp. 78-89. Leiden: E.J. Brill.
Clason, A.T. (Ed.) 1975. *Archaeozoological Studies*. Amsterdam: North-Holland Publishing Company.
Clason, A.T. 1979. *Wild and Domestic Animals in Prehistoric and Early Historic India*. Lucknow: the Ethnographic and Folk Culture Society.
——— 1984. Animal-Man Relationship in Southern Asia During the Holocene, in *South Asian Archaeology 1981* (B. Allchin Ed.), pp. 341-3. Cambridge: Cambridge University Press.
Clutton-Brock, J. 1965. *Excavations at Langhnaj, Part II: the Fauna*. Poona: Deccan College.
Conrad, R. 1966. *Die Haustiere in den Fruhen Kulturen Indiens*. Munchen: Franz Frank.
Cornwall, I.W. 1956. *Bones for the Archaeologist*. London: J.M. Dent & Sons Ltd.
Dales, G.F. and J.M. Kenoyer 1977. Shell Working at Ancient Balakot, Pakistan, *Expedition* 19 (2): 13-19.
Daniel, G. 1972. Editorial, *Antiquity* 46: 265.
Davis, S.J.M. 1987. *The Archaeology of Animals*. London: Batsford.
Dhavalikar, M.K., H.D. Sankalia and Z.D. Ansari (Eds.) 1988. *Excavation at Inamgaon*. Pune: Deccan College.
Driesch, A. von den 1976. *A Guide to the Measurement of Animal Bones from Archaeological Sites*. Cambridge (Mass.): Peabody Museum, Harvard University.
Eapen, J. 1960. A Report on the Animal Remains of Nevasa Excavation, in *From History to Prehistory at Nevasa (1954-56)* (H.D. Sankalia, S.B. Deo, Z.D. Ansari and S. Erhardt Eds.), pp. 531-6. Poona: Deccan College.
Efremov, J.A. 1940. Taphonomy: a New Branch of Palaeontology, *Pan American Geologist* 74: 81-93.
Epstein, H. and I.L. Mason 1984. Cattle, in *Evolution of Domesticated Animals* (I.L. Mason Ed.), pp. 6-27. London: Longman.
Fairservis, W.A. Jr. 1956. Excavations in the Quetta Valley, West Pakistan, *Anthropological Papers of the American Museum of Natural History* 45 (2).
Gadgil, M. and K.C. Malhotra 1983. Adaptive Significance of the Indian Caste System: an Ecological Perspective, *Annals of Human Biology* 10: 465-78.
George, J.C. 1955. Identification of Bones, in *Excavations at Nasik and Jorwe 1950-51* (H.D. Sankalia and S.B. Deo Eds.), pp. 142-3. Poona: Deccan College.
——— 1958. Identification of Bones from the Chalcolithic Layer, in *Excavations at Maheshwar and Navdatoli 1952-53* (H.D. Sankalia, B. Subbarao and S.B. Deo Eds.), pp. 256-7. Poona-Baroda: Deccan College and the M.S. University of Baroda.
Ghosh, N.C. 1986. The Chalcolithic Background of West Bengal, in *Indian Studies* (A. Ray, H. Sanyal and S. Ray Eds.), pp. 15-19. New Delhi: Books & Books.
Gilchrist, R. and H.C. Mytum 1986. Experimental Archaeology and Burnt Animal Bone from Archaeological Sites, *Circaea* 4 (1): 29-38.
Grayson, D.K. 1984. *Quantitative Zooarchaeology*. Orlando: Academic Press.
Grigson, C. 1978. Towards a Blueprint for Animal Bone Reports in Archaeology, in *Research Problems in Zooarchaeology* (D.R. Brothwell, K.D. Thomas and J. Clutton-Brock Eds.), pp. 121-8. London: Institute of Archaeology Occasional Paper 3.
——— 1980. The Craniology and Relationships of Four Species of *Bos*. 5. *Bos indicus* L, *Journal of Archaeological Science* 7: 3-32.
——— 1985. *Bos indicus* and *Bos namadicus* and the Problem of Autochthonous Domestication

in India, in *Recent Advances in Indo-Pacific Prehistory* (V.N. Misra and P. Bellwood Eds.), pp. 425-8. New Delhi: Oxford-IBH.

Gupta, H.P. 1976. Holocene Palynology from Meander Lake in the Ganga Valley, District Pratapgarh, U.P., *The Palaeobotanist* 25: 109-19.

Hecker, H.M. 1982. Domestication Revisited: Its Implications for Faunal Analysis, *Journal of Field Archaeology* 9: 217-36.

Hesse, B. and P. Wapnish 1985. *Animal Bone Archaeology*. Washington, D.C.: Taraxacum.

Higgs, E.S. (Ed.) 1972. *Papers in Economic Prehistory*. London: Cambridge University Press.

——— 1975. *Palaeoeconomy*. London: Cambridge University Press.

Higgs, E.S. and M.R. Jarman 1972. Criteria of Animal Domestication, in *Papers in Economic Prehistory* (E.S. Higgs Ed.). London: Cambridge University Press.

Hsu, T.C. and K. Benirschke 1967-1977. *An Atlas of Mammalian Chromosomes*, 1-10. Berlin: Springler.

IAR 1967-8. *Indian Archaeology—a Review*. New Delhi: Archaeological Survey of India.

Jarman, M.R., G.N. Bailey and H.N. Jarman (Eds.) 1982. *The Early European Agriculture*. London: Cambridge University Press.

Jarrige, J.-F. and R.H. Meadow 1980. The Antecedents of Civilization in the Indus Valley, *Scientific American* 243(2): 122-33.

Joshi, J.P. 1978. A Note on the Excavation at Bhagawanpura, *Puratattva* 8: 178-80.

Kane, V.S. 1989. Animal Remains from Rojdi, in *Harappan Civilization and Rojdi* (G.L. Possehl and M.H. Raval Eds.), pp. 182-4. New Delhi: Oxford-IBH.

Kenoyer, J.M. 1989. Socio-Economic Structures of the Indus Civilization as Reflected in Specialized Crafts and the Question of Ritual Segregation, in *Old Problems and New Perspectives in the Archaeology of South Asia* (J.M. Kenoyer Ed.): pp. 183-92. Madison: University of Wisconsin. Wisconsin Archaeological Reports 2.

Khan, F., J.R. Knox and K.D. Thomas 1991. *Explorations and Excavations in Bannu District, North-West Frontier Province, Pakistan, 1985-1988*. London: British Museum Occasional Paper 80.

Kiefer, N.M. and T.C. Cartwright 1968. Sex Chromosome Polymorphism in Domestic Cattle, *Journal of Heredity* 59 (1): 35-6.

Klein, R.G. and K. Cruz-Uribe 1984. *The Analysis of Animal Bones from Archaeological Sites*. Chicago: Chicago University Press.

Kolke, H. and N. Ohtaishi 1985. Prehistoric Hunting Pressure Estimated by the Age Composition of Excavated Sika Deer (*Cervus nippon*) Using the Annual Layer of Tooth Cement, *Journal of Archaeological Science* 12: 443-56.

Legge, A.J. 1978. Archaeozoology or Zooarchaeology?, in *Research Problems in Zooarchaeology* (D.R. Brothwell, K.D. Thomas and J. Clutton-Brock Eds.), pp. 129-32. London: Institute of Archaeology Occasional Paper 3.

Levine, M. 1986. The Vertebrate Fauna from Meare East 1982, *Somerset Levels Papers* 12: 61-71.

Maltby, J.M. 1985. Patterns in Faunal Assemblage Variability, in *Beyond Domestication in Prehistoric Europe* (G.W.W. Barker and C. Gamble Eds.), pp. 33-74. London: Academic Press.

Marshall, J. 1931. *Mohenjo-daro and the Indus Civilization*. London: Arthur Probsthain.

Meadow, R.H. 1979. Prehistoric Subsistence at Balakot: Initial Considerations of the Faunal

Remains, in *South Asian Archaeology 1977* (M. Taddei Ed.), pp. 275-315. Naples: Istituto Universitario Orientale, Seminario di Studi Asiatici.

——— 1980. Animal Bones: Problems for the Archaeologist Together with some Solutions, *Paleorient* 6: 65-77.

——— 1981. Early Animal Domestication in South Asia: a First Report of the Faunal Remains from Mehrgarh, Pakistan, in *South Asian Archaeology 1979* (H. Härtel Ed.), pp. 143-79. Berlin: Dietrich Reimer Verlag.

——— 1984a. Animal Domestication in the Middle East: a View from the Eastern Margin, in *Animals and Archaeology 3: Early Herders and Their Flocks* (J. Clutton-Brock and C. Grigson Eds.), pp. 309-37. Oxford: B.A.R. International Series 202.

——— 1984b. Notes on the Faunal Remains from Mehrgarh, with a Focus on the Cattle (*Bos*), in *South Asian Archaeology 1981* (B. Allchin Ed.), pp. 34-40. Cambridge: Cambridge University Press.

——— 1986. Faunal Exploitation in the Greater Indus Valley: a Review of Recent Work to 1980, in *Studies in the Archaeology of India and Pakistan* (J. Jacobson Ed.), pp. 43-64. New Delhi: Oxford-IBH.

——— 1987. Faunal Exploitation Patterns in Eastern Iran and Baluchistan: a Review of Recent Investigations, in *Orientalia Iosephi Tucci Memoriae Dicata* (G. Gnoli and L. Lanciotti Eds.), pp. 881-916. Rome: IsMEO.

——— 1989a. Continuity and Change in the Agriculture of the Greater Indus Valley: the Palaeoethnobotanical and Zooarchaeological Evidence, in *Old Problems and New Perspectives in the Archaeology of South Asia* (J.M. Kenoyer Ed.): Wisconsin Archaeological Reports, Vol. 2, pp. 61-74. Madison: University of Wisconsin.

——— 1989b. A Note on the Distribution of Faunal Remains During the Later Periods at Mehrgarh (Baluchistan, Pakistan), in *South Asian Archaeology 1985* (K. Frifelt and P. Sørensen Eds.), pp. 167-75. London: Curzon Press Ltd.

——— 1991. Faunal Remains and Urbanism at Harappa, in *Harappan Excavations 1986-1990* (R.H. Meadow Ed.), pp. 89-106. Madison, Wisconsin: Prehistory Press.

——— 1993. The Past, Present and Future of Bioarchaeological Studies in Pakistan with Special Reference to Mohenjo-daro and the Indus Civilization, *Pakistan Archaeology* 28: 183-215.

Meadow, R.H. and A. Patel 1997. A Comment on 'Horse Remains from Surkotada' by Sandor Bökönyi, *South Asian Studies* 13: 308-15.

Meadow, R.H. and M.A. Zeder (Eds.) 1978. *Approaches to Faunal Analysis in the Middle East.* Harvard: Peabody Museum Bulletin 2.

Miller, D. 1985. Ideology and the Harappan Civilization, *Journal of Anthropological Archaeology* 4: 34-71.

Mills, C.W. 1959. *The Sociological Imagination.* Oxford: Oxford University Press.

Mishra, H.M. 1982. The Ecology and Behaviour of Chital (*Axis axis*) in the Royal Chitwan National Park, Nepal [With Comparative Studies of Hog Deer (*Axis porcinus*), Sambar (*Cervus unicolor*) and Barking Deer (*Muntiachus muntjak*)]. Ph.D. Dissertation. Edinburgh: University of Edinburgh (British Library Microfilm).

Misra, V.N. 1971. Two Late Mesolithic Settlements in Rajasthan, *Journal of the University of Poona* (Humanities Section) 35: 59-77.

——— 1973. Problems of Palaeo-Ecology, Palaeo-Climate and Chronology of the Microlithic

Cultures of North-West India, in *Radiocarbon and Indian Archaeology* (D.P. Agrawal and A. Ghosh Eds.), pp. 58-72. Bombay: Tata Institute of Fundamental Research.

——— 1989. Stone Age India: an Ecological Perspective, *Man and Environment* XIV (1): 17-64.

——— 1997. Balathal, A Chalcolithic Settlement in Mewar, Rajasthan, India: Results of First Three Seasons' Excavation, *South Asian Studies* 13: 251-73.

Mithen, S. 1990. *Thoughtful Foragers*. Cambridge: Cambridge University Press.

Nagaraja Rao, M.S. and K.C. Malhotra 1965. *The Stone Age Hill Dwellers of Tekkalakota*. Poona: Deccan College.

Naik, S.N. 1978. Origin and Domestication of Zebu Cattle (*Bos indicus*), *Journal of Human Evolution* 7: 23-30.

Naik, S.N., P.K. Sukumaran and L.D. Sanghvi 1969. Haemoglobin Polymorphism in Indian Zebu Cattle, *Heredity* 24: 239-47.

Narain, A.K. and P.K. Agrawala 1978. *Excavations at Rajghat (1957-58, 1960-65)*. Varanasi: Banaras Hindu University.

Narain, L.A. 1970. Neolithic Settlement at Chirand, *Journal of Bihar Research Society* 56: 16-35.

——— 1972. A Study in the Techniques of the Neolithic Bone Tool Making at Chirand and Their Probable Uses, *Journal of Bihar Research Society* 58: 1-24.

Narayan, B. 1996. *Prehistoric Archaeology of Bihar*. Patna: K.P. Jaysawal Research Institute.

Nath, Bhola 1954-5. Animal Remains, *Ancient India* 10-11: 107-20.

——— 1957. Animal Remains from Maski, *Ancient India* 13: 111-20.

——— 1962-63. Animal Remains from Rangpur, *Ancient India* 18-19: 153-60.

——— 1967. Animal Remains from Adamgarh Rock Shelters, *Indian Museum Bulletin* 2: 28-38.

——— 1968a. Advances in the Study of Prehistoric and Ancient Animal Remains in India: a Review, *Records of the Zoological Survey of India* 61 (3-4), 1963: 1-63.

——— 1968b. Animal Remains from Brahmagiri (Mysore State, India), *Records of the Zoological Survey of India* 61 (3-4), 1963: 65-88.

——— 1968c. Animal Remains from Rupar and Bara Sites, Ambala District of East Punjab, India, *Bulletin of the Indian Museum* 3 (1-2): 69-116.

——— 1969. The Role of Animal Remains in the Early and Prehistoric Culture of India, *Bulletin of the Indian Museum* 4 (2): 102-10.

Nath, Bhola and M.K. Biswas 1969. Animal Remains from Alamgirpur, *Indian Museum Bulletin* 4 (1): 43-52.

Nath, Bhola and M.K. Biswas 1980. Animal Remains from Chirand, Saran District, Bihar, *Records of the Zoological Survey of India* 76: 115-24.

Nath, Bhola and G.V.S. Rao 1985. Animal Remains from Lothal Excavations, in *Lothal: a Harappan Port Town 1955-62*, Vol. II (S.R. Rao), pp. 636-50. New Delhi: Archaeological Survey of India.

Neumayer, E. 1983. *Prehistoric Indian Rock Paintings*. Delhi: Oxford University Press.

Noe-Nygaard, N. 1977. Butchering and Marrow Fracturing as a Taphonomic Factor in Archaeological Deposits, *Palaeobiology* 3: 218-37.

Olsen, S.J. 1971. *Zooarchaeology: Animal Bones in Archaeology and their Interpretation*. Addison-Wesley Modular Publications 2.

——— 1979. Archaeologically, What Constitutes an Early Domestic Animal?, in *Advances in Archaeological Method and Theory*, Vol. 2 (M.B. Schiffer Ed.), pp. 175-97. New York: Academic Press.

Paddayya, K. 1975. The Faunal Background of the Neolithic Culture of South India, in *Archaeozoological Studies* (A.T. Clason Ed.), pp. 329-34. Amsterdam: North Holland Publishing Company.

——— 1993. Ashmound Investigations at Budihal, Gulbarga District, Karnataka, *Man and Environment* XVIII (1): 57-87.

Patel, A. 1997. The Pastoral Economy of Dholavira: a First Look at Animals and Urban Life in Third Millennium Kutch, in *South Asian Archaeology 1995* (R. Allchin and B. Allchin Eds.), pp. 101-13. New Delhi: Oxford-IBH.

Pawankar, S.J. and P.K. Thomas 1997. Fauna and Subsistence Pattern in the Chalcolithic Culture of Western India with Special Reference to Inamgaon, *Anthropozoologica* 25-6, Section 5: 737-46.

Payne, S. 1972. Partial Recovery and Sample Bias: the Results of Some Sieving Experiments, in *Papers in Economic Prehistory* (E.S. Higgs Ed.), pp. 49-64. London: Cambridge University Press.

Perkins, D. 1964. Prehistoric Fauna from Shanidar, Iraq, *Science* 144: 1565-6.

——— 1969. Fauna of Çatal Hüyük: Evidence for Early Cattle Domestication in Anatolia, *Science* 164: 177-9.

Perkins, D. and P. Daly 1968. Hunter's Village in Neolithic Turkey, *Scientific American* 219: 97-106.

Possehl, G.L. 1992. The Harappan Civilization in Gujarat: the Sorath and Sindhi Harappans, *The Eastern Anthropologist* 45 (1-2): 117-54.

Possehl, G.L. and K.A.R. Kennedy 1979. Hunter-gatherer/Agriculturalist Exchange in Prehistory: an Indian Example, *Current Anthropology* 20 (3): 592-3.

Possehl, G.L., Y.M. Chitalwala, P. Rissman, G.E. Wagner, P. Crabtree and J. Longenecker 1985. Preliminary Report on the Second Season of Excavation at Rojdi: 1983-84, *Man and Environment* IX: 80-100.

Prasad, A.K. 1997. A Note on the Food Habits of the Neolithic People of Bihar, in *Indian Prehistory: 1980* (V.D. Misra and J.N. Pal Eds.), pp. 161-2. Allahabad: University of Allahabad.

Prashad, B. 1936. Animal Remains from Harappa, *Memoirs of the Archaeological Survey of India* 51: 1-60, 7 pls.

Prater, S.H. 1971. *The Book of Indian Animals*. Third Revised Edition. Bombay: Bombay Natural History Society.

Rackham, J. 1994. *Animal Bones*. London: British Museum Press.

Reddy, V.R. 1978. *A Study of the Neolithic Culture of Southwestern Andhra Pradesh*. Hyderabad: Government of Andhra Pradesh.

Reed, C.A. 1959. Animal Domestication in the Prehistoric Near East, *Science* 130 (3389): 1629-39.

——— 1969. The Pattern of Animal Domestication in the Prehistoric Near East, in *Domestication and Exploitation of Plants and Animals* (P.J. Ucko and G.W. Dimbleby Eds.), pp. 361-80. London: Duckworth.

——— 1983. Archaeozoological Studies in the Near East: a Short History (1960-1980), in *Prehistoric Archaeology Along the Zagros Flanks* (L.S. Braidwood, R.J. Braidwood, B. Howe, C.A. Reed and P.J. Watson Eds.), pp. 511-36. Chicago: The Oriental Institute.

Renfrew, C. 1978. *Before Civilization: the Radiocarbon Revolution and Prehistoric Europe*. London: Penguin Books.

Rissman, P.C. and Y.M. Chitalwala 1990. *Harappan Civilization and Oriyo Timbo*. New Delhi: Oxford-IBH.

Roberts, T.J. 1977. *The Mammals of Pakistan*. London: E. Benn.

Rowley-Conwy, P. 1980. Continuity and Change in the Prehistoric Economies of Denmark 3700 BC-2300 BC. Ph.D. Dissertation. Cambridge: University of Cambridge.

Roy, A. 1993. A Preliminary Study on Faunal Remains of Dholavira 1990-92. Ph.D. Dissertation. New Delhi: Institute of Archaeology.

Sahlins, M. 1974. *Stone Age Economics*. London: Tavistock.

Sahu, BP 1988. *From Hunters to Breeders*. New Delhi: Anamika Prakashan.

Schaller, G.B. 1967. *The Deer and the Tiger: a Study of Wildlife in India*. Chicago: University of Chicago Press.

Sewell, R.B.S. and B.S. Guha 1931. Zoological Remains, in *Mohenjodaro and the Indus Civilization*, Vol. 2 (J. Marshall Ed.), pp. 649-73, London: Arthur Probsthain.

Shaffer, J.G. and D.A. Lichtenstein 1989. Ethnicity and Change in the Indus Valley Cultural Tradition, in *Old Problems and New Perspectives in the Archaeology of South Asia* (J.M. Kenoyer Ed.), pp.117-26. Madison: University of Wisconsin.Wisconsin Archaeological Reports 2.

Shah, D.R. 1969. Animal Remains, in *Excavations at Ahar (Tambavati)* (H.D. Sankalia, S.B. Deo and Z.D. Ansari Eds.), pp. 237-45. Poona: Deccan College.

——— 1971. A Note on Unmodified Animal Remains from Bagor, *The Eastern Anthropologist* 24(3): 319-20.

——— 1973. Animal Remains from Kodekal Excavation, in *Investigations on the Neolithic Culture of Shorapur Doab* (K. Paddayya), pp. 92-5. Leiden: E.J. Brill.

——— 1980. Animal Remains from Kanewal, in *Excavations at Kanewal* (R.N. Mehta, K.N. Momin and D.R. Shah), pp. 74-6. Baroda: the M.S. University of Baroda Archaeological Series 17.

——— 1983. The Animal Remains, *in Excavations at Atranjikhera: Early Civilization of the Upper Ganga Basin*. Delhi: Motilal Banarsidass.

——— 1997. The Animal Remains, in *Excavations at Lal Qila: a Habitational OCP Site and Unique Copper Hoard from Kiratpur*, pp. 193-8. Jaipur: Publication Scheme.

Shah, D.R. and Kuldeep K. Bhan 1992. Faunal Remains, in *Excavation at Nageswar, Gujarat: a Harappan Shell Working Site on the Gulf of Kutch* (K.T.M. Hegde, K.K. Bhan, V.H. Sonawane, K. Krishnan and D.R. Shah), pp. 145-7. Baroda: the M.S. University of Baroda.

Sharma, A.K. 1974. Evidence of Horse from the Harappan Settlement at Surkotada, *Puratattva* 7: 75-6.

——— 1979-80. Excavations at Gufkral, *Puratativa* 11: 19-25.

——— 1980-81. Animal Bones from Gufkral: Evidence of Human and Non-human Activities, *Puratattva* 12: 31-6.

——— 1990. Animal Bone Remains, in *Excavation at Surkotada 1971-72 and Exploration in Kutch* (J.P. Joshi), pp. 372-83. New Delhi: Archaeological Survey of India.

Sharma, G.R. 1975. Seasonal Migrations and Mesolithic Lake Cultures of the Ganga Valley, in *K.C. Chattopadhyaya Memorial Volume*, pp. 1-20. Allahabad, Department of Ancient History, Culture and Archaeology, University of Allahabad.

Sharma, G.R., V.D. Misra, D. Mandal, B.B. Misra and J.N. Pal 1980. *Beginnings of Agriculture*. Allahabad: Abinash Prakashan.

Singh, P. (Ed.) 1994. *Excavations at Narhan—1984-89*. Varanasi: Banaras Hindu University.

Thapar, B.K. 1987. Fresh Light on the Neolithic Cultures of India, in *Archaeology and History: Essays in Memory of Shri A. Ghosh* (B.M. Pande and B.D. Chattopadhyaya Eds.), Vol. I, pp. 247-54. Delhi: Agam Kala.

Thomas, P.K. 1975. Role of Animals in the Food Economy of the Mesolithic Culture of Western and Central India, in *Archaeozoological Studies* (A.T. Clason Ed.), pp. 322-8. Amsterdam: North-Holland Publishing Company.

——— 1984a. The Faunal Background of the Chalcolithic Culture of Western India, in *Animals and Archaeology 3: Early Herders and Their Flocks* (J. Clutton-Brock and C. Grigson Eds.), pp. 355-61. Oxford: BAR International Series 202.

——— 1984b. Faunal Assemblage of Veerapuram, in *Veerapuram: a Type Site for Cultural Study in the Krishna Valley* (T.V.G. Sastri, M. Kasturi Bai and J.V.P. Rao Eds.), Appendix C, pp. i-xi. Hyderabad: Bhavani Printers.

——— 1988. Faunal Assemblage, in *Excavation at Inamgaon*, Vol. I, Part II (M.K. Dhavalikar, H.D. Sankalia and Z.D. Ansari), pp. 822-961. Pune: Deccan College.

——— 1989. Utilization of Domestic Animals in Pre- and Protohistoric India, in *The Walking Larder: Patterns of Domestication, Pastoralism and Predation* (J. Clutton-Brock Ed.), pp. 108-12. London: Unwin Hyman.

——— (n.d.) Development of Archaeozoology in India. Paper presented at the National Seminar on 'Indian Archaeology Since Independence: Retrospect and Prospects', held at the University of Allahabad (14-16 November 1998).

Thomas, P.K. and P.P. Joglekar 1990. Faunal Remains, in *Excavations at Kaothe* (M.K. Dhavalikar, V. Shinde and S. Atre Eds.), pp. 233-64. Pune: Deccan College.

——— 1994. Holocene Faunal Studies in India, *Man and Environment* XIX: 179-203.

——— 1996. Faunal Remains from Balathal, Rajasthan: a Preliminary Report, *Man and Environment* XXI (1): 91-7.

Thomas, P.K., P.P. Joglekar, V.D. Misra, J.N. Pandey and J.N. Pal 1995. A Preliminary Report of the Faunal Remains from Damdama. *Man and Environment* XX (1): 29-36.

——— 1996. Faunal Evidence for the Mesolithic Food Economy of the Gangetic Plain with Special Reference to Damdama. Paper presented at the International Union of Prehistoric and Proto-historic Sciences, Section 16, Colloquium XXXIII.

Ucko, P.J. and G.W. Dimbleby (Eds.) 1969. *Domestication and Exploitation of Plants and Animals*. London: Duckworth.

Uerpmann, H.-P. 1973. Animal Bone Finds and Economic Archaeology: a Critical Study of 'Osteo-archaeological' Methods, *World Archaeology* 4: 307-22.

Varma, S. 1991. Villages Abandoned: the Case of Mobile Pastoralism in Post-Harappan Gujarat, *Studies in History* (New Series) 7 (2): 279-300.

Wemmer, C.M. (Ed.) 1987. *Biology and Management of the Cervidae*. Washington, D.C.: Smithsonian Institution Press.

Williams, M.A.J. and K. Royce 1982. Quaternary Geology of the Middle Son Valley, North-central India: Implications for Prehistoric Archaeology, *Paleogeography, Paleoclimatology and Paleoecology* 38: 139-62.

——— 1983. Alluvial History of the Middle Son Valley, North-Central India, in *Palaeoenvironments and Prehistory in the Middle Son Valley* (G.R. Sharma and J.D. Clark Eds.), pp. 9-21. Allahabad: University of Allahabad.

Wilson, B., C. Grigson, and S. Payne (Eds.) 1982. *Ageing and Sexing Animal Bones from Archaeological Sites*. Oxford: BAR International Series 109.

Wood, E.M. 1997. What is the 'Postmodern' Agenda?, in *In Defence of History: Marxism and the Postmodern Agenda* (E.M. Wood and J.B. Foster Eds.), pp. 1-16. New York: Monthly Review Press.

Zeuner, F.E. 1963. *A History of Domesticated Animals*. London: Hutchinson.

Archaeometallurgical Studies in India: a Review

D.P. AGRAWAL

This essay reviews the archaeometallurgical studies in India. I have discussed below these studies in two periods: (1) Pre-Independence and (2) Post-Independence. Mainly copper, iron and zinc will be discussed. I agree with Tripathi and Mishra (1997) that the key to studying archaeometallurgy is through the study of tribal metallurgical practices. Even for the present-day requirements of the country, it may be good to support these tribal industries as small scale enterprises. This will not only cater to the local demands of iron but will be able to provide quality products.

COPPER

Pan-Asian Backdrop

Let me first give a pan-Asian view of early copper technology as a backdrop to the South Asian archaeometallurgy. Small beads and pins of hammered copper found at Ali Kosh in western Iran and Cayonu Tepesi in Anatolia date from ninth-seventh millennia BC and were made from native, unmelted copper. In Asia Minor, however, where copper was far less accessible, metallurgical development was very rapid. Cities and civilizations, which produce both wealth and demand, seem far more effective than natural resources in stimulating successful technical innovation. The earliest crucible furnace remains so far identified were found at Abu Matar, near the old city of Beersheba in Israel on a site used between 3300 and 3000 BC. The earliest vitrified copper bearing slags were found at Catal Huyuk in Anatolia at about 7000-6000 BC, and cast native copper was found at Sialk in Iran (4500 BC). Egyptian artefacts produced from cast and wrought native copper appear to date from the period between 5000 and 4000 BC. The technique of melting and casting native copper originated in Anatolia, and between 5000 and 4000 BC spread rapidly over much of the West Asia.

SMELTING OF COPPER ORES

Most of the copper artefacts produced after 3500 BC were extracted from ore as native copper became scarce. The earliest was extracted from oxide or carbonate ores which could be smelted in the primitive furnaces. In prehistory, as in modern times, the bulk of the world's supply of copper appears to have been obtained from chalcopyrite.

ALLOYING

The earliest Egyptian artefacts of arsenical copper were produced around 4000 BC in Predynastic times. It has been suggested that the Sumerians who made these artefacts came from the Caucasus and were instrumental in transferring the arts of metallurgy from the land of Elam (part of Iran) into Babylonia. The low tin bronze were the precursors of the later true bronzes containing 8-10 per cent tin. it appears that at Ur they suddenly discovered the concept of alloying, and rapidly developed and optimised the composition of bronze (Darling 1990). The true Bronze age in Egypt, when artefacts containing 8-10 per cent of tin were produced, did not begin until 2000 BC. About 3000 BC, the concept of bronze manufacture was acquired by the Sumerians. The earliest tin bronzes so far identified appear to date from the fourth millennium BC at the site of Tepe Giyan, in western Iran. Early Bronze Age artefacts have also been found in southern China, Thailand and Indonesia.

CASTING TECHNIQUES

During the early years of the third millennium foundry processes appear to have developed rapidly in Sumer. Before 3000 BC most of the copper artefacts from Ur were simply fabricated from sheet metal. By 2700 BC, however, very refined cast copper artefacts were being produced, probably by a version of shell moulding. The Egyptians also had developed the expertise of producing hollow copper and bronze statuary by 2500 BC, Many large Egyptian statues were cast with an internal sand core,which is still present in some of the figures which have been found. The *cire perdue* (lost wax processes) technique, had been mastered by Egyptian craftsmen before 2200 BC.

EAST ASIA

The Shang bronzes (1400 and 1027 BC) are now world famous for their artistic merit and technical virtuosity. These ritual objects, which were produced entirely by casting, were notable for the richness of their relief patterns and also for their mass and solidity, although some smaller wine vessels were also produced. One vessel weighed over 1.6 tonnes and had abviously been cast in a multipart mould. The high tin, but lead free, alloys would be easier to melt and cast in large quantities. Bronzes containing 20 per cent tin are invariably associated with the manufacture of bells.

SOUTH-EAST ASIA

For a long time, South-East Asia was considered a backwater for the development of metallurgy. But the evidence discovered recently has clearly established that this area is also an early centre of metallurgy (White 1997). Concerning the dating of bronze in the Ban Chiang sequence Tables 2 and 1 give pertinent results from the pottery programme. Previous charcoal based dating has been criticized due to ambiguity of association between the dated sample and cultural contexts. The dates reported here derive directly from rice tempered burial pottery with impeccable provenance. The carbon from rice temper comes from short-lived plant remains incorporated into clay fabric shortly after harvest during vessel manufacture and deposited into its archaeological context probably within a few years.

With the exception of two dramatically old dates which cannot be considered archaeologically meaningful (both from Early Period Phase III), five of the determinations are internally consistent both in terms of their relative phase assignment, and in terms of their position within superimposed sequences of graves. The early evidence of bronze at Ban Ching appears by Early Period II/III in both burial and non-burial contexts. The calibrated AMS dates, particularly the AA-12538, indicate an early 2nd millennium BC date for this part of the sequence (White 1997).

SOUTH ASIAN ARCHAEOMETALLURGY

Ores

No significant source of native copper is known in India. Copper ores show concentration in parts of Rajasthan, Madhya Pradesh, Andhra Pradesh, Karnataka, Gujarat and Bihar, but there are other areas such as Baluchistan, the Himalayan belt in Uttar Pradesh, etc., that were significant in protohistoric and historic periods. Large lead mines are known in Rajasthan, Kumaun (Uttar Pradesh) and Andhra Pradesh. Old copper workings have been reported at such places at Barudih, and take back the antiquity of copper mining in Singhbhum to the second millennium BC. That the metal resources of the Chhotanagpur plateau were opened up in the second millennium BC is suggested by the find of tin as an alloy in a small finger ring from the 'Chalcolithic' levels at Bahiri in Birbhum, West Bengal, dated *c.* 1000 BC.

The main Indian copper minerals are: (i) chalcopyrite, (ii) bornite and (iii) tetrahedrite (iv) covellite. Present mining areas for copper are mainly located in Rajasthan, Bihar, Andhra Pradesh and Kumoan (Uttar Pradesh), though there are several other minor deposits. The Singhbum belt extends over a region 130 km long and up to 8 km wide. In 1959 the reserves of copper ore were estimated to be 3.8 million tonnes with an average 2.47 per cent copper content. New explorations have brought to light copper ore resources of Patharghora, Surdha, Kendadih, Room-Sidheshar area. Guntur (Andhra Pradesh), South Arcot (Tamil Nadu) and Hassan (Karnataka) districts have good copper ore deposits. The Guntur belt is 4.8 km long. Ore deposits of Jabalpur are very poor. The veins of copper minerals are only 6" to 3' in width. The minerals are chalcopyrite and tetrahedrite. These ores are in the dolomite limestone regions. In Rajasthan, copper ore mines are located in practically all over. The most important of them is at Khetri-Singhana in Jaipur district. This belt stretches from Singhana to Raghunathpura, about 80 km. In this belt, in the Mardan-Kudan section there is a reserve of 28 million tonnes of ore with 0.8 per cent copper and in the Dariba area 0.5 million tonnes of ore deposit with 2.5 per cent copper.

The mineral found in these places is chalcopyrite which is usually disseminated in schists and phyllites.

The main occurrences of copper ores in Rajasthan are:

(i) Khetra Singhana (Jaipur district)
(ii) Kho-Dariba (Alwar district)
(iii) Delwara Kirovli (Udaipur district)
(iv) Debari (Udaipur district)

Sana Ullah (in Marshall 1931) considered the following probable sources of copper ores for the Indus Civilization: Baluchistan (Shah Ballaul, Raskuh and Kojak Amran); Afghanistan (Shah Maksud and Kalih Zeri); Persia (Anarak); Indore (Madhya Pradesh); Nellore and Krishna districts (Andhra Pradesh); Rupawati in Kathiawar, Amba Mata and Kumbaria in north Gujarat; and Nepal. He is, however, doubtful that they were worked before the Hellenistic times. Mallowan identified Magan (a copper supply centre) with the Zagros mountains and the mines of Persia. For the supply of Indus copper, Mackay thought Persia as more likely because both tin and copper ores occur plentifully in that region. An oxide ore from Mohenjo Daro excavations was analysed by Desch.

ANALYTICAL WORK

Sana Ullah (in Vatsa 1940) analysed 48 specimens from Harappa and tabulated them on the basis of the presence of arsenic, nickel and lead. He noted that nickel is generally below 0.5 per cent and seldom 1 per cent, but the proportion of arsenic is relatively high and at times excessive. Sumerian copper also contained similar proportions of nickel, but he said that it could be distinguished from the Harappan by its virtually being free from arsenic. It has been found that ores from Khetri, Alwar, Singhbhum and Afghanistan contain both nickel and arsenic, while those from Bilaspur and Nellore are entirely free of nickel.

P.C. Ray also followed Sana Ullah's views. The presence of lead in some of the copper objects is also noteworthy. Copper ores associated with lead occur in Rajputana and in Hazaribagh district, as also in Afghanistan and Baluchistan. Samples of copper ores from Khetri, Alwar and Singhbhum and Afghanistan contain both nickel and arsenic, while those from Bilaspur and Nellore are entirely free from nickel. It can therefore be concluded that Indus Valley copper most likely came from the Indian ores in the Rajputana district and Baluchistan, though Afghanistan and Persian sources cannot be ruled out.

POST-INDEPENDENCE PERIOD

The post-Independence era saw quite a few attempts to take archaeometallurgy studies further from where the earlier workers had left. Notable among such scholars are: Agrawal, Bhanuprakash, Bharadwaj, Hedge, Chakrabarti, Chattopadhyaya, Seshadri, Tripathi and a few others (see References). But it has to be admitted that the required systematic effort is still lacking. The work so far done is sporadic rather than exhaustive.

Mining Areas

To determine the mining areas used by different cultures is rather difficult and requires a large number of samples. So far only a few ore-samples could be obtained and examined. Chalcopyrites, both from Khetri and Singhbhum, pyrrhorite from Madras, and galena from Mohenjo Daro have been analysed.

It is important to note that Singhbhum pyrites showed absence of arsenic, antimony and lead, which are present in significant amounts in the Harappan artefacts.

A closer comparison of the impurity patterns of the spectroscopic analyses of the Harappan artefacts and various ores shows that there is a close correspondence with the Khetri ores. Singhbhum chalcopyrites and Madras pyrrhotite are quite dissimilar. So if we can base any conclusions on the few analyses done so far, Khetri belt is a more probable mining area for the Harappans. It is further supported by the use of mostly oxide and native minerals, which could be available in plenty in virgin mine. Singhbhum mines were too far-off and the thick forests intervened in between, and are thus precluded as a likely source.

A comparison of the spectroscopic analyses of the Chalcolithic artefacts with the Khetri ore shows a good correspondence. It is imperative that a much larger number of ore analyses are required to arrive at definite conclusions. At present we can only say that the Rajasthan ores were probably used by both the Harappan and the Chalcolithic people. This source alone can justify the import of 'copper from Meluha' in Mesopotamia.

Chemical Analysis

Lal (in Lal 1951) analysed an anthropomorphic figure from Bisuali and found 0.66 per cent nickel (copper - 98.77 per cent) in it. On this basis he said, 'small amount of nickel detected in the specimen represents an impurity derived from the copper ore. The fact is significant, as it shows that the ore from which the metal was smelted was of Indian origin. The Indian copper ores have generally arsenic or nickel or both as impurities, and these are considered the key elements in placing the source of raw material.' But nickel is not peculiar to India, and is quite common in Mesopotamian artefacts too. Though in Kish arsenic is rare, in Khafaje and Ur about 88 per cent artefacts contain arsenic and hence this cannot be used as a safe criterion for distinguishing the Mesopotamian from the Indus copper. Therefore, on the basis of nickel alone we cannot ascribe the artefact to Indian origins.

Hegde realized (Hegde 1964, 1986) the complexity of the problems of ore correlations. When copper is smelted from an ore, normally elements like gold, silver, tin, nickel, lead, cobalt, bismuth pass on to the constitution of the extracted metal, if these elements are present in the copper ore smelted, without much loss in their quantity, during the smelting process. Elements like iron, manganese, zinc, aluminium, chromium, molybdenum, vanadium, gallium, ziroconium, tungsten and titanium will also pass on to the constitution of the extracted metal, if they are present in the ore smelted. The difference between the former set of elements and the latter is that the elements in the former set pass on to the extracted metal with considerable loss in their quantity, often they are present in the extracted metal only in minute traces.

'Apart from these (two sets of) elements, elements like phosphorus, silicon, calcium arsenic, sulphur and antimony also at times pass on to the extracted metal, if they are present in the copper ore smelted' (Hegde 1965). He compares the impurity patterns of Ahar artefacts and Khetri ore on the basis of spectroscopic analyses and finds close parallelism. Absence of gold also, in his view, confirms the derivation of Ahar artefacts from Khetri ores.

Coghlan had (1960) proposed the following list of elements for ore correlations which the Ancient Mining and Metallurgy Committee accepted: gold, silver, arsenic, antimony, tin, lead, bismuth, iron, silicon, aluminium, nickel, cobalt, zirconium, manganese, beryllium, cadmium, tellurium, zinc, phosphorus, selenium, platinum, vanadium, chromium, molybdenum, tungsten, mercury, indium, germanium, rhodium, iridium, palladium, osmium, gallium, tantalum, titanium, magnesium and niobium.

Some research workers employ a statistical grouping of metals over wide cultural and geographical areas, rather than to a closer evolution in which analyses of the ores must run parallel to that of artefacts, in order to trace the mineral sources. Their approach gives speedy results and will be of value to archaeologists in giving an overall picture of cultures, manufacturing centres and trade routes. Coghlan's method (Coghlan 1960), which he admits is slower, aims at complete research right back to the parent ore. Clearly there is room, for both methods of approach to the related problem.

Coghlan, basing on his own and Pittioni's researches, contradicts Thomson:

> Impurity pattern does not vary except in quantity. The impurities pattern of the mineral will be found to appear in the smelted copper, and, under prehistoric conditions of production, this pattern should still be traceable in the mental, even if the end product has been more or less refined. It is this transmission of the 'impurities pattern' which gives us the key to he problems of linking ore and metal. (Coghlan 1960).

In the context of British metallurgy Tylecote observed that:

> Certain elements, such as silver and gold, will be concentrated during smelting and therefore will occur in a greater quantity in the smelted product than in the ore. Using rich ores, the concentration factories not likely to be much greater than about 2. Arsenic and antimony behave very similarly under smelting conditions and are therefore likely to be present in the smelted copper in the same ratio as in the ore. (Tylecote 1962)

On this basis he correlated the Kenmare, Kerry ores to the Irish artefacts. In the artefacts the arsenic and antimony ratio is 3:1 and in the ores 4:1.

A systematic study of both objects and ore deposits in Austria, of the problems connected with early mining, and the treatment and smelting of the ore was undertaken by Pittioni. Research has been concentrated on the regions of early exploitation in Salzburg and Tyrol, where all the major deposits of copper ore have now been examined. Care has been taken to analyse samples from different depths in the deposit so as to define correctly the range of impurities characteristic of the ore-body as a whole. By 1959, they had completed 2,000 analyses of ores from ancient smelting places. On this basis, for example, they could correlate the Voralpenland hoard of ingots to Slovakian ores and the Urnfield to copper deposits of the Beragrube near Schwaz. As noted before they have based their conclusions on the transmission of the 'impurities pattern' which gives us the key to the problems of linking ore and metal.

USE OF ORES IN ANTIQUITY

At Harappa the probability of the use of oxide ores is high. Even in the early levels of Mohenjo Daro sulphide ores (e.g. chalcopyrite) probably were being smelted. Though on the whole in Mohenjo Daro and Rangpur native and oxide ores were probably in common use.

Native copper and oxide minerals generally occur on the surface outcrops of ore-bodies. The preponderance of native and oxide forms thus may indicate use of fresh mines. Exclusive use of native or oxide minerals at Rangpur makes the use of fresh mines (e.g. Rupawati in Kathiawar) quite probable.

Large quantities of copper oxide ore (along with some lead) were recovered from a brick lined pit, 5' 6"x 4' 3" x 4' 6" in room 51 in the DK area of Mohenjo Daro (Mackay 1938). It was analysed by Desch. This discovery further proves the use of oxide ores for smelting by the Indus smiths, though they could obtain quite pure copper from sulphide ores right from the start.

Thus we can infer the availability of fresh mines which could provide native and oxide minerals to the Harappans, though they had the technology to smelt sulphide ores from the early phase itself. On the other hand the analyses of the Chalcolithic artefacts so far do not indicate any probability of the use of sulphide ores though there is a very high probability of the oxide ores being used.

Alloying

Copper is alloyed to improve its casting properties, as also its hardness and tensile strength. Metals when heated absorb gases. Pure copper has a tendency to 'gas' when cast, producing a porous casting. Addition of tin or arsenic considerably reduces this tendency as they function as deoxidising agents. Without alloying, complex casting is impossible.

Hardness of pure copper can be increased by hammering alone from 87 to 135 (Brinell hardness numbers) comparable to a 10 per cent tin-bronze. But to retain a sharp edge frequent hammering will be needed, which makes the tool too brittle, while work-hardening would make the bronze much harder than the pure metal in a comparable condition.

In the copper-arsenic alloy, up to 4 per cent of arsenic forms a solid solution. In solidifying from the molten state, first the portions of each crystal grain crystallize—that is to say, the nuclei of the primary branches or crystallites—which are richer in the metal with higher melting point (here copper) than the succeeding layers, and this gradual process goes on until the liquid metal of each portion solidifying last of all is rich in the metal with the lower melting point (here arsenic). Tin is soluble in copper up to 16 per cent only in the solid state; if tin is in excess of that, a second constituent. Between 8-16 per cent it is only as a result of annealing that homogenous solid solutions can be obtained. Solid solutions (in contrast to eutectics) have a greater hardness than any of the individual elements they are composed of, and yet have sufficient ductility to enable them to be worked both hot and cold. When cold worked the hardness of such solid solutions is increased still further.

About the definition of an alloy in ancient world there is considerable difference of opinion. Coghlan (Coghlan 1954) includes only alloys with 5-15 per cent tin as bronzes, below this limit he calls them accidental bronzes. Tylecote (1962) however includes all alloys containing more than 1 per cent tin in the category of bronzes. Thomson does not believe that the copper with less than 1 per cent of tin or arsenic could be deliberate alloys. It could only be due to the use of impure ores.

Not many analyses are available from Pre-Harappan sites. In Mundigak a low tin (1.06 per cent) bronze (?) is reported. Another object from Nal does not show any tin, but lead therein is 2.14 per cent. About 70 per cent of the Harappan tools were not alloyed. And only 14 per cent were alloyed correctly in the range of 8-12 per cent tin for optimum strength and ductility. In a bronze rod the tin percentage was more than 22. It is clear that though the alloying was understood, correct proportions should not be controlled. It may be due to the mixing of arsenic in ore form. Lollingite (iron-arsenic ore) is reported from Nal and could have been used.

I worked out the relative abundance of bronze from Mohenjo Daro upper and lower levels. It is more abundant (23 per cent tools of bronze) in the upper levels and less in the lower levels (6 per cent). It appears that mainly knives, axes and chisels were made of tin-bronze. But the fact that 70 per cent of the tools were of copper only that tin was scarce. From Rangpur only 6 artefacts show tin 2.6 to 11 per cent; three have nickel ranging between 1.8 to 5.8 per cent. None had lead or arsenic.

Out of the 177 analyses of artefacts from Mohenjo Daro and Harappa only 8 per cent tools show arsenic (1-7 per cent) alloying, 4 per cent show nickel (1-9 per cent) alloying and 6 per cent indicate lead (1-32 per cent) alloying. Even about 1 per cent of arsenic increases the hardness of copper from 124 to 177 (Brinell hardness numbers) in hammered condition. In view of this property, the fact that only 8 per cent tools were arsenic alloys may betray their ignorance of it or poverty of the metal. It is quite likely that arsenic was added only as a deoxidiser for closed castings, e.g. fulcrum bar.

The copper artefacts from the Chalcolithic sites show no arsenic; tin alloying is indicated. Lead is common and varies from 1-2 per cent and probably was a deliberate addition for better fusibility. As regards tin, a Jorwe axe has 1.78 per cent, a Nevasa chisel has 2.7 per cent all the three Navdatoli objects have it within 3-5 per cent, and the Somnath axe has the maximum, 12.8 per cent. It is clear that tin alloying was known to these people, though except for the Somnath few objects shows tin concentration in the optimum range of 8-12 per cent. Tin is significantly absent in the Ahar objects.

Thus we see that the high range of tin, lead and arsenic alloying of the Indus Civilization stands distinct from the other Chalcolithic objects. In the latter, arsenic alloying is absent and tin content does not exceed 5 per cent (excluding the Somnath axe).

B.B. Lal (Lal 1951) had emphasized that the Copper Hoards were of pure copper in contrast to the use of bronze in the western socketed axe, adze, etc. Smith (1905) however had mentioned the following examples of bronze:

(i)	Strachey celt from Jabalpur	13.3 per cent tin
(ii)	Elliot sword	3.83 per cent tin
(iii)	Norham harpoon	7.97 per cent tin
(iv)	Elliot harpoon	6.74 per cent tin

Lal (Lal 1951) analysed the Bisuali anthropomorph and found it to be unalloyed: copper - 98.77 per cent; nickel - 0.66 per cent. The five Copper Hoard specimens (Shahabad celt, Shahabad harpoon (?) fragment, Kamdera celt, Dhanbad celt, and Dargoma celt) examined by us also shows absence of tin. Smith's samples were taken mostly from British museums and their find spots too were not definitely known. Hence one can't rely on them much. Though the analyses of the artefacts from Copper revealed that half of them were alloyed with arsenic (Agrawal et al. 1981).

If we take into account the poor casting, the simple shapes, the relative scarcity of metal (as compared to the Harappans), the absence of sulphide ore-smelting and arsenic alloying, and the poor content of tin (less than 5 per cent) in the Chalcolithic bronzes, the contrast with the developed Harappan metallurgy becomes quite glaring.The distinct identities of the Harappan and the Chalcolithic metallurgical traditions preclude the probability of any direct transmission. There is a clear setback in the Chalcolithic technology.

On the basis of the available evidence we can thus tentatively infer that:

the Harappans used deliberate arsenic, lead and tin alloying;
the Banasians added lead only;
the Malwa and Jorwe people used lead and tin alloying; and
the Copper Hoards were alloyed with arsenic only.

IRON

It would be better to trace the history of studies on iron metallurgy by following the excellent historical account given by Chakrabarti (1992) (for details refer to Chakrabarti 1992). He has identified 4 phases—Phase I: AD 1795-1850; Phase II: 1850-1950; Phase III: 1950-75; and Phase IV: 1976 onwards.

The primary feature of the first phase was a scientific interest in understanding the properties and the manufacturing process of pre-industrial Indian steel which came to be known in Europe as wootz. This word was derived from the Kannadae term *ukku* meaning steel. The pre-industrial Indian steel had a reputation in Europe. Pearson's theory that this steel was made directly from the ore and that it was never in the state of wrought iron was subsequently proved wrong. David Mushet pointed out that wootz steel was never formed directly from the ore but by the fusion of fragments so small bars of malleable iron in a crucible with woody carbonaceous matter covered with leaves and clay.

Chakrabarti has mentioned a large number of reports on pre-industrial iron: Robert Rose's Account of the Process of Making Iron at Amdeah near Sambalpur (Orissa) in 1831; W. Cracroft's description of smelting of Iron in the Kasya Hills (Assam) in 1832; J.M. Heath's account of the south Indian process in 1832 and 1830; Legrand Jacob's report on Marcadieu's report on Kulu in 1855; Bal Gangadhar Shastree's report on Malvan in Ratnagiri district of Maharashtra in 1844; S.F. Hannay's report on upper Assam in 1857; James Abbott's account of gun-manufacture at Koteli near Sialkot (Punjab) in 1848; the reports of Henry Piddington, Welby Jackson; H. Torrens and W.E. Baker on Birbhum and Ranigun (West Bengal) in 1855, 1845, 1851 and 1854; and T.H. Newbold's examination of the nature, distribution and methods in 1846.

There was only a marginal interest in the origin and antiquity of Indian iron in this phase of research. Its interesting to note J. Stodart's trade card in London around 1820: 'surgeons's instruments, razors and other cutlery made from . . . a steel from India, preferred by Mr. Stodart to the best steel in Europe after years of comparative trial'.

In the second phase (*c.*1850-1950), the reports prepared in 1864 by John Percy classified the pre-industrial Indian smelting furnaces into three basic types. Thomas Turner, in 1893, gave a summary of the available evidence both on the distribution of ores and the pre-industrial smelting practices in the fourth volume of George Watt's *A Dictionary of the Economic Products of India*. In 1880, Valentine Ball in his *Jungle Life in India* gave an account of the iron-smelting practices of the tribal group of the Agarias in the Chhotanagpur plateau. A synoptic account of the east Indian iron industry with considerable emphasis on the pre-industrial practice was given by Charles Ritter Von Schwarz in 1901. Robert Hadfield's paper on the composition of early Indian iron objects in 1912 is a landmark. Lester's comment was: 'India produced the first manganese steel ages before the Western Hemisphere was acquainted with the use of iron.' John Hawkshaw, in his presidential address to the British Association for the Advancement of Science in 1875, remarked: 'India well rapid any advantage which she may have derived from the early civilized communities of the west if she were the first to supply them with iron and steel.' As late as 1913, Axel Sahlins wrote: 'India is the oldest iron-producing country of which we have definite knowledge.'

In this phase, there was also emphasis on the literary data. W.H. Schoff shows that the Seric iron of the Classical writers came from India and not from China. For the importation into the Roman world from some eastern source of the finest grade of steel then known, there is ample evidence, and it all points toward central India and not China. Ferrum Indicum appears in the list of articles subject to duty at Alexandria. In this phase there was also an attempt to systematize the whole range of evidence. The most significant attempt was made by Panchanan Neogi in 1914 but mention should also be made of the section on India iron in Ludwig Beck's monumental history of iron in 1884.

In the third phase, the first paper on the archaeological data was that of D.H. Gordon (1950) who thought iron could have been introduced in India between 600 and 700 BC. The archaeological discovery which went against the assumptions of Gordon and Wheeler was that of the Painted Grey Ware at Hastinapur and other sites. The date borders around 1000 BC. Koshambi in 1963 depending on the Suttanipata which, he thought, was the earliest of the Buddhist canons, put the date of the beginning of this metal in the Ganga Valley, at least in the middle Ganga Valley, at 800-700 BC. He thought that there was no iron in the Early Vedic period.

The current phase (1976 onwards) began with Chakrabarti's definitive study which indicated six early iron-using centres in the subcontinent: Baluchistan, the Northwest, the Indo-Ganga divide and the Upper Ganga Valley, eastern India, Malwa and Berar in central India and the Megalithic south India. I will not contest his conclusions here which were:

The iron in central and south India is earlier than the iron in the north-western periphery of India. The central Indian centre seems to be the earliest of the six early Indian centres.

Iron entered the Indian productive system by *c.* 800 BC.

All these early centres are either in or near the ore areas, thought Tripathi has contested this view (see below).

The evidence of pre-industrial smelting and rich ore deposits is very impressive in central and southern India which also seem to show the first evidence of Indian iron.

The first Indian iron tool-types do not significantly correspond to the iron tool-types known in west Asia.

There is an apparent continuity between the early and the contemporary (pre-industrial) traditions of iron metallurgy in India. On the basis of these points Dilip Chakrabarti thinks that India was a separate and possibly independent centre of the manufacture of early iron.

Dilip Chakrabarti's concluding observations are: the occurrence of iron in the Black-and-Red Ware deposit in Ahar in south-east Rajasthan and in what has been called pre-Northern-Black-Polished-Ware and post-Chalcolithic Black-and-Red Ware phases of Nagda, Eran, Dangwada and Prakash in Malwa and the periphery of Malwa decidedly goes beyond 1000 BC and at present the weight of the evidence takes it back to the middle of the second millennium. According to him, the issue is clinched by the discovery of iron at Lothal. Thus he seems to ascribe the beginnings of iron to the Harappans with which not many will agree!

In this connection, we had carried out some explorations and analyses which indicate that Kumaun could as well have been source of supply of iron to the Ganga Valley (Agrawal et al. 1991, 1995a, 1995b). Some of the old mining sites in Kumaun have high grade magnetite, goethite, and haemetite. From a site (Uleni), which had yielded iron slag, we radiocarbon dated a sample to *c.* 900 BC (Agrawal and Kharakwal 1997).

In contrast a Dilip Chakrabarti's views, which are mainly based on available literature, Tripathi and Mishra (1997), basing on their extensive fieldwork, has brought in an interesting ethnometallurgical approach to understand the iron archaeometallurgy. They say the early workers preferred low grade ores for technical reasons and:

> Most of the pre-industrial iron workers reside in close proximity to the mineral deposits like reiverine magnetitic sand. . . . Even today, in such areas where pre-industrial iron-working continues, not much mining is involved. (Tripathi and Mishra 1997: 59)

And iron produced by these traditional smelters is preferred by the local people to factory produced iron because of its high durability, ductility and capacity to provide a better cutting edge. She reports the following special features of pre-industrial metallurgy:

The Chhattisgarh tribes use 'sal' or teak wood to produce charcoal. This is a purer material with a lower sulphur and phosphorous content. The metal thus produced is naturally low in sulphur. The tribal smelters are almost 'religiously' particular about the type of wood they use to make charcoal for fuel.

Prolonged contact with charcoal in this process carburizes or hardens the iron, making it malleable and providing the object with a sharper and longer lasting working edge. She reports a close resemblance between the pre-industrial iron technology and the archaeological evidence. Some efforts have been to reconstruct these iron working processes by Gogte (1982), Hegde (1973,1991) and by the Tripathis (Tripathi and Tripathi 1997).

Quoting the examples of the Asur-Birjia, the Mahuli Agarias (producing white iron) and the Kamis of Darjeeling, she thinks that the tribal workers make a deliberate choice of ore, technique and product.

ZINC

Not much work was done on the archaeometallurgy of zinc in pre-Independence India. The following is mainly based on Craddock (1985, 1987, 1987-8, 1995) and his co-workers' (Craddock et al. 1985) publications.

The famous zinc mines are in Zawar which lies about 40 km south of Udaipur in Rajasthan, apart of the Precambrian metamorphic rocks of the Aravalli Hills. The zinc/lead ore is in dolomite formations sharply inclined into steep ridges above the valley bottom. The ancient mines followed the ore down from where it outcropped on the top of these hills. Remains of wooden stairways, haulage scaffolds, staging and drainage leets survive in the mines.

The earliest firm evidence for the production of metallic zinc on a regular basis come from India. There are references to burning a metal, rasa, to produce an eye salve, which should refer to zinc, placing its use in the last centuries of the first millennium BC. The *Rasaratnakara*, ascribed to Nagarjuna, the great Indian scientist who lived in the fourth century AD, describes both the production of brass by the familiar cementation process, and of metallic zinc. Furnaces (Koshthi) have been found at the ancient mines of Zawar in Rajasthan. The ore at Zawar is a mixed sphalerite (ZnS/galena) deposit.

The excavations at Zawar uncovered several almost intact banks of furnaces with the inverted retorts fired over a cool chamber where the zinc was collected. But the furnaces at Zawar were the industrial version of those outlined in the *Rasaratna-samuchchaya*, with banks of between three and seven furnaces, and each furnace held 36 retorts. These details of the smelting process are described in detail in Craddock et al. (1985). As zinc is a very volatile metal, it was a very difficult technical process to extract it from the ores.

> Maintaining these conditions had to be simultaneously maintained over 36 retorts in each furnace irrespective of whether they were in the centre or a corner. This must rank as one of the most skilled and sophisticated operations known from the pre-industrial world. (Craddock et al. 1985)

The earliest dates (Table 1) for Zawar are from the mines at Mochina and Zawar Mala which show that zinc and some lead was being mined between the sixth and first centuries BC. The earliest dates we have for zinc distillation are from a white heap which is of the twelfth century AD. Further Craddock, who has specialized on ancient zinc says:

> at first glance the Zawar industry is the most unusual phenomena, a fully fledged technology with neither antecedents nor successors—and apparently no contemporaries either, for even within India it seems unique. . . . Zinc required a much higher temperature and the total exclusion of air. The form of the Kosthi furnace for holding the retorts seems to have been inspired by the common spottery kiln. The arrangement is of course totally different: instead of a fire beneath to heat the pots stacked above through the perforated floor, in the Kosthi, the fire and retorts were in the upper chamber and the zinc was collected beneath . . . the Zawar process was certainly one of the most sophisticated and technically exacting process developed in the mediaeval world. one hesitates to use the term 'pre-industrial', for surely this process, with its appreciation of scientific techniques, and learning towards mass production, should properly be considered as an early example of an industrial process in the modern sense. (Craddock 1987)

CONCLUSIONS

Before drawing the conclusions let me summarize the evidence adduced above. The Pre-Harappans were very poor in metal. The evidence only indicates that copper has being used on a small scale either because of lack of known local ores or due to the inability of the Pre-Harappan societies to afford full-time metallurgists. We do not have enough data to derive typological correlations.

The Harappans, on the other hand, show a sudden upsurge in metallurgical activity. They have a profusion and variety of pots and pans indicating the knowledge of the techniques of 'sinking', raising, 'running on', etc. But no metal vessels are reported either from the Chalcolithic cultures, or the Copper Hoards. The Harappan and the Chalcolithic artefacts betray the knowledge of cold working and annealing also, which were probably not known to the Copper Hoards people. Quite developed casting methods, including cire-perude, were used by the Harappans. However, open moulds

TABLE 1. EARLY METAL WORKING SITES IN INDIA (Key: AD, BC = calibrated dates)

Site	Sample Nos.	Calib. Dates	Culture
Chigar Gunta mine	PRL-1188	AD 991	Gold mine
Chigar Gunta mine	PRL-1187	716, 743, AD 757	Gold mine
Ingaldhal Copper mines	BM-2364	AD 221	Copper mine
Ingaldhal Copper mines	PRL-252	381 BC	Copper mine
Ingaldhal Copper mines	PRL-1097	10 BC	Copper mine
Kolar mines	TF-1199	AD 725, 735, 766	Gold mine
Kolar mines	TF-879	AD 605	Mine
Kolar mines	MO-352	AD 605	Gold mine
Mailaram	TF-373	AD 1414	Copper mine
Dariba mines	TF-1117	372 BC	Mine
Dariba smelting area	BM-2492	66 BC	Lead/Silver, zinc smelting
Dariba smelting area	BM-2490	399 BC	Lead/Silver, zinc smelting
Dariba smelting area	BM-2491	331, 329, 200 BC	Lead/Silver, zinc Smelting
Khodarbia mine	PRL-927	None	Mine
Kumbaria	TF-1222	AD 1166	Copper mine
Kumbaria	TF-1221	AD 1414	Copper mine
Kumbaria	PRL-549	AD 1285	Copper mine
Rajpura Dariba	PRL-928	407 BC	Old mine shaft
Rajpura Dariba	PRL-210	1314 BC	Copper mine
Rajpura Dariba	PRL-208A	186 BC	Copper mine
Rajpura Dariba	PRL-209	AD 233	Copper mine
Zawar lead slag heap	BM-2484	1885, 1912,	Smelting
Zawarmala mine	BM-2065	None	Zinc mine
Zawarmala	BM-2578	None	Zinc mine smelting
Zawarmala mine	BM-2482	192 BC	Smelting
Zawarmala mine	PRL-934	AD 1272	Zinc mine
Zawarmala mine	PRL-935	AD 1225	Zinc mine
Zawarmala mine	PRL-932	410 BC	Zinc mine
Zawarmala mine	BM-2017	None	Zinc mine
Zawarmala mine	BM-2483	AD 1898, 1902, 1955	Zinc mine
Zawarmala mine	BM-2381	None	Smelting
Zawarmala mine	BM-2338	AD 1676,1747, 1799,1942,1922	Zinc mine
Zawarmala mine	BM-2148	196 BC	Zinc mine
Zawarmala mine	BM-2222	AD 1955	Zinc mine
Zawarmala mine	BM-2223	AD 1657	Zinc mine
Zawarmala mine	BM-2381 1799, 1942	AD 1676, 1747, 1955	Zinc mine
Zawarmala mine	PRL-933	666 BC	Zinc mine
Zawarmala mine	PRL-298	None	Lead smelting
Zawarmala mine	BM-2149	AD 77	Zinc mine
Zawar smelting area	BM-2486	AD 1666, 1790, 1949, 1952	Smelting
Zawar smelting area	BM-2485	AD 58	Smelting
Zawar smelting area	BM-2487	AD 72	Smelting
Zawar smelting area	BM-2488	AD 657	Smelting

were quite often used. The Chalcolithic people used only open moulds. But the Copper Hoards show the use of closed-casting as indicated by the harpoons and tell-tale ridges on some Gungeria axes. Closed-casting of pure copper is a difficult thing indeed to achieve; perhaps the lack of tin or the know-how precluded alloying in the Copper Hoards. In the metal forging technology the Harappans are the most advanced, then some of the Copper Hoards, and lastly the other Chalcolithic cultures. Alloying was practised both in the Harappan and Chalcolithic cultures, and also by the Copper Hoards people.

The Harappans have very distinctive types: the razors; the arrowhead; the barbed fish hooks; and the curved blade. They even had the first true saw and the first tubular drills which show their ingenuity. The Copper Hoards are distinguished by the anthropomorph, the antennae sword and the harpoon—so well adapted for a hunting nomadic life. The Chalcolithic cultures, however, have very simple types which are ubiquitous. In the metal repertoire there is nothing very characteristic of them.

The typology shows that the Harappans, the Chalcolithic culture and the Copper Hoards are distinct groups without any demonstrable affinities. The alleged links—like the Chandoli antennae dagger, the Lothal 'anthropomorph'—were shown to be technologically much different from their so-called counterparts in the other cultures.

Amongst the Chalcolithic cultures, the Banasians are distinguished by the lack of microliths and presence of definite metallurgical evidence; the Malwa by the use of 'microliths'; and the Jorwe by the use of ground stone axes. The evidence is too meagre for finer distinctions.

Finally, in the total metal inventory we saw that the Harappans led the rest in the abundance of metal, followed by the Copper Hoards. The other Chalcolithic cultures are poorer in this comparison too; but are far richer than the Neolithic cultures of the south.

The considerations of space, time, typology, and technology, all go against any possibility of links between these three disparate cultures. We showed earlier that the Chalcolithic cultures succeed the Harappan. The Copper Hoards may be later still. The three groups have distinct geographical distributions and, in fact, thrived in different ecological zones.

The richness of the Harappans in the metal is due to the agricultural surplus and the discovery of local mines: both the things are interdependent. A society without a fluid surplus cannot support metallurgical specialists. The large number of the so-called narrow axes and chisels could have been used as hoes. In the pliable fertile Indus plains, simple copper tools and even big chert blades could help cultivation. There are several chert blades, smoothed all over, which could also have been used as hoes mounted on sticks. An efficient village economy with agricultural surplus, with metal-technology, abundant source of metal and an optimum ecology could burst fast into urbanization—as it probably did in the Indus.

The Copper Hoards people too have a developed tool technology and abundant metal. Their individuality and isolation may indicate even independent origins of their metallurgy, though late. The wooded plateau and rich ores were ideal for such a discovery. But the ecology was not suitable for the growth of urbanization in the Doab. The thick monsoonal forests were rich in game and the rivers full of fish. Their took kit, of the antennae sword, the anthropomorph and the harpoon, was ideally suited for a hunting nomadic life. However, this metal technology does not indicate the presence of specialized craftsmen in the society but only itinerant smiths who were probably released from the kinship bonds.

Complete absence of metal pots and pans, despite abundance of the metal, does prove a nomadic existence. No permanent settlement mounds of the Copper Hoard Culture have so far been identified—nor are likely to be. To colonize the Doab only the iron-technology and abundance of iron were the answer.

Despite the claims of Dilip Chakrabarti, iron technology seems to begin only with the opening of the first millennium BC. The studies on iron are a few centuries old now in India but detailed systematic studies have not been made so far, despite laudable efforts of scholars like Dilip Chakrabarti and Vibha Tripathi. What one needs is detailed technological studies of early iron slags, mining, artefacts, and above all ethnoarchaeological studies.

In zinc production and in mastering the difficult technology of distilling zinc, there is no doubt that India led the world. The fact that early zinc smelting dates of Zawar go back to the last centuries of the first millennium BC, establishes the oldest dates for this technology in India.

REFERENCES

Agrawal, D.P. 1969. The Copper Hoards Problems: a Technological Angle, *Asian Perspectives* XII: 113-19.

——— 1969-70. The Metal Technology of the Indian Protohistoric Cultures: Its Archaeological Implications, *Puratattva* 3: 15-22.

——— 1970. Metal Technology of the Harappan Culture and Its Socio-Economic Implications, *Indian Journal of History of Science* 5 (2): 238-52.

——— 1971. *The Copper Bronze Age in India*. Delhi: Munshiram Manoharlal.

——— 1981. The Technology of the Indus Civilisation, in *New Perspectives in Indian Archaeology* (R.K. Sharma Ed.), pp. 83-112. New Delhi: Agam Kala.

——— 1982. The Indian Bronze Age Cultures and Their Metal Technology, in *Advances in World Archaeology* (F. Wendorf and A.E. Close Eds.), pp. 163-8. New York: Academic Press.

——— 1984. Metal Technology of the Harappans, in *Frontiers of the Indus Civilization* (B.B. Lal and S.P. Gupta Eds.), pp.163-8. New Delhi: Books & Books.

Agrawal, D.P., C. Margabandhu 1975-76. Ancient Gold Working: Some New ^{14}C Dates, *Puratattva* 139-149.

Agrawal, D.P. and C. Margabandhu 1975-6. Ancient Copper Workings: Some New ^{14}C Dates, *Indian Journal of History of Science* II (2): 133-6.

Agrawal, D.P. and J.S. Kharakwal 1998. Archaeology and Culture of the Central Himalayas. Delhi: Aryan Books International.

Agrawal, D.P., R.V. Krishnamurthy and Sheela Kusumgar 1977. New Data on the Copper Hoards and the Diamabad Bronzes, *Man and Environment* XI: 41-6.

——— 1979. On the Affiliation of the Daimabad Bronzes: Some Fresh Data, *International Symposium on Archaeometry and Prospection, Bonn* (I. Scollar Ed.): 8-13.

——— 1981. Arsenical Coppers in the Indian Bronze Age, in *Madhu; Recent Researches in Indian Archaeology and Art History* (M.S. Nagraja Rao Ed.), pp. 9-16. New Delhi: Agam Kala.

Agrawal, D.P., Diva Bhatt, Sudha Malaiya, Jeevan Kharakwal 1991. Archaeology of Kumaon: Problems and Prospects, *Man and Environment* XVI (1): 60-3.

Agrawal, D.P., Jeevan Kharakwal, Sheela Kusumgar and M.G. Yadava 1995a. Cist Burials of the Kumaun Himalayas, *Antiquity* 69 (264): 549-54.

Agrawal, D.P., R.V. Krishnamurthy, Sheela Kusumgar, L.A., Narain and M.N. Sarin 1974. Alloying in the Copper Hoards, *Bulletin of the Museum and Archaeology* 14: 14-18.

Agrawal, D.P., V.D. Gogte, J. Kharakwal, S. Kusumgar and M.G. Yadava 1995b. Was Kuman the Source of Early Iron, *Man and Environment* XX (1): 82-5.

Agrawal, R.C. and V. Kumar 1982, Ganeshwar-Jodhpura Culture: New Traits in Indian Archaeology, in *Harappan Civilisation* (G.L. Possehl Ed.), pp.156-62. Delhi: Oxford-IBH.

Bharadwaj, H.C. 1979. *Aspects of Ancient Indian Technology: a Research Based on Scientific Methods*. Delhi: Motilal Banarsidass.

Bhowmik, S.K. 1973-4. Chalcolithic Protohistoric Period Copper Metallurgy of Gujarat—a Preliminary Survey, *Bulletin of the Baroda Museum and Picture Gallery* 25: 37-53.

Biswas, A.K. 1991. Archaeo-materials in India: Some Residual Problems and Future Prospects, in *Indian Archaeometallurgy* (Vibha Tripathi Ed.). New Delhi: Sharda Publishing House.

Brooke, J.C. 1864. The Mines of Khetri in Rajputana, *Journal of the Asiatic Society of Bengal* 33: 419-29.

Caldwell, K.S. 1920. The Result of Analyses of Certain Ornaments Found in Asur Sites, *Journal of Bihar and Orissa Research Society* 6: 409-11.

Chakrabarti, D.K. 1979. The Problems of Tin in Early India: a Preliminary Survey, *Man and Environment* III: 61-74.

——— 1986. The Pre-industrial Mines of India, *Puratattva* 16: 65-72.

——— 1988. The Old Copper Mines of Eastern India, in *The Beggining of the Use of Metal and Alloys* (R. Maddin Ed.), pp. 203-44. Boston: MIT Press.

——— 1992. *The Early Use of Iron in India*. Bombay: Oxford University Press.

Chakrabarti, D.K. and Nayanjot Lahiri 1996. *Copper and Its Alloys in Ancient India*. Delhi: Munshiram Manoharlal.

Chattopadhyay, P.K. 1984. Archaeometallurgical Studies in Indian Subcontinent: a Survey of Metallography of Iron Objects, *Indian Journal of History of Science* 16 (4): 361-5.

Coggin Brown, J. and A.K. Dey 1955. *India's Mineral Wealth: a Guide to the Occurrences and Economics of the Useful Minerals of India, Pakistan and Burma.* Bombay: Oxford University Press.

Coghlan H.H. 1960. *Viking Fund Publications in Anthropology* 28.

Craddock, P.T. 1987. *The Early History of Zinc* (New Series), Vol. II (4): 183-91.

——— 1995. *Early Metal Mining and Production* , pp. 309-21. Edinburgh: Edinburgh University Press.

——— 1987/88. The Early History of Zinc and Brass, *Wiener Berichte uber Naturwissenschaft in der Kunst*: 225-45.

Craddock, P.T., I.C. Freestone, K.T.M. Hegde, L.K. Gurjar and V.H. Sonawne 1985. Early Zinc Production in India, *Mining Magazine* (January 1985): 45-51.

Darling, A.S. 1990. Non-Ferrous Metals, in *An Encyclopaedia of the History of Technology* (Ian Mcneil Ed.), pp. 47-144. London: Routledge.

Datta, A. and P.K. Chattopadhyay 1986. The Problems of Copper Hoards in West Bengal—a Reappraisal in the Light of Metallographic and Chemical Analysis, *Indian Museum Bulletin* 11: 61-7.

De, S. and P.K. Chattopadhyay 1989. Iron Objects from Pandurajar Dhibi: Archaeometallurgical Studies, *Steel India 12* (1): 33-41.

Ganorkar, M.C., V.P. Rao, P. Gayatri and T.A.S. Rao 1987. Scientific Study and Conservation of Coins, in *Numismatics and Archaeology* (P.L Gupta and A.K. Jha Eds.), pp. 114-24. Anjaneri: Indian Institute of Numismatic Studies.

Gogte, V.D. 1982. Megalithic Iron Smelting at Naikund: Discovery by Three Probe Resistivity Survey, in *Naikund Excavations 1978-1980* (S.B. Deo and A.P. Jamkhedkar Eds.), pp. 52-9. Bombay: Archaeology and Museums, Government of Maharashtra.

Gordon, D.H. 1958. *Prehistoric Background of Indian Culture.* Bombay: Madhuri Dhirajlal Deasi and Bhulabai Memorial Institute.

Harris, D.H. 1996. *The Origins and Spread of Agriculture and Pastoralism in Eurasia.* Washington, D.C.: Smithsonian Institution Press.

Hegde, K.T.M. 1964. Metallic Studies in Chalcolithic Objects, *Journal of the Oriental Institute* 14: 84-90.

——— 1965. Chalcolithic Period Copper Metallurgy in India. Ph.D. Dissertation. Baroda: M.S. University of Baroda.

——— 1986. Mining, Smelting and Smithery of Copper in Ancient India, in *Technology in Ancient and Medieval India* (A. Roy and S.K. Bagchi Eds.), pp. 35-50. Delhi: Indian National Science Academy.

Krishnan, M.V. 1976. *Cire Perdue Casting in India.* New Delhi: Kanak Publications.

Kuppuram, G. 1989. *Ancient Indian Mining Metallurgy and Metal Industries.* Delhi: Sundeep Prakashan.

Lal, B.B. 1951. Further Copper Hoards from the Gangetic Basin and a Review of the Problem, *Ancient India* 7: 20-39.

——— 1972. The Copper Hoard Culture of the Ganga Valley, *Antiquity* 46: 232-87.

Mackay, E.J.H. 1938. *Further Excavations at Mohenjodaro.* Delhi: Government of India.

——— 1943. *Chanhu-daro Excavations 1935-36.* Boston: Museum of Fine Arts.

Maddin, Robert 1986. The Beginning of the Use of Metals and Alloys, *Papers from the Second International Conference on the Beginning Metallurgy, Zhengzhou, China,* pp. 21-6. Boston: MIT Press.

Marshall, J.H. (Ed.) 1931. *Mohenjodaro and the Indus Civilisation.* London: Arthur Probsthain.

Mcneil, Ian (Ed.) 1990. *Encyclopaedia of the History of Technology.* London: Routledge.

Nautiyal, V., D.P. Agrawal and R.V. Krishnamurthy 1981. Some New Analysis on the Protohistorical Copper Artefacts, *Man and Environment* V: 48-51.

Neogi, P. 1917 and 1979. *Copper in Ancient India.* Patna: Janaki Prakashan.

Ottaway, B.S. 1975. Aspects of Early Copper Smelting, *Journal of the Historical Metallurgy Society* 9(1): 30-1.

Pal, P. 1975. *Bronzes of Kashmir.* Graz: Akademische Druck-u. Verlagsanstalt.

Rao. S.R. 1987. Mining and Metallurgy of Copper in Ancient India, in *Archaeology and History* (B.M. Pande and B.D. Chattopadhyaya Eds.), pp. 383-98. Delhi: Agam Kala.

Ray, P.C. 1902-3 and 1909. *History of Hindu Chemistry*. Culcutta: Bengal Chemical and Pharmaceutical Works Ltd.

Reeves, R. 1962. *Cire Perdue Casting in India*. New Delhi Crafts Museum.

Roy, A. and S.K. Bagchi (Eds.) 1986. *Technology in Ancient and Medieval India*. Delhi: Sundeep Prakashan.

Seshadri, R. 1992. The Composition and Smithery Techniques of Copper Artefacts from Nagwada: a Preliminary Study, *Man and Environment* XVII (1): 7-12.

Smith, V.A. 1905. The Copper Age and Prehistoric Bronze Implements of India, *Indian Antiquary* 34: 229-44.

Tripathi, Vibha and Arun K. Mishra 1997. Understanding Iron Technology and Ethnographic Model, *Man and Environment* XXII (1): 59-66.

Tirpathi, V. and B. Prakash 1986. Iron Technology in Ancient India, Metal and Materials, *Historical Metallurgy* 568-79.

Tylecote, R.F. 1962. *Metallurgy in Archaeology*. London: Edward Arnold Ltd.

Vatsa, M.S. 1940. *Excavations at Harappa*. Delhi: Government of India.

Wertime, A. Theodore and I.D. Muhly 1980. *The Coming of the Age of Iron*. New Haven and London: Yale University Press.

White, Joyce C. 1997. Note on New Dates for the Ban Chiang Cultural Tradition, *Bulletin of the Indo-Pacific Prehistory Association* 16: 103-6.

Yule, P. 1985. *Metalwork of the Bronze Age in India*. Munich: C.H. Beck'sche Verlagsbuchhandlung.

Progress of Archaeological Chemistry in India

ANUPAMA KSHIRSAGAR and B.C. DEOTARE

INTRODUCTION

Archaeology is considered as a social science in the arts faculty. However in the last few decades, its inclination towards the science faculty is undoubtedly well established. Archaeology is a natural bridge between the humanities and science. Now it is the only 'arts' subject which brings physical, earth, biological, mathematical and computer sciences together, while studying different aspects of ancient man. Aspects like prospection, chronology, environment or ancient technology are studied in archaeology and various scientific techniques are used for this purpose. The archaeological studies are mainly concerned with:

1. Discovery through explorations and excavations;
2. Interpretation of material remains discovered for understanding their significance and relevance to human development and;
3. Conservation of the objects excavated.

Application of all the sciences mentioned above is a relatively recent development in all these stages. While studying the past with the help of ancient remains, the archaeologist always puts some typical questions to the scientists: What is the composition of the object? How old is it? How was it made? Was it locally made or elsewhere? And where could it have come from? Chemistry plays an important role in answering these questions, in collaboration with archaeology, chemistry forms a new and distinctly interdisciplinary subject, Archaeological Chemistry, dealing with the chemical study of ancient materials. As a systematic science, chemistry is young in years, but archaeology is even younger. The composition, structure and properties of materials can be studied with the help of archaeological chemistry. The essence of this science rests in its ability to provide information about the properties of matter that are completely closed to visual observations. It therefore helps the archaeologist to seek that stored information which is beyond the scope of visual observations and is buried with the ancient material in the form of minerals and chemical elements.

Since no written records are available, it is only through the scientific studies of the material remains that we can understand what prehistoric people made, what were their resources and what was their scientific and technological knowledge. Archaeotechnological studies depend upon the unwritten records in the form of antiquities of stone, metal or clay objects of diverse compositions which have been buried. Every piece of antiquity, whether potsherd or a bead of glass, a terracotta or a piece of plaster or a brick, all these are the products of the contemporary technology. Various studies of these objects have been made to explain their composition, method of production and fabrication, determination of raw materials required for their production and the location of these raw materials in adjacent regions. As such a number of problems confront the archaeologist.

It is in this connection that experimental procedures with special reference to analytical chemistry, metallurgy and silicate technology are being increasingly utilized for solving the various archaeo-technological problems. The discovery of radioactive elements by which radioactive materials can provide 'clocks' for dating events, has added a new dimension to the chemical and physical approach to the solution of archaeological problems.

BEGINNING AND PROGRESS OF ARCHAEOLOGICAL CHEMISTRY

The primary motive of the early investigators in archaeological chemistry seems to have been out of personal curiosity. In Europe, chemists have shown an early interest in the chemical composition of ancient materials. The first significant results of chemical analysis of ancient objects were published at the end of the eighteenth century by M.H. Klaproth, a pioneer in the chemical investigations of antiquities, as well as in the field of chemical analysis as a whole. He determined the composition of Greek and Roman coins, other ancient metallic objects, and specimens of Roman glass (Klaproth 1796). Some distinguished chemists such as Sir H. Davy, J.J. Berzelius and M. Berthelot were concerned with the analysis of ancient materials (Davy 1815, 1817; Berzelius 1836; Berthelot 1906). Gobel (1842) was the first to suggest that the results of chemical analysis of archaeological materials could be of service to archaeology.

The first account of archaeological discoveries was published, which had an appendix describing the chemical composition of excavated artefacts (Layard 1853). This publication marks the beginning of collaboration between archaeology and chemistry. It is the earliest concrete evidence of the appreciation by archaeologists of the value of chemical information on materials and objects recovered from excavations.

Wocel (1853, 1856) for the first time, attempted a correlation between chemical composition and the possible provenance of ancient materials. He was also the first to suggest that approximate or relative dates of ancient metal objects might be estimated from their composition.

By the last quarter of the nineteenth century, archaeological excavations were being conducted in a systematic way. This led to wider appreciation of the services of chemistry. The results of chemical investigation began to appear in archaeological reports. Chemists' reports began to be published as separate articles in archaeological journals (Schliemann 1878).

The French mineralogist, Carnot (1892) was the first to investigate the fluorine content of ancient bones, by the end of the nineteenth century. He suggested that the results might be used as a means of dating such remains. After his work, much of the research on fluorine analysis was carried out in temperate regions of Europe and the United States in the last century. However, the validity of this method was not tested and proved until 1939 when Oakley and Montagu from Britain amplified and revived this method of relative dating for ancient bones. They successfully applied it to disprove the antiquity of the Galley Hill skeleton (Oakley and Montagu 1939).

The systematic application of chemical principles and techniques to the restoration and preservation of antiquities started only at the end of the nineteenth century. The pioneer in this field was Rathgen (1905) who set up a laboratory at the Staatlichen Museum in Berlin and later published the first book dealing with chemical procedures for the conservation of antiquities. The usefulness of chemistry in archaeology continued to grow in the first quarter of the twentieth century. The archaeological chemistry laboratories began to increase in number and through research, sober facts gradually replaced the process of guessing about the technical achievements in ancient civilizations. Electrolytic method for the restoration of ancient bronzes was first established by Fink and Eldridge in 1925 and is now widely used. Caley (1951) of Ohio State University has carried out pioneering work in this field since 1930 and provided a status to the subject by his systematic work. Caley's analytical work and his results stand out at one end as the basis of all future work in archaeochemistry. With the passage of time greater need was felt for such studies all over the world, without exception the archaeology departments have a chemistry department supporting an integrated archaeological research in conservation and restoration.

The new developments in scientific instrumentation and the usefulness of radioactive and nuclear techniques have brought about a revolution in archaeological methods, especially during the last 50 years. With the result archaeological chemistry claims an independent statuts for itself owing to increasing application of laboratory-based techniques. The revolution began with the development of radiocarbon dating by Wilard Libbey (Libby 1952). The method brought Nobel prize to W.F. Libby in 1960. It has given a sound chronological basis for Indian archaeology in particular by providing reliable time brackets to various cultural periods. This was an important contribution and radiocarbon dating is likely to remain the major technique for many years to come. Thus at present chemistry is playing an increasingly significant role in dating the anceint past.

ARCHAEOLOGICAL CHEMISTRY BEFORE INDEPENDENCE

The Archaeological Survey of India was reorganized in 1902 with the objective of looking after the cultural heritage of this vast country and exploring and excavating new sites with a view to revealing India's ancient past. Gradually the activities of the Survey increased rapidly, the need was felt for putting the preservation of ancient remains, antiquities and museum exhibits on a firm scientific basis. The Chemical Branch of the Survey was established in 1917 with the appointment of an Archaeological Chemist for scientific examination, chemical treatment and preservation of museum objects and antiquities recovered in explorations and excavations. The laboratory of the Archaeological

Chemist was initially set up in the Indian Museum, Calcutta, and later on shifted to Dehra Dun. The work in this laboratory was modelled on the lines of the British Museum Laboratory in London, where Sir Alexander Scott had developed important methods of chemical preservation of metals, alloys, terracotta, glass, faience, textiles, drawings and other types of antiquities. The application of such methods to the Indian material yielded exciting results and created considerable enthusiasm among art collectors, museum curators, archaeological officers and others interested in the preservation of India's cultural heritage. This resulted in a tremendous expansion of the activities of the Archaeological Chemist. Large scale chemical preservation of monuments was begun in 1937, when the decaying sculptures of the famous caves at Elephanta were chemically treated with very spectacular results. This type of preservation work has since been extended to a large number of monuments.

The growth and development of archaeological chemistry during the period of three decades from the establishment of the Chemical Branch of the Survey in 1917, i.e. till the declaration of Independence of India, could not remain isolated from the scientific progress in other countries. Numerous techniques of immense potential in the scientific conservation of ancient monuments and cultural remains of various kinds were being developed. These methods were adopted by the Chemical Branch in its own work because it was realized that the interpretation of ancient Indian techniques and materials could be carried out best by the application of the results of research in these various branches of science (Lal 1953).

The role played by analytical chemistry in resolving many archaeological problems such as the composition of metals and alloys (metallography), the techniques of manufacturing glass, terracotta and other allied problems, was recognized long ago by Western scientists, and the results of this analytical work have been summarized by Caley (1951). Though the science of archaeological chemistry is based on the pioneering work done by western scientists, the Archaeological Survey of India did not lag behind in the application of methods of analytical chemistry to archaeological problems. Intensive analytical work was carried out over three decades produced important and interesting results.

Archaeological chemists of the Archaeological Survey of India like for example, Sana Ullah, and Paramsivan (1939) have been the earliest workers in this field. They reported on the chemical composition of antiquities from Harappa, Mohenjo Daro, Taxila and other sites in the publications of the Archaeological Survey of India. By this time, around the 1940s, the Excavation Branch was re-established as a specialized nucleus for Indian archaeology. Together with prehistoric and epigraphic study, the task of conservation became a full-time responsibility of the Survey. *Ancient India* a serial publication of the Archaeological Survey of India always included a note on the preservation of antiquities which was contributed by Sana Ullah (1946), who by then had retired as Archaeological Chemist, whose experience of chemical conservation was unqestionable.

Sana Ullah has given basic instructions and details about the chemical/mechanical treatment of antiquities together with the list of equipments and chemicals required for an archaeological field laboratory at a major excavation. The instructions given by him, five decades back, are valuable and are still in practice, in addition to the benefit of modern instrumentation. The antiquities discovered during excavation are found deteriorated as a result of chemical and physical changes that have taken place during the long period of burial in the soil. This is the reason for the application of chemical methods for their preservation. These transformations depend upon the composition of the material, soil character and the age of the site. For pottery, crystallized salts derived from soil are removed by washing several times with distilled water or with certain chemical solution for specific incrustation, e.g. sodium hexametaphosphate solution is used to remove calcareous incrustation. Treatment of metallic objects requires chemical knowledge and considerable practical experience, he has added. Electrochemical reduction or treatment with mild acids have been suggested for metallic objects. For organic materials, mechanical treatment, impregnation, fumigation with thymol or carbon disulphide is suggested.

The earliest useful data on the chemical composition of antiquities is available in the form of *Annual Reports of the Archaeological Survey of India* and separate reports of major archaeological excavations, e.g. Excavations at Harappa, Mohenjo Daro and Taxila. Since 1946, excavation reports of the Archaeological Survey of India started appearing in *Ancient India,* formerly a bulletin published by the Archaeological Survey of India where some notes on the chemical composition of the antiquities have been reported. At present reports on the chemical treatment for the conservation of monuments, antiquities and the research in this subject continue to be published under the heading of Archaeological Chemistry in *Indian Archaeology—A Review*, the annual bulletin of the Archaeological Survey of India; *Puratattva,* journal of the Indian Archaeological Society, New Delhi; *Indian Journal of History of Science* a publication of Indian National Science Academy, New Delhi; and in other journals, like *Journal of Numismatic Society of India*; *Bharati* and *Bulletin of the Deccan College Post-Graduate and Research Institute.*

POST-INDEPENDENCE DEVELOPMENT OF ARCHAEOLOGICAL CHEMISTRY

There was a tremendous spurt in archaeological activities in Independent India. Many new archaeological sites were excavated. In addition to the Archaeological Survey of India, departments of Archaeology were set up by the state governments and universities. The efforts of these institutions brought out our cultural heritage in the form of a large number of archaeological sites such as Kalibangan, Lothal, Ahar, Navadatoli, Nashik, Eran, Hastinapura, etc., excavated by various organizations. Similarly sites like Nevasa, Langhnaj, Inamgaon, Chandoli were excavated by Deccan College, Pune.

These excavations brought to light a rich cultural heritage in the form of antiquities—the products of various industries and crafts from various archaeological sites in different regions of India. The scientific studies of the antiquities can throw useful light on ancient Indian technology—chemical and scientific practices and metallurgical and ceramic techniques. These studies are also important because it is from these practices and techniques that the present-day science and technology have developed. However, as compared to the rich material culture recovered from various Indian sites, very little work was done till the 1970s, to know ancient Indian technology through scientific examination.

B.B. Lal and O.P. Agrawal joined the Archaeological Survey of India in 1952 and worked on conservation together with some geochronological studies. O.P. Agrawal worked for conservation and has made a major contribution in conservation of our Indian Cultural heritage. Similarly Gairola (1950-60) carried out much of the analytical and conservation work of ancient remains from number of places. He analysed red paints, lime washes, plasters on Bhubaneswar and Konark temples to investigate the nature of extraneous coating on the temples (Gairola 1950). The red paint was found to be a simple mixture of local hematite (red ochre) and clay as against the earlier belief that it was composed of organic origins like unripe fruits, resin lac, bel fruit, etc. The white coatings on temples were found to be of lime. Gypsum was not found in plaster samples, unlike the much older plasters of Mohenjo Daro, Harappa and the Nile Valley sites in Egypt. This work initiated research on the ancient remains with the help of chemical analysis. Gairola (1952) has described the use of organic solvents for stain removing and use of vinyl acetate in spirit, toluene for surface coating for the preservation of some ancient paintings.

A note on skilful cleaning and preservation of Tibetan paintings and a bone object embedded in clay in the excavation at Rupar has been given by Gairola (1954-5). Use of methyl metacrylate in alcohol for joining the sheets as well as for impregnation and use of paraffin wax for filling the cracks in the bones has been suggested. Gairola (1956) found that the metal ware manufactured at Bidar was composed of zinc 92 per cent, copper 3.6 per cent and lead 1.3 per cent. Gairola (1957, 1960) did the preservation of fragile textile from Central Asia and Rajasthani miniature paintings and wall painting.

The results of chemical analysis used to appear as supplementary information in the appendix of the excavation reports or archaeological journals. The work in conservation and specific research problems carried out by B.B. Lal, as a Chief Archaeological Chemist in ASI, brought this interdisciplinary field in the main stream of archaeology. For example, Lal (1951) analysed one copper specimen from Bisauli. The object, made up of copper, which contained 98.77 per cent copper and 0.66 per cent nickel as an impurity, derived from copper ore showed that the ore from which the metal smelted was of Indian origin and was not made of bronze. This was an important conclusion about the ancient copper object, on the basis of chemical analysis.

Lal (1952) discussed the chemical constituents of a few Indian glass samples with a view to correlating glass industries of sites and establishing chronology with the help of internal evidence. A report on the analysis of glass samples of different colours from the sites, Taxila, Nalanda, Ahichchhatra and Arikamedu has been given. The data is useful for tracing the chronology and regional developments of ancient glass making. On the basis of this data, it is possible to trace the history of the glass industry.

Lal (1953) has reviewed the progress of archaeological chemistry in India in three decades after the establishment of the chemistry branch of the Archaeological Survey of

India. He has given a detailed report on the analytical work of pottery, ancient metallurgy and chemical conservation of monuments, paintings, etc. Some of the salient features about this are mentioned here.

Ceramics

The materials excavated at Mohenjo Daro and Harappa were chemically analysed. The results throw much light on the development of the material technology of protohistoric India. The specimens of glass glaze found at Taxila and other Buddhist sites were analysed and much information was obtained about the state of technical knowledge that existed in India during the historical period. The results of chemical analysis of glass specimens from Nalanda, Arikamedu, Ahichchhatra and other places were of great value in determining the composition and provenance of raw materials used in their manufacture.

Metallurgy

The application of chemical analysis in the investigation of metallurgical problems regarding the metal and alloy specimens recovered in the course of excavation has been also proved significant. The analysis of specimens from Mohenjo Daro and Harappa has shown that the ancient craftsman had attained a very high degree of skill in metallurgy. Bronze was well known and used on a fairly large scale, while the technique of its casting and working had also developed considerably.

Chemical conservation of ancient monuments was based on a firm scientific footing. The problems of preservation of stone monuments are extremely complicated in India because of their exposure to varied climatic conditions. The materials used in the construction of these monuments are of widely different nature. Also, they are exposed to varying climatic factors such as temperature, humidity, atmospheric pollution, salinity, etc., which are different in various parts of the country. As such it becomes necessary to examine the causes of decay before suitable preservative measures are devised. At this stage, the Chemical Branch of the ASI reinforced the petrographic investigation with the help of newly set up petrological section. The petrographic studies together with analytical data resulted in giving an insight into the causes of decay of stone. In this way, large scale chemical preservation was carried out at Elephanta, Karla, Bhaja and Kanheri in the Bombay State; Konark, Bhubaneswar, Udayagiri and Khandagiri in Orissa; Nalanda, Lauriya Nandangarh and Maner in Bihar; and Agra and Fatehpur Sikri in Uttar Pradesh. Together with this, large scale fungicidal treatment was successfully carried out at several sites by employing 1-2 per cent solution of zinc silicofluoride. The Chemical Branch, at this stage undertook the research for a suitable preservative for the consolidation of rock.

The mural paintings in the monuments needed the treatment and preservation. Suitable cleaning reagents, detergents and emulsions were evolved by research. The wall paintings at Ajanta, Ellora, Tanjore, Panamalai were scientifically surveyed to study the technique of the painting process at each place to find out suitable preservative methods.

In this report on archaeological chemistry and scientific studies, Lal (1953) at the end has mentioned the necessity to study the environmental conditions in which the various cultures flourished. He has further has pointed out that the chemical and mechanical study of the exposed deposits from various layers in the course of excavation is of great importance. For example, the phosphate content of soils from various layers is helpful in understanding the distribution of population. He has also mentioned the need of systematic work on the application of the fluorine test to the bone materials for determining the dates of prehistoric sites. This could be utilized to establish a chronological sequence and dating prehistoric sites.

In the 1970s, two projects on the chemical analysis of archaeological deposits and animal fossils from India were undertaken at Deccan College, Pune, and successfully completed. The details of these two will appear later in this chapter.

That chemical analysis if supplemented by some other technique can give further more information about the ancient technology. Chemical analysis revealed (Lal 1956) that brass and bronzes with high tin were used for casting images at Nalanda. The results are useful in understanding the composition of alloys employed and the sources of material used. However, to furnish material evidence regarding the metallurgical processes employed at Nalanda, systematic metallurgical examination of representative bronzes together with spectroscopic examination is necessary (Lal 1956).

The analysis sometimes can give an opposite answer as against the previous belief. Chemical analysis showed (Lal 1958) that the material from Arikamedu contains high percentage of alkali. This agrees with the alkali content of common glass. It was thought before that those people might have used fossil wood and not glass for this material. However, microscopic examination and chemical analysis showed that the rods of the glass like material unearthed at Arikamedu were composed of glass. It is further concluded that various metallic oxides have been used for producing glasses of different colours.

The soil chemical analysis can help in the environmental studies, was a new aspect in archaeological studies. For the first time, at Birbhanpur, soil samples from two trenches were microscopically examined, chemically analysed and subjected to mechanical analysis for studying the environmental conditions at Birbhanpur during the Mesolithic times (Lal 1958). The chemical analysis showed that there is a considerable leaching of alkalies, removal of silica and accumulation of aluminium and iron oxides, in the samples in the upper layers which overlie the implementiferrous horizon. This indicates a long period of the weathering. The ratio of SiO_2/Al_2O_3 confirms this conclusion.

The pre-microlithic phase is marked by intense weathering under hot and wet conditions. The weathering of the deposit overlying habitational layer, on the other hand, indicates milder conditions tending towards comparatively dry phase. Post-microlithic period is suggestive of a drier climate.

For a detailed geochronological investigation, with a view to studying the climatic conditions and environments prevailing at the site during prehistoric times, the mechanical, chemical and heavy mineral analysis was carried out by Lal and Lal (1961). In chemical analysis, maturity index (Al_2O_3/Na_2O+K_2O), Sa value (SiO_2/Al_2O_3), total soluble material, Fe_2O_3 and the leaching factor were determined.

The chemical character of the sediments depend upon the size of the grains and their maturity. A completely matured sand will contain only quartz, while the clay portion will be rich in alumina. Thus the order of the loss of oxides may be determined by a comparison of the chemical data of the fresh and weathered rocks. As alumina and soda are not likely to be added to or subtracted from the sediment during or after the process of deposition, the Al_2O_3/Na_2O+K_2O ratio is calculated. This ratio is taken as the maturity index of different layers in the process of weathering. In the trench BBP-1 (Birbhanpur I), maturity index is nearly constant in the upper three layers but increases in the lower layers. The total soluble material in arid soils is 30 per cent and in humid soils it is 15 per cent. According to soluble material in soils, it was concluded that the climate prevailing at the time of microlithic man was humid (Lal and Lal 1961).

In this progress of archaeological chemistry, we come across an example of a valuable collaborative picture of work between scientists and the excavator. Lal (1962 and 1963) has reported a compilation of the concerned ^{14}C dates of some protohistoric sites from Indo-Pakistan subcontinent.

The Harappan or Indus Civilization was ascribed in broad terms to the end of fourth and third millennia BC. However, sharper chronological precision was needed. Also, in the 1950s and 1960s, many new cultures came to light, e.g. the Painted Grey Ware Culture of the Ganga-Yamuna Doab, the Chalcolithic cultures of central India and the Deccan, the Neolithic culture of the north-west, etc. It was because of the invaluable help offered by radiocarbon dating, a rough chronological outline of these cultures was possible. This has been discussed and reported by Lal with radiocarbon dates available at the sites like Kot Diji, Damb Sadaat, Kalibangan, Lothal, Moḥenjo Daro, Ahar, Eran, Navadatoli, Nevasa Utnur and so on, in the subcontinent.

Conservation and preservation of ancient objects is an important task for the Archaeological Survey of India. The easy methods which can be adopted in the simple chemical laboratory have been discussed (Lal 1962, 1963). With some new instructions, most of these are similar to those adopted by the pioneer chemists in the ASI. The techniques required for preservation of portable objects depend upon the nature of material employed in their fabrication (i.e. metallic, non-metallic and organic mainly) and the causes of their decay and deterioration have been presented similarly, as mentioned by Sana Ullah (1946).

Metallic Objects

Gold is easily cleaned by washing in water containing a little ammonia. Cementation of mud and clay due to lime, if any, is removed by very dilute nitric acid. Silver is treated with 5 per cent aqueous citric acid which removes corrosion products. Lead object is treated with zinc and caustic soda or with dilute acetic acid. Iron object is treated with 10 per cent oxalic acid, with zinc and caustic soda, if heavily corroded.

Copper and bronze objects are treated with alkaline Rochelle salt solution. Fragile objects are treated with 10 per cent sodium bicarbonate solution for 10 to 15 days. Copper objects covered with calcareous incrustation are treated with sodium metaphosphate solution and so on.

All metallic objects are made free from any chemical solution by washing several times with plain water after the chemical treatment is over. They are dried and preserved with vinyl acetate or methyl methacrylate solution.

Siliceous, Calcareous Objects

Stone objects are affected by soluble salts and fungal growth and are covered with calcareous and other accretions. Steeping of the object in plain water for a week, results in the elimination of soluble salts. A highly decayed object is consolidated with 3 to 5 per cent vinyl acetate solution with a view to preventing its breaking up and disintegration.

Monuments

The chemical treatment and preservation of large monuments is complex because of the complicated nature of their decay, depending upon the varied climatic and environmental conditions, such as hilly or coastal region, growth of moss and lichen, as well as the fluctuations in temperature.

Use of asphalt and other damp proof courses around the foundations of walls have been suggested to minimize the capillary absorption of ground moisture. Impregnation of the surface with paraffin wax eliminate the solvent action of the rainwater for sometime, thereby providing protection from dampness. Methyl methacrylate resin dissolved in toluene is a better surface protector. Many organic solvents like acetone, benzene, toluene ether, xylene, etc., are used to eliminate oil and smoke stains from the stone surface. Use of 3 per cent calcium metaphosphate for removing hard calcareous incrustations or that of 10 per cent ammonium carbonate for removing gypsum incrustations is helpful. However, this should be followed by gentle scrubbing and thorough washing with pure salt free water.

Growth of moss or plants that take deep root in structure results in considerable damage to them. The elimination of moss is effected by the fungicidal treatment of surface with 1-2 per cent aqueous zinc silicofluoride, pentachlorophenol and copper naphthenate and the surface is coated with protective coating. Large plants with deep roots in structures are cut off and the roots are injected with sodium arsenate or sulphuric acid.

Application of preservatives to the surface has a temporary effect. Therefore, periodical applications of surface protective reagents like vinyl acetate, methyl methacrylate or paraffin wax are necessary for preservation.

Lime water is not a suitable material for the consolidation of decayed rock. It is suggested that where the rock is porous and friable, a very thin colloidal suspension of ochrous clays (red and yellow ocher) with 1 to 2 per cent methyl methacrylate resin solutions is spread, under pressure. Colloidal clays reduce the water absorption of the stone.

It is necessary that all the materials used in structural conservation of ancient monuments are free from soluble salts. Also, the concrete used in structural repairs should be impermeable to water.

Marble Structures

Surface accumulation of greasy matter like dust, dirt and smoke is cleaned with cloth soaked in a mixture of soft soap 10 gm water 100 cc and ammonia liquid 1 cc. The removal of thicker fatty accretions is effected with the help of organic solvents like rectified spirit, benzene, xylene, pyridine, etc.

Clay and Glass

The treatment of burnt clay objects is generally simple. Steeping in water results in the removal of most of the incrustations and soluble salts. For a fragile, porous object, a preliminary consolidation with vinyl acetate is necessary. Unburnt clay objects disintegrates with water treatment and strength can be imparted to them by controlled firing to about 600 °C. in a furnace. Glass objects are generally found weathered, porous and spongy due to decomposition by carbonated ground water. Alkalies leache out and silica accumulates. Object is impregnated with vinyl acetate solution. Accretions are eliminated with organic solvents such as alcohol and benzene. Precious and semi-precious stones, beads, pendants, generally are found in a good state of preservation.

Organic Materials

Wooden antiquities are susceptible to attack by insect pests, fungus and soluble salts resulting in thier deterioration. For protection against insects, the best treatment is fumigation with carbon disulphide. An object with cavities is impregnated with paraffin wax. Generally a preservative coating of 5 per cent vinyl acetate solution in toluene is useful. The wooden object, deteriorated due to certain fungi, is treated with a fungicide, 1 per cent mercuric chloride solution in alcohol. Elimination of soluble salts is satisfactorily done by the use of paper pulp. It is further preserved with a 5 per cent vinyl acetate resin solution in toluene.

A freshly excavated bone or ivory object is washed in plain water and is consolidated by impregnation with vinyl acetate. Soluble salts are drawn out by osmosis. Dull and stained ivory can be rendered white by the bleaching action of hydrogen peroxide. For mending an object like horn, 20 per cent solution of vinyl acetate is used.

The preservation of manuscripts, paintings and other ancient objects of paper is a difficult task. Accretions such as dust, dirt and excreta of insects is removed with camel hair brushes. Oily stains are removed with ether or benzene. Water marks are removed by distilled water containing a few drops of rectified spirit. Fungus on old paper can be destroyed by treatment with a solution of thymol in rectified spirit. Hydrogen peroxide solution of 10 per cent containing a few drops of ammonia is effective in eliminating stains on old paper. Moth affected objects and documents affected by insects should be subjected to thymol or carbon disulphide fumigation in a fumigation chamber.

Leather objects become hard and brittle with age. It can be kept in a good state of preservation by application of castor oil. Fumigation of these destroys all insects. Para-nitrophenol and pentachlorophenol have been found to be effective in checking of the recurrence of fungal growth on leather objects. Two per cent solution of santobrite in water or alcohol is suitable for impregnation. For eliminating danger from insects and vermines, a small quantity of paradichlorobenzene is kept in air tight show cases used for housing these objects.

Chemical preservation of typical paintings in India is described by Lal (1966). Paintings from different regions like Fatehpur Sikri, Agra, Vadodara, Chandrapur, Bijapur, Badami, Ajanta, Allahabad, Tanjavur, etc., were treated. He has discussed the causes of damage, need of conservation and the choice of preservatives and adhesives. A systematic scientific study was conducted with a view to determining the nature of materials used in execution of mural paintings. Pigments were analysed, composition of plaster was determined and nature of binding media was ascertained by chemical analysis. For the study of binding media, chromatography was found useful.

As usual, organic solvents like acetone, alcohol and ether for cleaning and vinyl acetate (3-5 per cent) for coating and protection was used. He mentions Polyvinyl acetate dissolved in toluene-ethyl alcohol mixture containing 1-2 per cent dibutyl phthalate is the chief preservative consolidant and adhesive currently in use on Indian wall paintings.

After the 1960s, the progress of archaeological chemistry was more towards the problem oriented research regarding the ancient cultures, in addition to the work of conservation of the cultural remains. This was possible because, apart from the chemistry section in the Archaeological Survey of India, as mentioned earlier, new departments of Archeology were set up by the state governments and premier universities. Archaeological exploration and excavations, teaching and research was taken up by such organizations. Additional chemistry laboratories were also engaged in this field. K.T.M. Hegde, H.C. Bhardwaj, D.P. Agrawal, O.P. Agrawal are amongst those who had pursued research with significant contribution and had given the present status to archaeological chemistry, in the last three to four decades. A brief account of the work by these scientists and the research carried out at Deccan College has been given below. As far as university departments of archaeology from Uttar Pradesh are concerned, Prakash and Rawat (1965), Prakash and Singh (1968) worked on the chemical studies of Indian archaeological antiquities. Over three decades beginning with the 1960s, K.T.M. Hegde of the M.S. University of Baroda worked on the ancient Indian metallurgy, ceramic technology, environmental archaeology and so on. He set up a chemistry laboratory and necessary infrastructure in the department for chemical and physical analysis and preservation of antiquities. He equipped this laboratory with advanced instruments to carry out metallurgical, petrological and chemical analysis of antiquities.

K.T.M. Hegde studied copper metallurgy of the Chalcolithic period and made technical studies on other archaeological materials (Hegde 1965) for his doctoral thesis. His work on the analysis of PGW and NBP is acknowledged as the most important contribution to ceramic studies in archaeology. In the field of environmental archaeology, Hegde in the 1970s work in Gujarat and Rajasthan in collaboration with the Cambridge team. It was a significant attempt to correlate the prehistoric cultures with environmental changes in the region (Allchin et al. 1978). He also used caliche concentrations in the alluvial and aeolian deposits as an evidence for the chronology of the stratigraphy, climatic change and their relation to the culture of early man. On the basis of radiocarbon dates of caliche, chronological framework for the alluvial stratigraphy of the plain of Gujarat has been constructed. Chemical analysis of the soil samples of buried soil within the dunes and calcified sand on the surface of the dunes was carried out. Since caliche indicates climatic change, carbonate, humus, iron, phosphate contents have been linked with the climatic fluctuation during the Late Quaternary period in Gujarat and Rajasthan (Hegde 1975-6).

The most important excavation carried out by Hegde was in 1983, in collaboration with the British Museum, London, at Zawar near Udaipur in Rajasthan. This brought to light concrete evidence of the 'vertical distribution' method used in zinc metallurgy in ancient India, firmly establishing the antiquity of the knowledge of zinc distillation in India. This disproved the popularly held belief that the vertical distillation of zinc started in Europe in the nineteenth century (Hegde et al. 1987).

The first radiocarbon laboratory was set up in 1962 at the Tata Institute of Fundamental Research, Bombay. Afterwards it was shifted to the Physical Research Laboratory, Ahmedabad. The Birbal Sahani Institute of Palaeobotany, Lucknow also has another unit of radiocarbon laboratory. D.P. Agrawal initially in TIFR and subsequently attached to PRL, determined a series of radiocarbon dates for a number of archaeological cultural periods from different archaeological sites in India (Agrawal and Kusumgar 1974 and 1990; Agrawal and Yadava 1992).

He undertook an integrated study of the Copper-Bronze Age, chronology, technology and ecology and proposed a model for proto-historic archaeology. Since absolute chronology based on the ^{14}C dating method provides a firm framework, he has given two phases of urbanization, one based on copper metallurgy and Indus plains, and the other on iron metallurgy and Indo-Ganga plains. (Agrawal 1967-8). As regards archaeo-technological studies he pointed out that the typological studies of artefacts should be supplimented by technological studies. He has discussed the salient features about the copper bronze technology involving extraction, alloying of the metal and the metal forging techniques of proto-historic cultures. The objects from Navadatoli, Chandoli, Somnath, Ahar, Nevasa were studied (Agrawal 1969-70). Thus ancient metal technology was his another field of research (Agrawal 1971). For calibration, he compared the radiocarbon dates of wood material and the dates obtained by dendrochronology (Agrawal and Kusumgar 1974) and discussed the problems about the corrections in ^{14}C dates. The Geological and archaeological evidence, together with the radiocarbon dates determined by him (Agrawal and Margabandhu 1975-6) from Kolar fields showed that these gold fields were exploited from the fifth century AD.

H.C. Bhardwaj, in the beginning, as a Chief Archaeological Chemist, Government of India, worked in the field of conservation and scientific archaeology. After 1964, while working in the Department of Ancient Indian Culture and Archaeology, Banaras Hindu University, he also undertook various studies in ancient Indian technology. A multidisciplinary approach involving archaeology, chemistry, indology, metallurgy, glass and ceramic technology taken by him brought to light the salient features of ancient Indian technology. Such type of studies revealed intellectual efforts made by Early Indians in exploiting natural mineral resources and making a variety of materials from ceramics, glasses, metals including copper, silver, gold, iron and their alloys. In addition to reporting on the chemical composition of various metals and alloys, the probable sources of the ores, methods of ore dressing, technique of smelting and extraction of metals from their ores, the temperature obtained, the role of fluxes, nature of slags, methods of purification of metals, process of fabrication, casting and forging techniques as used in the ancient period were enlightened. He analysed glass beads of different colours from Rajghat for silica, alumina, iron, copper, calcium, magnesium, nickel, sodium and potassium. These were soda lime silica glasses. He discussed the different colouring agents or chemical elements, such as iron for black, copper for blue, ferrous for green and copper, iron and nickel for opaque red colour (Bhardwaj 1967-8). He analysed chemically and metallographically the copper and bronze objects from Rajghat. The copper objects were found to contain minor impurities of other elements like lead, iron, nickel, calcium etc. (Bhardwaj 1968-9). A number of copper red glass from Mohenjo Daro, Rajghat, Taxila, Kausambi, Nalanda, Arikamedu were chemically analysed for the study of the copper red glass through the ages. He has concluded that the glass technology of 1700 BC had made significant contribution to the evolution of copper red glasses (Bhardwaj 1969-70). His studies on the ancient iron technology, gold coins from Rajghat excavations, chemical studies of glass, pottery and the chronological studies of copper coins have proved useful to the students of archaeology, metallurgy and historians of sciences and technology (Bhardwaj 1979). His significant contribution in ancient glass technology was reflected in the International Congress on Glass which was organized by him at New Delhi in 1986. Modern glass technologists realize that some aspects of glass, such as weathering with time, the prudent use of raw materials, recipes for colours, etc., can be understood by the study of ancient glass. In this connection, research in ancient glass technology with their chemical analyses was presented in this conference (Bhardwaj 1987). This gives full information on chemical analysis of ancient glasses. Ancient Indian glasses had a high alumina content and it was emphasized that most ancient glasses were made indigenously as against the belief that they were imported from West or Near West.

Conservation of our cultural property is the main and important aspect in archaeological chemistry. The distinguished name in this field is of O.P. Agrawal. In the beginning he was Head of National Museum's Conservation Laboratory, a pioneer laboratory of India. Then he was asked by Govt. of India to set up National Research Laboratory for Conservation of Cultural Property (NRLC) in 1976 at Lucknow. He is considered a pioneer in the conservation field and rendered services for the development of conservation not only in India (Agrawal and Dhavan 1990), but also in most countries of South and South-East Asia (Agrawal 1984). He founded the Indian National Trust for Art and Cultural Heritage (INTACH), which is aware of and working for the conservation of monuments, paintings, art and cultural heritage. He helped in the establishment of several conservation laboratories in various states, at places like Bangalore, Delhi, Bhubaneswar, etc., in India. He studied the factors for alterations and deterioration of the most famous monumental structure of Taj Mahal (Agruwal 1992-3). He was honoured with the International Award for Conservation in 1993, by the UNESCO for his dedicated and continued service to conservation.

ARCHAEOLOGICAL CHEMISTRY IN DECCAN COLLEGE, PUNE

The chemistry laboratory in the Archaeology Department of Deccan College was established with the inspiration by H.D. Sankalia. In the beginning, G.G. Mujumdar initiated studies on the atmospheric conditions and the firing temperature of the ancient pottery, some work on chemical conservation of the metallic objects and preliminary analysis like pH, calcium carbonate, organic carbon content of soils was carried out. He also carried out some experiments on the cowdung ash which were helpful in knowing the nature of Kupgal ashmound from Karnataka (Mujumdar and Rajaguru 1966). After joining this department in 1973, R.V. Joshi took initiative in the research of archaeological chemistry besides its routine analysis. By this time, in the 1980s, the archaeological research in India was becoming more and more multidisciplinary employing the methodology of physical and natural sciences. Joshi (1985) made a brief review of progress of archaeological chemistry in India after Independence. An account of the work on conservation of monuments and antiquities and chemical studies of antiquities has been summarized in this. He has mentioned that in the beginning cultural material studies involved simple chemical methods for cleaning stone and metal antiquities. Subsequently better results were achieved by elaborate methods with the available advanced scientific techniques. Experiments were also carried out on some selected monuments to study the effects of environment and air pollution. While mentioning the importance of chemical studies of metal objects, ores, slags, etc. Joshi emphasized that chemical analysis of these ancient materials is carried out for investigating ancient metallurgical processes involved in obtaining the metal used in the manufacture of various antiquities like weapons of war, agricultural implements and a variety of art objects. Chemical analysis of the ancient glass and ceramic can provide useful information about the manufacturing processes. All such studies throw considerable light on the socio-economic and cultural activities of the ancient peoples.

The research in these two lines, as Joshi has mentioned further, was enhanced mostly due to the work done by scientists, B.B. Lal, O.P. Agrawal, H.C. Bhardwaj, K.T.M. Hegde and D.P. Agrawal.

With these developments in mind, R.V. Joshi strongly felt the need for chemical studies of archaeological deposits and fossils since chemistry was playing an important role in enhancing the value of research for meaningful results. He provided a firm base for research in the archaeological chemistry laboratory of the Deccan College, with the successful completion of the projects on chemistry of soils and fluorine analysis of ancient bones which have assumed now an important role in scientific research in India. Sankalia

(1965) in the 1960s had sent some bone samples from Langhnaj excavation for dating by fluorine analysis to Oakley in Britain. However, he could not get the results. After two/three decades of this incidence, by fluorine has become a routine work of testing the ancient bones in the chemistry laboratory of the Deccan College.

Soil Chemistry of Ancient Habitational Deposits

Chemical studies of archaeological deposits can provide additional information on stratigraphy, settlement patterns, human activity areas and related ecological problems which till the 1970s had been based largely on the physical composition of archaeological debris and associated cultural materials. The human occupation of land causes chemical changes in the soil which is, therefore, recorded in the chemistry of the soil. Dwellings, settlements and areas surrounding them are characterized by phosphate rich organic waste resulting from human activity. The term 'anthrosol' is used for the soil which is influenced by various human activities. Joshi undertook a UGC project on the chemical analysis of archaeological deposits in India. They studied the enrichment of some chemical elements in the archaeological deposits of different cultural periods from different geographical regions in India (Joshi and Deotare 1983). The significance of soil analysis can be enlightened with the following conclusions:

1. Phosphorus ranges in habitational deposits from 0.2 to 1.0 per cent while the values are 0.04 to 0.1 per cent in non-habitational areas. Phosphorus content of more than 0.2 per cent is a sure indicator of ancient habitation or human interference at a particular locality.
2. The periods of maximum intensity of habitation can be recognized from the very high values of phosphate at the multicultural sites, e.g. the Early Jorwe Culture at Inamgaon, the Savalda Culture at Daimabad and Ramtirth Culture at Apegaon. The results of analysis from the two sites, Inamgaon and Daimabad have been compared since they belong to similar environment (Joshi et al. 1978-9). The elements like phosphorus, organic carbon, nitrogen, calcium carbonate in the habitational deposits are directly proportional to the extent, duration and intensity of habitation.
3. Periods of desertion or the gaps in habitation could be detected by low phosphate content in some habitational deposits at Rupar (Punjab), Dangwada (Madhya Pradesh) and Veerapuram (Andhra Pradesh).
4. Phosphate field test also helped to demarcate the extent of settlements at Chalcolithic Inamgaon and Megalithic Bhagimohari (Deotare 1983-4).
5. Distribution of soil phosphorus within different activity areas was used to distinguish subsections within the sites of Kuntasi (Gujarat) and Balathal (Rajasthan) by Kshirsagar (1991-2, 1996).
6. The higher nitrogen content of the sediments from courtyards as compared to that of the soils inside the houses at Chalcolithic Inamgaon indicated that the courtyards were used as cattle sheds as it is well known that the decomposition of animal excreta increases the nitrogen content of soils (Kshirsagar 1983).

Thus the chemistry of archaeological deposits plays an important role in different aspects about the ancient settlements. It has now become routine in the excavation process to collect soil samples during the course of excavation and to analyse them. Phosphorus analysis of soils from archaeological sites in Garhwal Himalaya and the Ganga Yamuna Doab has also been carried out to establish the correlation between different fractions of phosphorus (Nautiyal et al. 1992). They also determined the total and available phosphorus for the burial soils in order to investigate the conversion behaviour of phosphorus in the cist and urn burial complex at the sites in Kumaun Himalaya (Farswan and Nautiyal 1997).

BONE CHEMISTRY AS TOOL FOR DATING AND PALAEODIETARY STUDIES

The commonest feature of the archaeological record of a past human settlement is the variety of human and animal bones. Chemical analysis of ancient bones is useful in relative dating and for knowing their fossilization process and in palaeoenvironmental studies. The accumulation, depletion or alteration of a number of substances in ancient bones is a definable function of time. Such substances furnish useful dating information. The chemistry section of the Archaeology Department of Deccan College initiated this kind of investigation in this direction.

Taking into consideration the importance of this line of research, R.V. Joshi undertook another UGC project on the chemical analysis of archaeological animal fossils from India (Joshi and Kshirsagar 1986). The element fluorine gets accumulated in buried bones from ground waters as time passes. It was observed that fluorine/phosphate ratio is an indicator of the relative age of the buried bone. The analysis of a number of animal bone samples of different periods and from different regions of India proved fluorine method to be useful for relative dating (Kshirsagar 1993). A five years conventional distillation-titration method was replaced by modern Fluoride Electrode in Deccan College, for more accurate and quick results. Now we have a reference list of standard fluorine/phosphate ratios in bones from diverse environmental regions of India, for dating bones to be found in those regions in the archaeological context. On this basis, the bones found at the sites Uran, Chander (Maharashtra), Poredam (Kerala), Tiruvellur (Tamil Nadu) and some Mesolithic sites from Rajasthan, have been dated.

The important observations that are drawn from fluorine analysis can be summarized as follows:

1. The bones from archaeological sites can be dated to Late Holocene when ratio is less than 1.
2. The ratio increases to 2 to 3 in bones from the Early Holocene to Terminal Pleistocene period.
3. It is 3 to 6 in bones of the Upper Pleistocene period.
4. The bones from Late Middle Pleistocene and Earlier, up to Tertiary period have the ratio from 6.5 to 9.0, i.e. fluorine saturation occurs beyond the Late Middle Pleistocene period. The theoretical saturation value of this ratio is 8.92.

Thus, bones can be dated on the basis of the fluorine/phosphate ratio, in the time brackets as mentioned above, from the Late Holocene to Late Middle Pleistocene period. This is now a scientifically established technique that definitely helps to assign tentative time brackets to the bones from the undated site. These deductions are well supported by faunal studies.

In addition to the dating of ancient bones, the voluminous literature on bone chemical investigations for ancient diet, generated during the last two decades, represents one of the significant growth areas of archaeological chemistry. Quantitative analysis of certain trace elements (such as strontium, barium, zinc, copper, etc.) incorporated into bone mineral has been used to assess diet, nutrition, health status and pathology. Animal food is rich in zinc and copper, plant food in strontium, manganese, etc., the whole meal grain cereals and sea food is rich in selenium, these are some of the examples for dietary studies. The first author could participate in the project on palaeodiet in Sweden. Her main contribution was the successful extraction of selenium from archaeological bones by differential Cathodic Stripping polarograph (Kshirsagar 1987).

The trace element analysis of bones from archaeological sites has the potential to reveal different levels of food consumption in ancient societies. This is possible because some elements are incorporated into bones in a determinable relation to the amounts in which they are present in various foods. By calculating the concentration of such elements in ancient bones and comparing them with the evidence of food remains it is possible to differentiate between different kinds of food consumed, such as animal food, plant food, etc. A trace element analysis of human skeletal remains from Chalcolithic Inamgaon was carried out (Gogte and Kshirsagar 1988) on the basis of which it was possible to infer that the Late Jorwe people consumed more animal food and fish (as shown by greater concentrations of copper and zinc) in their diet than the Early Jorwe people. Possible differences in the social status of various individuals was also inferred from this analysis on bone samples from the Late Jorwe period. Dietary differences between males and females were, however, not detected.

STUDIES IN ANCIENT TECHNOLOGY

Apart from soil and bone analysis, studies on ancient glass as well as iron smelting technology was carried out at Deccan College. The resistivity method of recording electrical resistivity measurements was successfully applied to locating a Megalithic iron smelting site at Naikund (Gogte 1982). Further, an attempt was made to determine the efficiency of the iron smelting operation from chemical analysis. Change in the chemical composition of iron ore, slightly reduced iron ore, cinder and tapped slag was determined to get a better idea of the smelting operation. It was concluded that the megalithic smelters used about 10 to 12 kg iron ore for a single operation producing 3 to 4 kg of pure iron (Gogte et al. 1982).

The roots of today's advanced technology can be traced back in time through the chemical analysis of ancient glass. The International Congress on glass is a good example

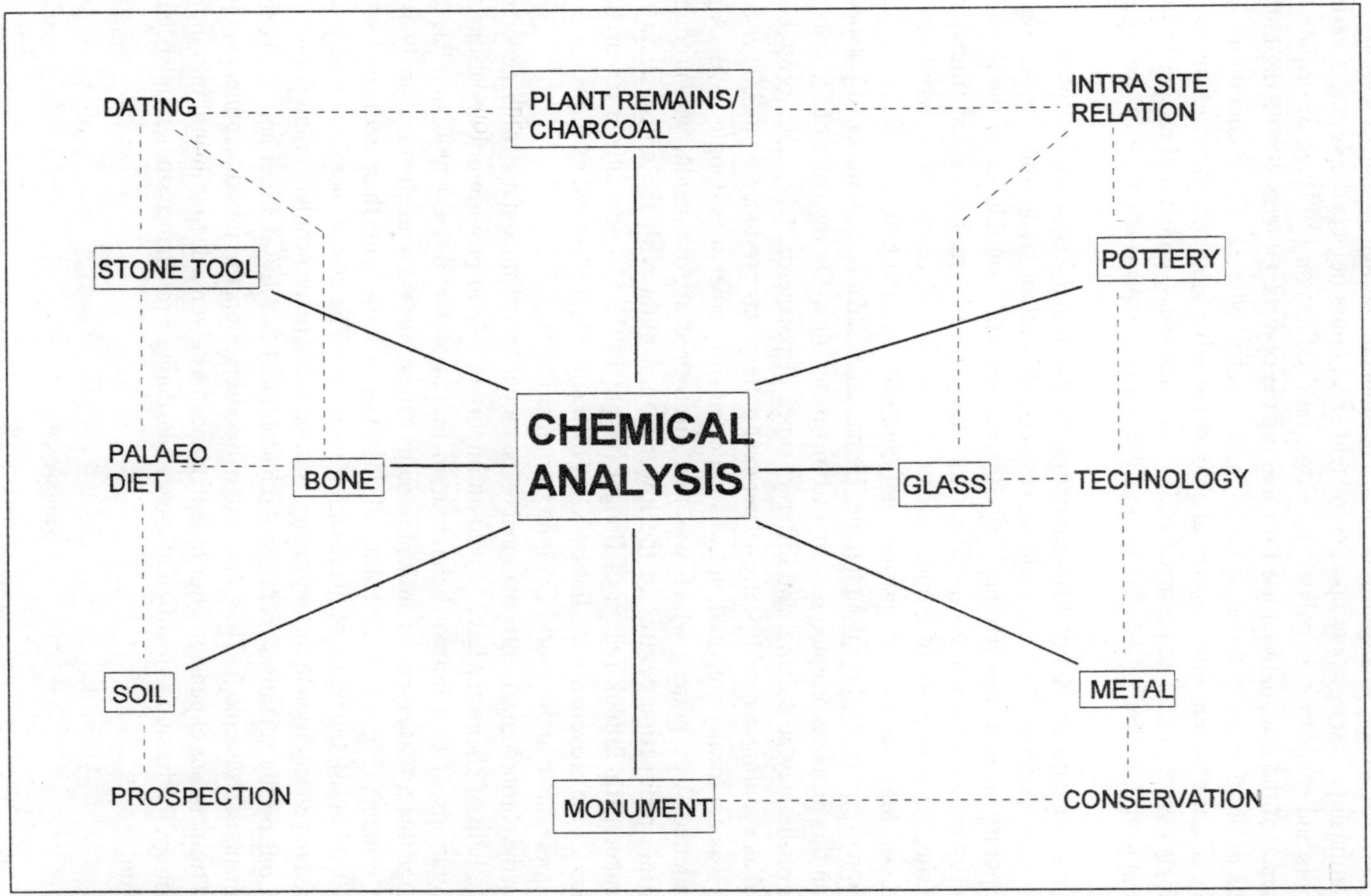

Fig. 1. Diverse applications of Archaeological Chemistry.

of this fact as already mentioned earlier. The analysis is also useful in establishing interrelationships among contemporary ancient sites. Glass objects displaying a variety of colours and shades were analysed by Gogte and Kshirsagar (1991) to determine the provenance of the raw material used for making the objects. Objects containing higher amounts of alumina were found to be of Indian origin, whereas those containing low amounts of alumina but with substantial amounts of other elements like lead, antimony and cobalt were exotic. The presence of iron in black glass, cobalt and copper in blue glass and lead in yellow glass were responsible for the respective colour of these glass objects.

Gogte's work on the X-ray diffraction and chemical analysis of ancient pottery has given a new dimension to the field of research in ancient trade and correlation of contemporary ancient sites (Gogte 1989). On the basis of resemblance of the impurity pattern (by trace element or X-ray diffraction analysis), in certain potsherds found at a distant site, the possibility of a trade link or a common source of raw material can be pointed out. Material with composition not compatible to indigenous sources suggests its foreign origin or import through trade. He has analysed a large number of potsherds based on this problem oriented research from various sites. On the basis of the mineral pattern of the clay at Balathal and different types of potsherds, he is able to establish Balathal as a trading centre. Locally 40 per cent pottery was produced while 60 per cent pottery was not locally prepared, but was imported from other sites (Gogte 1996). Also, the Rouletted Ware pottery which was first discovered at Arikamedu, was produced at multiple production centres in the lower Ganga plain with the epicentre in the Chandraketugarh-Tamluk region of Bengal (Gogte 1997). His specialized research in ceramics for the provenance studies by X-ray diffraction and chemical methods has been highly appreciated at the World Ceramic Congress (1995).

Thus, the chronological, compositional or locational data of ancient materials, generated with the help of chemistry have played an important role in providing foundations for interpretations of past human behaviour in Indian archaeology. Chemistry has the advantage that diverse types of ancient remains can be studied with chemical analysis of ancient remains (Fig. 1). Archaeological chemists in India with their dedicated work have helped in solving many of the research problems. The use of chemistry which was restricted to conservation in the beginning, was extended to the problem oriented research carried out by the scientists from the Archaeological Survey of India and University departments of archaeology. Thus, in addition to conservation, this interdisciplinary subject with its tremendous expansion after Independence has given a deeper insight into Indian archaeology, for the studies in different aspects like dating, provenance studies, prospection and so on.

REFERENCES

Allchin, B., A. Goudie and K.T.M. Hegde 1978. *The Prehistory and Palaeogeography of the Great Indian Desert*. London: Academic Press.

Agrawal, D.P. 1967-8. Protohistoric Chronology and Technical and Ecological Factors, *Puratattva* 1: 17-23.

——— 1969-70. The Metal Technology of the Indian Protohistoric Cultures: Its Archaeological Implications, *Puratattva* 3: 15-22.

——— 1971. *The Copper Bronze Age in India*. New Delhi: Munshiram Manoharlal.

——— 1975-6. Ancient Gold Workings: Some New ^{14}C Dates, *Puratattva* 8: 138 9.

Agrawal, D.P. and C. Margabandhu 1975-6. Ancient Gold Workings: Some New ^{14}C Dates, *Puratattva* 8: 138-9.

Agrawal, D.P. and Sheela Kusumgar 1974. On The Calibration of ^{14}C Dates, *Puratattva* 7: 70-3.

Agrawal, D.P. and S. Kusumgar 1990. ^{14}C Dating and Archaeology: an Indian Experience in *PACT: Proceedings of the Second International Symposium ^{14}C and Archaeology Groningen 1987* (W.G. Mook and H.T. Waterbolk Eds.), pp. 281-8. Groningen: University of Groningen.

Agrawal, D.P. and M.G.Yadava 1992. *Dating the Human Past*. Pune: The Indian Society for Prehistoric and Quaternary Studies.

Agrawal, O.P. 1984. *Conservation of Manuscripts, and Paintings of South and South-East Asia*. London: Butterworth.

——— 1992-3. Taj Mahal—Some Issues of Conservation, *Puratattva* 23: 40-7.

Agrawal, O.P. and Shashi Dhavan 1990. *Biodeterioration of Cultural Property*. New Delhi: Macmillan India Limited.

Berthelot, M. 1906. *Mem. Acad. Sci. Paris* 49: 4.

Berzelius, J. 1837. Ann. Word. Oldkundighedd 104.

Bhardwaj, H.C. 1967-8, Note on the Chemical Composition of Some Glass Beads from Rajghat, Varanasi, *Puratattva* 1: 42-6.

——— 1968-9. Rajghat Copper—a Metallurgical View, *Puratattva* 2: 30-4.

——— 1969-70. Copper Red Glasses Through the Ages, *Puratattva* 3: 3-14.

——— 1979. *Aspects of Ancient Indian Technology*. Banaras: Banaras Hindu University.

——— 1987. *Archaeometry of Glass* (H.C. Bhardwaj Ed.). Calcutta: Indian Ceramic Society. Central Glass & Ceramic Research Institute.

Caley, E.R. 1951. Early History and Literature of Archaeological Chemistry, *Journal of Chemical Education* XXVIII: 54-66.

Carnot, A. 1892. *Computes Rendus* 115: 243.

Davy, H. 1817. *Archaeologia* 18: 222.

Deotare, B.C.1983. Determination of the Extent of Settlement Area by Phosphate Analysis, *Bulletin of the Deccan College Research Institute* 42: 40-8.

——— 1984. Phosphate Spot Test at Megalithic Settlement of Bhagimohari, Maharashtra, *Bulletin of the Deccan College Research Institute* 43: 37-48.

Deotare, B.C., Anupama Kshirsagar and V.D. Gogte 1988. Archaeochemistry: the Study of Soils, Bones and Pottery, in *Excavations at Inamgaon* Vol. I (M.K. Dhavalikar, H.D. Sankalia and Z.D. Ansari Eds.), pp. 963-90. Pune: Deccan College.

Farswan,Y.S. and Vinod Nautiyal 1997. Investigation of Phosphorus Enrichment in the Burial Soil of Kumaun, Mid-Central Himalaya, India, *Journal of Archaeological Science* 24: 251-8.

Fink, C.G. and Eldridge, C.M. 1925. *The Restoration of Ancient Bronzes and Other Alloys*. New York: The Metropolitan Museum of Art.

Gairola, T.R. 1950.The Red Paint, Lime Washes and Plasters on Bhuvaneshwar and Konark Temples, *Ancient India* 6: 103-7.

——— 1952. On the Preservation of Some Paintings and Manuscripts, *Ancient India* 8: 93-8.

——— 1954-5. Preservation of Two Ancient Objects, *Ancient India* 10-11: 192-3.

——— 1956. Bidri Ware, *Ancient India* 12: 116-18.

——— 1957. Preservation of Fragile Textile from Central Asia and Rajasthani Miniature Painting, *Ancient India* 13: 143-5.

——— 1960. Preservation of Miniature and Wall Painting, *Ancient India* 16: 85-8.

Ganguli, M.M. 1912. *Orissa and Her Remains*. Calcutta.

Gobel, F. 1842. Uber Den Einfluss Der Chemie Auf Die Ermittelungder Volker Der Vorzeit Oder Resultate Der Chemischenuntersuchung Metallischer Alterthumer Insbesondere Der Den Ostseegouvernements Verkommenden Behufs Der Erm Ittelung Der Volker Von Welchen Sie Abstammen, Erlangen.

Goffer, Zvi 1980. *Archaeological Chemistry*. New York: John Wiley and Sons.

Gogte, V.D. 1980. Discovery of Megalithic Iron Smelting Site by Three Probe Resistivity Survey, *Bulletin of the Deccan College Research Institute* 39: 211-15.

——— 1989. Simple Methods of Chemical Analysis of Pottery: a Forgotten Art, in *Pottery Technology: Ideas and Approaches* (G. Bronitsky Ed.), pp. 101-16. Boulder-San Francisco-London: Westview Press.

——— 1995. Provenance Studies of Ceramics by X-Ray Diffraction and Chemical Methods, in *Proceedings of the 6th CIMTEC—World Ceramic Congress and Forum on New Materials* (P. Vincenzini Ed.), pp. 433-40. Florence: Techna Sri.

——— 1996. Chalcolithic Balathal—a Trading Centre as Revealed by The XRD Study of Ancient Pottery, *Man and Environment* XXI (1): 103-10.

——— 1997. The Chandraketugarh-Tamluk Region of Bengal: Source of the Early Historic Rouletted Ware from India and Southeast Asia, *Man and Environment* XXII(1): 69-86.

Gogte V.D., S.M. Kanetkar and A.A. Kshirsagar 1982. Efficiency of Megalithic Iron Smelting by Chemical Analysis, *Bulletin of the Deccan College Research Institute* 41: 68-71.

Hegde, K.T.M. 1965. Technical Studies in Chalcolithic Period Copper Metallurgy in India. Ph.D. Dissertation. Vadodara: the M.S. University, Baroda.

——— 1975-6. Use of Caliche as a Chronological and Environmental Tool in the Study of Late Quaternary Formations in Gujarat and Rajasthan, *Puratattva* 8: 37-43.

Hegde, K.T.M., P. Craddock and V.H. Sonawane 1987. Zinc Distillation in Ancient India, in *Proceedings of the 24th International Archaeology Symposium* (J. Olin Ed.). Washington: Smithsonian Institution.

Joshi, R.V., B.C. Deotare and A.A. Kshirsagar 1978-9. Chemistry of Deccan Chalcolithic Deposits from Daimabad and Inamgaon, *Puratattva* 10: 80-1.

——— 1985. Archaeological Chemistry in India: Some Aspects, Archaeological Perspectives of India Since Independence, *Puratattva* 111-14.

Joshi, R.V. and B.C. Deotare 1983. *Chemical Analysis of Archaeological Deposits from India*. Pune: Deccan College.

Joshi, Ramchandra and Anupama Kshirsagar 1986. *Chemical Studies of Archaeological Bones from India: Fluorine and Fossilization Process*. Pune: Deccan College.

Klaproth, M.H. 1796. *Philosophical Transactions of the Royal Society*: 395.

Kshirsagar, Anupama 1983. Nitrogen Contents of the Sediments from Chalcolithic Inamgaon, *Bulletin of the Deccan College Research Institute* 42: 99-101.

——— 1987. Selenium Determinations in Archaeological Bones by Differential Cathodic Stripping Voltametry, in *Laborative Archaeologi* 2, pp. 165-70. Stockholm: Universitets Reprocentral.

——— 1991-2. Soil Phosphorus Distribution within Human Activity Areas at Kuntasi, *Bulletin of the Deccan College Post-Graduate and Research Institute* 51-2: 497-500.

——— 1993. The Role of Fluorine in Chronometric Dating of Indian Stone Age Cultures, *Man and Environment* XVIII (2): 23-32.

——— 1996. Anthrosols from Balathal: a Chemical Study, *Man and Environment* XXI(1): 111-16.

Lal, B.B. 1951. Further Copper Hoards from Gangetic Basin and a Review of Problem, *Ancient India* 7: 20-39.

——— 1952. Examination of Some Ancient Indian Glass Specimens, *Ancient India* 8: 17-27.

——— 1953. Archaeological Chemistry and Scientific Studies, *Ancient India* 9: 119-206.

——— 1956. An Examination of Some Metal Images from Nalanda, *Ancient India* 12: 53-7.

——— 1958. Examination of Rods of Glass Like Material from Arikamedu, *Ancient India* 14: 139-42.

——— 1958. Birbhanpur: a Microlithic Site, *Ancient India* 14: 5-48.

——— 1962-3. A Picture Emerges—an Assessment of the ^{14}C Datings of the Protohistoric Cultures of the Indo-Pakistan Subcontinent, *Ancient India* 18 and 19: 208-21.

——— 1962-3. Chemical Preservation of Ancient Objects, *Ancient India* 18 and 19: 230-50.

——— 1966. Preservation of Mural Paintings, *Ancient India* 22: 83-101.

Lal, B.B. and S.B. Lal 1961. The Microlithic Site at Birbhanpur: a Geochronological Study, *Ancient India* 17: 37-45.

Layard, B. 1853. *Discoveries in the Ruins of Nineveh and Babylon*.

Libby, W.F. 1955. *Radiocarbon Dating*. Chicago: University of Chicago Press.

Mujumdar G.G. and S.N. Rajaguru 1966. *Ashmound Excavations at Kupgal*. Pune: Deccan College.

Nautiyal, Vinod., Y.S. Farswan and J.S. Rawat 1992. Phosphorus Analysis of Soils from Archaeological Sites in the Mid-Central Himalaya and Ganga-Yamuna Doab, *Man and Environment* XVII (1): 41-50.

Oakley, K.P. and M.F.A. Montagu 1949. A Reconsideration of the Galley Hill Skeleton, *Bulletin of the British Museum (Natural History), Geology* 1: 25-8.

Paramsivan, S. 1939, Technique of Painting Process in the Cave Temples of Ajanta and Ellora, *Annual Report (1936-37), Archaeological Deptt. of H.E the Nizam of Hyderabad.*

Prakash, S. and N.S. Rawat 1965. *Chemical Study of Some Indian Archaeological Antiquities, U.P.* New Delhi: C.S.I.R., Monograph 10.

Prakash, S. and R. Singh 1968. *Coinage in Ancient India*. New Delhi.

Rathgen, F. 1905. *Die Konservierung von Alterthumsfunden*. Berlin.

Sana Ullah Khan Bahadur Mohd. 1946. Preservation of Antiquities in the Field, *Ancient India* 1: 77-82.

Sankalia, H.D. 1965. *Excavations at Langhnaj, 1944-63. Part I, Archaeology.* Poona: Deccan College.

Schliemann, H. 1878. *Mycenae*. London: John Murray.

Wocel, J.E. 1855. *Sitz. Der Kaiser. Akad. Wiss, Wien, Phil. Hist. Classe* 16: 169.

Dating of Indian Stone Age and Quaternary Deposits

D.P. AGRAWAL

INTRODUCTION

When we talk of scientific dating, we often think of ^{14}C dating only. In fact, ^{14}C dating is the most important method, as far as archaeology is concerned, but its utility is constrained by its dating range which is less than 50 ka (thousand years). But once we enter the Stone Age, it becomes inadequate in its range and can not fully cover even the Upper Palaeolithic (see Tables 1-7). In recent years, many other physical dating techniques have been developed which can go back to million of years.

Such techniques have not only enabled us to date Stone Age assemblages but many Quaternary and palaeoclimatic events which are of direct relevance to Stone Age archaeology. Sankalia (1974: 137) conservatively dated the Acheulian to 50 ka, on the basis of Kalambo Falls' chronology. Much of the Stone Age Chronology was based on conjectures. The ^{14}C dates could date only the Upper Palaeolithic; the Middle Palaeolithic ^{14}C dates were generally much younger than expected as they were based on carbonate material which is no good for dating (Table 1). In 1982 D.P. Agrawal wrote:

> The ^{14}C dates show that most of the Middle Palaeolithic sites have come within a range of *c.* 37,000-11,000 B.P. But a wood sample from the Mula dam is outside the range of radiocarbon dating. This serves as a warning. In the case of samples older than 40,000 B.P. even a small amount of younger carbon can result in a finite age, i.e. one within the ^{14}C dating range being recorded. (Agrawal 1982: 37)

Earlier, the emphasis was on geological correlation which were tenuous and conjectural. Let us sample some statements. In 1974 H.D. Sankalia wrote:

> In our present knowledge, this would be the earliest occurrence of the handaxe in the Indian subcontinent. At one time De Terra equated this Second Interglacial terrace (T1) with the Narmada Lower group, and so also did Zeuner. But now it appears unwise to attempt such distant correlations, particularly when the Narmada Lower group is not independently dated.
>
> In the rest of peninsular India the conditions are still more difficult. Nowhere there is clear, undisputed stratigraphical evidene to support the typological development. We have advanced Acheulian handaxe-cleaver industry along with the Abbevillian and ordinary pebble tools. And if we date the Acheulian to the last Interglacial, as did Wainright's observation on the Lower Narmada, then it will belong to the Upper Pleistocene. We cannot at this stage determine the exact sub-phase of the Pleistocene but the evidence from the Potwar, West Punjab, is worth citing. Here occurs a highly advanced Acheulian handaxe-cleaver industry called Late Stellenbosch by Paterson and Drummond after the famous type site in South Africa which is also representative of the various

types. This view was further confirmed by Graziozi who has illustrated the tools photographically. Paterson assigns this (Middle and Upper) Stellenbosch industry to the second phase (U2) of the Upper Pleistocene, in other words to the Penultimate Interglacial in the Himalayas. And this approximately would be the period for the highly advanced handaxe-cleaver industry from Gujarat-Saurashtra, eastern Rajasthan, Madhya Pradesh (Lalitpur particularly), south Uttar Pradesh, Bihar, Orissa, West Bengal, Andhra, Karnataka, Tamil Nadu and Maharashtra. (Sanaklia 1974: 137)

At best the Stone Age industry was dated to the interglacial-glacial sequences which themselves were very much subjective. Nobody seemed to dare to take back our Stone Age industries more than a few hundred thousand years. For example, V.D. Krishnaswami in his review article said:

In any case the succession of the Ice Ages provides a real absolute chronometer, though the units of time it marks must be recknoned not in years or even centuries but in millennia and tens of millennia. Zeuner has recently expressed in years the duration of the Pleistocene glaciations, which gives the reader some notion of the magnitudes that may be involved. It is roughly estimated to be five hundred thousand years since the beginning of the Old Stone Age. (Krishnaswami 1953: 57)

Let us contrast it with what Leakey has to say about the present-day hominid chronology:

We assume that the human bush took root 7.5 Myr, but there is lack of fossil evidence between that point and 4 Myr. A single species of bipedal ape established the family and probably began an adaptive radiation. They were subsisting on apelike diets, but were ranging over larger areas in woodland country, not dense forest and not savannah. By 3 Myr the bipedal apes' teeth were less apelike, so presumably a shift in diet had begun. By 2 Myr some bipedal apes had become small-brain, large cheek-teeth, specialist plant eaters, others, large-brain, small cheek-teeth omnivores. Some filled niches in between. By 1.7 Myr—the time of Homo erectus—the large-brain, small cheek-teeth adaptation began to dominate, eventually it was the only occupied bipedal ape niche. We were the occupant. (Leakey and Levin 1993)

B.B. Lal uses the same geological chronometers. In 1956 B.B. Lal wrote:

The Potwar region in Pakistan has a somewhat different story to tell. Here, on the Indus, the Boulder Conglomerate, ascribable to the second Glaciation, has yielded only large-sized flakes, but neither the chopper-chopping-tools nor bifacial handaxes. Both these industries occur simultaneously in the next stage, Terrace I, assignable to the great Interglacial. This would mean that either both the industries are part and parcel of one and the same culture or they may have originated elsewhere independently and may have reached the region after commingling. Further, while most of the sites in the Indus valley show preponderance of chopper-chopping-tools, at Chauntra, on the Sohan, the outstanding industry was the bifacial one, although it is ascribed to a somewhat later stage. (Lal 1956: 86)

Comparing the Narmada industry R.V. Joshi said:

Against the three groups of deposits, each consisting of gravel and clay, as observed in the Narmada basin, the area under description has only two gravel-beds, which are underlain and overlain respectively by the silt-deposits. The non-fossiliferous nature of the deposits of the Damoh area precludes its comparison with those of the Narmada region strictly on the basis of stratigraphy. As a negative evidence, it may be stated that the Damoh area does not have very coarse and boudlery type of gravel bed comparable with Gravel I of the Narmada. But this may be due to the smaller size of the streams and their limited erosive and transporting capacities. The components of both the Gravel I and II of the Narmada are pebbles of quartzite, and very rarely fragments of trap appear only in the Gravel II. In the Damoh area, the first (lower) gravel is composed of pebbles of quartzites and sandstone, and only in the upper gravel appear pieces of disintegrated Deccan Trap and its secondary minerals. In the Narmada deposits, the sands replacing Gravel II contain an appreciable quantity of sediments derived from the Deccan trap.

From the lower group of the Narmada deposits come fresh tools of the Acheulian facies along with rolled tools of Abbevillean and early Acheulian characters. This, therefore, appears to be the true Acheulian horizon, which has been dated to the Middle Pleistocene from the associated fossil-remains. On the basis of the culture-contents this horizon, however, seems to be absent in the Damoh deposits.

The gravel of the second (upper) group of the Narmada has yielded fresh Late Sohan type of tools along with rolled tools of Abbevilleo-Acheulian facies. McCown and Banerjee noted the absence of Late Sohan tools and the presence of the Nevasian (Middle Palaeolithic) industry in this horizon.

The fossil-contents of this deposits are of Middle Pleistocene type. The true Nevasian horizon at Kalegaon on the Godavari river has yielded the fossil of *Bos namadicus* Falc. (Middle Pleistocene). Subbarao ascribes an Upper Pleistocene date for this horizon, while Banerjee considers the beginning of the Late Pleistocene period as appropriate for the deposits containing true Nevasian tools. The lower gravel of Damoh has yielded fresh retouched flakes with a plain obtuse-angled platform along with rolled specimens of Abbevilleo-Acheulian facies. These flakes are completely different from the large heavy Clactonian flakes of the lower group of the Narmada. Besides, the heavy choppers of the lower group of the culture-contents, this gravel of Damoh is comparable with the second gravel (upper group) of the Narmada. (Joshi 1961: 35)

These examples from well known prehistorians indicate that only a few decades back, it was just not possible to discuss objectively about absolute dates of our Stone Age cultures. New dating techniques have not only revolutionized our preceptions about the antiquity of man but also about the Ice Ages and their chronology. This has become possible because of the advent of TL, potassium-organ, fission-track, uranium-thorium palaeomagnetic and other techniques.

The use lake sediments for palaeoclimatic studies has made it possible to achieve much higher resolution both in climatic change sequences and also about their chronology. The sea sediments have provided much finer climatic sequences which are truly global in nature. We must admit that even today these techniques though available in India have not been used fully to build up our Stone Age sequences. Nevertheless much has been achieved which need to be noted.

In this article we propose to briefly discuss some of these techniques, mainly from the point of view of Stone Ages and Quaternary studies and what has been achieved and what more needs to be done.

TL DATING

Thermoluminescence, TL is the emission of light in excess of the incandescent glow that is produced when an electrically non-conducting solid is heated. It is due to the ionising radiation to which the solid has been subjected. Many naturally occurring materials, called TL phosphers, show this property of natural TL, when exposed to nuclear radiation (alpha, beta particles, gamma rays) emitted during the radioactive decay of uranium, thorium, potassium and rubidium. These radioactive elements occur as impurities in most rocks, clays and soils, and in many minerals. Cosmic rays also contribute but to a lesser extent (Wagner 1983). When alpha and beta particles or gamma rays traverse a mineral, they lose energy by interacting with the atoms. Ionisation, i.e. detachment of electrons from their parent atoms, is one result. Most of such detached electrons recombine immediately, but some are trapped in the imperfections in the lattice structure, and may stay there for millions of years. Their number depends on the accumulated radiation dose to which the mineral is exposed during its history and if the intensity of the radiation (i.e. the dose-rate) is known, it can be used as a measure of the elapsed time.

Heating the mineral frees the trapped electrons. Those which recombine with luminescent centres—another type of lattice imperfection—release their energy as light. This in fact is 'thermoluminescence' which can be detected with sensitive photo-multipliers. The intensity of TL glow as a function of the heating temperature is recorded as a 'glow curve'. Typically the part of the glow curve between 300 and 500 ^{0}C is of interest for archaeological dating. The reason for this is that the glow in this temperature range is emitted by electrons which have been in deep enough traps to ensure their long-term storage. Because the intensity of TL emission is proportional to the number of electrons released, and thus to the radiation dose accumulated, the total dose ('archaeodose') the mineral has absorbed since its last heating can be determined. As different materials have different TL sensitivities, therefore the TL signal after irradiating it with known artificial doses. TL age is therefore the duration of the natural radiation exposure.

We thus see that Thermoluminescence dating comprises two basic steps: the determination of the archaeodose which a sample has absorbed during its past, and the determination of the corresponding dose-rate. The age determined in this way dates the formation of the mineral or the event of its last heating to a temperature sufficiently high for any previous TL to be completely removed.

There are other variations of the basic TL technique like Electron Spin Resonance (ESR) Dating and other methods into which we need not go here. The calcite dating by ESR is a very useful application of ESR. Speleothems are secondary carbonate precipitates. These occur in limestone regions and caves; in such regions Palaeolithic occupations are often associated. Typically, speleothems have an age range of 10,000 to about 1 million years depending on sensitivity, annual dose and temperature. Palaeolithic occupations have been dated in a number of caves, mainly in France and Italy. In Greece, the dating of samples from Petralona cave has raised considerable controversy. Among the samples dated was about 1 gram obtained from the calcite encrustation on the hominid skull found on the site. This gave an age of 1,98,000±40,000 years.

Spring deposited travertine dating

Like speleothems, this is a carbonate precipitate, but it occurs on open-air sites and usually has a high concentration of organic components. The ESR dating of these deposits give the possible age, ranging for roughly 10,000 to 1 million years.

The TL technique is generally used for dating pottery

In India Ashok Singhvi's group at the Physical Research Laboratory, Ahmedabad has used the TL related techniques to date sand dunes, loess and carbonates in Rajasthan and I have used it in Kashmir. This helped in working out detailed climatic amelioration changes. For example, in Kashmir, the climatic amelioration of 18,000 years BP is associated with the formation of a buried soil and the Upper Paleolithic industry (Agrawal 1992). In Rajasthan, Singhvi et al. (1991) have dated various Palaeolithic industries in dune profiles. There are many other dating techniques which can be used for Stone Age and Quaternary studies.

OTHER PHYSICAL-CHEMICAL TECHNIQUES OF DATING

Nature records its history in a variety of archives: lacustrine sediments of lakes; riverine deposits; wind borne formations, like sand dunes and loess deposits; and of course sea-bottom deposits. Let us discuss some dating methods which have a long dating range.

Palaeomagnetic Dating

The Earth behaves like a magnet. The Earth's magnetic field has been measured for several centuries now. For the older record one has to study the fossil (remanent) magnetism in the Earth's rocks and sediments, which can date back to 170 million years (Agrawal 1992). Many natural materials are able to retain a signature of geomagnetic field despite later field changes or geological events. Scientists studying palaeomagnetism have been able to assemble global data of the ancient geomagnetic field by measuring global data of the ancient geomagnetic field by measuring direction and intensity changes in suitable rocks and sediments. It has been found that the Earth's global field has reversed its polarity several times in the past.

Palaeomagnetic reversals, when dated independently, provide a dating method based on polarity timescale (Thompson and Oldfield 1986). The standard equipment used for measuring magnetic remanence are Fluxgate Spinner Magnetometer, and Super-conduction magnetometer. We have used Schonstedt Spinner-Magnetometer as it provides a convenient and fast method of taking a large number of readings.

Palaeomagnetic sampling of the Kashmir Karewa sediments was done by establishing several hundred magnetic sites at an interval of one meter. These samples were measured for their natural remanent magnetisation (NRM) on the Schonstedt SSM-1 Magnetometer.

Dubjan and Hirpur 1 localities provide the bottom-most part of the sequence exposed by the river Rembiara (i.e. Remzones 1, 2, part of 3), Remzone 2, the massive 200 m thick conglomerate, along with the thick sand lenses, did not provide any fine grained materials for magnetic sampling and is therefore blank. From Remzone 3 onwards, there is a reasonably continuous record of magnetic polarity changes. Remzone 1 (lowermost part) showed a normal polarity. Remzone 2, comprising boulder conglomerate, is obviously a rapidly deposited sediment and in terms of time spanned may not be significant. Remzone 3 starts with a reversed polarity followed by a normal chron with two intervening reversals, identified by us as Kaena and Mammoth subchrons. If the lower part of N2 magnetozone is equated with the Cochiti subchron of the Gilbert chron, it will push back the origin of the Karewa sediments beyond 3.82 Ma. Fossils of *Equus*, *Elephas*, *Cervus*, etc., do not appear before the Matuyama chron.

Fission-track dating helped in connecting the two major Karewa profiles. Let us discuss this method now.

Fission Track Dating

This method is based on the observation of individual damage caused by heavy charged particles (in this case fission fragments of ^{238}U) which fission inside uranium bearing minerals. The trails (tracks) of such radiation damage are about 100 A^0 in width and require electron microscope to study them. It has been shown that in case of micas, fission-tracks can be enlarged by immersion of micas in hydroflouric acid (HF) for periods varying from a few seconds to a few minutes, and as a result, such damaged regions produce fine tabular holes which are readily seen in transmitted light in an optical microscope (Fleisher et al. 1975). Such tracks are found in a variety of minerals like quartz, mica, zircon, orthoclase, apatite, etc. In general tracks are produced by heavy particles, with atomic mass greater than 20, with energies of about 100 MeV. Therefore in these terrestrial minerals such heavy particles are most likely to be produced by spontaneous fission of ^{238}U. The fission-track age is calculated by the formulae given by Fleisher et al. (1975).

In Kashmir, volcanic ash samples were collected from the exposed section near Pakharpura (33° 48' 30" N; 74° 46'E) from Khaigam village and were dated by Kusumgar et al. (1985).

Potassium-Argon Dating

Potassium is one of the eight most abundant chemical elements found in the crust of the Earth and is a major constituent of many important rock-forming minerals, such as micas, feldspars and clay minerals. It has thus three naturally occurring isotopes ^{39}K, ^{40}K, ^{41}K. It is seen that 88.8 per cent of ^{40}K decays to stable ^{40}Ca (calcium with mass number 40) by emission of electron (beta particle) and 11.2 per cent of ^{40}K decay to ^{40}Ar by a process called electron capture (Faure 1986). Hence, in a mineral which contains potassium as one of its constituents will have growth of ^{40}Ar and ^{40}Ca due to the decay of ^{40}K to stable ^{40}Ar is a measure of the time passed since, the rock or mineral cooled down sufficiently to block the diffusion of argon gas out of the body. If the mineral is hot then gas will diffuse out. To date a potassium-bearing mineral, the concentration of potassium and the amount of ^{40}Ar produced from the decay is required to be measured. Potassium concentrations can be determined by one of several methods, including flame photometry, atomic absorption spectrometry, isotope dilution, X-ray fluorescence, gravimetric chemistry, or even neutron activation. The amount of ^{40}Ar is measured by means of isotope dilution method. The K-Ar method of dating is applicable to all K-bearing minerals of rocks satisfying the basic assumption. Most suitable minerals are biotite, muscovite, high-grade metamorphic rocks and feldspar from volcanic rocks.

Uranium and Thorium Dating

Uranium and thorium are members of the so called actinide series of elements. Uranium is found in nature in three forms ^{238}U, ^{235}U and ^{234}U. All three isotopes are radioactive. Thorium has six isotopes, and one of them ^{232}Th is found in primary form. Other five are found as shortlived intermediate products called daughters of ^{238}U, ^{235}U, and ^{232}Th (Faure 1986). ^{238}U, ^{235}U, and ^{232}Th are parent of a chain of radioactive daughters ending with stable isotopes of lead. The decay of ^{238}U, ends in stable ^{206}Pb and produced a series of daughters called the Uranium series. The decay of ^{235}U ends in stable ^{207}Pb producing the so called actinium series.

The half-lives of ^{238}U, ^{235}U and ^{232}Th are all very much longer than those of their daughters or decay products. In such situations a condition in radioactivity called secular equilibrium is established and decay rates or activites of the intermediate daughters are equal to those of their respective parents in a uranium and thorium bearing mineral.

The decay series of ^{238}U and ^{235}U contain radioactive isotopes of many different elements. These daughters of uranium and thorium may be separated from their parents and from each other in the course of normal geological processes such as chemical weathering, precipitation of minerals from aqueous solutions by biological and inorganic processes, adsorption on suspended clay minerals and even during the formation of magma at a depth in the Earth and the crystallization of lava flows on its surface.

Two kinds of situation arise that have been exploited by geochronologists.

(1) A member of the series is seperated from its parent which subsequently decays at a rate determined by its half life;
(2) A daughter nuclide is formed by decay of its parent (previously separated from its daughter) until radioactive equilibrium is re-established. This has been utilized by geochronologists.

This disequilibrium gives rise to several geochronometers which are capable of measuring geologic time ranging from a few years up to one million years or more. These geochronometers therefore provide information about Earth's history during the last million years and fill an important gap between the ^{14}C and K-Ar method of dating. Only the fission track method and certain cosmogenic radionuclides compete with them in this respect (Faure 1986). The disequilibrium methods of dating have been useful in the study of sediment and calcium carbonate deposited in the oceans and in lakes. One of the methods based on these isotopes are discussed here briefly.

$^{230}Th/^{238}U$ AND $^{230}Th/^{234}$ U RATIOS AS A DATING TOOL

Calcium carbonate deposited in oceans and in saline lakes contain appreciable concentrations of uranium. Thorium concentration is virutally zero. Hence, initial activity of thorium is zero in fresh deposits to ^{230}Th as the time passes, ^{230}Th activity will build up (Faure 1986).

The ratio of $^{230}Th/^{238}U$ will increase from zero value and will tend towards unity. This ratio can be used as a geochronometer. If ^{234}U is in secular equilibrium with ^{238}U, then the extent to which this ratio has known indicates the deposit time.

In India $^{230}Th/^{234}U$ was used to date the formation of Quaternary carbonate deposits of Saurashtra by Baskaran et al. (1989). Two distinct groups of such deposits have been found, viz., group-I age = 50-70 ka; group-II age =75-115 ka Sea level changes appear to be responsible for the occurrence of these carbonate deposits (Baskaran et al. 1989).

STONE AGE APPLICATION

The earliest stone age tools belonging to *Homo habilis* go back to 2.4 Ma (million years ago) and are expected to go further (Semaw et al. 1997). *Homo erectus* has been dated to 1.6 Ma in Africa. The only early K-Ar date in India has been reported from Bori, near Pune, and goes back to 1.4 Ma. It is a volcanic material overlying an Acheulian assemblage. Baskaran et al. (1989) have used U-Th dating technique on the Quaternary carbonate deposits of Saurashtra. They have reported two groups of such carbonate deposits; Group I has a range of 50-70 ka and Group II, 75-115 ka. Circumstantially, these dates have been used to define the chronology of the underlying Acheulian assemblage.

There are a few ^{14}C dates for the Middle Palaeolithic sites but they are generally too young to be taken into account. For example. PRL-293, PRL-13, BSI-163 (Table 1) are on shell material. At this range, a little contamination can make them look as if they are within the ^{14}C dating range. We had dated two wood samples from Mula dam (TF-217, 345, Table 1). Both were beyond the limit of ^{14}C range. One TL date for Didwana gives the range 144-350 ka. Similarly, TF-1002 from Dhom dam gives a date of greater than 35 Ka and is thus beyond the range of ^{14}C dating method.

In Kashmir (Kusumgar et al. 1985) fission-track dating technique has been used to date the Matuyama/Gauss magnetic reversal boundary to about 2.3 Ma. This is close to the globally accepted value of 2.4 Ma for this event. Its importance lies in the fact that this date marks the lower boundary of the Villafranchian fauna in South Asia.

CONCLUSION

Thus we see that a couple of decades back, it was understandable for our prehistorians to talk in vague and subjective terms about the time-frames of Stone Age cultures. But now most of the techniques like TL, fission track, K-Ar, palaeomagnetism, etc., are available in India and have been used for dating Quaternary deposits. In Kashmir both fission-track and palaeomagnetic methods have been used by us to date the advent of Villafranchian (present-day types) fauna to 2.4 Ma. K-Ar has been used to date an Acheulian level at Bori, near Poona. The validity of these dates has been debated (see Singhvi et al. 1998; Korisettar and Rajaguru 1998; Petraglia 1998).

There is a distinct possibility that the Toba volcanic ashes can be used to date some of our Stone Age cultures. The various volcanic ashes recorded in Pakistan can be used to date our Siwalik deposits and associated (?) Stone Age artefacts.

TABLE 1. STONE AGE CHRONOLOGY

Site Name	Sample No.	5568 years BP	Calib Dates	Culture	Material
Bhimbetka	PRL-787	15370+570, -530 BP	None	Middle Pal.	Charcoal
Bhimbetka	PRL-789	17670+490, -460 BP	None	Middle Pal.	Charcoal
Bhimbetka	PRL-788	17230+480, -440 BP	None	Middle Pal.	Charcoal
Dhamner	PRL-143	10130±250 BP	None	Middle Pal.	Shell
Dhom Dam	TF-1004	38470+8940 -4125 BP	None	Middle Pal.	Unknown
Didwana	Unknown TL	None	None	Middle Pal.	Unknown
Didwana	PRL-911	26210+2110 -1670 BP	None	Middle/Lower Pal.	Organic Matter
Didwana	Unknown U/Th	None	None	Middle/Lower Pal.	Unknown
Didwana	Unknown U/Th	None	None	Middle/Lower Pal.	Unknown
Didwana	Unknown U/Th	None	None	Middle Pal.	Unknown
Gerwa Well	PRL-710	26090+800, -720 BP	None	Middle Pal.	Calcium Carbonate
Kaldevan Halli	PRL-79	1560±120 BP	463,478, 530 bc	Middle Pal.	Shell
Mula Dam	TF-217	>39000 BP	None	Middle Pal.	Wood
Mula Dam	TF-345	31075+5550 -3254 BP	None	Middle Pal.	Wood
Nandipali	PRL-293	23670+690 -640 BP	None	Middle Pal.	Shell
Nandur Madmesh	BS-163	26600±430 BP	None	Middle Pal.	Shell
Prabhas Patan	PRL-30	20825+6670 -540 BP	None	Middle Pal.	Shell

KEY: BP = uncalibrated dates based on 5568 years half-life, bp/bc/ad = calibrated date.

TABLE 2. STONE AGE CHRONOLOGY (MESOLITHIC)

Site Name	Sample No.	5568 years BP	Calib dates	Culture	Material
Bhimbetka	PRL-535	1160±150 BP	886 ad	Microlithis	Charcoal
Bhimbetka	PRL-315	1760±180 BP	249 ad	Microlithis, Burial	Charcoal
Bhimbetka	PRL-321	370±130 BP	1480 ad	Microlithis	Charcoal
Bhimbetka	PRL-49	Modern	None	Microlithis, Burial	Charcoal
Bhimbetka	PRL-317	2490±100 BP	762, 678, 662 6627, 600 bc	Microlithis	Charcoal
Bhimbetka	PRL-18	2650±125 BP	813 bc	Microlithis,	Charcoal
Chauldari	BS-617	1350±100 BP	663 ad	Shell Midden	Charred/Uncharred Marine Shells
Chauldari	BS-600	2070±100 BP	101 bc	Shell Midde	Charred/Uncharred Marine Shells
Chauldari	BS-618	1570±100 BP	447 ad	Shell Midden	Charred/Uncharred Marine Shells
Chauldari	BS-599	2280±90 BP	387 bc	Shell Midden	Charred/Uncharred Marine Shells
Chauldari	BS-598	2070±100 BP	101 bc	Shell Midden	Charred/Uncharred Marine Shells
Chennur	BS-79	>40,000 BP	None	Microliths	Shell
Great Andaman	R-86	370±80 BP	1480 ad	Shell Miden	Charcoal
Great Andaman	R-84	430±80 BP	1445 ad	Shell Midden	Charcol
Great Andaman	R-85	430±90 BP	1445 ad	Shell Midden	Charcoal
Inamgaon	BS-146	11700±150 BP	None	Microliths	Shell
Kauvakoh	PRL-907	1040±130 BP	999 ad	Microliths	Soil
Langhnaj	TF-744	3875±105 BP	2452, 2427, 2397, 2374, 2366 bc	Microliths Inorg. Fraction	Bone
Lekhahia	TF-342	180±110 BP	1673, 1753, 1796, 1944, 1950 bc	Phase 4, Microliths and Pottery	Charcoal
Lekhahia	TF-344	Modern	None	Phase 4, Microliths and Pottery	Charcoal
Lekhahia	TF-417	3560±105 BP	1908 bc	Lekhahia I, Phase 3, Microliths and Pottery	Bone
Lekhahia	TF-419	4240±110 BP	2895 bc	Lekhahia I, Phase 1, Microliths	Bone
Mahada	BS-137	2880±250 BP	1044 bc	Mesolithic	Charred bone, carbonate
Mahada	BS-138	3840±130 BP	2315 bc	Mesolithic	Charred bone, carbonate
Mahada 2503 BC	BS-136	4010±110 BP	2569, 2538,	Mesolithic	Charred bone, carbonate
Mantai	BM-2341	3550±70 BP	1895 bc	Microliths	Charcoal
Mantai	BM-2340	3520±45 BP	1883 bc	Microliths	Charcoal
Nirgudsar	BS-43	39000±3200 BP	None	Microliths	Wood

(contd.)

Site Name	Sample No.	5568 years BP	Calib dates	Culture	Material
Oriyo Timbo	PRL-888/9	4720±160 BP	3510, 3396, 3388 bc	Period I, Microliths	Charcoal
Oriyo Timbo	PRL-886	4160±170 BP	2870, 2806, 2774, 2720 2702 bc	Period I, Microliths	Charcoal
Oriyo Timbo	PRL-876	4080±160 BP	2850, 2845, 2652, 2647, 2612 bc	Period I, Microliths	Charcoal
Paisra	BS-675	7420±110 BP	6223, 6195, 6187, bc	Mesolithic	Charcoal
Pava jig	BS-843	1530±70 BP	544 ad	Midden	Shell
Patiraja wela site	PRL-107	4500±170 BP	3307, 3255, 3177, 3163, 3134, 3112, 3110 bc	Microliths	Shells
Sarai Nahar Rai	TF-1356/59	2860±120 BP	1021 bc	Microliths	Charred and Semi-charred bone
Sarai Nahar Rai	TF-1104	10050±110 BP	None	Microliths	Human bone, Inorg.

KEY: BP = uncalibrated dates based on 5568 years half-life, bp/bc/ad= calibrated date.

TABLE 3. STONE AGE (ROCK ART)

Site Name	Sample No.	5568 years BP	Calib dates	Culture	Material
Tenmalai	BS-646	4420±110 BP	3040 bc	Microliths and Paintings	Wood charcoal
Tenmalai	BS-630	5210±110 BP	4032, 4026, 4001 bc	Microliths and Paintings	Wood Charcoal
Tenmalai	BS-525	4971±115 BP	3780, 3731, 3728 bc	Microliths and Painting	Wood Charcoal

KEY: BP = uncalibrated dates based on 5568 years half-life, bp/bc/ad= calibrated date.

TABLE 4. STONE AGE (NEOLITHIC KASHMIR)

Site Name	Sample No.	5568 years BP	Calib dates	Culture	Material
Burzahom	TF-123	4055±110 BP	2586 bc	Period IA Neolithic	Charcoal
Burzahom	TF-13	3690±125 BP	2130, 2074 2045 bc	Period IA Neolithic	Charcoal
Burzahom	TF-127	3935±110 BP	2465 bc	Period IB Neolithic	Charcoal
Burzahom	TF-14	3860±340 BP	2343 bc	Neolithic	Charcoal
Burzahom	TF-129	3670±90 BP	2114, 2086, 2039 bc	Neolithic	Charcoal
Burzahom	TF-15	3390±105 BP	1730, 1729, 1689 bc	Period IB Neolithic	Burnt Organic Material

(contd.)

Site Name	Sample No.	5568 years BP	Calib dates	Culture	Material
Burzahom	TF-10	2580±100 BP	797 bc	Neolithic	Charcoal
Burzahom	TF-128	4205±115 BP	2881, 2797, 2783 bc	Period IB Neolithic	Charcoal
Gufkral	BS-359	3864±115 BP	2347 bc	Period IB Neolithic .	Wood Charcoal
Gufkral	BS-356	3466±105 BP	1860,1847, 1770 bc	Period IB, Neolithic	Wood Charcoal
Gufrkal	BS-370	2709±105 BP	842 bc	Period IC, Neolithic	Wood Charcoal
Gufkral	BS-371	3466±95 BP	1860, 1847, 1770 bc	Period IC, Neolithic	Wood Charcoal
Gufkral	BS-358	3039±105 BP	1313 bc	Period IA, Aceramic Neolithic	Wood Charcoal
Gufkral	BS-360	3243±95 BP	1519 bc Neolithic	Period IC, Charcoal	Wood
Gufkral	BS-357	3369±105 BP	1681 bc	IB Period Neolithic	Wood Charcoal

KEY: BP = uncalibrated dates based on 5568 years half-life, bp/bc/ad= calibrated date.

TABLE 5. STONE AGE (NEOLITHIC PAKISTAN)

Site Name	Sample No.	5568 years BP	Calib dates	Culture	Material
Mehrgarh	Beta-2690	3590±60 BP	1997 bc	Period IV	Unknown
Mehrgarh	Beta-1719	13340±125 BP	14,191- 13, 789 bc, 2e 14,381- 13, 567 bc centre 13990 bc	Period IB	Unknown
Mehrgarh	Beta-1721	9385±120 BP	(1) 8827-8818, 8591-8542, 8539-8335, 8305-8261 bc (2) 8949-8090 bc; centre 8420 bc	Period IA	Unknown
Mehrgarh	LV-993	6110±90 BP	5190,5058 bc	Period IB	Unknown
Mehrgarh	Beta-2686	5860±70 BP	4777 bc	Period IA	Unknown
Mehrgarh	Beta-2688	5490+70 BP	4350 bc	Period IIA	Unknown
Mehrgarh	LY-1945	5360±310 BP	4235 bc	Period IIB	Unknown
Mehrgarh	Beta-7315	5620±100 BP	4465 bc	Period IIA	Unknown
Mehrgarh	Beta-2689	6500±78 BP	5474±5435, 5426 bc	Period III	Unknown
Mehrgarh	LV-994	6290±70 BP	5238 bc	Period IB	Unknown
Mehrgarh	LY-1946	33000±3000 BP	None	Period IB	Charcoal
Mehrgarh	Beta-1408	6925±80 BP	5749 bc	Period IA	Unknown
Mehrgarh	Beta-1407	7115±290 BP	5980 bc	Period IA	Unknown
Mehrgarh	Beta-1720	7115±120 BP	5980 bc	Period IIB	Unknown
Mehrgarh	LY-1950	8440±250 BP	(1) 7694-76651,	Period IB	Unknown

(contd.)

Site Name	Sample No.	5568 years BP	Calib dates	Culture	Material
			7648-7239, 7223-7200, 7180-7141, 7119-7096 bc (2) 8008-6758, 6739-6719 bc centre 7490 bc		
Mehrgarh	LV-906	5950±65 BP	4894, 4883	Period IB	Unknown
Mehrgarh	LV-907	6020±80 BP	4937, 4917,	Period IB	Unknown
Mehrgarh	LV-909	5940±55 BP	4892, 4887, 4841 bc	Period IB	Unknown
Mehrgarh	LY-1948	5720±730 BP	4653, 4648, 4581 bc	Period IA	Charcoal
Mehrgarh	LV-908	6090±70 BP	5046, 5019, 5004 bc	Period IB	Unknown
Mehrgarh	LY-1949	5530±180 BP	4360 bc	Period IA	Charcoal
Mehrgarh	Beta-7314	5400±90 BP	4318, 4285, 4246 bc	Period IIA	Unknown
Mehrgarh	LY-1947	5830±190 BP	4725 bc	Period IA	Charcoal
Mehrgarh	LY-1528	4190±140 BP	2877, 2800, 2780, 2712, 2708 bc	Period IV	Charcoal
Mehrgarh	LY-1529	3960±140 BP	2470 bc	Period VI	Charcoal
Mehrgarh	LV-910	5880±100 BP	4782 bc	Period IB	Unknown
Mehrgarh	LY-1527	3570±150 BP	1923 bc	Period VII	Charcoal
Mehrgarh	Beta-73166	5990±120 BP	4931,4928, 4901 bc	Period IA	Unknown
Rehman Dheri	PRL-675	4400±110 BP	3034 bc	Period I, Kechi beg	Charcoal
Rehman Dheri	PRL-676	4520±110 BP	3331,3226, 3185,3155, 3143 bc	Period I, Kechi beg	Charcoal
Rehman Dheri	WIS-1698	4190±70 BP	2877,2800, 2780,2712, 2708 bc	Period I Kechi beg	Unknown
Rehman Dheri	WIS-1697	4300±70 BP	2915 bc	Period I Kechi beg	Unknown
Said Qala	DIC-22	3620±220 BP	2018,2002, 1980 bc	Occupation No.1 (Damb Sadaat III)	Charcoal
Said Qala	DIC-20	3710±90 BP	2135,2052, 2050 bc	Occupation No.1 (Damb Sadaat II)	Charcoal
Said Qala	DIC-18	3800±220 BP	2278,2234, 2209 bc	Occupation No.3 (Damb Sadaat II)	Charcoal
Saraikhola	BM-1934R	4470±150 BP	3263,3246, 3102 bc	Period I Neolithic	Charcoal
Saraikhola	BM-1939R	4530±160 BP	3334,3219, 3189,3152, 3148 bc	Period I, Neolithic	Charcoal
Saraikhola	BM-1940R	4600±200 BP	3360 bc	Period I, Neolithic	Charcoal

(contd.)

Site Name	Sample No.	5568 years BP	Calib dates	Culture	Material
Saraikhola	BM-1935R	4370±250 BP	3023,2994, 2928 bc	Period I, Neolithic	Charcoal
Shahr-i Sokhta	P-2077	3950±60 BP	2468 bc	Shahr-i Sokhta II, Phase 5, proto-urban	Charcoal
Shahr-i Sokhta	R-627	4020±50 BP	2573,2535 2506 bc	Shahr-i Sokhta II, Phase 5-6, proto-urban	Charcoal
Shahr-i Sokhta	R-634	4050±50 BP	2584 bc	Shahr-i Sokhta II, Phase 6, proto-urban	Charcoal
Shahr-i Sokhta	P-2542	3990±60 BP	2559,2544, 2495 bc	Shahr-i Sokhta II, Phase 5-6 proto-urban	Charcoal
Shahr-i Sokhta	P-2543	4200±60 BP	2880, 2798, 2782 bc	Shahr-i Sokhta I, Phase 9-10, proto-urban	Charcoal
Shahr-i Sokhta	TUNC-24	3943±70 BP	2466 bc	Shahr-i Sokhta III, Phase 3-4	Charcoal
Shahr-i Sokhta	R-623	4050±50 BP	2584 bc	Shahr-i Sokhta II, Phase 5-6, Proto-urban	Charcoal
Shahr-i Sokhta	TUNC-27	3890±90 BP	2455, 2416, 2405 bc	Shahr-i Sokhta III, Phase 3-4, proto-state	Charcoal
Shahr-i Sokhta	R-405A	3960±50 BP	2470 bc	Shahr-i Sokhta II, Phase 5-6, Proto-urban	Charcoal
Shahr-i Sokhta	TUNC-22	3829±61 BP	2298 bc	Shahr-i Sokhta III, Phase 3-4, proto-urban	Charcoal
Shahr-i Sokhta	R-629	4200±50 BP	2880, 2798, 2782 bc	Shahr-i Sokhta I, Phase 8-9, Archaic	Charcoal
Shahr-i Sokhta	P-2081B	4150±70 BP	2867, 2808, 2772, 2723, 2699 bc	Shahr-i Sokhta II, Phase 6, Proto-urban	Charcoal
Shahr-i Sokhta	TUNC-26	4115±72 BP	2859, 2819, 2692, 2686, 2661, 2635, 2625 bc	Shahr-i Sokhta III, Phase 3-4, Proto-state	Charcoal
Shahr-i Sokhta	P-2084	4110±60 BP	2587, 2821, 2691, 2689, 2660, 2637, 2623 bc	Shahr-i Sokhta II, Phase 6, Proto-urban	Charcoal
Shahr-i Shokta	R-632	4100±50 BP	2855, 2824, 2657, 2640, 2619 bc	Shahr-i Sokhta II, Phase 6, proto-urban	Charcoal
Shahr-i Sokhta	P-2071	3970±60 BP	2483 bc	Shahr-i Sokhta IV, Phase 0	Charcoal

(contd.)

Site Name	Sample No.	5568 years BP	Calib dates	Culture	Material
Shahr-i Sokhta	TUNC-21	4065±65 BP	2598 bc	Post-urban Shahr-i Sokhta III, Phase 3-4, proto-state	Charcoal

KEY: BP = uncalibrated dates based on 5568 years half-life, bp/bc/ad= calibrated date.

TABLE 6. STONE AGE (NEOLITHIC PENINSULAR INDIA)

Site	Sample No.	5568 years BP	Calib. dates	Culture	Material
Gharluli	TF-1162	Modern	None	Late Neolithic	Charcoal
Hallur	TF-576	3280±105 BP	1570, 1528, bc	Period IB, Late Neolithic	Charcoal
Hallur	TF-580	3560±105 BP	1902 bc	Period IA, Early Neolithic	Charcoal
Hallur	TF-586	3055±95 BP	1379, 1343, 1319 bc	Period IB, Late Neolithic	Charcoal
Hallur	TF-575	2895±100 BP	1065 bc	Period II, Neolithic Iron Age Overlap	Charcoal
Marakatola	BS-42	660±95 BP	1287 bc	Neolithic	Charcoal
Numphuk	PRL-539	19310±920 BP	None	Neolithic	Charcoal
Paiyampalli	TF-349	3340±100 BP	1643 bc	Neolithic/ Meghalithic Transition	Charcoal
Paiyampalli	TF-829	985±105 BP	1023 ad	Late Southern Neolithic	Charcoal
Payampalli	TF-833	3215±210 BP	1513 bc	Late Southern Neolithic	Charcoal
Payampalli	TF-827	3570±105 BP	1923 bc	Neolithic/ Meghalithic Transition	Charcoal
Palvoy	TF-700	3390±95 BP	1730, 1729, 1689 bc	Neolithic/ Meghalithic	Charcoal Transition
Palvoy	TF-701	3805±100 BP	2281 bc	Early Southern Neolithic	Charcoal
Polakonda	BS-98	3255±120 BP	1522 bc	Southern Neolithic	Wood
Polakonda	BS-97	2045±90 BP	83 bc	Meghalithic Period	Wood Charcoal
Payatha Pattan	PRL-816	4190±140 BP	2877, 2800, 2780, 2712, 2708 bc	Aceramic Neolithic	Charcoal
Sangankallu	TF-354	3440±100 BP	1746 bc	Middle Southern Neolithic	Charcoal
Sangankallu	TF-359	3400±100 BP	1733, 1721, 1697 bc	Middle Southern	Charcoal

(contd.)

Site	Sample No.	5568 years BP	Calib. dates	Culture	Material
				Neolithic	
Sangankallu	TF-355	3435±100 BP	1745 bc	Late Southern Neolithic	Charcoal
Satanikota	BS-202	1440±100 BP	621 ad	Meghalithic	Charcoal
Satanikota	BS-201	1620±100 BP	420 bc	Meghalithic	Charcoal
Satanikota	BS-204	8960±120 BP	None	Meghalithic	Charcoal
Satanikota	BS-203	7520±140 BP	66410 bc	Meghalithic	Charcoal
T. Narasipur	TF-412	3645±105 BP	2033 bc	Southern Neolithic	Charcoal
T. Narasipur	TF-413	3345±105 BP	1672 bc	Southern Neolithic	Charcoal
Tekkalakota	TF-237	3465±105 BP	1859, 1848, 1769 bc	Neolithic Period	Charcoal
Tekkalakota	TF-239	3395±105 BP	1732, 1725, 1692 bc	Neolithic Period	Charcoal
Tekkalakota	TF-266	3625±100 BP	2023, 1998, 83 bc	Neolithic Period	Charcoal
Tekkalakota	TF-262	3460±135 BP	1851, 1850, 1761 bc	Neolithic Period	Charcoal
Terdal	TF-684	3775±95 BP	2200 bc	Southern Neolithic	Charcoal
Terdal	TF-683	3615±120 BP	2014, 016, 19766 bc	Southern Neolithic	Charcoal
Utnur	TF-168	3875±110 BP	2452, 2427, 2395, 2374, 2366 bc	Period IIIA Neolithic	Charcoal
Utnur	BM-54	4120±150 BP	28660, 2817, 2693, 2684, 2662, 2633, 2626 bc	Period I Neolithic	Charcoal
Utnur	TF-167	3890±110 BP	2455, 416, 2405 bc	Period IIA Neolithic	Charcoal

KEY: BP = uncalibrated dates based on 5568 years half-life, bp/bc/ad= calibrated date.

TABLE 7. STONE AGE (NEOLITHIC GANGA-YAMUNA DOAB AND EASTERN INDIA)

Site	Sample No.	5568 years BP	Calib. Dates	Culture	Material
Chirand	TF-1032	3600±150 BP	1961 bc	Period I, Neolithic	Charcoal
Chirand	TF-446	1930±105 BP	72 bc	NBP Period	Charcoal
Chirand	TF-1035	3125±100 BP	1418 bc	Period I, Neolithic	Charcoal
Chirand	TF-1031	3225±135 BP	1884 bc	Period I, Neolithic	Charcoal
Chirand	TF-1126	2290±120 BP	391 bc	Period I, Neolithic	Charcoal
Chirand	TF-1125	3365±150 BP	1679 bc	Period I, Neolithic	Charcoal

(contd.)

Site	Sample No.	5568 years BP	Calib. Dates	Culture	Material
Chirand	TF-1127	3230±95 BP	1516 bc	Period I, Neolithic	Charcoal
Chirand	TF-1034	3420±110 BP	1740 bc	Period I, Neolithic	Charcoal
Chirand	TF-1036	2485±120 BP	761,681,659, 596,633,577, 561 bc	Period I, Neolithic	Charcoal
Chirand	TF-1033	3390±110 BP	1730,1729, 1689 bc	Period I, Neolithic	Charcoal
Chirand	TF-334	2715±120 BP	890,845 bc	Period I, Neolithic	Charcoal
Chirand	BS-129	4540±110 BP	3338,3213, 3203 bc	Period III, Vindhyan Neolithic	Charcoal
Koldihwa	PRL-224	8280±210 BP	None	Neolithic ?	Charcoal
Koldihwa	PRL-56	820±100 BP	1225 ad	Chalcolithic	Charcoal
Koldihwa	PRL-227	2050±110 BP	92 bc	Chalcolithic-IC	Charcoal
Koldihwa	PRL-101	6295±180 BP	5240 bc	Neolithic	Charcoal
Koldihwa	PRL-100	7180±230 BP	6075, 6059, 6043, 6018, 6001 bc	Neolithic	Charcoal
Koldihwa	PRL-102	2380±105 BP	405 bc	Chalcolithic	Charcoal
Koldihwa	PRL-99	2900±150 BP	1092 bc	Chalcolithic	Charcoal
Koldihwa	PRL-223	3300±120 BP	1607,1554, 1544 bc	Neolithic	Charcoal
Kunjhun River	BETA-6414	4010±110 BP	2569, 2538, 2503 bc	Vindhyan Neolithic	Unkown
Kunjhun River	BETA-6415	46600±80 BP	3360 bc	Vindhyan Neolithic	Unknown
Kunjhun River	BETA-4879	3120±70 BP	1414 bc	Vindhyan Neolithic	Unknown
Mahagara	PRL-409	3260±150 BP	1523 bc	Neolithic	Charcoal
Mahagara	BS-128	3330±100 BP	1628 bc	Neolithic	Charcoal
Mahagara	PRL-407	3300±100 BP	1607, 1554, 1544 bc	Neolithic	Charcoal

KEY: BP = uncalibrated dates based on 5568 years half-life, bp/bc/ad= calibrated date.

REFERENCES

Agrawal, D.P. 1982. *The Archaeology of India*. London: Curzon Press.

Agrawal, D.P. and M.G. Yadava 1995. *Dating the Human Past*. Pune: The Indian Society for Prehistoric and Quaternary Studies.

Agrawal, D.P. and S. Kusumgar 1974. *Prehistoric Chronology and Radiocarbon Dating in India*. New Delhi: Munshiram Manoharlal.

Agrawal, D.P., R.N. Athavale, R.V. Krishnamurthy, S. Kusumgar, C.R.K. Murthy and V. Nautiyal 1979. Chronostratigraphy of Loessic and Lacustrine Sediments in the Kashmir Valley, *Acta Geologica Academias Scientiarium Hungaricae* 22 (1-4): 185-96.

Baskaran, M., G. Rajagopalan and B.L.K. Somayajulu 1989. $^{230}Th/^{234}U$ and ^{14}C Dating of the Quaternary Carbonate Deposits of Saurashtra, India, *Chemical Geology* (Isotope Geoscience Section) 79: 65-82.

Faure, Gunter 1986. *Principles of Isotope Geology*. New York: John Wiley and Sons.

Fleisher, R.L., P.B. Price, and R.M. Walker 1975. *Nuclear Tracks in Solids*. Berkeley: University of California Press.

Fleming, Stuart 1976. *Dating in Archaeology: a Guide to Scientific Techniques*. London: J.M. Dent and Sons Ltd.

Joshi, R.V. 1961. Stone Age Industries of the Damoh Area, Madhya Pradesh, *Ancient India* 17: 5-36.

Korisettar, R. and S.N. Rajaguru 1998. Quaternary Stratigraphy, Palaeoclimate and the Lower Palaeolithic of India, in *Early Human Behaviour in Global Context: the Rise and Diversity of the Lower Palaeolithic Record* (M.D. Petraglia and R. Korisettar Eds.), pp. 304-42. London-New York: Routledge.

Krishnaswami, V.C. 1953. Progress in Prehistory, *Ancient India* 9: 53-79.

Kusumgar, S., B.S. Kotlia, D.P. Agrawal and A. Sahni 1985. Magnetostratigraphy of the Karewa Fossiliferous Horizons from the Kashmir Valley, India, in *Climate and Geology of Kashmir and Central Asia* (D.P. Agrawal, S. Kusumgar and R.V. Krishnamurthy Eds.), pp. 27-8. New Delhi: Today and Tomorrows Printers and Publishers.

Kusumgar, S., N. Bhandari and D.P. Agrawal 1985. Fission-track Ages of the Romushi Lower Karewas, in *Climate and Geology of Kashmir: the Last Four Million Years* (D.P. Agrawal, S. Kusumgar and R.V. Krishnamurthy Eds.), pp. 245-7. New Delhi: Today and Tomorrow's Printers and Publishers.

Lal, B.B. 1956. Palaeoliths from the Beas and Banganga Valleys, Punjab, *Ancient India* 12: 58-92.

Leakey, Richard and Roger Lewin 1993. *Origins Reconsidered*. London: Abacus.

Petraglia, M.D. 1998. The Lower Palaeolithic of India and Its Bearing on the Asian Record, in *Early Human Behaviour in Global Context: the Rise and Diversity of the Lower Palaeolithic Record* (M.D. Petraglia and R. Korisettar Eds.), pp. 343-90. London-New York: Routledge.

Possehl, G.L. 1994. Radiometric Dates for South Asian Archaeology (Compiled by G.L. Possehl).

Sankalia, H.D. 1974. *Prehistory and Protohistory of India and Pakistan*. Pune: Deccan College.

Semaw, S., P. Renne, J.W.K. Harris, C.S. Feibel, R.L. Berner, N. Fesseha and K. Mowbray 1997. 2.5 Million-Year-Old Stone Tools from Gona, Ethiopia, *Nature* 385: 333-6.

Singhvi, A., G.A. Wagner and R. Korisettar 1998. Techniques for the Chronometry of the Palaeolithic: Evidence for Global Colonization, in *Early Human Behaviour in Global Context: the Rise and Diversity of the Lower Palaeolithic Record* (M.D. Petraglia and R. Korisettar Eds.), pp. 23-83. London-New York: Routledge.

Singhvi, A.K., D.P. Agrawal and K.S.V. Nambi 1991. Thermoluminescence Dating: an Update on Application to Indian Archaeology, in *Recent Advances in Marine Archaeology* (S.R. Rao Ed.), pp. 173-80. Goa: National Institute of Oceanography.

Thompson, R. and F. Oldfield 1986. *Environmental Magnetism*. London: Allen and Unwin.

Wagner, G.A. 1983. *Handbooks for Acheologists (No.1) Thermoluminescence Dating*. Strasbourgh: European Science Foundation.

Wehmiller, J.F. 1984. Relative and Absolute Dating of Quaternary Molluscs with Amino Acid Racemization: Evaluation, Applications, and Questions, in *Quaternary Dating Methods* (William C. Mahaney Ed.), pp. 171-94. New York: Elsevier Science Publishing Company Inc.

Contributors

D.P. AGRAWAL, 10 Jayantilal Park, Amli-Bhopal Road, Ahmedabad 380 054; email: dharma@ad1.vsnl.net.in

G.L. BADAM, Department of Archaeology, Deccan College, Pune 411 006

D.K. BHATTACHARYA, Department of Anthropology, University of Delhi, Delhi 110 007

DEEPRA BHATTACHARYA, Department of Archaeology, Deccan College, Deccan College, Yeravada, Pune 411 006

U.C. CHATTOPADHYAYA, Department of Ancient History Culture and Archaeology, University of Allahabad, Allahabad 211 002; email:ucc@mri.ernet.in

G.S. DASOG, Department of Soil Chemistry, University of Agricultural Sciences, Dharwad 580 005; email: root@zrclar08.kar.nic.in

B.C. DEOTARE, Department of Archaeology, Deccan College, Yeravada, Pune 411 006; email: <dakshina@pn2.vsnl.net.in>

DORIAN Q. FULLER, Department of Archaeology, University of Cambridge, Downing Street, Cambridge CB2 3DZ, UK; email: df203@hermes.cam.ac.uk

K.A.R. KENNEDY, Division of Biological Sciences, Section of Ecology and Systematics, Corsan Hall, Ithaca, New York 14853-2701, USA; email: kak10@cornell.edu

RAVI KORISETTAR, Department of History and Archaeology Karnatak University, Dharwad 580 003; email: karuni@bgl.vsnl.net.in

A.A. KSHIRSAGAR, Department of Archaeology, Deccan College, Yeravada, Pune 411 006, email: dakshina@pn2.vsnl.net.in

JOHN R. LUKACS, Department of Anthropology, University of Oregon, Eugene, Oregon 97403, USA; email: jrlukacs@oregon.uoregon.edu

V.M. MEHER-HOMJI, 20 D, Sagar Sangeet, 58, Colaba Road, Mumbai 400 005

Jitu Mishra, Department of Archaeology, Deccan College, Yeravada, Pune 411 006

Pradeep Mohanty, Department of Archaeology, Deccan College, Yeravada, Pune 411 006

R. Ramesh, Earth Sciences Division, Physical Research Laboratory, Ahmedabad 380 009, email: ramesh.@prl.ernet.in

Ripudaman Singh, Emeritus Professor, Department of Sociology and Anthropology, University of Windsor, Windsor, Ontario N9B 3P4 Canada. email: rsingh@server.uwindsor.ca

Aletha Tavares, Department of Archaeology, Deccan College, Yeravada, Pune 411 006

Index